Reshaping CyberSecurity With Generative AI Techniques

Noor Zaman Jhanjhi
School of Computing Science, Taylor's University, Malaysia

A volume in the Advances in
Information Security, Privacy,
and Ethics (AISPE) Book Series

Published in the United States of America by
    IGI Global
    Engineering Science Reference (an imprint of IGI Global)
    701 E. Chocolate Avenue
    Hershey PA, USA 17033
    Tel: 717-533-8845
    Fax: 717-533-8661
    E-mail: cust@igi-global.com
    Web site: http://www.igi-global.com

Library of Congress Cataloging-in-Publication Data

CIP PENDING

ISBN13: 9798369354155
Isbn13Softcover: 9798369354162
EISBN13: 9798369354179

British Cataloguing in Publication Data
A Cataloguing in Publication record for this book is available from the British Library.

All work contributed to this book is new, previously-unpublished material.
The views expressed in this book are those of the authors, but not necessarily of the publisher.

For electronic access to this publication, please contact: eresources@igi-global.com.

Table of Contents

Detailed Table of Contents

Chapter 1

Siva Raja Sindiramutty, Taylor's University, Malaysia
Krishna Raj V. Prabagaran, Universiti Malaysia Sarawak, Malaysia
Rehan Akbar, Florida International University, USA
Manzoor Hussain, Indus University, Pakistan
Nazir Ahmed Malik, Bahria University, Islamabad, Pakistan

Generative AI techniques have been popular since they can generate data or content that could be hardly distinguished from genuine ones. This chapter comprehensively reviews generative AI for cybersecurity and its definition, history, and applications in different fields. It covers basic ideas such as generative models, probability distributions, and latent spaces. Also, it goes into more detail on some of the more popular approaches like GANs, VAEs, and the combination of RL. The chapter explores the structure and training processes of GANs and VAEs and demonstrates their application in tasks such as image synthesis, data enhancement, and novelty detection. Also, it explores the interaction between RL and generative models and the challenges, including the exploration-exploitation trade-off. The chapter focuses on the development of generative AI with the help of DL and analyses the benefits of deep generative models and their usage in various fields. Evaluation measures and the problems with measuring generative models are discussed, focusing on the methods of improving the measurement accuracy. Finally, the chapter focuses on new directions, like transformer-based models and self-supervised learning, to look at the future of generative AI. The emphasis is made on understanding these techniques due to their versatility, and some ideas about the possible further developments of the findings for other fields and future studies and applications are provided.

Chapter 2

Ehtisham Safeer, UIIT, Pakistan

Reinforcement learning (RL) allows defense mechanisms to adapt to changing threats and has shown promise in tackling cyber security issues. This study presents a thorough introduction which includes foundations, uses, and difficulties to RL in cyber security. The efficacy of RL in making decisions is also emphasized in the introduction. Then the foundation for comprehending RL's use in cyber security, the fundamentals of the technology, and algorithm classifications is clarified. The study then delves into a number of RL applications in cyber security. Then a number of RL applications in cyber security and issues in RL is discussed. Along with prospects for improving cyber security safeguards through the application of RL methodologies, to successfully manage increasing cyber threats, future research directions are proposed with the integration of blockchain technology and generative adversarial networks (GANs). This work emphasizes the importance of RL in supporting cyber security and research to improve cyber defenses.

Chapter 3

Siva Raja Sindiramutty, Taylor's University, Malaysia
Krishna Raj V. Prabagaran, Universiti Malaysia Sarawak, Malaysia
N. Z. Jhanjhi, Taylor's University, Malaysia
Raja Kumar Murugesan, Taylor's University, Malaysia
Sarfraz Nawaz Brohi, University of the West of England, UK
Mehdi Masud, Taif University, Saudi Arabia

Protecting virtual assets from cyber threats is essential as we live in a digitally advanced world. Providing a responsible emphasis on proper network security and intrusion detection is imperative. On the other hand, traditional strategies need a supportive tool to adapt to the transforming threat space. New generative AI techniques like generative adversarial networks (GANs) and variational autoencoders (VAEs) are the mainstream technologies required to meet the gap. This chapter deals with how these models can enhance network security by inspecting the network traffic for anomalies and malicious behaviors detected through unsupervised learning, which considers strange or emerging phenomena. This survey features innovations in fault detection, behavior control, deep packet inspection, traffic classification, and examples of real-world intrusions detected by GAN-based systems. Furthermore, the chapter focuses on the challenges of adversarial attacks on models that require the development of solid defense mechanisms, such as generative adversarial networks. Ethics becomes the following matter on our list of discussions, given that privacy transparency and accountability are to be observed when working with generative AI technologies in network security. Finally, the authors examine trends that determine how cyber-attacks are dealt with comprehensively.

    Hafsa Shahid, International Islamic University, Islamabad, Pakistan
    Humaira Ashraf, Taylor's University, Malaysia
    N. Z. Jhanjhi, Taylor's University, Malaysia
    Qurat-ul Ain Zam Zam, International Islamic University, Islamabad,
        Pakistan

Security is a major problem in wireless sensor networks (WSN) because they are vulnerable to a variety of dangerous threats, the deadliest of which is the wormhole assault. These networks support functions like localization and other networking protocols. These networks are made up of many small sensors that collect and share data with central repositories. In such a setting, the detection of wormholes becomes more difficult because of low resource availability in detecting equipment. The authors propose to develop an algorithm for wormhole detection which performs efficiently within the given resource constraints in WSN environment. This research has initially performed a survey using systematic literature review (SLR) to study the schemes against wormhole attacks. Articles have been searched using reliable data sources and applied quality assessment measures to refine the article collection. The SLR has helped to find the shortcomings and limitations in the literature. This research elaborates a comparison of the wormhole attack prevention techniques based on results, findings, and limitations in each category of schemes in literature. Finally, the problem of high energy consumption is taken under consideration for the purpose of research. The proposed technique for handling wormhole has been designed to give good performance and consume less energy of the network. This method uses the transmission duration between the sender and recipient nodes to identify suspicious nodes. Then, it uses the hop count and hop interval time to detect suspicious nodes. The simulation's findings indicate a 100% packet delivery ratio and detection rate. Comparing the proposed technique to a good existing technique in the considered base article, it has enhanced throughput, lowered end-to-end delay, and consumed less energy.

Chapter 5

Deepak Varadam, Ramaiah University of Applied Sciences, India
Sahana P. Shankar, Ramaiah University of Applied Sciences, India
Nidhi N. P., Ramaiah University of Applied Sciences, India
Vinay Dubey, Ramaiah University of Applied Sciences, India
Aaditi Jadwani, Ramaiah University of Applied Sciences, India
Shaik Falak Taj, Ramaiah University of Applied Sciences, India
Sahil C. T. Uthappa, Ramaiah University of Applied Sciences, India
Aryan Bharadwaj, Ramaiah University of Applied Sciences, India

Various global institutions are exploring the potentials and hurdles of 6G communication networks to address the security shortcomings of existing 5G networks while capitalizing on the promises of 6G for heightened privacy and dependability. Artificial intelligence (AI) emerges as a solution with minimal drawbacks and reduced expenses. This chapter delves into diverse applications where AI integration can prove advantageous. AI has undergone substantial evolution, transitioning from network diagnosis and monitoring to optimizing large-scale systems. Advanced algorithms bolster network security by continuously updating and identifying vulnerabilities. Furthermore, AI facilitates the creation of innovative networking models like intent-based networking, streamlining network configuration based on user needs. The integration of AI with networks has witnessed increased usage, such as cost reduction in managing IoT data and enhanced efficiency in healthcare systems through fuzzy classifiers.

Chapter 6

Humaira Ashraf, Taylor's University, Malaysia
Uswa Ihsan, International Islamic University, Islamabad, Pakistan
Ata Ullah, Independent Researcher, Pakistan
Sayan Kumar Ray, Taylor's University, Malaysia
Navid Ali Khan, Taylor's University, Malaysia

Blockchain and AI have revolutionized how distributed systems can work. Combining blockchain and generative ai to enhance data integrity and cooperation in the treacherous field may find innovative ways blockchain and generative AI can develop distributed systems in terms of data integrity, transparency, scalability, security, cooperation, and decision-making. Through an investigation, it is understood how blockchain secures AI models, makes them more transparent and traceable, decentralizes training, and makes distributed models more efficient and scalable. Examples from real applications across worlds will guide how blockchain and generative AIs are used in fields such as health, finance, film, supply chains, and electrical transmission.As a result, different sources' knowledge is adopted as proven to propel the process of supplementing blockchain and AI towards a future of intelligent, flexible, and secure distributed systems.

Chapter 7

Azeem Khan, University Islam Sultan Sharif Ali, Brunei
Noor Jhanjhi, TUSB, Malaysia
Ghassan Ahmed Ali Abdulhabeb, University Islam Sultan Sharif Ali,
*   Brunei*
Sayan Kumar Ray, TUSB, Malaysia
Mustansar Ali Ghazanfar, University of East London, UK
Mamoona Humayun, Independent Researcher, UK

Generative artificial intelligence (GenAI) is a part of artificial intelligence which has the ability to generate content in various formats ranging from text to videos and images to audio formats. GenAI has the ability to inherently learn from large datasets and can produce results that can be of optimal use in case of cybersecurity. In the current digital landscape, we see a plethora of electronic gadgets connected to this seamless network of devices connected online. These seamless network of devices which were earlier unable to connect due to lack of ip addresses are now able to connect and are improving the quality of human life ranging from home appliances to health domain. From here we see emergence of smart networks which at one side is a boon but at the same time they have the risk of exploitation with unexpected cyberattacks. Hence, this chapter is an effort to highlight the issues concerning cyberthreats and advice on how GenAI can be utilized to mitigate these risks. This chapter focused on applying generative AI to secured IoT devices. By discussing the core concepts of IoT security, such as device authentication and access control, the chapter demonstrated how the next-generation generative AI models, including GANs and VAEs, can boost anomaly detection for device security. The chapter also provided examples of real-life use cases to illustrate how generative AI can be used to optimize the energy grid, protect data privacy, and strengthen cybersecurity efforts. Additionally, this chapter presented the key issues related to ethical considerations pertaining to privacy, bias, and accountability in the development and deployment of responsible AI. Moreover, it introduced the legal aspects of privacy legislation, data protection, and cybersecurity compliance. Finally, the chapter outlined some of the future trends in generative AI for IoT security to name a few are enhanced threat detection, privacy-preserving multimedia processing, and secure communications. The chapter then encourages organizations to start using generative AI to enable systems to become proactive about IoT security and reduce the massive onslaught of cyber threats while navigating an ever-evolving digital landscape.

Chapter 8

Basheer Riskhan, Albukhary International University, Malaysia
Halawati Abd Jalil Saufan, Albukhary International University,
Malaysia
Jazuli Bello Ladan, Albukhary International University, Malaysia
Md Amin Ullah Sheikh, Albukhary International University, Malaysia
Khalid Hussain, Albukhary International University, Malaysia
Manzoor Hussain, Indus University, Pakistan

A combination of technical expertise, creativity, and problem-solving skills is needed to succeed in the complicated and demanding profession of programming. As a result, there are several challenges that programmers may run against when creating software or computer systems. The literature on how to optimize and reduce the problems and difficulties in computer programming is reviewed in this chapter. The issue has a global scope and keeps becoming worse on a local scale. Even though there are numerous instructional tools available to support the teaching and learning of computer programming, the issue still exists. Computer introduction courses had high failure and dropout rates even from the beginning. This situation's justification includes the student's inability to solve problems. To overcome the challenges of learning computer programming, these two factors must be taken into account concurrently. This chapter will find out the ways to minimize these challenges.

Chapter 9

    Siva Raja Sindiramutty, Taylor's University, Malaysia
    Krishna Raj V. Prabagaran, Universiti Malaysia Sarawak, Malaysia
    N. Z. Jhanjhi, Taylor's University, Malaysia
    Mustansar Ali Ghazanfar, University of East London, UK
    Nazir Ahmed Malik, Bahria University, Islamabad, Pakistan
    Tariq Rahim Soomro, Institute of Business Management, Karachi,
       Pakistan

Protecting AI in web applications is necessary. This domain is a composite of technology and huge scope with good prospects and immense difficulties. This chapter covers the landscape of security issues with advancing generative AI techniques for integration into web development frameworks. The initial section is on security in web development—a conversation on the subtleties of generative AI-based methods. In a literal stance, the chapter offers 13 ways to approach it. Among the threats are those that introduce security issues related to generative AI deployments, which illustrate why it is vital for defenders and infrastructure owners to implement mitigation measures proactively. This chapter pertains to the security and privacy of data and lessons for securing and preventing vulnerability. The chapter explores attacks, model poisoning, bias issues, defence mechanisms, and long-term mitigation strategies. Additionally, Service A promotes transparency, explainability, and compliance with applicable laws while structuring a development methodology and deployment methods/operation. The text outlines how to respond and recover from incidents as it provides response frameworks for everyone involved in managing security breaches. Finally, it addresses trends, possible threats, and lessons learned from real-world case studies. In order to contribute to addressing these research needs, this chapter sheds light on the security considerations associated with AI for web development and suggests recommendations that can help researchers, practitioners, and policymakers enhance the security posture of popular generative AI advancements used in generating web applications.

Siva Raja Sindiramutty, Taylor's University, Malaysia
Krishna Raj V. Prabagaran, Universiti Malaysia Sarawak, Malaysia
Rehan Akbar, Florida International University, USA
Manzoor Hussain, Indus University, Pakistan
Nazir Ahmed Malik, Bahria University, Islamabad, Pakistan

Generative AI, which is equipped with unique capabilities, is about to put the world of secure user interface (UI) design upside down and turn it into something full of endless possibilities in which users will be able to use the same opportunities and experienced solutions to protect their interaction in digital from any future security threats. This chapter takes a deep plunge into the merger of the generative AI with the secure user interface design, on the whole, presenting a complete exposition of the principals involved, methodologies applied, practical embodiment, and ultimate ramifications. The beginning will explore the building blocks of UI design principles and the user-centred iterative approach, wherein a robust framework for understanding Generative AI as a critical part of building secure, intuitive, and engaging user experiences is implemented. Further, it provides an overview of different types of generative AI approaches that could be deployed for secure UI design, such as GANs, VAEs, and autoregressive models, with their capabilities expanding the scope of security measures, which include authentication protocols, encryption, and user access rights while retaining usability and aesthetic appeal. Moreover, it surveys instance applications of the generative AI that support the Secure design of GUI, among the automatic generation of safe layout patterns, the dynamic change of the interface according to emerging threats, and the creation of cryptographic keys and secure symbols.

Khalid Hussain, Albukhary International University, Malaysia
Md Amin Ullah Sheikh, Albukhary International University, Malaysia
Thiha Naing, Albukhary International University, Malaysia
Manzoor Hussain, Indus University, Pakistan
Noor Ul Amin, Taylor's University, Malaysia

Web application penetration testing is known as pretesting. It is a critical process for identifying and addressing security vulnerabilities in web applications. Statistics show that 88% of organizations worldwide experienced phishing attempts in 2019. The most significant security violation was predictable resource location attacks were 34%, SQL attacks at 20%, and code injection attacks at 10%, together generating 64% of total web application attack activity. Also, 75% of IT leaders lack confidence in their web application security. The study of the literature review emphasizes the lack of security issues in web applications and some proposals about penetration testing procedures. The method sections talk about detailed procedures from scratch for doing web app pen tests. In the discussion section, the authors talk about some suggestions that organizations can follow to make their websites more secure and unauthorized access. In conclusion, conducting web application penetration testing in the proper way can play a crucial role in securing web applications.

Chapter 12

Siva Raja Sindiramutty, Taylor's University, Malaysia

Krishna Raj V. Prabagaran, Universiti Malaysia Sarawak, Malaysia

Noor Zaman Jhanjhi, Taylor's University, Malaysia

Raja Kumar Murugesan, Taylor's University, Malaysia

Nazir Ahmed Malik, Bahria University, Islamabad, Pakistan

Manzoor Hussain, Indus University, Pakistan

The chapter discusses how ethics and transparency relate to creating secure web models for AI. AI plays a role in secure web development, and the authors consider ethics and transparency as two critical aspects of this subject, which influences users, stakeholders, or society. The examination begins with AI principles, which include fairness, accountability, and privacy requirements. They then get into the problems with secure web models. In this chapter, they break down bias and fairness concerns at the source and find ways to resolve them in web models. This relates to trust and accountability, where transparency and explainability are highlighted. They also provide case studies showing the effectiveness of transparent and explainable AI in increasing user engagement. They also delve into decision-making frameworks to help navigate the ethical dilemmas in AI web development. It then represents the conversation on the atmospherics of empowerment tools, such as monitoring and evaluation guidelines for mobilisation implementation practice and governance. To sum up, the authors underline the ethical and transparent views for us to do AI-driven web development. Therefore, they urge all stakeholders to make ethics and transparency the cornerstones of responsible webs.

Chapter 13

Venkat Narayana Rao T., Sreenidhi Institute of Science and Technology,
India
Harsh Vardhan G., Sreenidhi Institute of Science and Technology, India
Krishna Sai A. N., Sreenidhi Institute of Science and Technology, India
Bhavana Sangers, Sreenidhi Institute of Science and Technology, India

The relationship between the fields of generative (AI) and cybersecurity offers both opportunity and danger as technology continues to grow at an unimaginable rate. The emergence of 5G networks and the spread of internet of things (IoT)-connected devices are changing the challenging landscape in the field of cybersecurity. The predictions point to an increase in complex cyberattacks using AI-driven strategies like adversarial machine learning and deepfake methods. Simultaneously, content manipulation are being revolutionized by the rise of generative AI technologies such as deep learning and GANs (generative adversarial networks). The AI-generated synthetic media contributes to existing problems with digital trust and authenticity by posing moral questions about identity theft and disinformation. In conclusion, managing the intersection of cybersecurity and generative AI requires proactive steps to fully utilize AI's potential while minimizing its inherent risks. This chapter includes solutions like anomaly detection systems and AI-powered threat intelligence.

The chapter presents a comprehensive exploration of the changing dynamics at the intersection between the rapidly growing landscape of the interconnectivity of various devices—the internet of things—and the innovations piloted by advancements in generative artificial intelligence. In the following background-focused analysis, the significance of the enactment of new levels of security details in this fast-growing and virulently expansive landscape is emphasized, with generative AI ultimately serving as the highlight. The conversation consequently shifts to threats. This includes a detailed depiction of new cybersecurity threats rooted in advancements in AI, featuring AI malicious actors and incidents, such as the increasingly popular phenomenon of ransomware-as-a-service as mirror illustrations of the dynamic and multifaceted character of these threats. The class further proceeds to more in-depth detail about the most contemporary generative AI platforms such as generative adversarial networks, variational autoencoders, and reinforcement learning—all relevant in identifying emerging solutions to advance strategies in cybersecurity. The conversation simultaneously conducts an opportunity and threat analysis of the merger between these platforms and cybersecurity with regard to ethics, regulations, and overall adversarial touchpoints and tactics. The chapter concludes with a call for unity in discourse and action between the relevant industry, academia, and government stakeholders as a summary of the essential cross-disciplinary aspect that must drive the narrative in confronting and overcoming the threats to and from generative AI research. Having presented the narrative structure, this chapter has allowed a comprehensive coverage of the major issues and opportunities at the heart of the cybersecurity-generative AI combination. Additionally, it has provided a forum to call for collaborative and fortified efforts regarding the securing and defending of the uncertainties that the rapidly changing and more unpredictable digital landscape has in store for the world.

Preface

In an era where technological advancement accelerates with unprecedented speed and cyber threats become increasingly sophisticated, the cybersecurity landscape faces formidable challenges. Traditional defense mechanisms, while foundational, are often outpaced by the dynamic and adaptive nature of modern attacks. Yet, amidst these challenges, a promising frontier emerges: Generative AI.

We are delighted to present *Reshaping CyberSecurity With Generative AI Techniques*, a definitive guide to understanding and harnessing the transformative power of generative AI in the realm of cybersecurity. This book serves as a comprehensive exploration into how cutting-edge generative AI technologies are revolutionizing cybersecurity practices and defenses.

As editors, our goal is to illuminate the intersection of artificial intelligence and cybersecurity, revealing how generative AI can not only enhance traditional defense mechanisms but also forge entirely new approaches to safeguarding our digital world. Each chapter is a deep dive into how these technologies address and mitigate evolving cyber threats, from adversarial attacks and malware to data breaches and insider threats.

We have meticulously curated contributions from leading experts, researchers, and practitioners who provide invaluable insights and practical guidance. Their work spans theoretical foundations, practical applications, and real-world case studies, offering readers a well-rounded perspective on integrating generative AI into their cybersecurity strategies.

This book is crafted for a diverse audience: cybersecurity professionals, researchers, technology enthusiasts, industry leaders, and consultants. Whether you are an analyst seeking to enhance your toolkit, a researcher exploring new academic frontiers, or a decision-maker aiming to fortify your organization's defenses, this book will equip you with the knowledge and tools necessary to navigate and excel in the rapidly evolving field of cybersecurity.

The objectives of *Reshaping CyberSecurity With Generative AI Techniques* are multi-faceted:

1. **Educational Empowerment**: To provide a thorough understanding of generative AI techniques and their applications in cybersecurity, enabling readers to leverage these technologies effectively.
2. **Practical Guidance**: To offer actionable insights on implementing generative AI solutions for real-world cybersecurity challenges, from threat detection to incident response.
3. **Enhanced Defense Capabilities**: To explore how generative AI can advance defense mechanisms against various cyber threats, providing advanced tools for proactive security.
4. **Innovation and Adaptation**: To inspire innovation in cybersecurity practices by showcasing the transformative potential of generative AI and encouraging readers to embrace emerging technologies.
5. **Collaborative Learning**: To foster a community of learning and knowledge exchange among cybersecurity professionals, researchers, and enthusiasts, promoting collaboration and shared insights.

Our journey through this book will lead us to explore groundbreaking techniques such as Generative Adversarial Networks (GANs), Variational Autoencoders (VAEs), and Reinforcement Learning, among others. We will examine their roles in threat detection, anomaly identification, and building resilient systems. Additionally, we address ethical considerations, privacy-preserving methods, and future trends in cybersecurity and generative AI.

We invite you to embark on this journey with us, discovering the frontiers of cybersecurity innovation and uncovering the boundless possibilities that generative AI offers. As we delve into each chapter, we hope you find both inspiration and practical knowledge that will empower you to contribute to a more secure digital future.

Chapter 1: Overview of Generative AI Techniques for Cybersecurity

In this foundational chapter, we explore the landscape of generative AI techniques and their transformative impact on cybersecurity. Generative AI encompasses methods capable of producing data and content that mimic real-world examples, offering promising applications in various domains. This chapter provides a comprehensive examination of generative models, including Generative Adversarial Networks (GANs) and Variational Autoencoders (VAEs), alongside Reinforcement Learning (RL) techniques. We delve into the core concepts, such as probability distributions and latent spaces, and illustrate how these models are utilized in tasks like image generation, data augmentation, and anomaly detection. By detailing the structure, training procedures, and collaborative efforts between RL and generative models, this chapter sets the stage for understanding how these advanced techniques can address modern cybersecurity challenges.

Chapter 2: Reinforcement Learning Approaches in Cybersecurity

Reinforcement Learning (RL) has emerged as a potent tool for adapting to evolving cyber threats, and this chapter provides a thorough introduction to its role in cybersecurity. We cover the foundational principles of RL, including algorithm classifications and decision-making efficacy. The chapter further investigates various applications of RL in cybersecurity, addressing both its benefits and challenges. We explore how RL can be integrated with other technologies, such as blockchain and GANs, to enhance cyber defenses. The chapter concludes with a discussion on future research directions and the potential of RL methodologies to bolster security measures against emerging threats.

Chapter 3: Generative AI in Network Security and Intrusion Detection

As digital assets become increasingly critical, safeguarding network security and detecting intrusions are paramount. This chapter examines how generative AI techniques, particularly GANs and VAEs, can enhance network security by identifying anomalies and malicious activities through unsupervised learning. We review advancements in fault detection, behavior control, and deep packet inspection, highlighting real-world applications where GAN-based systems have successfully detected intrusions. Additionally, we address the challenges posed by adversarial attacks on generative models and discuss the development of robust defense mechanisms.

Chapter 4: Reshaping Cybersecurity of Wireless Sensor Networks Using Energy-Optimized Approach Against Wormhole Attack

Wireless Sensor Networks (WSNs) face significant security challenges, with wormhole attacks being particularly dangerous. This chapter proposes an energy-optimized algorithm for detecting wormhole attacks in WSNs, where resource constraints make detection difficult. By focusing on efficient detection mechanisms within limited resources, the chapter presents a novel approach to enhancing the security of WSNs and mitigating one of the most severe threats in this domain.

Chapter 5: AI in 6G Network Security and Management

With the advent of 6G networks, the integration of Artificial Intelligence (AI) is becoming crucial for addressing security shortcomings of 5G networks and enhancing privacy and reliability. This chapter explores various applications of AI in 6G network security, from network diagnosis and monitoring to optimization and innovative models like Intent-Based Networking. By highlighting how AI can improve efficiency and reduce costs in managing IoT data and healthcare systems, the chapter underscores the transformative potential of AI in next-generation network security and management.

Chapter 6: Blockchain and Generative AI for Securing Distributed Systems

Blockchain and generative AI are revolutionizing distributed systems, offering enhanced data integrity, transparency, and security. This chapter investigates how the combination of these technologies can improve the scalability and efficiency of distributed systems. By examining real-world applications in sectors such as health, finance, and supply chains, we illustrate how blockchain can secure AI models and enhance their performance. The chapter provides insights into how these technologies can collaboratively advance the future of distributed systems.

Chapter 7: Securing IoT Devices Using Generative AI Techniques

The proliferation of Internet of Things (IoT) devices presents significant security challenges. This chapter explores how generative AI techniques can be applied to enhance the security of IoT devices. By addressing core concepts such as device authentication and access control, the chapter provides practical advice on using generative AI to mitigate cyber risks associated with the growing network of connected devices. The focus is on leveraging AI's capabilities to safeguard IoT environments from emerging threats.

Chapter 8: Reshaping Secure Coding Through Generative AI Approach to Minimizing Programming Challenges

Programming presents numerous challenges, particularly for novice coders. This chapter reviews how generative AI can address and minimize these challenges in secure coding. By analyzing existing literature and proposing innovative solutions, the chapter aims to enhance problem-solving skills in programming and reduce the difficulties associated with software development. The exploration of generative AI's role in optimizing coding practices provides valuable insights for improving programming education and practice.

Chapter 9: Security Considerations in Generative AI for Web Applications

Integrating generative AI into web applications introduces both opportunities and security challenges. This chapter delves into the critical security considerations of using generative AI within web engineering frameworks. We outline 13 key areas of focus, including threat landscapes, data security, and privacy concerns. The chapter provides strategies for protecting sensitive information, addressing adversarial attacks, and mitigating vulnerabilities, emphasizing the need for proactive defense measures in the development of secure web applications.

Chapter 10: Generative AI for Secure User Interface (UI) Design

Generative AI is poised to revolutionize Secure User Interface (UI) design by offering innovative solutions to enhance security while maintaining usability. This chapter explores the integration of generative AI with UI design, detailing various approaches such as GANs and VAEs. We discuss how these techniques can be applied to improve authentication protocols, encryption, and user access rights, ensuring secure interactions in digital environments. The chapter provides a comprehensive overview of how generative AI can transform UI design to address future security challenges.

Chapter 11: Reshaping Cybersecurity Practices by Optimizing Web Application Penetration Testing

Web application penetration testing is vital for identifying and addressing security vulnerabilities. This chapter highlights the importance of thorough penetration testing procedures and their role in enhancing web application security. We review statistical data on common attack vectors and provide detailed methodologies for conducting effective penetration tests. The chapter also offers recommendations for organizations to strengthen their web security practices and prevent unauthorized access.

Chapter 12: Ethics and Transparency in Secure Web Model Generation

Ethics and transparency are crucial in the development of AI-driven secure web models. This chapter explores the ethical considerations and transparency issues related to AI in web development. We discuss fundamental ethical principles such as fairness, accountability, and privacy, and examine the challenges of bias and fairness within web models. The chapter also addresses privacy protection and regulatory compliance, emphasizing the importance of transparency and explainability in building trust and accountability in secure web model generation.

Chapter 13: Future Trends and Trials in Cybersecurity and Generative AI

The evolving landscape of cybersecurity and generative AI presents both opportunities and risks. This chapter examines emerging trends and potential challenges, including the impact of AI-driven strategies like adversarial machine learning and deepfake methods. We explore how generative AI technologies, such as deep learning and GANs, contribute to issues of digital trust and authenticity. The chapter concludes with strategies for leveraging AI's potential while mitigating its risks, focusing on anomaly detection and AI-powered threat intelligence.

Chapter 14: Future Trends and Challenges in Cybersecurity and Generative AI

The final chapter offers an in-depth analysis of future trends and challenges at the intersection of cybersecurity and generative AI. We focus on the dynamic nature of cybersecurity threats driven by advancements in AI and the Internet of Things (IoT). The chapter highlights emerging threats, such as ransomware-as-a-service, and discusses the need for advanced security measures to address these evolving challenges. By examining the interplay between generative AI innovations and cybersecurity practices, we provide insights into navigating the future landscape of cyber threats and defenses.

As we reach the conclusion of *Reshaping CyberSecurity With Generative AI Techniques*, we stand at a pivotal moment in the evolution of cybersecurity. The journey through this book reveals a landscape transformed by the convergence of generative AI and advanced security practices. Traditional methods, while foundational, often fall short in the face of rapidly evolving threats. Generative AI, with its ability to create and adapt, offers a new paradigm for tackling these challenges.

Our exploration began with a broad overview of generative AI techniques, laying the groundwork for understanding how these technologies—such as Generative Adversarial Networks (GANs) and Variational Autoencoders (VAEs)—can be harnessed to enhance cybersecurity. We delved into how Reinforcement Learning (RL) can adapt defenses to shifting threats, and examined the role of these technologies in network security, intrusion detection, and securing distributed systems.

We also highlighted the specific challenges faced in different contexts, from the vulnerability of Wireless Sensor Networks (WSNs) to the intricate demands of 6G network security and management. Each chapter provided not only theoretical insights but also practical applications and case studies that showcase the transformative potential of generative AI across various domains.

Our discussion extended to the integration of blockchain with generative AI, illustrating how these technologies can secure distributed systems and enhance data integrity. We explored how generative AI techniques can be applied to the burgeoning field of Internet of Things (IoT) security, and how these methods can address programming challenges and optimize web application penetration testing.

Furthermore, ethical considerations and transparency emerged as crucial themes, especially in the context of AI-driven secure web model generation. We addressed the need for fairness, accountability, and privacy, emphasizing the importance of transparent practices in building trust and ensuring effective security measures.

Looking to the future, we confronted the emerging trends and trials at the intersection of cybersecurity and generative AI. As the digital landscape continues to evolve, so too must our strategies and defenses. The potential of AI to drive both innovation and risk underscores the need for proactive, informed approaches to cybersecurity.

In closing, this book aims to empower readers with the knowledge and tools to navigate the rapidly changing world of cybersecurity. Whether you are a cybersecurity professional, researcher, or enthusiast, we hope that the insights provided here inspire and guide you as you contribute to a more secure digital future. The integration of generative AI into cybersecurity practices represents not just an enhancement of existing methods, but a significant leap forward in safeguarding our digital world against ever-more sophisticated threats.

Welcome to the forefront of cybersecurity innovation—reshaped and fortified by the power of generative AI.

Noor Zaman Jhanjhi
School of Computing Science, Taylor's University, Malaysia

Chapter 1
Overview of Generative AI Techniques for Cybersecurity

Siva Raja Sindiramutty
https://orcid.org/0009-0006-0310-8721
Taylor's University, Malaysia

Krishna Raj V. Prabagaran
Universiti Malaysia Sarawak, Malaysia

Rehan Akbar
https://orcid.org/0000-0002-3703-5974
Florida International University, USA

Manzoor Hussain
Indus University, Pakistan

Nazir Ahmed Malik
https://orcid.org/0000-0002-0118-4601
Bahria University, Islamabad, Pakistan

ABSTRACT

Generative AI techniques have been popular since they can generate data or content that could be hardly distinguished from genuine ones. This chapter comprehensively reviews generative AI for cybersecurity and its definition, history, and applications in different fields. It covers basic ideas such as generative models, probability distributions, and latent spaces. Also, it goes into more detail on some of the more popular approaches like GANs, VAEs, and the combination of RL. The chapter explores the structure and training processes of GANs and VAEs and demonstrates

DOI: 10.4018/979-8-3693-5415-5.ch001

their application in tasks such as image synthesis, data enhancement, and novelty detection. Also, it explores the interaction between RL and generative models and the challenges, including the exploration-exploitation trade-off. The chapter focuses on the development of generative AI with the help of DL and analyses the benefits of deep generative models and their usage in various fields. Evaluation measures and the problems with measuring generative models are discussed, focusing on the methods of improving the measurement accuracy. Finally, the chapter focuses on new directions, like transformer-based models and self-supervised learning, to look at the future of generative AI. The emphasis is made on understanding these techniques due to their versatility, and some ideas about the possible further developments of the findings for other fields and future studies and applications are provided.

INTRODUCTION TO GENERATIVE AI

Definition of Generative AI

Generative AI stands out as a form of intelligence setting itself apart from conventional approaches that focus on analyzing data to draw conclusions and make decisions. Unlike its counterparts generative AI is geared towards creating content, like text, images or music. These sophisticated algorithms are crafted to recognize patterns and characteristics within a dataset and generate data resembling it. Operating at a level of Machine Learning (ML) techniques such as learning generative AI excels at approximating probabilistic distributions to yield remarkably lifelike outcomes. Its ability to spark creativity and produce works across domains has garnered significant attention and acclaim. Generative AI models function by learning from datasets to grasp the structure and features of the information. Effectively trained these models can generate samples that rival the quality of the original dataset. Among the employed techniques in AI is GANs as described by Dash et al. (2023). GANs comprise two networks. The generator and the discriminator. That train harmoniously in tandem. While the generator focuses on creating data samples the discriminator strives to differentiate between generated data driving a continuous enhancement, in the quality of generated outputs. In AI there is another known technique called VAEs, which was introduced by Ye and Borş in 2023. VAEs can create a representation of the input data and produce samples using this hidden space. These models are commonly applied in tasks like generating images or detecting anomalies. The components of AI can be seen in Figure 1 provided below.

Figure 1. Elements in Hybrid Generative AI

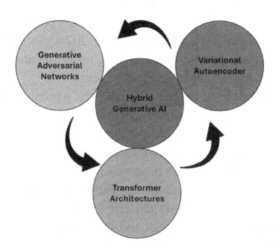

Moreover, transformer based models such, as the GPT series developed by Ope-nAI as discussed in Cao et al. (2023) demonstrate abilities in creating contextually relevant text. By utilizing self-attention mechanisms these models effectively capture long distance connections in input data allowing them to produce high quality text for a range of tasks like language translation, summarization and dialog generation. Apart from these established methods, ongoing research and advancements, in AI field are exploring new architectures and training approaches to enhance the quality and variety of generated content. In general generative AI holds promise across applications from promoting creative content creation to supporting data augmentation and generating data for training machine learning models.

Importance of Generative AI in Various Domains

Generative AI plays a role, in fields by creating fresh and authentic content. It is particularly valuable in art, entertainment, healthcare and cybersecurity. In the realm of art and entertainment generative AI aids in producing captivating content spanning images, music and written pieces. Artists and musicians can leverage AI techniques to explore realms of creativity that enhance their artistic endeavors. A notable example is Googles DeepDream application, which utilizes AI to transform images into remarkable pieces of art. Within healthcare generative AI is instrumental in diagnostics and image analysis for imaging, drug design and the evolving concept of medicine. Generative models prove beneficial in generating medical images for training diagnostic algorithms to address data scarcity issues while maintaining privacy standards (Paladugu et al., 2023; Krishnan et al., 2021). Moreover, these algorithms expedite drug discovery by crafting structures with desired characteristics that propel the drug development process forward. In the field of cybersecurity generative AI contributes to producing phishing emails. Malware samples for training defense systems (Shibli et al., 2024). Such simulations bolster an organizations security posture by mimicking cyber threats thus enhancing its overall preparedness, against potential cyber attacks.

Furthermore generative AI is revolutionizing the gaming industry by creating worlds and intelligent non player characters (NPCs) (Filipović, 2023; Sindiramutty et al., 2023). Game developers leverage AI algorithms to craft environments, character traits and storylines that elevate the gaming experience, for players. Additionally within the realm of natural language processing (NLP) generative AI models like GPT play a role in language translation, text generation and interactive agents (Tan et al., 2023). These advanced models generate text that mirrors human language, facilitate translation between languages and power chatbots and voice activated assistants. Through its applications, across sectors generative AI empowers businesses and organizations to explore new opportunities boost efficiency and provide enhanced user interactions.

Historical Overview and Evolution of Generative AI Techniques

Generative AI techniques have made progress, over time thanks to advancements in machine learning algorithms, computing power and the availability of amounts of data. This evolution showcases how generative AI has evolved from models to deep learning architectures. The early days of modeling can be traced back to the 1950s and 1960s when pioneers began using models like Markov chains and Hidden Markov Models (HMMs) to generate sequences such as text and speech. These initial efforts laid the foundation for developments in AI. The later years of the 1980s and 1990s brought about models like Restricted Boltzmann Machines and Variational Autoencoders (VAE). RBMs, introduced by Smolensky in 1986 allowed for data representation learning and sample generation. Meanwhile VAEs, proposed by Kingma and Welling in 2013 offered a modeling approach that enabled the creation of high quality samples. A significant milestone in AI history was marked by the introduction of Generative Adversarial Networks (GANs), by Karapantelakis et al. (2023).

GANs have transformed the field by presenting modeling as a competition involving two networks; a generator and a discriminator. The generator produces output while the discriminator distinguishes between fake samples (Gaur et al., 2023; Sindiramutty et al. et al., 2023). Through training GANs have learned to produce quality and more diverse outputs than previous techniques (Maqsood et al., 2022; Azam et al., 2023). Recently deep learning architectures, like recurrent networks have played a significant role in enhancing generative AI. Models such as Convolutional GANs (DCGANs) for generating images and recurrent GANs (RNN GANs) for sequences have been developed (Deep & Verma, 2023). Transformer based models like OpenAI's GPT series have showcased capabilities in generating text that's syntactically and semantically coherent.

Generative AI methods find applications in fields including computer vision, natural language processing, healthcare, robotics among others (Ali et al., 2024). These models are utilized for tasks such, as image generation, text generation, drug discovery, data augmentation which have expedited advancements in both research and industry sectors. The field of AI is set to progress as researchers work on enhancing the quality, diversity and comprehensibility of the generated content. Anticipate methods, in architecture, training and utilization of AI to spark increased innovation and adoption moving forward.

Chapter Contributions: Enlist 5 to 6 Key Points

Foundational Understanding

This chapter will try to provide a broad understanding of generative AI and its foundations: generative models, probability distributions, and latent spaces.

Technique Deep Dive

It provides a detailed look at the most widely used generative AI approaches, such as GANs, VAEs, and the incorporation of RL. Readers receive information on the architecture of these techniques, training methods, and real-life uses.

Applications Across Domains

The application of generative AI is diverse, encompassing numerous fields such as image generation, data augmentation, dimensionality reduction, anomaly detection, natural language processing, and gameplay. By providing examples, readers realise what generative AI means and how it can be applied in different spheres.

Evaluation and Challenges

Focusing on the pivotal issue of model assessment, the chapter describes the vocabulary of standard measures and issues such as mode collapse, sample quality, and diversity. Approaches for increasing the accuracy of evaluations are currently being discussed to use generative AI methods optimally.

DL Advancements

The chapter focuses on the centrality of DL in the advancement of generative AI. This paper focuses on the differentiation between shallow and deep generative models and their strengths and weaknesses. Other works explore the state-of-the-art deep generative models and review their impact on different fields.

Future Directions

Concluding with a forward-looking perspective, the chapter delves into emerging techniques like transformer-based models, self-supervised learning, and meta-learning. It outlines the potential applications and implications of these advancements, encouraging readers to remain informed about the evolving landscape of generative AI for innovative research and practical implementations.

Chapter Organization

In this chapter, we set off on a tour of generative AI, starting with Section 2, which covers probability distributions, latent space, and model architecture. Section three explores GANs with a focus on the functions of the generator and discriminator networks as well as the uses of GANs. Section 4 explains the VAEs and how they can learn the latent representations and decode the information—section 5 combines Reinforcement Learning (RL) with generative models and explains its pros, cons, and uses. Section 6 delves, into AI specifically exploring Deep Learning (DL) methodologies and examining models and their impacts. Moving on to Section 7 the focus shifts to assessment metrics and hurdles while Section 8 delves into endeavors like transformer based models and self supervised learning. Finally Section 9 wraps up the section, by summarizing discoveries and underlining the significance of AI across diverse domains to bolster future studies and practical implementations.

GENERATIVE MODELS: FOUNDATIONS AND PRINCIPLES

Explanation of Generative Models

Generative models belong to a category of machine learning techniques that focus on grasping the distribution of existing data and the capacity to generate data instances. They cover a range of fields, like creating images generating text and developing drugs. These models identify the patterns and structures within the training dataset allowing them to produce samples that closely resemble the dataset. One prominent example of models is GAN, introduced by Srivastava and Kumar in 2024. GANs consist of two networks. The generator and the discriminator. Engaged in a competitive dynamic akin, to a game. In this case, the generator creates fake samples while the discriminator learns to distinguish between real and fake ones. This adversarial relationship enables the generation of high-quality synthetic data by GANs. VAEs, introduced by Kingma and Welling in 2013, are another important class of generative models (Hu, 2023; Azam, Tan, et al., 2023). VAEs learn a probabilistic encoding of the input data and generate new samples by drawing from the encoded latent space. They combine principles from autoencoders and variational inference to effectively learn the data-generating distribution. Another class of generative models is autoregressive models that have also received attention, some of which are PixelCNN and WaveNet (Zhang et al., 2023; Azam, Tajwar, et al., 2023). Given the previous samples, these models build data gradually and are useful when creating large data sets such as images and audio. It is evident from Figure 2 that Generative AI is important.

Figure 2. Importance of Generative AI

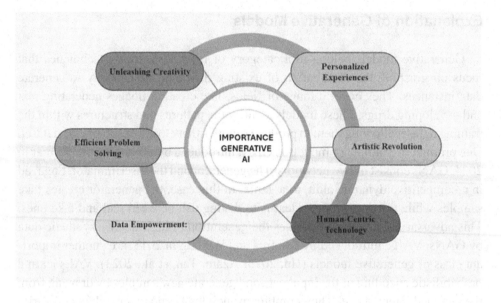

Furthermore, flow-based models have appeared as one of the potential directions within generative modelling. Some models, Real NVP and Glow, developed by Del Debbio et al. (2021), use an invertible transformation between the data and latent space, allowing efficient sampling and density estimation. Generative models are uniquely positioned in the spectrum of applications of DL across different areas, ranging from image synthesis to the discovery of new chemical compounds. By analysing the generative model's initial data distribution, they can generate new and valuable samples for research in ML and AI, making them essential tools.

Key Concepts Such as Probability Distributions, Latent Space, and Sampling

Probability Distributions: Understanding and modelling the data distribution is critical in generative modelling. Probability distribution defines the chance of different occurrences or events (Ermagun et al., 2024; Ananna et al., 2023). Generative models attempt to learn the probability distribution of data to create new samples as close as possible to the training data set. Different generative models assume different forms of this distribution and use different approaches to estimate or sample from it.

Latent Space: It is noteworthy to mention that latent space is related to a lower-dimensional space that contains all the details of complex data. In generative models such as VAEs, the model learns a representation of input data (Ye & Borş, 2024).

This latent space consists of considerable features or attributes of the data in a condensed manner. The model can generate new data by sampling from this space, thus allowing it to spawn new data. The latent space representations allow the data manifold to be stored, transformed, interpolated, and generally navigated easily.

Sampling: Sampling involves the creation of new data points from a learned probability distribution function. In generative models, it is possible to release the model to generate new data instances that resemble the training data by sampling from the acquired distribution. The choice of the sampling methodologies may also depend on the specific generative model that is used. For instance, in GANs, sampling entails creating fake samples from the generator network (Byeon et al., 2024). However, in models such as PixelCNN that follow an autoregressive architecture, sampling is done successively, where a data point is produced based on the previous ones (Courville, 2024). Sampling is one of the fundamental processes in generative modelling and is irreplaceable when generating a range of realistic samples.

Probability distributions, latent space, and sampling are core ideas in generative modelling. These concepts help generate realistic and diverse synthetic data by capturing the distribution of data, learning useful representations in the latent space, and generating new data samples through sampling. These concepts are the foundation of various generative models and approaches widely used in tasks like image generation, text generation, and synthetic data generation. The generative model is introduced in Figure 3.

Figure 3. Introduction to Generative Models

Generative Models	Components of Generative Model	Types of Generative Models	Variational Autoencoders (VAEs):
• Generative models are a class of machine learning models designed to learn and mimic the underlying distribution of a given dataset	• Generative models typically consist of two main components: a generator and a discriminator.	• Autoregressive models • Variational autoencoders (VAEs) • Generative adversarial networks (GANs) • Flow-based model	• VAEs are generative models that learn a low-dimensional latent space representation of the input data.
Generative Adversarial Networks (GANs):	**Autoregressive Models**	**Flow-Based Models**	**Evaluation Metrics for Generative Models**
• Generative models that learn to generate data by playing a minimax game between the generator and the discriminator..	• Generative models that model the conditional probability distribution of each variable in a sequence given previous variables.	• Flow-based models are generative models that learn a bijective mapping between a latent space and the data space	• Inception Score • Frechet Inception Distance (FID) • Precision and Recall • Perceptual Metrics • Likelihood-based Metrics

Types of Generative Models: Explicit vs. Implicit, Autoregressive Models, Flow-Based Models, etc.

Generative models belong to the class of ML algorithms, which are expected to synthesise data similar to the actual examples. These models can be broadly classified into two categories: both direct and indirect. Generative models that operate explicitly, like VAEs, estimate the probability distribution of data. They carefully identify the hidden data distribution and produce new samples based on the acquired distribution (C. Hu et al., 2024). On the other hand, implicit generative models such as GAN are excellent in sampling from the data distribution without necessarily defining the distribution. Instead, they sharpened their skills in constructing samples by making a generator network to generate data that looks like true samples to a discriminator network.

Autoregressive models are the other category of generative modelling where the conditional probability of each data element is modelled based on the previous data elements. PixelRNN and PixelCNN are some of the most notable examples that paint images with detail, pixel by pixel, by predicting the distribution of the pixel in question concerning the previously generated pixels (Sampath et al., 2021). In contrast, flow-based models change a simple distribution, such as Gaussian, for a complex distribution that resembles the actual data distribution through a series of reversible transformations. RealNVP and Glow are two of the flow-based models that are widely known for their ability to produce high-quality images (Zhou et al., 2024).

Thus, every generative model has strengths and weaknesses based on the given task and data set. For example, autoregressive models are great in sequence and image generation with the presence of identifiable spatial relations, but their sample generation can be slow because of their sequential nature. Some implicit generative models, such as GANs, possess high sample generation rates. However sometimes the model may experience an issue known as mode collapse, where the generator gets stuck on producing a set of examples (Shi et al., 2022). Flow based models are valued for their ability to accurately estimate likelihood and invertibility. Nonetheless they can be time consuming, during both training and sampling processes particularly when dealing with data (Papamakarios et al., 2019). Generative modeling encompasses a range of methods each with its strengths and weaknesses. It is crucial to understand the characteristics of different generative models in order to choose the most suitable approach, for a specific task.

GENERATIVE ADVERSARIAL NETWORKS (GANS)

Explanation of the GAN Architecture

GANs represent an advancement, in the field of intelligence. They comprise two networks. The generator and the discriminator. Engaged in a learning battle (Hardy et al., 2019). The primary goal of GANs is to produce data samples, such as images or text that closely resemble data. This innovative architecture has gained recognition for its ability to generate looking data across a range of domains. The generator network is responsible for creating data samples from input noise. It accomplishes this by transforming input noise vectors through a mapping process. While the initial samples generated may not be of quality successive iterations enhance the generators capacity to produce high quality data. Conversely the discriminator network distinguishes between fake data produced by the generator network. It can differentiate samples from those generated artificially during training sessions. Throughout training the discriminator hones its ability to discern between fabricated data. At the heart of GANs lies the competition, between these two networks. Generator and discriminator (Cai et al., 2021). During training the generator strives to create samples that deceive the discriminator into perceiving them as real while the discriminators primary objective is to classify samples.

The competitive dynamic, between these two networks drives a cycle of performance enhancement. In this process the generator hones its ability to generate data while the discriminator improves its skill in distinguishing from fake samples. One common challenge in training GANs is finding the balance between the generator and discriminator networks (Jabbar et al. 2021). When the networks are not balanced it can result in training issues or the generator producing samples. Researchers have suggested approaches to address this problem, such, as modifying network structures using regularization methods and refining training techniques (Chakraborty et al., 2024; Azam et al., 2023). GANs comprise a system where interconnected generator and discriminator networks learn together. With enhancements GANs can create data samples across domains proving useful for tasks like image creation, data expansion and generating data, for machine learning model training. An overview of GAN technology is presented in Figure 4.

Figure 4. Introduction to Generative Adversarial Network

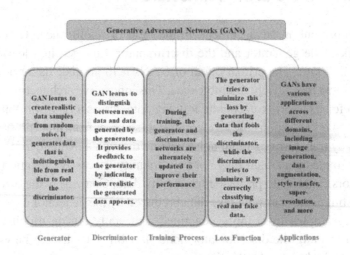

Role of Generator and Discriminator Networks

In the world of GANs introduced by Goodfellow and his team in 2014 there are two players; the generator and discriminator networks. GANs involve these two networks interacting dynamically. The generators job is to create data samples that resemble a distribution while the discriminators role is to distinguish between fake data. This competitive setup encourages refinement. The generation of data, within a domain. During training the generator learns to recognize patterns and structures in noise generated data samples (Wang et al., 2018). As time passes the generator improves its ability to create samples that can deceive the discriminator effectively.

On the hand the discriminator network is trained to differentiate between samples using a dataset that includes both real and generated examples. This process sharpens its capability to identify differences and offers feedback to enhance the performance of generators. The interaction between these two networks resembles a game; where the generator strives to outsmart the discriminator while the latter aims to avoid misclassifications (Chivukula, 2020). This tug of war leads to enhancement until a balance is reached, ideally resulting in generated samples that're indistinguishable from ones. A variety of applications make use of generator and discriminator networks across fields such, as image creation, text generation and drug discovery (Shamsolmoali et al., 2021).

In the field of image creation GANs are utilized to generate images and artistic renditions as to improve image clarity as highlighted by T. Wang in 2018. Similarly GANs exhibit promise in crafting semantically sound text passages, within text creation processes (Meena et al., 2023). These networks play roles in GAN operations by working in opposition to produce samples that mirror the distribution of real data; their applications are varied.

Training Process and Adversarial Training

GANs are trained through a collaboration, between the generator and discriminator networks which involves training. This technique, introduced by X. Cao and colleagues in 2023 sets up a competition, between the two networks to enhance their performance iteratively. In the training phase the generator network produces data samples based on noise inputs. These generated samples are then assessed by the discriminator. Initially both the generator and discriminator networks start with initialization. However as training progresses the discriminator improves its ability to differentiate between fake samples. Simultaneously the generator aims to produce samples that closely resemble data. This dynamic creates a feedback loop where the discriminator helps refine the synthesis process of the generator while also benefiting from this improvement.

The training of GANs involves a minimax game where the generator aims to maximise the probability of fooling the discriminator. At the same time, the discriminator aims at minimising the probability of misclassifying samples (Han et al., 2024). This adversarial relationship drives both networks towards improvement until a steady state is reached, which should ideally be the creation of data samples that are very hard to distinguish from real ones. Adversarial training allows GANs to learn complex data distributions without the need to model them probabilistically (Mangla et al., 2022). However, the GANs acquire knowledge about the underlying structure of the data through the generator and discriminator's competition process. However, adversarial training can be problematic regarding mode collapse and instability. Mode dropout occurs when the generator is obsessed with generating a small set of samples other than other modes in the data distribution. Researchers have devised various techniques to mitigate these challenges, including architectural adjustments, regularisation strategies, and more stable training methodologies. Adversarial training constitutes a fundamental facet of the GAN training process, fostering an iterative exchange between the generator and discriminator networks, ultimately producing high-fidelity synthetic data samples.

Applications of GANs in Image Generation, Data Augmentation, and More

GANs have had an impact, in fields, such as generating images and improving datasets. Lets explore some of the ways GANs are utilized in these domains;

GANs have transformed the landscape of image creation by producing a range of visuals. StyleGAN has been really important, in creating faces while BigGAN is great at generating high quality images across categories like animals, objects and landscapes. These Generative Adversarial Networks (GANs) are super useful for diversifying training data by generating samples that closely resemble data. This helps improve the performance and adaptability of machine learning models. GANs can also create images with features and characteristics to improve models in medical imaging. One cool thing about GANs is their ability to transform images from one category to another like turning input images into styles or artistic interpretations using techniques such as CycleGAN. Another handy tool in this area is Pix2Pix, which is commonly used for converting sketches into images and generating satellite imagery from maps.

When it comes to improving image quality GANs use techniques like resolution enhancement to turn low resolution images into high resolution ones with sharpness and detail through learned transformations. There have been advancements in this field with models like SRGAN (Demiray et al., 2021) and ESRGAN (Yu et al. 2022) showing improvements over interpolation methods. In terms of video synthesis GANs have progressed to the point where they can generate videos frame by frame. Specialized models such, as VideoGAN (Aldausari, 2022) are designed specifically for creating videos with motion and dynamic scenes. New advancements, in technology have opened doors for use in video production, animation and editing. In essence GANs have contributed to progress in image editing, data improvement and similar activities by providing the ability to generate, enhance and alter content, across domains.

VARIATIONAL AUTOENCODERS (VAES)

Introduction to Autoencoders and Their Limitations

Autoencoders are networks used to reconstruct input data through an encoding decoding process. They consist of an encoder and a decoder that compress the input data into a representation aiming to reproduce the input. Autoencoders are applied in tasks such, as image enhancement, dimension reduction and anomaly detection by extracting data features (J. Wang et al., 2023).. However they face challenges related to limitations in the hidden space size that can restrict the complexity and richness of representations (Jaiswal et al. 2023).. Another issue is effectively capturing data distributions when dealing with structures or dependencies in the input data. The performance of autoencoders heavily depends on selecting hyperparameters designing architecture and utilizing high quality training data efficiently(Bengio, 2012; Wen et al., 2023).. An important concern is their susceptibility to overfitting during training on datasets, where the model unintentionally captures patterns or noise from the training data affecting performance, on data. Furthermore autoencoders may struggle in capturing features within the data for representation (Zhao et al., 2024).

Essentially when it comes to using autoencoders, for learning tasks it's important for both researchers and practitioners to recognize and address their limitations (J. Zhou, 2023; Sindiramutty, Jhanjhi, Tan, Khan, Gharib, & Yun, 2023).. These limitations include issues like fixed space sizes, complexities in modeling data distributions sensitivity to hyperparameters and design choices susceptibility to overfitting and the difficulties, in obtaining representations. Overcoming these challenges requires research efforts focused on enhancing the architecture and training methods of autoencoders to boost their robustness and flexibility.

Explanation of VAE Architecture

VAEs, also known as a network framework, in machine learning play a role in generating data points that resemble those present in a dataset. This framework comprises two components: the encoder and the decoder. The encoder processes input data to transform it into a space where each point serves as an input encoding. In contrast the decoder reconstructs the input data based on these points within the space (Bhalodia, 2020; Sindiramutty et al., 2023). By adopting this method VAEs can grasp the distribution of input data, within the space enabling them to generate data points through sampling from this distribution. In VAE applications both the encoder and decoder are constructed using networks. The encoder network receives input data. Gradually reduces its dimensionality by passing through layers of neurons until it reaches the designated space. On the hand the decoder network reconstructs the input by traversing layers of neurons that progressively increase dimensionality based on points (Lei et al., 2020; Sindiramutty et al., 2024). These networks undergo training utilizing a loss function that evaluates how well the data aligns with the provided input. Figure 5 provides an overview of autoencoders.

Figure 5. Introduction to VAE

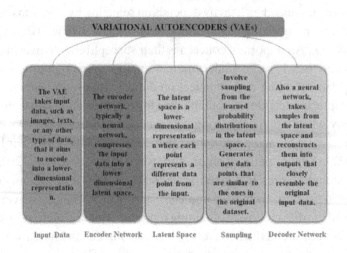

Variational Autoencoders (VAEs) rely on inference to comprehend components enabling them to grasp the probability distribution parameters that mirror the data distribution in the space. This process involves maximizing a constraint known as Evidence Lower Bound (ELBO) which focuses on the log likelihood of the data. Optimizing ELBO, in VAEs helps capture features in the space while maintaining control over the distribution to prevent overfitting issues (Alemi, 2018; Sindiramutty, Tan et al. 2024). Despite their effectiveness VAEs encounter challenges, in representing data distributions in spaces and generating high quality samples when trained on diverse datasets. Addressing these limitations necessitates research efforts dedicated to enhancing VAE structures and training methods. VAEs serve as tools for learning tasks that align with a given dataset by utilizing encoder and decoder networks for inference purposes. While VAEs are successful they face hurdles in representing data distributions and producing top tier samples underscoring the need for research and advancements, in this area.

Learning Latent Representations and Decoding Process

In the field of machine learning autoencoders have roles in capturing data representations and performing decoding tasks. The process begins with the encoder, which converts input data into a condensed form called the space. This space captures features of the input data in a format. During training the encoder network aims to map input data to this space to preserve information while minimizing loss

(Akçay et al., 2019). After encoding the input data into the space the decoder takes over. Working alongside the encoder the decoder network retrieves points from this space. Strives to reconstruct the input data. Through layers of neurons the decoder progressively refines representations from this space with a goal of replicating the input data as possible. Both encoder and decoder networks undergo training to reduce differences, between input data and reconstructed output (Quan et al., 2018; Sindiramutty, Tee et al. 2024). Learning latent representations and decoding is steered by optimization algorithms like stochastic descent (SGD). Throughout training continual adjustments are made to parameters of both encoder and decoder networks in order to minimize a loss function.

Typically this loss function assesses discrepancies, between input data and its reconstruction, motivating networks to grasp representations that facilitate decoding. However a significant challenge, in learning latent representations and decoding is striking a balance between compression and accuracy during reconstruction. This entails discovering a representation that retains information while filtering out details within the space. Additionally factors like the choice of architecture, network depth and hyperparameters contribute to determining the quality of obtained representations and the accuracy of decoding (Du et al., 2022; Sindiramutty et al., 2024). Essentially acquiring representations and decoding processes are components of designs. While the encoder compresses input data into a concise latent space by capturing features the decoders goal is to reconstruct data based on this representation. Through optimization both the encoder and decoder networks learn to data for various applications such, as data compression, denoising and generative modeling.

Applications of VAEs in Image Generation, Dimensionality Reduction, and Anomaly Detection

The usage of Variational Autoencoders (VAEs) has seen a rise, in the creation of images. By grasping the data distribution during training VAEs have the capability to produce samples that mirror the data. This functionality holds significance in fields such as computer graphics where image creation plays a role. VAEs facilitate the development of top notch images proving beneficial for tasks like image completion, style alteration and content generation (J. Wang, 2023).

Another notable application of VAEs lies in dimensionality reduction. By condensing data into a lower dimensional latent space VAEs simplify the representation and visualization of complex datasets. This reduction in dimensionality not aids in visualization. Also enhances the efficiency of tasks such as classification and clustering. Through capturing attributes while eliminating noise and unnecessary details VAEs learn representations of input data (Detlefsen et al., 2022). VAEs have displayed promise in detecting anomalies. By familiarizing themselves with the input data distribution they can accurately pinpoint outliers or anomalies that significantly deviate from the established distribution. Anomalies are typically identified based on their probability, within the learned distribution space. VAEs, which are recognized for their capability to spot irregularities, in sectors such as finance, manufacturing and cybersecurity contribute to uncovering fraud and identifying faults (Ruff et al., 2021). Apart from their effectiveness in producing images and simplifying data dimensions VAEs stand out in anomaly detection by forming compact data representations in a space. With progress in this field VAEs are anticipated to have a range of important applications, across various industries.

REINFORCEMENT LEARNING IN GENERATIVE MODELS

Overview of RL

Reinforcement Learning (RL) is subset of Machine Learning, where an agent learns to make decisions by engaging with its environment to reach a goal or maximize rewards. It functions similar, to a trial and error method, where the agent gains insights from its experiences through feedback whether negative rewards (Varghese & Mahmoud, 2020; Sindiramutty, 2023). RL has garnered attention due to its ranging applications in areas such as robotics, gaming, finance and healthcare. In RL the agent learns by interacting with an environment and observing the outcomes healthcare (Zafar et al., 2023; Kok et al., 2022). The objective is to establish a strategy. A roadmap from state to action. That maximizes rewards over time. This process comprises three components; the agent itself the environment it operates in and the rewards it earns. The agent hones its decision making skills by engaging with the environment through actions and adjusting its tactics based on feedback (rewards). This learning journey enables the agent to uncover strategies by balancing between exploration and exploitation. A pivotal algorithm, in RL is Q learning, introduced by Jin in 2018. Q learning trains an action value function that anticipates the reward expected from taking action in a state.

The policy gradient technique is a method that focuses on teaching the policy by adjusting its parameters to maximize expected rewards. Sutton and Bartoss book, "RL; An Introduction" explores RL algorithms making it a valuable resource, for grasping RL principles. Deep reinforcement learning (DRL) merges RL with learning methods to manage state and action spaces (Gupta et al., 2021; Verma et al., 2021).

Zhang Wang introduced a technique known as Deep Q Networks (DQN) that utilizes networks to estimate the effectiveness of actions, for achieving success in mastering Atari games. In a vein the Deep Deterministic Policy Gradient (DDPG) algorithm expands on the policy gradient approach for action spaces enabling applications in robotics and autonomous systems. Despite its promise reinforcement learning (RL) encounters obstacles such as sampling challenges dilemmas in exploration versus exploitation and issues with training stability in RL models. Current research endeavors are dedicated to overcoming these hurdles and advancing RL methodologies. The interdisciplinary aspects of RL draw insights from disciplines like neuroscience, psychology and control theory underscoring its significance in system development. RL offers a framework for guiding agents to make decisions within environments. Through its applications and ongoing research efforts RL holds the potential to drive changes, across industries.

Integration of RL With Generative Models

Reinforcement learning (RL) and generative models have proven to be valuable, in fields such as robotics, gaming and natural language processing (Luketina et al., 2019; Fatima et al., 2019). Recent studies have focused on combining these approaches to capitalize on their strengths and develop systems that excel in tasks like manipulation thereby enhancing robots efficiency in real world scenarios. By merging RL with models researchers have achieved improvements in performance such as training robots to manipulate objects with agility and precision (Tanwani, 2018).. This integration enables robots to generate training data for RL algorithms without the need for data collection efforts. In the realm of natural language processing the integration of RL with models has led to advancements. Scientists have devised models that utilize reinforcement learning to improve text generation by incorporating user feedback ultimately enhancing the quality and relevance of the generated content. Through this incorporation of reinforcement learning, into these models they are able to refine their outputs based on user interactions resulting in responses (Keneshloo et al., 2019; Hussain et al., 2019).. Researchers have also delved into utilizing reinforcement learning alongside models, for generating and modifying images. Methods like training, through reinforcement learning have been used to guide models in creating images with characteristics (M & Jayagopal 2020).

This strategy allows for the creation of images that fulfill defined criteria by leveraging input from the reinforcement learning agent. In general the integration of reinforcement learning with models shows promise across domains such as robotics, natural language processing and image generation. Through the fusion of these approaches researchers can create systems of adapting through interactions, with users or their surroundings driving progress in AI technology. Figure 6 demonstrates the application of reinforcement learning to the model.

Figure 6. RL for Generative Model

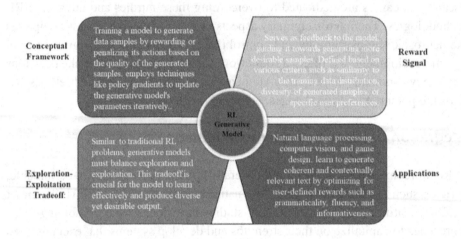

Conceptual Framework — Training a model to generate data samples by rewarding or penalizing its actions based on the quality of the generated samples, employs techniques like policy gradients to update the generative model's parameters iteratively.

Reward Signal — Serves as feedback to the model, guiding it towards generating more desirable samples. Defined based on various criteria such as similarity to the training data distribution, diversity of generated samples, or specific user preferences.

RL Generative Model

Exploration-Exploitation Tradeoff — Similar to traditional RL problems, generative models must balance exploration and exploitation. This tradeoff is crucial for the model to learn effectively and produce diverse yet desirable output.

Applications — Natural language processing, computer vision, and game design, learn to generate coherent and contextually relevant text by optimizing for user-defined rewards such as grammaticality, fluency, and informativeness

Exploration-Exploitation Tradeoff in RL-Based Generative Models

In the field of reinforcement learning (RL) finding a balance, between using known strategies to maximize rewards and trying out actions is crucial. This dilemma also arises in RL models, where agents have to decide whether to stick with paths (exploitation) or explore areas to enhance the diversity and quality of samples (exploration). To tackle this challenge methods like epsilon policies and Thompson sampling can be employed to promote both exploration and exploitation. These techniques can be tailored in RL models to generate samples while maintaining consistency with the training data distribution. For instance researchers have suggested incorporating an exploration bonus term into Variational Autoencoders (VAEs) to stimulate sample generation. Another method involves integrating uncertainty estimation into the model allowing it to determine when to explore data regions or exploit existing ones based on uncertainty levels (Bai et al., 2023; Adeyemo et al., 2019).Bayesian generative models are skilled, at handling prediction uncertainty assisting in decision making during exploration phases. Moreover learning techniques facilitate adjusting the exploration strategy based on experiences(Cassenti & Kaplan 2021; Sankar et al., 2020)..

These techniques allow for adjusting the balance between exploring possibilities and utilizing ones based on the specific task or setting thus improving the effectiveness of learning in generative models that use reinforcement learning (as discussed by YuChao et al., 2021; Almusaylim et al., 2020). It is crucial to address the exploration exploitation dilemma to maintain a harmony, between sample variety and richness. By incorporating exploration strategies assessing uncertainty and applying learning approaches researchers can develop models that produce high quality outputs across different tasks and domains.

Applications of RL in Generating Sequences, Game Playing, and More

Reinforcement Learning (RL) is often used in creating sequences for tasks, like Natural Language Processing (NLP) such as generating text, translating languages and improving dialogue systems. Techniques such as Recurrent Neural Networks (RNNs) and Transformers are trained using RL algorithms to generate text sequences. For instance RL boosts the precision of machine translation by encouraging the model to produce translations (Chen et al., 2024). Similarly RL driven models in music composition help create melodies or harmonies that meet constraints or preferences (Sturm et al., 2018).

The progress made in gaming advancements due, to Reinforcement Learning is apparent in instances such as AlphaGo and AlphaZero. These models make use of RL techniques and deep reinforcement learning (DRL) to excel in strategies through gameplay whether it's against themselves or human players (Gonzalez, 2021). For example DeepMinds AlphaGo achieved victories over world champion Go players by studying gameplay data and honing its tactics through self play and RL methods. Moreover RL based gaming expands beyond board games to encompass video games, robotics applications and simulations where agents learn to navigate environments and accomplish objectives. Reinforcement Learning transcends sequence generation by excelling in gaming. In the realm of robotics robots can acquire skills like handling objects moving within spaces and adapting to real world scenarios using techniques such as reinforcement learning (RL) (Franceschetti et al., 2022). RL also plays a role in recommendation systems by helping agents comprehend user preferences and provide suggestions. Furthermore RL finds application in sectors like finance, healthcare, autonomous vehicles and various other domains to aid decision making processes and formulate strategies through interactions with the environment. By learning from experiences and adjusting to circumstances RL emerges as a tool, for addressing decision making challenges across fields.

DL APPROACHES TO GENERATIVE AI

Deep Generative Models: Deep Belief Networks, Deep Boltzmann Machines

Advance generative models, like Deep Boltzmann Machines (DBMs) and Deep Belief Networks (DBNs) have captured the interest of the machine learning community due to their capability to comprehend data distributions and produce examples. These models hold promise in fields such as image creation, language modeling and recommendation system development(Pala et al., 2017)... Deep Belief Networks comprise variables that depict data features at levels and utilize a layer by layer learning approach known as Contrastive Divergence (CD) during their training phase (Hua et al., 2015; Khalil et al., 2021). On the hand Deep Boltzmann Machines are structured with hidden units arranged in layers. Employ a Markov Chain Monte Carlo (MCMC) sampling technique for both training and inference tasks (De Oliveira, 2024). A key benefit of models like DBNs and DBMs is their capacity to identify patterns and relationships, within datasets enabling them to generate samples (Abukmeil et al., 2021; L. Gaur et al., 2021).. These models acquire data representations where each layer captures characteristics.

This structured setup enables models to capture data patterns making them suitable for tasks such, as generating images and refining data.Moreover these models showcase a skill, for dealing with data by utilizing insights gathered during training (Biffi et al., 2020; Ghosh et al., 2020). This feature proves beneficial in datasets such as diagnostics or sensor data analysis. Additionally deep generative models have shown prowess in scenarios with labeled data by making use of the knowledge gained through work (Shokrollahi et al., 2023). Models like Deep Belief Networks and Deep Boltzmann Machines act as tools for understanding data distributions generating samples thanks to their structures ability to handle missing information and effectiveness in situations with labeled data. As research advances in this field we anticipate developments, in modeling that will enhance their capabilities and widen their range of uses.

Challenges and Benefits of DL in Generative Modeling

DL has brought about changes, in how we approach data analysis and understanding distributions as mentioned by Foster in 2022. While deep generative modeling offers advantages it also presents challenges. One key issue is the training requirements for these models. The intricate structures of models such as DBMs and DBNs involve layers that add complexity during both training and inference stages as noted by Voulodimos et al. In 2018. To tackle this challenge optimizing techniques through parallelization methods and access to computing resources are often crucial. Furthermore deep generative models frequently face mode collapse. A scenario where the model struggles to capture the range of data distribution leading to diversity, in generated samples. This can impact the quality of the samples produced.

Restrict the usefulness of these models. To tackle this challenge common strategies include incorporating regularization methods, refining model structures and adjusting training procedures to explore aspects of the data space. Despite these obstacles deep generative models offer advantages across domains according to Ranzato et al. In 2011. One key benefit is their ability to learn data representations that help us better understand patterns and relationships, within datasets. The structured nature of these models enables systems to create samples that closely resemble the original training data used.

Moreover these state of the art generative models demonstrate a knack, for managing data making them well suited for scenarios where data quality may be compromised (Wu, 2021). They excel in extracting insights from data using learning techniques thereby reducing the reliance on datasets and human oversight. These advanced generative models have found application in tasks such as creating images generating text and aiding in drug discovery endeavors (Bian & Xie 2021). Their ability to produce outputs has AI technology, pharmaceutical research and strategies for enhancing datasets. Despite facing challenges like complexity and mode collapse the benefits of modeling to capture data distributions and create samples outweigh these hurdles. Ongoing research advancements and innovative learning approaches will help address these obstacles and unleash the potential of models across fields. Figure 7 illustrates the advantages of utilizing learning methods, for AI applications.

Figure 7. Benefits of Approaches to Generative AI

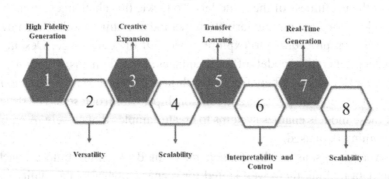

Benefits Of Deep Learning Approaches To Generative AI

Comparison of Shallow vs. Deep Generative Models

Various types of models such, as ones offer methods to represent data distributions. Shallow generative models consist of a layer of variables while deep generative models include layers that can effectively capture data structures (Salakhutdinov, 2015). Simple and efficient shallow models like Gaussian mixture models (GMMs) and restricted Boltzmann machines (RBMs) are widely recognized in the field (X. Jin et al., 2014). GMMs utilize Gaussian components to model clustered data making them suitable for datasets (Najar et al. 2017). On the hand RBMs can manage data distributions through learning. May encounter difficulties capturing intricate patterns in high dimensional data due to their limited structure. In contrast deep generative models like belief networks (DBNs) and variational autoencoders (VAEs) utilize layers of variables to learn representations of data. DBNs stack RBMs to identify features, in the data; meanwhile VAEs employ encoder decoder networks to grasp a space that accurately reflects the structure of the data and efficiently generates samples. One benefit of these models is their ability to understand data patterns and produce examples.

Their structured design allows them to understand connections, across levels of complexity making them useful for tasks that involve creativity such as creating visuals generating text and designing molecules. However there are challenges associated with these models. Training deep neural networks requires amounts of data and computational power. Fine tuning them can be difficult due to the nature of the tuning process. Additionally deep models are more prone to overfitting especially when trained on data and deciphering the acquired patterns can be complex due to their architecture. Both shallow and deep generative models have their advantages and limitations. Shallow models provide simplicity and efficiency. May struggle with recognizing data patterns. On the hand deep models excel at capturing nuances in data but require more computational resources and meticulous fine tuning. Understanding the trade-offs, between these approaches is crucial when choosing a model for a project.

Applications of Deep Generative Models in Natural Language Processing, Image Generation, and More

Deep learning models have found use in both natural language processing and image creation. Lets explore some of the applications, in these fields.

Sophisticated generative models such as Recurrent Neural Networks (RNNs) Generative Adversarial Networks (GANs) and Variational Autoencoders (VAEs) are frequently utilized for tasks such as generating text, summarizing content and crafting dialogues. Sequence to sequence models, often leveraging deep learning architectures like Transformers employ methods to translate text across languages. Deep generative models play a role in adjusting text styles to allow for changes in sentiment or formality while preserving the core message. These generative models can also provide responses to questions based on input text making them valuable for developing question answering systems and chatbots. GANs are particularly adept at generating images by learning from datasets. Their applications range from creating artwork and designing avatars to enhancing image quality. Advanced models now possess the ability to alter images in styles, such as converting sketches into photographs or transforming scenes into settings (Wu et al., 2022). Face generation techniques using GANs and VAEs are employed to create faces that benefit industries, like video games, virtual reality and identity protection (Liu et al., 2021).

Cutting edge models are helping in drug discovery by creating structures with characteristics, which speeds up the process of developing medications (Cheng et al., 2021).. They can also generate music by producing melodies inspired by existing compositions providing resources, for musicians and music producers (Herremans et al., 2017).. Additionally advanced models focused on detecting abnormalities analyze data patterns to pinpoint irregularities or outliers in datasets. This technology is used in applications such as fraud detection enhancing network security and ensuring product quality in manufacturing processes (Chalapathy et al., 2019). In essence deep generative models play a role in fields like natural language processing and image creation. Their ability to recognize patterns in data and generate examples has driven progress across domains from understanding languages to fostering creativity. As research, on learning progresses we look forward to seeing advancements and practical applications of these models.

EVALUATION METRICS AND CHALLENGES

Joint Evaluation Metrics for Generative Models

Generative models are utilized across fields, like NLP, computer vision and ML. It's crucial to assess the performance and trustworthiness of these models through metrics. One common metric is the Inception Score (IS) which gauges the quality and diversity of generated images by examining predictions, from the Inception V3 classifier and class label distribution. Another significant metric is the Fréchet Inception Distance (FID) which evaluates how the feature representations of generated images match labels (G. Meena et al. 2023).

In classification tasks metrics, like Precision and Recall are commonly used for evaluation purposes (Soloveitchik et al., 2021). Precision refers to the ratio of identified instances, among those retrieved while recall indicates the proportion of instances that were successfully retrieved. Moreover perplexity is often utilized to gauge the performance of language models by assessing their ability to accurately predict a given sample based on its context (Powers, 2020). Lastly Variational Information Maximization (VIM) assesses model quality by maximizing the information shared between generated samples and the target distribution (Pan, 2020).

These assessments aid, in assessing the effectiveness of models in areas. It's important to recognize that no one measure can fully capture all aspects of models. This is why it's typical to utilize a variety of measures for assessment. Moreover the choice of measures may vary depending on the task at hand and the data available. Hence it is crucial, for researchers and professionals to select measures thoughtfully based on their objectives and requirements. Assessing model performance is crucial to guarantee their efficiency and dependability.

Through the use of established evaluation criteria like Inception Score, Fréchet Inception Distance, Precision, Recall, Perplexity and Variational Information Maximization researchers and professionals can gain insights, into the quality and variety of generated samples, which drives progress in this field.

Challenges In Evaluating Generative Models: Mode Collapse, Sample Quality, Diversity, and More

Evaluating the performance of models can be quite a challenge, due to complexities. One major issue is mode collapse, where the model struggles to capture the range of data leading to limitations in its outputs. To tackle this the model needs to generate a set of samples that accurately represent the data distribution. Another hurdle involves assessing the quality of samples. Metrics like Inception Score and Fréchet Inception Distance offer some insights into quality and diversity. May not fully account for aspects such as realism and semantic coherence (Maturana et al. 2023). Creating high quality samples requires an approach that combines metrics with assessments, from experts.

Evaluating sample diversity poses its challenges. It is important for generative models to produce samples that accurately represent the data they are trained on. However assessing diversity is not straightforward as it involves considering both uniqueness and novelty while avoiding repetition. Creating metrics, for this purpose is key to improving the performance of these models. Additionally evaluating models in areas such as natural language generation comes with its complexities. Ensuring accuracy, coherence and relevance within context is crucial in this scenario. Nevertheless current evaluation metrics may not fully capture these subtleties leading to differences, between automated assessments and human evaluations. Closing this gap requires tailored evaluation methods that cater to the needs of each field.

In order for researchers to effectively assess models they must overcome obstacles such, as mode collapse evaluating the quality of samples measuring diversity and customizing evaluations for domains (Bandi et al., 2023). Overcoming these challenges involves using methods like metrics, subjective evaluations and taking into account domain factors. By conquering these hurdles researchers can drive progress in modeling. Unlock potentials, in the fields of artificial intelligence and machine learning.

Strategies for Improving Evaluation and Addressing Challenges

Enhancing our assessment of models includes utilizing techniques to gauge their effectiveness. One method is to define criteria, for evaluating aspects of generative model performance. To address challenges like mode collapse researchers can examine metrics like Coverage GAN (Krukowski et al., 2008) to assess the similarity between generated samples and the data distribution. Furthermore integrating input, from user studies and expert assessments can offer perspectives on sample quality, diversity and consistency.

Human reviewers have the task of analyzing created examples, for their authenticity, significance and practicality in assignments. By merging evaluations with automated measurements we can gain an insight into the efficiency of models. It's essential to expand our understanding of the elements that lead to model collapse and other obstacles in modeling to enhance model dependability. Research endeavors that concentrate on recognizing these challenges and applying approaches such, as regularization techniques (Sajeeda & Hossain 2022) or alternative training methodologies can enhance the resilience of models.

Additionally fostering collaboration and knowledge exchange among researchers is crucial for advancing the evaluation and mitigation of modeling challenges. Researchers can compare models and evaluation methods using datasets, benchmarking platforms and reproducible research practices. This facilitates the identification of practices and areas, for enhancement. Improving assessment methods and tackling obstacles, in modeling approaches involve developing evaluation criteria that consider input acknowledging limitations of models and promoting teamwork among researchers. Through a blend of metrics qualitative evaluations and cross disciplinary collaborations experts can push the boundaries of modeling. Open up fresh opportunities in the realms of artificial intelligence and machine learning. Figure 8 showcases evaluation benchmarks, for models.

Figure 8. Common Evaluation Metrics for a Generative Model

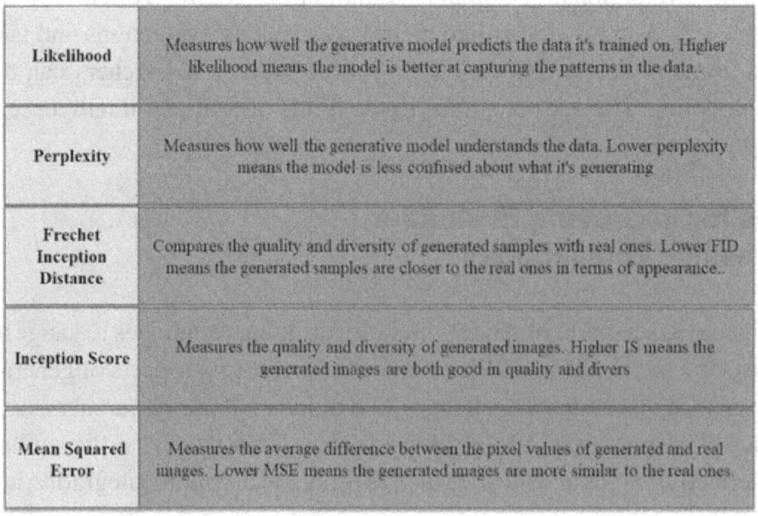

Likelihood	Measures how well the generative model predicts the data it's trained on. Higher likelihood means the model is better at capturing the patterns in the data.
Perplexity	Measures how well the generative model understands the data. Lower perplexity means the model is less confused about what it's generating
Frechet Inception Distance	Compares the quality and diversity of generated samples with real ones. Lower FID means the generated samples are closer to the real ones in terms of appearance.
Inception Score	Measures the quality and diversity of generated images. Higher IS means the generated images are both good in quality and divers
Mean Squared Error	Measures the average difference between the pixel values of generated and real images. Lower MSE means the generated images are more similar to the real ones

FUTURE DIRECTIONS AND EMERGING TECHNIQUES

Recent Advancements and Trends in Generative AI

The progress, in intelligence development has greatly impacted fields, including the creation of images text generation and music composition. A significant milestone in this progress was the introduction of GANs by Goodfellow and colleagues in 2014. GANs comprise two networks. The generator and the discriminator. Working together to produce data while distinguishing between generated samples. This framework has driven advancements in image generation enabling the creation of images from scratch.

Another notable trend is the emergence of transformer based models, such as OpenAIs GPT series introduced by Pakhale in 2023. These models utilize self attention mechanisms to understand relationships. Have shown performance across various natural language processing tasks like text generation, translation and summarization. The launch of GPT 3 marked an achievement with its scale and capabilities showcasing the potential of large scale pre training for tasks as highlighted by Hadi et al. In 2023. Moreover there have been improvements in conditional generation techniques where specific attributes or input signals influence the output generated. For instance StyleGAN developed by Dang & Nguyen in 2023 provides control over image features, like expressions, hairstyles and lighting settings.

This leads to the development of applications such, as systems for fashion and facial expression imitation technologies. Similarly text generation models like CTRL (Chan et al., 2020) give users the ability to influence the style and content of generated text using control codes resulting in outcomes. Additionally reinforcement learning techniques have been integrated with models to allow agents to interact with their environments and learn from feedback. This combination has progress in gaming, robotics and autonomous systems (Rao, 2024). Integrating capabilities with reinforcement learning AI systems can showcase adaptable behaviors paving the way for research and practical applications. Recent advancements in AI involving developments, in GANs, transformer based models conditional generation approaches and reinforcement learning have driven advancements in industries. Set the foundation for creating more sophisticated and intelligent AI systems.

Exploration of Emerging Techniques Such as Transformer-Based Models, Self-Supervised Learning, and Meta-Learning

In times there have been advancements, in the field of artificial intelligence particularly in transformer based models used for supervised learning and meta learning. Transformer models are becoming increasingly recognized for their ability to effectively handle long range dependencies in data through self attention mechanisms (Choi & Lee 2023). This feature allows them to prioritize input elements and demonstrate performance in processing text data excelling across natural language tasks (H. Srivastava et al., 2023). A new method called self supervised learning has emerged as a way to train AI models without the need for human labeled data. In this approach models learn from examples. Labels are created from data through tasks like predicting masked tokens in sentences, a method that has been successful, in training language models and aiding transfer learning to tasks with labeled data (Mohamed et al., 2022).

Learning to learn, also known as " Meta learning, " is growing in popularity as it enables AI systems to adapt to tasks and environments by leveraging knowledge from experiences (Min et al., 2023). By improving their ability to learn efficiently meta learning models leverage past experiences to quickly acquire skills or knowledge making them well suited for situations with training data or changing conditions (Hospedales et al., 2021). These methods have shown results in fields such as natural language processing, computer vision and reinforcement learning.

Transformer based models have proven to be quite effective, in tasks that involve understanding and creating language (J. Et al., 2021). Moreover self supervised learning methods have facilitated the training of AI models on datasets improving their ability to adapt and endure. The promise of these learning approaches lies in the creation of AI systems that can quickly adapt to tasks and environments paving the way for intelligent agents. Delving into transformer based models through self supervised learning and meta learning represents a field, in AI research with the potential to advance AI capabilities across domains.

Potential Applications and Implications of Future Generative AI Techniques

AI technologies, like GANs and Transformer models have shown promise in fields by empowering machines to create content such as images, text, audio and videos collaboratively. One exciting application of AI is seen in the healthcare industry where it can produce images to enhance disease diagnosis using machine learning data. Furthermore generative AI has the capacity to spark creativity, in art, music and literature by pushing boundaries (Kaur et al., 2020). In the domain of natural language processing generative AI holds the potential to transform communication and translation through text generation (Doshi & Hauser 2023; Fatima Tuz Zahra et al., 2020).

Advance language models such, as GPT 3 have the ability to generate responses that imitate conversations making them useful for interacting with chatbots and virtual assistants. Additionally in the field of vehicle development generative AI can simulate driving scenarios to improve the training of self driving algorithms for outcomes (Zhang & Chen et al. 2023). However with the adoption of intelligence it is important to consider ethical dilemmas (S. Chen et al., 2019). One significant issue is the misuse of these technologies, for spreading information and creating deepfakes that can have societal impacts (Vasist & Krishnan 2022).

Additionally there are concerns regarding data security and privacy when AI models are trained on datasets that might unintentionally retain information. The integration of AI, into decision making processes, such as in hiring or loan approvals could exacerbate biases in the training data resulting in outcomes and discriminatory practices (Raso et al., 2018).. While advancements in generative AI show promise for driving innovation across industries it is crucial to recognize and tackle the challenges and repercussions that accompany them to ensure use. By addressing these issues and harnessing AI capabilities ethically we can unleash its potential, for progress.

CONCLUSION

Importance of Understanding Different Generative AI Techniques for Their Applications in Various Domains

Various industries have needs and constraints that require tailored solutions. Skilled professionals knowledgeable, in AI techniques can customize models to address requirements whether it involves generating images, text or other forms of data. Generative AI approaches provide problem solving strategies for a variety of challenges. By understanding methodologies experts can select the appropriate technique for a particular task enhancing productivity and effectiveness. Leveraging generative AI promotes innovation and creativity by facilitating the development of content. Proficiency in diverse techniques empowers creators to explore ways of delivering content that resonates with audiences and inspires concepts. Generative AI methods can generate data to complement existing datasets in fields grappling with issues like data scarcity or imbalance thereby enhancing model robustness and generalization capabilities. Some generative AI techniques, such as GANs may face challenges like mode collapse or limited diversity, in generated outputs. Being aware of these obstacles enables professionals to implement strategies that ensure the generation of a range of outputs.

Generative AI methods are applied in healthcare, entertainment and finance (P. Gupta et al. 2024). Understanding these methods encourages experts to leverage AI for advantages. The utilization of AI technology brings up issues such, as fakes, biases in generated content and the potential misuse of synthetic data. Professionals versed in AI methods are better prepared to handle these issues ensuring that AI applications benefit society positively (Lee, 2024). The field of AI is constantly evolving, with new techniques and advancements emerging. Proficiency, in these strategies enables experts to keep up with advancements that foster a culture of creativity and improvement in AI implementations (Vartiainen & Tedre 2024; Taj & Jhanjhi 2022). Essentially mastering AI methods is crucial for unleashing the capabilities of AI across fields. It empowers professionals to customize solutions to tackle problems effectively promote thinking and approach issues with care—all of which contribute to advancement and influence, in AI driven endeavors.

Implications for Future Research and Practical Implementations of Generative AI Techniques

Advancements, in AI technology have been making strides in fields from producing visuals to composing music and writing content.

Researchers are exploring further into this field uncovering chances, for exploration and practical uses. A major emphasis lies in enhancing the transparency and manageability of AI models. Although these models produce outcomes comprehending their operations and directing the generation process poses difficulties. Improving transparency could empower researchers to grasp the workings of these models facilitating adjustments and interventions (Tursunalieva et al. 2024; Singhal et al., 2020).

When it comes to AI it's important to address the impacts it brings. With the advancements, in these models concerns about misuse like creating videos or spreading information are becoming more prominent. It's crucial for us to focus on reducing these risks and setting guidelines for their use. Additionally there are opportunities in industries to leverage AI techniques. For instance in the healthcare field generative models can aid in producing images to assist in diagnosing and planning treatments (Rudroff, 2024; Almusaylim et al., 2018). Similarly in the domain these methods can serve as a wellspring of ideas, for art, music and literature – promoting innovation. It's imperative to delve into exploring how AI can contribute to content creation moving forward.

By using information provided by users and their preferences AI systems can tailor content to match interests leading to user engagement, on platforms such as recommendation systems and personalized advertising. It is crucial to ensure that these models are strong and adaptable. Although current models excel at creating content within guidelines they may face challenges with inputs. Future research should focus on developing strategies that allow models to generate results, across scenarios and inputs. Essentially future AI studies should aim to improve clarity, tackle obstacles, explore applications enhance personalization capabilities and strengthen resilience and flexibility. Overcoming these challenges could empower AI to advance fields and spark transformations.

REFERENCES

Abukmeil, M., Ferrari, S., Genovese, A., Piuri, V., & Scotti, F. (2021). A survey of Unsupervised Generative Models for exploratory data analysis and representation learning. *ACM Computing Surveys*, 54(5), 1–40. DOI:10.1145/3450963

Adeyemo, V. E., Abdullah, A., Jhanjhi, N. Z., Supramaniam, M., & Balogun, A. O. (2019). Ensemble and Deep-Learning Methods for Two-Class and Multi-Attack Anomaly Intrusion Detection: An Empirical Study. *International Journal of Advanced Computer Science and Applications*, 10(9). Advance online publication. DOI:10.14569/IJACSA.2019.0100969

Akçay, S., Atapour-Abarghouei, A., & Breckon, T. P. (2019). Skip-GANomaly: Skip Connected and Adversarially Trained Encoder-Decoder Anomaly Detection. *2019 International Joint Conference on Neural Networks (IJCNN)*. DOI:10.1109/IJCNN.2019.8851808

Aldausari, N. (2022). *Cascaded Siamese Self-Supervised Audio to Video GAN*. https://openaccess.thecvf.com/content/CVPR2022W/MULA/html/Aldausari_Cascaded_Siamese_Self-Supervised_Audio_to_Video_GAN_CVPRW_2022_paper.html

Alemi, A. (2018, February 15). *An information-theoretic analysis of deep latent-variable models*. OpenReview. https://openreview.net/forum?id=H1rRWl-Cb

Ali, R. S. E., Meng, J., Khan, M. E. I., & Jiang, X. (2024). Machine Learning Advancements in Organic Synthesis: A focused exploration of artificial intelligence applications in chemistry. *Artificial Intelligence Chemistry.*, 2(1), 100049. DOI:10.1016/j.aichem.2024.100049

Almusaylim, Z. A., Jhanjhi, N. Z., & Alhumam, A. (2020). Detection and Mitigation of RPL rank and version number attacks in the Internet of Things: SRPL-RP. *Sensors (Basel)*, 20(21), 5997. DOI:10.3390/s20215997 PMID:33105891

Almusaylim, Z. A., Jhanjhi, N. Z., & Jung, L. T. (2018). Proposing A Data Privacy Aware Protocol for Roadside Accident Video Reporting Service Using 5G In Vehicular Cloud Networks Environment. *2018 4th International Conference on Computer and Information Sciences (ICCOINS)*. DOI:10.1109/ICCOINS.2018.8510588

Amankwah-Amoah, J., Abdalla, S., Mogaji, E., Elbanna, A. R., & Dwivedi, Y. K. (2024). The impending disruption of creative industries by generative AI: Opportunities, challenges, and research agenda. *International Journal of Information Management*, 102759, 102759. Advance online publication. DOI:10.1016/j.ijinfomgt.2024.102759

Ananna, F. F., Nowreen, R., Jahwari, S. S. R. A., Costa, E., Angeline, L., & Sindiramutty, S. R. (2023). Analysing Influential factors in student academic achievement: Prediction modelling and insight. *International Journal of Emerging Multidisciplinaries Computer Science & Artificial Intelligence*, 2(1). Advance online publication. DOI:10.54938/ijemdcsai.2023.02.1.254

Azam, H., Dulloo, M. I., Majeed, M. H., Wan, J. P. H., Xin, L. T., & Sindiramutty, S. R. (2023). Cybercrime Unmasked: Investigating cases and digital evidence. *International Journal of Emerging Multidisciplinaries Computer Science & Artificial Intelligence*, 2(1). Advance online publication. DOI:10.54938/ijemdcsai.2023.02.1.255

Azam, H., Dulloo, M. I., Majeed, M. H., Wan, J. P. H., Xin, L. T., Tajwar, M. A., & Sindiramutty, S. R. (2023). Defending the digital Frontier: IDPS and the battle against Cyber threat. *International Journal of Emerging Multidisciplinaries Computer Science & Artificial Intelligence*, 2(1). Advance online publication. DOI:10.54938/ijemdcsai.2023.02.1.253

Azam, H., Tajwar, M. A., Mayhialagan, S., Davis, A. J., Yik, C. J., Ali, D., & Sindiramutty, S. R. (2023). Innovations in Security: A Study of Cloud Computing and IoT. *International Journal of Emerging Multidisciplinaries Computer Science & Artificial Intelligence*, 2(1). Advance online publication. DOI:10.54938/ijemdcsai.2023.02.1.252

Azam, H., Tan, M., Pin, L. T., Syahmi, M. A., Qian, A. L. W., Jingyan, H., Uddin, H., & Sindiramutty, S. R. (2023). Wireless Technology Security and Privacy: A Comprehensive Study. *Preprint*. DOI:10.20944/preprints202311.0664.v1

Bai, C., Liu, P., Liu, K., Wang, L., Zhao, Y., Han, L., & Wang, Z. (2023). Variational dynamic for Self-Supervised Exploration in deep Reinforcement learning. *IEEE Transactions on Neural Networks and Learning Systems*, 34(8), 4776–4790. DOI:10.1109/TNNLS.2021.3129160 PMID:34851835

Bandi, A., Adapa, P. V. S. R., & Kuchi, Y. E. V. P. K. (2023). The power of Generative AI: A review of requirements, models, Input–Output formats, evaluation metrics, and challenges. *Future Internet*, 15(8), 260. DOI:10.3390/fi15080260

Bao, H., Li, D., Wang, W., Yang, N., Piao, S., & Wei, F. (2023). Fine-tuning pretrained transformer encoders for sequence-to-sequence learning. *International Journal of Machine Learning and Cybernetics*. Advance online publication. DOI:10.1007/s13042-023-01992-6

Bengio, Y. (2012). Practical Recommendations for Gradient-Based Training of Deep Architectures. In *Lecture Notes in Computer Science* (pp. 437–478). DOI:10.1007/978-3-642-35289-8_26

Bhalodia, R. (2020). *DPVAES: Fixing sample generation for regularized VAEs.* https://openaccess.thecvf.com/content/ACCV2020/html/Bhalodia_dpVAEs_Fixing_Sample_Generation_for_Regularized_VAEs_ACCV_2020_paper.html

Bian, Y., & Xie, X. (2021). Generative chemistry: Drug discovery with deep learning generative models. *Journal of Molecular Modeling*, 27(3), 71. Advance online publication. DOI:10.1007/s00894-021-04674-8 PMID:33543405

Biffi, C., Cerrolaza, J. J., Tarroni, G., Bai, W., De Marvao, A., Oktay, O., Ledig, C., Folgoc, L. L., Kamnitsas, K., Doumou, G., Duan, J., Prasad, S. K., Cook, S. A., O'Regan, D. P., & Rueckert, D. (2020). Explainable anatomical shape analysis through deep hierarchical generative models. *IEEE Transactions on Medical Imaging*, 39(6), 2088–2099. DOI:10.1109/TMI.2020.2964499 PMID:31944949

Bond-Taylor, S., Leach, A., Long, Y., & Willcocks, C. G. (2022). Deep Generative Modelling: A comparative review of VAEs, GANs, normalizing flows, Energy-Based and autoregressive models. *IEEE Transactions on Pattern Analysis and Machine Intelligence*, 44(11), 7327–7347. DOI:10.1109/TPAMI.2021.3116668 PMID:34591756

Brakel, P., Dieleman, S., & Schrauwen, B. (2012). Training Restricted Boltzmann Machines with Multi-tempering: Harnessing Parallelization. In *Lecture Notes in Computer Science* (pp. 92–99). DOI:10.1007/978-3-642-33266-1_12

Byeon, H., Shabaz, M., Shrivastava, K., Joshi, A., Keshta, I., Oak, R., Singh, P., & Soni, M. (2024). Deep learning model to detect deceptive generative adversarial network generated images using multimedia forensic. *Computers & Electrical Engineering*, 113, 109024. DOI:10.1016/j.compeleceng.2023.109024

Cai, Z., Xiong, Z., Xu, H., Wang, P., Li, W., & Pan, Y. (2021). Generative adversarial networks. *ACM Computing Surveys*, 54(6), 1–38. DOI:10.1145/3459992

Cao, D., Jia, F., Arık, S. Ö., Pfister, T., Yi, Z., Ye, W., & Yan, L. (2023). TEMPO: prompt-based generative pre-trained transformer for time series forecasting. *arXiv (Cornell University)*. https://doi.org//arxiv.2310.04948DOI:10.48550

Cao, X., Sun, G., Yu, H., & Guizani, M. (2023). PerFED-GAN: Personalized federated learning via generative adversarial networks. *IEEE Internet of Things Journal*, 10(5), 3749–3762. DOI:10.1109/JIOT.2022.3172114

Cao, Y., Li, S., Liu, Y., Zhang, Y., Dai, Y., Yu, P. S., & Sun, L. (2023). A Comprehensive Survey of AI-Generated Content (AIGC): A History of Generative AI from GAN to ChatGPT. *arXiv (Cornell University)*. https://doi.org//arxiv.2303.04226DOI:10.48550

Cassenti, D. N., & Kaplan, L. (2021). *Robust uncertainty representation in human-AI collaboration*. SPIE., DOI:10.1117/12.2584818

Chakraborty, T., Reddy K S, U., Naik, S. M., Panja, M., & Manvitha, B. (2024). Ten Years of Generative Adversarial Nets (GANs): A survey of the state-of-the-art. *Machine Learning: Science and Technology*, 5(1), 011001. DOI:10.1088/2632-2153/ad1f77

Chalapathy, R., Toth, E., & Chawla, S. (2019). Group anomaly detection using deep generative models. In *Lecture Notes in Computer Science* (pp. 173–189). DOI:10.1007/978-3-030-10925-7_11

Chan, A., Ong, Y., Pung, B. T. W., Zhang, A., & Fu, J. (2020). COCON: A Self-Supervised Approach for Controlled Text Generation. *arXiv (Cornell University)*. https://doi.org//arxiv.2006.03535DOI:10.48550

Chen, S., Leng, Y., & Labi, S. (2019). A deep learning algorithm for simulating autonomous driving considering prior knowledge and temporal information. *Computer-Aided Civil and Infrastructure Engineering*, 35(4), 305–321. DOI:10.1111/mice.12495

Chen, Y., Chawla, S., Mousadoust, D., Nichol, A., Ng, R. T., & Isaac, K. V. (2024). Machine Learning to Predict the Need for Postmastectomy Radiotherapy after Immediate Breast Reconstruction. *Plastic and Reconstructive Surgery. Global Open*, 12(2), e5599. DOI:10.1097/GOX.0000000000005599 PMID:38322813

Chen, Z., Gan, W., Wu, J., Hu, K., & Lin, H. (2024). Data Scarcity in Recommendation Systems: A survey. *ACM Transactions on Recommender Systems*. DOI:10.1145/3639063

Cheng, Y., Gong, Y., Liu, Y., Song, B., & Zou, Q. (2021). Molecular design in drug discovery: A comprehensive review of deep generative models. *Briefings in Bioinformatics*, 22(6), bbab344. Advance online publication. DOI:10.1093/bib/bbab344 PMID:34415297

Chivukula, A. S. (2020). *Game theoretical adversarial deep learning algorithms for robust neural network models*. https://opus.lib.uts.edu.au/handle/10453/140920

Choi, S. R., & Lee, M. (2023). Transformer Architecture and Attention Mechanisms in Genome Data Analysis: A Comprehensive review. *Biology (Basel)*, 12(7), 1033. DOI:10.3390/biology12071033 PMID:37508462

Courville, A. (2024, January 31). *Sequential decision modeling in uncertain conditions*. https://papyrus.bib.umontreal.ca/xmlui/handle/1866/32582

Dang, M. H., & Nguyen, T. N. (2023). Digital Face Manipulation Creation and Detection: A Systematic review. *Electronics (Basel)*, 12(16), 3407. DOI:10.3390/electronics12163407

Dash, A., Ye, J., & Wang, G. (2023). A review of Generative Adversarial Networks (GANs) and its applications in a wide variety of disciplines: From Medical to Remote Sensing. *IEEE Access : Practical Innovations, Open Solutions*, 1, 1. Advance online publication. DOI:10.1109/ACCESS.2023.3346273

De Oliveira, A. C. N. (2024). Learning the optimal representation dimension for restricted Boltzmann machines. *Performance Evaluation Review*, 51(3), 3–5. DOI:10.1145/3639830.3639833

Deep, G., & Verma, J. (2023). Textual alchemy. In *Advances in computational intelligence and robotics book series* (pp. 124–143). DOI:10.4018/979-8-3693-0502-7.ch007

Del Debbio, L., Rossney, J. M., & Wilson, M. G. (2021). Efficient modeling of trivializing maps for lattice $\phi 4$ theory using normalizing flows: A first look at scalability. *Physical Review. D*, 104(9), 094507. Advance online publication. DOI:10.1103/PhysRevD.104.094507

Demiray, B. Z., Sit, M., & Demir, İ. (2021). D-SRGAN: DEM Super-Resolution with Generative Adversarial Networks. *SN Computer Science*, 2(1), 48. Advance online publication. DOI:10.1007/s42979-020-00442-2

Detlefsen, N. S., Hauberg, S., & Boomsma, W. (2022). Learning meaningful representations of protein sequences. *Nature Communications*, 13(1), 1914. Advance online publication. DOI:10.1038/s41467-022-29443-w PMID:35395843

Doshi, A. R., & Hauser, O. P. (2023). Generative artificial intelligence enhances creativity. *Social Science Research Network*. DOI:10.2139/ssrn.4535536

Du, C., Du, C., Huang, L., Wang, H., & He, H. (2022). Structured neural decoding with multitask transfer learning of deep neural network representations. *IEEE Transactions on Neural Networks and Learning Systems*, 33(2), 600–614. DOI:10.1109/TNNLS.2020.3028167 PMID:33074832

Du, H., Li, Z., Niyato, D., Kang, J., Xiong, Z., Huang, H., & Mao, S. (2024). Diffusion-based reinforcement learning for edge-enabled AI-Generated Content services. *IEEE Transactions on Mobile Computing*, 23(9), 1–16. DOI:10.1109/TMC.2024.3356178

Ermagun, A., Smith, V., & Janatabadi, F. (2024). High urban flood risk and no shelter access disproportionally impacts vulnerable communities in the USA. *Communications Earth & Environment*, 5(1), 2. Advance online publication. DOI:10.1038/s43247-023-01165-x

Fatima-Tuz-Zahra, Jhanjhi, N. Z., Brohi, S. N., & Malik, N. A. (2019). Proposing a Rank and Wormhole Attack Detection Framework using Machine Learning. *2019 13th International Conference on Mathematics, Actuarial Science, Computer Science and Statistics (MACS)*. DOI:10.1109/MACS48846.2019.9024821

Fatima-Tuz-Zahra, Jhanjhi, N. Z., Brohi, S. N., Malik, N. A., & Humayun, M. (2020). Proposing a Hybrid RPL Protocol for Rank and Wormhole Attack Mitigation using Machine Learning. *2020 2nd International Conference on Computer and Information Sciences (ICCIS)*. DOI:10.1109/ICCIS49240.2020.9257607

Filipović, A. (2023). *The role of artificial intelligence in video game development.* Questa Soft. https://www.ceeol.com/search/article-detail?id=1201751

Foster, D. (2022). *Generative Deep learning.* O'Reilly Media, Inc.

Franceschetti, A., Tosello, E., Castaman, N., & Ghidoni, S. (2022). Robotic arm control and task training through deep reinforcement learning. In *Lecture notes in networks and systems* (pp. 532–550). DOI:10.1007/978-3-030-95892-3_41

Gaur, A., Raghuvanshi, C. S., & Sharan, H. O. (2023). Smart prediction farming using deep learning and AI techniques. In *Practice, progress, and proficiency in sustainability* (pp. 152–170). DOI:10.4018/979-8-3693-1722-8.ch009

Gaur, L., Afaq, A., Solanki, A., Singh, G., Sharma, S., Jhanjhi, N. Z., My, H. T., & Le, D. (2021). Capitalizing on big data and revolutionary 5G technology: Extracting and visualizing ratings and reviews of global chain hotels. *Computers & Electrical Engineering*, 95, 107374. DOI:10.1016/j.compeleceng.2021.107374

Ghosh, G., Kavita, , Verma, S., Jhanjhi, N. Z., & Talib, M. N. (2020). Secure surveillance system using chaotic image encryption technique. *IOP Conference Series. Materials Science and Engineering*, 993(1), 012062. DOI:10.1088/1757-899X/993/1/012062

Gonzalez, K. (2021, June 1). *Enhanced Monte Carlo Tree Search in Game-Playing AI: Evaluating DeepMind's Algorithms.* https://espace.rmc-cmr.ca/jspui/handle/11264/1502

Gupta, P., Ding, B., Guan, C., & Ding, D. (2024). Generative AI: A systematic review using topic modelling techniques. *Data and Information Management*, 100066(2). Advance online publication. DOI:10.1016/j.dim.2024.100066

Gupta, S., Singal, G., & Garg, D. (2021). Deep Reinforcement Learning Techniques in Diversified Domains: A survey. *Archives of Computational Methods in Engineering*, 28(7), 4715–4754. DOI:10.1007/s11831-021-09552-3

Hadi, M. U., Tashi, Q. A., Qureshi, R., Shah, A., Muneer, A., Irfan, M., Zafar, A., Shaikh, M. B., Akhtar, N., Wu, J., & Mirjalili, S. (2023). Large Language Models: A Comprehensive Survey of its Applications, Challenges, Limitations, and Future Prospects. *TechRxiv*. DOI:10.36227/techrxiv.23589741.v4

Han, M., Zhu, T., & Zhou, W. (2024). Fair Federated Learning with Opposite GAN. *Knowledge-Based Systems*, 111420, 111420. Advance online publication. DOI:10.1016/j.knosys.2024.111420

Hao, J., Yang, T., Tang, H., Bai, C., Liu, J., Meng, Z., Liu, P., & Wang, Z. (2023). Exploration in deep reinforcement learning: From Single-Agent to Multiagent Domain. *IEEE Transactions on Neural Networks and Learning Systems*, ●●●, 1–21. DOI:10.1109/TNNLS.2023.3236361 PMID:37021882

Hardy, C., Merrer, E. L., & Séricola, B. (2019). MD-GAN: Multi-Discriminator Generative Adversarial Networks for Distributed Datasets. *2019 IEEE International Parallel and Distributed Processing Symposium (IPDPS)*. DOI:10.1109/IPDPS.2019.00095

Hernandez-Trinidad, A., Murillo-Ortíz, B., Guzmán-Cabrera, R., & Córdova–Fraga, T. (2023). Applications of Artificial intelligence in the classification of magnetic resonance images: Advances and Perspectives. In *IntechOpen eBooks*. DOI:10.5772/intechopen.113826

Herremans, D., Chuan, C., & Chew, E. (2017). A functional taxonomy of music generation systems. *ACM Computing Surveys*, 50(5), 1–30. DOI:10.1145/3108242

Hospedales, T. M., Antoniou, A., Micaelli, P., & Storkey, A. (2021). Meta-Learning in Neural Networks: A survey. *IEEE Transactions on Pattern Analysis and Machine Intelligence*, 1, 1. Advance online publication. DOI:10.1109/TPAMI.2021.3079209 PMID:33974543

Hu, C., Wu, J., Sun, C., Chen, X., Nandi, A. K., & Yan, R. (2024). Unified Flowing Normality Learning for Mechanical Anomaly Detection in Continuous Time-Varying Conditions. *SSRN*. DOI:10.2139/ssrn.4719411

Hu, T. (2023, December 15). *Complexity matters: Rethinking the latent space for generative modeling*. https://proceedings.neurips.cc/paper_files/paper/2023/hash/5e8023f07625374c6fdf3aa08bb38e0e-Abstract-Conference.html

Hua, Y., Guo, J., & Zhao, H. (2015). Deep Belief Networks and deep learning. *Proceedings of 2015 International Conference on Intelligent Computing and Internet of Things*. DOI:10.1109/ICAIOT.2015.7111524

Humayun, M., Alsaqer, M., & Jhanjhi, N. Z. (2022). Energy optimization for smart cities using IoT. *Applied Artificial Intelligence*, 36(1), 2037255. Advance online publication. DOI:10.1080/08839514.2022.2037255

Hussain, S. J., Ahmed, U., Liaquat, H., Mir, S., Jhanjhi, N. Z., & Humayun, M. (2019). IMIAD: Intelligent Malware Identification for Android Platform. *2019 International Conference on Computer and Information Sciences (ICCIS)*. DOI:10.1109/ICCISci.2019.8716471

Hutson, J., Lively, J., Robertson, B., Cotroneo, P., & Lang, M. (2023). Of Techne and Praxis: Redefining creativity. In *Springer series on cultural computing* (pp. 21–36). DOI:10.1007/978-3-031-45127-0_2

Jabbar, A., Li, X., & Omar, B. (2021). A survey on Generative Adversarial Networks: Variants, applications, and training. *ACM Computing Surveys*, 54(8), 1–49. DOI:10.1145/3463475

Jaiswal, G., Rani, R., Mangotra, H., & Sharma, A. (2023). Integration of hyperspectral imaging and autoencoders: Benefits, applications, hyperparameter tunning and challenges. *Computer Science Review*, 50, 100584. DOI:10.1016/j.cosrev.2023.100584

Jin, C. (2018). *Is Q-Learning provably efficient?*https://proceedings.neurips.cc/paper_files/paper/2018/hash/d3b1fb02964aa64e257f9f26a31f72cf-Abstract.html

Jin, X., Li, H., & Zhou, S. (2014). An overview of deep generative models. *IETE Technical Review*, 32(2), 131–139. DOI:10.1080/02564602.2014.987328

Karapantelakis, A., Alizadeh, P., Al-Abassi, A., Dey, K., & Níkou, A. (2023). Generative AI in mobile networks: A survey. *Annales des Télécommunications*. Advance online publication. DOI:10.1007/s12243-023-00980-9

Kaur, S., Singla, J., Nkenyereye, L., Jha, S., Prashar, D., Joshi, G. P., El–Sappagh, S., Islam, M. S., & Islam, S. M. R. (2020). Medical Diagnostic Systems Using Artificial intelligence (AI) Algorithms: Principles and Perspectives. *IEEE Access : Practical Innovations, Open Solutions*, 8, 228049–228069. DOI:10.1109/ACCESS.2020.3042273

Keneshloo, Y., Shi, T., Ramakrishnan, N., & Reddy, C. K. (2019). Deep reinforcement learning for Sequence-to-Sequence models. *IEEE Transactions on Neural Networks and Learning Systems*, 1–21. DOI:10.1109/TNNLS.2019.2929141 PMID:31425057

Khalil, M. I., Jhanjhi, N. Z., Humayun, M., Sivanesan, S., Masud, M., & Hossain, M. S. (2021). Hybrid smart grid with sustainable energy efficient resources for smart cities. *Sustainable Energy Technologies and Assessments*, 46, 101211. DOI:10.1016/j.seta.2021.101211

Khennouche, F., Elmir, Y., Himeur, Y., Djebari, N., & Amira, A. (2024). Revolutionizing generative pre-traineds: Insights and challenges in deploying ChatGPT and generative chatbots for FAQs. *Expert Systems with Applications*, 246, 123224. DOI:10.1016/j.eswa.2024.123224

Kok, S., Abdullah, A., & Jhanjhi, N. Z. (2022). Early detection of crypto-ransomware using pre-encryption detection algorithm. *Journal of King Saud University. Computer and Information Sciences*, 34(5), 1984–1999. DOI:10.1016/j.jksuci.2020.06.012

Krishnan, S., Thangaveloo, R., Rahman, S. B. A., & Sindiramutty, S. R. (2021). Smart Ambulance Traffic Control system. *Trends in Undergraduate Research*, 4(1), c28–c34. DOI:10.33736/tur.2831.2021

Krukowski, S., Kempisty, P., & Strąk, P. (2008). Role of chlorine in the dynamics of GaN(0001) surface during HVPE GaN growth—Ab initio study. *Journal of Crystal Growth*, 310(7–9), 1391–1397. DOI:10.1016/j.jcrysgro.2007.11.099

Lee, P. (2024, February 10). *Synthetic data and the future of AI*. https://papers.ssrn.com/sol3/papers.cfm?abstract_id=4722162

Lehrberger, J., & Bourbeau, L. (1988). *Machine translation: Linguistic characteristics of MT systems and general methodology of evaluation*. John Benjamins Publishing. DOI:10.1075/lis.15

Lei, X., Sun, L., & Xia, Y. (2020). Lost data reconstruction for structural health monitoring using deep convolutional generative adversarial networks. *Structural Health Monitoring*, 20(4), 2069–2087. DOI:10.1177/1475921720959226

Lim, W., Yong, K. S. C., Theng, L. B., & Tan, C. L. (2024). Future of Generative Adversarial Networks (GAN) for Anomaly Detection in Network Security: A review. *Computers & Security*, 139, 103733. DOI:10.1016/j.cose.2024.103733

Liu, M., Huang, X., Yu, J., & Mallya, A. (2021). Generative Adversarial networks for image and video synthesis: Algorithms and applications. *Proceedings of the IEEE*, 109(5), 839–862. DOI:10.1109/JPROC.2021.3049196

Liu, Z., Ma, C., She, W., & Xie, M. (2024). Biomedical image Segmentation using Denoising Diffusion Probabilistic Models: A Comprehensive Review and analysis. *Applied Sciences (Basel, Switzerland)*, 14(2), 632. DOI:10.3390/app14020632

Luketina, J., Nardelli, N., Farquhar, G., Foerster, J., Andreas, J., Grefenstette, E., Whiteson, S., & Rocktäschel, T. (2019). A survey of Reinforcement Learning informed by Natural language. *arXiv (Cornell University)*. /arxiv.1906.03926DOI:10.24963/ ijcai.2019/880

Luleci, F., & Çatbaş, F. N. (2023). A brief introductory review to deep generative models for civil structural health monitoring. *AI in Civil Engineering*, 2(1), 9. Advance online publication. DOI:10.1007/s43503-023-00017-z PMID:37621778

M, R. K., & Jayagopal, P. (2020). Generative adversarial networks: a survey on applications and challenges. *International Journal of Multimedia Information Retrieval*, 10(1), 1–24. DOI:10.1007/s13735-020-00196-w

Mangla, M., Shinde, S. K., Mehta, V., Sharma, N., & Mohanty, S. N. (2022). *Handbook of Research on Machine Learning: Foundations and Applications*. CRC Press. DOI:10.1201/9781003277330

Maqsood, R., Abid, F., & Farooq, G. (2022). Cycle Consistency and Fine-Grained Image to Image Translation in Augmentation: An Overview. *Social Science Research Network*. DOI:10.2139/ssrn.4157023

Maturana, C. N. V., Orozco, A. L. S., & Villalba, L. J. G. (2023). Exploration of metrics and datasets to assess the fidelity of images generated by generative adversarial networks. *Applied Sciences (Basel, Switzerland)*, 13(19), 10637. DOI:10.3390/ app131910637

Meena, D., Katragadda, H., Narva, K., Rajesh, A. N., & Sheela, J. (2023). Text-Conditioned Image Synthesis using TAC-GAN: A Unique Approach to Text-to-Image Synthesis. *2023 2nd International Conference on Automation, Computing and Renewable Systems (ICACRS)*. DOI:10.1109/ICACRS58579.2023.10404459

Meena, G., Mohbey, K. K., & Kumar, S. (2023). Sentiment analysis on images using convolutional neural networks based Inception-V3 transfer learning approach. *International Journal of Information Management Data Insights*, 3(1), 100174. DOI:10.1016/j.jjimei.2023.100174

Megahed, M., & Mohammed, A. (2023). A comprehensive review of generative adversarial networks: Fundamentals, applications, and challenges. *Wiley Interdisciplinary Reviews: Computational Statistics*. Advance online publication. DOI:10.1002/ wics.1629

Min, B., Ross, H., Sulem, E., Veyseh, A. P. B., Nguyen, T. H., Sainz, O., Agirre, E., Heintz, I., & Roth, D. (2023). Recent advances in natural language processing via large pre-trained language models: A survey. *ACM Computing Surveys*, 56(2), 1–40. DOI:10.1145/3605943

Mohamed, A., Lee, H., Borgholt, L., Havtorn, J. D., Edin, J., Igel, C., Kirchhoff, K., Li, S., Livescu, K., Maaløe, L., Sainath, T. N., & Watanabe, S. (2022). Self-Supervised Speech Representation Learning: A review. *IEEE Journal of Selected Topics in Signal Processing*, 16(6), 1179–1210. DOI:10.1109/JSTSP.2022.3207050

Najar, F., Bourouis, S., Bouguila, N., & Belghith, S. (2017). A Comparison Between Different Gaussian-Based Mixture Models. *2017 IEEE/ACS 14th International Conference on Computer Systems and Applications (AICCSA)*. DOI:10.1109/AICCSA.2017.108

Pakhale, K. (2023). Large language models and information retrieval. *Social Science Research Network*. DOI:10.2139/ssrn.4636121

Pala, Z., Yamli, V., & Ünlük, İ. H. (2017). Deep Learning researches in Turkey: An academic approach. *2017 XIIIth International Conference on Perspective Technologies and Methods in MEMS Design (MEMSTECH)*. DOI:10.1109/MEMSTECH.2017.7937546

Paladugu, P., Ong, J., Nelson, N. G., Kamran, S. A., Waisberg, E., Zaman, N., Kumar, R., Dias, R. D., Lee, A. G., & Tavakkoli, A. (2023). Generative Adversarial Networks in Medicine: Important Considerations for this Emerging Innovation in Artificial Intelligence. *Annals of Biomedical Engineering*, 51(10), 2130–2142. DOI:10.1007/s10439-023-03304-z PMID:37488468

Pan, B. (2020, November 21). *Adversarial mutual information for text generation*. PMLR. https://proceedings.mlr.press/v119/pan20a.html

Papamakarios, G., Nalisnick, E., Rezende, D. J., Mohamed, S., & Lakshminarayanan, B. (2019). Normalizing flows for probabilistic modeling and inference. *arXiv (Cornell University)*. http://export.arxiv.org/pdf/1912.02762

Park, J. H., Park, S., & Shim, H. (2019). Semantic-aware neural style transfer. *Image and Vision Computing*, 87, 13–23. DOI:10.1016/j.imavis.2019.04.001

Powers, D. (2020). Evaluation: from precision, recall and F-measure to ROC, informedness, markedness and correlation. *arXiv (Cornell University)*. https://doi.org//arxiv.2010.16061DOI:10.48550

Quan, T. M., Nguyen-Duc, T., & Jeong, W. (2018). Compressed sensing MRI reconstruction using a generative adversarial network with a cyclic loss. *IEEE Transactions on Medical Imaging*, 37(6), 1488–1497. DOI:10.1109/TMI.2018.2820120 PMID:29870376

Ranzato, M., Susskind, J. M., Mnih, V., & Hinton, G. E. (2011). On deep generative models with applications to recognition. *CVPR*, 2011, 2857–2864. Advance online publication. DOI:10.1109/CVPR.2011.5995710

Rao, P. V. (2024, February 7). *Deep Reinforcement Learning: Bridging the Gap with Neural Networks*. https://www.ijisae.org/index.php/IJISAE/article/view/4792

Raso, F., Hilligoss, H., Krishnamurthy, V., Bavitz, C., & Levin, K. (2018). Artificial Intelligence & Human Rights: Opportunities & Risks. *Social Science Research Network*. DOI:10.2139/ssrn.3259344

Rudroff, T. (2024). Artificial Intelligence's transformative role in illuminating brain function in long COVID patients using PET/FDG. *Brain Sciences*, 14(1), 73. DOI:10.3390/brainsci14010073 PMID:38248288

Ruff, L., Kauffmann, J. R., Vandermeulen, R. A., Montavon, G., Samek, W., Kloft, M., Dieterich, T. G., & Müller, K. (2021). A unifying review of deep and shallow anomaly detection. *Proceedings of the IEEE*, 109(5), 756–795. DOI:10.1109/JPROC.2021.3052449

Saad, M. M., O'Reilly, R., & Rehmani, M. H. (2024). A survey on training challenges in generative adversarial networks for biomedical image analysis. *Artificial Intelligence Review*, 57(2), 19. Advance online publication. DOI:10.1007/s10462-023-10624-y

Sajeeda, A., & Hossain, B. (2022). Exploring generative adversarial networks and adversarial training. *International Journal of Cognitive Computing in Engineering*, 3, 78–89. DOI:10.1016/j.ijcce.2022.03.002

Salakhutdinov, R. (2015). Learning deep generative models. *Annual Review of Statistics and Its Application*, 2(1), 361–385. DOI:10.1146/annurev-statistics-010814-020120

Sampath, V., Maurtua, I., Martín, J. J. A., & Gutierrez, A. (2021). A survey on generative adversarial networks for imbalance problems in computer vision tasks. *Journal of Big Data*, 8(1), 27. Advance online publication. DOI:10.1186/s40537-021-00414-0 PMID:33552840

Sankar, S., Ramasubbareddy, S., Luhach, A. K., Deverajan, G. G., Alnumay, W. S., Jhanjhi, N. Z., Ghosh, U., & Sharma, P. K. (2020). Energy efficient optimal parent selection based routing protocol for Internet of Things using firefly optimization algorithm. *Transactions on Emerging Telecommunications Technologies*, 32(8), e4171. Advance online publication. DOI:10.1002/ett.4171

Shamsolmoali, P., Zareapoor, M., Granger, É., Zhou, H., Wang, R., Celebi, M. E., & Yang, J. (2021). Image synthesis with adversarial networks: A comprehensive survey and case studies. *Information Fusion*, 72, 126–146. DOI:10.1016/j.inffus.2021.02.014

Shi, Z., Peng, S., Xu, Y., Liao, Y., & Shen, Y. (2022). Deep Generative Models on 3D Representations: a survey. *arXiv (Cornell University)*. https://doi.org//arxiv .2210.15663DOI:10.48550

Shibli, A., Pritom, M. M. A., & Gupta, M. (2024). AbuseGPT: Abuse of generative AI ChatBots to create smishing campaigns. *arXiv (Cornell University)*. /arxiv.2402. 09728DOI:10.1109/ISDFS60797.2024.10527300

Shokrollahi, Y., Yarmohammadtoosky, S., Nikahd, M. M., Dong, P., Li, X., & Gu, L. (2023). A comprehensive review of Generative AI in healthcare. *arXiv (Cornell University)*. https://doi.org//arxiv.2310.00795DOI:10.48550

Sindiramutty, S. R. (2023). Autonomous Threat Hunting: a future paradigm for AI-Driven Threat intelligence. *arXiv (Cornell University)*. https://doi.org//arxiv.2401 .00286DOI:10.48550

Sindiramutty, S. R., Jhanjhi, N. Z., Ray, S. K., Jazri, H., Khan, N. A., & Gaur, L. (2023). Metaverse. In *Advances in medical technologies and clinical practice book series* (pp. 93–158). DOI:10.4018/978-1-6684-9823-1.ch003

Sindiramutty, S. R., Jhanjhi, N. Z., Ray, S. K., Jazri, H., Khan, N. A., Gaur, L., Gharib, A. H., & Manchuri, A. R. (2023). Metaverse. In *Advances in medical technologies and clinical practice book series* (pp. 24–92). DOI:10.4018/978-1-6684-9823-1.ch002

Sindiramutty, S. R., Jhanjhi, N. Z., Tan, C. E., Khan, N. A., Gharib, A. H., & Yun, K. J. (2023). Applications of blockchain technology in supply chain management. In *Advances in logistics, operations, and management science book series* (pp. 248–304). DOI:10.4018/978-1-6684-7625-3.ch009

Sindiramutty, S. R., Jhanjhi, N. Z., Tan, C. E., Khan, N. A., Shah, B., & Gaur, L. (2023). Securing the digital supply chain cyber threats and vulnerabilities. In *Advances in logistics, operations, and management science book series* (pp. 156–223). DOI:10.4018/978-1-6684-7625-3.ch007

Sindiramutty, S. R., Jhanjhi, N. Z., Tan, C. E., Tee, W. J., Lau, S. P., Jazri, H., Ray, S. K., & Zaheer, M. A. (2024). IoT and AI-Based Smart Solutions for the Agriculture Industry. In *Advances in computational intelligence and robotics book series* (pp. 317–351). DOI:10.4018/978-1-6684-6361-1.ch012

Sindiramutty, S. R., Tan, C., Tee, W. J., Lau, S. P., Balakrishnan, S., Kaur, S. D. A., Jazri, H., & Aslam, M. (2024). Modern smart cities and open research challenges and issues of explainable artificial intelligence. In *Advances in computational intelligence and robotics book series* (pp. 389–424). DOI:10.4018/978-1-6684-6361-1.ch015

Sindiramutty, S. R., Tan, C. E., Lau, S. P., Thangaveloo, R., Gharib, A. H., Manchuri, A. R., Khan, N. A., Tee, W. J., & Muniandy, L. (2024). Explainable AI for cybersecurity. In *Advances in computational intelligence and robotics book series* (pp. 31–97). DOI:10.4018/978-1-6684-6361-1.ch002

Sindiramutty, S. R., Tee, W. J., Balakrishnan, S., Kaur, S., Thangaveloo, R., Jazri, H., Khan, N. A., Gharib, A. H., & Manchuri, A. R. (2024). Explainable AI in healthcare application. In *Advances in computational intelligence and robotics book series* (pp. 123–176). DOI:10.4018/978-1-6684-6361-1.ch005

Singhal, V., Jain, S. P., Anand, D., Singh, A., Verma, S., Kavita, , Rodrigues, J. J. P. C., Jhanjhi, N. Z., Ghosh, U., Jo, O., & Iwendi, C. (2020). Artificial Intelligence Enabled Road Vehicle-Train Collision Risk Assessment Framework for Unmanned railway level crossings. *IEEE Access : Practical Innovations, Open Solutions*, 8, 113790–113806. DOI:10.1109/ACCESS.2020.3002416

Sohail, S. S., Farhat, F., Himeur, Y., Nadeem, M., Madsen, D. Ø., Singh, Y., Atalla, S., & Mansoor, W. (2023). *Decoding ChatGPT: a taxonomy of existing research, current challenges, and possible future directions. arXiv*. Cornell University., DOI:10.1016/j.jksuci.2023.101675

Soloveitchik, M., Diskin, T., Morin, E., & Wiesel, A. (2021). Conditional frechet inception distance. *arXiv (Cornell University)*. https://doi.org//arxiv.2103.11521DOI: 10.48550

Srinivasan, K. (2021, June 16). *Performance comparison of deep CNN models for detecting driver's distraction*. https://papers.ssrn.com/sol3/papers.cfm?abstract_id =3868549

Srivastava, H., Bharti, A. K., & Singh, A. (2023). Context-Aware Vision Transformer (Cavit) for Satellite Image Classification. *SSRN*. DOI:10.2139/ssrn.4673127

Srivastava, R., & Kumar, P. (2024). Deep-GAN: An improved model for thyroid nodule identification and classification. *Neural Computing & Applications*, 36(14), 7685–7704. Advance online publication. DOI:10.1007/s00521-024-09492-6

Sturm, B. L., Ben-Tal, O., Monaghan, Ú., Collins, N., Herremans, D., Chew, E., Hadjeres, G., Deruty, E., & Pachet, F. (2018). Machine learning research that matters for music creation: A case study. *Journal of New Music Research*, 48(1), 36–55. DOI:10.1080/09298215.2018.1515233

Sun, J., Wang, X., Xiong, N., & Shao, J. (2018). Learning sparse representation with variational Auto-Encoder for anomaly detection. *IEEE Access : Practical Innovations, Open Solutions*, 6, 33353–33361. DOI:10.1109/ACCESS.2018.2848210

Taj, I., & Jhanjhi, N. Z. (2022). Towards Industrial Revolution 5.0 and Explainable Artificial Intelligence: Challenges and opportunities. *International Journal of Computing and Digital Systems*, 12(1), 285–310. DOI:10.12785/ijcds/120124

Tan, T. F., Thirunavukarasu, A. J., Campbell, J. P., Keane, P. A., Pasquale, L. R., Abràmoff, M. D., Kalpathy–Cramer, J., Lum, F., Kim, J. E., Baxter, S. L., & Ting, D. S. W. (2023). Generative artificial intelligence through ChatGPT and other large language models in ophthalmology. *Ophthalmology Science*, 3(4), 100394. DOI:10.1016/j.xops.2023.100394 PMID:37885755

Tanwani, A. K. (2018). Generative Models for Learning Robot Manipulation Skills from Humans. *Generative Models for Learning Robot Manipulation Skills From Humans*. DOI:10.5075/epfl-thesis-8320

Toshevska, M., & Gievska, S. (2022). A review of text style transfer using Deep learning. *IEEE Transactions on Artificial Intelligence*, 3(5), 669–684. DOI:10.1109/TAI.2021.3115992

Tursunalieva, A., Alexánder, D., Dunne, R., Li, J., Riera, L. G., & Zhao, Y. (2024). Making Sense of Machine Learning: A review of interpretation techniques and their applications. *Applied Sciences (Basel, Switzerland)*, 14(2), 496. DOI:10.3390/app14020496

Varghese, N. V., & Mahmoud, Q. H. (2020). A survey of Multi-Task Deep Reinforcement Learning. *Electronics (Basel)*, 9(9), 1363. DOI:10.3390/electronics9091363

Vartiainen, H., & Tedre, M. (2024). How Text-to-Image Generative AI is Transforming Mediated Action. *IEEE Computer Graphics and Applications*, 44(2), 1–12. DOI:10.1109/MCG.2024.3355808 PMID:38285567

Vasist, P. N., & Krishnan, S. (2022). Deepfakes: An integrative review of the literature and an agenda for future research. *Communications of the Association for Information Systems*, 51, 590–636. DOI:10.17705/1CAIS.05126

Verma, S., Kaur, S., Rawat, D. B., Chen, X., Alex, L. T., & Jhanjhi, N. Z. (2021). Intelligent framework using IoT-Based WSNs for wildfire detection. *IEEE Access : Practical Innovations, Open Solutions*, 9, 48185–48196. DOI:10.1109/AC-CESS.2021.3060549

Voulodimos, A., Doulamis, A., & Protopapadakis, E. (2018). Deep Learning for Computer Vision: A Brief review. *Computational Intelligence and Neuroscience*, 2018, 1–13. DOI:10.1155/2018/7068349 PMID:29487619

Wang, J. (2023, December 15). *FaceComposer: a unified model for versatile facial content creation*. https://proceedings.neurips.cc/paper_files/paper/2023/hash/2b4caf39e645680f826ae0a9e7ae9402-Abstract-Conference.html

Wang, J., Wang, J., Wang, S., & Zhang, Y. (2023). Deep learning in pediatric neuroimaging. *Displays*, 80, 102583. DOI:10.1016/j.displa.2023.102583

Wang, J. X. (2021). Meta-learning in natural and artificial intelligence. *Current Opinion in Behavioral Sciences*, 38, 90–95. DOI:10.1016/j.cobeha.2021.01.002

Wang, T. (2018). *High-Resolution image synthesis and semantic manipulation with conditional GANs*. https://openaccess.thecvf.com/content_cvpr_2018/html/Wang_High-Resolution_Image_Synthesis_CVPR_2018_paper.html

Wang, Z. (2016, June 11). *Dueling network architectures for deep reinforcement learning*. PMLR. http://proceedings.mlr.press/v48/wangf16.html

Wang, Z., Wang, J., & Wang, Y. (2018). An intelligent diagnosis scheme based on generative adversarial learning deep neural networks and its application to planetary gearbox fault pattern recognition. *Neurocomputing*, 310, 213–222. DOI:10.1016/j.neucom.2018.05.024

Waqas, A., Bui, M. M., Glassy, E. F., Naqa, I. E., Borkowski, P., Borkowski, A., & Bouaynaya, N. (2023). Revolutionizing digital pathology with the power of generative artificial intelligence and foundation models. *Laboratory Investigation*, 103(11), 100255. DOI:10.1016/j.labinv.2023.100255 PMID:37757969

Wen, B. O. T., Syahriza, N., Xian, N. C. W., Wei, N., Shen, T. Z., Hin, Y. Z., Sindiramutty, S. R., & Nicole, T. Y. F. (2023). Detecting cyber threats with a Graph-Based NIDPS. In *Advances in logistics, operations, and management science book series* (pp. 36–74). DOI:10.4018/978-1-6684-7625-3.ch002

Wu, A. N., Stouffs, R., & Biljecki, F. (2022). Generative Adversarial Networks in the built environment: A comprehensive review of the application of GANs across data types and scales. *Building and Environment*, 223, 109477. DOI:10.1016/j.buildenv.2022.109477

Wu, Y. (2021). Robust Learning-Enabled Intelligence for the Internet of Things: A survey from the perspectives of noisy data and adversarial examples. *IEEE Internet of Things Journal*, 8(12), 9568–9579. DOI:10.1109/JIOT.2020.3018691

Xu, L., Zhou, T., Wang, Y., Wang, Y., Cao, Q., Du, W., Yang, Y., He, J., Qiao, Y., & Shen, Y. (2023). Towards the Unification of Generative and Discriminative Visual Foundation Model: a survey. *arXiv (Cornell University)*. https://doi.org//arxiv.2312.10163DOI:10.48550

Ye, F., & Borş, A. G. (2023). Lifelong generative adversarial autoencoder. *IEEE Transactions on Neural Networks and Learning Systems*, 1–15. DOI:10.1109/TNNLS.2023.3281091 PMID:37410645

Ye, F., & Borş, A. G. (2024). Self-Supervised Adversarial Variational learning. *Pattern Recognition*, 148, 110156. DOI:10.1016/j.patcog.2023.110156

Yu, C., Liu, J., Nemati, S., & Yin, G. (2021). Reinforcement Learning in Healthcare: A survey. *ACM Computing Surveys*, 55(1), 1–36. DOI:10.1145/3477600

Yu, L., Yousif, M. Z., Zhang, M., Hoyas, S., Vinuesa, R., & Lim, H. (2022). Three-dimensional ESRGAN for super-resolution reconstruction of turbulent flows with tricubic interpolation-based transfer learning. *Physics of Fluids*, 34(12), 125126. Advance online publication. DOI:10.1063/5.0129203

Zafar, I., Anwar, S. M. S., Kanwal, F., Yousaf, W., Nisa, F. U., Kausar, T., Ain, Q. U., Unar, A., Kamal, M. A., Rashid, S., Khan, K. A., & Sharma, R. (2023). Reviewing methods of deep learning for intelligent healthcare systems in genomics and bio-medicine. *Biomedical Signal Processing and Control*, 86, 105263. DOI:10.1016/j.bspc.2023.105263

Zhang, C., Chen, J., Li, J., Peng, Y., & Mao, Z. (2023). Large language models for human-robot interaction: A review. *Biomimetic Intelligence and Robotics*, 3(4), 100131. DOI:10.1016/j.birob.2023.100131

Zhang, C., Zhang, C., Zheng, S., Qiao, Y., Li, C., Zhang, M., Dam, S. K., Thwal, C. M., Tun, Y. L., Huy, L. L., Kim, D., Bae, S., Lee, L., Yang, Y., Shen, H. T., Kweon, I. S., & Hong, C. S. (2023). A Complete Survey on Generative AI (AIGC): Is ChatGPT from GPT-4 to GPT-5 All You Need? *arXiv (Cornell University)*. https://doi.org//arxiv.2303.11717DOI:10.48550

Zhang, R., Guo, J., Chen, L., Fan, Y., & Cheng, X. (2021). A Review on Question Generation from Natural Language Text. *ACM Transactions on Information Systems*, 40(1), 1–43. DOI:10.1145/3468889

Zhao, H., Li, H., Maurer-Stroh, S., & Cheng, L. (2018). Synthesizing retinal and neuronal images with generative adversarial nets. *Medical Image Analysis*, 49, 14–26. DOI:10.1016/j.media.2018.07.001 PMID:30007254

Zhao, Z., Alzubaidi, L., Zhang, J., Duan, Y., & Gu, Y. (2024). A comparison review of transfer learning and self-supervised learning: Definitions, applications, advantages and limitations. *Expert Systems with Applications*, 242, 122807. DOI:10.1016/j.eswa.2023.122807

Zhou, J. (2023, October 13). *Retrieval-based Disentangled Representation Learning with Natural Language Supervision*. OpenReview. https://openreview.net/forum?id=ZlQRiFmq7Y

Zhou, Z., Bao, Z., Jiang, W., Huang, Y., Peng, Y., Shankar, A., Maple, C., & Shitharth, S. (2024). Latent Vector Optimization-Based Generative image steganography for consumer electronic applications. *IEEE Transactions on Consumer Electronics*, 1(1), 4357–4366. Advance online publication. DOI:10.1109/TCE.2024.3354824

Chapter 2
Reinforcement Learning Approaches in Cyber Security

Ehtisham Safeer

UIIT, Pakistan

ABSTRACT

Reinforcement learning (RL) allows defense mechanisms to adapt to changing threats and has shown promise in tackling cyber security issues. This study presents a thorough introduction which includes foundations, uses, and difficulties to RL in cyber security. The efficacy of RL in making decisions is also emphasized in the introduction. Then the foundation for comprehending RL's use in cyber security, the fundamentals of the technology, and algorithm classifications is clarified. The study then delves into a number of RL applications in cyber security. Then a number of RL applications in cyber security and issues in RL is discussed. Along with prospects for improving cyber security safeguards through the application of RL methodologies, to successfully manage increasing cyber threats, future research directions are proposed with the integration of blockchain technology and generative adversarial networks (GANs). This work emphasizes the importance of RL in supporting cyber security and research to improve cyber defenses.

DOI: 10.4018/979-8-3693-5415-5.ch002

I. INTRODUCTION

A. Overview of Reinforcement Learning in Cyber Security

RL in machine learning makes decisions that refer to strategies for enhancing performance via trial and error (Qi et al., 2022). RL techniques have shown to be quite successful in the last few decades in resolving challenging issues in a variety of industries, such as vision in computers, robotics, and gaming. Rejuvenation in RL is superior to that of human performance. The agent's capacity to automate features acquisition and complete end-to-end learning is credited with this method's effectiveness. RL is goal-oriented and hypothesis-based, and it occurs when events, observations, and incentives are employed as inputs (Nguyen et al., 2020).

Figure 1. Representation of the RL Model

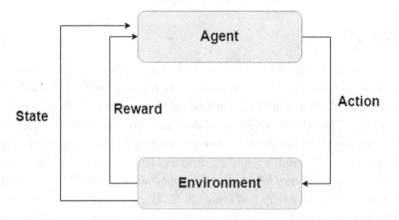

As modern civilization becomes more dependent on Information Technology (IT) systems including autonomous ones malicious actors also aggressively take advantage of these systems. Indeed, cyber risks are always changing, and as per Gartner, attackers will possess the necessary skills to cause injury or even death to humans. Defense mechanisms must be able to quickly respond to the changing settings and dynamic threat landscape in order to prevent such accidents and reduce the multitude of hazards that can target present and future IT systems (Süzen, 2020).

RL is a unique kind of machine learning in which a collection of observations, actions, and incentives provides the input. RL stands for goal-oriented interaction-based learning. RL picks up knowledge from, and while interacting with, the outside world. It makes use of agents, or systems, that enhance performance in response to their interactions with the surroundings. Through interactions with their surroundings, agents learn a series of actions or input information that maximizes the reward signal as determined by the reward function through reinforcement learning. In reinforcement learning, algorithms use trial and error to identify patterns in the unlabeled unprocessed information and then award human experts based on those findings (Piplai et al., 2020)

Figure 2. RL Explanation as ML

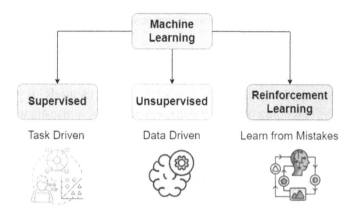

Among the traits of RL are that the learner is not provided instruction for what to do, thus there's a need to figure things out via try and error should investigate and seize chances while there's a chance for a reward that will come later. RL considers the problem of a focused on objectives agent communicating in an uncertain environment in its entirety (Suchithra et al., 2023).

B. Importance of RL in Cyber Security

The threat posed by cyber attacks is only increasing due to the development in intelligent and successful targeted assaults that occur globally. RL enables adaptable safety measures, enabling them to identify and respond instantly to evolving security threats. There is an urgent need to address this issue with cyber security specialists who are adequately skilled and motivated to avoid, detect, react to, or even mitigate the impact of such threats ((Rjoub et al., 2023).

C. Scope and Objectives of the Article

Scope

This article explores the application of RL strategies to computer security to defenses against unpredictable attacks. This study offers details on the possible disadvantages and effectiveness of these methods for safeguarding digital data. It examines RL algorithm and their applications. This study also highlighted how they could enhance cyber security protocols in various fields.

Objectives

The objectives of this article are the application of RL methods in cyber security and effectiveness in fending off new threats. Additionally, it investigates the possibilities and challenges of applying RL to enhance security measures.

II. FUNDAMENTALS OF REINFORCEMENT LEARNING

A. Explanation of RL Concepts

In RL, a "Agent" is an independent variable that has to find its goal through specific conditions to reach its objectives ((Cam, 2020). The observable qualities and the results of the agent's operates are referred to as the "Environment" (Luketina et al., 2019). "Actions" are the things that an agent is capable of doing. It selects these activities in accordance with internal guidelines to optimize accumulative "rewards" which are indications from the Environment (Zhang et al., 2021).

Figure 3. Learning Action Values of Reinforcement Learning

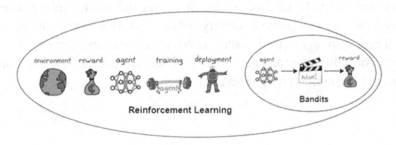

B. Types of RL Algorithms

RL algorithms can be generally classified into many sorts. Here are a few of the main categories.

Value Based Approaches

These algorithms try to calculate the worth of doing a certain action or existing in a certain state. Q-Learning, Double Deep Q-Networks (DDQN), and Deep Q-Networks (DQN) are a few examples. Value-based approaches acquire value functions, which stand for the projected total benefit of doing a specific action in a specific condition (Zang et al., 2020).

Policy Gradient Techniques

Unlike value-based techniques, policy-based algorithms figure out the best course of action by mapping states to actions (Ni et al., 2022). Examples include Trust Region Policy Optimization (TRPO) and Policy Gradient techniques like REINFORCE. In order to maximize the projected cumulative benefit, policy-based techniques explicitly parameterize the policy and change its parameters.

Actor Critic Methods

These algorithms include elements of policy-based and value-based methodologies. They keep two distinct parts: an actor who becomes familiar with the policy and a critic who assesses the actor's decisions (Kumar et al., 2023). Proximal Policy Optimization (PPO) and Advantage Actor-Critic (A2C) are two examples.

Model Based Approaches

RL algorithms that are model-based acquire a model of the dynamics of their environment and utilize it for action planning. Usually, they entail learning a transition model that, given the present state and action, forecasts the next state and reward (Moerland et al., 2023). Dyna-Q and Model Predictive Control (MPC) are two examples.

Deep Reinforcement Learning

These algorithms handle high-dimensional state and action spaces by combining RL approaches with deep neural networks. Deep RL techniques have shown impressive results in applications including natural language processing, robotics control, and video game play (Azar et al., 2023). Asynchronous Advantage Actor-Critic (A3C), Deep Q-Networks (DQN), and Deep Deterministic Policy Gradients (DDPG) are a few examples.

Q-Learning

With Q-learning, an agent gains decision-making skills by calculating the benefit of a specific course of action in a given situation. The projected cumulative reward of performing each action in each condition is stored in a Q-table, also known as a Q-function, which is used to achieve this. The agent eventually learns by making mistakes and experimenting as it engages with the surroundings. It then utilises this table to determine which course of action is optimal in each given state. There are different types of variants of q-learning each intended to solve particular problems or enhance performance in various contexts. Some of them are discussed as following.

Deep Q-Networks (DQN): To handle highly dimensional state spaces, DQN blends deep neural networks with Q-learning is used. It can learn directly from unprocessed sensory inputs, such as pixels on a screen. To stabilise training, DQN included target networks along with replay.

Double Q-learning: By separating action selection from action evaluation, double Q-learning tackles the problem of overestimation bias in conventional Q-learning techniques. It keeps track of two sets of Q-values, using one for action selection and the other for evaluation.

Duelling Q-Networks: The agent is able to better understand the worth of each action in relation to the state by using Duelling Q-Networks. Learning efficiency is increased by this architecture, particularly in settings where there are many of activities but not enough crucial ones.

Prioritized Experience Replay (PER): Experiences saved in the replay buffer are ranked in order of significance for learning via Prioritised Experience Replay.

Distributional Q-learning: deDistributional Q-learning represents the distribution of returns. Learning a distribution provides the agent with a deeper comprehension of the uncertainty around various courses of action, which may result in more sound decision-making.

Inverse Reinforcement Learning

Inverse RL looks to expert demonstrations to learn the underlying reward function. It is frequently applied in contexts of imitation learning, when the objective is to imitate the actions of an expert actor.

Since each kind of RL algorithm has advantages and disadvantages, it can be used to various problem domains and scenarios. Based on variables including task complexity, data availability, and computational capacity, researchers and practitioners select the best method (Arora et al., 2021).

Figure 4. RL Algorithms

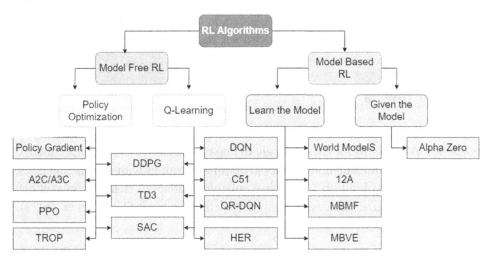

C. Application of RL

RL finds applications in a wide range of domains. Below is a discussion of its use in several fields:

Gaming

With applications ranging from modern video games to traditional card, RL is becoming increasingly common in the gaming industry. Moreover, adaptive non-player characters are made in games using RL (Sivamayil et al., 2023).

Robotics

Robot computerizations depend on RL. When RL techniques are implemented on a robot, it can learn to perform complex tasks such as grabbing objects, shifting, and even travelling around landscapes. RL enables machines to gain knowledge from their experiences and adapt to shifting environments, increasing their adaptability and capacity to manage real-world scenarios (Du et al., 2023).

Autonomous Vehicles

Road-safe and road-effective driverless automobile creation uses RL. RL techniques discover how to drive by analyzing sensor inputs, road circumstances, and routing targets. These algorithms enable cars to acquire knowledge from humans driving behaviors over time to improve their decision-making skills (Hambly et al., 2023).

Financial Trading

RL is utilized in automated trading to enhance investment approaches and managing portfolios. Algorithms for RL are taught to make trade choices based on, economic trends and market information in order to optimize earnings with minimizing risks. Trading algorithms built on an RL base are able to adapt to changing market circumstances and seize chances in highly turbulent economies (Tiwari et al., 2023).

Healthcare

The use of RL facilitates pharmaceutical exploration, medical testing, and customized treatment planning. RL techniques are taught to generate customized treatment alternatives for every patient based on medical data and performance. In order to maximize the choice and layout of therapeutic applicants, RL is utilized in the development of drugs to simulate chemical reactions and evaluate efficiency (Mohamadi et al., 2024).

Logistics

RL helps improve the management of supply chains, inventory control and logistics. RL algorithms are taught to make judgments regarding inventory levels, paths to transportation, and manufacturing schedules in order to minimize costs and maximize efficiency. Logistics management systems built on RL underpinnings are adaptable enough to deal with unanticipated circumstances and shifts in consumer demand (Jendoubi et al., 2023).

Natural Language Processing (NLP)

RL is employed in NLP activities such as creating languages, translators, and conversation systems. RL techniques generate coherent and culturally specific material by interacting with syntax models and observing user response. RL-based NLP platforms can improve their ability to produce and comprehend speech in time (Mijwil et al., 2023).

Energy Administration

RL is employed for maximizing energy circulation and use in smart grids and systems that generate electricity from renewable resources. RL calculations can adjust to changes in generation, warehouses. Expenditure based on pattern of demand, the prediction of the weather, and layout conditions. RL based systems for energy management has the potential to improve network reliability, efficacy, as well as longevity (Eze et al., 2023)

Figure 5. RL Applications in Various Fields

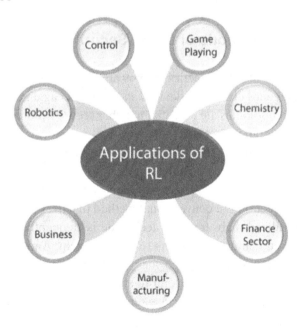

III. CYBER SECURITY THREAT LANDSCAPE

A. Risks and Difficulties in Cyber Security

There are numerous hazards and cyber security problems in today's online environment. The environment is changing; hostile actors are taking advantage of weaknesses and state actors are engage in hacking. Ransomware, Trojan horses, and other malware are among the most frequent threats because they may breach data security, corrupt entire systems, and interfere with regular corporate operations. They utilize shady websites or emails to lure consumers into disclosing important information, hackers continue to be a serious security risk (Krüger et al., 2021).Even if data leaks are the result of insiders or outsiders, they nevertheless compromise confidentiality and trust, resulting in monetary losses and harm to a the individual's reputation. The World Wide Web's rapid expansion has given rise to new threats that raise concerns about privacy and security. Artificial intelligence (AI) are examples of future breakthroughs that bring both opportunities and threats (Kilincer et al., 2021). Because of this, professionals in cyber security are concentrating increasingly on strengthened cryptography and AI-driven assaults against quantum computers. In order to sufficiently safeguard digital ownership and lower risks, countering these sophisticated attacks necessitates a proactive strategy that involves strong security mechanisms, constant surveillance of user information, and engagement with stakeholders (Ahmet et al., 2021).

B. Conventional Methods of Cyber Security

Conventional cyber security tactics employ an amalgamation of techniques and approaches to safeguard electronic devices and networks against diverse forms of breaches. These technologies are essential to cyber security protocols and One important tactic is penetration security, which involves monitoring all network traffic that comes and goes through the network by putting up safeguards and intrusion detection systems (IDS). Access limitations are also commonly used to prevent unauthorized users from accessing assets and private information (Wu et al., 2021). Signature-based detection is a conventional method that uses particular patterns to identify and neutralized malware. This technique is frequently used by antivirus software to locate and eliminate dangers from the system. Anomaly identification approaches, on the other hand, search for odd or suspicious activity that differs from routine operations and might point to an assault or compromise of security (Majadas et al., 2024). Encryption is an essential part of traditional cyber security, encryption techniques offer protection and privacy while making it more difficult for unauthorized parties to access or change sensitive data (Zhang et al., 2020).

C. Limitations of Traditional Approaches

The following are examples of the quickly evolving cyber threat landscape that often find difficult to keep up with:

Stabilized Security

Static security is used by many classical technologies to identify known hazards and restrict access based on pre-established policies. But threats that evolve quickly, such zero-day exploits or polymorphic malware, cannot be handled by current defenses since they can alter their behavior or signature to evade detection (Hore et al., 2023).

Absence of Awareness

Without contextual awareness, it can be difficult to discern between suspicious and non-suspicious behavior that can lead to false positives or miss real threats (Huang et al., 2022).

Limited Monitoring and Vision

Conventional methods are only able to offer restricted monitoring and vision of the whole attack surface in large, distributed systems or cloud infrastructures. Organizations may find it challenging to recognize threats and take necessary action when there is a lack of thorough monitoring and visibility, which may result in weaknesses that attackers may exploit (Jung et al., 2022).

Over-Reliance on Reactive Measures

Reactive technologies comprise a number of conventional methods that place more emphasis on responding to security breaches after they happen than on taking preventative action beforehand. While recovery from incidents and response play a crucial role in cyber security, businesses that rely solely on reactive tactics run the risk of suffering harm and interruption from successful attacks (Qi et al., 2022).

Problems and General Management

Many tools and technologies used in traditional cyber security solutions can be challenging to install, set up, and keep up without a lot of manual labor and specialized knowledge. Due to operational costs, misconfiguration, and coverage gaps brought on by this complexity, companies may find it challenging to maintain a robust security posture (Zhang et al., 2020).

IV. REINFORCEMENT LEARNING TECHNIQUES IN CYBER SECURITY

RL techniques are increasingly explored and applied in cybersecurity to address various challenges. Some of them are discussed as following.

Deep Reinforcement Learning

Deep reinforcement learning (DRL) techniques, like Deep Q-Networks (DQN) or Deep Deterministic Policy Gradients (DDPG), can be used to identify malware by teaching them to distinguish between benign and dangerous files or network traffic. (Li, 2023) These techniques can learn representations that capture pertinent aspects of malware behaviors and process complex, high-dimensional input data.

Adversarial Reinforcement Learning

The goal of adversarial reinforcement learning techniques is to increase the robustness of reinforcement learning agents against hostile attacks. This method can be applied to cybersecurity to create malware classifiers or intrusion detection systems that can withstand evasion efforts meant to trick or avoid detection (Bhardwaj et al., 2024).

Multi-Agent Reinforcement Learning for Network Security

Network security scenarios containing numerous interacting entities, like routers, firewalls, and attackers, can benefit from the application of multi-agent reinforcement learning (MARL) approaches. Through MARL, agents can acquire tactics for collaboration, rivalry, or compromise in order to thwart attacks and enhance network efficiency (Ju et al., 2023).

Reinforcement Learning for Vulnerability Assessment

RL can be applied to vulnerability assessment in order to minimise the risk of exploitation. RL works by simulating the actions of an attacker and teaching it how to prioritise security patches or configurations (Ghanem et at., 2023). In order to find flaws and strengthen defences, RL agents can mimic the actions of attackers and learn how to exploit vulnerabilities in a controlled setting.

These are just a few examples of how RL techniques are being applied in cyber-security. As cybersecurity threats continue to evolve, the integration of RL with traditional security approaches developing more adaptive and resilient defence systems.

V. REINFORCEMENT LEARNING APPLICATIONS IN CYBER SECURITY

A. Intrusion Detection Systems (IDS)

Among the intrusion detection strategies that have surfaced in recent years, intrusion detection systems (IDS) are a relatively new technology. In order to identify any odd or suspicious patterns that can indicate security flaws, these systems monitor system logs, network activity (Schwarting, 2023). IDS can be broadly divided into two types: networking-based IDS, which examines network traffic in real-time to identify suspicious behavior, and a host-based IDS, which monitors activity within particular systems or hosts for signs of illicit activity or unauthorized access IDS system's main role in network is to help computer systems to prepare and deal with the network attacks.

Figure 6. RL in Cyber Security

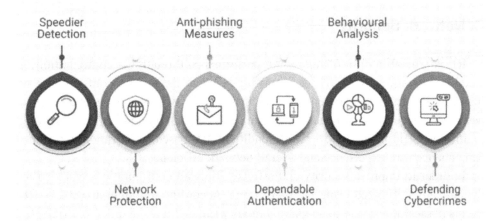

RL techniques for anomaly detection in numerous cyber security fields is used by enabling agents to adapt and learn from shifting patterns of typical behavior, It offers a dynamic and adaptable technique for identifying abnormalities in complicated structures. These algorithms learn from encounters, RL-based anomaly detection systems are able to improve their comprehension of typical behavior over time. By modelling the environment, including states, actions, and features, RL agents are able to recognize unusual patterns in the system (Burhani et al., 2023).

B. Vulnerability Management

IT systems may have security issues that RL i can resolve. RL algorithms can be used to continuously examine devices for potential vulnerabilities. that help with decision-making and use information. Prioritizing vulnerabilities according to their possible impact on the business's operations and materials is a skill that RL agents acquire. RL-based systems can maximize resource distribution by dynamically altering their configuration. As a result, they can prioritize reducing the most significant security threats while managing the trade-offs and impact (Carta et al., 2023). Effective trade-offs can be balanced by RL-based patching systems through continual learning and adaptation. RL agents optimize vulnerability mitigation procedures by utilizing past data and real-time feedback. RL-based prioritizing systems improve and adapt their decision-making procedures via ongoing learning. By guaranteeing that resources are distributed effectively to address the most critical security vulnerabilities first, this improves the resilience of cyber security (Sharifani et al., 2023).

C. Network Security

RL is crucial in optimizing system performance through the configuration of suitable network settings. These algorithms change the system configuration to increase performance. Efficiency and security are the two main goals of RL-based network configuration management (Zhang et al., 2020). By continuously adapting to shifting traffic patterns and network conditions, RL-based optimization algorithms can enhance user experience and overall network efficiency.

In order to improve security and efficacy, firewall configurations can also be dynamically optimized using RL algorithms. According to Tan et al. (2023), RL agents possess the ability to adaptively modify firewall rules in order to efficiently obstruct harmful traffic while permitting legitimate communication. This feature empowers intelligent firewall management platforms to recognize and react to new threats independently, as well as optimize rule sets for maximum effectiveness.

D. Phishing and Social Engineering Detection

Platforms for behavioral profiling using RL can detect complex threats and other anomalies that might evade traditional security measures (Schwarting, 2023). This technique educated the staff members using RL-based simulations, which involves creating dynamic, using RL algorithms. Staff members can practice identifying and responding to a variety of security hazards and scenarios in a safe setting by using these simulated attacks (Kabanda et al., 2023).

VI. CHALLENGES AND OPPORTUNITIES

A. Data Scarcity, Imbalanced Rewards, and Transferability

Applications of RL encounter significant challenges because of unequal rewards and limited data. The inability of an agent to fully investigate its data-rich environs may result from this scarcity. It distorts the learning process and increases the difficulty of the agent reaching a consensus on the optimal set of rules. Transferability of RL algorithms is the ability of agents to adjust acquired knowledge and skills from one context to another (Burhani et al., 2023). Because transportable enables agents to effectively apply their prior knowledge to new tasks, RL-based solutions are more scalable and effective.

B. Ethical Considerations and Privacy Concern

In the field of RL, privacy and ethical issues are major concerns, especially as these systems proliferate across a range of industries. Because RL algorithms are frequently trained on enormous volumes of data, concerns about data privacy, permission, and potential biases in the training set are raised (Satapathy et al., 2023). Moreover, if RL agents are not properly created and supervised, their decision-making in real-world settings may unintentionally reinforce or worsen underlying social prejudices. Transparent and dependable RL systems that include procedures for verifying fairness and equity and auditing decision-making processes are desperately needed (Kaddoura et al., 2023).

C. Adversarial Attacks and Robustness Concern

Adversarial attacks entail the deliberate alteration of input information which is the one major cyber security challenge is the possibility of adversarial assaults against RL-based systems. The integrity and dependability of RL systems may be compromised by these attacks. These represent only a handful of the ways in which cybersecurity is using RL techniques to improve threat detection, response, and mitigation. Combining RL with conventional security techniques could lead to defence systems that are more adaptable and durable as cyberattacks keep getting more sophisticated. Strong defenses are needed to lessen the effects of conflicting perturbations and strengthen the resistance of RL-based system against malevolent exploitation (Sharifani et al., 2023).

D. Explainablility and Interpretability

In RL-based systems, explainability and interpretability pertain to how well humans can understood the choices and actions of the RL agent. These ideas are becoming more and more significant, particularly when RL is used in industries like healthcare, banking, and autonomous systems where openness, responsibility, and trust are critical.

E. Scalability and Resource Requirements

When designing and implementing RL-based systems, scalability and resource requirements are important factors that take into account. The ability of a system to manage growing data volumes, computational challenge, and environmental challenges while preserving performance is referred to as scalability. Large datasets are frequently used in RL algorithms to train intricate models, which can necessitate substantial computational resources like memory, processing power, and storage. Scaling RL systems to tackle real-world tasks with extensive state and action spaces requires effective algorithms and distributed computational frameworks.

VI. FUTURE WORK AND RESEARCH TRENDS

To increase strengthen RL-based defensive systems one major trend is integrate which is generative adversarial networks (GANs) because to new developments in reinforcement learning. Another trend is the use of meta-learning approaches that allowing RL agents to swiftly adjust to new and developing dangers. Block chain technology, opens us exciting new possibilities for cyber security that created by fusing the unchangeable and decentralized properties with the learning powers of RL. Where RL agents might enhance the detection and response to threats across different businesses while maintaining data from shared block chain network (Gasmi et al., 2023).

CONCLUSION

RL shows up as an evolving and viable cyber security strategy that makes it possible for systems to react instantly to evolving threats and defensive strategies facilitating adaptive security measures. The potential of RL approaches in detection of intrusions, risk management, and network security, is explored in this article. The efficacy and morality of RL-based security measures can be improved. These algorithms hold great significance in the field of cyber security that enables security systems to predict and counteract harmful acts in real-time by constantly learning and reacting to emerging threats. RL also promotes a resilient culture where systems are capable of withstanding the complexity of today's threat landscape.

REFERENCES

Ahmet, E. F. E., & Abaci, İ. N. (2022). Comparison of the host based intrusion detection systems and network based intrusion detection systems. *Celal Bayar University Journal of Science*, 18(1), 23–32.

Arora, S., & Doshi, P. (2021). A survey of inverse reinforcement learning: Challenges, methods and progress. *Artificial Intelligence*, 297, 103500. DOI:10.1016/j.artint.2021.103500

Azar, A. T., Koubaa, A., Ali Mohamed, N., Ibrahim, H. A., Ibrahim, Z. F., Kazim, M., Ammar, A., Benjdira, B., Khamis, A. M., Hameed, I. A., & Casalino, G. (2021). Drone deep reinforcement learning: A review. *Electronics (Basel)*, 10(9), 999. DOI:10.3390/electronics10090999

Bai, M., & Fang, X. (2024). Machine Learning-Based Threat Intelligence for Proactive Network Security. *Integrated Journal of Science and Technology, 1*(2).

Bhardwaj, M., Xie, T., Boots, B., Jiang, N., & Cheng, C. A. (2024). Adversarial model for offline reinforcement learning. *Advances in Neural Information Processing Systems*, 36.

Burhani, H., Shi, X. Q., Jaegerman, J., & Balicki, D. (2023). Scope Loss for Imbalanced Classification and RL Exploration. *arXiv preprint arXiv:2308.04024.*

Cam, H. (2020). Cyber resilience using autonomous agents and reinforcement learning. *Artificial Intelligence and Machine Learning for Multi-Domain Operations Applications*, 2, 35. Advance online publication. DOI:10.1117/12.2559319

Carta, T., Romac, C., Wolf, T., Lamprier, S., Sigaud, O., & Oudeyer, P. Y. (2023). Grounding large language models in interactive environments with online reinforcement learning. In *International Conference on Machine Learning* (pp. 3676-3713). PMLR.

Chen, D., Wawrzynski, P., & Lv, Z. (2021). Cyber security in smart cities: A review of deep learning-based applications and case studies. *Sustainable Cities and Society*, 66, 102655. DOI:10.1016/j.scs.2020.102655

Du, Y., Chen, J., Zhao, C., Liao, F., & Zhu, M. (2023). A hierarchical framework for improving ride comfort of autonomous vehicles via deep reinforcement learning with external knowledge. *Computer-Aided Civil and Infrastructure Engineering*, 38(8), 1059–1078. DOI:10.1111/mice.12934

Eze, V. H. U., Ugwu, C. N., & Ugwuanyi, I. C. (2023). A Study of Cyber Security Threats, Challenges in Different Fields and its Prospective Solutions: A Review. *INOSR Journal of Scientific Research*, 9(1), 13–24.

Gasmi, R., Hammoudi, S., Lamri, M., & Harous, S. (2023). Recent Reinforcement Learning and Blockchain Based Security Solutions for Internet of Things: Survey. *Wireless Personal Communications*, 132(2), 1307–1345. DOI:10.1007/s11277-023-10664-1

Ghanem, M. C., Chen, T. M., & Nepomuceno, E. G. (2023). Hierarchical reinforcement learning for efficient and effective automated penetration testing of large networks. *Journal of Intelligent Information Systems*, 60(2), 281–303. DOI:10.1007/s10844-022-00738-0

Habbal, A., Ali, M. K., & Abuzaraida, M. A. (2024). Artificial Intelligence Trust, Risk and Security Management (AI TRiSM): Frameworks, applications, challenges and future research directions. *Expert Systems with Applications*, 240, 122442. DOI:10.1016/j.eswa.2023.122442

Hambly, B., Xu, R., & Yang, H. (2023). Recent advances in reinforcement learning in finance. *Mathematical Finance*, 33(3), 437–503. DOI:10.1111/mafi.12382

Han, D., Mulyana, B., Stankovic, V., & Cheng, S. (2023). A survey on deep reinforcement learning algorithms for robotic manipulation. *Sensors (Basel)*, 23(7), 3762. DOI:10.3390/s23073762 PMID:37050822

Hore, S., Shah, A., & Bastian, N. D. (2023). Deep VULMAN: A deep reinforcement learning-enabled cyber vulnerability management framework. *Expert Systems with Applications*, 221, 119734. DOI:10.1016/j.eswa.2023.119734

Huang, Y., Huang, L., & Zhu, Q. (2022). Reinforcement learning for feedback-enabled cyber resilience. *Annual Reviews in Control*, 53, 273–295. DOI:10.1016/j.arcontrol.2022.01.001

Hwang, I., Wakefield, R., Kim, S., & Kim, T. (2021). Security awareness: The first step in information security compliance behavior. *Journal of Computer Information Systems*, 61(4), 345–356. DOI:10.1080/08874417.2019.1650676

Ismagilova, E., Hughes, L., Rana, N. P., & Dwivedi, Y. K. (2022). Security, privacy and risks within smart cities: Literature review and development of a smart city interaction framework. *Information Systems Frontiers*, 24(2), 1–22. DOI:10.1007/s10796-020-10044-1 PMID:32837262

Jendoubi, I., & Bouffard, F. (2023). Multi-agent hierarchical reinforcement learning for energy management. *Applied Energy*, 332, 120500. DOI:10.1016/j.apenergy.2022.120500

Ju, Y., Chen, Y., Cao, Z., Liu, L., Pei, Q., Xiao, M., Ota, K., Dong, M., & Leung, V. C. (2023). Joint secure offloading and resource allocation for vehicular edge computing network: A multi-agent deep reinforcement learning approach. *IEEE Transactions on Intelligent Transportation Systems*, 24(5), 5555–5569. DOI:10.1109/TITS.2023.3242997

Jung, B., Li, Y., & Bechor, T. (2022). CAVP: A context-aware vulnerability prioritization model. *Computers & Security*, 116, 102639. DOI:10.1016/j.cose.2022.102639

Kabanda, G., Chipfumbu, C. T., & Chingoriwo, T. (2023). A Reinforcement Learning Paradigm for Cybersecurity Education and Training. *Oriental Journal of Computer Science and Technology*, 12-45.

Kadakia, Y. A., Suryavanshi, A., Alnajdi, A., Abdullah, F., & Christofides, P. D. (2024). Integrating machine learning detection and encrypted control for enhanced cybersecurity of nonlinear processes. *Computers & Chemical Engineering*, 180, 108498. DOI:10.1016/j.compchemeng.2023.108498

Kaddoura, S., & Al Husseiny, F. (2023). The rising trend of Metaverse in education: Challenges, opportunities, and ethical considerations. *PeerJ. Computer Science*, 9, e1252. DOI:10.7717/peerj-cs.1252 PMID:37346578

Kilincer, I. F., Ertam, F., & Sengur, A. (2021). Machine learning methods for cyber security intrusion detection: Datasets and comparative study. *Computer Networks*, 188, 107840. DOI:10.1016/j.comnet.2021.107840

Krüger, P. S., & Brauchle, J. P. (2021). *The European Union, cybersecurity, and the financial sector: A primer. Carnegie Endowment Int*. Peace Publications Dept.

Kumar, H., Koppel, A., & Ribeiro, A. (2023). On the sample complexity of actor-critic method for reinforcement learning with function approximation. *Machine Learning*, 112(7), 2433–2467. DOI:10.1007/s10994-023-06303-2

Li, S. E. (2023). Deep reinforcement learning. In *Reinforcement learning for sequential decision and optimal control* (pp. 365–402). Springer Nature Singapore. DOI:10.1007/978-981-19-7784-8_10

Luketina, J., Nardelli, N., Farquhar, G., Foerster, J., Andreas, J., Grefenstette, E., Whiteson, S., & Rocktäschel, T. (2019). A survey of reinforcement learning informed by natural language. *Proceedings of the Twenty-Eighth International Joint Conference on Artificial Intelligence*. https://doi.org/DOI:10.24963/ijcai.2019/880

Majadas, R., García, J., & Fernández, F. (2024). Clustering-based attack detection for adversarial reinforcement learning. *Applied Intelligence*, 54(3), 1–17. DOI:10.1007/s10489-024-05275-7

Mijwil, M., Unogwu, O. J., Filali, Y., Bala, I., & Al-Shahwani, H. (2023). Exploring the top five evolving threats in cybersecurity: an in-depth overview. *Mesopotamian Journal of Cybersecurity,* 57-63.

Moerland, T. M., Broekens, J., Plaat, A., & Jonker, C. M. (2023). Model-based reinforcement learning: A survey. *Foundations and Trends® in Machine Learning, 16*(1), 1-118.

Mohamadi, N., Niaki, S. T. A., Taher, M., & Shavandi, A. (2024). An application of deep reinforcement learning and vendor-managed inventory in perishable supply chain management. *Engineering Applications of Artificial Intelligence*, 127, 107403. DOI:10.1016/j.engappai.2023.107403

Nguyen, T. T., & Reddi, V. J. (2023). Deep reinforcement learning for cyber security. *IEEE Transactions on Neural Networks and Learning Systems*, 34(8), 3779–3795. DOI:10.1109/TNNLS.2021.3121870 PMID:34723814

Ni, Y., Issa, M., Abraham, D., Imani, M., Yin, X., & Imani, M. (2022). Hdpg: Hyperdimensional policy-based reinforcement learning for continuous control. In *Proceedings of the 59th ACM/IEEE Design Automation Conference* (pp. 1141-1146). DOI:10.1145/3489517.3530668

Oh, S. H., Kim, J., Nah, J. H., & Park, J. (2024). Employing Deep Reinforcement Learning to Cyber-Attack Simulation for Enhancing Cybersecurity. *Electronics (Basel)*, 13(3), 555. DOI:10.3390/electronics13030555

Piplai, A., Ranade, P., Kotal, A., Mittal, S., Narayanan, S. N., & Joshi, A. (2020). Using knowledge graphs and reinforcement learning for malware analysis. *2020 IEEE International Conference on Big Data (Big Data)*. DOI:10.1109/BigData50022.2020.9378491

Qi, J., Yang, C. H., & Chen, P. (2022). Exploiting low-rank tensor-train deep neural networks based on riemannian gradient descent with illustrations of speech processing. https://doi.org/DOI:10.31219/osf.io/gdqnz

Qi, W., Ma, C., Xu, H., Zhao, K., & Chen, Z. (2022). A comprehensive analysis method of spatial prioritization for urban flood management based on source tracking. *Ecological Indicators*, 135, 108565. DOI:10.1016/j.ecolind.2022.108565

Rangaraju, S. (2023). Ai sentry: Reinventing cybersecurity through intelligent threat detection. *EPH-International Journal of Science And Engineering*, 9(3), 30–35. DOI:10.53555/ephijse.v9i3.211

Rjoub, G., Bentahar, J., Abdel Wahab, O., Mizouni, R., Song, A., Cohen, R., Otrok, H., & Mourad, A. (2023). A survey on explainable artificial intelligence for cybersecurity. *IEEE Transactions on Network and Service Management*, 20(4), 5115–5140. DOI:10.1109/TNSM.2023.3282740

Satapathy, P., Hermis, A. H., Rustagi, S., Pradhan, K. B., Padhi, B. K., & Sah, R. (2023). Artificial intelligence in surgical education and training: Opportunities, challenges, and ethical considerations–correspondence. *International Journal of Surgery*, 109(5), 1543–1544. DOI:10.1097/JS9.0000000000000387 PMID:37037597

Schwarting, R. K. (2023). Behavioral analysis in laboratory rats: Challenges and usefulness of 50-kHz ultrasonic vocalizations. *Neuroscience and Biobehavioral Reviews*, 152, 105260. DOI:10.1016/j.neubiorev.2023.105260 PMID:37268181

Sharifani, K., & Amini, M. (2023). Machine learning and deep learning: A review of methods and applications. *World Information Technology and Engineering Journal*, 10(07), 3897–3904.

Shichun, Y., Zheng, Z., Bin, M., Yifan, Z., Sida, Z., Mingyan, L., Yu, L., Qiangwei, L., Xinan, Z., Mengyue, Z., Yang, H., Fei, C., & Yaoguang, C. (2023). Essential technics of cybersecurity for intelligent connected vehicles: Comprehensive review and perspective. *IEEE Internet of Things Journal*, 10(24), 21787–21810. DOI:10.1109/JIOT.2023.3299554

Sivamayil, K., Rajasekar, E., Aljafari, B., Nikolovski, S., Vairavasundaram, S., & Vairavasundaram, I. (2023). A systematic study on reinforcement learning based applications. *Energies*, 16(3), 1512. DOI:10.3390/en16031512

Suchithra, J., Robinson, D., & Rajabi, A. (2023). Hosting capacity assessment strategies and reinforcement learning methods for coordinated voltage control in electricity distribution networks: A review. *Energies*, 16(5), 2371. DOI:10.3390/en16052371

Süzen, A. A. (2020). A risk-assessment of cyber attacks and defense strategies in industry 4.0 ecosystem. *International Journal of Computer Network and Information Security*, 12(1), 1–12. DOI:10.5815/ijcnis.2020.01.01

Tan, H., Ye, T., Rehman, S., ur Rehman, O., Tu, S., & Ahmad, J. (2023). A novel routing optimization strategy based on reinforcement learning in perception layer networks. *Computer Networks*, 237, 110105. DOI:10.1016/j.comnet.2023.110105

Tiwari, P., Lakhan, A., Jhaveri, R. H., & Gronli, T. M. (2023). Consumer-centric internet of medical things for cyborg applications based on federated reinforcement learning. *IEEE Transactions on Consumer Electronics*, 69(4), 756–764. DOI:10.1109/TCE.2023.3242375

Vashishtha, L. K., Singh, A. P., & Chatterjee, K. (2023). HIDM: A hybrid intrusion detection model for cloud based systems. *Wireless Personal Communications*, 128(4), 2637–2666. DOI:10.1007/s11277-022-10063-y

Wang, M., Qin, Y., Liu, J., & Li, W. (2023). Identifying personal physiological data risks to the Internet of Everything: The case of facial data breach risks. *Humanities & Social Sciences Communications*, 10(1), 1–15. DOI:10.1057/s41599-023-01673-3 PMID:37192941

Wu, T., & Ortiz, J. (2021). Rlad: Time series anomaly detection through reinforcement learning and active learning. *arXiv preprint arXiv:2104.00543*.

Zang, X., Yao, H., Zheng, G., Xu, N., Xu, K., & Li, Z. (2020). MetaLight: Value-based meta-reinforcement learning for traffic signal control. *Proceedings of the AAAI Conference on Artificial Intelligence*, 34(01), 1153–1160. DOI:10.1609/aaai.v34i01.5467

Zhang, C., Cai, Y., Huang, L., & Li, J. (2021). Exploration by maximizing Renyi entropy for reward-free RL framework. *Proceedings of the AAAI Conference on Artificial Intelligence*, 35(12), 10859–10867. DOI:10.1609/aaai.v35i12.17297

Zhang, C., Odonkor, P., Zheng, S., Khorasgani, H., Serita, S., Gupta, C., & Wang, H. (2020). Dynamic dispatching for large-scale heterogeneous fleet via multi-agent deep reinforcement learning. In *2020 IEEE International Conference on Big Data (Big Data)* (pp. 1436-1441). IEEE. DOI:10.1109/BigData50022.2020.9378191

Zhang, X., Ma, Y., Singla, A., & Zhu, X. (2020, November). Adaptive reward-poisoning attacks against reinforcement learning. In *International Conference on Machine Learning* (pp. 11225-11234). PMLR.

Chapter 3
Generative AI in Network Security and Intrusion Detection

Siva Raja Sindiramutty
https://orcid.org/0009-0006-0310
-8721

Taylor's University, Malaysia

Raja Kumar Murugesan
https://orcid.org/0000-0001-9500
-1361

Taylor's University, Malaysia

Krishna Raj V. Prabagaran
Universiti Malaysia Sarawak, Malaysia

Sarfraz Nawaz Brohi
University of the West of England, UK

N. Z. Jhanjhi
https://orcid.org/0000-0001-8116
-4733

Taylor's University, Malaysia

Mehdi Masud
https://orcid.org/0000-0001-6019
-7245

Taif University, Saudi Arabia

ABSTRACT

Protecting virtual assets from cyber threats is essential as we live in a digitally advanced world. Providing a responsible emphasis on proper network security and intrusion detection is imperative. On the other hand, traditional strategies need a supportive tool to adapt to the transforming threat space. New generative AI techniques like generative adversarial networks (GANs) and variational autoencoders (VAEs) are the mainstream technologies required to meet the gap. This chapter deals with how these models can enhance network security by inspecting the network traffic for anomalies and malicious behaviors detected through unsupervised learning, which considers strange or emerging phenomena. This survey features innovations in fault detection, behavior control, deep packet inspection, traffic classification, and examples of real-world intrusions detected by GAN-based systems. Furthermore, the chapter focuses on the challenges of adversarial attacks on models that require the

DOI: 10.4018/979-8-3693-5415-5.ch003

development of solid defense mechanisms, such as generative adversarial networks. Ethics becomes the following matter on our list of discussions, given that privacy transparency and accountability are to be observed when working with generative AI technologies in network security. Finally, the authors examine trends that determine how cyber-attacks are dealt with comprehensively.

INTRODUCTION

Overview of the Significance of Network Security and Intrusion Detection in Protecting Digital Assets

Securing networks and monitoring intrusions is essential because this is one of the most vital parts of cyber protection. Digital networks' security concerns have become necessary because they are the core of modern business communications. Confidential information and operational stability will derange if the networks are unprotected (Kumar & Khan, 2024). The network security protocols govern pro-active approaches to disallow unauthorized access, damaging intrusions, or other malicious activities that may affect reliability, confidentiality, and data availability (Rachakonda et al., 2024).

Employment of Intrusion Detection Systems (IDS), which continuously work to detect and stop abnormal traffic, is an imperative part of network security as these devices monitor and identify any possible penetrations in traffic flow within the organization's infrastructure. As sophisticated as IDS might be, it can be used to conduct real-time analysis, thus providing a platform in which it is possible to detect malware attacks, unauthorized access attempts, and denial-of-service attacks before any serious harm can be done to the business, hence giving the businesses enough time to take corrective action before it is too late. Monitoring the activity patterns of a particular company's digital assets may be accomplished by this technology. In so doing, the concerns will easily be in the position to proactively deal with any vulnerability that the hackers may be trying to utilize, which in turn will prevent data or financial loss that unlawful activities like cyber-attacks may cause (Ali et al., 2024; Konar et al.,2023). The application of sound techniques used in protecting networks from intrusions aids organizations in the legal compliance department when they deal with critical information, such as customer details, by protecting people's rights regarding security. Having a complex and high-security framework presents the unequivocal message of treating as sacred client content, which in turn promotes the client's trust in the service, and the service provider reduces this risk of reputation being tarnished due to downtimes induced by the laxity of information security (Alalmaie et al., 2024; Khalil et al., 2021).

Systems must require regular upgrades of their network security measures to keep pace with the development of cyber threats. This action involves applying numerous defense mechanisms, continuous network traffic scanning and analysis, and investing in cybersecurity training of workers, focusing on the safe way the sensitive data should be handled and stored. Employing intrusion detection techniques alongside a dependable network security system is essential to protect crucial digital assets from potential breaches. By thoroughly integrating these technologies and robust prevention protocols into operations, companies can heighten their resiliency against unauthorized access attempts by hackers seeking sensitive information - thereby reinforcing defenses against future attacks or infiltrations.

Introduction To Generative AI Techniques and Their Potential Applications in Network Security

Generative AI techniques, used in various spheres, are the major players in producing authentic data, visual, or other outputs that look just like natural objects. Including these techniques alongside network security provides many advantages concerning enhancing security mechanisms and arresting possible threats. Alongside constantly evolving cyber-attacks, it is also challenging to navigate the complexities of digital networks; consequently, it is essential to take preventive measures using generative AI techniques.

Generative AI applications can help network security detect abnormalities via the modeling approach, whose techniques like GANs enable the understanding of regular network activity patterns and identify deviations that may refer to possible intrusions or security threats (Agrawal et al., 2024). In addition, practitioners and cybersecurity experts could benefit from applying generative AI approaches to generate synthetic datasets that can train advanced intrusion detection systems that can detect highly novel attack patterns. Moreover, it equipped with sophisticated tools that can detect phishing attempts between employees and customers, in addition to setting up the websites and emails meant for such practices, powered by the advancements in this technology, organizations will have an added protective layer on their awareness campaigns over this topic and more as (Banafa, 2023) suggests. Unlikewise employed are Generator Poisoning Attacks, which adjust adversarial examples, setting up an opportunity where the machine learning-based security system resilience against advanced manipulation becomes its weight, which could also enable threat sensors to function differently in various conditions (Zhang, 2024; Almusaylim et al., 2020). Apart from detecting and mitigating the threats, it also comprises a highly potential key to improve the strength of encryption techniques and cryptographic keys through Deep Learning algorithms (Mehmood et al., 2021; Gaur et al., 2020).

Further exploration in this area can lead to continued advancements in network security solutions that safeguard critical infrastructure and confidential information. Generative AI strategies can enhance threat detection measures and cybersecurity training for professionals and fortify existing encryption methods - all crucial components needed for reimagining overall network security tactics. Timely research into advancing artificial intelligence technology is imperative to avoid evolving risks cyber adversaries pose while preserving effective defense mechanisms.

Chapter Contributions

1. **Introduction to Generative AI Techniques:** The chapter describes the generative AI method by GANs, VAEs, and DL arrangements. It describes a possibility for these models to overcome the limitations of ordinary intrusion detection techniques, namely, by enabling extraction of the very complex network patterns that can lead to the identification of unusual activity deemed as a cyber threat.

2. **Addressing Limitations of Traditional Methods:** Performing the Dissection of the Weakness of the Traditional Detection Services: A thorough study of signature-based intrusion detection shows that they struggle with the detection of new and advanced threats, which necessitates better technologies to be brought in. The comparison of these perspectives with the capabilities of generative AI implies the risk of the conception of more protected and adaptive systems for the detection of unauthorized attempts at break-ins.

3. **Enhancing Anomaly Detection and Behavior Analysis:** The section investigates the progress through the combination of the machinery of anomaly detection and behavioral analysis that is made possible by generative AI. It gives a glimpse into the role of unsupervised learning tools capable of generating models that may be used for security purposes by their potential to identify emerging threats and patterns of machine attacks.

4. **Utilizing Deep Packet Inspection:** The chapter exemplifies how generative AI can conduct deep packet inspection and classify traffic streams. This is an example of how these approaches can derive meaningful objects from traffic networks, enabling the detection of malicious patterns and evil tactics.

5. **Mitigating Adversarial Attacks:** The chapter describes the methods of reducing the effect of adversarial attacks on generative AI models at the generative modeling level. These strategies are in place to improve the intrusion detection system capabilities and manage threats. One can amend and appraise the defense mechanisms of more comprehensive AI solutions to contend with malign actors through investigation methods.

Chapter Organisation

Introduction to Network Security and Generative AI: Firstly, it mentions the significance of digital asset protection using network security and intrusion detection as ways of ensuring the security of the respective asset. Besides, it uses AI technology for many purposes, such as statistics, network security enhancements, etc. It explains the implications of IoT in the fingerprinting area. The point has been made, but it is worth noting that more investigations will be carried out in future conversations.

Fundamentals of Network Security: Principles of network security in general will be further expounded in the second section, emphasizing network architecture, protocols, and standard attack methods. The second part of the chapter points out the necessity of incorporating IDS and IPS into a system to replace the old security strategies with more effective measures.

Challenges in Traditional Intrusion Detection: In this section, we will discuss, analyze, and evaluate signature-based approaches for identifying intruded limitations. We focus on obstructing on-time recognition of existing and future cyber threats through network communications, prompting the application of different generative AI approaches.

Generative AI Techniques for Intrusion Detection: The applicable Generative AI techniques for Intrusion Detection are covered here. It elucidates these relationships and the applications that VAEs, DNN architectures, and Generative GANs can use, for instance, in cybersecurity and intrusion detection. The idea is to provide insight into how the models can be employed until the network traffic analysis is accomplished to detect anomalies and identify involved malicious activities.

Anomaly Detection and Behavior Analysis: This segment delves into the application of Artificial Intelligence Generative AI approaches in the context of anomaly detection and behavior analysis for network security. It highlights this aspect as the most valuable advantage of unsupervised learning applications: the ability to discover threats that have never been known before or emerged as new threats. In this way, intrusion detection systems become more agile, a positive outcome. A helpful difficulty with the Sentence is the word "which" used in a context.

Deep Packet Inspection and Traffic Classification: This part dives into how generative AI can maximize the operation of deep packet inspection and traffic classification with the best performance. Insignificant network packets are mainly extracted using feature extraction techniques to affect anomalous activities. This effectively is important because it reduces the number of false positives, which is an issue in many current threat detection systems.

Adversarial Attacks and Defenses: This part will review the AI generative models' vulnerability to the adversarial attacks focused on the network security systems and suggest approaches to dealing with these challenges, as well as raise the efficiency of deployment of intrusion detection systems based on the generative AI.

Case Studies and Use Cases: This paragraph provides a variety of live examples of how generative AI is used in network security and breach detection in real-world applications. It evaluates and reviews the cases of 'good practices' and performance ratings of intrusion detection systems based on generative AI.

Ethical and Legal Considerations: The chapter finishes by exploring the morality and law related to generative AI roleplaying in network security. Among them, privacy, transparency, accountability, and a detailed discussion of relevant laws and controlling mechanisms hinged on data protection and network security will be discussed.

Future Directions and Emerging Trends: The chapter examines the prospects for generative AI representing network security and intrusion detection by evaluating trends and reviewing the possible future directions. Next-generation networking technology is described as reshaping the cybersecurity landscape by providing insights into its effects on cybersecurity.

Conclusion: The final part of the chapter is a summary of the central part of this, as well as other essential lessons about dealing with intruders in network security. The part is of complete significance as it shows how generative AI can be applied to network security or intrusion detection systems. This, moreover, summons managers to use these systems to protect against the threats created daily by technology.

FUNDAMENTALS OF NETWORK SECURITY

Explanation of Core Concepts in Network Security, Including Network Architecture, Protocols, and Common Attack Vectors

Defending information systems and data from intrusion, deduction, and obstruction attacks is essential in network security. Basic concepts such as network architecture, protocols, and common vulnerable points must be known to enforce efficient defense mechanisms that operators can use in the future. In simple terms, network architecture is the degree of complexity, connectivity, and structure, including its composing sub-elements and their relationships. This comprises several strategies: like the OSI model; these seven layers include physical, data link, Network, transport, sessions, presentations, and applications layers; each layer is responsible for specific functions to ensure smooth and safeguarded network transmission, citing (Hasan et al., 2024; Sankar et al., 2020). Regulations of protocols, which are communications between systems and devices, are how they function. TCP/IP protocols are already there to ensure the integrity of the data transmission process, while SSL/TLS encrypts the information to remain secure in the communication channel (Ma, 2024).

Network security threats are mounting on hand with the exploitation of vectors by attackers to gain unauthorized access and corrupt the networks. Another example is Malware, which can be viruses or worms programmed to corrupt and steal user data (Kim et al., 2024). One more evil is an arrangement of phishing scams, an extinguisher of valuable data, like login or credit card passwords (Ali & Zaharon, 2022), while denying of service deals with flooding the network traffic and harms legitimate user access (Abedin & Hajek, 2023). With a man-in-the-middle-attack technique, the group of cybercriminals work through the channel four entities are sharing information via -whence they can overhear or purposely distort message exchanges (Elrawy et al., 2023). Empowering government authorities is a more than one-size-fits-all approach. It involves adopting multiple strategies to combat the threat actors who use the internet to wreak havoc. Two of the essential security measures applied are a firewall that employs predetermined rules for checking incoming and outgoing traffic (Kizza, 2024 a), intrusion detection systems that detect suspicious actions on the system, registering them to the supervisors (Möller, 2023; Wassan et al., 2021) and encryption algorithms such as symmetric/asymmetric cryptography. In conclusion, understanding network architecture, protocols, and common attack vectors is essential for establishing robust network security defenses. Organizations can safeguard their networks and data against evolving threats by implementing appropriate measures and protocols.

Overview of the Importance of Intrusion Detection Systems (IDS) and Intrusion Prevention Systems (IPS) in Network Defense

Safety for networks has become an essential issue in the modern digital era, as interconnected computers make it easy to convey data from one end to the other. This is so creative that we must have IDS and IPS functions despite the changes brought about by the cyber threats. IDS works as a watchful eye that constantly monitors your Network for uninvited access or any form of irregular activity that can be recognized as an abnormal pattern to promptly inform administrators of the emergence of anomalies. Then, IPS is proactive in its approach, adopted by scanning the traffic and responding immediately if detected. Any intrusions would be quickly handled either by blocking or reducing them so that damage could be caused entirely by their being prevented.

Classification and intelligible interpretation of network connectivity data for immediate threat detection and response becomes a reality through the application of IDS and IPS (Jonnala et al., 2024; Shahid et al., 2021). the systems constantly monitor the network activity and then safely identify abnormal behavior patterns like port scans, the pronouncement of power words, and error data transfer patterns (Javadpour et al., 2024), which help to make the right decision before penetrating the system and reducing the possibility of cyber-attacks. Rather than keep the practice of very particular rules, for instance, HIPAA or PCI DSS, where attack infiltration occurs, examine the beginning sentence: "The specific impact of AI on particular departments will vary depending on their specific tasks and sectors."

Having human malware and virus activity constantly remedied by the identification and response process provided by IDS and IPS may be a likely option to lessen the burden of security operators. This is because the fast-growing complexity of cyber threats blinds many scientists, making unencumbered monitoring practice no longer feasible. Leveraging algorithms and machine learning principles, these systems can swiftly identify suspicious activities, thus outperforming manual procedures for network traffic assessment. This is where the higher efficiency levels lie (Repetto, 2023; Ghosh et al., 2020). Implementing IDS and IPS into defense strategies establishes multiple layers of protection for an overall increase in resilience against attacks that may surpass initial perimeter defenses such as firewalls. Consequently, vulnerabilities are reduced through early identification while mitigating worst-case scenarios from worsening ones before they affect operational efficiencies or customer trust (Sewak et al.,2022). To summarise, IDS and IPS play an essential role in modern network defense approaches by offering real-time threat recognition, proactive prevention measures, adherence to regulatory requirements, visiting the workload for security personnel, and adding overall endurance against cyber-attacks. Figure 1 shows the Importance of the Intrusion Detection System in the network.

Figure 1. Importance of intrusion detection systems (IDS) and intrusion prevention systems (IPS) in network defense

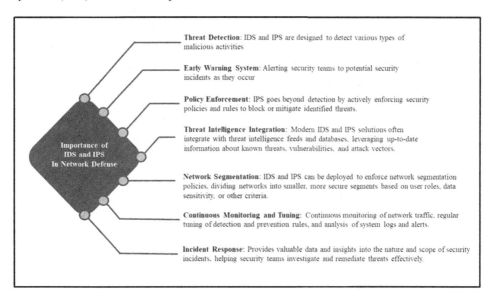

CHALLENGES IN TRADITIONAL INTRUSION DETECTION

Discussion on the Limitations of Traditional Signature-Based Intrusion Detection Methods

Standard intrusion detection has for many years successfully alerted of computer network breaches by pointing to malicious traffic of known type. Hence, the technology itself must be optimized when dealing with cybersecurity. The other way it works is by deploying standard attack patterns and never new attacks, as the old ones have yet to develop new features to look out for. Also, signature-based systems have been known to generate false positives because the existing algorithms cannot differentiate between showy features of Malware and actual legit functionalities (Martins et al., 2022; Azam et al. Et Al., 2023).

The evolution of malware variants is a daunting hurdle, as it is almost impossible for the traditional pattern-matching and signature-based methods to continue to be effective against Code that constantly mutates to avoid detection (Rani & Reeja, 2019). Defending against these vectors is challenging as they evade detection when used by insiders or when they feature a high level of obscurity or encryption. Large networks scale signature-based systems well due to their inability to handle traffic and cyber-attack events (Kozik et al., 2018; Almusaylim et al., 2018). More importantly, such systems will not be able to reveal every type of encrypted traffic as you need to inspect payloads first to decrypt them – and the processing of encrypted communications may leave any malicious activity hidden within the encrypted channels. In addition, a common approach to bypass any static signatures is to use evasion techniques like fragmentation. Attackers execute malicious Code in pieces that easily bypass the detection above mechanisms (Caviglione et al.,2021; Humayun et al.,2022).

Traditional intrusion detection methods (IDM) that labor on signature detection have their obstacles when transforming into a modern cyber world in one word. These deficiencies cover susceptibility to unidentified and polymorphic attacks, high false positive detection, an inability to detect toxic menaces in both encrypted or original payloads, scalability issues, and attackers' ability to bypass detection by evasion tactics. Therefore, present efforts are concentrating on combining signature-based methodologies with alternative techniques such as anomaly identification, machine learning (ML), and behavioral analysis to safeguard networks against potential assaults better. This merger methodology holds enormous prospects for offering more robust defenses characterized by the adaptability required against ever-evolving online hazards.

Identification of Challenges Related to Detecting New and Advance Cyber Threats in Network Traffic

Cybersecurity staff confront the problem of choosing between dense network traffic for searching new and advanced cyber dangers, as the dangers change the whole time, and the networks' complex architectures give them a tough time. The tremendous scale of ordinary traffic poses one of the most critical challenges for traditional detection techniques that consequently risk being quickly overloaded (Erhan et al., 2021). Cyber hackers keep perfecting their means by employing new evasion strategies to avoid conventional antimalware methods (Diogenes & Ozkaya, 2019; Singhal et al., 2020). Thus, among typical security protocols, signature-based approaches find it challenging to remain current (Raparthi, 2020).

Hiding malicious activity in the flow of legitimate traffic is a vital objection. Thus, it hinders distinguishing anomalies from suitable activities (Lelah et al., 2023). For instance, an attacker may resort to data encryption or cover its intention by using covert communication routes, thus reducing the chances of being discovered (Gardiner et al., 2014). IoT devices, ubiquitous and lacking adequate security standards with a high possibility of being exploited as well, are one of the recent factors that have increased the risk level (Majeed et al., 2021). Thus, there are challenges in training

ML models for anomaly detection as labeled datasets that are supposed to be needed in the training process are nonexistent (Patel et al., 2021). Again, the ML models concerning accuracy would also involve distinguishing between normal behavior and abnormal activity, requiring high-quality data. However, the situation gets worse along with cyber threats, and the risk of becoming outdated increases, ultimately causing rewriting of the detection model every so often; this strategy requires massive consumption of computational resources; only professionals have the experience and knowledge to establish this type of solutions in challenging situations (Tajwar et al., 2023). This calls for integrating human intuition with advanced AI and ML technologies to nail down such issues. Creating new disclosure strategies and sharing threat information among professionals, researchers, and industry representatives participating in collaboration are now unavoidable.

Cultivating a highly skilled workforce well-versed in the fight against contemporary cyber threats demands investment in cybersecurity education and training programs, as Al-Daajeh et al. (2022) emphasized. Acknowledging the difficulties of identifying emerging and advanced cyber hazards in network activity highlights the importance of ongoing ingenuity and cooperation among cybersecurity experts. Through joint efforts to tackle these obstacles, entities can reinforce their ability to withstand evolving digital dangers and adequately protect their network framework. Figure 2 shows Challenges Related to Detecting New and Advanced Cyber Threats in Network Traffic.

Figure 2. Challenges Related to Detecting New and Advanced Cyber Threats in Network Traffic

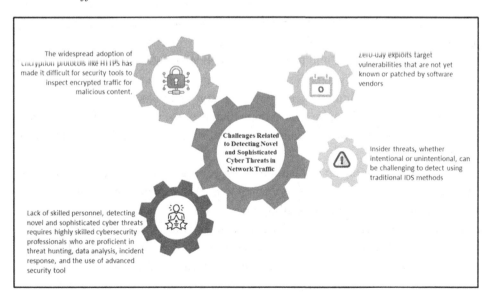

GENERATIVE AI TECHNIQUES FOR INTRUSION DETECTION

Introduction to Generative AI Models Suitable for Intrusion Detection, Such as GANs, VAEs, and DL Architectures

Over the past few years, cybersecurity has entered a new period of change because of the incredible innovations of the AI generative model, which alerts of possible attacks. Generative Adversarial Networks (GANs), Variational Autoencoders (VAEs), and several other deep learning architectures are shining a hopeful light regarding realizing security threats within computer systems. This is indeed a remarkable AI-driven technology explicitly created to understand and imitate standard network patterns, hence capable of identifying unusual activities that might indicate potential attacks being planned (Azam et al., 2023; Taj &Jhanjhi, 2022).

Goodfellow et al. (2014) introduced GANs, which are designed with generators and discriminators of neural networks that use a game theory application to identify the created samples of accurate data and tell the differences between genuine and fake samples. Moreover, VAEs from Kingma and Welling are generative probabilistic models able to detect deviations based on reconstruction errors by calculating the probability representation to determine the abnormality of the standard system. Emerging deep learning architectures like CNNs and RNNs have been used to find intrusions as they identified complicated patterns in network traffic data (Ashraf et al., 2020). An advantage of incorporating artificial intelligence (AI) based security mechanisms is their autonomous dynamic capability when they are faced with new threats; they do not need to contrive manually but continuously learn by adapting on their own (Ananna et al., 2023; He et al., 2023). Such algorithms, since, in reality, can detect the intricate connections in massive data sets without relying solely on a set of 'hard and fast rules' boost the efficiency of eco-friendliness compared to classical computing techniques! Representational abstraction allows this sort of deep learning technology to be fast-tracked by monitoring unsafe/safe online; thus, decision-making is lightning speed. Even Jackson's team has shown effectiveness in monitoring and applying response immediately, most of the time to allow direct communication or information transmission to responsible agencies when an attack is assumed.

Moreover, enhancing an infrastructure improvement requiring such scalability/ capacity reasoning makes it more practical than ever. Hnamte and Hussain (2023) showcased how well-suited DL methodologies impact extensive intrusion detection across wide-spectrum networks/devices concurrently despite having different environments. Integrating generative AI models like GANs, VAEs, and DL architectures presents an immense opportunity to improve intrusion detection capabilities in cybersecurity. By utilizing advanced ML techniques, these models can seamlessly identify unusual behaviors that are signs of potential security violations, leading to fortified network defenses against emerging threats. This marks a crucial step towards upgrading our existing cyber defense mechanisms significantly.

Explanation of How Generative AI Can Be Used to Analyse Network Traffic Patterns, Detect Anomalies, and Identify Malicious Activity

An unmatched feature of AI-based technology is that it can investigate, find subtle irregular patterns, and identify malicious intent. With DL (Deep Learning) and probabilistic modeling, generative AI models can develop typical traffic patterns and facilitate easy detection of deviation from them. A pragmatic approach can be training an algorithm with synthetic data that looks precisely like the actual network traffic and more easily learns structures/patterns behind it. GAN can be used to generate training data that the models will use for anomaly detection, as Boppana and Bagade (2023) demonstrate in the context of network traffic GAN.

Generative AI can beat traditional rule-based systems to find anomalies too subtle to detect in other systems. These algorithms, which are learning-based, can be termed intelligent in that every time they are being run, they keep making corrections. Static approaches to threat defense are gradually being replaced by dynamically evolving network environments where new network threats keep emerging. The group of Zhang et al. (2023) recommends the utilization of anomaly detection in network traffic through recurrent neural networks (RNNs), which are highly capable of this activity. AI technology through generative AI has made it easy to identify malicious behavior by monitoring the traffic for unique attributes against typical traffic using the labeled dataset, which contains samples of known attacks, thus providing live data matching and giving alerts. This study by Choudhry et al. (2023) reveals that VAEs employed in detecting suspicious indicators supportive of evil activities become the primary factor to be considered while enhancing security operations.

Additionally, it is a consideration of the scalability of the generative artificial intelligence that is essential to analyze the enormous data of the networks in contemporary computer networks. Such networks generate data sets with a significant volume that need to be processed and analyzed in real-time; therefore, scaling must be addressed. The deep learning model class samples helped Goodfellow et al. (2014) investigate the generation of network traffic intricacy. Thus, such deep learning models can be used in cybersecurity because they manage complex, concealed data. To sum up, generative AI holds great potential for examining network traffic patterns, recognizing aberrations, and pinpointing nefarious behaviors. Its ability to assimilate information and adjust to changing conditions makes it an essential tool in cybersecurity operations - bolstering detection abilities and expanding scalability measures to shield against new hazards that may crop up within networks.

ANOMALY DETECTION AND BEHAVIOR ANALYSIS

Exploration of How Generative AI Techniques Can Enhance Anomaly Detection and Behavior Analysis in Network Security

Due to the ever-changing threat landscape, network security plays a crucial role in today's interconnected digital world. Within network security systems, anomaly detection and behavior analysis are critical to identifying deviations from standard patterns that indicate potential threats or malicious activities (Aljawarneh et al., 2018) and emerging as promising avenues for enhancing network security, generative AI techniques employ ML algorithms to model and understand complex data patterns (Mohan et al., 2022).

The remarkable capabilities of generative AI techniques, such as GANs and VAEs, are evidenced by their ability to craft synthetic data that closely mirrors real-world data distributions. These models grasp the typical behavior of network entities through training on extensive volumes of network traffic data and flag anomalies by identifying deviations from established patterns. For example, GANs have successfully produced realistic network traffic data and enhanced anomaly detection model training while improving adaptability to unseen attack patterns (Abdelmoumin et al., 2022). In terms of behavior analysis, generative AI plays a crucial role in generating diverse scenarios for normal and abnormal network behaviors; this aids robust testing and evaluation efforts when simulating various attack scenarios, assisting security analysts with vulnerability identification -- allowing them to devise effective defense strategies accordingly (Zografopoulos et al., 2021). Furthermore, generated datasets can enrich limited labeled datasets while enhancing supervised learning algorithms' performance aimed at detecting anomalous activities or behaviors related specifically within perspective cybersecurity context information domains concerning physical networks infrastructures ICT systems contingent operationalized resilience cyber-attack counter measurements strategic technical-tactic types responses decisions loops causing impacts inside businesses/organizations environment reducing losses as well ensuring business continuity preventing reputation damages due regulatory non-compliance reasons, etc. (Fan et al., 2021)

Generative AI models are effective at learning intricate data representations, leading to improved detection of advanced cyber threats such as zero-day attacks and stealthy intrusions. By identifying subtle patterns in network traffic data that may be difficult for traditional rule-based or signature-based methods to detect, these models offer heightened capabilities necessary for staying ahead of emerging threats in dynamic cybersecurity environments. Consequently, exploring generative AI techniques shows immense potential for enhancing anomaly detection and behavior analysis in network security by leveraging the power of ML to model complex data distributions and generate synthetic information – providing invaluable tools that strengthen resilience while increasing efficacy across a wide range of systems. Figure 3 shows how generative AI techniques can enhance anomaly detection and behavior analysis in network security.

Figure 3. How Generative AI Techniques Can Enhance Anomaly Detection and Behavior Analysis in Network Security

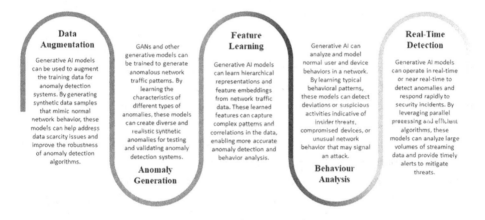

Discussion on the Advantages of Unsupervised Learning Approaches for Detecting Unknown and Emerging Threats

An impressive feature of unsupervised learning techniques to serve out here is identifying threat sources that are either unknown or emerging, even in complex and dynamic environments. Unlike supervised learning, which is critically choosy and needs labeled data for training, unsupervised learning can enhance options for unstructured data free of preconceived labels, letting it discover the unknown. It accurately shows its skills in directing hidden patterns and anomalies in large datasets and subsequently detecting the potential hazards at the early stage (Usama et al., 2019). K-means clustering, or a hierarchical clustering algorithm that is unsupervised, can be used to group like data and the outliers that appear as danger signs are therefore identified by analysts (Sinaga & Yang, 2020).

Unsupervised learning is one of the most effective approaches that help machine learning models to outperform when customizing their models to the databases by assimilating new data and making required readjustments in their models (Bouchama & Kamal, 2021). Therefore, it is phenomenal, for which we should thank AI technologies, as only they will be successful in rapidly changing environments (Shukla, 2023; Azam et al., 2023). Besides, unsupervised learning would also be capable of analyzing a vast array of formats of information, including text, images, and network traffic, which would aid in complete threat detection (Naeem, Immaculate Ismael & Zhen Yi et al., 2023; Sindiramutty & Zhianjhi, Chun Feng, & Xinmin & Tee & Lau et al., 2024), One more advantage that offers is the extraordinary capacity of algorithms for learning, which includes the ability to discover new correlations that was never connected with a unique dataset before (Khoo et al., 2023). Heuristics such as principal component analysis [PCA] are commonly used in PCA/autoencoders to represent the features via advanced techniques. This, in turn, helps increase the accuracy in identifying potential hazards with the time the credibility rates are high during high-risk scenarios, according to Suelekhshahrezaee et al. (2023).

The unsupervised learning technique is a benefit because of its scalability, which makes the rapid analysis of massive data sets possible in real-time (Shi et al., 2023). This feature is particularly advantageous for organizations that struggle with vast amounts of data from various sources, enabling them to detect emerging threats promptly and efficiently (Allioui & Mourdi, 2023). Unsupervised learning methods offer numerous benefits in identifying unknown or emergent hazards. These include uncovering concealed patterns and correlations within diverse data types while adapting well in evolving contexts. At an organizational level, these approaches can significantly enhance threat detection capabilities by scaling up effectively when analyzing large-scale datasets, thus mitigating risks better amidst today's ever-evolving security landscape. Figure 4 shows the advantages of unsupervised learning approaches for detecting unknown and emerging threats.

Figure 4. Advantages of Unsupervised Learning Approaches for Detecting Unknown and Emerging Threats

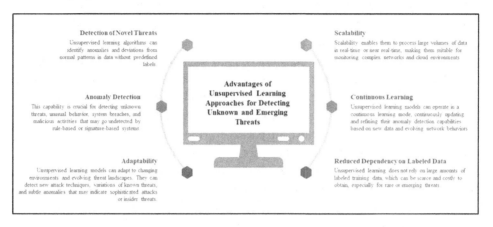

DEEP PACKET INSPECTION AND TRAFFIC CLASSIFICATION

Explanation: How Generative AI Can Be Used for Deep Packet Inspection and Traffic Classification

Generative AI can be considered when performing tasks such as deep packet inspection (DPI) and traffic classification. DPI works at the packet level, decoding data and going through the networks to learn about its content and origin. While doing this, the Network divided the data flow into several streams: protocol, traffic load, threat level, etc. As the only tool capable of inputting system commands via algorithms to the data and generating sophisticated predictions, the Generated AI could amplify both processes with high accuracy in finding the deep structure of network traffic by realizing the complicated system of inputs and outputs. Models are practiced in varied data sets regarding the type of traffic network. Thus, they detect slight differences in day-to-day patterns, such as the structure of a payload or the communication behavior. This consequently empowers the surveillance systems to be more accurate at distinguishing among entities within the traffic that are encrypted or obfuscated against every digital data that is circulated across the computer networks (Liu et al., 2023; Sindiramutty et al., 2024).

Generative AI replaces automated pattern recognition and feature extraction activities as part of DPI systems, boosting their effectiveness. To do this task, DL is used to gain the irrelevance of known rules and patterns from raw data, and generative models are adaptable in their ability to evolve and eliminate new risks and protocol changes (Zaman et al., 2023). Secondly, general AI eliminates performance weaknesses involved with processing large volumes or complexities, a drawback of traditional traffic classification solutions, by parallel processing huge data volumes in real time (Chen & Yan, 2024). The anticipatory anomaly detection that incorporates expected routines with Generative Models permits, to a great extent, the production of a new generation of hazard detection systems, consequently preventing network breaches, decreasing cyberattack risk, and providing uniform safety for the Network. To begin with, in Generative AI, we are talking about a finer mesh of traffic classification between the deep packet and the traffic inspection. In addition, Generative AI boasts a range of benefits, including data analytics that is highly accurate, efficient, and scalable in traffic management. The critical factor that sets Generative AI apart is the combination of advanced algorithms with intense data inspection, offering a whole new range of options. Figure 5 shows how generative AI can be used for deep packet inspection and traffic classification.

Figure 5. How Generative AI Can Be Used for Deep Packet Inspection and Traffic Classification

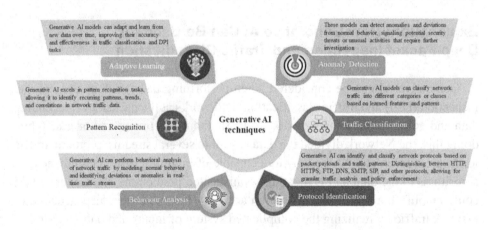

Showcase of Techniques for Extracting Meaningful Features From Network Packets and Identifying Suspicious Behavior

Some state-of-the-art approaches to network security improvement should be demonstrated by showing how to find network packets' main features and detect Wireshark examples that may be misleading. Threats keep changing in the rapidly moving cyber world; it is mandatory to set up robust detection mechanisms.

This showcase illustrates that taking preventive measures like anticipating emerging threats and relentlessly fighting for resolution can help reduce existing risks. The other significant method highlighted here is Deep Packet Inspection (DPI), which monitors packet content to gather significant details about communicational patterns and payload data (Ji et al., 2024). The DPI provides an excellent opportunity to study the payloads in close and accurate detail. This way, abnormal activities can be detected quickly by identifying intrusion attempts, data exfiltration, etc. Using machine learning (ML) algorithms is another critical area in which network traffic is also analyzed. From historical data, ML models can then extract essential information. This, in turn, enables them to recognize patterns characteristic of criminal activities and identify them earlier - thus facilitating case screening (Rajasekaran et al., 2023; Sindiramutty et al., 2024). Machine learning capabilities involve an ability to distinguish between proper operational states and malicious networks through assessing datasets that have been previously tagged during training drills.

The Behavior-based Analysis is the monitoring of various network activities and lets instances that differ from the established baselines be known (Wang et al., 2023). An average behavior profile would include all the security-relevant behaviors that may show deviation from normal operations in a specific location. This deviation would be a cause for proactive measures. Feature engineering is off as it relies on methods like statistical analysis, frequency-based features, protocol-specific attributes, etc., to process the crucial features required for machine learning in the Network. Such engineered entities add a basis for the Network's performance after they facilitate the identification process of suspicious activities.

Moreover, the advantage of such a clustering technique has been specified that it does not need explicit user knowledge or administrator interaction; therefore, it can precisely observe network behaviors and any unusual patterns from different flows since sometimes it is challenging to identify outliers initially (Rele & Patil, 2023). Clustering methods have a substantial upside for the likes of network administrators since they are potent tools for sifting accurately through activity that might be deemed harmful, deviating away from the typical communication patterns among clusters and swiftly removing any loopholes or faults, which in turn will result in reduced reporting of problems on disparate environments, which rarely stem from horrible system configurations or malicious attacks. In the Showcase Technique that will help in network packet feature extraction and how it can be used to find suspicious behavior concerns, the importance of new approaches in improving network security is highlighted. Adopting technologies like DPI, complex ML algorithms, behavioral analysis, salient feature extraction, and clustering can help organizations build defenses against developing cyber threats while protecting valuable data assets and sensitive national infrastructure. Figure 6 shows techniques for extracting meaningful features from network packets and identifying suspicious behavior.

Figure 6. Techniques for Extracting Meaningful Features From Network Packets and Identifying Suspicious Behavior

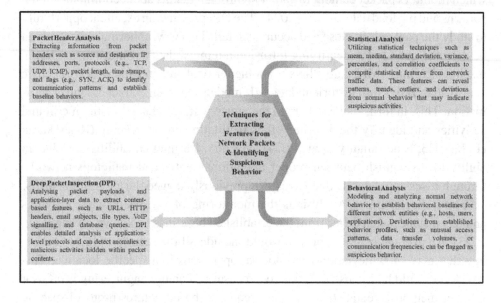

ADVERSARIAL ATTACKS AND DEFENSES

Examination of Adversarial Attacks Targeting Generative AI Models Used in Network Security

Generative AI models are a must-have for security restitution, and they could be applied to investigate and neutralize threats (Striuk & Kondratenko, 2023). However, late works have insinuated these models' shortcomings in terms of how they withstand adversary attacks. Adversarial attacks are intentional attacks that demonstrate the power of manipulating AI systems using carefully tailored data that escapes automatic checking (Khan & Ghafoor, 2024). This fundamental threat has generated considerable anxiety because of its power to erode the reliability of integral artificial intelligence system elements used in the cyber sphere.

One of the most complicated problems is that generative AI models are prone to adversarial examples (inputs deliberately designed to mislead the generation system) and their negative repercussions. The studies have proved that multiple methods have been developed for instances of this kind. One example is the Fast Gradient Sign Method (FGSM), which disturbs the input data, resulting in the wrong classification value. Modern machine learning techniques such as GANs suggest different ways to build credible data for a successful attack that rivals the one created by the human eye. In addition to being misclassified, the generative AI systems are used as a club for creating negative implications beyond themselves. Additionally, it comes through another avenue affecting the performance of IDS and malware detection processes in the network-specific domain where adversaries use it to achieve a non-detection state. Instead of malware infection, a more thorough approach requires tackling the flaws embedded in the advanced malware techniques that may compromise the defense mechanisms, thus weakening the systems against attacks!

A concerted effort is needed to mitigate the security flaws present in generative AI models used in network security, including creating sound security systems against targeted attacks and a comprehensive evaluation of the model's resistance to adversarial attacks. Among the new techniques, adversarial training is based on generating noisy data to improve model robustness (Goyal et al., 2023). Besides, detections and counteractivities of hostile surroundings can be further extended through achievements in feature squeezing and input transformations (Anjaria & Shah, 2024). Focus on diligence and active procedures should be implemented to identify potential vulnerabilities and protect these systems from present and future threats. Understanding inherent vulnerabilities within the technology can enable stakeholders to apply more effective safeguards while utilizing defensive measures that promote increased resiliency throughout all stages of an attack sequence. Figure 7 shows adversarial attacks targeting generative AI models used in network security.

Figure 7. Adversarial Attacks Targeting Generative AI Models Used in Network Security

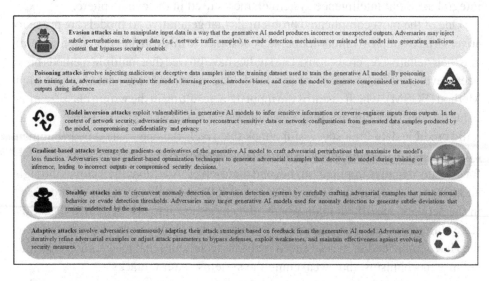

Strategies for Defending Against Adversarial Attacks and Improving the Robustness of Generative AI-Based Intrusion Detection Systems

Enhancing the sturdiness and integrity of IDS fusion with generative AI is one of the most challenging problems since it may involve numerous potential exploits of adversarial hacking to compromise the efficacy of this advanced technology.

Detection systems, one of the indispensable components of any IDS, are a crucial part of any IDS framework. It can take care of different kinds of attacks holistically, such as anomaly detection and signature-based detections, which are enabled by the ML algorithms (Saeed et al., 2023). Thus, incorporating ensemble learning tactics helps the imbrication of IDS by availing of many model outputs yet reducing the impact of every one of the vulnerabilities (Alqahtani & Kumar, 2024; Sindiramutty, 2023). Integrating GAN for data synthesis with IDS would scale countermeasure capacities against adversary attacks (Saravanan et al., 2023) and provide abounding variation and massive samples that can be used for training deep learning models. This innovation not only strengthens the ability to reduce the risk of generalization but also helps to radically improve the knowledge of new attack scenarios and enhance their recognition. Implementing the proper explanation and interpretability within the design of IDS can complement the ability to spot and react to the misleading techniques the adversaries are using. Interpretable designs make it possible to see the essence of decision-making systems, and analysts can also point out the vulnerable points and inputs they can add to make it possible to survive intrusions. Besides the fact that including adversarial training in the development process of IDS can create a robust IDS against evasion attacks through exposure to such techniques in learning that will enhance effectiveness in deployment situations that are needed to be robust to unpredicted features, the IDS could learn resilient features that are enhancing effectiveness.

It would be better to have a multifaceted policy with dynamic security capability to defend against attacks and build steady, robust, generative AI systems capable of intrusion detection. It will have to merge different thresholds of detection analyses, artificial data enhancement strategies and techniques with explanations, and personally developed adversarial procedures. Blending these varying tactics will be an essential boost to organizations' new strategy formulation success. Figure 8 shows strategies for defending against adversarial attacks and improving the robustness of generative AI-based intrusion detection systems.

Figure 8. Strategies for Defending Against Adversarial Attacks and Improving the Robustness of Generative AI-Based Intrusion Detection Systems

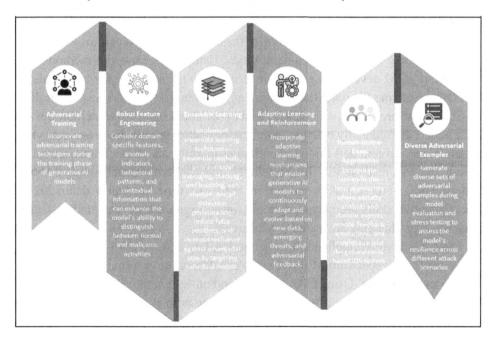

CASE STUDIES AND USE CASES

Showcase of Real-World Examples and Use Cases Demonstrating the Application of Generative AI In Network Security and Intrusion Detection

Generative AI makes a real buzz in network security and intrusion detection by outstandingly detecting extremely complex cyber-attacks. One critical case involves the anomaly detection GAN, built upon two neural networks (the generator and discriminator) that whip together genuine and fake instances (Singh et al., 2024). Speculative systems detect diversions authentically through their data training processes, which is the network data typically with their deviations reflecting intrusions or malicious activities (Bukhari et al., 2024; Sindiramutty et al., 2024). Generative AI will be applicable in perfecting fake data to improve intrusion detection systems as well. The VAE with latent space features to generate new examples is employed to address the datasets' lack of labeled data. So, the VAE's model can be used to augment datasets with a high probability of incomplete paraphrases (Mumuni et al., 2024). Through this strategy, the IDS are strengthened, thereby allowing them to have a generalization ability against potential new risk scenarios that could not have been considered before.

Generative AI facilitates a narrative for the test of potential scenarios as a means of understanding the system's vulnerabilities. Using different battle methods and test scenarios, AI developers can generate multiple intricate offensive patterns to accurately examine the operational efficiency of defense systems (Azadmanesh et al., 2024). The preventive act helps prevent cyber-attacks and fix vulnerabilities on prior notice, consequently offering organizations better preparedness against cyber threats. Generative models through continuous learning and data stream adaptation support network resiliency as these intelligent mechanisms gradually increase their understanding of these attacks and prevent them over time (Roshan & Zafar, 2024). These adaptive skills are necessary tools for an organization, especially when it comes to ever-changing advanced cyber threats.

The generative AI application of network safety and intrusion detection proffers a whole new spectrum of novel ideas to address the constantly evolving and devious cyber climate. Using GANs, VAEs, and other generative approaches could benefit companies in detecting anomalies, training with synthetic data, producing a scheduled attack scenario, an adaptive defense tactic, and identifying emerging cybersecurity issues.

Analysis of Successful Implementations and Performance Evaluations of Generative AI-Based Intrusion Detection Systems

GANs have been identified as especially helpful in positioning intrusion detection systems (IDS), which have needed enhancement in recent years. This section describes success based on Generative AI intelligence availability through IDS evaluations. The study by Kholgh and Kostakos in 2023 shows that GANs are great at generating synthetic network data that resembles the actual world traffic in such a way that IDS models trained to be complex are more complete. Moreover, GAN inference provides the scope for a diverse set of attack scenarios that can be generated, ensuring a greater resilience of a detection system against new threats- as stated by Ranka et al. (2024) and Jhanjhi et al. (2024). Another example of contraction is that by calling RNN in collaboration with GANS, generative AI systems can create an intrusion detection system. To augment this objective, short-term forecasting takes advantage of the transfer learning using historical data and, in the process, ensconces temporal dependencies in network traffic with unparalleled accuracy. By mental ability, Gonzalez et al. (2023) beat the competition with innovative approaches. They also used sequential learning capabilities to minimize the rate of false identifications, which made the RNN model generate top-notch results.

Generative AI datasets' effectiveness for debugging IDs denotes the necessity for a broad spectrum of training datasets. Le et al. (2023) cite novel results that stress the significance of extensive data collection in different networking environments and possible attack scenarios to increase the model's robustness and generalization capabilities. Moreover, the paper by Wu et al. indicates that the necessity to constantly retrain and adjust emerging attack strategies and lessen the chances for concept drifts must be addressed. The scalability of its systems based on Generative AI was showcased through the distributed architecture framework by Syed et al., where the computing workload was split across multiple nodes, thus allowing for real-time massive network traffic handling in their study in this (Syed et al., 2023). This feature is far more effective in establishing such systems in networks that comprise high throughput rates and low-latency coupling. This, in return, ensures quick response times and, thus, efficient detection of these threats.

Conclusively, the triumph of implementing and assessing Generative AI-based IDS highlights its capacity to strengthen cybersecurity measures. By incorporating GANs with other advanced methods, such as RNNs, these systems demonstrate reliability, precision, and scalability in detecting various network breaches.

ETHICAL AND LEGAL CONSIDERATIONS

Discussion on Ethical Considerations Related to Using Generative AI In Network Security, Including Privacy, Transparency, and Accountability

The ethical considerations that arise from integrating AI technologies within a network security setting include privacy, transparency, and accountability (Bale et al., 2024). DL algorithms, which are an integral part of generative AI, have unprecedentedly surmounted cybersecurity challenges by not only preventing but also identifying threats toward cybersecurity (Yigit et al., 2024). However, it may be imperative to look for possible shortcomings to maintain ethical guidelines. It is imperative to conserve the most basic privacy rights amidst these systems for the ability to analyze vast amounts of data, which not only gender information but also can be susceptible (Rial, 2024). Thus, it is paramount to find the equilibrium between successfully identifying the threat and protecting citizens' confidence that their clean private life will be preserved in all the stages between introducing this technology and its seamless functionality.

Transparency of ethics must be balanced in the development of the algorithms of generative AI. This sophisticated algorithm may be incapable of providing a simple explanation to a non-expert, thereby slowing down the process of assuring accuracy and fairness. To strengthen system accountability and create user trust, designers must prioritize transparency at the design and operation stages (Oluwafemi Oloyede, 2024; Sindiramutty and Jhanjhi et al., 2024). What is under question in AI in cybersecurity is who takes on the accountability of any fallacies that might result from erroneous instructions or impartiality in decision-making capacities that only advanced technologies can provide (Berber & Srećković, 2023). The culture that welcomes both developers' and users' punishments emerging anew from the implementation of generative AI technology ensures secure and stable deployments of the pains associated with this place (King, 2024).

To address these concerns and humanize the development as well as the use of generative AI for network security (Ferrara, 2023), inclusive and decent datasets need to be provided, as well as diverse representation in training the models. That will help eradicate stereotypes, putting a value on equality in the results.

Ethical frameworks should incorporate principles of justice and fairness to ensure the responsible use of this technology in safeguarding digital infrastructures (Alam, 2023). When utilizing generative AI for network protection purposes, different ethical considerations, such as privacy concerns, need addressing through transparency measures, and accountability protocols must also be enacted. By adhering strictly to these guidelines consistently throughout the implementation phase, stakeholders thus unlock the full potential offered by AI technologies without impacting their core values or principles.

Overview of Legal Frameworks and Regulations Governing Network Security Practices and Data Protection

With the science of technology getting advanced every day around the world, it has become obligatory for organizations to back data and network security completely. These numerous regulations have been introduced to mitigate cyber time risks and provide high levels of privacy in a world where everyone wants to connect (Kshetri, 2017). The General Data Protection Regulation (GDPR), which the European Union undertook at the beginning of 2016, is a legislative regulation example, among others. Data management is an area in which organizations have to monitor their operations, such as data repositories, processing, and storage. Such organizations should consider publishing their data management processes while practicing these activities (Sharma,2019).

The Code of Standards on the security of the payment card industry (PCI DSS) stipulates security measures for organizations dealing with payment card trans-actions, protects cardholders' data, and guards against breaches (Morse & Raval, 2008). While within California, these businesses are beholden to the regulations specified within the California Consumer Privacy Act (CCPA), which entail proper collection, use, and information sharing; consumers, on the other hand, are highly protected by these standards, and in addition, they have an opportunity to control their personal information by also keeping their privacy intact. In China's case where, the Cybersecurity Law intends to raise the levels of protection surrounding critical infrastructure with concerns the fields of primary sensitive information, a doing which has been promoted by (Van Der Mei et al., 2024) and through the same time, the law has also been created to enforce rules that regulate cyberspace activities with a sole purpose to achieve national safety along the safely.

Legal frameworks and regulations, however, are the fundamentals of creating safety and compliance in the digital world. Consequently, companies can achieve such goals as data breaches, protecting the privacy rights of individuals, and high stakeholder trust through meeting security standards. The development of local cybersecurity threats and regulations will inevitably be tracked regularly; otherwise, organizations may need help to avert cyber-attacks and protect their information. Establishing such protocols will assist in formulating global cybersecurity standards and thereby support organization security systems against potential cyber-attacks. At the same time, there will be accountability for those who compromise the online environment through compliance adherence.

FUTURE DIRECTIONS AND EMERGING TRENDS

Exploration of Emerging Trends and Future Directions in Generative AI for Network Security and Intrusion Detection

As per paramount research by Mohammed and Hossain (2024), the integration of artificially intelligent technology transforms privacy and network intrusion detection to a considerable level. On the other hand, deep reinforcement learning (DRL) also has a prominent place for DRL techniques widely used for different tasks within this domain. DRL teaches AI agents efficient strategies by interacting with the environment and receiving feedback; it is a dynamically structured approach for acting in the case of emerging dangers (Reddy et al., 2024). DRL is an approach that IDS can develop while progressing in detecting security breaches in an organization (Mohanad et al., 2024). Among other things, introducing graph neural networks (GNNs) is a further promising direction toward increasing the reliability of information security measures (Sindiramutty et al., 2024; Masood & Zafar, 2024). GNN models work miraculously well when tackling complicated connection-oriented problems where data shape is structured as in networks - just like a computer network with many links. The like introduction of GNN in a current IDS also speeds up the recognition of irregular behavior patterns or harmful activity carried out through different connection topologies current throughout the stack of specific nodes in any targeted infrastructure, which in turn makes the coverage of such an IDS more comprehensive compared to most penetration tests.

Self-supervised learning is becoming increasingly crucial in fortifying network security attributes. Such systems let AI models teach themselves from data without a label, even if they are new, and respectively, they perform better if there are smaller amounts of labeled data (Jannat et al., 2024). This is where such technology outweighs the supervised method when the cases involve the scarcity of labeled data and the high costs of data labeling. AI technologies development in network security and intrusion detection as well as future IDS systems by using GANs, DRL, and GNNs, which incorporate self-supervised learning solutions, are significant opportunities for cyber security advancements (Xu & Wang, 2024; Sindiramutty et al., 2024) amid digitalization. We may witness crucial breakthroughs grounded in technologies, including the

Predictions for How Generative AI Will Continue to Shape the Landscape of Network Defense And Cybersecurity

AI and machine learning are setting the stage for DNS, or cyberattack prevention changes that no one may have thought possible. The future of cyber security is still unshaped; various speculations are possible of how the current technology's improvements might reshape security strategies and practices in the upcoming years.

Generative AI will provide cyber-attackers with a capability upgrade, making highly advanced Malware that could be challenging to detect by traditional security systems (Munir et al., 2024; Wen et al., 2023). Building a shield faces great difficulty because as soon as the defense camp develops its strategies, it must be swiftly able to increase the efficiency of these strategies. While generative AI shows prospective applications on the offensive side, it is also applicable for automating surveillance, threat detection, and response purposes (Dhoni & Kumar, 2023; Sindiramutty et al., 2023). Machines look for meaningful data patterns collected for anomalies that might suggest attacks; the defenders can then use this knowledge to develop more proactive defense techniques (Abdullah,2019). Among the significant threats that are likely to come along with AI is the counterfeiting of messaging or websites, whereby the fake will not be distinguishable from the original, thus making phishing attacks even more challenging to detect (Yazan, 2019); this emphasizes the need for users to understand how to spot persuasive influence tactics which are known as social engineering attacks.

Generative AI by adversarial ML could apply to the security systems of artificial intelligence by detecting arising vulnerabilities. Those adversarial examples allowed researchers to find anything wrong embedded within algorithms, and then they could create more sophisticated defense mechanisms. Furthermore, AI's generativity can help improve errors and save time when monitoring insights. It is a platform on which analysts can rely to obtain the tactics used by malign actors. Thus, as they emerge, better preparedness and neutralizing threat strategies can be seen as more feasible (Magnusson, 2023; Sindiramutty et al., 2023;).

CONCLUSION

Summary of Key Insights and Takeaways From the Chapter

Generative AI is the latest component that adds sophistication to network security by network IDS integration, potentially improving extant cybersecurity systems and guarding against cyber-attacks. It first clarifies the essential role of IDS in keeping cyber networks safe in the current world, where everything is related to the digital ecosystem. However, as hackers upgrade their skills, they keep redesigning their modules and introduce newer and unforeseen attack vectors, which traditional signature-based technology needs help to detect. Creeping AI applications showed a way of handling the barriers of network security. GANs and VAEs models are in play now, and businesses can sink into traffic pattern details more to pick up anomalies and criminal behavior now. Natural language also contributes advanced anomaly detection and behavior analysis while profiting from unsupervised learning through natural language processing. This allows security personnel to discover previously unknown threat variations. Also, deep packet inspection and traffic classifiers help with detection and response. These techniques can analyze the features of network packets and indicate where the wrong signals are before there is a problem.

Nevertheless, the paper stresses that cyberattacks that exploit AI vulnerabilities (which are common problems) should be handled just as well. Adequate grasp on and operationalization of effective methods to counter these intrusions is imperative to the credibility and workability of intrusion detection systems dependent on generative AI. Various technological applications suitable for network security are illustrated appropriately through examples and instances in this chapter. In this regard, the effectiveness of artificial intelligence solutions in real-world scenarios is demonstrated, and with this democracy, specific ethical, legal, and moral issues regarding confidentiality, transparency, and accountability were extensively touched when deploying artificial intelligence-based security solutions. The concluding part captures outstanding traits to be fashioned in the future. The spotlight is on Gen Security through the general Network. This audit will keep evolving emerging threats in anticipation of being able to respond immediately to changing tactics.

Staying proactive through utilizing capabilities provided by GAN can help them stay ahead in combating contemporary cyber adversaries, ultimately ensuring resilience throughout an organization's infrastructure protection mechanisms. Converting Passive Voice was initially used, But it was converted into Active voice-' the author emphasis.' Initial Sentence Reframed: The author emphasizes the need to address vulnerabilities caused by generic artificial intelligence, like adversarial attacks, which target these models specifically. Suppose organizations aim to ensure reliability and efficiency within the intrusion detection system. In that case, they should take essential measures toward understanding and implementing more robust defenses, especially against aerial attacks.

Reflection on the Transformative Potential of Generative AI for Network Security and Intrusion Detection

Being an eye-opening solution with wide-ranging applications, the merger of generative AI into network security and intrusion detection systems will lead to a radical revolution in cybersecurity in the future. These techniques transform the paradigm for detecting and fighting cybercrime using deep learning networks to enable unsupervised learning and dynamic response to new attack patterns beyond signature-based methods' limits. The flexible take on this concern is vital to deal with the progressive and greedier cyber threats constantly developed by cybercriminals. Another great opportunity of generative AI is that you can spot deviations and jumps without setting up specific estimates or standards. Unlike the customary approach, this shows more resilience to cyber-attacks – by proactively detecting new attack paths as the market evolves – and not after an event. Besides this, Generative AI has advanced information security from a mere breach detection level to an analytical, behavioral mode that can foresee breach possibilities and hence offer additional proactive virtual guards before the occurrence or actual breach, thereby redefining what was previously known as IDS, i.e., Intrusion Detection Systems, into PGS, i.e., Proactive Guardians guarding Networks Security successfully.

While the possible opportunities for utilizing generative AI in network security, intrusion detection, and other fields will take much work, they pose challenges. From the manipulative attacks launched at such deals to their defense, they have become a severe danger to the effectiveness of such systems. As a result, there is a pressing need for continuous efforts in the research and development programs to avert abuse of the systems by malevolent agents and enhance systems' resilience against changing threats. Taking advantage of state-of-the-art machine learning (ML) approaches, organizations can bolster their defenses via generative AI technology-enabling them, in turn, to adapt to swiftly emerging cybersecurity hazards, the same as protecting all of their valuable digital assets more proficiently and quickly than ever before. With time, this advanced technology will play a crucial role in shaping this data security landscape in the future.

Call to Action for Organisations to Leverage Generative AI Technologies to Enhance Their Network Security Posture and Defend Against Evolving Cyber Threats

Organizations are encouraged to engage generative AI technologies and their security capacity effectively and respond to continuously evolving digital threats and other hack attacks. They should concede that the future military force will be very different from the military tactics of yesterday, which have uncovered flaws still in existence in the present crisis. With the help of generative AI, companies can easily find the attack before it even happens with more accuracy and efficacy than adversaries because they are more technologically advanced than adversaries. Adequate investment of funds in professionals such as skillful data scientists or partnering experienced providers that will provide AI-driven security solutions is essential to effectively applying this technology to intrusion detection systems. Overall, it is imperative to have an unshakable resolve towards creating a dynamic defense infrastructure that is strong and steady enough to confront any unplanned events caused by malicious intelligence of cybercriminals coming up with newer approaches irrespective of whichever long-term path the organizations adopt for their organization. A culture of innovation and cooperation must be established in every company. Such collaboration stimulates the interdepartmental squads to investigate new technologies, exchange information, and resource generative AI to the maximum of its security development. These collaborative efforts enhance organizational capacities and promote prompt reaction to evolving risks that might arise. Businesses need to emphasize research through involvement in trade forums, emerging projects, and associations with academic or independent research organizations by means of strategic partnerships in order to stay abreast with the latest developments of generative AI that come up every day. Interactions with all the community members can be an excellent way to adopt the latest innovations for a good cybersecurity posture that will ensure good business continuity.

However, when considering legal aspects, organizations must be diligent when considering technologies. This includes maintaining transparency in decision-making processes, safeguarding user privacy, and ensuring compliance with standards. By addressing these considerations and mitigating risks associated with intelligence-driven solutions, organizations can build trust among stakeholders. Upholding principles is critical to preventing public relations outcomes linked to implementation issues from software malfunctions or breaches due to errors in managing safety protocols on secure network infrastructures. Surveillance activities can be enhanced through real-time monitoring using tools like automation scripts and cloud-based machine learning models seamlessly integrated into business operations platforms. These technologies aid in analyzing data trends and predicting behaviors in business sectors while reducing operational costs and enhancing fraud detection capabilities.

In conclusion, the current moment demands measures. Embracing generative AI technologies and prioritizing cybersecurity measures enable entities to protect their assets against cyber threats in our interconnected world. Let us seize this opportunity to strengthen our defenses and move towards a resilient future.

REFERENCES

Abdelmoumin, G., Whitaker, J., Rawat, D. B., & Rahman, A. (2022). A Survey on Data-Driven Learning for Intelligent Network Intrusion Detection Systems. *Electronics (Basel)*, 11(2), 213. DOI:10.3390/electronics11020213

Abdullah, A. (2019). International Journal of Computing and Digital Systems. *International Journal of Computing and Digital Systems* [Preprint]. https://doi.org/ .DOI:10.12785/ijcds

Abedin, M. Z., & Hajek, P. (2023). *Cyber security and business intelligence: Innovations and Machine Learning for Cyber Risk Management*. Taylor & Francis. DOI:10.4324/9781003285854

Agrawal, G., Kaur, A., & Myneni, S. (2024). A review of generative models in generating synthetic attack data for cybersecurity. *Electronics (Basel)*, 13(2), 322. DOI:10.3390/electronics13020322

Akanfe, O., Lawong, D., & Rao, H. R. (2024). Blockchain technology and privacy regulation: Reviewing frictions and synthesizing opportunities. *International Journal of Information Management*, 76, 102753. DOI:10.1016/j.ijinfomgt.2024.102753

Al-Daajeh, S. H., Saleous, H., Alrabaee, S., Barka, E., Breitinger, F., & Raymond Choo, K.-K. (2022). The role of national cybersecurity strategies on the improvement of cybersecurity education. *Computers & Security*, 119, 102754. DOI:10.1016/j.cose.2022.102754

Alalmaie, A. Z., Nanda, P., & He, X. (2024) 'Zt-Nids: Zero Trust - Network Intrusion Detection System Validation Based on Attack Simulations,' *SSRN* [Preprint]. DOI:10.2139/ssrn.4762072

Alam, A. (2023). Developing a Curriculum for Ethical and Responsible AI: a university course on safety, fairness, privacy, and ethics to prepare next generation of AI professionals. *Lecture notes on data engineering and communications technologies*, 879–894. DOI:10.1007/978-981-99-1767-9_64

Ali, M. M., & Zaharon, N. F. M. (2022). Phishing—A Cyber fraud: The types, implications and governance. *International Journal of Educational Reform*, 33(1), 101–121. DOI:10.1177/10567879221082966

Ali, S., Li, Q., & Yousafzai, A. (2024). Blockchain and federated learning-based intrusion detection approaches for edge-enabled industrial IoT networks: A survey. *Ad Hoc Networks*, 152, 103320. DOI:10.1016/j.adhoc.2023.103320

Aljawarneh, S., Aldwairi, M., & Yassein, M. B. (2018). Anomaly-based intrusion detection system through feature selection analysis and building hybrid efficient model. *Journal of Computational Science*, 25, 152–160. DOI:10.1016/j.jocs.2017.03.006

Allioui, H., & Mourdi, Y. (2023). Exploring the Full Potentials of IoT for Better Financial Growth and Stability: A Comprehensive Survey. *Sensors (Basel)*, 23(19), 8015. DOI:10.3390/s23198015 PMID:37836845

Almusaylim, Z. A., Jhanjhi, N. Z., & Alhumam, A. (2020). Detection and Mitigation of RPL rank and version number attacks in the internet of things: SRPL-RP. *Sensors (Basel)*, 20(21), 5997. DOI:10.3390/s20215997 PMID:33105891

Almusaylim, Z. A., Jhanjhi, N. Z., & Jung, L. T. (2018). Proposing A Data Privacy Aware Protocol for Roadside Accident Video Reporting Service Using 5G In Vehicular Cloud Networks Environment. *2018 4th International Conference on Computer and Information Sciences (ICCOINS)* [Preprint]. DOI:10.1109/ICCOINS.2018.8510588

Alqahtani, H., & Kumar, G. (2024). Machine learning for enhancing transportation security: A comprehensive analysis of electric and flying vehicle systems. *Engineering Applications of Artificial Intelligence*, 129, 107667. DOI:10.1016/j.engappai.2023.107667

Alzaabi, F., & Mehmood, A. (2024). *A Review of Recent Advances, Challenges and Opportunities in Malicious Insider Threat Detection using Machine Learning Methods*. IEEE Access. DOI:10.1109/ACCESS.2024.3369906

Ananna, F. F., Nowreen, R., Al Jahwari, S. S. R., Costa, E. A., Angeline, L., & Sindiramutty, S. R. (2023). Analysing Influential factors in student academic achievement: Prediction modelling and insight. *International Journal of Emerging Multidisciplinaries Computer Science & Artificial Intelligence*, 2(1). Advance online publication. DOI:10.54938/ijemdcsai.2023.02.1.254

Anjaria, B., & Shah, J. (2024) *Exploring magnitude perturbation in adversarial attack & defense*. https://ijisae.org/index.php/IJISAE/article/view/4589

Asharf, J., Moustafa, N., Khurshid, H., Debie, E., Haider, W., & Wahab, A. (2020). A review of intrusion detection systems using machine and deep learning in Internet of Things: Challenges, solutions and Future Directions. *Electronics (Basel)*, 9(7), 1177. DOI:10.3390/electronics9071177

Azadmanesh, M., Ghahfarokhi, B. S., & Talouki, M. A. (2024) 'Privacy in generative models: attacks and defense mechanisms,' in *Springer eBooks*, pp. 65–89. DOI:10.1007/978-3-031-46238-2_4

Azam, H., Pin, L.T., Syahmi, M.A., Qian, A.L.W., Jingyan, H., & Uddin, H. (2023) Wireless Technology Security and Privacy: A Comprehensive Study. Preprints [Preprint]. DOI:10.20944/preprints202311.0664.v1

Azam, H., Dulloo, M. I., Majeed, M. H., Wan, J. P. H., Xin, L. T., & Sindiramutty, S. R. (2023). Cybercrime Unmasked: Investigating cases and digital evidence. *International Journal of Emerging Multidisciplinaries Computer Science & Artificial Intelligence*, 2(1). Advance online publication. DOI:10.54938/ijemdcsai.2023.02.1.255

Azam, H., Dulloo, M. I., Majeed, M. H., Wan, J. P. H., Xin, L. T., Tajwar, M. A., & Sindiramutty, S. R. (2023). Defending the digital Frontier: IDPS and the battle against Cyber threat. *International Journal of Emerging Multidisciplinaries Computer Science & Artificial Intelligence*, 2(1). Advance online publication. DOI:10.54938/ijemdcsai.2023.02.1.253

Azam, H., Tajwar, M. A., Mayhialagan, S., Davis, A. J., Yik, C. J., Ali, D., & Sindiramutty, S. R. (2023). Innovations in Security: A study of cloud Computing and IoT. *International Journal of Emerging Multidisciplinaries Computer Science & Artificial Intelligence*, 2(1). Advance online publication. DOI:10.54938/ijemdcsai.2023.02.1.252

Azam, Z., & Islam, Md. M. (2023). Comparative analysis of intrusion detection systems and Machine Learning-Based model analysis through Decision Tree. *IEEE Access*, 11, 80348–80391. DOI:10.1109/ACCESS.2023.3296444

Babu, C. V.S. & P, A. (2023) Adaptive AI for dynamic cybersecurity systems. *Advances in computational intelligence and robotics book series*, 52–72. DOI:10.4018/979-8-3693-0230-9.ch003

Bai, M., & Fang, X. (2024) *Machine Learning-Based Threat intelligence for proactive network security*. https://ijstindex.com/index.php/ijst/article/view/4

Bale, A. S. (2024) *The impact of generative content on individuals privacy and ethical concerns*. https://www.ijisae.org/index.php/IJISAE/article/view/3503

Banafa, A. (2023). *Transformative AI: Responsible, Transparent, and Trustworthy AI Systems*. River Publishers Series in Computing and Information Science and Technology.

Banu, G. K., & Demirci, M. (2024) *A robust machine learning based IDS design against adversarial attacks in SDN*. https://open.metu.edu.tr/handle/11511/108348

Berber, A., & Srećković, S. (2023). When something goes wrong: Who is responsible for errors in ML decision-making? *AI & Society*. Advance online publication. DOI:10.1007/s00146-023-01640-1

Boppana, T. K., & Bagade, P. (2023). GAN-AE: An unsupervised intrusion detection system for MQTT networks. *Engineering Applications of Artificial Intelligence*, 119, 105805. DOI:10.1016/j.engappai.2022.105805

Bouchama, F., & Kamal, M. (2021) *Enhancing Cyber Threat Detection through Machine Learning-Based Behavioral Modeling of Network Traffic Patterns.* https://research.tensorgate.org/index.php/IJBIBDA/article/view/76

Braghin, C., Lilli, M., & Riccobene, E. (2023). A model-based approach for vulnerability analysis of IoT security protocols: The Z-Wave case study. *Computers & Security*, 127, 103037. DOI:10.1016/j.cose.2022.103037

Bukhari, S. A.. (2024). *Secure and privacy-preserving intrusion detection in wireless sensor networks: Federated learning with SCNN-Bi-LSTM for enhanced reliability.* Ad Hoc Networks. DOI:10.1016/j.adhoc.2024.103407

Caviglione, L., Choras, M., Corona, I., Janicki, A., Mazurczyk, W., Pawlicki, M., & Wasielewska, K. (2021). Tight Arms Race: Overview of current malware threats and trends in their detection. *IEEE Access : Practical Innovations, Open Solutions*, 9, 5371–5396. DOI:10.1109/ACCESS.2020.3048319

Chaudhari, P., Chin, J.-J., & Mohamad, S. M. (2024). An In-Depth analysis on efficiency and vulnerabilities on a Cloud-Based searchable symmetric encryption solution. *Journal of Informatics and Web Engineering*, 3(1), 265–276. DOI:10.33093/jiwe.2024.3.1.19

Chen, Y.-b., & Yan, Q. (2024) 'Privacy-Preserving diffusion model using homomorphic encryption,' *arXiv (Cornell University)* [Preprint]. https://doi.org//arxiv.2403.05794.DOI:10.48550

Choudhry, N., Abawajy, J., Huda, S., & Rao, I. (2023). A comprehensive survey of machine learning methods for surveillance Videos anomaly Detection. *IEEE Access : Practical Innovations, Open Solutions*, 11, 114680–114713. DOI:10.1109/ACCESS.2023.3321800

Crepax, T. (2024) 'Global Privacy Control and Portability of Privacy Preferences Through Browser Settings: A Comparative Study of Techno-Legal Challenges Under the Ccpa/Cpra and the Gdpr,' *SSRN* [Preprint]. DOI:10.2139/ssrn.4710372

Davis, J. J., & Clark, A. E. (2011). Data preprocessing for anomaly based network intrusion detection: A review. *Computers & Security*, 30(6–7), 353–375. DOI:10.1016/j.cose.2011.05.008

Dhoni, P., & Kumar, R. (2023) 'Synergizing Generative AI and Cybersecurity: Roles of Generative AI Entities, Companies, Agencies, and Government in Enhancing Cybersecurity,' *Tech Rxiv* [Preprint]. DOI:10.36227/techrxiv.23968809.v1

Diogenes, Y., & Ozkaya, E. (2019) *Cybersecurity? Attack and defense strategies.* https://international.scholarvox.com/catalog/book/docid/88877993

Duy, P., Khoa, N. H., Hien, D. T. T., Hoang, H. D., & Pham, V.-H. (2023). Investigating on the robustness of flow-based intrusion detection system against adversarial samples using Generative Adversarial Networks. *Journal of Information Security and Applications*, 74, 103472. DOI:10.1016/j.jisa.2023.103472

Elrawy, M. F., Hadjidemetriou, L., Laoudias, C., & Michael, M. K. (2023). 'Detecting and classifying man-in-the-middle attacks in the private area network of smart grids,' *Sustainable Energy. Grids and Networks*, 36, 101167. DOI:10.1016/j. segan.2023.101167

Erhan, L., Ndubuaku, M., Di Mauro, M., Song, W., Chen, M., Fortino, G., Bagdasar, O., & Liotta, A. (2021). Smart anomaly detection in sensor systems: A multi-perspective review. *Information Fusion*, 67, 64–79. DOI:10.1016/j.inffus.2020.10.001

Fan, C., Liu, Y., Liu, X., Sun, Y., & Wang, J. (2021). A study on semi-supervised learning in enhancing performance of AHU unseen fault detection with limited labeled data. *Sustainable Cities and Society*, 70, 102874. DOI:10.1016/j.scs.2021.102874

Ferrara, E. (2023). Fairness and Bias in Artificial intelligence: A brief survey of sources, impacts, and mitigation strategies. *Sci*, 6(1), 3. DOI:10.3390/sci6010003

Gardiner, J. C., Cova, M., & Nagaraja, S. (2014) 'Command & Control: Understanding, Denying and Detecting - A review of malware C2 techniques, detection and defences,' *arXiv (Cornell University)* [Preprint]. https://doi.org//arxiv.1408 .1136.DOI:10.48550

Gaur, L., Afaq, A., Solanki, A., Singh, G., Sharma, S., Jhanjhi, N. Z., My, H. T., & Le, D.-N. (2021). Capitalizing on big data and revolutionary 5G technology: Extracting and visualizing ratings and reviews of global chain hotels. *Computers & Electrical Engineering*, 95, 107374. DOI:10.1016/j.compeleceng.2021.107374

Ghosh, G., Kavita, , Verma, S., Jhanjhi, N. Z., & Talib, M. N. (2020). Secure surveillance system using chaotic image encryption technique. *IOP Conference Series. Materials Science and Engineering*, 993(1), 012062. DOI:10.1088/1757-899X/993/1/012062

Gibert, D.. (2023). *'Query-Free Evasion Attacks Against Machine Learning-Based Malware Detectors with Generative Adversarial Networks,' arXiv*. Cornell University. [Preprint], DOI:10.1109/EuroSPW59978.2023.00052

González, G. G.. (2023). *One model to find them all deep learning for multivariate Time-Series anomaly detection in mobile network data*. IEEE Transactions on Network and Service Management., DOI:10.1109/TNSM.2023.3340146

Goyal, S., Doddapaneni, S., Khapra, M. M., & Ravindran, B. (2023). A survey of Adversarial Defenses and Robustness in NLP. *ACM Computing Surveys*, 55(14s), 1–39. DOI:10.1145/3593042

Hamid, K., Iqbal, M. W., Aqeel, M., Liu, X., & Arif, M. (2023). Analysis of Techniques for Detection and Removal of Zero-Day Attacks (ZDA). *Communications in Computer and Information Science*, 1768, 248–262. DOI:10.1007/978-981-99-0272-9_17

Hasan, K. M. B. (2024). Blockchain technology meets 6 G wireless networks: A systematic survey. *Alexandria Engineering Journal*, 92, 199–220. DOI:10.1016/j.aej.2024.02.031

He, K., Kim, D.-S., & Asghar, M. R. (2023). Adversarial Machine Learning for Network Intrusion Detection Systems: A Comprehensive survey. *IEEE Communications Surveys and Tutorials*, 25(1), 538–566. DOI:10.1109/COMST.2022.3233793

Hnamte, V., & Hussain, J. (2023). Dependable intrusion detection system using deep convolutional neural network: A Novel framework and performance evaluation approach. *Telematics and Informatics Reports*, 11, 100077. DOI:10.1016/j.teler.2023.100077

Humayun, M., Ashfaq, F., Jhanjhi, N. Z., & Alsadun, M. K. (2022). Traffic management: Multi-Scale vehicle detection in varying weather conditions using YOLOV4 and spatial pyramid pooling network. *Electronics (Basel)*, 11(17), 2748. DOI:10.3390/electronics11172748

Hussain, S. J. (2019) 'IMIAD: Intelligent Malware Identification for Android Platform,' *2019 International Conference on Computer and Information Sciences (ICCIS)* [Preprint]. DOI:10.1109/ICCISci.2019.8716471

Jannat, F.-E. (2024) 'OCT-SelfNet: A Self-Supervised Framework with Multi-Modal Datasets for Generalized and Robust Retinal Disease Detection,' *arXiv (Cornell University)* [Preprint]. https://doi.org//arxiv.2401.12344.DOI:10.48550

Javadpour, A. (2024). *A comprehensive survey on cyber deception techniques to improve honeypot performance.* Computers & Security., DOI:10.1016/j.cose.2024.103792

Ji, I. H., Lee, J. H., Kang, M. J., Park, W. J., Jeon, S. H., & Seo, J. T. (2024). Artificial Intelligence-Based Anomaly Detection Technology over Encrypted Traffic: A Systematic Literature Review. *Sensors (Basel)*, 24(3), 898. DOI:10.3390/s24030898 PMID:38339615

Jonnala, J. (2024) *Advancing Cybersecurity: a comprehensive approach to enhance threat detection, analysis, and trust in digital environments.* https://www.ijisae.org/index.php/IJISAE/article/view/4302

Keshk, M., Koroniotis, N., Pham, N., Moustafa, N., Turnbull, B., & Zomaya, A. Y. (2023). An explainable deep learning-enabled intrusion detection framework in IoT networks. *Information Sciences*, 639, 119000. DOI:10.1016/j.ins.2023.119000

Khalil, M. I., Jhanjhi, N. Z., Humayun, M., Sivanesan, S. K., Masud, M., & Hossain, M. S. (2021). Hybrid smart grid with sustainable energy efficient resources for smart cities. *Sustainable Energy Technologies and Assessments*, 46, 101211. DOI:10.1016/j.seta.2021.101211

Khan, M., & Ghafoor, L. (2024) *Adversarial machine learning in the context of network Security: Challenges and solutions.* https://thesciencebrigade.com/jcir/article/view/118

Kholgh, D. K., & Kostakos, P. (2023). PAC-GPT: A Novel approach to generating synthetic network traffic with GPT-3. *IEEE Access : Practical Innovations, Open Solutions*, 11, 114936–114951. DOI:10.1109/ACCESS.2023.3325727

Khoo, L., Lim, M. K., Chong, C. Y., & McNaney, R. (2024). Machine Learning for Multimodal Mental Health Detection: A Systematic Review of Passive Sensing Approaches. *Sensors (Basel)*, 24(2), 348. DOI:10.3390/s24020348 PMID:38257440

Kim, J., Seo, M., Lee, S., Nam, J., Yegneswaran, V., Porras, P., Gu, G., & Shin, S. (2024). Enhancing security in SDN: Systematizing attacks and defenses from a penetration perspective. *Computer Networks*, 241, 110203. DOI:10.1016/j.comnet.2024.110203

King, D. (2024). *Legal & Humble AI: Addressing the Legal, Ethical, and Societal Dilemmas of Generative AI.* Ingene Publishers.

Kizza, J. M. (2024a) 'Firewalls,' in *Texts in computer science*, 265–294. DOI:10.1007/978-3-031-47549-8_12

Kizza, J. M. (2024b) 'System Intrusion Detection and Prevention,' in *Texts in computer science*, 295–323. DOI:10.1007/978-3-031-47549-8_13

Konar, S., Mukherjee, G., & Dutta, G. (2024) 'Understanding the relationship between trust and faith in Micro-Enterprises to cyber hygiene,' in *Advances in business information systems and analytics book series*, 125–148. DOI:10.4018/979-8-3693-0839-4.ch006

Kozák, M. (2024) 'Creating valid adversarial examples of malware,' *Journal of Computer Virology and Hacking Techniques* [Preprint]. .DOI:10.1007/s11416-024-00516-2

Kozik, R., Pawlicki, M., & Choraś, M. (2018). Cost-Sensitive distributed machine learning for NetFlow-Based Botnet activity detection. *Security and Communication Networks*, 2018, 1–8. DOI:10.1155/2018/8753870

Kshetri, N. (2017). Blockchain's roles in strengthening cybersecurity and protecting privacy. *Telecommunications Policy*, 41(10), 1027–1038. DOI:10.1016/j.telpol.2017.09.003

Kumar, R. and Khan, R.A. (2024) 'Securing military computing with the blockchain,' *Computer Fraud & Security*, 2024(2). .DOI:10.12968/S1361-3723(24)70007-4

Le, T.-T.-H., Wardhani, R. W., Putranto, D. S. C., Jo, U., & Kim, H. (2023). Toward enhanced attack detection and explanation in intrusion detection System-Based IoT environment data. *IEEE Access : Practical Innovations, Open Solutions*, 11, 131661–131676. DOI:10.1109/ACCESS.2023.3336678

Lelah, T. A. (2023). Abuse of Cloud-Based and Public Legitimate Services as Command-and-Control (C&C) Infrastructure: A Systematic Literature Review. *Journal of Cybersecurity and Privacy*, 3(3), 558–590. DOI:10.3390/jcp3030027

Liu, J., Wang, L., Hu, W., Gao, Y., Cao, Y., Lin, B., & Zhang, R. (2023). Spatial-Temporal Feature with Dual-Attention Mechanism for Encrypted Malicious Traffic Detection. *Security and Communication Networks*, 2023, 1–13. DOI:10.1155/2023/7117863

Ma, Z. (2024) 'The investigation of communications protocol,' in *Advances in intelligent systems research*, 576–582. DOI:10.2991/978-94-6463-370-2_58

Magnusson, O. (2023) *Cyber threat emulation.* https://odr.chalmers.se/items/62874e36-08b6-4d7b-92b5-705e91cc26f4

Mandal, S. (2023) 'Defense Against Adversarial Attacks using Convolutional Auto-Encoders,' *arXiv (Cornell University)* [Preprint]. https://doi.org//arxiv.2312.03520 .DOI:10.48550

Martins, I., Resende, J. S., Sousa, P. R., Silva, S., Antunes, L., & Gama, J. (2022). Host-based IDS: A review and open issues of an anomaly detection system in IoT. *Future Generation Computer Systems*, 133, 95–113. DOI:10.1016/j.future.2022.03.001

Masood, S., & Zafar, A. (2024). Deep-efficient-guard: Securing wireless ad hoc networks via graph neural network, [Preprint]. *International Journal of Information Technology : an Official Journal of Bharati Vidyapeeth's Institute of Computer Applications and Management*. Advance online publication. DOI:10.1007/s41870-023-01702-z

Mehmood, A.. (2024). *Advances and Vulnerabilities in Modern Cryptographic Techniques: A comprehensive survey on cybersecurity in the domain of Machine/Deep Learning and Quantum Techniques*. IEEE Access., DOI:10.1109/ACCESS.2024.3367232

Mohammed, S. D., & Hossain, G. (2024) 'ChatGPT in Education, Healthcare, and Cybersecurity: Opportunities and Challenges,' *2024 IEEE 14th Annual Computing and Communication Workshop and Conference (CCWC)* [Preprint]. DOI:10.1109/CCWC60891.2024.10427923

Mohan, P. V., Dixit, S., Gyaneshwar, A., Chadha, U., Srinivasan, K., & Seo, J. T. (2022). Leveraging Computational intelligence Techniques for defensive deception: A review, recent advances, open problems and future directions. *Sensors (Basel)*, 22(6), 2194. DOI:10.3390/s22062194 PMID:35336373

Mohanad, M., Hazzaa, F., Mohanad Sameer, , Jamal Fadhil, , Sekhar, R., Pritesh, , & Parihar, S. (2024). Intrusion Detection in Software-Defined Networks: Leveraging Deep Reinforcement Learning with Graph Convolutional Networks for Resilient Infrastructure. *Research Gate*, 15(1), 78–87. DOI:10.54216/FPA.150107

Möller, D. P. F. (2023) 'Intrusion Detection and Prevention,' in *Advances in information security*, 131–179. DOI:10.1007/978-3-031-26845-8_3

Morse, E. A., & Raval, V. (2008). PCI DSS: Payment card industry data security standards in context. *Computer Law & Security Report*, 24(6), 540–554. DOI:10.1016/j.clsr.2008.07.001

Mulyanto, M., Leu, J.-S., Faisal, M., & Yunanto, W. (2023). Weight embedding autoencoder as feature representation learning in an intrusion detection systems. *Computers & Electrical Engineering*, 111, 108949. DOI:10.1016/j.compeleceng.2023.108949

Mumuni, A., Mumuni, F., & Gerrar, N. K. (2024) 'A survey of synthetic data augmentation methods in computer vision,' *arXiv (Cornell University)* [Preprint]. https://doi.org//arxiv.2403.10075.DOI:10.48550

Munir, Md. S. (2024) 'A zero trust framework for realization and defense against generative AI attacks in power grid,' *arXiv (Cornell University)* [Preprint]. https://doi.org//arxiv.2403.06388.DOI:10.48550

Naeem, S., Ali, A., Anam, S., & Ahmed, M. M. (2023). An Unsupervised Machine Learning Algorithms: Comprehensive Review. *International Journal of Computing and Digital Systems*, 13(1), 911–921. DOI:10.12785/ijcds/130172

Naseer, F. (2024) 'Automated assessment and feedback in higher education using Generative AI,' in *Advances in educational technologies and instructional design book series*, pp. 433–461. DOI:10.4018/979-8-3693-1351-0.ch021

Oloyede, J. O. (2024) 'Ethical Reflections on AI for Cybersecurity: Building trust,' *Social Science Research Network* [Preprint]. https://doi.org/DOI:10.2139/ssrn.4733563

Pang, G., Shen, C., Cao, L., & Hengel, A. V. D. (2021). Deep learning for anomaly detection. *ACM Computing Surveys*, 54(2), 1–38. DOI:10.1145/3439950

Payá, A. S., Arroni, S., García-Díaz, V., & Gómez, A. (2024). Apollon: A robust defense system against Adversarial Machine Learning attacks in Intrusion Detection Systems. *Computers & Security*, 136, 103546. DOI:10.1016/j.cose.2023.103546

Puttagunta, M. K., Subban, R., & Babu, C. N. K. (2023). Adversarial examples: Attacks and defences on medical deep learning systems. *Multimedia Tools and Applications*, 82(22), 33773–33809. DOI:10.1007/s11042-023-14702-9

Rachakonda, L. P., Siddula, M., & Sathya, V. (2024) 'A comprehensive study on IoT privacy and security challenges with focus on spectrum sharing in Next-Generation networks(5G/6G/beyond),' *High-Confidence Computing*, p. 100220. DOI:10.1016/j.hcc.2024.100220

Rajasekaran, A. S. (2023) 'Cybersecurity Measures Using Machine Learning for Business Applications,' *2023 4th International Conference on Computation, Automation and Knowledge Management (ICCAKM)* [Preprint]. DOI:10.1109/ICCAKM58659.2023.10449580

Rani, S. S., & Reeja, S. R. (2019) 'A survey on different approaches for malware detection using machine learning techniques,' in *Lecture notes on data engineering and communications technologies*, pp. 389–398. DOI:10.1007/978-3-030-34515-0_42

Ranka, P., Shah, A., Vora, N., Kulkarni, A., & Patil, N. (2024). Computer Vision-Based Cybersecurity Threat Detection System with GAN-Enhanced Data Augmentation. *Communications in Computer and Information Science*, 2031, 54–67. DOI:10.1007/978-3-031-53728-8_5

Raparthi, M. (2020). *Examining the use of Artificial Intelligence to Enhance Security Measures in Computer Hardware, including the Detection of Hardware-based Vulnerabilities and Attacks.* EEL. [Preprint], DOI:10.52783/eel.v10i1.991

Reddy, B. S. R. (2024) 'Reinforcement Learning for Zero-Day Vulnerability Detection in IoT Devices: A Proactive approach,' *Research Square(Research Square)* [Preprint]. DOI:10.21203/rs.3.rs-4086508/v1

Rele, M., & Patil, D. (2023) 'Intrusive Detection Techniques Utilizing Machine Learning, Deep Learning, and Anomaly-based Approaches,' *2023 IEEE International Conference on Cryptography, Informatics, and Cybersecurity (ICoCICs)* [Preprint]. DOI:10.1109/ICoCICs58778.2023.10276955

Repetto, M. (2023). Adaptive monitoring, detection, and response for agile digital service chains. *Computers & Security*, 132, 103343. DOI:10.1016/j.cose.2023.103343

Rial, R. C. (2024). *AI in analytical chemistry: Advancements, challenges, and future directions.* Talanta., DOI:10.1016/j.talanta.2024.125949

Roshan, K., & Zafar, A. (2024). AE-Integrated: Real-time network intrusion detection with Apache Kafka and autoencoder. *Concurrency and Computation*, 36(11), e8034. Advance online publication. DOI:10.1002/cpe.8034

Saeed, M. M., Saeed, R. A., Abdelhaq, M., Alsaqour, R., Hasan, M. K., & Mokhtar, R. A. (2023). Anomaly detection in 6G networks using machine learning methods. *Electronics (Basel)*, 12(15), 3300. DOI:10.3390/electronics12153300

Salekshahrezaee, Z., Leevy, J. L., & Khoshgoftaar, T. M. (2023). The effect of feature extraction and data sampling on credit card fraud detection. *Journal of Big Data*, 10(1), 6. Advance online publication. DOI:10.1186/s40537-023-00684-w

Sankar, S. (2020). Energy efficient optimal parent selection based routing protocol for Internet of Things using firefly optimization algorithm. *Transactions on Emerging Telecommunications Technologies*, 32(8), e4171. Advance online publication. DOI:10.1002/ett.4171

Saravanan, T., Deepa, S. N., & Sasikumar, P. (2023). Advanced EGAN-IDS Framework for Resilience against Adversarial Attacks using Multi-headed Attention Module. *Procedia Computer Science*, 230, 203–213. DOI:10.1016/j.procs.2023.12.075

Sewak, M., Sahay, S. K., & Rathore, H. (2022). Deep reinforcement learning in the advanced Cybersecurity Threat Detection and Protection. *Information Systems Frontiers*. Advance online publication. DOI:10.1007/s10796-022-10333-x

Shahid, H. (2021). Energy Optimised Security against Wormhole Attack in IoT-Based Wireless Sensor Networks. *Computers, Materials & Continua*, 68(2), 1967–1981. DOI:10.32604/cmc.2021.015259

Sharma, S. (2019). *Data Privacy and GDPR handbook*. John Wiley & Sons. DOI:10.1002/9781119594307

Shi, Y., Lian, L., Shi, Y., Wang, Z., Zhou, Y., Fu, L., Bai, L., Zhang, J., & Zhang, W. (2023). Machine Learning for Large-Scale Optimization in 6G wireless networks. *IEEE Communications Surveys and Tutorials*, 25(4), 2088–2132. DOI:10.1109/COMST.2023.3300664

Shukla, S. (2023) 'Synergizing machine learning and cybersecurity for robust digital protection.,' *Research Square* [Preprint]. DOI:10.21203/rs.3.rs-3571854/v1

Sinaga, K. P., & Yang, M.-S. (2020). Unsupervised K-Means clustering algorithm. *IEEE Access: Practical Innovations, Open Solutions*, 8, 80716–80727. DOI:10.1109/ACCESS.2020.2988796

Sindiramutty, S. R. (2023) 'Autonomous Threat Hunting: a future paradigm for AI-Driven Threat intelligence,' *arXiv (Cornell University)* [Preprint]. https://doi.org//arxiv.2401.00286.DOI:10.48550

Sindiramutty, S. R., Jhanjhi, N. Z., Tan, C., Khan, N. A., & Shah, B. (2024) 'Cybersecurity measures for logistics industry,' in *Advances in information security, privacy, and ethics book series*, 1–58. DOI:10.4018/979-8-3693-3816-2.ch001

Sindiramutty, S.R., Jhanjhi, N.Z., Tan, C.E., Khan, N.A., & Gharib, A.H. (2023) 'Applications of blockchain technology in supply chain management,' in *Advances in logistics, operations, and management science book series*, 248–304. .DOI:10.4018/978-1-6684-7625-3.ch009

Sindiramutty, S.R., Jhanjhi, N.Z., Tan, C.E., Khan, N.A., & Shah, B. (2023) 'Securing the digital supply chain cyber threats and vulnerabilities,' in *Advances in logistics, operations, and management science book series*, 156–223. .DOI:10.4018/978-1-6684-7625-3.ch007

Sindiramutty, S. R., Jhanjhi, N. Z., Tan, C. E., Khan, N. A., & Shah, B. (2024) 'Future trends and emerging threats in drone cybersecurity,' in *Advances in information security, privacy, and ethics book series*, 148–195. DOI:10.4018/979-8-3693-0774-8.ch007

Sindiramutty, S. R., Jhanjhi, N. Z., Tan, C. E., Tee, W. J., & Lau, S. P. (2024) 'IoT and AI-Based Smart Solutions for the Agriculture Industry,' in *Advances in computational intelligence and robotics book series*, 317–351. DOI:10.4018/978-1-6684-6361-1.ch012

Sindiramutty, S. R., & Tan, C. (2024) 'Modern smart cities and open research challenges and issues of explainable artificial intelligence,' in *Advances in computational intelligence and robotics book series*, 389–424. DOI:10.4018/978-1-6684-6361-1.ch015

Sindiramutty, S. R., Tan, C., & Wei, G. W. (2024) 'Eyes in the sky,' in *Advances in information security, privacy, and ethics book series*, 405–451. DOI:10.4018/979-8-3693-0774-8.ch017

Sindiramutty, S.R., Tan, C.E., & Goh, W.W. (2024) 'Securing the supply chain,' in *Advances in information security, privacy, and ethics book series*, 300–365. .DOI:10.4018/979-8-3693-3816-2.ch011

Sindiramutty, S. R., Tan, C. E., & Lau, S. P. (2024) 'Explainable AI for cybersecurity,' in *Advances in computational intelligence and robotics book series*, 31–97. DOI:10.4018/978-1-6684-6361-1.ch002

Sindiramutty, S. R., Tan, C. E., & Shah, B. (2024) 'Ethical considerations in drone cybersecurity,' in *Advances in information security, privacy, and ethics book series*, 42–87. DOI:10.4018/979-8-3693-0774-8.ch003

Sindiramutty, S. R., Tee, W. J., Balakrishnan, S., Kaur, S., & Thangaveloo, R. (2024) 'Explainable AI in healthcare application,' in *Advances in computational intelligence and robotics book series*, 123–176. DOI:10.4018/978-1-6684-6361-1.ch005

Singh, R., Sethi, A., Saini, K., Saurav, S., Tiwari, A., & Singh, S. (2024). Attention-guided generator with dual discriminator GAN for real-time video anomaly detection. *Engineering Applications of Artificial Intelligence*, 131, 107830. DOI:10.1016/j.engappai.2023.107830

Singhal, V., Jain, S. S., Anand, D., Singh, A., Verma, S., Kavita, , Rodrigues, J. J. P. C., Jhanjhi, N. Z., Ghosh, U., Jo, O., & Iwendi, C. (2020). Artificial Intelligence Enabled Road Vehicle-Train Collision Risk Assessment Framework for Unmanned railway level crossings. *IEEE Access : Practical Innovations, Open Solutions*, 8, 113790–113806. DOI:10.1109/ACCESS.2020.3002416

Striuk, O., & Kondratenko, Y. (2023) 'Generative Adversarial Networks in Cybersecurity: analysis and response,' in *Studies in computational intelligence*, 373–388. DOI:10.1007/978-3-031-25759-9_18

Sun, N., Ding, M., Jiang, J., Xu, W., Mo, X., Tai, Y., & Zhang, J. (2023). Cyber Threat Intelligence Mining for Proactive Cybersecurity Defense: A survey and New Perspectives. *IEEE Communications Surveys and Tutorials*, 25(3), 1748–1774. DOI:10.1109/COMST.2023.3273282

Syed, S. A., Sharma, D. K., & Srivastava, G. (2023). Modeling Distributed and Configurable Hierarchical Blockchain over SDN and Fog-Based Networks for Large-Scale Internet of Things. *Journal of Grid Computing*, 21(4), 64. Advance online publication. DOI:10.1007/s10723-023-09698-3

Taj, I., & Jhanjhi, N. Z. (2022). Towards Industrial Revolution 5.0 and Explainable Artificial Intelligence: Challenges and opportunities. *International Journal of Computing and Digital Systems*, 12(1), 285–310. DOI:10.12785/ijcds/120124

Tyagi, A. K., Hemamalini, V., & Soni, G. (2023) 'Digital health communication with Artificial Intelligence-Based Cyber Security,' in *Advances in medical technologies and clinical practice book series*, 178–213. DOI:10.4018/978-1-6684-8938-3.ch009

Usama, M., Qadir, J., Raza, A., Arif, H., Yau, K. A., Elkhatib, Y., Hussain, A., & Al-Fuqaha, A. (2019). Unsupervised machine learning for networking: Techniques, applications and research challenges. *IEEE Access : Practical Innovations, Open Solutions*, 7, 65579–65615. DOI:10.1109/ACCESS.2019.2916648

Van Der Mei, A. P. (2024). Research on Information Security Protection in the context of Post-epidemic tourism Revival. *International Journal of Education and Humanities*, 12(2), 44–48. DOI:10.54097/zwbmyt93

Wang, Y., Wang, X., Arifoglu, D., Lu, C., Bouchachia, A., Geng, Y., & Zheng, G. (2023). A survey on Ambient Sensor-Based Abnormal Behaviour Detection for Elderly People in Healthcare. *Electronics (Basel)*, 12(7), 1539. DOI:10.3390/electronics12071539

Wassan, S. (2021) 'Amazon Product Sentiment Analysis using Machine Learning Techniques,' *International Journal of Early Childhood Special Education (INT-JECSE)*, 30(1), 695. https://doi.org/.DOI:10.24205/03276716.2020.2065

Wen, B. O. T. (2023) 'Detecting cyber threats with a Graph-Based NIDPS,' in *Advances in logistics, operations, and management science book series*, 36–74. DOI:10.4018/978-1-6684-7625-3.ch002

Wu, Y. (2024) 'Online Adaptive Ensemble Enhanced Anomaly Detection for Addressing Concept Drift in IoT Systems,' *TechRiv* [Preprint]. DOI:10.36227/techrxiv.23304461.v2

Xu, B., & Wang, S. (2024) 'Examining Windows File System IRP Operations with Machine Learning for Ransomware Detection,' *Research Square(Research Square)* [Preprint]. DOI:10.21203/rs.3.rs-4032456/v1

Yazan, A. (2019) 'International Journal of Computing and Digital Systems,' *International Journal of Computing and Digital Systems* [Preprint]. https://doi.org/ .DOI:10.12785/ijcds

Yigit, Y. (2024) 'Review of Generative AI methods in Cybersecurity,' *arXiv (Cornell University)* [Preprint]. https://doi.org//arxiv.2403.08701.DOI:10.48550

Zaman, M., Upadhyay, D., & Lung, C.-H. (2023). Validation of a Machine Learning-Based IDS design framework using ORNL datasets for power system with SCADA. *IEEE Access : Practical Innovations, Open Solutions*, 11, 118414–118426. DOI:10.1109/ACCESS.2023.3326751

Zhang, Q., Chen, B., Zhang, T., Cao, K., Ding, Y., Gao, T., & Zhao, Z. (2023). Generative Adversarial Network-Based Anomaly Detection and Forecasting with Unlabeled Data for 5G Vertical Applications. *Applied Sciences (Basel, Switzerland)*, 13(19), 10745. DOI:10.3390/app131910745

Zhang, Z. (2024) 'Reinforcement Learning-Based Approaches for Enhancing Security and Resilience in Smart Control: A survey on attack and defense methods,' *arXiv (Cornell University)* [Preprint]. https://doi.org//arxiv.2402.15617.DOI:10.48550

Zografopoulos, I., Ospina, J., Liu, X., & Konstantinou, C. (2021). Cyber-Physical Energy Systems Security: Threat modeling, risk assessment, resources, metrics, and case studies. *IEEE Access : Practical Innovations, Open Solutions*, 9, 29775–29818. DOI:10.1109/ACCESS.2021.3058403

Chapter 4
Reshaping Cybersecurity of Wireless Sensor Networks Using Energy– Optimized Approach Against Wormhole Attack

Hafsa Shahid
International Islamic University, Islamabad, Pakistan

Humaira Ashraf
https://orcid.org/0000-0001-5067-3172
Taylor's University, Malaysia

N. Z. Jhanjhi
https://orcid.org/0000-0001-8116-4733
Taylor's University, Malaysia

Qurat-ul Ain Zam Zam
International Islamic University, Islamabad, Pakistan

ABSTRACT

Security is a major problem in wireless sensor networks (WSN) because they are vulnerable to a variety of dangerous threats, the deadliest of which is the wormhole assault. These networks support functions like localization and other networking protocols. These networks are made up of many small sensors that collect and share data with central repositories. In such a setting, the detection of wormholes becomes more difficult because of low resource availability in detecting equipment. The

DOI: 10.4018/979-8-3693-5415-5.ch004

authors propose to develop an algorithm for wormhole detection which performs efficiently within the given resource constraints in WSN environment. This research has initially performed a survey using systematic literature review (SLR) to study the schemes against wormhole attacks. Articles have been searched using reliable data sources and applied quality assessment measures to refine the article collection. The SLR has helped to find the shortcomings and limitations in the literature. This research elaborates a comparison of the wormhole attack prevention techniques based on results, findings, and limitations in each category of schemes in literature. Finally, the problem of high energy consumption is taken under consideration for the purpose of research. The proposed technique for handling wormhole has been designed to give good performance and consume less energy of the network. This method uses the transmission duration between the sender and recipient nodes to identify suspicious nodes. Then, it uses the hop count and hop interval time to detect suspicious nodes. The simulation's findings indicate a 100% packet delivery ratio and detection rate. Comparing the proposed technique to a good existing technique in the considered base article, it has enhanced throughput, lowered end-to-end delay, and consumed less energy.

1. INTRODUCTION

Wireless sensor networks (WSNs) represent a cutting-edge technology in today's world, offering versatility that makes them deployable across various scenarios. Telecommunications, satellite communication, traffic monitoring, space communication, weather monitoring, forest monitoring, fire detection, underwater networks, military systems, smart homes, and the Internet of Things (IoT) are just a few of the areas of modern life that these networks have revolutionized (Li et al., 2011). Of all the several kinds of WSNs, mobile sensor networks are the most developed and fastest-growing. Mobile sensor nodes, which are low-resource devices primarily intended to gather and wirelessly send data to a base station in charge of keeping an eye on the sensor nodes and carrying out necessary procedures, make up these networks (Akyildiz et al., 2002).

The precise location of nodes plays a critical role in these systems. Since sensor nodes typically lack GPS capabilities due to limited energy availability, Localization methods are used to continually monitor the geographical position of sensor nodes (Halder & Ghosal, 2016; Singh & Sharma, 2015). In some localization techniques, GPS-equipped anchor nodes are utilized to track the unidentified locations of sensor nodes (Han et al., 2016).

Figure 1. Wireless Sensor Network Architecture

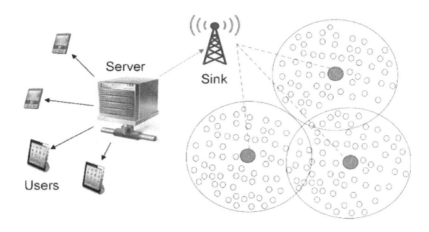

(Shahid et al., 2021)

The decentralized nature of WSN raises significant security concerns. It is vulnerable to numerous security threats focused on node capture and hacking, which can compromise data and security (Pandey & Tripathi, 2010). The wormhole assault is one of the worst dangers that wireless sensor networks face. Because it may be started without jeopardizing any genuine nodes in the network and without the attacker needing any shared keys, this attack presents a serious issue. Depending on the attack's nature and the region it starts in, the system's response to it may differ. The wormhole attack transmits bogus coordinates to the system, tricking it into believing the node is somewhere else when it is launched during the localization protocol. However, if it is started inside of the routing protocol, data breach may occur.

Wormhole attacks typically manifest in two forms: internal and external. The internal wormhole attack is initiated through the use of an encapsulation method (Maidamwar, 2012). Here, after reaching the first malicious node, the packet is wrapped and sent over the safe network path. But the wormhole tunnel's jumps remain unaccounted for. The packet is de-encapsulated and the hop count is increased by one once it reaches the last node of the wormhole tunnel, as illustrated in Figure 2.

Figure 2. Hop Count-based Internal wormhole attack

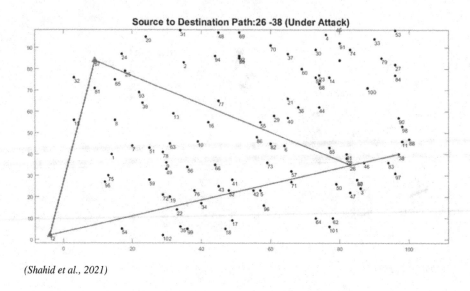

(Shahid et al., 2021)

Figure 3 illustrates an external wormhole assault in which the attacker is not a member of the system. At both ends of the wormhole tunnel, a high-speed out-of-band link is built to provide the appearance of a neighborhood between two distant nodes (Luo et al., 2019; Maidamwar, 2012). Using the packet relay technique, the attacker launches this kind of attack by sending a packet between two distant nodes while pretending to be their neighbors.

Figure 3. High power transmission-based External wormhole attack

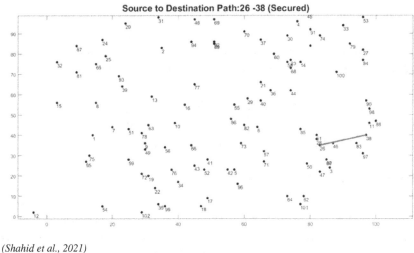

(Shahid et al., 2021)

In literature, many techniques have been proposed to tackle this deadly attack in WSNs. A rich literature is available to study and analyze for the implications of more research which would lead to providing better solutions. There are many survey articles which provide researchers with helpful information in a very comprehensive manner. The author provides a thorough analysis of the benefits and drawbacks of the various wormhole detection and prevention strategies currently in use (Dutta & Singh, 2019). A critical review of existing surveys against wormhole attack with the help of their limitations as well as a comparison among their significant parameters has been presented in Farjamnia et al. (2019). Abd El-mawla et al. (2019) and Patel et al. (2017) explain types of wormhole attacks in detail along various countermeasures existing in literature. Survey articles like those mentioned above have aggregated information about existing techniques against wormhole attack. These articles have provided researchers with an analytical and critical perspective to study wormhole attack avoidance, detection and handling in WSNs.

In this research, SLR has been performed on the existing literature for mitigating wormhole attack during year 2014 to 2020. Various types of techniques have been included, applicable to static as well as dynamic mobile sensor network. By the end of SLR, For easy study, it offers a parameter-based comparison of wormhole attack avoidance strategies in a table with the article references. This section highlights the gaps and shortcomings in the existing literature which defines scopes for future work and lay foundation for further research in the field.

1.1. Motivation for Research

- The detailed study of literature describes numerous security techniques exist in wireless sensor networks to prevent wormhole attacks, but they lack in one aspect or other.
- Simpler techniques lack in performance aspects and the more efficient techniques consume high energy as well which is a vital and critical resource in sensor network.
- This analysis has provided motivation for developing a technique giving high performance while consuming least energy possible, providing a resource optimized and efficient security solution for sensor networks.

1.2. Problem Statement

Wormhole attack is a critical security issue in resource constrained wireless sensor networks. Existing security techniques have limitations such as high energy consumption (Aliady & Al-Ahmadi, 2019; Shukla et al., 2018), low detection rate (Singh et al., 2016; Wu et al., 2014), poor packet delivery ratio (Amish & Vaghela, 2016; Scholar & Yadav, 2019; Sharma & Joshi, 2017), high end to end delay (Aliady & Al-Ahmadi, 2019; Amish & Vaghela, 2016; Karthigadevi et al., 2018) and low throughput (Aliady & Al-Ahmadi, 2019; Okunlola et al., 2017; Shukla et al., 2018). Thus, there is a need for an efficient and energy optimized algorithm against wormhole attacks.

1.3. Research Question

Following research questions have been generated to lay foundation for the proposed research:

RQ 1: How can wormhole attack be efficiently detected and handled in resource constrained WSN?
RQ 2: How can wormhole detection algorithm be made less complicated to consume less energy?
RQ 3: How can wormhole detection algorithm be made efficient to give enhanced throughput and reduced delay from end to end?

1.4. Aim of Research

To develop an efficient and low energy consuming security technique against wormhole attacks while producing increased throughput and decreased end to end delay in resource constrained wireless sensor network

1.5. Objectives of Research

- To simplify wormhole detection technique and reduce energy consumption of security algorithm.
- To find suspicious nodes and then wormhole links in WSN
- To eliminate wormhole links and reestablish secure communication links
- To avoid processing overhead to produce reduced end-to-end delay and enhanced throughput

2. SYSTEMATIC LITERATURE REVIEW

The systematic literature review is a step by step process which begins with a research question. It involves collecting articles from significant sources, refining the collection based on quality assessment criteria, examining the qualifying papers in-depth, extracting relevant information, and creating goals that might address the research issue (Kitchenham et al., 2009). The SLR process involves; i) Research question, ii) Data sources, iii) Data retrieval, iv) Study selection, v) Quality evaluation measures, vi) Quality assessment, vii) Findings of SLR and viii) Results of critical analysis. Initially, research question is formulated, which justifies the need of proposed research and explains the reason for which the research is being conducted. The existing available articles about the specific area are searched, for which the data sources are decided. Available data on the subject has been extracted using the formulated keyword string based on Boolean search methods. Article refinement process is then started by finding the qualifying articles based on previously specified standards for inclusion and exclusion. The qualified articles are expected to be the most refined and relevant form of data on which the detailed study and critical analysis will be performed (Kitchenham et al., 2009). Figure 4 shows the phases and steps of systematic literature review.

2.1. Process of SLR

2.1.1. Research Question

The research questions for the proposed research have been described in Chapter 1 Introduction. They have been considered for the initiation of the presented SLR study.

Figure 4. Systematic Literature Review

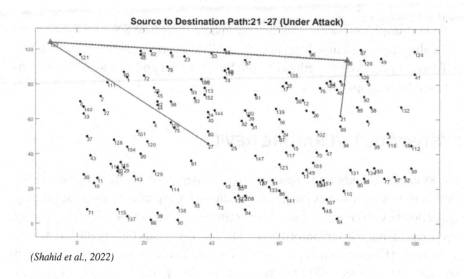

(Shahid et al., 2022)

2.1.2. Data Sources and Data Retrieval

Articles under study are obtained from the following libraries including IEEE (http://www.ieeexplore.ieee.org/), Elsevier (https://www.elsevier.com/), Springer (https://link.springer.com/), Science Direct (http://www.sciencedirect.com/), and https://scholar.google.com.pk/. Search strings are defined by following these steps; i) identify keywords by analyzing research question; ii) Consider synonyms as well; iii) linking the OR between synonyms & AND between main keywords like ((WSN OR "wireless sensor network") AND (prevention OR "securing" OR "detection" OR handling OR "recovery") AND ("wormhole "OR "attack")).

2.1.3. Study Selection

Selective inclusion of articles is carried out for research using the following standards; i) Online published and available article; ii) Published during 2014-2020; iii) Full text of article must be in English and available; iv) Must have discussed the security tactics against wormhole in mobile WSN; v) Survey or Review articles, helpful for better understanding. Articles have been excluded as per following criteria; i) All types of network other than WSN; ii) Redundant or duplicated material; iii) Irrelevant to the objective; iv) Does not contain all parts of specifically required information. Figure 5 shows how choosing studies leads to improving the process of gathering articles.

Figure 5. Study Selection Process

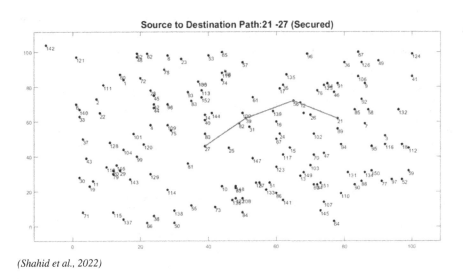

(Shahid et al., 2022)

2.1.4. Quality Evaluation and Assessment

Firstly, set of rules is defined, each against specific characteristic of an article. Ranks are assigned to these rules and a point system is defined against each rank. Then against each number of points a quality evaluation result statement is defined. This system helps to individually assess each article and find out whether the article is relevant to the topic under study and matches the required criteria of needed information. It helps to decide whether the article should be included for detailed study. Following Table 1 illustrates the criteria defined for evaluation of the quality of articles using ranks and points

Table 1. Quality Evaluation Criteria using Ranks and Points

Rules	Rank	Points	Quality Evaluation
None	0	0	0
Wormhole Attack in WSN	1	1	Poor
Wormhole attack prevention	2	1	Average
Wormhole attack Detection	3	1	Average
Wormhole handling	4	1	Average
Wormhole prevention and detection	5	2	Good
Wormhole Attack + Detection + Prevention + Handling in WSN	6	3	Excellent

Each article is assessed by matching the rule it follows and give corresponding rank to that article. Then points are assigned to the article for the achieved rank. These points lead rea to measuring the quality of article by finally giving evaluation result according to the points. Table 2 explores the detailed Quality assessment and evaluation of selected articles. This system allows to effectively evaluate the quality of each article without the need to perform detailed study on it. This helps to refine the data collection by including the most relevant articles which are fulfilling the required information criteria in the best way. These refined articles are then proceeded to become the base of presented literature review and detailed critical analysis.

Table 2 Quality Assessment and Evaluation of Selected Articles

Research articles	Rank	Points	Evaluation
DEA (Céspedes-Mota et al., 2018)	0	0	Poor
RSSL (Chen et al., 2018)	1	1	Poor
TBA-MANET (Panwar et al., 2020)	1	1	Poor
TRM (Wu et al., 2014)	3	1	Average
ANN (Shaon & Ferens, 2015)	3	1	Average
NCI (Patel & Aggarwal, 2016)	3	1	Average
NDPV (Okunlola et al., 2017)	5	2	Good
NIAPC (Patel et al., 2019)	3	1	Average
WDUST (Harsanyi et al., 2018)	3	1	Average
CREDND (Luo et al., 2019)	6	3	Excellent
EPSMAW (Aliady & Al-Ahmadi, 2019)	5	2	Good

continued on following page

Table 2 Quality Assessment and Evaluation of Selected Articles Continued

Research articles	Rank	Points	Evaluation
AOMDV-RTT (Amish & Vaghela, 2016)	5	2	Good
EIGRP-RTT (Karthigadevi et al., 2018)	5	2	Good
TBWM (Kori, 2019)	4	1	Average
MAODV (Bhagat & Panse, 2017)	3	1	Average
MHTPW (Sharma & Joshi, 2017)	3	1	Average
Poster (Minohara & Nishiyama, 2016)	3	1	Average
WRHT (Singh et al., 2016)	3	1	Average
SPRT (Padmanabhan & Manickavasagam, 2017)	2	1	Average
DMLE (Kumar et al., 2017)	6	3	Excellent
ESR (Naidu & Himaja, 2017)	4	1	Average
TESRP (Shukla et al., 2018)	5	2	Good
EFM (Scholar & Yadav, 2019)	5	2	Good
IPS (Scholar et al., 2020)	5	2	Good
LITS (Bhushan & Sahoo, 2018)	5	2	Good
AWDV-hop (Li et al., 2018)	5	2	Good
EDAK (Athmani et al., 2019)	5	2	Good
HKP-HD (Ahlawat & Dave, 2018)	1	1	Poor
PPKP (Zeng & Yao, 2020)	2	1	Average
VCL-MAPS (Patel & Patel, 2018)	3	1	Average
CLVF (Jagadeesan & Parthasarathy, 2019)	5	2	Good

2.2. Literature Review

The results of the literature review are supplied in the form of the extracted article data and the analysis done on it. This information will be organized and explained in the literature review part making it convenient to study and understand. By studying the literature, It is discovered that several kinds of strategies are used to prevent wormhole attacks. Each sub section explores detailed explanation followed by a table describing the literature review of that category. This table includes technique name, its experimental results, findings and its gaps or limitations.

2.2.1. Neighborhood Information-Based Techniques

Every node in a wireless sensor network environment keeps track of its neighbors and has the information it needs about them. This information of network's connectivity is useful for detecting wormhole attacks in WSN. Such techniques have been explained ahead and a literature review of those articles has been presented in Table 3. Transmission Range-based Method (TRM) depends on the local neighborhood data of the nodes to detect the wormholes by using the medium of transmission range of packets. Simulation has been performed for 100 nodes; rate of detection is 100% (Wu et al., 2014). No special hardware is needed so this approach can be applied to real-world scenarios with large transmission range, it also works efficiently in dynamic topology. It is applicable in case of closed wormholes only. In case of sparse network, detection rate decreases. No detection rate is shown for other types of wormholes. ANN is an Artificial Neural Network-based method which applies ANN training to node neighbor count information to detect wormhole uniform as well as non-uniform network environment. Results for 500 nodes show 98.25% Average accuracy of detection, 1.71% 0.02% false negative rate and false positive rate. Shows an increase in without adding to the communication overhead, detection rates and a reduced false positive rate (Shaon & Ferens, 2015). This technique shows better detection rate for uniform networks as compared with detection rate for non-uniform networks. Network Neighborhood and Connectivity Information (NCI) uses to identify the existence of wormholes, sensor nodes' connection and neighborhood information. Results show 97.15% packet delivery ratio, 95% detection accuracy and throughput as 84kbps. This technique effectively identifies wormhole attacks without requiring new hardware and with little storage costs. (Patel & Aggarwal, 2016). Dynamic WSNs cannot be served by this method.

Neighbor discovery and path verification method (NDPV) uses information in the AODV protocol-based environment against wormhole attack. Simulation results for 70 nodes show that packet delivery ratio is approx. 80%, throughput is 3.5 kbps and delay from end-to end is 0.8 seconds. This method has been implemented using a modified AODV procedure and is not required specialized hardware (Okunlola et al., 2017). Its low packet delivery ratio and processing overhead are caused by the detection technique it runs for each node. The AODV routing protocol serves as the foundation for Neighborhood Information and Alternate Path Calculation (NIAPC). Simulation results for up to 100 nodes show that detection accuracy is 99%. Packet delivery ratio is 98.10% and throughput is 84.70kbps (Patel et al., 2019). Results have shown competitive detection rates without excessive storage requirements. However, for wormholes launched over shorter distances, the False negative rate is high.

A technique based on spanning trees solely makes use of the node neighborhood's connection information. For implementation, two deployment models have been used with $\lambda = 5,6,7$. Results with Random placement model show that Average false positive is 9.0+ and Average recall is 0.92 to 0.99. Results with Perturbed grid model show that Average false positive is 1.6 and Average recall is 1.0 (Harsanyi et al., 2018). This technique requires only connectivity information for detection of wormholes. It doesn't raise costs because it doesn't require any more hardware. An increase in wormhole count has no effect on performance. It works well for wormhole paths that are longer, but the false positive rate rises for wormholes that are shorter. In order to defend against wormhole attacks, the Credible Neighbor Discovery (CREDND) protocol uses hop difference and local monitoring based on neighbor information. Simulation is performed for 800 – 1700 nodes & 2- 10 internal & external wormholes were launched. Results show that detected number of bogus links is 0 – 30 approx. Without the need for an extra hardware node, both internal and exterior wormholes were found, saving time and energy. If every node adheres to a separate distribution protocol but has a distinct communication range, this technique may not perform well (Luo et al., 2019). Energy-saving measures that are secure against Wormhole (EPSMAW) is founded on neighborhood and connectivity information implemented using AODV routing protocol. Simulations results for up to 150 nodes show that Energy consumption has fell to 97.5%, Throughput is 36.409 kbps and End-to-End delay is 2 sec. By using two checking steps, this technique aims to reduce false positives in sparse networks with fewer nodes. It doesn't result in transmission overhead or call for extra hardware (Aliady & Al-Ahmadi, 2019). Malicious nodes can still create a fake neighborhood list to trick the detection algorithm, and it hardly ever finds wormhole tunnels with fewer than four hops.

Table 3. Literature Review of Neighbourhood Information-Based Techniques

Technique	Results	Findings	Limitations
TRM (Transmission range-based method) (Wu et al., 2014)	The average rate of detection is 88%.	Not requiring any unique hardware needed Works efficiently in dynamic topology Applicable in real-world scenarios with large transmission range	Applicable only for closed wormholes (Dutta & Singh, 2019). Communication overhead increased (Luo et al., 2019). For spare network, detection rate and efficiency decreases (Mukherjee et al., 2016). Limited support for mobile networks (Padmanabhan & Manickavasagam, 2017)
ANN (Artificial Neural Network training) (Shaon & Ferens, 2015)	1.71% False positive rate 0.02% False negative rate Average accuracy of detection: 98.25%	Boost the number of detections Reduced rate of erroneous positives No extraneous communication overhead	Increased detection rate for networks that are uniform, not non-uniform (Dutta & Singh, 2019)

continued on following page

Table 3. Continued

Technique	Results	Findings	Limitations
NCI (Neighborhood &Connectivity Info. based method) (Patel & Aggarwal, 2016)	97.15% Packet delivery ratio 95% Detection accuracy Throughput = 84kbps	Minimized storage cost No additional hardware needed	Not relevant for dynamic WSN (Dutta & Singh, 2019) For short-length wormholes, a false negative occurs. (Patel & Aggarwal, 2016)
NDPV (Neighbor discovery and path verification) (Okunlola et al., 2017)	Avg. exposure accuracy: 98% Packet delivery ratio: 80% approx. Throughput: 3.5 kbps End-to-End Delay: 0.8 sec	No specialized hardware needed	False positive needs to reduce (Okunlola et al., 2017) Low Packet delivery ratio (Dutta & Singh, 2019)
NIAPC (Neighbor Info. & Alternate path calculation) (Patel et al., 2019)	Detection accuracy is 99% Packet delivery ratio is 98.10% Throughput is 84.70kbps	Enhanced rate of detection No need for extra storage	a higher false positive for wormholes launched along shorter paths (Patel et al., 2019)
WDUST (Wormhole detection using Spanning Trees) (Harsanyi et al., 2018)	*Random placement model:* Avg false positive 9.0+ Avg recall is 0.92 to 0.99 *Perturbed grid model:* Avg false positive is 1.6 Avg recall is 1.00	Just connectivity information is needed; no further hardware is needed. Performance not affected by increasing wormholes	Higher false +ve for wormholes that are shorter (Harsanyi et al., 2018)
CREDND (Credible neighbor discovery protocol) (Luo et al., 2019)	No. of detected bogus links = 0 – 30 approx.	finds both external and internal wormholes Not requiring any extra hardware Node energy is conserved	If every node has a distinct communication range and adheres to different distributions, performance will suffer (Luo et al., 2019)
EPSMAW (Energy Preserving secure measure against wormhole) (Aliady & Al-Ahmadi, 2019)	Detection rate is 100% Energy consumption max.129 joules Throughput is 36.409 kbps End-to-End delay is 2 sec	In sparse networks, lessen false positives No need for further hardware Absence of overhead transmission	Malicious nodes create fake neighborhood lists to trick detection systems; wormhole tunnels with fewer than four hops are rarely found (Aliady & Al-Ahmadi, 2019)

2.2.2. Techniques Based on Round Trip Time

AODV-based RTT mechanism uses round-trip time (RTT) mechanism to detect wormholes. Simulation results for 45 nodes show that Packet delivery fraction is 0.7892, The average end-to-end delay is 80.8036 seconds, while the average throughput is 216.7 bits/sec. System overhead and end-to-end latency are reduced without the requirement for specialist hardware. This approach is limited to stationary nodes and is ineffective in dynamic environments. Additionally, it cannot manage the delays brought on by traffic or queues (Amish & Vaghela, 2016). To find the shortest path and find malicious nodes, another author employs a round-trip time variation technique based on the EIGRP protocol. The simulation findings indicate that the throughput is 216, the average end-to-end delay is 89.632, and the packet delivery fraction is 0.812 for a 500 m × 500 m region with up to 50 nodes. Although this method is simpler and produces superior performance outcomes, it still has to be improved upon and contrasted with other currently used methods (Karthigadevi et al., 2018). The two-tier Round-Trip Time notion is used in the AODV protocol to achieve trust-based wormhole mitigation (TBWM). Simulation was performed for 450 nodes and results were compared with two schemes. The results explore that packet delivery ratio is 3% better than scheme 1 and 3.3% better than scheme 2 and Throughput is almost the same as schemes 1 and 2 of this article. The AODV routing protocol performs better with proposed scheme by 0.0168% than scheme 1 and 0.0218% than scheme 2 of the article. It does not require additional hardware or tight clock synchronization. Throughput still needs to be improved (Kori, 2019). Table 4 explores the literature review of articles with techniques based on round trip time.

Table 4. Summary of Round-Trip Time-Based Schemes

Technique	Results	Findings	Limitations
AOMDV based RTT (Amish & Vaghela, 2016)	Packet delivery fraction is 0.7892 Average throughput is 216.7 bits/sec Average end to end delay is 80.8036 seconds	Minimized end-to-end delay lower overhead of the system No specialist hardware is required.	Applicable to stationary nodes and not in dynamic environment (Dutta & Singh, 2019) Doesn't handle delays caused by queuing or congestion (Dutta & Singh, 2019)
EIGRP based RTT (Karthigadevi et al., 2018)	Throughput is 216 kbps Average end to end delay is 89.632 ms Packet delivery fraction is 81.2%	Less complicated	Low effectiveness in identifying malicious nodes (Karthigadevi et al., 2019)

continued on following page

Table 4. Continued

Technique	Results	Findings	Limitations
TBWM (trust-based wormhole mitigation) (Kori, 2019)	Packet delivery ratio is 91.6% Throughput is 222.5 kbps	No additional hardware required No tight clock synchronization required	Throughput desires to be enhanced (Kori, 2019)

2.2.3. Transmission Power-Based Techniques

The Modified AODV protocol is implemented by the MAODV technology, which measures the transmission power of the malicious nodes to identify them. Simulation results for up to 80 nodes show that Throughput is up to 88.88 kbps, End to end delay is 75.74 Msec and Packet delivery ratio is 98.69%. Validation of nodes is performed based on ID. The delay of this method is increased (Bhagat & Panse, 2017). Using the AODV protocol, MHTPW (Mitigation of High transmission power-based wormholes) mitigates wormhole attacks by utilizing high power transmission. Throughput decreases from 118 to 82 b/s, packet delivery ratio drops from 27% to 22%, end-to-end delay increases from 9 to 55 ms, and average jitter increases from 2 to 55 ms, according to simulations conducted for up to 100 nodes. There is a reduction in end-to-end delay and an improvement in throughput and packet delivery ratio. Initial checking before adding neighbor nodes takes time and increases delay in communication (Sharma & Joshi, 2017). Table 5 describes in detail the literature review of techniques based on Transmission power.

Table 5. Summary of Transmission Power-Based Schemes

Technique	Results	Findings	Limitations
MAODV (modified AODV protocol) (Bhagat & Panse, 2017)	Throughput is up to 88.88 kbps End to end delay is 75.74 Msec Packet delivery ratio is 98.69%	Validation of nodes based on ID	Delay increased (Abd El-mawla et al., 2019)
MHTPW (mitigation of High transmission power-based wormholes) (Sharma & Joshi, 2017)	Throughput drops from 118 to 82 b/s Packet delivery ratio drops 27% to 22% End to end delay rises from 9 to 55 ms Average jitter rises from 2 to 55 ms	Increased packet delivery ratio and throughput Delay from beginning to end is decreased	Initial checking increases latency in communication (Qadri et al., 2020)

2.2.4. Statistical Method-Based Techniques

The duty cycling sensor network's poster mechanism uses information about delays in synchronized transmission to identify wormholes. This method has performed in a simulation considering of real sensor network as it considers actual behavior of wireless sensor network. Only the wormhole types that were initiated by hidden, cooperative node pairs are displayed in this paper's detection results (Minohara & Nishiyama, 2016). The watchdog and Delphi methods are used by the wormhole-resistant hybrid technique (WRHT) to determine the likelihood that a wormhole exists. The average detection accuracy, according to simulation data for 500 nodes, is 87.3%. Wormholes of various kinds can be found using this technique without the need for further hardware. Nevertheless, the autonomous application of watchdog and Delphi techniques reduces performance (Singh et al., 2016). The sequential probability ratio test is used in the SPRT-based approach to find network wormholes. The average detection rate for a 500-node simulation is 99%, the average false positive rate ranges from 0.2 to 7.5%, and the average detection time for a node density variation is 18.9 seconds. This technique used a small number of nodes in a high mobility environment to discover wormholes more quickly. Nevertheless, its false-positive rate is considerable (Padmanabhan & Manickavasagam, 2017). Range-free localization is used in conjunction with the Distance & Maximum Likelihood Estimation (DMLE) approach. It utilizes base station and anchor nodes to apply distance estimation method and MLE to make localization accurate and wormhole free. Simulation is carried out for 100 - 200 unknown nodes with 10 - 40 anchor nodes where 1 – 10% wormholes are launched. The findings indicate that the localization error rate decreases from 0.6 to 0.3 and the percentage of localization error caused by wormholes increases from 45 to 180 approximately. Because the technique spares the resource-constrained unknown nodes from computational strain, location estimate is less complicated and more precise. Despite this, detection rates still require improvement, and a high anchor to sensor node ratio raises network costs (Kumar et al., 2017).

Euclidean Range System (ERS) strategy uses data from nodes about their base stations. It uses Euclidean distance system to detect and handle wormhole attack. It secures the connections at signal node intervals and make them efficient. Simulation was carried out in NS2 using 50 nodes. Theoretical results suggest that the proposed scheme was able to detect wormhole however, no statistical results have been given in the paper. This method shows increased latency (Naidu & Himaja, 2017). Two sequence numbers are applied using the sequence number method-based scheme and the trust and energy-aware Secure Routing Protocol (TESRP). One for source and other for destination, to the Trust-based routing protocol to prevent wormhole attack. Simulation for up to 60 nodes show that Packet delivery Ratio is 100%, End to end delay is 14 ms, Residual energy is 45 joules and Throughput is 36.5 kbps. TESRP protocol has been made secure from wormhole attack after being applied with security algorithm and sequencing concept. It is still prone to node capture attacks (Shukla et al., 2018). Encapsulation and Fragmentation of message (EFM) method proposes encapsulating the message and appending an additional four bits of information, which will be de-capsulated upon arrival at the destination. It also recommends breaking up the message into smaller pieces and sending them over several channels (Dogra et al., 2022; Jabeen et al., 2023; Julie et al., 2020; Singh et al., 2020). In this way least number of fragments would fall into the wormhole thus preserving data confidentiality. Simulation results for up to 10 nodes show 45% packet delivery ratio. According to statistics given in paper, for 30% of the nodes, the packet delivery ratio is equal to zero (Scholar & Yadav, 2019). Intrusion Prevention System (IPS) has been modifies and implemented with the AODV routing protocol in (Scholar et al., 2020). In this method, wormhole is detected, the credentials of the malicious node are obtained and broadcasted over the network as to prevent other nodes from establishing connection with this wormhole node. IPS system is supposed to prevent data compromise in case of wormholes . But not all the nodes especially distant ones are concerned about a wormhole emerging in a specific area hence, informing all nodes about each malicious node found will be an unnecessary amount of communication resulting in possible increase in overhead and cost. Table 6 illustrates in detail the summary of techniques based on Statistical methods.

Table 6. Summary of Techniques Based on Statistical Methods

Technique	Results	Findings	Limitations
Poster (Minohara & Nishiyama, 2016)	There hasn't been any results evaluation.	Examines the real-world actions of WSN	Lack of results evaluation
WRHT (wormhole-resistant hybrid technique) (Singh et al., 2016)	Detection accuracy: 87.4%	finds every kind of wormhole	By using watchdog and Delphi techniques independently, the detection rate is reduced (Dutta & Singh, 2019).
SPRT (sequential probability ratio test) (Padmanabhan & Manickavasagam, 2017)	Average rate of detection: 90–100% True positive rate: 0.2-2.5% Average time to detect: 18.9 seconds	finds wormholes more quickly uses a minimal number of nodes	needs a clock synchronization module, which raises the price. Detection rates must be raised. Hardware costs rise with a high anchor to sensor node ratio (Kumar et al., 2017).

continued on following page

Table 6. Continued

Technique	Results	Findings	Limitations
DMLE (distance & maximum likelihood estimation) (Kumar et al., 2017)	Localization error rate reduces: 0.6 – 0.3 Wormhole induced localization error % increases: 45 – 180%	Accurate Location estimation Reduced complexity No computational load on nodes	Requires clock synchronization module which increases cost Detection rates need improvement High anchor to sensor node ratio increases hardware cost (Kumar et al., 2017)
ERS (Euclidean Range System) (Naidu & Himaja, 2017)	Wormholes are detected	Determine the attacker's distance in a dispersed node configuration.	Increased latency (Farjamnia et al., 2019)
TESRP and sequence number method (Shukla et al., 2018)	Packet Delivery Ratio: 100% End-to-End Delay: 14 ms Residual Energy: 50.3 joule Throughput: 38 kbps	Improved prevention of wormhole	However vulnerable to node capture attacks (Shukla et al., 2018)
EFM (encapsulation & fragmentation method) (Scholar & Yadav, 2019)	Average Packet Delivery Ratio: 45%	Avoids information compromise	Needs to advance Packet Delivery Ratio (Scholar & Yadav, 2019)
IPS (intrusion prevention system) (Scholar et al., 2020)	End to End Delay: 0.24 ms Throughput: 88.5 kbps Packet Delivery Ratio: 93% NRL: 0.1 – 0.4	Successfully found wormhole stopped more wormholes	Overhead in communication brought on by recurrent broadcasting (Scholar et al., 2020)
Technique	Results	Findings	Limitations
Poster (Minohara & Nishiyama, 2016)	There hasn't been any results evaluation.	Contemplates actual behaviour of WSN	Only wormholes launched by cooperative and out-of-sight node pairs are detected (Dutta & Singh, 2019).
WRHT (wormhole-resistant hybrid technique) (Singh et al., 2016)	Detection accuracy: 87.4%	finds every kind of wormhole No need for further hardware	Independent use of watchdog and Delphi methods resulted in a drop in the detection rate (Dutta & Singh, 2019).
SPRT (sequential probability ratio test) (Padmanabhan & Manickavasagam, 2017)	Avg. detection rate: 90 – 100%. False positive: 0.2 – 7.5% Avg detection time for varying node density: 18.9 sec	finds wormholes more quickly uses a minimal number of nodes Operates in a situation with high mobility	High false-positive (Padmanabhan & Manickavasagam, 2017)

continued on following page

Table 6. Continued

Technique	Results	Findings	Limitations
DMLE (distance & maximum likelihood estimation) (Kumar et al., 2017)	The localization error rate decreases from 0.6 to 0.3, whereas the approximate localization error percentage caused by wormholes rises from 45 to 180%.	Precise location estimation Decreased intricacy Nodes are not under any computational stress	demands a clock synchronization module, raising the price (Li & Wang, 2019) The rate of detection has to be raised [S]. Hardware costs are increased by a high anchor to sensor node ratio (Kumar et al., 2017)
ERS (Euclidean Range System) (Naidu & Himaja, 2017)	Wormholes are found The paper contains no statistics.	Determine the attacker's distance in a dispersed node configuration.	Increased latency (Farjamnia et al., 2019)
TESRP and sequence number method (Shukla et al., 2018)	Average results: Packet delivery Ratio: 100% End to end delay: 14 ms Residual energy: 50.3 joule Throughput: 38 kbps	Improved prevention of wormhole	However vulnerable to node capture attacks (Shukla et al., 2018)
EFM (encapsulation & fragmentation method) (Scholar & Yadav, 2019)	Normal packet delivery ratio 45%	Prevents data compromise	Needs to advance Packet delivery ratio (Scholar & Yadav, 2019)
IPS (intrusion prevention system) (Scholar et al., 2020)	End to end delay: 0.24 ms Throughput: 88.5 kbps Packet delivery ratio: 93% approx.. NRL: 0.1 – 0.4	Successfully found wormhole stopped more wormholes	Overhead in communication brought on by recurrent broadcasting (Scholar et al., 2020)

2.2.5. Techniques Based on Hop Count and Weight

Wormholes are detected via Location Information and Time Synchronization (LITS) using straightforward hardware and no intricate computations. Suspicious nodes are identified using increasing latency. Verification for wormhole presence is performed on suspicious nodes using two replay-able control messages and time synchronization (Bhushan & Sahoo, 2018). The clock synchronization module needed for this technology raises the network's cost. In contrast, localization based on WDV-hop provides protection against wormhole. This algorithm looks for suspicious nodes, assesses their localization errors, and removes them if it determines they are hostile. Regarding 100 nodes: The likelihood of finding a wormhole is 95.4%. approximate localization error is decreased by 34% compared to Neighbor Discovery based (NDDV-hop algorithm), 7% compared to Label Based (LBDV-hop), and 80% compared to DV-hop. When there is an uneven distribution of nodes, this approach has higher localization error and false positive detection (Li et al., 2018). Table 7 explains in detail the literature review of ho-count and weight-based techniques.

Table 7. Literature Review of Techniques Based on Hop-Count and Weight

Technique	Results	Findings	Limitations
LITS (location information and time synchronization) (Bhushan & Sahoo, 2018)	effectively stopped wormholes No statistical information was provided.	makes use of basic hardware No intricate computations	costs more since it needs a clock synchronization module (Li & Wang, 2019)
AWDV-hop (Li et al., 2018)	Wormhole detection probability is 95.4% approx. Localization error is reduced by: 80% than (DV-hop), 7% than Label Based (LBDV-hop), 34% than Neighbor Discovery based (NDDV-hop algorithm)	Enhanced rate of detection Decreased mistake in localization	Increased latency Increased model's complexity Beacon configuration based on low frequency (Farjamnia et al., 2019)

2.2.6. Authentication Key-Based Techniques

Every time a message is transmitted, an Efficient Dynamic Authentication and Key (EDAK) management and creation procedure generates a new key without transmitting additional information. Legitimate sensor nodes are identified using local information via the dynamic matrix key DMK technique. DMK requires between 3.00 KB and 148.59 KB of total network storage. Encryption and decryption are the only two symmetric operations that EDAK performs for computational complexity. It only runs two hash algorithms. The extra data delivered is merely one byte in the event of transmission overhead. It doesn't require a secure channel or sharing phase because it produces dynamic keys from pre-existing data. It may be used with big networks because of its greater scalability and versatility. Freshness and data integrity should be part of it (Athmani et al., 2019). In order to lower the likelihood of a node capture attack, the hybrid key pre-distribution scheme (HKP-HD) combines the q-composite scheme and polynomial scheme. Two hundred nodes have been simulated (Ahlawat & Dave, 2018). Channel shifting is used in the Polynomial Pool-based Key-Predistribution (PPKP) technique to thwart wormhole attacks. Using a polynomial pool-based key predistribution technique, paired keys are established across the initial common channel. After that, data transmission is switched to a channel that is chosen at random. This prevents wormhole attacks by giving the adversary the appearance that communication is occurring over a different channel than itself (Zeng & Yao, 2020). Only when communication is first established are security measures implemented; if an attacker manages to get access to the network's existing channel information, the network is vulnerable to both internal and external wormhole attacks. Table 8 illustrates summary of Authentication Key based techniques.

Table 8. Literature Review of Techniques Based on Authentication Key

Technique	Results	Findings	Limitations
EDAK (Athmani et al., 2019)	*Memory consumption:* Network storage required is 3.00 KB to 148.59 KB *Computational complexity:* Executes only Two symmetric (encryption and decryption) operations and maximum two hashing algorithms *Communication overhead:* The additional data that is transferred is merely one byte in size.	uses preexisting data to generate dynamic keys; no secure channel or sharing phase is needed. Enhanced adaptability and expandability Suitable for extensive networks	Needs to include data integrity and freshness (Abd El-mawla et al., 2019)
HKP-HD (Ahlawat & Dave, 2018)	Node seizure ratio: 0.125 Likelihood of key compromise: 0.5	Key compromise opportunity reduced No communique overhead No garage overhead	Not appropriate for high mobility network and VANET (Bhatt et al., 2020)
PPKP (polynomial pool-based Key predistribution) (Zeng & Yao, 2020)	The likelihood of a wormhole assault caused by several channels: 0.57	safe correspondence Improved security and key distribution	Applied only at initiation (Zeng & Yao, 2020)

2.2.7. Techniques Based on Mobile Agent and Cloud Verification

Visiting Centre Local (VCL) based Mobile Agent Packet Structure (MAPS) is the method which uses the Sinalgo simulator. It relies on a mobile agent introduced in the system which is meant to distinguish the malicious nodes from the normal nodes. When wormhole attack is launched for 200 nodes for 0.8 seconds, there is 28% rise in energy ingesting and 43% rise in packet drop ratio. Packet delivery rate is improved, and energy consumption is reduced. Maintaining reliable communication and enhancing the lifetime of network. This method does not work in mobile sensor node environment or for different types of attacks (Patel & Patel, 2018). A technique uses Cross-layer verification framework (CLVF) against wormhole attack. As per simulation results Compared with existing LBIDS technique, CLVF for 250 nodes and 50 rounds gives 10% lesser malevolent nodes, 97% energy conservation,

26 msec end-to-end delay and 474 kbps throughput. CLVF shows better results as compared to the existing technique in terms of the comparison parameters. Performance of CLVF eventually degrades in comparison to LBIDS technique. In order to understand network behavior, the reduction factor is taken to be greater than 1 (Jagadeesan & Parthasarathy, 2019). Table 9 explains the detailed literature review of methods founded on Mobile agent and cloud confirmation.

Table 9. Literature Review of Methods Based on Mobile Agent and Cloud Confirmation

Technique	Results	Findings	Limitations
VCL-MAPS (visiting Center Local-based Mobile Agent Packet Structure) (Patel & Patel, 2018)	Energy consumption increased by 28%, and the packet drop ratio increased by 43%.	Improved packet delivery rate Reduced energy consumption Continues to communicate with reliability lengthens the network's lifetime	Increased energy consumption (Qadri et al., 2020)
CLVF (cross layer verification framework) (Jagadeesan & Parthasarathy, 2019)	Compared with existing LBIDS technique:10% less malicious nodes 97% energy Preservation Throughput is up to 6400 packets End to end delay is max. 26ms	Better results than a comparable technique in terms of the comparison parameters	Performance finally degrades (Jagadeesan & Parthasarathy, 2019). Does not fit to multi-cast routing protocols (Sagwal & Singh, 2018)

2.3. Analysis of Schemes

The most significant parameters have been listed for the comparison of different articles based on their techniques used. These variables aid in assessing the technique's overall efficacy, deficiencies, and efficiency. It goes on to say that detection rate, PDR, latency, and throughput are the primary parameters utilized in wormhole attack prevention strategies. Table 10 explores that mostly the detection rate is mentioned between 88% to 100% in (Li et al., 2018; Padmanabhan & Manickavasagam, 2017; Patel & Aggarwal, 2016; Shaon & Ferens, 2015; Singh et al., 2016; Wu et al., 2014) whereas other schemes have not calculated this metric. EPSMAW (Aliady & Al-Ahmadi, 2019) dominates with 100% detection rate. PDR varies from 80 to 100% but the schemes (Sharma & Joshi, 2017) and (Scholar & Yadav, 2019) provide 22% and 45%. TESRP (Shukla et al., 2018) claims 100% PDR. It has been noted that end-to-end latency varies depending on the communication paradigm for various methods where high delays are 89.632msec, 0.8 sec and 2sec by MAODV (Bhagat & Panse, 2017), NDPV (Okunlola et al., 2017) and EPSMAW (Aliady & Al-Ahmadi,

2019), respectively. Highest delay is 80.1 sec in (Amish & Vaghela, 2016). The throughput values are diversely ranged between 3.5 kbps to 474 kbps in (Aliady & Al-Ahmadi, 2019; Bhagat & Panse, 2017; Harsanyi et al., 2018; Jagadeesan & Parthasarathy, 2019; Karthigadevi et al., 2018; Kori, 2019; Okunlola et al., 2017; Patel et al., 2019; Scholar et al., 2020; Shukla et al., 2018). The schemes in (Amish & Vaghela, 2016; Naidu & Himaja, 2017; Sharma & Joshi, 2017) have throughput values as 216.7 bit/sec, 92.5 bit/sec and 2000 bit/sec, respectively.

Table 10. Analysis of Metrics Used in Wormhole Attacks-Based Schemes

Technique	Routing protocol	Detection rate %	Packet delivery ratio %	End to end delay	Throughput	Energy consumption
Techniques based on Neighborhood Information:						
TRM (Wu et al., 2014)	-	88%	-	-	-	-
ANN (Shaon & Ferens, 2015)	-	98.25%	-	-	-	-
NCI (Patel & Aggarwal, 2016)		95%	97.15%	-	84 kbps	
N NDPV (Okunlola et al., 2017)	AODV	-	80%	0.8 sec	3.5 kbps	-
NIAPC (Patel et al., 2019)	AODV	98%	98.10%	-	84.70kbps	-
WDUST (Harsanyi et al., 2018)	-	-	-	-	-	-
CREDND (Luo et al., 2019)	-	-	-	-	-	-
EPSMAW (Aliady & Al-Ahmadi, 2019)	AODV	100%	-	1 sec	36.409 kbps	73 joules
Techniques based on Round Trip Time:						
AOMDV-RTT (Amish & Vaghela, 2016)	AOMDV	-	78.92%	80.1 sec	216.7 bit/sec	-
EIGRP-RTT (Karthigadevi et al., 2018)	EIGRP	-	81.2%	89.632msec	216 kbps	-
TBWM (Kori, 2019)	AODV	-	91.6%	-	222.5 kbps	-
Techniques based on transmission power:						

continued on following page

Table 10. Continued

Technique	Routing protocol	Detection rate %	Packet delivery ratio %	End to end delay	Throughput	Energy consumption
MAODV (Bhagat & Panse, 2017)	AODV	-	98.69%	75.74 msec	88.88 kbps	-
MHTPW (Sharma & Joshi, 2017)	AODV	-	22%	55 msec	92.5 bit/sec	-
Techniques based on Statistical methods:						
Poster (Minohara & Nishiyama, 2016)	-	-	-	-	-	-
WRHT (Singh et al., 2016)	AODV	87.4%	-	-	-	-
SPRT (Padmanabhan & Manickavasagam, 2017)	-	99%	-	-	-	-
DMLE (Kumar et al., 2017)	-	-	-	-	-	-
ERS (Naidu & Himaja, 2017)	AODV	-	-	-	2000bit/sec	-
TESRP (Shukla et al., 2018)	TESRP	-	100%	14 msec	38 kbps	50 joules
EFM (Scholar & Yadav, 2019)	AODV	-	45%	-	-	-
IPS (Scholar et al., 2020)	AODV	-	93%	0.24 msec	88.5 kbps	-
Techniques based on Hop Count and Weight:						
LITS (Bhushan & Sahoo, 2018)	OLSR	-	-	-	-	-
AWDV-hop (Li et al., 2018)	AWDV	95.4%	-	-	-	-
Techniques based on Authentication key:						
EDAK (Athmani et al., 2019)	-	-	-	-	-	-
HKP-HD (Ahlawat & Dave, 2018)	-	-	-	-	-	-
PPKP (Zeng & Yao, 2020)	-	-	-	-	-	-
Methods grounded on Mobile Agent and Cloud Confirmation:						

continued on following page

Table 10. Continued

Technique	Routing protocol	Detection rate %	Packet delivery ratio %	End to end delay	Throughput	Energy consumption
VCL-MAPS (Patel & Patel, 2018)	-	-	-	-	-	-
CLVF (Jagadeesan & Parthasarathy, 2019)	-	-	-	26msec	474 kbps	-

3. PROPOSED SCHEME

A low-weight and energy-efficient method has been suggested for wormhole attack detection in wireless sensor networks (WSNs). As seen in Figure 6, this approach determines suspicious links by measuring the transmission time between sender and recipient nodes. Next, the suspicious nodes or the detection algorithm is executed. By utilizing the hop time stamp to assess the hop count and gap, wormholes can be found. Important terminology and variables utilized in the method that will be detailed later are mentioned in Table 11.

Table 11. Notation Table

Rt	Received time by destination node
St	Send time stamp by source node
Dt	Duration of travel by packets
Hi	Hop interval stamp
Tt	Transmission threshold
Th	Hop interval threshold
S	Suspicious flag
W	Wormhole existence flag
M	Malicious node flag
Ns	Sender node (which sent the packet last time)
Nr	Reciever node (which has just received packet now)
R	Rate of transmission
d	Geographical distance between source and destination
dn	Distance of node from farthest neighbor

3.1. Phase 1: Finding Suspicious Nodes

3.1.1. Algorithm 1

Table 12. Algorithm for Finding Suspicious Nodes

Step 0	Install the sensor network, set up the nodes, and initiate contact.
Step 1	Establish a threshold for transmission time., $Tt = R * d$
Step 2	Include the hop time stamp at each hop and embed the source and destination addresses, St, with the data packets.
Step 3	For arriving packets from Ns at node Nr, Mark stamp Rt
Step 4	Find duration of travel by packets, $Dt = Rt - St$
Step 5	Check if $(Dt > Tt)$
	then:
Step 6	Mark suspicious flag $S=$ "TRUE", suspicious node found
Step 7	An method for detecting calls from questionable nodes Ns and Nr
	Else:
Step 7	Consider path Safe and allow continue communication

3.1.2. Flowchart 1

Figure 6. Finding Suspicious Nodes and Links

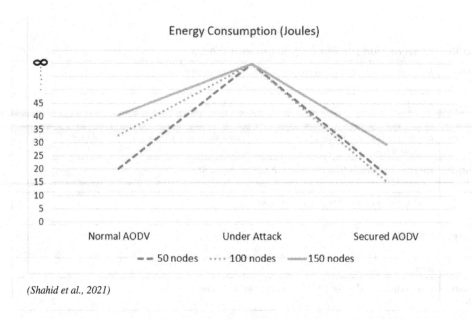

(Shahid et al., 2021)

A detection method is triggered for the suspicious nodes to identify wormholes when a link is determined to be suspicious. The two-step detection process starts by looking up the hop count. If it is not 1, then this path is regarded as having several hops and is hence valid; nevertheless, if hop count is 1, the algorithm then determines whether the hop interval time exceeds the threshold. If it does then the presence of wormhole is confirmed, malicious nodes are identified as shown in figure 7. The wormhole nodes are de-linked, secure path is re-routed between source and destination to re-establish secure communication and malicious nodes are then reconfigured.

3.2. Phase 2: Detection and Handling of Wormhole Attack

3.2.1. Algorithm 2

Table 13. Algorithm for Wormhole Detection and Management Links and Nodes

Step 0	Access the other end of the suspicious sender node Ns. Nr and the data they provide,

continued on following page

Table 13. Continued

Step 1	Decide on a hop interval threshold, Th = dn * R	
Step 2	Check if ((Hc == 1) is True	
	then	
Step 3	*Checkif(Hi>Th)* *then*	
Step 4		*Mark **W** = "TRUE"*
	else	
Step 4		*Mark **W**= "FALSE"*
Step 5	*Check **if** (W== "TRUE")*	
	Then	
Step 6		*Delink track among **Ns** and **Nr***
Step 7		*Re-establish communication by protected route*
Step 8		*Allow **Ns** and **Nr** to reconfigure*
	Else	
Step 9		*deem the route safe and permit the continuation of the conversation*

3.2.2. Flowchart 2

Figure 7. Detection of Malevolent Nodes and Wormhole Links

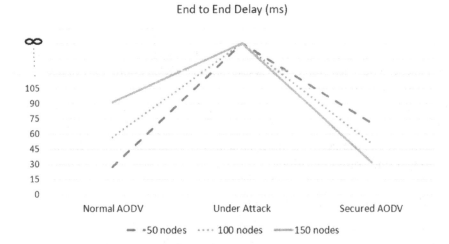

End to End Delay (ms)

4.1. Simulation and Experimentation

M ATLAB R2019a was utilized to execute the network simulation, and the AODV routing protocol was employed. Random wormholes have been launched in our network simulation. Visualization network simulation and results of proposed wormhole detection algorithm have been elaborated ahead.

4.1.1. Simulation Environment

The important constraints involved in the simulation experimentation and their values have been given in the following Table 14.

Table 14. Parameter Values for Simulation Environment

Routing protocol	AODV
Network area	100m x 100m
Network size	50, 100, 150 nodes
Transmission range	20 meters
Packet size	500 bytes
Sensor positioning	Random
Mobility	Static
Simulation time	500 seconds

4.1.2. Experiment

Following series of graphs elaborate the whole experiment step wise in which it can be observed how wormhole attack compromises the system, how it is detected, and network security is enhanced.

Three different network sizes—50,100, and 150 nodes—have been used for the experiment. Two graphics are used to demonstrate the simulation for each pair of nodes: one depicts the network under attack, while the other shows the wormhole removed and safe communication.

4.1.2.1. Simulation for 50 Node Network Size

Figure 8. shows a network under wormhole attack with 50 nodes, with node 11 serving as the source and node 20 as the destination. There is a random wormhole path from node 6 to node 46. It is evident that communication security has been jeopardized.

Figure 8. Network of 50 Nodes Under Attack and Security Compromised

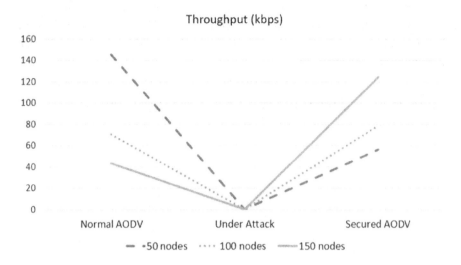

Figure 9 illustrates the removal of the wormhole link, the marking of malicious nodes 16 and 46 for reconfiguration, and the establishment of a secure communication channel between source node 11 and destination node 20.

Figure 9. Wormhole Link Eliminated, and Secure Path Established

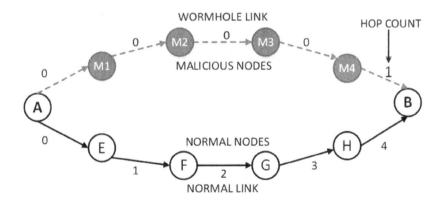

Simulation for 100 Node Network Size

A network with 100 nodes that is subject to a wormhole assault is shown in the figure.10 where node 15 is the destination and node 45 is the source. There is a random wormhole path from node 82 to node 31. It is evident that communication security has been jeopardized.

Figure 10. Network of 100 Nodes Under Attack and Security Compromised

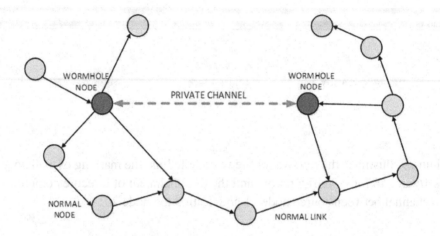

Figure 11 illustrates the removal of the wormhole link, the marking of malicious nodes 82 and 31 for reconfiguration, and the establishment of a secure path between source node 45 and destination node 15.

Figure 11. Wormhole Link Eliminated, and Secure Path Established

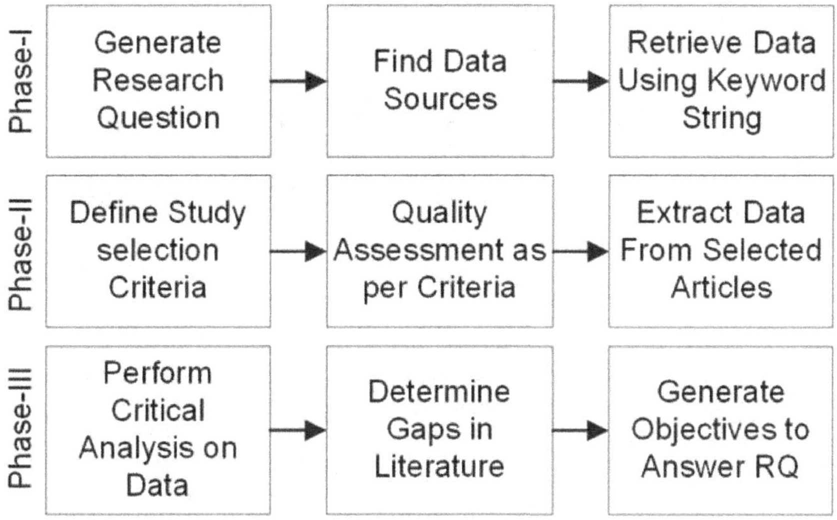

Phase-I	Generate Research Question	→	Find Data Sources	→	Retrieve Data Using Keyword String
Phase-II	Define Study selection Criteria	→	Quality Assessment as per Criteria	→	Extract Data From Selected Articles
Phase-III	Perform Critical Analysis on Data	→	Determine Gaps in Literature	→	Generate Objectives to Answer RQ

Simulation for 150 Node Network Size

A network with 100 nodes that is subject to a wormhole assault is shown in the figure.12 where the destination is node 140 and the source is node 108. There is a random wormhole path from node 2 to node 85. It is evident that communication security has been jeopardized.

Figure 12. Network of 150 Nodes Under Attack and Security Compromised

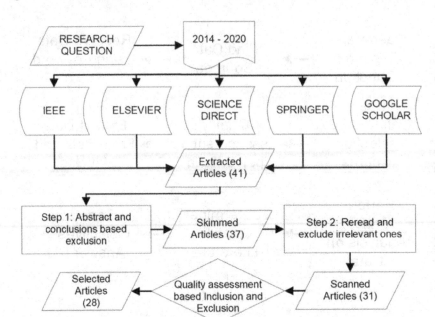

Figure 13 illustrates the removal of the wormhole link, the marking of malicious nodes 2 and 85 for reconfiguration, and the establishment of a secure communication channel between source node 108 and destination node 140.

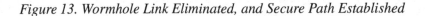

Figure 13. Wormhole Link Eliminated, and Secure Path Established

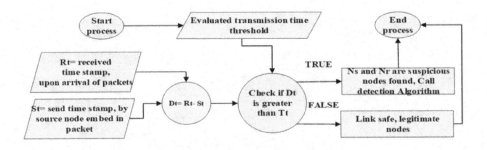

4.2. Results Evaluation Parameters and Analysis

This section explains the significant parameters considered for evaluating the performance of proposed technique. This is followed by a parameter-based comparison of proposed technique results with results of technique in base paper EPSMAW (Aliady & Al-Ahmadi, 2019).

4.2.1. Evaluation Measures

For evaluation of proposed technique, considered The characteristics include energy consumption (joules), packet delivery ratio (%), detection rate (%), throughput (kbps), and end-to-end delay (seconds).

4.2.1.1. Detection rate: It is the ratio of the total number of wormholes launched in the network to the number of wormholes accurately recognized by the security algorithm (Zhang & Xiao, 2019). It is a gauge of how well the network's security system is working. The following formula, where DR stands for detection rate, Wd for number of detected wormholes, and Wt for total number of launched wormholes, is used to evaluate it. It is expressed in percentage terms.,

$$DR = \frac{Wd}{Wd + Wt}$$

4.2.1.2. Packet delivery ratio: it is the proportion of all packets sent during a communication session that are successfully delivered to all packets communicated (Khan & Ramesh, 2019). An increase in the packet delivery ratio boosts the network's performance. It is expressed as a percentage and assessed using the formula below, in where PDR stands for packet delivery ratio, Pt for transmitted packets, and Pr for received packets during a communication round,

$$PDR = \frac{\sum Pr}{\sum Pt}$$

4.2.1.3. Throughput: it is the quantity of correctly received packets per second in a sensor network transmission between the source and destination nodes (Khan & Ramesh, 2019). A higher throughput indicates superior communication speed and improved network performance. It is evaluated using the following formula, where Th stands for throughput, sec for seconds, and Pr for packets received. It is measured in kbps (kilobits per second),

$$Th = \frac{\sum Pr}{sec}$$

4.2.1.4.*End to end delay:* It is the amount of time packets need to travel from their source to their destination. If it's not zero, processing and waiting time are applied to it. This parameter represents the network's performance and speed (Khan & Ramesh, 2019). Usually measured in milliseconds (ms), it is assessed using the following formula: N is the total number of nodes; λ is the number of hops; D is the delay; Ti is the time delay by considered packet; and td is the transmission delay,

$$D = \lambda * T_i + td *(N-1)$$

4.2.1.5.*Energy consumption:* A finite resource in sensor networks is energy. Since sensor nodes run on batteries, transmitting data uses up a significant portion of their energy. It is necessary to provide algorithms for sensor network functions like routing, location, security, etc. that are efficient and low energy consumers (Aliady & Al-Ahmadi, 2019). The following formula (Casares-Giner et al., 2019), where ET is transmitting energy, ER is receiving energy, λ is the number of hops on the routed path, d is the distance between sender and recipient, and E is the energy consumed, can be used to calculate the amount of energy consumed in a sensor network,

$$E = \sum (\lambda * (E_T *(d) + E_R))$$

4.2.2. Results

The results of the proposed scheme have been described for each parameter elaborated in the previous section. It is followed by a comparison of results and evaluation in the next section.

- **Detection Rate Result**: Proposed technique gives 100% Detection Rate which is parallel in performance with base paper
- **Packet delivery ratio Result:** Proposed Technique has given 100% Packet Delivery Ratio which is parallel to the results of base paper.
- **False Positive:** False positive values for proposed techniques are reduced to negligible extent as compared to few techniques in literature (Aliady & Al-Ahmadi, 2019; Luo et al., 2019; Wu et al., 2014), values for proposed scheme are 0.0187, 0.1642, 0.0364 for 50, 100 and 150 nodes, respectively

Energy Consumption

Energy consumption is the most important parameter of proposed technique as energy is a critical resource in sensor network. It has been attempted to reduce the energy consumption of proposed security algorithm in comparison with the technique of considered base paper. Following Figure.14 shows the results of proposed technique in a line graph.

Figure 14. Energy Consumption Results

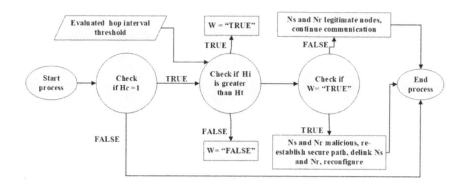

Following Table 15. describes the energy consumption results for normal, under attack and secured system.

Table 15. Energy Consumption Results Comparison

	For 50 nodes	For 100 nodes	For 150 nodes
Normal AODV	20.2013	32.8597	40.584
Under Attack	0	0	0
Secured AODV	18.0171	15.3733	29.5155

End to End Delay

Regarding a sensor network's performance, this is a crucial parameter. The suggested method is intended to provide a reduced end-to-end delay. The results graph in Figure.15 shows end to end delay caused for a normal, under attack and secured network with 50, 100 and 150 nodes respectively.

Figure 15. End to End Delay Results

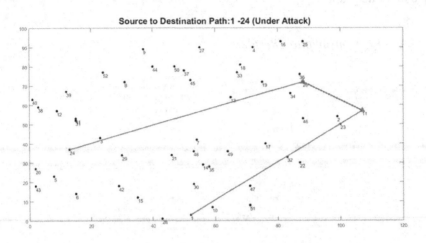

Following Table 16. describes end to end delay (milliseconds) results for normal, under attack and secured system with 50, 100 and 150 nodes.

Table 16. End to End Delay Results Comparison

	For 50 nodes	For 100 nodes	For 150 nodes
Normal AODV	27.5113	56.6762	91.7236
Under Attack	∞	∞	∞
Secured AODV	70.8106	50.5852	32.0956

Throughput

A wireless sensor network's throughput is a crucial component in assessing its performance. Proposed security technique has been designed to produced increased throughput in a secured system along with less consumption of energy. The graph in Figure.16 shows throughput results of a system in state of normal, under attack and secured by proposed scheme for 50, 100 and 150 nodes respectively.

Figure 16. Throughput Results

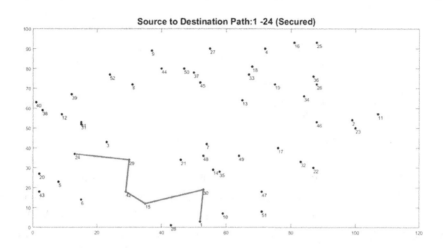

Following Table 17. Describes throughput (kbps) results for normal, under attack and secured system with 50, 100 and 150 nodes.

Table 17. Throughput Results Comparison

	For 50 nodes	For 100 nodes	For 150 nodes
Normal AODV	145.3134	70.5467	43.6205
Under Attack	∞	∞	∞
Secured AODV	56.4888	79.0745	124.6277

4.2.3 Results Comparison

Results of proposed technique have been compared with results of base paper EPSMAW (Aliady & Al-Ahmadi, 2019) and presented the comparison in Table.18. the detection rate of proposed technique is 100% and packet delivery ratio is 100%, both are equal to those of EPSMAW (Aliady & Al-Ahmadi, 2019).

Table 18. Comparison of Proposed Technique With Our Base Paper

Parameters	Proposed Technique			EPSMAW (Aliady & Al-Ahmadi, 2019)		
	50 nodes	100 nodes	150 nodes	50 nodes	100 nodes	150 nodes
Energy consumption (Joules)	18.1	15.4	29.6	70	21	129
End to end delay (ms)	70.9	50.6	32.1	1700	200	1000
Throughput (kbps)	56.5	79.1	124.7	14.42	39.7128	36.409

It is evident that the suggested algorithm operates effectively in terms of energy consumption across the three scenarios (Khan et al., 2022; Lim et al., 2019; Shah et al., 2023). The suggested approach's optimum energy consumption scenarios involve 50 and 100 nodes, and our maximum energy consumption for 150 nodes is just 33 joules—a significant decrease from our EPSMAW (Aliady & Al-Ahmadi, 2019). The suggested technique yields a delay of less than 0.1 seconds in all three scenarios, which is even less than the best-case value of 0.2 of EPSMAW (Aliady & Al-Ahmadi, 2019). The end-to-end latency of the proposed strategy is significantly improved and decreased. In comparison to the best-case value of EPSMAW, the throughput (kbps) of the suggested method is likewise enhanced and increased in all three circumstances (Alex et al., 2022; Aliady & Al-Ahmadi, 2019).

5. CONCLUSION

Wireless Sensor Networks (WSNs) face various security threats, with the wormhole attack being particularly troublesome. To combat this challenge, extensive research and development efforts have been ongoing to devise reliable solutions. The goal of the planned exploration is to develop a technique against the wormhole attack that not only conserves energy but also delivers superior performance.

To begin with, a systematic literature review was conducted, extracting significant data and critically analyzing existing techniques against the wormhole attack. The review included a thorough classification of the literature and then compared different strategies depending on parameters. These factors were used to assess each technique's overall efficacy as well as its weaknesses and efficiency. High resource consumption, rising network costs, communication or processing overhead, and non-compliance with the evolving requirements of dynamic sensor networks are some of the major drawbacks noted in the literature assessment.

Addressing the issue of high energy consumption is a focal point of the proposed research. The strategy intended to counter wormhole assaults is to maximize efficiency while lowering energy usage in the network. Transmission time data between sender and recipient nodes is first analyzed in order to identify suspicious nodes. These suspect nodes are then subjected to detection utilizing hop count hop interval duration.

Simulation results of the proposed scheme demonstrate a 100% detection rate and packet delivery ratio. Moreover, the technique exhibits increased throughput and decreased end-to-end delay while consuming a significantly lower percentage of energy compared to existing techniques outlined in the base paper

Future Work

Wireless sensor networks are prone to many security threats and attacks. In future, more types of node capture attacks are to be explored and attempt to simplify methods of security against them. It is intended to utilize meta-heuristics approach for optimizing security algorithms and resource usage while ensuring good performance and more reliability.

REFERENCES

Abd El-mawla, N., Badawy, M., & Arafat, H. (2019). Security And Key Management Challenges Over WSN (A Survey). *Int. J. Comput. Sci. Eng. Surv.*, 10(01), 15–34. DOI:10.5121/ijcses.2019.10102

Aherwadi, N., Mittal, U., Singla, J., Jhanjhi, N. Z., Yassine, A., & Hossain, M. S. (2022). Prediction of fruit maturity, quality, and its life using deep learning algorithms. *Electronics (Basel)*, 11(24), 4100. DOI:10.3390/electronics11244100

Ahlawat, P., & Dave, M. (2018). An attack resistant key predistribution scheme for wireless sensor networks. *Journal of King Saud University. Computer and Information Sciences.*

Akyildiz, I. F., Su, W., Sankarasubramaniam, Y., & Cayirci, E. (2002). Wireless sensor networks: A survey. *Computer Networks*, 38(4), 393–422. DOI:10.1016/S1389-1286(01)00302-4

Alex, S. A., Jhanjhi, N. Z., Humayun, M., Ibrahim, A. O., & Abulfaraj, A. W. (2022). Deep LSTM model for diabetes prediction with class balancing by SMOTE. *Electronics (Basel)*, 11(17), 2737. DOI:10.3390/electronics11172737

Aliady, W. A., & Al-Ahmadi, S. A. (2019). Energy preserving secure measure against wormhole attack in wireless sensor networks. *IEEE Access : Practical Innovations, Open Solutions*, 7, 84132–84141. DOI:10.1109/ACCESS.2019.2924283

Amish, P., & Vaghela, V. B. (2016). Detection and Prevention of Wormhole Attack in Wireless Sensor Network using AOMDV Protocol. *Procedia Computer Science*, 79, 700–707. DOI:10.1016/j.procs.2016.03.092

Athmani, S., Bilami, A., & Boubiche, D. E. (2019, March). EDAK: An Efficient Dynamic Authentication and Key Management Mechanism for heterogeneous WSNs. *Future Generation Computer Systems*, 92, 789–799. DOI:10.1016/j.future.2017.10.026

Bhagat, S., & Panse, T. (2017). A detection and prevention of wormhole attack in homogeneous Wireless sensor Network. Proceedings of 2016 International Conference on ICT in Business, Industry, and Government, ICTBIG, 1–6.

Bhatt, R., Maheshwary, P., Shukla, P., Shukla, P., Shrivastava, M., & Changlani, S. (2020, January). Implementation of Fruit Fly Optimization Algorithm (FFOA) to escalate the attacking efficiency of node capture attack in Wireless Sensor Networks (WSN). *Computer Communications*, 149, 134–145. DOI:10.1016/j.comcom.2019.09.007

Bhushan, B., & Sahoo, G. (2018). Detection and defense mechanisms against wormhole attacks in wireless sensor networks. Proceedings - 2017 3rd International Conference on Advances in Computing, Communication and Automation (Fall), ICACCA 2017, 1–5.

Casares-Giner, V., Navas, T. I., Flórez, D. S., & Hernández, T. R. V. (2019). End to end delay and energy consumption in a two tier cluster hierarchical Wireless Sensor Networks. *Information (Basel)*, 10(4), 1–29. DOI:10.3390/info10040135

Céspedes-Mota, A., Castañón, G., Martínez-Herrera, A. F., Cárdenas-Barrón, L. E., & Sarmiento, A. M. (2018). Differential evolution algorithm applied to wireless sensor distribution on different geometric shapes with area and energy optimization. *Journal of Network and Computer Applications*, 119, 14–23. DOI:10.1016/j.jnca.2018.06.006

Chen, D., Zhang, Q., Wang, N., & Wan, J. (2018). An Attack-resistant RSS-based Localization Algorithm with L1 Regularization for Wireless Sensor Networks. Proceedings of 2018 2nd IEEE Advanced Information Management, Communicates, Electronic and Automation Control Conference, IMCEC 2018, 1048–1051. DOI:10.1109/IMCEC.2018.8469253

Dogra, V., Verma, S., Verma, K., Jhanjhi, N. Z., Ghosh, U., & Le, D. N. (2022). A comparative analysis of machine learning models for banking news extraction by multiclass classification with imbalanced datasets of financial news: challenges and solutions.

Dutta & Singh. (2019). Wormhole attack in wireless sensor networks: A critical review. Advances in Intelligent Systems and Computing, 702, 147–161.

Farjamnia, G., Gasimov, Y., & Kazimov, C. (2019, April). Review of the Techniques Against the Wormhole Attacks on Wireless Sensor Networks. *Wireless Personal Communications*, 105(4), 1561–1584. DOI:10.1007/s11277-019-06160-0

Halder & Ghosal. (2016). A survey on mobility-assisted localization techniques in wireless sensor networks. Journal of Network and Computer Applications, 60, 82–94.

Han, Jiang, Zhang, Duong, Guizani, & Karagiannidis. (2016). A Survey on Mobile Anchor Node Assisted Localization in Wireless Sensor Networks. IEEE Communications Surveys and Tutorials, 18(3), 2220–2243.

Harsanyi, K., Kiss, A., & Sziranyi, T. (2018). Wormhole detection in wireless sensor networks using spanning trees. *2018 IEEE International Conference on Future IoT Technologies, Future IoT 2018*, 1–6. DOI:10.1109/FIOT.2018.8325596

Jabeen, T., Jabeen, I., Ashraf, H., Jhanjhi, N. Z., Yassine, A., & Hossain, M. S. (2023). An intelligent healthcare system using IoT in wireless sensor network. *Sensors (Basel)*, 23(11), 5055. DOI:10.3390/s23115055 PMID:37299782

Jagadeesan, S., & Parthasarathy, V. (2019, January). Design and implement a cross layer verification framework (CLVF) for detecting and preventing blackhole and wormhole attack in wireless ad-hoc networks for cloud environment. *Cluster Computing*, 22(S1), 299–310. DOI:10.1007/s10586-018-1825-8

Julie, E. G., Nayahi, J. J. V., & Jhanjhi, N. Z. (Eds.). (2020). *Blockchain Technology: Fundamentals, Applications, and Case Studies*. CRC Press.

Karthigadevi, K., Balamurali, S., & Venkatesulu, M. (2018). Wormhole attack detection and prevention using EIGRP protocol based on round trip time. *J. Cyber Secur. Mobil.*, 7(1), 215–228. DOI:10.13052/2245-1439.7115

Karthigadevi, K., Balamurali, S., & Venkatesulu, M. (2019). Based on Neighbor Density Estimation Technique to Improve the Quality of Service and to Detect and Prevent the Sinkhole Attack in Wireless Sensor Network. *IEEE International Conference on Intelligent Techniques in Control, Optimization and Signal Processing, INCOS 2019*, 1–4. DOI:10.1109/INCOS45849.2019.8951406

Khan, M. K. U., & Ramesh, K. S. (2019). Effect on Packet Delivery Ratio (PDR) & Throughput in Wireless Sensor Networks Due to Black Hole Attack. *International Journal of Innovative Technology and Exploring Engineering*, 8(12S), 428–432. DOI:10.35940/ijitee.L1107.10812S19

Khan, N. A., Jhanjhi, N. Z., Brohi, S. N., Almazroi, A. A., & Almazroi, A. A. (2022). A secure communication protocol for unmanned aerial vehicles. *CMC-Computers Materials & Continua*, 70(1), 601–618. DOI:10.32604/cmc.2022.019419

Kitchenham, B., Pearl Brereton, O., Budgen, D., Turner, M., Bailey, J., & Linkman, S. (2009). Systematic literature reviews in software engineering - A systematic literature review. *Information and Software Technology*, 51(1), 7–15. DOI:10.1016/j.infsof.2008.09.009

Kori, S. (2019). Distributed Wormhole Attack Mitigation Technique in WSNs. *Int. J. Comput. Netw. Inf. Secur.*, 11(5), 20–27.

Kumar, G., Rai, M. K., & Saha, R. (2017). Securing range free localization against wormhole attack using distance estimation and maximum likelihood estimation in Wireless Sensor Networks. *Journal of Network and Computer Applications*, 99, 10–16. DOI:10.1016/j.jnca.2017.10.006

Li, J., & Wang, D. (2019, April). The security dv-hop algorithm against multiple-wormhole-node-link in WSN. *KSII Transactions on Internet and Information Systems*, 13(4), 2223–2242.

Li, J., Wang, D., & Wang, Y. (2018). Security DV-hop localisation algorithm against wormhole attack in wireless sensor network. *IET Wireless Sensor Systems*, 8(2), 68–75. DOI:10.1049/iet-wss.2017.0075

Li, L., Hu, X., Chen, K., & He, K. (2011). The applications of WiFi-based Wireless Sensor Network in Internet of Things and Smart Grid. Proceedings of the 2011 6th IEEE Conference on Industrial Electronics and Applications, ICIEA, 789–793. DOI:10.1109/ICIEA.2011.5975693

Lim, M., Abdullah, A., Jhanjhi, N. Z., & Khan, M. K. (2019). Situation-aware deep reinforcement learning link prediction model for evolving criminal networks. *IEEE Access : Practical Innovations, Open Solutions*, 8, 16550–16559. DOI:10.1109/ACCESS.2019.2961805

Luo, X., Chen, Y., Li, M., Luo, Q., Xue, K., Liu, S., & Chen, L. (2019). CRED-ND: A Novel Secure Neighbor Discovery Algorithm for Wormhole Attack. *IEEE Access : Practical Innovations, Open Solutions*, 7(c), 18194–18205. DOI:10.1109/ACCESS.2019.2894637

Maidamwar, P. (2012, October). A Survey on Security Issues to Detect Wormhole Attack in Wireless Sensor Network. Int. J. AdHoc Netw. *Syst.*, 2(4), 37–50.

Minohara, T., & Nishiyama, K. (2016). Poster: detection of Wormhole attack on wireless sensor networks in duty-cycling operation. *Proceedings of the 2016 International Conference on Embedded Wireless Systems and Networks*, 281–282.

Mukherjee, S., Chattopadhyay, M., Chattopadhyay, S., & Kar, P. (2016). Wormhole Detection Based on Ordinal MDS Using RTT in Wireless Sensor Network. *Journal of Computer Networks and Communications*, 2016, 1–15. DOI:10.1155/2016/3405264

Naidu & Himaja. (2017). Handling wormhole attacks in WSNs using location based approach. Advances in Intelligent Systems and Computing, 507, 43–51.

Okunlola, M., Siddiqui, A., & Karami, A. (2017, September). A Wormhole Attack Detection and Prevention Technique in Wireless Sensor Networks. *International Journal of Computer Applications*, 174(4), 1–8. DOI:10.5120/ijca2017915376

Padmanabhan, J., & Manickavasagam, V. (2017). Scalable and Distributed Detection Analysis on Wormhole Links in Wireless Sensor Networks for Networked Systems. *IEEE Access : Practical Innovations, Open Solutions*, 6, 1753–1763. DOI:10.1109/ACCESS.2017.2780188

Pandey, A., & Tripathi, R. C. (2010, June). A Survey on Wireless Sensor Networks Security. *International Journal of Computer Applications*, 3(2), 43–49. DOI:10.5120/705-989

Panwar, A., Panwar, B., Rao, D. S., & Sriram, G. (2020). *A Trust Based Approach for Avoidance of Wormhole Attack in MANET.*

Patel & Aggarwal. (2016). Detection of Hidden Wormhole Attack in Wireless Sensor Networks Using Neighbourhood and Connectivity Information. Int. J. AdHoc Netw. Syst., 6(1), 1–10.

Patel, M., Aggarwal, A., & Chaubey, N. (2017, April). Wormhole Attacks and Countermeasures in Wireless Sensor Networks: A Survey. *Int. J. Eng. Technol.*, 9(2), 1049–1060. DOI:10.21817/ijet/2017/v9i2/170902126

Patel, Aggarwal, & Chaubey. (2019). Detection of wormhole attack in static wireless sensor networks. Advances in Intelligent Systems and Computing, 760, 463–471.

Patel, M. A., & Patel, M. M. (2018). Wormhole Attack Detection in Wireless Sensor Network. *Proceedings of the International Conference on Inventive Research in Computing Applications, ICIRCA 2018*, 269–274. DOI:10.1109/ICIRCA.2018.8597366

Qadri, Y. A., Ali, R., Musaddiq, A., Al-Turjman, F., Kim, D. W., & Kim, S. W. (2020). *The limitations in the state-of-the-art counter-measures against the security threats in H-IoT* (Vol. 7). Cluster Comput.

Sagwal, R., & Singh, A. K. (2018). Power Efficient and Light Weight Approach for Secure Multicast Tree Construction in MANETs. 2018 9th International Conference on Computing, Communication and Networking Technologies, ICCCNT. DOI:10.1109/ICCCNT.2018.8494002

Scholar, M. T., Kant, R., & Sen, A. D. (2020). Collaborative Decision for Wormhole Attack Prevention in WSN. *Int. J. Sci. Res. Eng. Trends*, 6(2).

Scholar, M. T., & Yadav, B. (2019). Predication and Root Selection of Worm Hole Attack in WSN. *Int. J. Sci. Res. Eng. Trends*, 5(6), 1937–1944.

Shah, I. A., Jhanjhi, N. Z., & Laraib, A. (2023). Cybersecurity and blockchain usage in contemporary business. In *Handbook of Research on Cybersecurity Issues and Challenges for Business and FinTech Applications* (pp. 49–64). IGI Global.

Shahid, H., Ashraf, H., Javed, J., Humayun, M., Jhanjhi, N. Z., & AlZain, M. A. (2021). Energy optimized security against wormhole attack in iot-based wireless sensor networks. *Computers, Materials & Continua*, 68(2), 1967–1981. DOI:10.32604/cmc.2021.015259

Shahid, H., Ashraf, H., Ullah, A., Band, S. S., & Elnaffar, S. (2022). Wormhole attack mitigation strategies and their impact on wireless sensor network performance: A literature survey. *International Journal of Communication Systems*, 35(16), e5311. DOI:10.1002/dac.5311

Shaon, M. N. A., & Ferens, K. (2015). *Wireless Sensor Network Wormhole Detection using an Artificial Neural Network*. ICWN.

Sharma, M. K., & Joshi, B. K. (2017). A mitigation technique for high transmission power based wormhole attack in Wireless Sensor Networks. Proceedings of 2016 International Conference on ICT in Business, Industry, and Government, ICTBIG.

Shukla, R., Jain, R., & Vyavahare, P. D. (2018). Combating against wormhole attack in trust and energy aware secure routing protocol (TESRP) in wireless sensor network. *International Conference on Recent Innovations in Signal Processing and Embedded Systems, RISE 2017*, 555–561.

Siddiqui, F. J., Ashraf, H., & Ullah, A. (2020). Dual server based security system for multimedia Services in Next Generation Networks. *Multimedia Tools and Applications*, 79(11), 7299–7318. DOI:10.1007/s11042-019-08406-2

Singh, A. P., Pradhan, N. R., Luhach, A. K., Agnihotri, S., Jhanjhi, N. Z., Verma, S., Kavita, , Ghosh, U., & Roy, D. S. (2020). A novel patient-centric architectural framework for blockchain-enabled healthcare applications. *IEEE Transactions on Industrial Informatics*, 17(8), 5779–5789. DOI:10.1109/TII.2020.3037889

Singh, R., Singh, J., & Singh, R. (2016). WRHT: A Hybrid Technique for Detection of Wormhole Attack in Wireless Sensor Networks. *Mobile Information Systems*, 2016, 1–13. DOI:10.1155/2016/8354930

Singh, S. P., & Sharma, S. C. (2015). Range Free Localization Techniques in Wireless Sensor Networks: A Review. *Procedia Computer Science*, 57, 7–16. DOI:10.1016/j.procs.2015.07.357

Wu, G., Chen, X., Yao, L., Lee, Y., & Yim, K. (2014). An efficient wormhole attack detection method in wireless sensor networks. *Computer Science and Information Systems*, 11(3), 1127–1142. DOI:10.2298/CSIS130921068W

Zeng, B., & Yao, L. (2020). Design of a secure communication scheme using channel shifting in wireless sensor networks. *IOP Conference Series. Earth and Environmental Science*, 428(1), 012026. DOI:10.1088/1755-1315/428/1/012026

Zhang, R., & Xiao, X. (2019). Intrusion detection in wireless sensor networks with an improved NSA based on space division. *Journal of Sensors*, 2019(1), 1–20. DOI:10.1155/2019/5451263

Chapter 5
AI in 6G Network Security and Management

Deepak Varadam

https://orcid.org/0000-0002-6079
-4805

*Ramaiah University of Applied
Sciences, India*

Sahana P. Shankar

https://orcid.org/0000-0001-8977
-9898

*Ramaiah University of Applied
Sciences, India*

Nidhi N. P.

*Ramaiah University of Applied
Sciences, India*

Vinay Dubey

*Ramaiah University of Applied
Sciences, India*

Aaditi Jadwani

*Ramaiah University of Applied
Sciences, India*

Shaik Falak Taj

*Ramaiah University of Applied
Sciences, India*

Sahil C. T. Uthappa

*Ramaiah University of Applied
Sciences, India*

Aryan Bharadwaj

*Ramaiah University of Applied
Sciences, India*

ABSTRACT

Various global institutions are exploring the potentials and hurdles of 6G communication networks to address the security shortcomings of existing 5G networks while capitalizing on the promises of 6G for heightened privacy and dependability. Artificial intelligence (AI) emerges as a solution with minimal drawbacks and reduced expenses. This chapter delves into diverse applications where AI integration can prove advantageous. AI has undergone substantial evolution, transitioning from network diagnosis and monitoring to optimizing large-scale systems. Advanced

DOI: 10.4018/979-8-3693-5415-5.ch005

algorithms bolster network security by continuously updating and identifying vulnerabilities. Furthermore, AI facilitates the creation of innovative networking models like intent-based networking, streamlining network configuration based on user needs. The integration of AI with networks has witnessed increased usage, such as cost reduction in managing IoT data and enhanced efficiency in healthcare systems through fuzzy classifiers.

INTRODUCTION

Various global institutions are exploring the potentials and hurdles of 6G communication networks to address the security shortcomings of existing 5G networks while capitalizing on the promises of 6G for heightened privacy and dependability. Artificial Intelligence (AI) emerges as a solution with minimal drawbacks and reduced expenses. This article delves into diverse applications where AI integration can prove advantageous.

AI has undergone substantial evolution, transitioning from network diagnosis and monitoring to optimizing large-scale systems. Advanced algorithms bolster network security by continuously updating and identifying vulnerabilities. Furthermore, AI facilitates the creation of innovative networking models like Intent-Based Networking, streamlining network configuration based on user needs.

The integration of AI with networks has witnessed increased usage, such as cost reduction in managing IoT data and enhanced efficiency in healthcare systems through fuzzy classifiers. Nonetheless, manual network configuration remains a bottleneck for extensive and intricate networks, underscoring the necessity for future technologies like 6G, promising AI-driven solutions to surmount current limitations.

Despite the advent of 5G, its societal impacts remain largely uncharted, with limited research elucidating its architecture and services. Edge AI emerges as a pivotal component of both 5G and 6G technologies, optimizing bandwidth and latency by distributing computations between the cloud and network components. However, integrating AI with edge computing poses challenges due to inherent disparities in their architectures.

AI systems excel in pinpointing network issues and optimizing resource allocation, particularly in managing large-scale IoT systems where edge computing offers decentralized control and context awareness. Challenges persist in coordinating communication and resource usage for concurrent applications, necessitating AI-driven algorithms for decentralized system control and resource sharing.

LITERATURE REVIEW

The evolution of cloud computing, spanning from early client-server programs in 1958 to today's diverse infrastructures, has become indispensable for various sectors like enterprises, government agencies, and academia, thanks to advances in serverless computing and adaptable virtual machines (Kavitha et al., 2021). The convergence of cloud computing with artificial intelligence (AI) is reshaping the technological landscape, impacting safety protocols and resource management. Meanwhile, the Internet of Things (IoT) contributes to both innovative applications and privacy concerns. AI methods like deep learning and classification algorithms enhance IoT security in dynamic networks. This study explores the symbiotic relationship between cloud computing, IoT, and AI, emphasizing their transformative potential across industries. AI aids safety measures by identifying patterns and implementing sophisticated security protocols, such as machine learning-integrated firewalls. Addressing evolving security challenges in cloud computing is crucial, especially with the combined potential of AI and IoT, which can revolutionize various sectors, including intelligent cities, by improving decision-making and fostering economic growth through computational methods and IoT data utilization.

In contemporary times, the widespread integration of computer systems underscores the critical importance of information security. Individuals and organizations alike recognize the imperative nature of safeguarding their data against various threats, elevating the significance of cybersecurity (Ramasamy et al., 2021). Despite substantial investments in cybersecurity hardware, software, and services, security breaches remain a persistent challenge. To bolster defense mechanisms, embracing modern technologies such as artificial intelligence (AI) becomes indispensable. Notably, according to a notable IDC analysis, businesses were projected to allocate $101.6 billion towards cybersecurity by 2020, underscoring the crucial need to protect sensitive data. Nonetheless, existing risks persist, underscoring the necessity for more robust security measures. In today's rapidly evolving digital environment, artificial intelligence (AI) has become a central driving force behind advancements in digital security (Raimundo & Rosário, 2021). Particularly in the wake of challenges arising from the pandemic, AI significantly impacts system security, addressing a wide array of issues including system openness, decision-making, quality control, and web security. The interdisciplinary nature of AI research holds broad technological implications for enhancing system security across various domains such as economics, medicine, and transportation. This global trend of investing in AI technology reflects the pressing need to combat rising security threats in everyday life, including digital, business, and societal applications. Heightened cybersecurity measures are imperative given the proliferation of malicious threats in the digital realm. The demand for AI-powered decision support systems is escalating, especially in the face of increasing complexity in business environments and amidst the ongoing global pandemic. In the rapidly evolving tech landscape, the fusion of artificial intelligence (AI) and big data analytics is revolutionizing the security of internet-connected devices, particularly in the domain of big data systems (Dai & Boroomand, 2021). As technology modernizes our lives, it simultaneously ushers in new security challenges, prompting researchers to harness the potential of big data and AI techniques.

Amid the fourth industrial revolution, Artificial Intelligence (AI) emerges as a central figure, utilizing data as its primary resource (Meurisch & Mühlhäuser, 2021). The year 2020 witnessed an extraordinary surge in data creation, with individuals generating 1.7 megabytes of data every second, while 26 billion interconnected devices diligently gathered, processed, and distributed information. This convergence of computation, data, and the physical realm heralded the advent of AI-driven user services, termed AI services, aimed at providing highly customized experiences. However, these AI services rely on two crucial prerequisites: (R1) a continuous stream of personal data and (R2) the need for localized, low-latency processing on Internet of Things (IoT) devices, which often conflicts with concerns about intellectual property. Balancing personalization and privacy presents an ongoing challenge encapsulated in the personalization-privacy paradox, compounded by the complexity of protecting intellectual property rights. Despite numerous proposed data protection approaches, a lack of common understanding and unresolved trust assumptions hinder effective integration and comparison. Encouraging providers to adopt data protection measures requires suitable incentives, such as personalized advertising or cost-efficient scaling. Ultimately, safeguarding proprietary AI algorithms and models at a local level is crucial to foster provider adoption of these approaches, signaling a need for deeper specialization in AI services and data decentralization. This article offers a fresh perspective on data protection within personalized AI services, addressing key challenges and paving the way for future interdisciplinary research.

The convergence of artificial intelligence (AI) and cybersecurity is highlighted as essential in the context of the Fourth Industrial Revolution (Industry 4.0) (Sarker et al., 2021). There's a growing need to utilize AI in safeguarding Internet-connected systems from a rising array of cyber threats, including malicious attacks and unauthorized access. AI's involvement encompasses various facets such as machine learning, deep learning, natural language processing, knowledge representation, and rule-based expert systems modeling, offering multifaceted solutions to contemporary cybersecurity challenges. Traditional security measures like antivirus software and firewalls may fall short in addressing the dynamic nature of cyber threats, making AI's automation and advanced decision-making capabilities crucial. The surge in data generation due to heavy reliance on technology, particularly the Internet of Things and cloud computing, has exacerbated the threat landscape with various malicious activities. To counteract this, leveraging AI's potential in intrusion detection, fraud detection, prediction of cyber-attacks, access control management, and anomaly detection is paramount. Amidst rapid technological progress, cybersecurity confronts a dynamic threat landscape encompassing data breaches, server intrusions, identity theft, and cryptographic system vulnerabilities (Srivastava et al., 2021). The integration of Artificial Intelligence (AI) and Machine Learning (ML) across various sectors amplifies these risks. AI's widespread application, from healthcare diagnostics to facial recognition, introduces new security challenges alongside promising synergies with cybersecurity. To counter evolving threats, cybersecurity systems must leverage AI and knowledge-based tools to safeguard extensive datasets and user information effectively. AI plays a pivotal role in intelligently identifying and mitigating security threats swiftly. It emerges as a potent asset in modern cybersecurity, offering superior flexibility, adaptability, and resilience compared to traditional solutions.

In today's rapidly evolving cybersecurity landscape, the magnitude and complexity of security threats have surpassed the capabilities of manual management and traditional security technologies (Das & Sandhane, 2021). Fixed decision-making algorithms struggle to keep pace with modern threats, necessitating the integration of artificial intelligence (AI) and machine learning. AI plays a crucial role in various cybersecurity aspects, especially through neural networks, to protect networks and address diverse challenges effectively. Real-world incidents like the Conficker virus highlight the urgent need for innovative cyber defense strategies. AI's adaptive decision-making and knowledge-intensive tools are vital for countering emerging offensive tactics and establishing protected perimeters dynamically. Its applications in decision support, situational awareness, and expert machine development contribute to strengthening cybersecurity. The healthcare industry has experienced significant progress due to the integration of advanced technologies such as Artificial Intelligence (AI), Machine Learning (ML), Internet of Things (IoT), and cloud computing (Seh et al., 2021). To address these critical security issues, experts and researchers are actively exploring various tools, techniques, and strategies. Research studies focused on healthcare data breaches highlight the need for proactive security mechanisms capable of identifying abnormal user behavior during data access. Furthermore, the potential of Machine Learning techniques in bolstering healthcare data privacy and security is continually growing. A novel conceptual framework based on Machine Learning has been introduced to detect suspicious user access to Electronic Health Records (EHRs). To assess the effectiveness of both supervised and unsupervised ML approaches in creating a dynamic digital healthcare data security environment, the article utilizes a fuzzy-based Analytical Network Process (ANP).

In the cybersecurity domain, the identification and prevention of cyber anomalies and attacks are of paramount importance (Sarker, 2021). "Cyber Learning" stands out as a machine learning-based cybersecurity framework that integrates correlated feature selection and provides an extensive empirical examination of various machine learning-based security models. Within Cyber Learning, a binary classification model can be applied to detect anomalies, while a multi-class classification model can identify a broad spectrum of cyber-attacks like Denial of Service (DoS), Backdoor, and Worms, among others.

The advancement of wellness systems has become possible by the application of utility cloud services, AI, ML and wireless sensor devices (Attaallah et al., 2022). Diagnosing a disease early, more accessibility results in these software systems. Regardless of these achievements, there is a serious concern about health and wellness data violation by cyber criminals. Recent statistics have shown data breach to be rising in the previous couple of years. The motive is to solve these problems by the application of big data security.

Artificial Neural Networks (ANNs) derived deep learning is crucial for modern security systems (Ghillani, 2022). While employing AI in cyber risk analytics offers numerous advantages, it also poses drawbacks. Various neural network architectures like Convolutional Neural Networks (CNNs), Recurrent Neural Networks (RNNs), auto-encoders, and deep transfer learning are adept at handling diverse cyber threats. Specific algorithms such as Stochastic Gradient Descent (SGD), Limited Memory BFGS (L-BFGS), and Adaptive Moment Estimation (Adam) contribute significantly to addressing cybersecurity issues. AI integration in healthcare promises enhanced effectiveness, accuracy, and safety, drawing substantial investments from both the public and private sectors (Bak et al., 2022). However, accessing data is crucial for leveraging this technology. Despite the dominance of the "consent approach" in European countries, it undermines the value of data-intensive medicine and poses potential harm to patients.

The burgeoning demand for internet services, exacerbated by the COVID-19 pandemic, has made organizations vulnerable to cyber threats due to poor cloud infrastructure (Wang et al., 2022). This exposes them to risks of data breaches and theft, including sensitive information like credit card and social security numbers stored on platforms like Dropbox or Google Drive. With the estimated cost of a data breach at USD 3.68 million, businesses must fortify themselves against cloud-related dangers. Concurrently, the increasing popularity of drones, or Unmanned Aerial Vehicles (UAVs), across commercial, military, and personal sectors necessitates robust cybersecurity measures.

Machine Learning (ML), a subset of Artificial Intelligence (AI), focuses on developing software capable of learning from data, identifying patterns, and making logical decisions autonomously (Wazid et al., 2022). Cybersecurity involves safeguarding digital systems and data from malicious attacks. The convergence of ML and cybersecurity encompasses two main perspectives: employing ML in cybersecurity practices and utilizing ML to enhance cybersecurity measures. In today's global culture where internet has become the main source of communication and commerce (Saura et al., 2022). At the same time, possibilities that artificial intelligence (AI) brings to governments in terms of evolving collective behavior analysis, vital concerns related to citizens' privacy have come up. This paper conducted an in-depth review taking into consideration citizens' privacy. According to the results, this paper classified and discussed strategies used by governments that may affect collective behavior. The paper is concluded with a discussion of the development of regulations revolving around the ethical design of citizen data collection, where implications for governments are displayed at regulating security, and data privacy. In today's advancements of wire free communications, a large portion of the information is part of a huge network which connects many devices across the world (Gupta et al., 2022). The possibilities of electronics are increasing day by day, which then results in more information shared. Among the most vital use of technology has been the way we do business. New technology influence the entire costing of products and pricing strategy (Liu et al., 2022). Business means buying and/or selling in exchange of money. The business which involves electronic business is known to be e-commerce. In the Aviation and Aeronautical industries, is a mechanical system that is a union of communication and information devices and the daily usage of these systems has raised worries about cyber security (Ukwandu et al., 2022). Moreover, the concern is getting more and more highlighted and serious as there is rapid growth in the industries in the usage of electronic-enabled aircraft and modern as well as well-equipped airports. The main motive of this paper is to find common threats, motivations, and breach types, and see the sensitivity of aviation infrastructure which is the most common topic in the recent attack scenarios. IT infrastructure is the most common part of this industry which has been attacked quite frequently and the threat it faces is unauthorized access to hackers. To guess the cyber-attack tendency in the upcoming time we need to analyze the scope of attacks and the existing threats. With the fast development of blockchain technology in the recent years, its application in instances that require privacy, such as health area, have become encouraged and widely discussed (de Moraes Rossetto et al., 2022). This paper presents an architecture to make sure the privacy of health-related data, which are stored and shared within a blockchain network, through using mix-up method with the RSA, and AES algorithms. Many advances related to blockchain technology have been recently considered, notably: the advent of blockchain 2.0, the blockchain network Ethereum.

A very innovative framework is introduced that integrates metaverse, artificial intelligence (AI), and blockchain technology to reshape the healthcare industry (Ali et al., 2023). This architecture has mainly three environments. They are doctor's space, patient's space and the metaverse realm. Also, it is important to note that all these environments are in a virtual set-up. Medical professionals and patients are presented by various avatars within the setup. In the doctor's space, medical professionals and patients interact with each other. This will provide them with a virtual healthcare experience. In the patient's space, patients join the Metaverse and communicate with medical professionals, which can be closely related to in person consultations. Metaverse serves as a centre here, backed up by Blockchain technology. In healthcare, blockchain network is being used to store and exchange patient records between hospital, laboratories, pharmacies, and doctors. Blockchain technology ensures data security, data transparency and data integrity. All the interactions happening in the network, EHR, medical records and any sensitive information about the patient are stored within the metaverse. Cybersecurity depends crucially on AI and ML (Muneer et al., 2023). Cyber-event detection model may involve the incorporation of state-of-the-art machine learning technologies and real-time network data analytics. Therefore, phishing attack detection, classification models, or Intrusion Detection Systems (IDS) is the solution. That way, IDSs can detect suspicious behavior through the use of AI and find out about unauthorized access in networks. Data security and cyber security are to be ensured in the field of energy harvesting systems (Mohammadi & Sohn, 2023). The systems are susceptible to several attacks, including data, tempering and eavesdropping, which can cause sensitive information to leak and interfere with the flow of energy. The system can be strengthened by the integration of AI techniques such as Federated, learning and machine learning. By doing so system reliability is eventually increased as they improve threat detection, predictive maintenance and real time monitoring. A Smart Grid refers to a communication-enabled electricity supply network that can sense and respond locally to grid disruptions (Simoes et al., 2023). Smart grid will integrate artificial intelligence technology with ML for better data safety and cybersecurity. Integration of Information Technology (IT) with Operational Technology (OT) brings in a lot of challenges. Cyber-attacks on smart grids can be caused by the integration between IT and OT as smart grids rely on such communications, control and monitoring technologies. Application of artificial intelligence and machine learning in the healthcare industry comes with a lot of benefits such as disease prediction, diagnosis prevention and monitoring (Khan et al., 2023). However, concerns such as data security, privacy of Electronic Health Records (EHRs) and the risk of data breaches cannot be overlooked.

The analysis takes a closer look at the relationship between artificial intelligence (AI) and smart contract (SC) security (Krichen, 2023). Highlighting coding errors, hackings, and other incidents like the infamous DAO (Decentralized Autonomous Organization) hack, the Parity wallet breach, and other noteworthy events, says a lot about the financial risks they pose. Then AI is introduced as an ally for this issue. The importance of data security and how it is linked to cyber security through AI and ML is discussed (Roy et al., 2023). The importance of having strong data governance procedures to protect digital data from theft, corruption, and unwanted access for the duration of its existence is highlighted. As the world is becoming progressively digital, the demand for robust cybersecurity measures is higher than ever (Bharadiya, 2023). Due to cyber-attacks, it turns out that there have been many unfortunate events like financial losses, damage to personal data and public safety risks. The traditional security methods are excruciating to keep up with the evolving threat landscape. These methods usually generate more false positives, making investigations time-consuming and expensive. There are many security and privacy-related issues come with metaverse-enabled healthcare systems such as protecting personal information, when collecting, exchanging, and using health data (Letafati & Otoum, 2023). At first, data security in the metaverse's access layer is evaluated, and then privacy and security concerns in the context of clinical machine learning for E-health are explored. The privacy of social exchanges between patients in Metaverse-enabled healthcare platforms is also tested. The Financial industry increasingly controls encrypting private consumers Personally Identifiable Information (PII) and Non-public Personal Information (NPI) data (Mishra, 2023). Failure to protect adequately could also lead to heavy fines and indirect costs of losses due to data breaches. Using Python program and Advanced Encryption Standard (AES) algorithm for key management including data encryption and decryption. Real–time predictions, using the K-nearest neighbour (KNN) algorithm underline the significance of real-time risk reduction ratios and data privacy. Artificial Intelligence (AI) offers effective solutions to combat the escalating security threats, particularly in cyber security applications. However, the focus has primarily been on practical implementations of AI in cyber security, neglecting its visual analysis applications. With the integration of AI, the structure of cyber security has undergone significant changes. This study examines the utilization of AI in cyber security and its diverse applications. Artificial Neural Networks (ANNs) are instrumental in various cyber-related domains such as cloud security and biometric recognition.

Recent times have posed significant challenges in protecting data, primarily due to two main issues: the compartmentalization of organizations and concerns regarding data security and privacy (Abbas et al., n.d.). A viable solution to these challenges is federated learning, which ensures both safety and security. Federated learning presents a novel and efficient approach to safeguarding data. This paper aims to introduce the features, architecture, and fundamental concepts of federated learning, highlighting its potential to address these challenges and its diverse applications. It is anticipated that federated learning will bridge the gaps between different organizations, enabling them to securely share confidential data without apprehension. The discussion will encompass the comprehensive framework of federated learning, including horizontal learning, vertical learning, and transfer learning. By leveraging federated learning, a data network can be established among various industries, promoting knowledge sharing while preserving privacy. The ultimate goal is to integrate federated learning into all aspects of life.

In the current era dominated by 5G and its successor technologies, there's a burgeoning focus on bolstering cyber network security, particularly through the integration of Artificial Intelligence (AI) and Machine Learning (ML) applications in peripheral devices (Yang, Liu, Chen et al, n.d.). This article explores the intersection of security and AI from two perspectives: AI and ML for device functionalities, and security measures for AI systems themselves.

Most of the AI algorithms use data to build a system that digs for precious features, yet there is a trust issue between the different stakeholders who control the data thus making the usage of this data in cyberspace difficult to verify or sanction (Porambage et al., n.d.). As an outcome, it is tough to allow data sharing in complex cyberspace. A feasible solution for these problems is "SecNet" which is a framework that allows us to secure and safeguard data storing, computing, and sharing.

Ensuring transparency in AI systems presents a significant challenge, as they must both detect suspicious activity and remain transparent to consumers (Wang et al., n.d.). A solution gaining traction is the use of counterfactual statements to elucidate algorithmic decisions, particularly in light of the "right to explanation" principle. Counterfactuals are favored for their comprehensibility among both laypeople and experts. This paper examines the pros and cons of explanations within modern AI systems and their impact on security, privacy, fairness, and safety. It explores the opportunities and challenges posed by counterfactual statements in AI systems, emphasizing the importance of data integrity and security. Securing AI systems is a complex task with multifaceted outcomes, necessitating a focus on transparency in future developments. Counterfactual statements are poised to play a crucial role in this endeavor, enhancing the security and accountability of AI systems.

Giving security to AI systems enhances the problems that are connected with giving security to software systems in a zone that we can't solve (Sokol, n.d.). An attacker can attack the system in many ways. AI algorithms provide a strong vector for an attacker to change the properties and output of the system and implementation of AI in software can be very hard sometimes. Furthermore, AI-enabled systems frequently depend on taking the input data into a data representation whose account can't be kept by humans. Problems make fundamental aspects of verification and validation not tractable for AI systems. AI algorithms face these challenges but this is particularly correct for deep learning models. For the data that is approachable to the public this incapability to find out whether a system will perform the task or not. A software system that has substantial legal or financial ramifications for users or consumers of the products of that system ought to meet higher standards. Securing AI systems requires new threat modeling of data which can affect how the systems are designed. Machine learning attacks like unpathetic inputs and data poisoning are based on the opponent taking the upper hand in the acceptance of the input space for an AI system.

Machine learning algorithms are increasingly utilized to create distinctive network traffic identification systems, especially for detecting prevalent threats like Denial of Service (DoS) attacks and phishing emails (Pons & Ozkaya, n.d.). These systems are trained using datasets comprising both benign and malicious samples to discern patterns of criminal behavior from typical user behavior. The Bag of Words (BoG) method, commonly employed in spam email detection, utilizes keywords or features to differentiate between normal and spam emails, often provided by network administrators or experts. However, with hackers continuously evolving and employing sophisticated techniques, sensitive information within e-government systems remains vulnerable, prompting the need for enhanced security measures.

In safeguarding cyberspace, essential automation is crucial as humans alone cannot determine the processing speed and data quantity required (Yang, Elisa, & Eliot, n.d.). The emergence of the Internet of Things (IoT) and interconnected devices presents challenges for cyber security experts, with cyber breaches on the rise. Effective security measures are essential to prevent unauthorized access to sensitive information. Artificial Intelligence (AI) plays a significant role in enhancing cyber defense by facilitating proactive threat detection and improving security processes across different layers of data networks. AI-enabled systems learn from each attack, enabling them to detect even subtle deviations from normal behavior, thereby reducing the cybersecurity threats faced by businesses worldwide. The integration of AI and Machine Learning (ML) is widespread in various industries due to advancements in computing power, storage capacity, and data availability. AI-driven systems not only enhance access times but also analyze network behavior deeply to identify patterns associated with cyber threats. Given the escalating challenges of cybercrime, rapid advancements in AI technology are imperative to bolster cybersecurity measures in both cyberspace and the market.

Multimedia applications like Computer Vision (CV), Multimedia Messaging Service (MMS), and Natural Language Processing (NLP) have seen significant growth across various sectors, including business, commerce, and cyber defense, owing to advancements in Artificial Intelligence (AI) (Tolani & Tolani, n.d.). However, utilizing AI for overall national security presents significant challenges due to its lack of transparency, often functioning as opaque "black boxes" that require expert understanding to interpret. Despite this complexity, AI plays a crucial role in identifying potential malicious activities within national defense systems. By examining each level of AI system execution, a secure and reliable environment can be established, surpassing human-set standards. AI not only simplifies tasks but also complicates endeavors for hackers, emerging as a formidable adversary for criminals. AI applications in cyber networks predominantly rely on decision-making and predictive capabilities, leveraging machine learning, data fusion, and sensor integration. The Internet of Things (IoT) is introduced at the outset of the article as a quickly developing technology having applicability across many industries. It highlights the proliferation of IoT devices and the challenges associated with securing them due to their heterogeneous nature and limited resources. The primary security concerns identified are Confidentiality, Integrity, and Availability (CIA).

In order to better understand the Internet of Things, this study will concentrate on three main areas: computing, communication, and authentication (Wu et al., 2020). The IoT, as a distributed network combining various sensor devices with the internet, has witnessed advancements in sensing technologies, transmission methods, and data computing. IoT three tier Architecture comprising of three layers: terminal perception, network transport, and application service.

Overall, this paper has a comprehensive survey of the security challenges in IoT and explores the potential of AI, particularly ML and DL, in enhancing IoT security. The outlines specify threats and corresponding AI solutions, emphasizing the need for further research to address challenges introduced by the integration of AI into IoT security.

Safdar et al. (2020) explores how artificial intelligence can revolutionize a number of industries, with a focus on healthcare—particularly radiology. Despite the promising benefits, concerns among radiologists about workforce impact exist. Ethical considerations, such as bias in AI algorithms, data ownership complexities, and patient privacy, are highlighted.

The sections delve into issues like bias in datasets and the data hunger of machine learning, emphasising the need for responsible AI development.

The increasing deployment of IoT devices, while offering significant benefits, raises concerns about security vulnerabilities and potential cyber threats (Zewdie & Girma, 2020). This paper discusses the necessity for robust cybersecurity, the role of AI/ML in enhancing security, and the challenges associated with AI adoption in cloud computing. The paper focus some ideas about cyber threats and challenges about security vulnerabilities

IoT Growth: The proliferation of IoT devices is highlighted, with predictions of a substantial increase in connected devices globally by 2025.

Hybrid Detection Model: A methodical strategy is suggested to address and alleviate cyber risks to Internet of Things devices on cloud computing platforms, utilizing AI/ML approaches such as supervised learning, unsupervised learning, and reinforcement learning.

Drawbacks of AI/ML: Despite the advantages, the paper acknowledges potential drawbacks of AI, including its susceptibility to attacks, high cost, limitations in replicating human intuition, and dependence on accurate training datasets.

It is observed that in order to create a globally connected environment, this article investigates how 6G networks can integrate satellite and terrestrial wireless communications (Li, Su, Li, Zhang, & Wang, 2020). Using artificial intelligence to enable intelligent and flexible network service creation is a fundamental 6G design principle. However, the deployment of intelligent services in 6G networks necessitates managing enormous volumes of data for computation, analysis, and storage, which presents security risks like hostile actors tampering with data and contaminating it. In order to demonstrate the effectiveness of blockchain technology in guaranteeing data security, the paper also offers a case study centered on an indoor navigation system. An approach to evaluate and improve the caliber of intelligent services is the combination of blockchain technology and artificial intelligence. The authors conclude by discussing a number of unresolved concerns about data security in the upcoming 6G networks and emphasizing the necessity for more research and development in this area.

The interconnectedness of big data processing, cloud computing, artificial intelligence, and the Internet of Things as cutting-edge technologies influencing multiple sectors is covered in this study (Chen, 2020). The technologies here collaborate and create interdisciplinary studies and applications across fields such as business, education, healthcare, and industry. IoT links physical devices to the virtual world, generating substantial data, while cloud computing processes this data and facilitates intelligent decision-making through big data analysis and machine learning. The introduction covers the progress of cloud computing, including Software as a Service, Platform as a Service, and Infrastructure as a Service, as well as the historical development from the internet's communication network. Lingering around, there is emphasis on the role of service-oriented computing, cloud computing, and their expansion into diverse cloud computing units.

Cloud computing provides scalable computing capacity, leading to the emergence of big data and its processing. The narrative here highlights the acceleration of data generation through IoT devices and social networks. The evolution of artificial intelligence from cybernetics to present-day big data and machine learning-based AI is also traced.

The special issue drives more into the in-depth studies covering analysis, modelling, simulation, and applications found in IoT, cloud computing, big data processing, and artificial intelligence that are interdisciplinary fields.

Explores the integration of Artificial Intelligence (AI) functionalities into wireless cellular networks, focusing on the potential transformation of network design, infrastructure management, cost reduction, and user performance improvement (Challita et al., 2020).

For the success of AI deployment this paper lists some key aspects given below:

Future wireless networks must support flexible and programmable data pipelines for the volume, velocity, and variety of real-time data and algorithms capable of real-time decision making.

Future communication networks must be designed to support exchange of data, models, and insights, and it is the responsibility of the AI agents to include any necessary user data.

The summary encompasses diverse applications of AI in the wireless domain, categorising them into areas such as the physical layer, mobility management, wireless security, and localization. Use case examples are highlighted, showcasing the practical applications of AI to enhance different aspects of wireless cellular networks.

Mohammed (2020) delves into the utilization of artificial intelligence (AI) to tackle cybersecurity challenges, shedding light on the risks associated with the digital revolution, such as data mining and profiling. It underscores the necessity for enhanced digital identity management and verification, proposing blockchain technology as a viable solution for securing digital identities. The author emphasizes the pivotal role of AI in mitigating cyber threats, emphasizing its proactive and data-driven capabilities. Key areas where AI can be instrumental in cybersecurity are outlined, including the identification of emerging threats, combating bots, predicting breach risks, and enhancing endpoint protection. The paper also touches upon AI's applications in spam, fraud, and botnet detection. While acknowledging AI's advantages in cybersecurity, such as adaptability to evolving threats and improved predictive intelligence, potential drawbacks are also discussed. These include resource and financial requirements for AI system development, as well as the risk of inaccurate findings without access to diverse and large datasets.

In Xue et al. (2020), the researchers explore the concept of backdoor attacks in machine learning, a type of attack where a specific trigger is embedded in the training data or pre-trained models. This trigger, when activated, causes the model to misclassify instances in a stealthy manner.

The concept basically holds two stages: A training phase that consists of an algorithm that learns from data to form a model with parameters, and a test phase where the model is given a task to carry out and give a predictable label for the data inputted. Furthermore the algorithm is divided into NN algorithms and non-NN algorithms.

The exploration of backdoor attacks underscores the importance of addressing vulnerabilities in training data and pre-trained models. As machine learning continues to advance, mitigating the risks associated with these stealthy attacks becomes crucial for ensuring the robustness and security of machine learning applications.

Gupta et al. (2020) explores the challenges arising from the proliferation of data generated by smart devices, known as Big Data (BD), and the limitations of traditional data analytics methods in handling this immense volume. In response, the paper investigates the potential of Machine Learning (ML) and Deep Learning (DL) models in identifying and mitigating attacks during data analytics processes.

In line with the aforementioned theme, the paper proposes a Secure Data Analytics (SDA) architecture based on DL and ML, presenting a taxonomy and threat model. The motivation behind this proposal is to address security issues in data analytics and establish defense mechanisms against attacks not confined to the database. Contributions encompass a systematic review of SDA utilizing ML and DL models, a suggested SDA-ML architecture, and a comprehensive examination of research challenges.

Feng et al. (2020) discusses the critical intersection of artificial intelligence, security, and government strategy, particularly during the 2020 COVID-19 pandemic. It emphasises the role of AI in data analysis for predicting and managing the pandemic's impact, highlighting the need for robust AI security. The potential consequences of security attacks on AI models are underscored, especially when inaccurate predictions can lead to significant loss of life. The paper explores various technical challenges, such as cyber security issues in AI technology, the security of robotic systems (e.g., Robot Operating System), and the application of AI in biometrics. Non-technical challenges, including social, political, and privacy considerations, are also discussed. The privacy implications of contact tracing apps and the trade-off between economic recovery and personal privacy are explored.

The paper calls for a balanced approach between AI, cyber security, and governmental strategies, considering both technical and non-technical challenges. It highlights the ongoing need for a better trade-off between AI, cyber security, and government considerations, particularly in the context of the evolving challenges posed by the pandemic.

EVOLUTION OF 6G NETWORK

The emergence of 6G wireless networks introduces a novel realm encompassing objectives, Key Performance Indicators (KPIs), and challenges stemming from Key Enabling Techniques (KETs) (Rasti et al., 2021). These include Reconfigurable Intelligent Surfaces, integrated underwater-terrestrial-air-space networks, Non-Orthogonal Multiple Access, dynamic network slicing, multi-band networks, ultra-massive spatially modulated MIMO, and Artificial Intelligence (AI). Notably, managing resources poses significant issues due to these KETs, necessitating a shift from conventional optimization-based methods to AI and machine learning solutions. Particularly, in 6G networks catering to ultra-reliable low-latency communication (eURLLC) and enhanced mobile broadband (FeMBB) services, challenges such as cooperative network selection and subchannel assignment arise. Addressing these challenges, a proposed approach utilizes deep reinforcement learning (DRL) techniques like double DQN, dueling DQN, and deep Q-network (DQN), demonstrating the efficacy of dueling DQN in achieving superior results and faster convergence rates within the multi-band network architecture. 6G envisions a distributed, fully autonomous, and highly adaptable user-centric system encompassing satellite, aerial, terrestrial, underwater, and subterranean communications, targeting peak data speeds of 1 Tbps, ultra-low latency, energy efficiency, and diverse application adaptability. Despite the myriad complexities posed by the incorporation of cutting-edge technology in 6G networks, addressing resource management challenges through innovative machine learning and AI solutions is imperative for successful adoption. The proposed DRL-based solution for the combined network selection and subchannel allocation problem illustrates the efficacy of these methods in resource management within 6G networks.

Since the inception of first-generation (1G) networks in the 1980s, mobile communication networks have undergone significant transformations (Solyman & Yahya, 2022). Each subsequent generation, building upon the accomplishments and challenges of its predecessors, has witnessed remarkable advancements in capabilities and services. As we stand on the brink of a new era, the anticipation and excitement surrounding the sixth-generation (6G) networks, promising further breakthroughs and potentials, are palpable.

The evolution began with the analog technology of 1G, emphasizing voice-centric services. This paved the way for second-generation (2G) networks utilizing Time Division Multiple Access (TDMA) for digital transition. Third-generation (3G) networks introduced technologies like Wideband Code Division Multiple Access (CDMA) and High-Speed Packet Access (HSPA), enabling faster internet access and enhanced multimedia capabilities. Fourth-generation (4G) networks, particularly Long-Term Evolution (LTE), incorporated Orthogonal Frequency Division Multiplexing (OFDM) for improved performance and data throughput.

5G represents the pinnacle of mobile communication technology, lauded for its exceptional data rates, minimal latency, and extensive connectivity capabilities, facilitating diverse applications from the Internet of Things (IoT) to augmented reality.

While 6G holds promise, it also presents challenges such as spectrum limitations, complex circuit design, and the need for efficient frequency mapping. Intelligence-related issues include the complexity of unsupervised learning and the requirement for rapid and energy-efficient processing. Network architectural considerations involve scalability, interference, and scheduling, alongside crucial elements like modeling, energy efficiency, and topology optimization.

From the inception of first-generation (1G) networks in the 1980s to the imminent arrival of 6G enhancements, wireless communication networks have undergone remarkable evolution (Alraih et al., 2022). Each generation, spanning roughly a decade, has brought significant advancements in capabilities and services, building upon the achievements and challenges of its predecessors. First-generation (1G) networks pioneered voice services, while second-generation (2G) networks initiated the transition to digital technologies. Third-generation (3G) networks saw enhancements in internet access and multimedia capabilities, while fourth-generation (4G) networks, primarily based on Orthogonal Frequency Division Multiplexing (OFDM), and revolutionized data services.

The advent of fifth-generation (5G) networks introduced key performance indicators (KPIs) set by the International Telecommunication Union (ITU), driving advancements in technologies like massive MIMO and millimeter-wave communications. Looking ahead, 6G networks are poised to operate at higher frequencies, featuring advanced technologies such as terahertz communications and artificial intelligence integration.

In essence, 6G wireless networks promise expanded coverage, faster data rates, lower latency, and innovative features like AI, aiming to facilitate ubiquitous mobile broadband communication and foster the development of an intelligent mobile society. With continued advancements in mobile communication technologies, the potential for societal transformation looms large.

AI APPLICATIONS IN INDUSTRY 4.0

The surge in cyber-attacks, both in volume and complexity, poses a significant challenge for companies and organizations, particularly in terms of their readiness to tackle such threats. Recognizing this pressing issue, cybersecurity experts have turned to Artificial Intelligence (AI) as a potential solution. Specifically, Machine

Learning (ML), a subset of AI, offers promising capabilities for detecting and combating malware, which is increasingly difficult to identify using traditional security measures. ML algorithms have the capacity to learn the patterns and behaviors of malware, as well as anticipate its potential evolution, thereby enhancing detection capabilities.

Moreover, AI-powered systems can go beyond detection to take proactive measures, such as remediation of threats and categorization of events, thus reducing the burden on cybersecurity professionals and allowing them to focus on more strategic tasks.

In the context of 6G networks, which are envisioned to be highly complex and dynamic, AI holds significant promise in optimizing performance, facilitating knowledge discovery, and enabling intelligent decision-making. AI techniques can enhance sensing and detection capabilities in 6G networks, enabling the collection of large volumes of diverse and dynamic data from physical environments. This includes identifying radio frequency utilization, spectrum sensing, intrusion detection, interference detection, and impulse corruption detection, among other functionalities.

Considering the heterogeneous nature of industrial systems, it is beneficial to classify autonomous actions using a graduated model of autonomy, which can vary based on specific application requirements. By employing a taxonomy of system autonomy based on AI, a six-level model of automated decision-making can be established, tailored to industrial processes.

However, it's important to acknowledge that this paper provides a high-level overview of the potential of AI in conjunction with 6G networks and industries, aiming to highlight its significance without delving into specific details or graphical representations. Additional information or visual aids may be provided upon request for further clarity.

SECURITY THREATS IN 6G NETWORK AND CHALLENGES

In this section, the security concerns are associated with 6G networks, analyzing the transition from 5G and the challenges stemming from architectural and technological changes. As 6G networks evolve, they are anticipated to shift from small to "tiny" configurations, marked by complex deployments involving mesh cells, dual connectivity, and Device-to-Device (D2D) communication becoming standard. The proliferation of suspicious networks presents a notable threat, escalating the risk landscape for distributed networks interconnected via mesh connectivity. There's a critical need to rethink security planning, particularly regarding sub-network definitions, as current measures struggle to manage the array of applications within individual sub-networks across the extensive network surface. A promising strategy for 6G involves implementing hierarchical mechanisms to differentiate communication and security levels between sub-networks and the broader network surface. Radio Access Network (RAN) convergence establishes a robust layer of RAN functions, potentially concentrated and complemented by core functions like user plane and control plane microservices at the network edge. Key targets for attackers include User Plane Management Systems (UPMS) and Control Plane Management Systems (CPMS), impacting numerous radio units served by small services. Some 6G networks adopt frameworks like zero-touch and Service Management (ZSM) architecture to facilitate features such as minimal operational costs and rapid service deployment, yet complete automation with individual learning capabilities may inadvertently introduce attack vulnerabilities. Protecting data privacy becomes increasingly complex due to the imperative for automation with minimal human intervention in zero-touch networks. Discussions persist regarding the implementation of automated machine manners in fully automated 6G networks, revealing various security challenges in network management system deployments.

AI SECURITY SOLUTIONS IN 6G ENVIRONMENT

In the rapidly evolving landscape of technology and mobile communication systems, the advent of 6G brings about various security challenges and considerations (Je et al., 2021). These include network openness, the handling of personal user data, and integration of AI, virtualization/containerization, and the potential impact of quantum computing. Open-source designs like O-RAN enhance interoperability but also increase security risks, necessitating robust authentication and access control measures. Privacy concerns related to 6G services underscore the importance of secure identification and compliance with data privacy regulations. The utilization of AI introduces risks such as adversarial machine learning (AML), which can be mitigated through techniques like trustworthy AI inference systems and anomaly detection procedures. Virtualization and containerization offer operational benefits but require measures like secure visualization layers and intrusion detection systems to address security vulnerabilities.

Security problems are certain in this evolving world of 6G networks, especially when the system envisions the Internet of Everything (IoE) with billions of different devices (Siriwardhana et al., 2021). To take care of all these complex security Concerns, a multifaceted strategy that leverages AI is required. (As mentioned below).

i.   Continuity from 5G security technologies:

It will remain significant in the 6G contexts to build on the basis of 5G, network software technologies such as Software Defined Networking (SDN), Network Function Virtualisation (NFV), Multi -access Edge Computing (MEC) and networking remains significant in the 6G context. However it is important to note that they come with security risks such as SDN controller assaults, NFV platform vulnerabilities and MEC risks from physical security flaws.

ii. Local 6G networks and diverse security levels:

6G expands local networks to include in – body networks, drones and environmental sensor networks, all of which might cooperate at various degrees of security. If this network unfortunately, has poor protection, will provide access points to attackers and compromise the network's confidence.

iii. AI-centric 6G technologies:

Because 6G depends heavily on AI to achieve completely autonomous networks, AI systems can be a target for a lot of assaults. Poisoning assaults, data manipulation, and logic corruption can be dangerous to machine learning systems. Another revolutionary technology called Blockchain is vulnerable to 51% assaults, particularly in the age of quantum computing.

iv. AI as Defender:

Application of AI in 6G system serves a dual purpose as both a possible target for assaults and defense against growing threats. AI's involvement in 6G requires intelligent security and privacy requirements that cover pre-6G security architecture, technology and privacy.

v. Preserving privacy with AI:

Through edge based federated learning, intelligent beam forming algorithms and dynamic identification of privacy – preserving parts, AI can be used for privacy preservation. Techniques like homomorphic encryption and differential privacy ensure that large scale data analysis does not compromise individual privacy.

Two Critical AI applications - indoor positioning and autonomous vehicles have been emphasised as a part of the solution (Li, Su, Li, Zhang, & Wang, 2020).

Indoor positioning solution:

This solution is AI-powered in 6G. It is a device used in emergency situations to quickly find / locate people. This device is particularly used in situations like fire rescue operations and ensures that people involved in such situations are safe and sound.

Autonomous Vehicle Solution

The integration of 6G and AI allows the complicated connectivity required for autonomous cars in cities. The system is determined by onboard sensors, real-time data transmission, and dynamic adaptation to road circumstances. The continuous flow of 6G and AI collaboration produces effective autonomous vehicle scheduling and operation.

Blockchain for Security

Blockchain technology is like a ray of hope to give answers to security and challenges. In centralised AI models. Using encryption methods, the technology offers decentralised and safe data sharing. It addresses privacy and trust concerns and thus, offers a safe platform for AI applications in the 6G context (Shankar, Supriya, Varadam et al, 2023).

FUTURE DIRECTION

The advent of 5G technology by 2023 is anticipated but may not fully meet escalating user demands and functionalities, necessitating the introduction of 6G promptly. Ongoing research on AI holds promise across diverse domains. Edge-native AI offers tailored, context-aware, and localized techniques, particularly benefiting urban computing and smart cities. In the forthcoming 6G era, edge-native AI will play a pivotal role in daily computing and smart technology. The paper initially discusses 5G achievements and challenges, then delves into potential 6G applications, technologies, and AI-based wireless applications, emphasizing the need for ultra-high throughput, low latency, reliability, and energy efficiency. Advanced network infrastructures and technologies such as cloud computing, optical wireless networks, and THz spectrum communications will be essential. Future applications will generate vast data, necessitating advanced AI technologies. Additionally, the paper outlines various technologies applicable to 6G communication, highlighting the importance of accommodating stringent quality of service requirements for future applications (Shankar et al., 2022).

DISCUSSION

Concerning the preceding discussion, it is fair to say that the most strong and emerging technology of recent times or the modern world is the 6G network without a doubt. The combination of Artificial intelligence with a 6G network transformed communication features in terms of decision-making and scattering. But it will take a long time before we reach our desired 6G network by that time the current network i.e. 5G will proceed to develop over the coming time. As we move from one generation to another in terms of technology or communication we change a lot. Eventually, the ultimate goal of 6G is to provide connectivity requirements for the 2025s and beyond. New applications will demand some new and modern technologies like convergence of communication, quantum computing, automated devices powered by artificial intelligence, modern AI techniques, and smart surfaces (Shankar, Varadam, Bharadwaj, Saxena et al, 2023). Thus we want a 6G network to support new and upcoming modern applications like extended reality, intelligent healthcare systems, and smart grids. So there is a need to address the safety-related issues in the 6G network (Shankar, Varadam, Bharadwaj, Dayananda et al, 2023). The main and major threats and the best possible solution to protect the 6G network have also been discussed in this paper.

CONCLUSION

5G technology is expected to be globally established by 2023, but it may struggle to meet the increasing demands of users and functionalities, necessitating the introduction of 6G. Research on AI across various domains shows promising results. Edge-native AI offers customized, context-aware, and localized techniques for platform providers, network operators, and end-users, empowering edge applications with enhanced capabilities. These solutions will drive innovations in urban computing and smart cities. In the future 6G era, edge-native AI will play a significant role in everyday computing and smart technology. While research on 6G systems is still in its early stages, this paper outlines potential applications, technologies, and requirements. It emphasizes the need for ultra-high throughput, low latency, high reliability, and minimal power consumption in future applications, necessitating advanced technologies like cloud computing, optical wireless networks, and THz spectrum communications. Additionally, advanced AI techniques and algorithms will be essential for managing large datasets generated by future applications.

REFERENCES

Abbas, Ahmed, Shah, Omar, & Park. (n.d.). Investigating the applications of AI in cyber security. Academic Press.

Ali, S., Abdullah, , Armand, T. P. T., Athar, A., Hussain, A., Ali, M., Yaseen, M., Joo, M.-I., & Kim, H.-C. (2023). Metaverse in healthcare integrated with explainable ai and blockchain: Enabling immersiveness, ensuring trust, and providing patient data security. *Sensors (Basel)*, 23(2), 565. DOI:10.3390/s23020565 PMID:36679361

Alraih, S., Shayea, I., Behjati, M., Nordin, R., Abdullah, N. F., Abu-Samah, A., & Nandi, D. (2022). Revolution or evolution? Technical requirements and considerations towards 6G mobile communications. *Sensors (Basel)*, 22(3), 762. DOI:10.3390/s22030762 PMID:35161509

Attaallah, A., Alsuhabi, H., Shukla, S., Kumar, R., Gupta, B. K., & Khan, R. A. (2022). Analyzing the Big Data Security Through a Unified Decision-Making Approach. *Intelligent Automation & Soft Computing*, 32(2), 1071–1088. DOI:10.32604/iasc.2022.022569

Bak, M., Madai, V. I., Fritzsche, M. C., Mayrhofer, M. T., & McLennan, S. (2022). You can't have AI both ways: Balancing health data privacy and access fairly. *Frontiers in Genetics*, 13, 1490. DOI:10.3389/fgene.2022.929453 PMID:35769991

Bharadiya, J. P. (2023). AI-Driven Security: How Machine Learning Will Shape the Future of Cybersecurity and Web 3.0. *American Journal of Neural Networks and Applications*, 9(1), 1–7.

Blasch, Sung, Nguyen, Daniel, & Mason. (n.d.). Using Artificial Intelligence Strategies in National Security and Safety Standards. Academic Press.

Challita, U., Ryden, H., & Tullberg, H. (2020). When machine learning meets wireless cellular networks: Deployment, challenges, and applications. *IEEE Communications Magazine*, 58(6), 12–18. DOI:10.1109/MCOM.001.1900664

Chen, Y. (2020). IoT, cloud, big data and AI in interdisciplinary domains. *Simulation Modelling Practice and Theory*, 102, 102070. DOI:10.1016/j.simpat.2020.102070

Dai, D., & Boroomand, S. (2021). A review of artificial intelligence to enhance the security of big data systems: State-of-art, methodologies, applications, and challenges. *Archives of Computational Methods in Engineering*, 1–19.

Das, R., & Sandhane, R. (2021, July). Artificial intelligence in cyber security. In Journal of Physics: Conference Series (Vol. 1964, No. 4, p. 042072). IOP Publishing. DOI:10.1088/1742-6596/1964/4/042072

de Moraes Rossetto, A. G., Sega, C., & Leithardt, V. R. Q. (2022). An Architecture for Managing Data Privacy in Healthcare with Blockchain. *Sensors (Basel)*, 22(21), 8292. DOI:10.3390/s22218292 PMID:36365991

Feng, X., Feng, Y., & Dawam, E. S. (2020). Artificial Intelligence Cyber Security Strategy. *2020 IEEE Intl Conf on Dependable, Autonomic and Secure Computing, Intl Conf on Pervasive Intelligence and Computing, Intl Conf on Cloud and Big Data Computing, Intl Conf on Cyber Science and Technology Congress (DASC/PiCom/CBDCom/CyberSciTech)*. IEEE.

Ghillani, D. (2022). Deep learning and artificial intelligence framework to improve the cyber security. *Authorea Preprints*. DOI:10.22541/au.166379475.54266021/v1

Gupta, C., Johri, I., Srinivasan, K., Hu, Y. C., Qaisar, S. M., & Huang, K. Y. (2022). A systematic review on machine learning and deep learning models for electronic information security in mobile networks. *Sensors (Basel)*, 22(5). DOI:10.3390/s22052017 PMID:35271163

Gupta, R., Tanwar, S., Tyagi, S., & Kumar, N. (2020). Machine learning models for secure data analytics: A taxonomy and threat model. *Computer Communications*, 153, 406–440. DOI:10.1016/j.comcom.2020.02.008

Je, D., Jung, J., & Choi, S. (2021). Toward 6G security: Technology trends, threats, and solutions. *IEEE Communications Standards Magazine*, 5(3), 64–71. DOI:10.1109/MCOMSTD.011.2000065

Kavitha, S., Bora, A., Naved, M., Raj, K. B., & Singh, B. R. N. (2021). An internet of things for data security in cloud using artificial intelligence. *International Journal of Grid and Distributed Computing*, 14(1), 1257–1275.

Khan, B., Fatima, H., Qureshi, A., Kumar, S., Hanan, A., Hussain, J., & Abdullah, S. (2023). Drawbacks of artificial intelligence and their potential solutions in the healthcare sector. *Biomedical Materials & Devices*, 1(2), 1–8. DOI:10.1007/s44174-023-00063-2 PMID:36785697

Krichen, M. (2023). Strengthening the security of smart contracts through the power of artificial intelligence. *Computers*, 12(5), 107. DOI:10.3390/computers12050107

Letafati, M., & Otoum, S. (2023). On the privacy and security for e-health services in the metaverse: An overview. *Ad Hoc Networks*, 150, 103262. DOI:10.1016/j.adhoc.2023.103262

Li, W., Su, Z., Li, R., Zhang, K., & Wang, Y. (2020). Blockchain-based data security for artificial intelligence applications in 6G networks. *IEEE Network*, 34(6), 31–37. DOI:10.1109/MNET.021.1900629

Li, W., Su, Z., Li, R., Zhang, K., & Wang, Y. (2020). Blockchain-based data security for artificial intelligence applications in 6G networks. *IEEE Network*, 34(6), 31–37. DOI:10.1109/MNET.021.1900629

Liu, X., Ahmad, S. F., Anser, M. K., Ke, J., Irshad, M., Ul-Haq, J., & Abbas, S. (2022). Cyber security threats: A never-ending challenge for e-commerce. *Frontiers in Psychology*, 13, 927398. DOI:10.3389/fpsyg.2022.927398 PMID:36337532

Meurisch, C., & Mühlhäuser, M. (2021). Data protection in AI services: A survey. *ACM Computing Surveys*, 54(2), 1–38. DOI:10.1145/3440754

Mishra, S. (2023). Exploring the Impact of AI-Based Cyber Security Financial Sector Management. *Applied Sciences (Basel, Switzerland)*, 13(10), 5875. DOI:10.3390/app13105875

Mohammadi, M., & Sohn, I. (2023). *AI based energy harvesting security methods: A survey*. ICT Express. DOI:10.1016/j.icte.2023.06.002

Mohammed, I. A. (2020). Artificial intelligence for cybersecurity: A systematic mapping of literature. *Artificial Intelligence*, 7(9), 1–5.

Mohanta, B. K., Jena, D., Satapathy, U., & Patnaik, S. (2020). Survey on IoT security: Challenges and solution using machine learning, artificial intelligence and blockchain technology. *Internet of Things : Engineering Cyber Physical Human Systems*, 11, 100227. DOI:10.1016/j.iot.2020.100227

Muneer, S. M., Alvi, M. B., & Farrakh, A. (2023). Cyber Security Event Detection Using Machine Learning Technique. *International Journal of Computational and Innovative Sciences*, 2(2), 42–46.

Pons & Ozkaya. (n.d.). Priority Quality Attributes for Engineering AI-enabled Systems. Academic Press.

Porambag, Gur, Osorio, Liyanage, & Ylianttila. (n.d.). 6G Security Challenges and Potential Solutions. Centre for Wireless Communications, University of Oulu.

Porambage, Kumar, Liyanage, Partala, Loven, Ylianttila, & Seppanen. (n.d.). Comparison between AI for edge security and security for edge AI through Sec-EdgeAI at Oulu.fi. University of Oulu.

Raimundo, R., & Rosário, A. (2021). The impact of artificial intelligence on Data System Security: A literature review. *Sensors (Basel)*, 21(21), 7029. DOI:10.3390/s21217029 PMID:34770336

Ramasamy, S. S., Vijayalakshmi, S., Gayathri, S. P., & Chakpitak, N. (2021). Data Security Essentials for the Convergence of Blockchain, AI, and IoT. In Convergence of Blockchain, AI, and IoT (pp. 137-156). CRC Press.

Rasti, M., Taskou, S. K., Tabassum, H., & Hossain, E. (2021). Evolution toward 6G wireless networks: A resource management perspective. arXiv preprint arXiv:2108.06527.

Roy, P., Chadrasekaran, J., Lanus, E., Freeman, L., & Werner, J. (2023). A Survey of Data Security: Practices from Cybersecurity and Challenges of Machine Learning. arXiv preprint arXiv:2310.04513.

Safdar, N. M., Banja, J. D., & Meltzer, C. C. (2020). Ethical considerations in artificial intelligence. *European Journal of Radiology*, 122, 10876. DOI:10.1016/j.ejrad.2019.108768 PMID:31786504

Sarker, I. H. (2021). CyberLearning: Effectiveness analysis of machine learning security modeling to detect cyber-anomalies and multi-attacks. *Internet of Things: Engineering Cyber Physical Human Systems*, 14, 100393. DOI:10.1016/j.iot.2021.100393

Sarker, I. H., Furhad, M. H., & Nowrozy, R. (2021). Ai-driven cybersecurity: An overview, security intelligence modeling and research directions. *SN Computer Science*, 2(3), 1–18. DOI:10.1007/s42979-021-00557-0

Saura, J. R., Ribeiro-Soriano, D., & Palacios-Marqués, D. (2022). Assessing behavioral data science privacy issues in government artificial intelligence deployment. *Government Information Quarterly*, 39(4), 101679. DOI:10.1016/j.giq.2022.101679

Seh, A. H., Al-Amri, J. F., Subahi, A. F., Agrawal, A., Kumar, R., & Khan, R. A. (2021). Machine learning based framework for maintaining privacy of healthcare data. *Intelligent Automation & Soft Computing*, 29, 697–712. DOI:10.32604/iasc.2021.018048

Shankar, S. P., Supriya, M. S., Varadam, D., Kumar, M., Gupta, H., & Saha, R. (2023). A comprehensive study on algorithms and applications of artificial intelligence in diagnosis and prognosis: AI for healthcare. In Digital Twins and Healthcare: Trends, Techniques, and Challenges (pp. 35-54). IGI Global.

Shankar, S. P., Varadam, D., Agrawal, H., & Naresh, E. (2022). Blockchain for IoT and Big Data Applications: A Comprehensive Survey on Security Issues. Advances in Industry 4.0. *Concepts and Applications*, 5, 65.

Shankar, S. P., Varadam, D., Bharadwaj, A., Dayananda, S., Agrawal, S., & Jha, A. (2023). Enhancing DevOps Using Intelligent Techniques: Application of Artificial Intelligence and Machine Learning Techniques to DevOps. In Cases on Enhancing Business Sustainability Through Knowledge Management Systems (pp. 251-274). IGI Global.

Shankar, S. P., Varadam, D., Bharadwaj, A., Saxena, T., Mohta, R., & Shankar, A. (2023). Artificial Intelligence for Defence: A Comprehensive Study on Applying AI for the Airforce, Navy, and Army. In Emerging Trends, Techniques, and Applications in Geospatial Data Science (pp. 244-262). IGI Global.

Simoes, M., Elmusrati, M., Vartiainen, T., Mekkanen, M., Karimi, M., Diaba, S., . . . Lopes, W. (2023). Enhancing data security against cyberattacks in artificial intelligence based smartgrid systems with crypto agility. arXiv preprint arXiv:2305.11652.

Siriwardhana, Y., Porambage, P., Liyanage, M., & Ylianttila, M. (2021, June). AI and 6G security: Opportunities and challenges. In 2021 Joint European Conference on Networks and Communications & 6G Summit (EuCNC/6G Summit) (pp. 616-621). IEEE.

Sokol. (n.d.). Counterfactual Explanations of ML Predictions: Opportunities and Challenges for AI Safety. Academic Press.

Solyman, A. A. A., & Yahya, K. (2022). Evolution of wireless communication networks: From 1G to 6G and future perspective. *Iranian Journal of Electrical and Computer Engineering*, 12(4), 3943.

Srivastava, S., Benny, B., Ma'am, M. P. G., & Ma'am, N. B. (2021). *Artificial Intelligence (AI) and It's Application in Cyber Security (No. 5791)*. EasyChair.

Tolani & Tolani. (n.d.). Use of artificial intelligence in cyber defence. Academic Press.

Ukwandu, E., Ben-Farah, M. A., Hindy, H., Bures, M., Atkinson, R., Tachtatzis, C., Andonovic, I., & Bellekens, X. (2022). Cyber-security challenges in aviation industry: A review of current and future trends. *Information (Basel)*, 13(3), 146. DOI:10.3390/info13030146

Wang, Dong, Wang, & Yin. (n.d.). Protecting data using AI and Blockchain. Academic Press.

Wang, C. N., Yang, F. C., Vo, N. T., & Nguyen, V. T. T. (2022). Wireless communications for data security: Efficiency assessment of cybersecurity industry—A promising application for UAVs. *Drones (Basel)*, 6(11), 363. DOI:10.3390/drones6110363

Wazid, M., Das, A. K., Chamola, V., & Park, Y. (2022). Uniting cyber security and machine learning: Advantages, challenges and future research. *ICT Express*, 8(3), 313–321. DOI:10.1016/j.icte.2022.04.007

Wu, H., Han, H., Wang, X., & Sun, S. (2020). Research on artificial intelligence enhancing internet of things security: A survey. *IEEE Access : Practical Innovations, Open Solutions*, 8, 153826–153848. DOI:10.1109/ACCESS.2020.3018170

Xue, M., Yuan, C., Wu, H., Zhang, Y., & Liu, W. (2020). Machine learning security: Threats, countermeasures, and evaluations. *IEEE Access : Practical Innovations, Open Solutions*, 8, 8. DOI:10.1109/ACCESS.2020.2987435

Yang, Elisa, & Eliot. (n.d.). Providing privacy and securing E-government in smart cities. Department of Computer and Information Sciences, Northumbria University.

Yang, Q., Liu, Y., Chen, T., & Tong, Y. (n.d.). The concept and applications of federated machine learning. *ACM Transactions on Intelligent Systems and Technology*, 10(2), 12.

Zewdie, T. G., & Girma, A. (2020). IoT security and the role of ai/ml to combat emerging cyber threats in cloud computing environment. *Issues in Information Systems*, 21, 4.

Chapter 6
Blockchain and Generative AI for Securing Distributed Systems

Humaira Ashraf

https://orcid.org/0000-0001-5067-3172

Taylor's University, Malaysia

Uswa Ihsan

International Islamic University, Islamabad, Pakistan

Ata Ullah

Independent Researcher, Pakistan

Sayan Kumar Ray

Taylor's University, Malaysia

Navid Ali Khan

Taylor's University, Malaysia

ABSTRACT

Blockchain and AI have revolutionized how distributed systems can work. Combining blockchain and generative ai to enhance data integrity and cooperation in the treacherous field may find innovative ways blockchain and generative AI can develop distributed systems in terms of data integrity, transparency, scalability, security, cooperation, and decision-making. Through an investigation, it is understood how blockchain secures AI models, makes them more transparent and traceable, decen-

DOI: 10.4018/979-8-3693-5415-5.ch006

tralizes training, and makes distributed models more efficient and scalable. Examples from real applications across worlds will guide how blockchain and generative AIs are used in fields such as health, finance, film, supply chains, and electrical transmission. As a result, different sources' knowledge is adopted as proven to propel the process of supplementing blockchain and AI towards a future of intelligent, flexible, and secure distributed systems.

1. INTRODUCTION

A blockchain is a type of computer network that keeps a record of all transactions. Currently, the technology is mostly used to make smart contracts, cryptocurrencies like Bitcoin, and nonfungible tokens (NFT) like digital artworks.

Figure 1. Blockchain Working (GeeksforGeeks, n.d.)

tokens   (NFT)   like   digital   artworks.

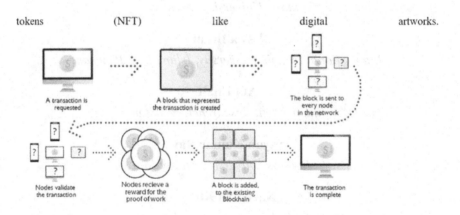

Needless to say that technology is changing rapidly, and we are introduced to new things almost every week. AI and blockchain are disrupting or set to disrupt every facet of business and life. These technologies will revolutionize everything from entertainment to health. However, whereas each technology is sufficient on its own, a group of new and emerging systems may provide incredible, transformative possibilities and benefits. Blockchain is a stable, decentralized database-sharing technology, while generative AI enables machines to learn and be creative. Merging of the two produces intelligent, flexible, and secure systems. Many firms desire to use these solutions to diminish expenses, enhance efficiency, and halt data breaches. Individual technologies progresses, but when more technologies combine, the impacts on enterprise and business are more beneficial.

AI is a new technology that can be a game-changer in the way customers relate with businesses. It can also result in significant cost and income savings. For the AI solutions to work effectively, data is necessary. Companies need to ensure they meet the completeness and the variability, fairness, and sufficiency of the information (Humayun et al., 2022; Humayun et al., 2020; Kumar et al., 2021). When a company makes the choice to use AI, I tell them to develop a robust data strategy and define data requirements, acquire or gather relevant high-quality data, and store, manage, and secure it.

A digital landscape, on the other hand, could be made possible by generative AI and blockchain technology. Using blockchain is one way to maintain the safety of the data used in AI models. Utilizing blockchain's distributed ledger technologies can help improve support for your data's vulnerability (Alferidah & Jhanji, 2020; Hanif et al., 2022; Ray et al., 2012; Yazdi et al., 2014). This added protection helps minimize the risks of unauthorized access, adjustment, and compromise while also boosting the accuracy and trustworthiness of AI outputs. This is how blockchain accomplishes it:

1. **immortal information storage**: blockchain operates by storing data in a network of nodes without becoming — or owned — by anyone. Each cube includes a mystery that safeguards it from being tampered with or modified.
   I. **Decentralization:** Unlike traditional databases, blockchain does not have a single point of control. Information is stored on several nodes, making the blockchain resistant to possible attacks or failures. Even if a few nodes are down, data is secure because multiple copies of it exist in the network.
2. **Security through Cryptography:** Blockchain relies on cryptography to secure data. Later, when you do something or enter data, It is encrypted and connected to what came before. As a result, you get a chain that can never be broken. This type of encryption has correct and secure data. To allow only certain people to view data that is stored on blockchain, it uses public-private key pairs.
   II. **Protection against Unauthorized Access:** Since it is almost impossible to access information with blockchain technology, To modify data on a blockchain network, you must attack many nodes at once, which is incredibly risky. Still, that is beside the point.
   III. **Enhanced Dependability and Precision:** Due to strong security, generative AI models can utilize actual, good data. AI findings come out more dependable because the security is robust (Ray et al., 2013). Data that is kept protected and scrutinize can be applied to reliable and precise AI models.

Figure 2. Benefits of Interlinking (Blockchain and AI) (Coinmonks, n.d.)

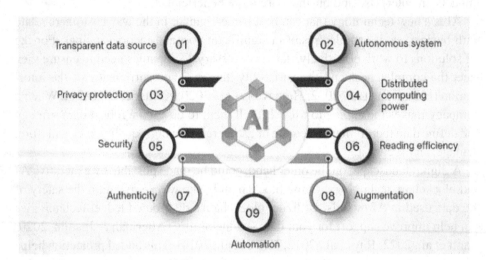

2. MAINTAINING PROVENANCE AND TRANSPARENCY

Ensuring transparency and traceability of the data that are employed to train these models is a key point, yet it remains difficult. It is why blockchain technology is used as a potential solution. Immutable blockchains generate an unambiguous, easily traceable history, which identifies the provenance of the utilized data (Shah, Jhanjhi, & Ray, 2024; Shah, Jhanjhi, & Ray, 2024) . It means that users and other interested parties can validate the credibility and provenience of the used information, helping make better generative AI outcomes.

Here's how blockchain technology addresses this challenge in a more human-friendly way:

I. **Immutable Record Keeping:** Blockchains are digital ledgers that can't be changed. Once data is recorded, it stays put, ensuring a clear history of transactions or data entries. This feature is very safe and transparent, which is important for applications where trust is important.
II. **Auditable Trail:** With blockchain's immutable ledger technology, we can keep a record of what happened. This trail lets users follow the data's origin, processing, and use throughout its lifecycle. It's like having a history book for your data, making sure it's accurate and reliable.

III. **Transparency for Verification:** Blockchain's transparency allows users to validate the accuracy and reliability of data used in generative AI models. Access to the complete history of data transactions stored on the blockchain ensures data integrity. Users can trust the results produced by AI models because they know the data is authentic and reliable.

IV. **Enhanced Dependability of AI Results:** By using blockchain technology, we can keep track of data and make AI results more reliable. Users can trust AI-generated outputs because they're based on real data sources.

2.1. Encouraging Distributed Training and Implementation

Blockchain's decentralized design opens up new avenues for developing and deploying generative AI models (Jabeen et al., 2022; Mushtaq et al., 2023; Ray et al., 2015; Ullah et al., 2021). By leveraging blockchain's distributed nature, training procedures can span across a network of nodes, reducing reliance on centralized servers and data centers. This decentralized approach enhances scalability, resource efficiency, and participant involvement, making generative AI more accessible and economically viable (Alex et al., 2022; Ashraf et al., 2023; Ashraf ct al., 2019; Dogra et al., 2022).

Here's a breakdown of how blockchain facilitates this process in a more human-friendly way:

I. **Decentralized Training**: Instead of relying solely on centralized servers and data centers, blockchain's decentralized architecture enables training to take place across a network of nodes. This distributed approach utilizes the computational power of multiple nodes, allowing for parallel processing and faster model training.

II. **Reduced Dependency on Centralized Infrastructure:** Traditional centralized systems often face limitations in scalability and resource availability. However, blockchain's distributed architecture allows for a more efficient utilization of resources across the network, reducing risks associated with centralized infrastructure constraints.

III. **Improved Scalability and Resource Efficiency:** Distributed training on a blockchain platform offers better scalability and resource efficiency compared to centralized approaches. By dynamically allocating computational resources based on demand, blockchain ensures optimal resource utilization, leading to faster training times and improved scalability of generative AI models.

IV. **Increased Participant Involvement:** Blockchain's decentralized approach encourages more participation in the development and implementation of generative AI models. Nodes in the network can actively contribute computational resources to the training process, making AI development more accessible to everyone. This increased participation fosters collaboration and innovation within the AI community, resulting in the creation of more diverse and robust models.

V. **Wider Accessibility and Economic Viability:** By distributing resources, blockchain technology is making generative AI training more accessible and cost-effective. This decentralized approach reduces barriers to entry for AI development, allowing individuals and organizations with limited resources to participate in model training. The democratization of AI development promotes innovation and competition, ultimately leading to cost reduction and making generative AI more economically feasible.

3. IMPROVING EFFICIENCY AND SCALABILITY

Generative AI often demands large training datasets and considerable processing power. Yet, blockchain technology offers a scalable solution capable of meeting these needs. By tapping into the distributed computing power of blockchain, generative AI models can efficiently handle massive datasets, speeding up both training and inference operations. This scalability leads to faster processing times, improved performance, and creates new opportunities for generative AI applications (Rajmohan et al., 2020; Ravi et al., 2021; Shah, Jhanjhi, & Ray, 2024).

Here's a simplified breakdown of how blockchain achieves this:

I. **Scalability for Large Datasets:** Generative AI models typically require substantial datasets and processing power. However, blockchain technology has the potential to provide the scalability and flexibility needed to handle these requirements efficiently. With its distributed architecture, blockchain can enable the efficient management of massive datasets, avoiding the bottlenecks often encountered in centralized systems (Julie et al., 2020; Singh et al., 2020).

II. **Utilization of Distributed Computing Power:** The decentralized nature of blockchain technology allows for the utilization of distributed computing power across the network. This approach enables generative AI models to leverage the combined computational resources of multiple nodes within the blockchain network. Consequently, training and inference operations can be completed more quickly, leading to faster processing times and improved performance.

III. **Expedited Training and Inference Operations:** Distributed computing power can speed up both training and inference operations of generative AI models. With blockchain technology, tasks can be executed concurrently across multiple nodes, significantly reducing the time required for generating AI outputs and training. This acceleration in processing enhances overall efficiency and enables real-time or near-real-time applications of generative AI.

IV. **Improved Performance:** Blockchain technology's scalability accelerates processing and improves the performance of generative AI models. These models benefit from access to a larger pool of computational resources, allowing algorithms to achieve higher accuracy and produce more sophisticated outputs. This improved performance contributes to the effectiveness and reliability of generative AI applications across various domains.

V. **Opportunities for New Applications:** Blockchain technology has the potential to transform generative AI applications by efficiently managing vast datasets and expediting processing. This capability opens up innovative solutions in areas such as image generation, natural language processing, and predictive modeling, where complex algorithms are needed to address challenges effectively.

4. ENHANCING COOPERATION AND INTEROPERABILITY

Blockchain technology helps people communicate with AI models. It makes it easy to share data and work together. This interoperability not only encourages innovation but also improves the precision and efficiency of generative AI systems. Let's simplify how blockchain facilitates this:

I. **Standardized Data Sharing:** Blockchain protocols and smart contracts build trust and collaboration among stakeholders by allowing secure data exchange. This standard approach makes data sharing transparent and reliable, which makes for a good environment for cooperation

II. **Facilitating Cooperation and Integration:** Blockchain establishes a common platform for communication and collaboration, simplifying cooperation and integration between different parties and generative AI models. By providing a standardized approach to data exchange, blockchain enables seamless interaction and interoperability, allowing diverse models to collaborate effectively towards common objectives.

III. **Utilizing Diverse Datasets and Expertise:** Blockchain interoperability enables the use of diverse datasets and expertise from multiple sources. Blockchain gives people access to a lot of data and skills, which encourages innovation and creativity in AI development. Collaboration among different stakeholders can lead to better AI models.

IV. **Encouraging Innovation:** Blockchain's interoperability promotes innovation in generative AI by allowing people to share ideas, data, and resources. This helps people work together and makes it easier to start, which makes AI better.

V. **Improving Accuracy and Performance:** Blockchain can help AI systems work better by allowing people to work together and communicate with each other. When resources and expertise are pooled, AI models can use different datasets and insights to make their outputs more accurate and reliable.

5. ARTIFICIAL INTELLIGENCE AT THE LEADING EDGE: GENERATIVE ROBOTICS

Generative AI is more advanced than traditional AI models. Generative AI can create new data that wasn't in the training set. This innovation allows more complex tasks like autonomous decision-making, advanced analytics, and content creation. Deep learning can make machines think like humans, which could make machines better than they already are...

Here's an elaboration on its key points:

I. **Advancement Beyond Traditional AI Models:** Generative robotics is a big step up from traditional AI models. Conventional AI uses existing data to make predictions or judgments, but generative AI can create new data that was not part of the original training set. This ability allows us to tackle tasks that require autonomous decision-making, advanced analytics, and creative content creation.

II. **Creation of New Data:** Generative AI's ability to create new data sets it apart from other AI approaches. This technology lets robots and AI systems respond to changing environments in real-time. This ability is important for tasks like navigating unpredictable environments, problem-solving, and responding to unexpected events.

III. **Facilitating Autonomous Decision-Making:** Generative robotics allows AI systems to make autonomous decisions based on the generated data. Unlike rule-based systems that follow predefined instructions, generative AI can analyze the current context and create appropriate responses or actions on its own. This ability is very useful for things that need quick decisions, like cars that drive themselves, robots that work, and smart factories.

IV. **Enabling Advanced Analytics**: Generative AI creates data samples that are diverse and realistic. These examples of data can be used to teach AI models better, find hidden patterns, and make better predictions. With generative AI techniques, organizations can get deeper insights into complex datasets and make data-driven decisions with greater confidence.

V. **Empowering Content Creation**: Generative AI has the potential to transform content creation by automatically creating text, images, videos, and other multimedia content. Using advanced computer programs, generative AI can act like humans and make great, original content at a large scale. This ability is useful for many different industries like entertainment, advertising, and digital media.

VI. **Redefining Machine Capabilities**: Generative robotics, powered by deep learning and generative AI techniques, has the potential to redefine the limits of machine capabilities. By imitating human-like cognitive functions, such as creativity, imagination, and intuition, generative AI expands the scope of tasks that machines can perform autonomously. This paradigm shift heralds a new era of AI-driven innovation and automation across industries.

6. ENHANCED TRUSTWORTHINESS OF AI SYSTEMS THROUGH OPEN DATA TRAILS

More transparency and audibility are inherent to Generative AI models when they are implemented in a blockchain setting. Data integrity and traceability are critical in industries such as healthcare, where errors can have fatal consequences—increased accountability results from the blockchain's unchangeable recording of every decision or change made by the AI.

Here's a detailed explanation:

I. **Transparency and Auditability**: Using Generative AI models and blockchain technology together makes things easier to see and check. Blockchain's system keeps track of every transaction or change to the data in a way that cannot be changed and is easy to understand. This openness lets people know where the data used in AI models came from and when it was used, which helps people trust the decision-making process.

II. **Data Integrity and Traceability**: In industries like healthcare, where errors can have serious consequences, keeping data integrity and traceability is important. Using Generative AI models on a blockchain platform keeps data safe by using cryptographic hashing and decentralized storage. This makes sure that the information cannot be changed or changed, so it can be traced back to its source and how it was used.

III. **Increased Accountability**: Blockchain technology makes AI more accountable. This makes it easy for people involved to find out what went into the data, how the model was trained, and what the AI did. They can hold the people responsible for any mistakes or mistakes. This increased accountability encourages AI systems to follow ethical and regulatory standards, which in turn strengthens trust in AI systems.

IV. **Risk Mitigation in Critical Industries**: In industries like healthcare, finance, and autonomous vehicles, where AI decisions have a direct impact on human lives, it is crucial to have trustworthy AI models. Blockchain-enabled Generative AI can enhance trustworthiness by mitigating the risks of data manipulation, unauthorized access, and algorithmic biases. With the help of blockchain-based solutions, fatal errors or misinterpretations can be prevented, ensuring the safety and reliability of these critical industries

V. **Improved Decision-Making and Performance**: The use of open data trails in AI decision-making processes provides transparency and auditability. This transparency facilitates better comprehension and assessment of AI models, leading to improved decision-making and performance optimization. Furthermore, the capacity to trace data lineage enhances data quality and reliability, further enhancing AI system performance.

7. BOOSTING SECURITY PROCEDURES: AN ADAPTIVE DEFENSE SYSTEM

AI's predictive skills along with blockchain's immutability create a proactive security paradigm as opposed to a reactive one. Real-time network behavior analysis, vulnerability prediction, prompting prompt preventive action, and transparent blockchain recording of these occurrences are all made possible by generative AI algorithms.

a. Here's a detailed explanation of each aspect:

II. **Predictive Capabilities of AI**: AI's predictive skills enable the identification of potential security threats before they occur. By analyzing patterns in network behavior and identifying anomalies, AI algorithms can anticipate and predict security vulnerabilities or attacks in real time.

III. **Immutability of Blockchain**: Blockchain's immutability ensures that once data is recorded, it cannot be altered or tampered with retroactively. This feature provides a transparent and tamper-proof record of security-related events, such as network breaches or attempted attacks.

IV. **Proactive Security Paradigm**: The combination of AI's predictive capabilities and blockchain's immutability shifts security procedures from a reactive to a proactive paradigm. Instead of responding to security incidents after they occur, organizations can take preemptive measures based on AI predictions and insights, thereby mitigating risks before they escalate.

V. **Real-Time Network Behavior Analysis**: AI algorithms continuously analyze network behavior in real time, identifying suspicious activities or deviations from normal patterns. This proactive monitoring allows security teams to detect and respond to potential threats promptly, minimizing the impact of security breaches or attacks.

VI. **Vulnerability Prediction**: AI-powered security systems can predict potential vulnerabilities in networks, systems, or applications based on historical data and ongoing analysis. By identifying weak points in advance, organizations can proactively address security gaps and strengthen their defense mechanisms.

VII. **Prompt Preventive Action**: AI predictions prompt preventive action, enabling organizations to implement security measures or countermeasures in a timely manner. This proactive approach helps prevent security incidents or limit their impact, reducing the likelihood of data breaches, unauthorized access, or other cyber threats.

VIII. **Transparent Blockchain Recording**: The transparent recording of security-related events on the blockchain enhances accountability and transparency. Any security incidents, preventive actions, or responses are recorded on the blockchain in a tamper-proof manner, providing a clear audit trail for investigation and compliance purposes.

Uses of Blockchain and Generative AI in the Actual World

Through the analysis of medical photos and data, blockchain combined with generative AI allows for accurate disease diagnosis. Diagnostic capabilities are improved while patient privacy is protected by the blockchain's decentralized and secure structure.

(a) Healthcare:

1. **Enclitic:** Regenerative AI models that can recognize and diagnose illnesses are being created by the healthcare startup Enclitic utilizing blockchain technology. More accurate diagnoses than with conventional techniques can be achieved with their models, which are trained on extensive databases of medical pictures and data.
2. **Medi Ledger:** Tracking and exchanging medical records is made possible by the blockchain-based platform Medi Ledger. Using vast datasets of medical information, this platform can be utilized to train generative AI models, potentially increasing the models' precision.

(b) Finance:

Generative AI models, which are empowered by blockchain systems with databases of past financial information, allow for more accurate predictions in the financial markets. Therefore, it allows better risk management and investment decisions:

"Financial technologist Symbiont is developing a similar model, training its system on databases of past financial data to enable it forecast markets more efficiently than traditional methods.

Financial technology, R3, is a financial services platform built on the blockchain . This platform can be used to train generative AI models on big financial data sets, which could enhance the models' accuracy.

(c) Entertainment:

Generative AI models on the blockchain can be used to create new types of art and entertainment by learning from vast libraries of pre-existing material. This becomes an expressive potentiality for artists and authors.

1. **SingularityNET:** Users can develop, share, and sell AI models on this decentralized network. Using this platform, generative AI models capable of producing original works of art and entertainment can be developed.
2. **Veritaste:** A blockchain-based technology called Veritaste is used to confirm the legitimacy of digital content. By tracking the source of entertainment and art, this platform can aid in the fight against plagiarism and counterfeiting.

(d) Real-Time Monitoring and Self-Aware Decision-Making in the Supply Chain:

At the moment, there are already quite promising uses of blockchain technology for complete visibility and traceability of the supply chain from beginning to end. Generative AI can take this to the next level by producing judgments on the fly to handle unforeseen supply chain interruptions, optimize routes, and save money. For example, a smart contract could automatically execute new orders if new smart AI algorithms anticipate that specific composites will become scarce at some point. An adaptable and proactive supply chain network will need to be formed.

(e) Energy Sector: Distribution of Renewable Energy and Grid Management:

The proper and efficient interaction and delivery of energy can be ensured by blockchain and supported. A generative AI algorithm can optimize energy grid distributions in the real world, taking into account the factors of supply and demand as well as the outdoor temperature, among other things . Thus, an energy grid can be rebuilt on a scale that is far much more decentralized, unleashing new levels of efficiency, and the network can automatically adapt to conditions, accelerating the transition to renewable energy sources.

REFERENCES

Alex, S. A., Jhanjhi, N. Z., Humayun, M., Ibrahim, A. O., & Abulfaraj, A. W. (2022). Deep LSTM model for diabetes prediction with class balancing by SMOTE. *Electronics (Basel)*, 11(17), 2737. DOI:10.3390/electronics11172737

Alferidah, D. K., & Jhanjhi, N. Z. (2020, October). Cybersecurity impact over bigdata and iot growth. In *2020 International Conference on Computational Intelligence (ICCI)* (pp. 103-108). IEEE. DOI:10.1109/ICCI51257.2020.9247722

Ashraf, H., Hanif, M., Ihsan, U., Al-Quayed, F., Humayun, M., & Jhanjhi, N. Z. (2023, March). A Secure and Reliable Supply chain management approach integrated with IoT and Blockchain. In *2023 International Conference on Business Analytics for Technology and Security (ICBATS)* (pp. 1-9). IEEE. DOI:10.1109/ICBATS57792.2023.10111371

Ashraf, H., Ullah, A., Tahira, S., & Sher, M. (2019). Efficient Certificate Based One-pass Authentication Protocol for IMS. *Journal of Internet Technology*, 20(4), 1133–1143.

Coinmonks. (n.d.). Blockchain and AI: A powerful combination for fraud detection. Medium. https://medium.com/coinmonks/blockchain-and-ai-a-powerful-combination-for-fraud-detection-d8c3000c7360

Dogra, V., Verma, S., Verma, K., Jhanjhi, N. Z., Ghosh, U., & Le, D. N. (2022). A comparative analysis of machine learning models for banking news extraction by multiclass classification with imbalanced datasets of financial news: challenges and solutions.

Forbes Business Council. (2023, June 12). Converging generative AI with blockchain technology. Forbes. https://www.forbes.com/sites/forbesbusinesscouncil/2023/06/12/converging-generative-ai-with-blockchain-technology/?sh=420546cb6112

GeeksforGeeks. (n.d.). How does the blockchain work? https://www.geeksforgeeks.org/how-does-the-blockchain-work/

Hanif, M., Ashraf, H., Jalil, Z., Jhanjhi, N. Z., Humayun, M., Saeed, S., & Almuhaideb, A. M. (2022). AI-based wormhole attack detection techniques in wireless sensor networks. *Electronics (Basel)*, 11(15), 2324. DOI:10.3390/electronics11152324

Humayun, M., Ashfaq, F., Jhanjhi, N. Z., & Alsadun, M. K. (2022). Traffic management: Multi-scale vehicle detection in varying weather conditions using yolov4 and spatial pyramid pooling network. *Electronics (Basel)*, 11(17), 2748. DOI:10.3390/electronics11172748

Humayun, M., Jhanjhi, N., & Alamri, M. (2020). IoT-based Secure and Energy Efficient scheme for E-health applications. *Indian Journal of Science and Technology*, 13(28), 2833–2848. DOI:10.17485/IJST/v13i28.861

Jabeen, T., Jabeen, I., Ashraf, H., Jhanjhi, N., Mamoona, H., Mehedi, M., & Sultan, A. (2022). A monte carlo based COVID-19 detection framework for smart healthcare. *Computers, Materials & Continua*, 70(2), 2365–2380. DOI:10.32604/cmc.2022.020016

Julie, E. G., Nayahi, J. J. V., & Jhanjhi, N. Z. (Eds.). (2020). *Blockchain Technology: Fundamentals, Applications, and Case Studies*. CRC Press.

KPMG. (2023). Blockchain + artificial intelligence =? [Blog post]. https://kpmg.com/us/en/articles/2023/blockchain-artificial-intelligence.html

Kumar, M. S., Vimal, S., Jhanjhi, N. Z., Dhanabalan, S. S., & Alhumyani, H. A. (2021). Blockchain based peer to peer communication in autonomous drone operation. *Energy Reports*, 7, 7925–7939. DOI:10.1016/j.egyr.2021.08.073

Mushtaq, M., Ullah, A., Ashraf, H., Jhanjhi, N. Z., Masud, M., Alqhatani, A., & Alnfiai, M. M. (2023). Anonymity assurance using efficient pseudonym consumption in internet of vehicles. *Sensors (Basel)*, 23(11), 5217. DOI:10.3390/s23115217 PMID:37299944

Najmi, K. Y., AlZain, M. A., Masud, M., Jhanjhi, N. Z., Al-Amri, J., & Baz, M. (2023). A survey on security threats and countermeasures in IoT to achieve users confidentiality and reliability. *Materials Today: Proceedings*, 81, 377–382. DOI:10.1016/j.matpr.2021.03.417

Rajmohan, R., Kumar, T. A., Pavithra, M., & Sandhya, S. G. (2020). Blockchain: Next-generation technology for industry 4.0. In *Blockchain Technology* (pp. 177-198). CRC Press.

Ravi, N., Verma, S., Jhanjhi, N. Z., & Talib, M. N. (2021, August). Securing vanet using blockchain technology. *Journal of Physics: Conference Series*, 1979(1), 012035. DOI:10.1088/1742-6596/1979/1/012035

Ray, S. K., Liu, W., Sirisena, H., Ray, S. K., & Deka, D. (2013, November). An energy aware mobile-controlled handover method for natural disaster situations. In *2013 Australasian telecommunication networks and applications conference (ATNAC)* (pp. 130-135). IEEE. DOI:10.1109/ATNAC.2013.6705369

Ray, S. K., Sarkar, N. I., Deka, D., & Ray, S. K. (2015, January). LTE-advanced based handover mechanism for natural disaster situations. In *2015 International Conference on Information Networking (ICOIN)* (pp. 165-170). IEEE. DOI:10.1109/ICOIN.2015.7057876

Ray, S. K., Sirisena, H., & Deka, D. (2012, November). Fast and reliable target base station selection scheme for Mobile WiMAX handover. In *Australasian Telecommunication Networks and Applications Conference (ATNAC) 2012* (pp. 1-6). IEEE. DOI:10.1109/ATNAC.2012.6398054

Shah, I. A., Jhanjhi, N. Z., Amsaad, F., & Razaque, A. (2022). The role of cutting-edge technologies in industry 4.0. In *Cyber Security Applications for Industry 4.0* (pp. 97–109). Chapman and Hall/CRC. DOI:10.1201/9781003203087-4

Shah, I. A., Jhanjhi, N. Z., & Ray, S. K. (2024). Enabling Explainable AI in Cybersecurity Solutions. In *Advances in Explainable AI Applications for Smart Cities* (pp. 255–275). IGI Global. DOI:10.4018/978-1-6684-6361-1.ch009

Shah, I. A., Jhanjhi, N. Z., & Ray, S. K. (2024). Artificial Intelligence Applications in the Context of the Security Framework for the Logistics Industry. In *Advances in Explainable AI Applications for Smart Cities* (pp. 297–316). IGI Global. DOI:10.4018/978-1-6684-6361-1.ch011

Shah, I. A., Jhanjhi, N. Z., & Ray, S. K. (2024). IoT Devices in Drones: Security Issues and Future Challenges. In *Cybersecurity Issues and Challenges in the Drone Industry* (pp. 217-235). IGI Global.

Singh, A. P., Pradhan, N. R., Luhach, A. K., Agnihotri, S., Jhanjhi, N. Z., Verma, S., Kavita, , Ghosh, U., & Roy, D. S. (2020). A novel patient-centric architectural framework for blockchain-enabled healthcare applications. *IEEE Transactions on Industrial Informatics*, 17(8), 5779–5789. DOI:10.1109/TII.2020.3037889

Tripathi, M. (n.d.). How blockchain revolutionizes generative AI. LinkedIn. https://www.linkedin.com/pulse/how-blockchain-revolutionizes-generative-ai-mukul-tripathi/

Ullah, A., Azeem, M., Ashraf, H., Jhanjhi, N. Z., Nkenyereye, L., & Humayun, M. (2021). Secure critical data reclamation scheme for isolated clusters in IoT-enabled WSN. *IEEE Internet of Things Journal*, 9(4), 2669–2677. DOI:10.1109/JIOT.2021.3098635

Yazdi, E. T., Moravejosharieh, A., & Ray, S. K. (2014, February). Study of target tracking and handover in Mobile Wireless Sensor Network. In *The International Conference on Information Networking 2014 (ICOIN2014)* (pp. 120-125). IEEE. DOI:10.1109/ICOIN.2014.6799677

Chapter 7
Securing IoT Devices Using Generative AI Techniques

Azeem Khan
https://orcid.org/0000-0003-2742
-8034
University Islam Sultan Sharif Ali,
Brunei

Noor Jhanjhi
https://orcid.org/0000-0001-8116
-4733
TUSB, Malaysia

Ghassan Ahmed Ali Abdulhabeb
University Islam Sultan Sharif Ali,
Brunei

Sayan Kumar Ray
TUSB, Malaysia

Mustansar Ali Ghazanfar
University of East London, UK

Mamoona Humayun
Independent Researcher, UK

ABSTRACT

Generative artificial intelligence (GenAI) is a part of artificial intelligence which has the ability to generate content in various formats ranging from text to videos and images to audio formats. GenAI has the ability to inherently learn from large datasets and can produce results that can be of optimal use in case of cybersecurity. In the current digital landscape, we see a plethora of electronic gadgets connected to this seamless network of devices connected online. These seamless network of devices which were earlier unable to connect due to lack of ip addresses are now able to connect and are improving the quality of human life ranging from home appliances to health domain. From here we see emergence of smart networks which at one side is a boon but at the same time they have the risk of exploitation with unexpected cyberattacks. Hence, this chapter is an effort to highlight the issues concerning

DOI: 10.4018/979-8-3693-5415-5.ch007

cyberthreats and advice on how GenAI can be utilized to mitigate these risks. This chapter focused on applying generative AI to secured IoT devices. By discussing the core concepts of IoT security, such as device authentication and access control, the chapter demonstrated how the next-generation generative AI models, including GANs and VAEs, can boost anomaly detection for device security. The chapter also provided examples of real-life use cases to illustrate how generative AI can be used to optimize the energy grid, protect data privacy, and strengthen cybersecurity efforts. Additionally, this chapter presented the key issues related to ethical considerations pertaining to privacy, bias, and accountability in the development and deployment of responsible AI. Moreover, it introduced the legal aspects of privacy legislation, data protection, and cybersecurity compliance. Finally, the chapter outlined some of the future trends in generative AI for IoT security to name a few are enhanced threat detection, privacy-preserving multimedia processing, and secure communications. The chapter then encourages organizations to start using generative AI to enable systems to become proactive about IoT security and reduce the massive onslaught of cyber threats while navigating an ever-evolving digital landscape.

1. INTRODUCTION

The Internet of Things has brought exponential growth and transformation to our daily lives. Smart homes, connected cities, and everywhere in-between these ever-present devices drive data and, with it, innovation, and convenience (Khan, Jhanjhi, Haji, & Omar, 2024; Mughal, Ullah, Cheema, Yu, & Jhanjhi, 2024). However, due to the widespread and accessible devices, a large critical problem has been created: how to secure and protect an ever-growing number of devices. Because today's security tools are traditional and slow to react, these devices are opportunities for attackers. This chapter is an effort to investigate on how generative AI can change the levers of IoT security and elucidates generative AI by examining how GenAI models can aid in the development of responsive security measures. This developing model, possibly including responsive threat recognition, mitigation and creating synthetic data to secure development, validation, and holds promise for the future of IoT security (Marjani, Jhanjhi, Hashem, & Hajibeigy, 2021).

IoT digital landscape though comprises numerous advantages for improving quality of life but at the same time there is an inherent concern that these devices(Sayan K Ray, Pawlikowski, & Sirisena, 2009) are not devoid of challenges. The sections below enlighten on those intricacies with which the whole IoT digital landscape can be protected and put on sustainable development path (Khan, Jhanjhi, Humayun, & Ahmad, 2020; Ponnusamy, Humayun, Jhanjhi, Yichiet, & Almufareh, 2022).

- **Overview of the proliferation of IoT devices and the importance of securing them against cyber threats.**

The Internet of Things may be defined as objects that were previously only available in the physical world which are now assigned with an internet address (Ponnusamy, Sharma, Nadeem, Guan, & Jhanjhi, 2021). From thermostats and refrigerators to automobiles and clothing, a vast, interconnected system is being built. Analysts anticipate that within a few years, billions of these items will be in use, dramatically altering how people live, work, and engage with their surroundings. While this indicates a promising future with numerous automations and conveniences, it also raises new security risks (Shah, Jhanjhi, & Ray, 2024).

Unsecured IoT devices pave a way in for intruders to creep in this whole ecosystem, if this ecosystem in comprised of basic passwords, obsolete firmware, and nearly no security concern at all, all these loopholes can be exploited and attacked by hackers (Annadurai et al., 2022). Sometimes, this exploitation might destroy vital infrastructure managed by these inter-connected IoT devices. To name a few infrastructures are power plants and transportation systems, where these intruders can carry out a massive cyberattacks (Ashraf, Nawaz, & Jhanjhi, 2024). On the other hand, individuals and organisations alike should know the risk of managing such devices and protect personal information that is of critical nature. Hence, apart from the obvious benefits, we need to comprehend that IoT devices landscapes are still at risk, which can be mitigated with the introduction of GenAI in the IoT landscape (Gyamfi, Ansere, Kamal, Tariq, & Jurcut, 2023).

- **Introduction to generative AI techniques and their potential applications in IoT security.**

Generative Artificial Intelligence acronymized as GenAI can be defined as a type of artificial intelligence that can generate output in various formats such as text, image, audio, or video with the given input based on user request. The capability of generating new content is provided by generative models that work with the inbuilt algorithms that are inherent in its ecosystem. These models are trained with massive, large data sets to create new data. It has numerous applications in various domains. Cybersecurity is also an area where GenAI can be used to mitigate cyberattacks and secure the whole IoT ecosystem (Vemuri, Thaneeru, & Tatikonda, 2024).

In cybersecurity GenAI models has made it possible to continuously observe and easily identify suspicious behaviours of entities in IoT ecosystem, at a faster rate and with more accuracy in comparison to traditional cybersecurity procedures (Hossain, Ray, & Lota, 2020). To cite an example, for instance, based on the pattern of historical data, GenAI can predict potential cyber threats, allowing all interested parties involved in this ecosystem to establish early preventive measures to safeguard and protect their systems against potential cyberattacks. Moreover, GenAI can be used to generate synthetic data that fully mirrors real-world datasets to train machine learning models in cybersecurity applications without compromising data privacy (A. Almusaylim & Jhanjhi, 2020).

GenAI has various applications in the development of reliable cybersecurity solutions. GenAI in IoT security landscape can provide new opportunities for many organizations to enhance their security level at the same time helping all stakeholders involved to establish protective measures to safeguard interconnected entities in IoTs ecosystem, as compared to the past this feature was scanty (Zhihan, 2023).

- **Chapter contributions in 4 to 7 main points**

The chapter Securing IoT Devices Using GenAI Techniques has been a vital contribution to the realm of cybersecurity. Through an investigation into the relationship between GenAI and the security threats faced by IoT devices in today's world, this chapter provides a broad spectrum of understanding and practical application to a wide audience. This effort will serve as a basis for academic researchers, students, industry practitioners, policy makers and organizations interested in the latest strides in cybersecurity measures, and it will be a beacon of guidance for regulators involved in harnessing this technology. This chapter delves into the capabilities of generative AI and how such technologies could significantly transform and enhance IoT ecosystem security measures.

The chapter's contribution is significant, ranging from a thorough cybersecurity study, which will give academia a substantial body of knowledge to implement and investigate the GenAI impact on IoT security, to practical implications, which industry-based viewers will benefit from. Thus, the chapter can act as a hands-on guide to establish GenAI in IoT environments that can help to manage threats and optimize model abilities. Further lessons for industry practitioners will result in numerous policy-making impacts relating to the instructions to set GenAI in the IoT security frameworks and follow the regulation. As a final point, this chapter can act as an expert guideline on what GenAI can do and how it can be used to secure IoT devices. To conclude, the chapter will be a guideline for all the stakeholders who will manage to deal with the intricacies of the IoT devices' security in a massive digitally connected realm, which can pass them closer to a safer and more secure IoT digital landscape.

- **Chapter organization.**

In this comprehensive chapter entitled "Securing IoT Devices Using Generative AI Techniques," Section 1 introduces the emergence of advanced security solutions in the context of the rapidly expanding IoT domain, setting the stage for the detailed exploration of generative AI's role in IoT security. Section 2 lays the foundation by describing the essential security frameworks surrounding IoT devices, preparing readers for the complicated series of concepts that follow. In Section 3, the chapter advances the narrative by discussing numerous issues that address IoT security, e.g., the varying types of devices and advanced cyber threats. These are the contexts in which GenAI can be employed.

This discussion is followed by Sections 4–8, constitutes the technical core of the work. Section 4 introduces GenAI, framing it as a key solution for security issues in IoT and other domains and simulating cyberattacks to train efficient security models. Sections 5 and 6 probes into the details related to how GenAI can help detect intrusions and anomalies while authenticating devices and controlling their access to the cloud, having a firm grasp of peculiar patterns of occurrences.

Section 7 uncovers the processes and features of using GenAI for detecting and defending against malwares, while Section 8 explains the peculiarities of privacy-preserving techniques that balance higher security and functionality. In Sections 9–12, the discussion arrives at the conclusions first practically and then via forecasting. The sections reveal case studies in real-life conditions and the ethical and legal matters of implementing IoT security. In this regard, generative AI is depicted as an overarching concept thereof, which brings structure to real-life enactments of IoT security models that are liable to evolve in the changing context of cyber threats and serves as a useful guideline for academics, industrialists, and policymakers.

2. FUNDAMENTALS OF IOT SECURITY

Internet of Things acronymized as IoT, is defined as proliferation of interconnected devices embedded with sensors, connectivity, identification, actuators, and gateways (Humayun, Jhanjhi, Alsayat, & Ponnusamy, 2021). Sensors are one of the key components of this entire IoT ecosystem from where the data is sensed or generated, they are sources of data or also known as datapoints, this data is sent through the gateways which are basically provides data to be sent to cloud for storage, this entire ecosystem is connected to internet or other communication technologies with unique Internet Protocol(IP) addresses that represents identification of this interconnected devices and actuators are those components that are responsible to take act, hence to conclude the entire ecosystem of IoT is comprised of sensors, connectivity with unique addresses, gateways and actuators (Tomer & Sharma, 2022). As depicted in Figure 1, IoT digital landscape has varied diverse application domains, to name a few are from environment monitoring, home automation, healthcare, smart cities, transportation, logistics, retail, public sector services, consumer wearables to industrial automation.

Figure 1. Navigating IoT: A Comprehensive Overview (Farhan et al., 2017)

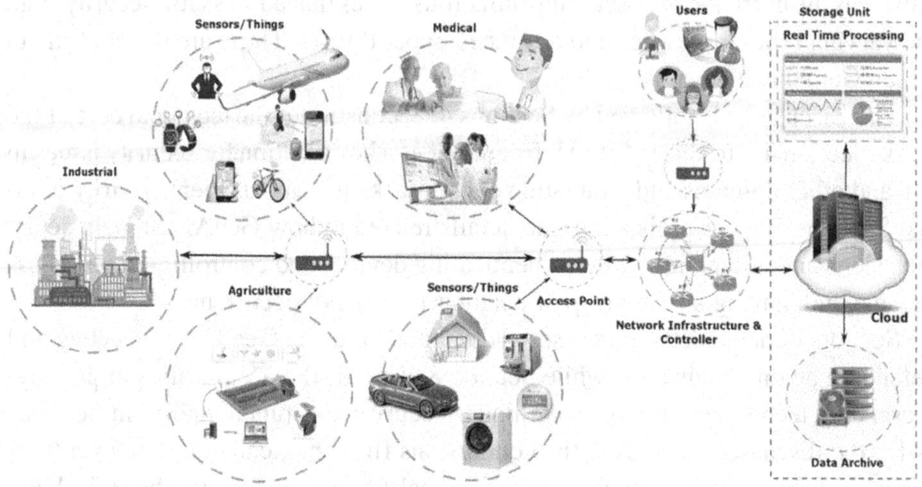

The foundation of broad spectrum of IoT security comprises systems and principles aimed to safeguard interconnected devices and networks that make up the entire IoT digital landscape. Securing interconnected IoT devices from cyberthreats involves protecting the devices integrity through secure data transmission, ensuring privacy and reliability (Alferidah & Jhanjhi, 2020; David & Eldon, 2022). These security mechanisms can be achieved through implementation of robust encryption methods like Advance Encryption Standards (AES), comprehensive risk management strategies to be adopted throughout organizations (Oh & Shon, 2023). Through the implementation of the above mechanisms, the entire ecosystem of IoT security designed will be adaptable and adequately addressed (Val, 2023). Apart from it this entire ecosystem also requires secure authentication protocols for authenticating device identification to prevent unauthorized access of devices in this interconnected plethora of network. Apart from it, another crucial aspect in this sphere is the deployment of regular software updates and patches to tackle new vulnerabilities and potential threats thereby enhancing security of the entire IoT digital landscape (Sayan Kumar Ray, Sinha, & Ray, 2015).

- **Explanation of core concepts in IoT security, including device authentication, access control, and data encryption.**

The security of IoT devices comprises a set of principles and practices aimed at protecting and safeguarding the plethora of interconnected devices and data within the Internet of Things ecosystem with minimal human intervention. Key core concepts in IoT security include:

- **Device Authentication**: As IoT ecosystem, comprises plethora of devices connected and this process will be in continuum with the increase of the ecosystem, since it constitutes numerous devices hence their authentication is required as sometimes this whole network is controlled remotely so the key challenge here will be to know whether the device belongs to specific network or not, necessitating a proper device authentication mechanism. The process includes validating the identity of IoT devices linked to the network and ensuring that solely authorized devices are able to connect to the network. To achieve this authentication of devices, various techniques like digital certificates, biometric authentication, and secure keys are employed for authenticating devices and deterring unauthorized access (Kumar et al., 2022).
- **Access Control:** The procedures governing access and overseeing the allocation of permissions and privileges to users and devices within an IoT network are encapsulated in this mechanism. It is accomplished through the implementation of the Role-based access control acronymised as RBAC, the second mechanism least privilege principle and the third multi-factor authentication. These strategies are commonly applied to confine unauthorized access (Figueroa-Lorenzo, Añorga, & Arrizabalaga, 2019).
- **Data Encryption:** The utilization of this technique is essential in safeguarding sensitive data exchanged between IoT devices and networks. To accomplish this Robust encryption algorithms such as Advanced Encryption Standards are required and they are utilized to encrypt data, thereby, ensuring confidentiality and integrity throughout the process of data transmission and storage (Saleh, Abdullah, & Saher, 2022).

Overview of Common Security Vulnerabilities and Attack Vectors Targeting IoT Devices

As discussed earlier, IoT devices are connected massively to an organizations network and are susceptible to various security vulnerabilities and attack vectors that can compromise their integrity and expose sensitive data. The security vulnerabilities that are most common in this whole ecosystem are as follows:

- **Default or weak passwords**: The Seamless network of interconnected IoT devices do often come with default or weak passwords, which make these interconnected devices vulnerable to brute force attacks and unauthorized access. Hence, implementing strong, unique passwords through policy enforcements are of paramount significance with which the security personnel can mitigate this risk and pave the way for smooth functioning of this whole ecosystem(joo Fong, Abdullah, Jhanjhi, & Supramaniam, 2019).
- **Insecure Network Services**: As discussed earlier, vulnerabilities in network services used by IoT devices can be exploited by attackers to gain unauthorized access or launch denial-of-service attacks. To regulate these inconsistencies and safeguard this whole ecosystem regular updating and securing network services are indispensable and through this mechanism only they can help prevent such vulnerabilities(Durakovskiy, Gavdan, Korsakov, & Melnikov, 2021).
- **Lack of Secure Update Mechanisms**: one of the critical aspects of these interconnected IoT devices is that if they lack secure update mechanisms then they are at risk of remaining vulnerable to known exploits or security flaws. Thus, to address Lack of secure update mechanisms, establishing over-the-air security (OTA) update processes is of paramount significance that can ensures that devices receive timely security patches thereby making the whole network robust(Tarek et al., 2022).
- **Insufficient Privacy Protection**: This mechanism elucidates that inadequate privacy measures can lead to unauthorized data collection and exposure of sensitive user information. Hence, implementing data anonymization, encryption, and privacy policies are indispensable to enhance privacy protection in IoT environments(Alex, Jhanjhi, & Ray, 2023).

Figure 2. Principles of Cybersecurity in IoT: Essential Insights (Padraig, 2016)

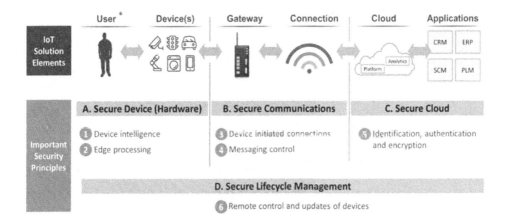

To sum up the above discussion as depicted in Figure 2, it can be concluded that the comprehension of these core concepts and vulnerabilities are essential for developing robust IoT security strategies that can mitigate risks, protect data integrity, and ensure the secure operation of interconnected devices in the IoT digital landscape.

3. CHALLENGES IN IOT SECURITY

As depicted in Figure 3, IoT security faces multifaceted challenges, including the vast diversity of devices and their widespread deployment, which complicates the enforcement of standard security protocols. Additionally, the constrained computational power of many IoT devices limits the feasibility of implementing sophisticated security measures, making them vulnerable to cyber-attacks. These challenges necessitate innovative solutions to safeguard the expanding IoT landscape (Essamlali, Nhaila, & El Khaili, 2024).

Figure 3. Complexities of IoT Security Challenges (Odeh & Abu Taleb, 2023)

Discussion on the Unique Challenges of Securing IoT Devices, Such as Resource Constraints, Heterogeneity, and Scale

As described in Figure 3, there are numerous unique challenges faced by IoT devices pertaining to small, medium, and large-scale organizations hence they need to bound themselves to the principles as depicted in the figure 3. Thus, Securing IoT devices presents a unique set of challenges due to the diverse nature of these interconnected devices. To name a few such key challenges include as described below:

1. **Resource Constraints**: As the name suggests, IoT devices are resource constrained and often operate with limited resources such as processing power, memory, and energy. Hence, securing these devices without compromising their functionality and efficiency poses a significant challenge, which can be addressed using state of the art solutions (Alkinani, Almazroi, & Khan, 2021).
2. **Heterogeneity**: As a matter of fact, the whole IoT digital landscape consists of devices not from the same manufacturer. Thus, the entire IoT ecosystem comprises a wide range of devices from different manufacturers with varying

communication protocols and security standards, hence, to ensuring interoperability and consistent security measures across heterogeneous devices is a complex task, which needs to be considered in this whole digital landscape (Lam, Mitra, Gondesen, & Yi, 2022).

Figure 4. Cybersecurity Principles for Enterprises, Businesses, and ISPs (Valkenburg & Bongiovanni, 2024)

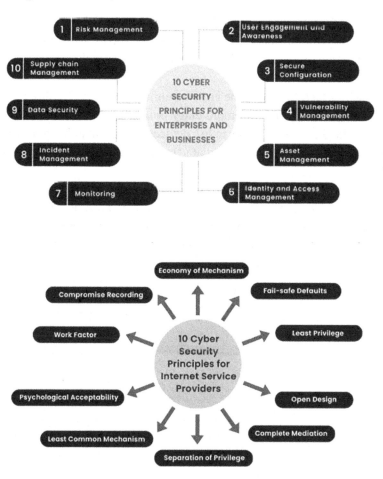

3. **Scale**: As we see the IoT digital ecosystem is on high rise as thousands of devices are being added to this landscape every now and then hence, the sheer scale of IoT deployments, involving thousands or even millions of devices, amplifies

the challenge of managing security at such a large scale, thus, securing a vast network of interconnected devices while maintaining efficiency and effectiveness is a major impediment which needs to be addressed for a sustainable ecosystem of this entire digital landscape (Naranjo, Espinoza, & Vivar, 2023).

Identification of Emerging Threats and Trends in IoT Security Landscape

There are numerous threats that are at the door of IoT digital landscape which is evident form Figure 6. Hence, as IoT technology evolves, new threats and trends emerge in the security landscape. Some notable trends and threats include:

1. **Increased Attack Surface**: The growing number of connected devices expands the attack surface, providing more entry points for cybercriminals to exploit. Attackers target vulnerabilities in IoT devices to gain unauthorized access, disrupt operations, or steal sensitive data (Imene Safer, Geert, Roel, & Wilfried, 2022).
2. **Ransomware Targeting IoT**: Ransomware attacks on IoT devices are on the rise, where hackers encrypt device data and demand ransom for decryption. This trend poses a significant threat to IoT security and highlights the need for robust encryption and backup strategies (McIntosh et al., 2023).

Figure 5. Navigating the Evolving Risks of IoT Security (Hatton, 2023)

3. **Supply Chain Attacks**: Cybercriminals target vulnerabilities in the supply chain of IoT devices to inject malware or compromise devices before they reach end-users. Securing the entire supply chain, from manufacturing to deployment, is crucial to prevent supply chain attacks (Khan, Jhanjhi, Ray, Amsaad, & Sujatha, 2024).

4. **Regulatory Compliance**: Increasing regulatory requirements and standards for IoT security, such as the General Data Protection Regulation (GDPR) which is a European Union law that regulates how companies collect, process, and protect the personal information of EU residents. and industry-specific regulations, add complexity to ensuring compliance. Organizations must navigate these regulations while implementing effective security measures to protect IoT devices and data.

As discussed above as there are numerous threats associated with IoT devices and it entire ecosystem hence, firm and consistent security mechanisms are inevitable to secure this seamless digital landscape thus by addressing these unique challenges and staying vigilant against emerging threats, organizations can enhance the security posture pertaining to IoT deployments and mitigate security risks associated with the dynamic IoT security landscape.

4. GENERATIVE AI TECHNIQUES FOR IOT SECURITY

GenAI makes use of neural networks to identify hidden patterns and structures from the existing data, thereby, it is able to create new content. To identify these hidden patterns GenAI can make use of the following techniques: viz Generative Adversary Network (GAN), transformers or Variational Autoencoders (VAEs) each underlies with distinct ability to generate new content. As depicted in Figure 7 it has various applications in diverse IoT domain where cybersecurity is considered to one of the crucial areas where it can be used at optimum level to have a robust security mechanism which can protect the entire IoT digital landscape. These Generative AI techniques stand at the forefront of addressing IoT security challenges as well by simulating cyber-attacks which can enhance system preparedness and resilience. These techniques enable the creation of dynamic security measures that can adapt to evolving threats, offering a proactive approach to safeguarding IoT ecosystems against sophisticated cyber-attacks (Mahmood, Akif, Ashraf, & Jhanjhi, 2024).

Figure 6. Creating Intelligent IoT Ecosystems with Generative AI (Wang et al., 2024)

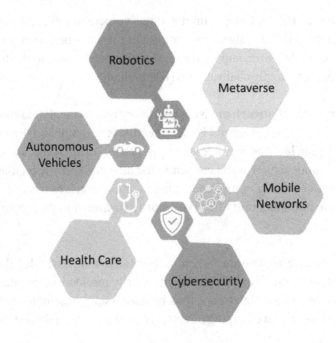

Introduction to Generative AI Models Suitable for IoT Security, Such as GANs, VAEs, and Deep Learning Architectures

GenAI is considered to be a tool to create new content, hence, Generative AI models, such as Generative Adversarial Networks (GANs), Variational Autoencoders (VAEs), and deep learning architectures, play a pivotal role in enhancing IoT security by leveraging advanced techniques for anomaly detection and threat identification. These models are tailored to address the unique challenges of securing interconnected IoT devices.

1. **Generative Adversarial Networks (GANs)**: GANs basically consist of two neural networks, namely the generator, and the discriminator, both these are engaged in a competitive game to generate realistic data samples, where one generates the content known as generator and the other one known as discriminator checks it with original and continuously provides feedback to generator unless and until desired level is reached (Hongbo, 2023; Rayeesa, Rumaan, & Kaiser, 2023). In IoT digital landscape security, GANs can be utilized to create synthetic data for training anomaly detection models and simulating potential cyber threats (Ashfaq, Jhanjhi, Khan, & Das, 2023).

2. **Variational Autoencoders (VAEs)**: The second technique is known as Variational Autoencoders (VAEs). These techniques are based on probabilistic models that learn the underlying structure of data and generate new data points based on this learned distribution (Asperti, Evangelista, & Loli Piccolomini, 2021). In the context of IoT security, VAEs can be employed to detect anomalies in device behaviour by reconstructing normal patterns and flagging deviations. Thereby providing secure and robust mechanisms for a sustainable IoT digital landscape.

3. **Deep Learning Architectures**: Deep learning architectures, including CNNs and RNNs, play a vital role in processing complicated IoT data and deriving meaningful insights. The utilization of these architectures for anomaly detection mechanisms will help easily identify patterns of malicious behaviour and improve device security through advanced pattern detection (Hosseini, Lu, Kamaraj, Slowikowski, & Venkatesh, 2020).

Explanation of How Generative AI Can Be Used to Detect Anomalies, Identify Malicious Behavior, and Enhance Device Security

GenAI models has the ability to determine cyberthreats in advance by applying machine learning techniques that help them advance in getting trained with datasets and apply it to diverse applications to name a few are discussed below:

1. **Anomaly Detection**: The Gen AI model can detect anomalies in the IoT system by learning the normal patterns of IoT device data and finding other types of data as anomalies; these anomalies are outliers of data that can represent a threat to the security system and can be used to secure security to all the connected devices (Konatham, Simra, Amsaad, Ibrahem, & Jhanjhi, 2024).
2. **Identification of Malicious Behaviour**: based on real-time data stream analysis from IoT devices, Gen AI could detect patterns specific to malicious behaviour, including unauthorized access or abnormalities of data transmission. Deep learning architecture and generative models were often employed for improving security practitioner's ability to identify the problem and eliminate the risk before it took effect (Bukhari, Agarwal, Koundal, & Zafar, 2023).
3. **Enhancement of Device Security**: The application of generative AI techniques can drastically enhance the device security because of real-time monitoring, threat detection technologies and response. An excellent model can train to create a safe authentication system, intrusion detection detection system, and IoT devices' security techniques (Ghelani, 2022).

Therefore, by utilizing generative AI capabilities such as GANs, VAEs, and deep learning system architectures, organisations can increase their IoT security, recognize abnormalities, forecast negative behaviour, and enhance their device shielding powers against dangerous cyber criminals.

5. ANOMALY DETECTION AND INTRUSION DETECTION

In the context of securing IoT devices, the deployment of Generative AI methods in anomaly and intrusion detection systems is a new and effective approach to protecting digital ecosystems. Generative AI-powered anomaly detection requires continuous, close monitoring and analysis of IoT device behaviour to identify and "flag" deviations from normal patterns. It predicts possible security violations and systems errors. However, this function cannot be implemented without assistance due to the IoT networks' increasing complexity and distribution, which makes traditional security methods ineffective. Generative AI's abilities are conditioned by the increase in the available power due to vast databases – it can detect even the smallest anomalies that might escape human or algorithm-driven threat assessment (Ndashimye, Sarkar, & Ray, 2021).

Generative AI not only helps to find the suggestions of a hostile interference but also allows to make the detection of false alerts. It may almost eliminate the role of human errors in the anomaly detection process. Intrusion detection refers to Generative AI as a solution that learns patterns of data influencing intrusion or compromise within the IoT infrastructure. It creates synthetic data for regular and malicious activity features, which helps to prepare IDS systems to distinguish between benign anomalies and actual threats with a close effectiveness. Thus, an AI-specialized system is prepared, and the threat can be managed promptly.

Since data generating algorithms may autonomously respond after a breach is detected, Generative AI can minimize the impact of any potential breach by instantly reacting and limiting danger. Thus, Generative AI tools for anomaly and intrusion detection are critical for the security of IoT devices in the context of a forward-looking cybersecurity threat landscape.

Exploration of How Generative AI Techniques Can Enhance Anomaly Detection and Intrusion Detection in IoT Environments

When it comes to securing Internet of Things devices, the implementation of Generative AI, including Generative Adversarial Networks, is a major breakthrough in the domains of anomaly and intrusion detection. These Gen AIs support the development of dynamic models that can generate data closely representing device operations and potential cybersecurity threats. They enable the most effective training of anomaly detection that allows systems to automatically detect deviations from acceptable normal behaviour, thus detecting potential safety threats or operational anomalies (Yu, Wang, & Wang, 2024).

Traditional methods often fail because IoT devices are autonomous and produce big data. Gen AIs are critical here because they can analyse the data and are generally better analytical tools. Generative AI has another advantage when it comes to intrusion detection. It enables systems to simulate attacks and learn to block the simulated attacks. This ability to continuously evolve in the face of new and emerging threats guarantees that protective layers are always up to date. This tool can predict how the next attack can look, and this predicts the ability to be a step ahead of the attacker is highly beneficial. Moreover, Generative AI also allows for more precise detection between real and false threats. This option will improve the overall security of IoT security by allocating more resources to crack down false threats (M. Hasan, Islam, Zarif, & Hashem, 2019).

Discussion on the Advantages of Unsupervised Learning Approaches for Detecting Abnormal Behavior and Potential Security Threats

Unsupervised learning approaches are advantageous, a vital component of the GenAI techniques, offering several benefits for detecting abnormal behaviour and potential security threats in IoT environments. The advantages are listed as follows:

- **Flexibility**: It happens since unsupervised learning does not require labelled data for training. Hence, it is easier to adapt to different and changing IoT environments where labelled data is limited. unsupervised learning more economically viable, as obtaining unlabelled data is inexpensive.
- **Scalability**: As Unsupervised learning algorithms are scalable as they have the ability to analyse large volumes of data generated by IoT devices, thereby, enabling companies to detect comprehensively anomalies over the network making them ideal for identifying abnormal behaviour and potential security threats in real-time.
- **Adaptability**: Lastly, Unsupervised learning approaches can adapt to changing patterns and emerging threats in IoT environments, providing a dynamic and proactive security framework for anomaly and intrusion detection.

Hence, by taking advantage of generative AI techniques and unsupervised learning approaches, IoT security can be fortified by organisations by identifying anomalies, detecting potential security threats, and safeguarding the integrity and confidentiality of data that is being transmitted and processed in interconnected IoT environments.

6. DEVICE AUTHENTICATION AND ACCESS CONTROL

Generative AI can develop innovative methods for authenticating devices and controlling access to prevent unauthorized entities from accessing the IoT network. As discussed earlier in IoT digital landscape the device is considered to be the core component of an IoT system: as it communicates with other devices as well as with users and performs all assigned tasks. Hence, for the IoT system to work properly and securely, a device must be recognized and restricted by the system. Since no unauthorized party can access an IoT network, the system is protected against data breaches, securing the whole IoT digital landscape.

Showcase Techniques for Using Generative AI to Improve Device Authentication Mechanisms and Access Control Policies

GenAI provides efficient devices authentication mechanism and effective access control policies. Generative AI improves access control and devices authentication system by learning and identifying the legitimate user and devices. Below are some of the ways the generative AI can improve devices authentication and access control:

1. **Behavioural Biometrics**: Generative AI analyses human behavioural data such as keystrokes, touchscreen, device movement, and learning data to develop a unique behavioural biometric profile for access control. Generative AI improvement to authentication is attributed to its knowledge and learning of normal and abnormal behaviour and varied environmental contexts to provide suitable access control. It alerts security personnel after determining that the normal user has been compromised through the magnitude of behavioural rule that has been broken. It applies Learnable rules for model adaptation from historical data as indicated in. It, therefore, improves authentication accuracy through learning and knowledge of normal behaviour to detect anomalies and adjust the access control (Yampolskiy & Govindaraju, 2008).

2. **Dynamic Authentication Models**: Generative AI creates dynamic authentication models that adapt to the surrounding environment as well as user behaviour. The dynamic model learns the use of distinguishing patterns among others and the set of features to model the user access. It also learns the environment where the users are and thus determines the access. Generative AI creates a dynamic model that adjusts the access control privilege in real-time. It improves access control by ensuring the system has an adaptive access pattern to authorized users (Lien & Vhaduri, 2023).

3. **Contextual Access Policy Management**: Contextual policy access management allows the organization to regulate policy based on the surroundings and risks. The generative AI takes data of the user's access, surrounding and the devices. Generative AI models the data by establishing the rules among users and devices and the rule to access data. It consistently monitors the user's access and learns when a model is not behaving like a role-based rule it has learned. The AI manages the policy depending on the user's access and behaviour it learns to suite policy management (Mazhar et al., 2023).

Analysis of How Generative AI Models Can Help Identify and Authenticate Legitimate Users and Devices

There are four main approaches that can be used by generative AI models to help identify and authenticate legitimate users and devices. They involve the following models:

- **Learning Patterns**: Generative AI models can learn from the historical data and user interactions in order to be able to identify patterns that are unique for the legitimate users and devices. This way, they can reach accurate authentication.
- **Anomaly Detection:** Generative AI models can analyse deviations from the normal behaviours, thus identifying the attempts to access while still being suspicious. The main signs are abnormal deviations and suspicious activities. This is one of the most effective ways of identifying the potential threats and preventing the access to the unauthorized devices and users.
- **Continuous Learning:** Generative AI models can continuously learn from the user behaviours and the interactions with the device. Hence, after a certain period, the AI models will definitely be much more accurate in detailed examination of the device.
- **Adaptive Access Control:** generative AI models can dynamically adapt access controls by considering contextual information, user behaviour, and the risk factors. In this way, only appropriate entities will gain access (Humayun et al., 2024).

Thus, to conclude the above discussion organizations can enhance device authentication and authorization mechanisms by strengthening access control policies, and through ensuring secure and reliable authentication of legitimate users and devices that are interconnected in entire IoT digital landscape.

7. MALWARE DETECTION AND DEFENSE

GenAI plays a vital role in the battle against malware since it helps recognize and eliminate newfound threats from the IoT digital landscape. Power-driven by learning and adaption, Gen AI systems avail in combating different threats produced disparate tactics. Mainly, these AI-powered systems can identify fresh variations and modifications of malware, which keeps cyber corporations on strong defence for other IoT appliances and their affiliated networks. GenAI-based approaches present state-of-the-art mechanisms and tactics for malware recognition, which help organizations analyse network operations, firmware integrity, and system performance to combat the issue effectively. The subsequent sections below discuss elaborately these AI-based approaches.

Overview of Generative AI-Based Approaches for Detecting and Mitigating Malware Targeting IoT Devices

Generative AI has tremendous potential to aid malware detection and defence efforts for Internet of Things devices. By leveraging sophisticated algorithms, it can scrutinize network patterns, check firmware for anomalies, and analyse system behaviours—giving security teams insight they need. This enables pre-emptive identification and handling of malware infections, thereby sheltering the integrity and safety of interconnected ecosystems. By capitalizing on AI-fostered approaches for malware identification and defences in IoT environments, organizations can substantially reinforce their security stance, intercept attacks beforehand, and ensure resilience against evolving digital dangers plaguing interconnected gadgets. The adaptive nature of AI could also help automatic countermeasures stay one step ahead of evolving hacks, plugging security holes before the next wave of IoT threats emerges (Smmarwar, Gupta, & Kumar, 2024).

Showcase of Techniques for Analyzing Network Traffic, Firmware Integrity, and System Behavior to Detect and Respond to Malware Infections

To begin, there exists condensed discussions surrounding generative AI approaches for detecting and mitigating malware designed to target IoT devices. Initially, these techniques are employed for Network Traffic Analysis purposes. Generative AI models can be applied to analyse network traffic, where they monitor network to scrutinize network activities, searching out anomalies that have crossed the line and moved into IoT networks such as malware. This task is accomplished by learning from historical data and by observing current network activity. These Gen AI models avail in revealing suspicious behaviour, unusual data flows and attempts to access unauthorized information hinting possible malware presence.

Generative AI can recognize normal communication patterns, they are then able to differentiate between good or null data, and on the other hand they are also able to check the infected traffic. In addition, generative AI can be used for monitoring firmware Integrity. Thus, organizations can observe the integrity of firmware in IoT devices to discover approved changes or contrivance indicating the presence of malware. By comparing anticipated firmware behaviour to actual changes which have occurred, generative models recognize variations and sound the alarm calling for further investigation and prevention. To accomplish this task, generate AI can detect unauthorized changes or detecting malicious insertions into device firmware.

Lastly, generative AI can perform System Behaviour Analysis. In this activity Gen AI models appraise system behaviour and user interactions, looking for abnormal activity hinting at malware infiltration in IoT devices. Thus, these models enhance capabilities for malware detection and enable timely responses against security threats. Thus, to conclude, generative AI undoubtedly plays a critical role in strengthening malware detection and providing protection for multitudes of connected IoT devices within seamless digital landscapes (Zola, Segurola-Gil, Bruse, Galar, & Orduna-Urrutia, 2022). (Bakhshi, Ghita, & Kuzminykh, 2024). (Moudgil, Hewage, Hussain, & Sadiq, 2023).

8. PRIVACY-PRESERVING TECHNIQUES

Generative AI-based privacy-preserving techniques aim to ensure that user data is well-secured and at the same time IoT systems operate effectively. They utilize complex techniques, including encryption and anonymization of data, to protect any confidential information. More specifically, privacy-preserving techniques enable IoT devices to operate and interact with other systems without revealing the information they process. For example, services like cameras can function fully and constantly exchange information while ensuring that the video feed remains private. These methods are essential in in today's changing digital landscape where protecting data is extremely important and at the same time enabling devices that are connected to this seamless network interact to serve their purpose.

Exploration of Privacy-Preserving Techniques Using Generative AI to Protect Sensitive Data and User Privacy in IoT Environments

Data privacy using generative AI in IoT deploy a series of methods to prevent exposure of user data such as anonymization of real data, synthetic data, and homomorphic encryption. Several generative models and differential privacy models provide a way to anonymize data or to generate realistic non-real datasets. Deployment of trained generative AI models allows these synthetic datasets to be used for training and best practices with late offline training integrated into the model. IoT systems use homomorphic encryption to perform complex computations on encrypted data safely and efficiently. The resulting computation mimics operations being performed on the plaintext. AI models have limited availability to replace real-world data with synthetic versions when the practical sources of real-world data are replaced.

These artificial intelligence models trained using advanced methods balance operation with privacy. Usage of these models allows IoT systems to use models instead of real data without noticeable operational degradation. The operation of privacy preservation models should be applied in real time as these data points are produced in the data stream of data produced by these IoT devices. Continuous operation ensures that generative AI methods never exceed the performance of the IoT system. At the same time, this makes the system worthy of a privacy-preserving scheme. Using generative AI to preserve privacy significantly reduces the risk of data of each user participating in the system being found and used. However, the method must be continually upgraded with its exposure to new threats and technology in the worst-case scenario. This poses a significant risk of being too computationally intensive and utilizing too many resources, especially in the smaller IoT devices. The balance of computational overhead and optimal method performance is used to maximize data protection.

Discussion on Techniques for Data Anonymization, Differential Privacy, and Secure Data Sharing

Generative AI is one of the innovative technologies that can help protect sensitive data and user privacy in the IoT environment through privacy-preserving techniques. The generative AI models maintain data security and confidentiality, allowing data sharing to be safe. The application of generative AI in exploring different privacy-preserving techniques includes the following points:

1. **Data Anonymization**: It ensures that the sensitive details are converted into a form that cannot be associated with real users. Generative AI helps create synthetic data that stays statistically similar to the original dataset and avoids including personal information. Capturing privacy by preserving theory and utility is possible due to generative AI (M. P. Neves & de Almeida, 2024).
2. **Differential Privacy**: Generative AI promotes differential privacy. Differential privacy helps ensure individual privacy while analysing aggregate data. Data privacy can set the standard for Internet of Things data analysis by enabling general unawareness. Artificial noise or query perturbations inserted by generative AI ensures that individual contributions are unknown to the organization analyse their data (F. Neves, Souza, Sousa, Bonfim, & Garcia, 2023).
3. **Secure Data Sharing**: Generative AI enables secure data sharing by creating synthetic data that preserves the patterns and trends of source data. Synthetic data can share so it cannot expose organizations to the risk of sharing private

data. Generative AI facilitates secure data that preserves the underlying patterns and characteristics of the original dataset without compromising data confidentiality (Lee et al., 2021).

9. CASE STUDIES AND USE CASES

Generative AI has been instrumental in addressing specific security challenges, providing real-world examples. This section followed by discussion below, provides a thorough real-world examples, providing insights to readers, providing a valuable reference for deploying solutions pertaining to Gen AI.

Showcase Real-World Examples and Use Cases Demonstrating the Application of Generative AI in Securing IoT Devices

Generative AI has substantially improved IoT security across a range of domains by generating synthetic data, anonymizing sensitive information, and preparing systems for potential attacks. A few concrete examples of the ways in which generative AI secures connected devices include: by training generative models to emulate actual sensor readings, systems can test their defences against tampering while preserving the anonymity of the real-world dataset. The overarching goal of these initiatives is to prevent the formation of botnets in factories or track the behaviour of established users in smart homes and offices. By employing an array of approaches, IoT security is being permanently and positively transformed by generative AI, making infrastructure tougher to compromise or misuse authorities. To illustrate this further, consider the following examples and use cases of generative AI in practical use to secure IoT devices.

1. Healthcare IoT Security

Use Case: Enhancing Patient Data Privacy

- **Scenario**: In the current scenarios, hospitals heavily leverage smart devices, such as monitors and trackers, to collect enormous amounts of patient-sensitive information continuously. Generative AI models can be beneficial in this scenario, as the hospitals can use them to generate synthetic data similar to the real one from the statistical perspective, but without any identifying details. This way, the research and progress can be implemented while protecting patient confidentiality entirely (Tayyab et al., 2023).

- **Impact**: This application not only safeguards patient confidentiality but also ensures compliance with strict data protection laws such as General Data Protection Regulation (GDPR) which is is a comprehensive data protection law that came into effect on May 25, 2018, in the European Union (EU). It's designed to give individuals control over their personal data and to simplify the regulatory environment for international business by unifying the regulation within the EU. and Health Insurance Portability and Accountability Act (HIPAA) which was enacted by the U.S. Congress in 1996. It has two main purposes: to provide continuous health insurance coverage for workers and their families when they change or lose their jobs, and to establish standards for electronic exchange, privacy, and security of health information.

2. Smart Home Security

Use Case: Anomaly Detection in Smart Home Devices

- **Scenario**: IoT devices are all around the modern smart home: from smart locks to smart cameras. The range of IoT devices available for home use is huge and generating data continuously. Generative AI-based systems learn user's normal device usage patterns and can point to any deviations from this model. These deviations can signal either a cyber-attack, fraud, or device functionality failures.
- **Impact**: Being able to detect these anomalies promptly helps homeowners take quick action to mitigate potential threats, thereby enhancing the security of their smart home setups.

3. Automotive Industry

Use Case: Securing Connected Vehicles

- **Scenario**: Modern vehicles are packed with IoT sensors and devices. These devices track the condition of the cars in real time. The problem with these devices is that there are too many connected cars in the world to always have a specialist available to read and analyse data. The generative AI usage model and spot on for defining the normal behaviour of these devices and search for abnormalities in the data. These abnormalities can signal cyber-attacks but also device or engineering issues in the car itself. Immediate detection of abnormalities in this case is crucial for saving lives and adjusting the systems handling the automation of vehicle management.

- **Impact**: This immediate detection is critical for maintaining the safety and functionality of connected vehicles, essential for preventing accidents and ensuring the safety of passengers.

4. Manufacturing Sector

Use Case: Protecting Industrial IoT (IIoT) Devices

- **Scenario**: In the manufacturing process, IoT devices play a crucial role in overseeing and managing industrial processes. Companies use generative AI systems to simulate tens of possible failure and threat scenarios. These scenarios help prepare the system to monitor and detect potential problems with the critical devices on the production line. These devices can be industrial robots or sensors, and the unusual patterns in their work can cost the company millions of dollars if no immediate action is taken after a failure or malfunction.
- **Impact**: This capability prevents unexpected breakdowns, promoting uninterrupted industrial operations and productivity.

5. Energy Sector

Use Case: Grid Security Enhancement

1. **Scenario**: IoT is a crucial part of the modern electricity grids – smart grids, that help optimize energy consumption and distribution. The generative AI models work 24/7 on top of electricity grids data and can detect abnormal patterns in data that signal an attack. Immediate response to grid attack improves the chances of security services responsible for grid maintenance to stop it before any damage is made (M. K. Hasan, Abdulkadir, Islam, Gadekallu, & Safie, 2024).
    - **Impact**: This proactive approach helps keep the energy grid stable and reliable, protecting it from both physical and cyber threats in an interconnected world.

6. Public Safety

Use Case: Surveillance and Monitoring

- **Scenario**: Public spaces are becoming more and more covered with IoT surveillance cameras. Generative AI models allow for differentiating normal from suspicious activity in a most efficient manner, and immediately informs police officers when something suspicious is happening (Boopathy et al., 2024).
- **Impact**: This improved surveillance capability aids in crime prevention and enhances the rapid response to public incidents, boosting overall public safety and security.

CONCLUSION

Thus, to conclude, the above examples clearly present generative AI's increasing and essential role in strengthening IoT devices' security. Through the synthesis of data, detection of anomalies, and offering immediate answers, generative AI secures IoT frameworks and the operating capacities to underpin them. The significance and centrality of generative AI in the field of cybersecurity continue to expand with the increasing IoT development and implementation landscape size. Indeed, it is the ideal and advanced tool for the complex and delicate challenges that characterize the current experience.

Analysis of Successful Implementations and Performance Evaluations of Generative AI-Based IoT Security Solutions

1. **Efficiency Optimization**: AI systems now autonomously optimize processes to maximize effectiveness over time. By continually examining usage patterns, these solutions have streamlined energy consumption for connected appliances and infrastructure without human intervention (Humayun, Alsaqer, & Jhanjhi, 2022).
2. **Privacy Protection**: Emerging techniques in generative technology safeguard sensitivity while allowing protected data use. Through anonymizing identifiers and differentially private algorithms, user confidentiality remains intact, even as insights aid network administration and problem solving effectively (Humayun et al., 2020).

3. **Security Enhancement**: Machine learning models have significantly strengthened defences against infiltration and compromise. By proactively scanning interconnected platforms for known vulnerabilities and abnormal activity indicators, pre-emptive responses can isolate dangers before harm occurs. Offline training improves real-time detection for a digitally safer environment, optimizing protection (Jayanthi et al., 2023).

As a result, organizations have achieved notable progressions in efficiency, privacy preservation, and security fortification through judicious applications of Generative AI techniques. Successfully executing thoughtfully designed generative AI-based solutions have exhibited tangible benefits in optimizing energy grids fluidly, sheltering data privacy conscientiously, and reinforcing cybersecurity measures comprehensively across IoT ecosystems.

Ethical and Legal Considerations

This section of the chapter underscores the importance of ethical and legal considerations for the prudent implementation of generative AI for IoT security. Developing precise guidelines and frameworks is crucial to ensure that AI technologies are used in a safe, responsible, and respectful manner while protecting privacy and personal data and eliminating the risk of malicious use across the entire digital IoT space (Chakraborty, 2023).

Discussion on Ethical Considerations Related to Using Generative AI in IoT Security, Including Privacy, Bias, and Accountability

Below, we delve deeply into the complex ethical issues surrounding the apt application of generative AI in IoT security, such as privacy, bias, and accountability:

1. **Privacy**: As AI systems evolve the ability to synthesize data in novel ways subtly, security measures must robustly anonymize information to safeguard user privacy and block unauthorized access to personal details completely. Failing to do so risks revealing identities. Generative AI raises serious privacy concerns because of its potential to generate synthetic data that could inadvertently disclose sensitive information if privacy protections are insufficient. To protect user privacy and prevent any unauthorized infiltration of personal data absolutely, companies must rigorously develop and implement data anonymization techniques thoughtfully (Maria & Oya, 2022).

2. **Bias**: Generative models may imitate and reinforce biases found within the data source. As a result, they hold the potential to also create discriminatory or inequitable outcomes. It remains the responsibility of developers to address biases in models to sustain fair decision-making and prevent the reinforcement of existing biases in IoT security practices. As such, bias in AI algorithms must be addressed to ensure fair decision-making and equitable practices. Biases found within IoT security data contribute to scenarios in which generative models may produce discriminatory or unfair outcomes (Fletcher, Nakeshimana, & Olubeko, 2021).

3. **Accountability**: The extensive application of generative AI for security will pose difficult questions of responsibility, accountability, transparency, and oversight for independent systems. Organizations should build frameworks to help determine who can be held answerable accountable for the decisions and activities carried out by AI-driven solutions. Using generative AI for IoT security will further complicate the challenge of answering the question of who should be answerable for what the top algorithms elect. Building liable frameworks will help address the difficult question of who should be answerable while also considering responsibility, transparency, oversight, and other AI-driven security solutions (Malhotra & Misra, 2022).

Overview of Legal Frameworks and Regulations Governing IoT Security Practices and Data Protection

The proliferation of IoT devices in various sectors, ranging from healthcare to home automation, has led to serious concerns regarding security and data protection. Indeed, such devices usually gather and transmit sensitive information, and strong legal frameworks and regulations are necessary to ensure that such data is adequately protected and treated while also respecting user privacy. Here are some of the key legal frameworks and regulations outlining the sustainable IoT security and data protection practices:

1. **Data Protection Regulations**: Strict legal frameworks like the General Data Protection Regulation (GDPR) in the EU, the California Consumer Privacy Act (CCPA) and Health Insurance Portability and Accountability Act (HIPAA) in the US enforce rigorous rules for information safekeeping and individual privacy. Firms employing creative AI in IoT security must abide by such regulations to shelter user details and ensure openness in information dealing practices (Milossi, Alexandropoulou-Egyptiadou, & Psannis, 2021). Below is the elaborate discussion on these data protection regulations:

2. **General Data Protection Regulation:** it is a fundamental EU regulation that sets a high threshold for data protection. It argues that data processors and controllers must be transparent, secure, and answerable to their users and consumers and grants individuals' substantial power over their personal data. Specifically, the GDPR requires IoT devices providers to thoroughly ensure data protection already at the design stage and throughout data processing the process. Further, it requires explicit consent for data collection and further processing, privacy by default principle and data anonymization wherever possible, and timely notification of authorities and the public of a data breach.

3. **California Consumer Privacy Act:** This act is a regulation similar to the scope of the GDPR aimed to provide Californian residents with rights over the data businesses collect on them. Specifically, the regulation entitles the customers to information about data collection, rights to request deletion, and right to opt-out of personally collected data sales. IoT businesses that collect data on Californian residents must adhere to these rules by not selling the data and enabling the above-mentioned rights and adequately protecting personal data information from unauthorized access, destruction, or disclosure through internal and external cybersecurity.

4. **Health Insurance Portability and Accountability Act:** This act, protects the privacy and security of health information in the U.S., which is a law that affects IoT devices in the healthcare sector such as wearable health monitors and connected medical devices. Covered entities and their business associates ensure that health information is safe from unauthorized access and breaches through risk assessments and implementation of risk management policies, encryption, and secure communication channels.

5. **IoT Cybersecurity Improvement Act of 2020:** This U.S. law is drafted to improve the cybersecurity standards of IoT devices purchased and used federal agencies.

6. **The National Institute of Standards and Technology:** This is required to publish relevant standards and guidelines regarding proper security, use, and management of these devices. Manufactures should ensure their IoT devices are patchable, without known vulnerabilities, and provide users with mechanisms to reset default passwords and security.

7. **Network and Information Systems Directive in the EU:** The Directive aims to create a high level of cybersecurity across the EU through measures to strengthen member states national capabilities, improve cooperation among them, and implement security measures for organizations in charge of offering services. The NID covers key digital service providers and the operators of essential services that have become increased users of IoT in areas such as energy, transport, water, and health sectors.

Apart from these legal frameworks cybersecurity laws and ethical guidelines are also inevitable to secure this plethora of connected digital device landscape, hence, below is the brief discussion dedicated to cybersecurity laws and ethical guidelines:

1. **Cybersecurity Laws**: Various cybersecurity laws and directions necessitate organizations to execute strong protection steps to shield IoT devices and systems from cyber dangers. Imaginative AI answers should adjust to cybersecurity laws to lessen risks, deter information breaches, and uphold the integrity of IoT ecosystems (Alexandrou, 2021; Azinheira, Antunes, Maximiano, & Gomes, 2023).

2. **Ethical Guidelines**: Ethical guidelines, such as those outlined by industry associations and AI ethics boards, provide principles for responsible AI development and deployment. Organizations leveraging generative AI in IoT security should adhere to ethical guidelines to promote fairness, accountability, and transparency in their AI-driven practices (Elgesem, 2023).

To sum up the whole discussion above, it is concluded that the legal frameworks and regulations are critical in developing and implementing strong security measures as IoT devices become more ingrained in essential functions of society. Compliance protects against financial fines, while also providing a means of ensuring consumer reliance as relevant organizations make all necessary advancements to ensure the security of their personal data against potential cyber threats. The above referenced legislation members are ever-changing due to new challenges and technology trends, indicating the ever-changing landscape of IoT security and data protection.

10. FUTURE DIRECTIONS AND EMERGING TRENDS

As IoT devices are becoming more and more common in personal and commercial settings, Generative AI has become a breakthrough in revolutionizing the security of digitally connected IoT landscape. Self-managing security systems are likely to surge in the coming years which can instantly manage and even predict security challenges. The use of blockchain for decentralized security and zero trust architectures that continuously verify the reliability of IoT systems are also on high rise, promising more secure and robust defenses. Additionally, Gen AI models that can learn and defensively reconfigure themselves are becoming more common.

Exploration of Emerging Trends and Future Directions in Generative AI for IoT Security

The following trends and directions underscore how GenAI is being implemented into IoT security:

1. **Better Prediction and Prevention:** There is better prediction and prevention as GenAI shifts from reacting to incidents to predicting and preventing them through data-based machine learning and understanding of past data. As a result, some cyber threats can be terminated even before they fully materialize. Thus, the IoT security system becomes much more robust, and preventive compared to what it used to be. Future trends indicate that generative AI will play a crucial role in enhancing threat detection capabilities to detect and mitigate cyber threats in real-time, through the implementation of proactive cybersecurity measures which can combat evolving cyber threats effectively (Imene Safer et al., 2022).

2. **Self-Learning Systems**: These systems imply the development of self-learning algorithms in GenAI technologies, including smart contracts. They would learn from continuous data integration without human involvement, continuously updating and adapting in response to changing threats. This approach is safer, more decentralized, and fail-safe. Thus, Generative AI will continue to be instrumental in safeguarding sensitive multimedia data while maintaining privacy and confidentiality in IoT environments (Fazzinga, Galassi, & Torroni, 2021; Nazish, Adnan, Muhammad, Ala, & Junaid, 2023).

3. **Blockchain for Enhanced Security:** Blockchain Technology is utilized for enhanced security referring to the combination of GenAI and Blockchain that can strengthen the verification processes and data storage. It makes everything more secure and safer through decentralized operations.

4. **Federated Learning and Data Privacy:** Federated learning and data privacy mean a trend whereby AI trains on devices without the need for actual data exposure. Federated learning is a trend that supports privacy by allowing AI models to learn from vast amounts of data without seeing the data itself. This method trains shared GenAI models on various devices while keeping all the sensitive data localized, significantly reducing privacy risks.

5. **Implementing Zero Trust:** Zero trust models are critical as they don't automatically trust any entity inside or outside the network unless their legitimacy is proven. Implementing Zero Trust is critical because GenAI applications watch every activity and react proactively to any suspect activity in real-time to stop any unauthorized security breaches. GenAI at the network edge implies relocating AI capabilities and applications away from centralized systems to decentralized locations.

6. **Secure Communication Protocols**: Future directions in generative AI for IoT security involve the development of secure communication protocols for transferring multimedia data in IoT-Edge environments. By incorporating AI-driven encryption and authentication, generative AI will enhance the security of data transmission, ensuring the integrity and confidentiality of multimedia content (Durakovskiy et al., 2021).

Predictions for How Generative AI Will Continue to Shape the Landscape of IoT Security and Cybersecurity

Generative AI is expected to deeply revolutionize IoT security and cybersecurity by ensuring extensive upgradable capabilities on threat detection, mitigations, and interventions. With GenAI expected to become more autonomous due to the increase in cybersecurity threats in the coming years, decentralized security with integration with blockchain and edge computing will ensure strong and real-time infrastructures that can handle these threats. Consequently, predictive, and adaptive approaches for securing IoT devices will be the new norm while ensuring a robust and more resilient security approach for the foreseeable future, securing the IoT devices from increased attacks. Below are few predictions discussed at length:

1. **Proactive Threat Mitigation**: Generative AI will change the cybersecurity paradigm from being reactive to proactive on security threats. Through predicting and preventing security breaches based on the patterns and trends in historical cybersecurity, generative AI will help organizations counter future threats before they happen (Sun et al., 2023).
2. **Efficiency and Scalability**: Generative AI will enhance the efficiency and scalability of cyber threat detection and response by accelerating analyst workflows and enabling in-depth analysis of security incidents. Through the automation of data analysis and incident summarization, generative AI will streamline cybersecurity operations and improve the overall effectiveness of security teams (Changwu, Zeqi, Bifei, & Xin, 2023; Gill et al., 2022).
3. **Innovative Security Solutions**: The incorporation of generative AI into the internet of things represents an innovative approach to enhancing cybersecurity by providing more robust protection of connected devices from malicious actors. Although the incorporation of artificial intelligence into the extensive network of sensors and appliances that make up the internet of things will surely encourage the advancement of defensive techniques, ranging from anomaly detection to privacy-preserving algorithms, the full extent of its security advantages is still unclear. Modifying the evaluation of internet of things systems and integrating AI

oversight of device transmissions continues to transform and refine the ultimate impact on information and communication technology security processes, as well as the messages transported through the internet of things' digital landscape (Wu, Han, Wang, & Sun, 2020).

Thus, to conclude, Gen AI will significantly change the paradigm of IoT and cybersecurity through improving the surveillance and privacy of ICT systems and ensuring pre-emptive security measures enhanced threat detection and ensured data privacy measures.

11. CONCLUSION

This chapter presents a detailed analysis of the critical role of generative AI in enhancing IoT security. While it has prioritized the inevitable role of GenAI in addressing the current and predicted complexities of the numbers and forms of cyber threats in modern enterprises. This chapter has also highlighted the rapid development of ethical and legal frameworks that are critical in shaping the use of GenAI. However, its benefits will only be realized through responsible and ethical use. All critical stakeholders, including policymakers, technology developers, and end-users, must fill knowledge and power gaps as they use the technology responsibly to protect IoT devices and energies from threats while maintaining ethical standards. In conclusion, taking a proactive innovation approach, using the right regulations, and implementing risk management strategies could improve securing IoT environments' adaptation to threats currently and in the future.

Summary of Key Insights and Takeaways From the Chapter

The following are the key insights and takeaways from this chapter:

1. **Foundational Role of GenAI:** one of the foundational functions of GenAI in cybersecurity is the use of advanced methods to invent additional data points due to identified models. It improves the ability to predict and detect real-time threats and, therefore, results in reducing the response period to the current and potential threats.
2. **Enhanced Threat Detection and Management:** Incorporation of GenAI into IoT devices makes these systems a better threat to anticipate and manage. GenAI will analyse very complexed data that carries a very high level of capacity to detect very minimal abnormalities that can point on a threat emerging.

3. **Balancing Benefits and Risks:** Despite the potential positives associated with Generalized AI, its application introduces hazards that necessitate addressing, like misuse and privacy issues. The implementation of this system mandates comprehensive awareness and mitigation of these risks to oversee it in a principled and lawful framework.

4. **Ethical and Legal Considerations:** As Generalized AI rises, ethical and legal considerations must be managed delicately. The considerations involve data privacy, information security, and international legal definitions, comprising GDPR and HIPAA standards. Organizations must handle these lawful requirements cautiously to ensure the accountable and effective use of Generalized AI.

5. **Revolutionizing IoT Security:** Generalized AI has enabled a transformation in applying security to the Internet of Things by progressing threat discovery. Lengthier sentences mixed among shorter ones can help illustrate varying complexity. While risks exist, diligently addressing privacy and managing legal issues responsibly can optimize AI's benefits. GenAI also enhances data transmissions, secure encrypted transactions, and protection of some privacy across interconnected systems. The utilization of GenAI in IoT systems has enabled the anticipation and prediction of threats through a combination of predictive analytical algorithms and real-time threat intelligence.

Reflection on the Transformative Potential of Generative AI for Securing IoT Devices

Transforming the paradigm of the defence from defensive AI to predictive AI and proactive, facilitative algorithms, GenAI has revolutionized cybersecurity on the front of Internet of Things. By quickly analyzing vast amounts of data, it can detect irregularities that are partially concealed and just imply a danger or violation and which, soon, will become a security hole that will be exploited. The capability of generative AI to learn and receive new intelligence and assault models is of primary significance because that is how it adjusts to and overcomes the cybercriminals' evolving strategies. Generative AI power propels intelligent manoeuvre to produce intelligent surmises and develop possible scenarios and provides knowledge base from which to create tailored security measures to be ready to recognize rapidly evolving threats. Generative AI guarantees a new level of secured integrated data by generating synthetic user information to efficiently teach the model, an essential layer for the next item of growing systems integration. In summary, accurate strategic use of generative AI which is planted to include essential value not only on security and meaning, but also comply and trust, will be a critical factor and a must-have for IOT security. Additionally, generative AI is an essential integrated data security by synthesizing user data to educate the model. This allows for high levels of data coverage, a factor which is particularly important in the field of increasing integration of systems. In conclusion, strategic deployment of generative AI not only enhances security and purport, but also maintains compliance and trust, making it a vital part of Internet of Things security.

Call to Action for Organizations to Leverage Generative AI Technologies to Enhance the Security and Resilience of IoT Ecosystems

It's absolutely critical for organizations seeking to enhance the security and reliability of their IoT ecosystems to adopt GenAI technologies. In development, however, if we are to truly realize what GenAI can achieve, organizations should not just install tools but also need widespread training in GenAI professions and resources. This may necessitate partnerships aimed at innovation. Organizations need to cultivate a culture of security. Through lifelong learning and capacity development, on top of average, GenAI concomitantly adapts itself in response to new threats of terrorizing enterprises. In addition, organizations need real-time feedback from on-site security analysts, as seen in the analytical and identification functionality of Google Glasses and OpenCV. They also must have an editing function that can automatically adjust to and fend off new attacks while they are taking place. Therefore, establishing a foundation for the technology and promoting widespread GenAI use is the strategic approach that ventures adopt.

It is recommended that organizations incorporate generative AI solutions to reinforce the safety and sustainability of their IoT environments. By utilizing generative AI technologies to strengthen threat detection and mitigation, identify irregularities, and safeguard data, companies may improve their overall cybersecurity posture and battle the challenges posed by quick-evolving cyber threats. To incorporate generative AI into their company's security standards, businesses should spend in training, skills, and cooperation. It is no longer only an innovation but an essential safety element. With the degree of innovation and interconnectedness now accessible, corporates cannot afford not to." Organizations have more reasons to enable generative AI now and emerge the future of their IoT environments.

REFERENCES

Alex, S. A., Jhanjhi, N. Z., & Ray, S. K. (2023). *Blockchain Based E-Medical Data Storage for Privacy Protection.* Paper presented at the International Conference on Mathematical Modeling and Computational Science. DOI:10.1007/978-981-99-3611-3_10

Alexandrou, A. (2021). *Cybercrime and information technology: The computer network infrastructure and computer security, cybersecurity laws, Internet of Things (IoT), and mobile devices.* CRC Press. DOI:10.4324/9780429318726

Alferidah, D. K., & Jhanjhi, N. (2020). *Cybersecurity impact over bigdata and iot growth.* Paper presented at the 2020 International Conference on Computational Intelligence (ICCI). DOI:10.1109/ICCI51257.2020.9247722

Alkinani, M. H., Almazroi, A. A., & Khan, N. A. (2021). 5G and IoT based reporting and accident detection (RAD) system to deliver first aid box using unmanned aerial vehicle. *Sensors (Basel)*, 21(20), 6905. DOI:10.3390/s21206905 PMID:34696118

Almusaylim, , Z., & Jhanjhi, N. (2020). Comprehensive review: Privacy protection of user in location-aware services of mobile cloud computing. *Wireless Personal Communications*, 111, 541–564. DOI:10.1007/s11277-019-06872-3

Annadurai, C., Nelson, I., Devi, K. N., Manikandan, R., Jhanjhi, N., Masud, M., & Sheikh, A. (2022). Biometric authentication-based intrusion detection using artificial intelligence internet of things in smart city. *Energies*, 15(19), 7430. DOI:10.3390/en15197430

Ashfaq, F., Jhanjhi, N. Z., Khan, N. A., & Das, S. R. (2023). *Synthetic Crime Scene Generation Using Deep Generative Networks.* Paper presented at the International Conference on Mathematical Modeling and Computational Science. DOI:10.1007/978-981-99-3611-3_43

Ashraf, H., Nawaz, M., & Jhanjhi, N. (2024). ML-Based Detection of Sybil Attack on MANETS.

Asperti, A., Evangelista, D., & Loli Piccolomini, E. (2021). A survey on variational autoencoders from a green AI perspective. *SN Computer Science*, 2(4), 301. DOI:10.1007/s42979-021-00702-9

Azinheira, B., Antunes, M., Maximiano, M., & Gomes, R. (2023). A methodology for mapping cybersecurity standards into governance guidelines for SME in Portugal. *Procedia Computer Science*, 219, 121–128. DOI:10.1016/j.procs.2023.01.272

Bakhshi, T., Ghita, B., & Kuzminykh, I. (2024). A Review of IoT Firmware Vulnerabilities and Auditing Techniques. *Sensors (Basel)*, 24(2), 708. DOI:10.3390/s24020708 PMID:38276399

Boopathy, P., Liyanage, M., Deepa, N., Velavali, M., Reddy, S., Maddikunta, P. K. R., Khare, N., Gadekallu, T. R., Hwang, W.-J., & Pham, Q.-V. (2024). Deep learning for intelligent demand response and smart grids: A comprehensive survey. *Computer Science Review*, 51, 100617. DOI:10.1016/j.cosrev.2024.100617

Bukhari, O., Agarwal, P., Koundal, D., & Zafar, S. (2023). Anomaly detection using ensemble techniques for boosting the security of intrusion detection system. *Procedia Computer Science*, 218, 1003–1013. DOI:10.1016/j.procs.2023.01.080

Chakraborty, S. (2023). AI and ethics: Navigating the moral landscape. In *Investigating the Impact of AI on Ethics and Spirituality* (pp. 25-33).

Changwu, H., Zeqi, Z., Bifei, M., & Xin, Y. (2023). An Overview of Artificial Intelligence Ethics. *IEEE Transactions on Artificial Intelligence*, 4(4), 799–819. DOI:10.1109/TAI.2022.3194503

David, E., & Eldon, S. (2022). AI Technologies, Privacy, and Security. *Frontiers in Artificial Intelligence*, 5, 826737. Advance online publication. DOI:10.3389/frai.2022.826737 PMID:35493613

Durakovskiy, A. P., Gavdan, G. P., Korsakov, I. A., & Melnikov, D. A. (2021). About the cybersecurity of automated process control systems. *Procedia Computer Science*, 190, 217–225. DOI:10.1016/j.procs.2021.06.027

Elgesem, D. (2023). *The AI Act and the risks posed by generative AI models*. Paper presented at the CEUR Workshop Proceedings.

Essamlali, I., Nhaila, H., & El Khaili, M. (2024). Advances in machine learning and IoT for water quality monitoring: A comprehensive review. *Heliyon*, 10(6), e27920. DOI:10.1016/j.heliyon.2024.e27920 PMID:38533055

Farhan, L., Shukur, S. T., Alissa, A. E., Alrweg, M., Raza, U., & Kharel, R. (2017). *A survey on the challenges and opportunities of the Internet of Things (IoT)*. Paper presented at the 2017 Eleventh International Conference on Sensing Technology (ICST). DOI:10.1109/ICSensT.2017.8304465

Fazzinga, B., Galassi, A., & Torroni, P. (2021). *A Preliminary Evaluation of a Privacy-Preserving Dialogue System*. Paper presented at the CEUR Workshop Proceedings.

Figueroa-Lorenzo, S., Añorga, J., & Arrizabalaga, S. (2019). A role-based access control model in modbus SCADA systems. A centralized model approach. *Sensors (Basel)*, 19(20), 4455. Advance online publication. DOI:10.3390/s19204455 PMID:31615147

Fletcher, R. R., Nakeshimana, A., & Olubeko, O. (2021). Addressing Fairness, Bias, and Appropriate Use of Artificial Intelligence and Machine Learning in Global Health. *Frontiers in Artificial Intelligence*, 3, 561802. Advance online publication. DOI:10.3389/frai.2020.561802 PMID:33981989

Ghelani, D. (2022). Cyber security, cyber threats, implications and future perspectives: A Review. *Authorea Preprints*. DOI:10.22541/au.166385207.73483369/v1

Gill, S. S., Xu, M., Ottaviani, C., Patros, P., Bahsoon, R., Shaghaghi, A., & Abraham, A. (2022). AI for next generation computing: Emerging trends and future directions. *Internet of Things : Engineering Cyber Physical Human Systems*, 19, 100514. DOI:10.1016/j.iot.2022.100514

Gyamfi, E., Ansere, J. A., Kamal, M., Tariq, M., & Jurcut, A. (2023). An Adaptive Network Security System for IoT-Enabled Maritime Transportation. *IEEE Transactions on Intelligent Transportation Systems*, 24(2), 2538–2547. DOI:10.1109/TITS.2022.3159450

Hasan, M., Islam, M. M., Zarif, M. I. I., & Hashem, M. M. A. (2019). Attack and anomaly detection in IoT sensors in IoT sites using machine learning approaches. *Internet of Things : Engineering Cyber Physical Human Systems*, 7, 100059. Advance online publication. DOI:10.1016/j.iot.2019.100059

Hasan, M. K., Abdulkadir, R. A., Islam, S., Gadekallu, T. R., & Safie, N. (2024). A review on machine learning techniques for secured cyber-physical systems in smart grid networks. *Energy Reports*, 11, 1268–1290. DOI:10.1016/j.egyr.2023.12.040

Hatton, M. (2023). key aspects of the evolving IoT security threat landscape. Retrieved from https://transformainsights.com/blog/evolving-iot-security-threat-landscape

Hongbo, Z. (2023). *Challenges, Corresponding Solutions, and Applications of Generative Adversarial Networks*. Highlights in Science Engineering and Technology., DOI:10.54097/hset.v57i.9991

Hossain, M. A., Ray, S. K., & Lota, J. (2020). SmartDR: A device-to-device communication for post-disaster recovery. *Journal of Network and Computer Applications*, 171, 102813. DOI:10.1016/j.jnca.2020.102813

Hosseini, M.-P., Lu, S., Kamaraj, K., Slowikowski, A., & Venkatesh, H. C. (2020). Deep learning architectures. *Deep learning: concepts and architectures*, 1-24.

Humayun, M., Alsaqer, M. S., & Jhanjhi, N. (2022). Energy optimization for smart cities using iot. *Applied Artificial Intelligence*, 36(1), 2037255. DOI:10.1080/088 39514.2022.2037255

Humayun, M., Jhanjhi, N., Alruwaili, M., Amalathas, S. S., Balasubramanian, V., & Selvaraj, B. (2020). Privacy protection and energy optimization for 5G-aided industrial Internet of Things. *IEEE Access : Practical Innovations, Open Solutions*, 8, 183665–183677. DOI:10.1109/ACCESS.2020.3028764

Humayun, M., Jhanjhi, N., Alsayat, A., & Ponnusamy, V. (2021). Internet of things and ransomware: Evolution, mitigation and prevention. *Egyptian Informatics Journal*, 22(1), 105–117. DOI:10.1016/j.eij.2020.05.003

Humayun, M., Tariq, N., Alfayad, M., Zakwan, M., Alwakid, G., & Assiri, M. (2024). Securing the Internet of Things in Artificial Intelligence Era: A Comprehensive Survey. *IEEE Access : Practical Innovations, Open Solutions*, 12, 25469–25490. DOI:10.1109/ACCESS.2024.3365634

Imene Safer, C., Geert, V., Roel, W., & Wilfried, V. (2022). AI privacy preserving robots working in a smart sensor environment. 300-306. DOI:10.1109/ICM-LA55696.2022.00049

Jayanthi, E., Ramesh, T., Kharat, R. S., Veeramanickam, M. R. M., Bharathiraja, N., Venkatesan, R., & Marappan, R. (2023). Cybersecurity enhancement to detect credit card frauds in health care using new machine learning strategies. *Soft Computing*, 27(11), 7555–7565. DOI:10.1007/s00500-023-07954-y

Joo Fong, T., Abdullah, A., Jhanjhi, N., & Supramaniam, M. (2019). The coin passcode: A shoulder-surfing proof graphical password authentication model for mobile devices. *International Journal of Advanced Computer Science and Applications, 10*(1).

Khan, A., Jhanjhi, N., Humayun, M., & Ahmad, M. (2020). The role of IoT in digital governance. In *Employing Recent Technologies for Improved Digital Governance* (pp. 128–150). IGI Global. DOI:10.4018/978-1-7998-1851-9.ch007

Khan, A., Jhanjhi, N., Ray, S. K., Amsaad, F., & Sujatha, R. (2024). Ethical and Social Implications of Industry 4.0 in SCM. In *Convergence of Industry 4.0 and Supply Chain Sustainability* (pp. 234-274): IGI Global.

Khan, A., Jhanjhi, N. Z., Haji, D. H. T. B. A., & Omar, H. A. H. B. H. (2024). Internet of Things (IoT) Impact on Inventory Management: A Review. *Cybersecurity Measures for Logistics Industry Framework*, 224-247.

Konatham, B., Simra, T., Amsaad, F., Ibrahem, M. I., & Jhanjhi, N. Z. (2024). A Secure Hybrid Deep Learning Technique for Anomaly Detection in IIoT Edge Computing. *Authorea Preprints*. DOI:10.36227/techrxiv.170630909.96680286/v1

Kumar, V., Malik, N., Singla, J., Jhanjhi, N., Amsaad, F., & Razaque, A. (2022). Light weight authentication scheme for smart home iot devices. *Cryptography*, 6(3), 37. DOI:10.3390/cryptography6030037

Lam, K. Y., Mitra, S., Gondesen, F., & Yi, X. (2022). ANT-Centric IoT Security Reference Architecture - Security-by-Design for Satellite-Enabled Smart Cities. *IEEE Internet of Things Journal*, 9(8), 5895–5908. DOI:10.1109/JIOT.2021.3073734

Lee, H., Kim, J., Ahn, S., Hussain, R., Cho, S., & Son, J. (2021). Digestive neural networks: A novel defense strategy against inference attacks in federated learning. *Computers & Security*, 109, 102378. DOI:10.1016/j.cose.2021.102378

Lien, C.-W., & Vhaduri, S. (2023). Challenges and opportunities of biometric user authentication in the age of iot: A survey. *ACM Computing Surveys*, 56(1), 1–37. DOI:10.1145/3603705

Mahmood, S., Akif, F., Ashraf, H., & Jhanjhi, N. (2024). Defense Mechanism Against Attacks Promoting Spread Of Wrong Information.

Malhotra, P., & Misra, A. (2022). *Accountability and responsibility of artificial intelligence decision-making models in Indian policy landscape.* Paper presented at the CEUR Workshop Proceedings.

Maria, C., & Oya, B. (2022). AI Ethics—A Bird's Eye View. *Applied Sciences (Basel, Switzerland)*, 12(9), 4130–4130. DOI:10.3390/app12094130

Marjani, M., Jhanjhi, N. Z., Hashem, I. A. T., & Hajibeigy, M. T. (2021). The role of iiot in smart industries 4.0. In *The Nine Pillars of Technologies for Industry 4.0* (pp. 91-116). Institution of Engineering and Technology.

Mazhar, T., Talpur, D. B., Shloul, T. A., Ghadi, Y. Y., Haq, I., Ullah, I., Ouahada, K., & Hamam, H. (2023). Analysis of IoT security challenges and its solutions using artificial intelligence. *Brain Sciences*, 13(4), 683. DOI:10.3390/brainsci13040683 PMID:37190648

McIntosh, T., Liu, T., Susnjak, T., Alavizadeh, H., Ng, A., Nowrozy, R., & Watters, P. (2023). Harnessing GPT-4 for generation of cybersecurity GRC policies: A focus on ransomware attack mitigation. *Computers & Security*, 134, 103424. DOI:10.1016/j.cose.2023.103424

Milossi, M., Alexandropoulou-Egyptiadou, E., & Psannis, K. E. (2021). AI Ethics: Algorithmic Determinism or Self-Determination? The GPDR Approach. *IEEE Access : Practical Innovations, Open Solutions*, 9, 58455–58466. DOI:10.1109/ ACCESS.2021.3072782

Moudgil, V., Hewage, K., Hussain, S. A., & Sadiq, R. (2023). Integration of IoT in building energy infrastructure: A critical review on challenges and solutions. *Renewable & Sustainable Energy Reviews*, 174, 113121. DOI:10.1016/j.rser.2022.113121

Mughal, M. A., Ullah, A., Cheema, M. A. Z., Yu, X., & Jhanjhi, N. (2024). An intelligent channel assignment algorithm for cognitive radio networks using a tree-centric approach in IoT. *Alexandria Engineering Journal*, 91, 152–160. DOI:10.1016/j. aej.2024.01.071

Naranjo, F. V., Espinoza, J. L. A., & Vivar, S. M. (2023). Exploring the Fusion of Blockchain and AI for Enhanced Practices in IoT Ecosystems: Opportunities and Challenges. *Fusion: Practice and Applications*, 13(2), 52–61. DOI:10.54216/ FPA.130205

Nazish, K., Adnan, Q., Muhammad, B., Ala, A.-F., & Junaid, Q. (2023). Privacy-preserving artificial intelligence in healthcare: Techniques and applications. *Computers in Biology and Medicine*, 158, 106848–106848. DOI:10.1016/j.compbiomed.2023.106848 PMID:37044052

Ndashimye, E., Sarkar, N. I., & Ray, S. K. (2021). A Multi-criteria based handover algorithm for vehicle-to-infrastructure communications. *Computer Networks*, 185, 107652. DOI:10.1016/j.comnet.2020.107652

Neves, F., Souza, R., Sousa, J., Bonfim, M., & Garcia, V. (2023). Data privacy in the Internet of Things based on anonymization: A review. *Journal of Computer Security*, 31(3), 261–291. DOI:10.3233/JCS-210089

Neves, M. P., & de Almeida, A. B. (2024). Before and Beyond Artificial Intelligence: Opportunities and Challenges. In *Law, Governance and Technology Series* (Vol. 58, pp. 107-125).

Odeh, A., & Abu Taleb, A. (2023). Ensemble-Based Deep Learning Models for Enhancing IoT Intrusion Detection. *Applied Sciences (Basel, Switzerland)*, 13(21), 11985. DOI:10.3390/app132111985

Oh, S., & Shon, T. (2023). *Cybersecurity Issues in Generative AI*. Paper presented at the 2023 International Conference on Platform Technology and Service (PlatCon). DOI:10.1109/PlatCon60102.2023.10255179

Padraig, S. (2016). Understanding IoT Security – Part 1 of 3: IoT Security Architecture on the Device and Communication Layers. Retrieved from https://iot-analytics.com/understanding-iot-security-part-1-iot-security-architecture/

Ponnusamy, V., Humayun, M., Jhanjhi, N., Yichiet, A., & Almufareh, M. F. (2022). Intrusion Detection Systems in Internet of Things and Mobile Ad-Hoc Networks. *Computer Systems Science and Engineering*, 40(3). Advance online publication. DOI:10.32604/csse.2022.018518

Ponnusamy, V., Sharma, B., Nadeem, W., Guan, G. H., & Jhanjhi, N. (2021). Green IoT (G-IoT) Ecosystem for Smart Cities. *Role of IoT in Green Energy Systems*, 1

Ray, S. K., Pawlikowski, K., & Sirisena, H. (2009). *A fast MAC-layer handover for an IEEE 802.16 e-based WMAN.* Paper presented at the AccessNets: Third International Conference on Access Networks, AccessNets 2008, Las Vegas, NV.

Ray, S. K., Sinha, R., & Ray, S. K. (2015). *A smartphone-based post-disaster management mechanism using WiFi tethering.* Paper presented at the 2015 IEEE 10th conference on industrial electronics and applications (ICIEA). DOI:10.1109/ICIEA.2015.7334248

Rayeesa, M., Rumaan, B., & Kaiser, J. G. (2023). Deep Generative Models: A Review. *Indian Journal of Science and Technology*, 16(7), 460–467. DOI:10.17485/IJST/v16i7.2296

Saleh, M., Abdullah, A., & Saher, R. (2022). Message security level integration with iotes: A design dependent encryption selection model for iot devices. *IJCSNS*, 22(8), 328.

Shah, I. A., Jhanjhi, N. Z., & Ray, S. K. (2024). IoT Devices in Drones: Security Issues and Future Challenges. In *Cybersecurity Issues and Challenges in the Drone Industry* (pp. 217-235). IGI Global.

Smmarwar, S. K., Gupta, G. P., & Kumar, S. (2024). Android malware detection and identification frameworks by leveraging the machine and deep learning techniques: A comprehensive review. *Telematics and Informatics Reports*, 14, 100130. DOI:10.1016/j.teler.2024.100130

Sun, N., Ding, M., Jiang, J., Xu, W., Mo, X., Tai, Y., & Zhang, J. (2023). Cyber threat intelligence mining for proactive cybersecurity defense: A survey and new perspectives. *IEEE Communications Surveys and Tutorials*, 25(3), 1748–1774. DOI:10.1109/COMST.2023.3273282

Tarek, M., Rateb, J., Abdulatif, A., Sidra, A., Salim El, K., Salah, Z., & Muhammad, R. (2022). Privacy-preserving federated learning cyber-threat detection for intelligent transport systems with blockchain-based security. *Expert Systems: International Journal of Knowledge Engineering and Neural Networks*, 40(5), e13103. Advance online publication. DOI:10.1111/exsy.13103

Tayyab, M., Marjani, M., Jhanjhi, N., Hashem, I. A. T., Usmani, R. S. A., & Qamar, F. (2023). A Comprehensive Review on Deep Learning Algorithms: Security and Privacy Issues. *Computers & Security*, 131, 103297. DOI:10.1016/j.cose.2023.103297

Tomer, V., & Sharma, S. (2022). Detecting IoT attacks Using an Ensemble Machine Learning Model. *Future Internet*, 14(4), 102. Advance online publication. DOI:10.3390/fi14040102

Val, T. (2023). Data Generation with Variational Autoencoders and Generative Adversarial Networks. DOI:10.3390/engproc2023033037

Valkenburg, B., & Bongiovanni, I. (2024). Unravelling the three lines model in cybersecurity: A systematic literature review. *Computers & Security*, 139, 103708. DOI:10.1016/j.cose.2024.103708

Vemuri, N., Thaneeru, N., & Tatikonda, V. M. (2024). Adaptive generative AI for dynamic cybersecurity threat detection in enterprises.

Wang, X., Wan, Z., Hekmati, A., Zong, M., Alam, S., Zhang, M., & Krishnamachari, B. (2024). IoT in the Era of Generative AI: Vision and Challenges. *arXiv preprint arXiv:2401.01923*.

Wu, H., Han, H., Wang, X., & Sun, S. (2020). Research on artificial intelligence enhancing internet of things security: A survey. *IEEE Access : Practical Innovations, Open Solutions*, 8, 153826–153848. DOI:10.1109/ACCESS.2020.3018170

Yampolskiy, R. V., & Govindaraju, V. (2008). Behavioural biometrics: A survey and classification. *International Journal of Biometrics*, 1(1), 81–113. DOI:10.1504/IJBM.2008.018665

Yu, R., Wang, Y., & Wang, W. (2024). AMAD: Active learning-based multivariate time series anomaly detection for large-scale IT systems. *Computers & Security*, 137, 103603. DOI:10.1016/j.cose.2023.103603

Zhihan, L. (2023). *Generative Artificial Intelligence in the Metaverse Era*. Cognitive Robotics., DOI:10.1016/j.cogr.2023.06.001

Zola, F., Segurola-Gil, L., Bruse, J. L., Galar, M., & Orduna-Urrutia, R. (2022). Network traffic analysis through node behaviour classification: A graph-based approach with temporal dissection and data-level preprocessing. *Computers & Security*, 115, 102632. DOI:10.1016/j.cose.2022.102632

Chapter 8
Reshaping Secure Coding Through Generative AI Approach to Minimizing Programming Challenges

Basheer Riskhan

Albukhary International University, Malaysia

Halawati Abd Jalil Saufan

Albukhary International University, Malaysia

Jazuli Bello Ladan

Albukhary International University, Malaysia

Md Amin Ullah Sheikh

Albukhary International University, Malaysia

Khalid Hussain

https://orcid.org/0000-0002-3714-8696

Albukhary International University, Malaysia

Manzoor Hussain

Indus University, Pakistan

ABSTRACT

A combination of technical expertise, creativity, and problem-solving skills is needed to succeed in the complicated and demanding profession of programming. As a result, there are several challenges that programmers may run against when creating software or computer systems. The literature on how to optimize and reduce the problems and difficulties in computer programming is reviewed in this chapter. The issue has a global scope and keeps becoming worse on a local scale. Even though there are numerous instructional tools available to support the teaching and learning of computer programming, the issue still exists. Computer introduction courses had high failure and dropout rates even from the beginning. This situation's justifica-

DOI: 10.4018/979-8-3693-5415-5.ch008

tion includes the student's inability to solve problems. To overcome the challenges of learning computer programming, these two factors must be taken into account concurrently. This chapter will find out the ways to minimize these challenges.

1. INTRODUCTION

1.1. Background

Programming knowledge is becoming more and more important in today's digital world across a variety of professions, thus it's critical for students to understand the basics of programming languages. However, students frequently run into a number of problems and difficulties while studying programming. This introduction seeks to give a thorough overview of the typical programming problems and difficulties encountered by students, emphasizing the need to remove these obstacles to support efficient learning and skill development (Mallick et al., 2023).

Students, especially those who are new to coding, may find programming to present a unique set of obstacles that are intimidating. The complexity of programming languages itself is one of the main difficulties. Beginners face major obstacles in the form of syntax mistakes, logical flaws, and comprehending the complexities of algorithms (Doe, 2019). Another degree of complexity is added by the fact that programming languages and frameworks are continually evolving, so it's important for students to keep up with the current developments in the industry (Mallick et al., 2023).

The absence of appropriate mentoring and assistance is another problem that students frequently encounter. Programming calls for a disciplined approach, and without the right assistance, students may find it difficult to wade through the plethora of internet knowledge. Their growth may be hampered and exacerbated by a lack of mentors with suitable experience, outdated resources, or outdated materials (Smith & Johnson, 2020).

In addition, a lack of possibilities for real-world application may make it difficult for students to comprehend programming ideas. Although theoretical understanding is necessary, programming is essentially practical, therefore students need chances to put what they have learned to use in practical situations. Without real-world projects or assignments, students could struggle to understand the applications of the theories they learn, which would hinder their potential to become competent programmers (Brown et al., 2018).

Furthermore, programming calls for excellent analytical and problem-solving capabilities. Many students struggle to turn big challenges into smaller, more manageable tasks, which makes it difficult to design and implement workable solutions. Students' progress and overall proficiency may be hampered by the lack of a problem-solving mindset and the inability to address programming issues methodically (Johnson, 2021).

In this paper, we are going to conduct a survey with the aid of a questionnaire in order to go through the topic and find a solution to the issues.

1.2 Problem Statement

For students seeking degrees in computer science, software engineering, and related professions, programming is a critical skill. Yet, school students deal with a variety of problems and difficulties in programming that might hinder their understanding and overall academic success. High-level programming ideas that are difficult to understand, poor time management, a lack of support from peers and teachers, and a lack of resources are a few examples of these problems. Students may also run into additional difficulties with algorithm analysis and implementation techniques due to the increased demand for optimization in programming. These difficulties may cause irritation, a lack of excitement, and poor academic results. Thus, there is a critical need to research optimization solutions that can enhance students' learning outcomes and handle the problem of programming issues and challenges.

1.3 Objective of the Research

The objective of this research is to:

- Understand programming languages by examining their concepts, features, and applications.
- Identify and analyze challenges students face when learning programming languages, including syntax, logical reasoning, algorithmic thinking, and staying updated with evolving technologies.
- Explore challenges faced by lecturers in teaching programming languages, such as addressing diverse student backgrounds, delivering complex concepts effectively, and providing adequate guidance and support.
- Investigate techniques and strategies to overcome student challenges in learning programming languages, including practical projects, mentorship programs, collaborative learning, and problem-solving training.
- Explore techniques and strategies for lecturers to overcome challenges in teaching programming languages, such as creating engaging materials, interactive learning environments, comprehensive feedback, and leveraging technology-enhanced teaching methods

1.4 Significance of the Research

Both programming students and lecturers at Albukhary International University can benefit greatly from this study. This project attempts to improve programming students' achievement by concentrating on the difficulties faced by programming students and investigating potential solutions.

This research's significance can be summarized as follows:

Student-Centered Approach: This study prioritizes the needs and experiences of its participants by looking at the difficulties that programming students face. It will highlight the particular challenges they face, including grammar, logical thinking, algorithmic thinking, and remaining current with changing technologies. Teachers will be able to successfully meet students' individual needs by adjusting their teaching strategies and support systems if they are aware of these difficulties.

Enhanced Learning Outcomes: The research's findings will aid in the creation of methods and strategies that will enable students to get past the difficulties they have when learning programming languages. Students are likely to benefit from greater learning results, more self-assurance, and stronger problem-solving abilities by putting these methods into practice. This will thus have a favorable effect on their academic performance and potential programming careers in the future.

Lecturer Training and Development: The study's emphasis on the difficulties experienced by lecturers when teaching programming languages will provide important insights into the pedagogical facets of programming education. It will deal with difficulties including catering to students from a variety of backgrounds, effectively communicating difficult ideas, and offering sufficient direction and support. Understanding these difficulties enables the research to offer suggestions for professor growth and training, allowing them to deliver more interesting and useful programming courses.

Institutional Improvement: The research findings may help Albukhary International University improve its programming curriculum. This study can guide curriculum development, instructional design, and support services inside the institution by identifying the difficulties faced by students and lecturers and offering solutions. It may result in the adoption of more student-centered strategies, the use of cutting-edge teaching techniques, and the development of a welcoming learning environment.

The research is significant because it has the potential to better institutional practices, encourage additional programming education research, and support lecturers in their efforts to support students in their learning.

2. LITERATURE REVIEW

2.1. What Programming Languages Are All About

Computer science education revolves around programming, which helps students develop their problem-solving skills and refine their analytical talents.

A programming language is a formal language used to instruct computers to perform specific tasks or operations through written instructions known as code. According to the Computer Science Department at the University of Illinois at Urbana-Champaign, programming languages provide a way to precisely describe computation and algorithms, enabling software developers to create complex systems that can perform automated tasks (University of Illinois, n.d.). There are many programming languages available, each with its own unique syntax and features, including Python, Java, C++, JavaScript, and Ruby. The choice of programming language depends on the specific requirements of the project and the preference of the developer. Understanding programming languages is crucial for software development, computer science, and technology fields in general.

Multiple companies, including web development, data analysis, artificial intelligence, and game creation, use programming languages. While languages like R and Python are frequently used for data analysis to draw conclusions from large datasets, HTML, CSS, and JavaScript are frequently utilized in web development to produce interactive and dynamic web pages. Programming languages like Python, Java, and C++ are frequently used in the field of artificial intelligence to create machine learning algorithms, systems for natural language processing, and computer vision applications. The production of games for multiple platforms uses languages like C++, C#, and Java, which is another field where programming languages are essential.

2.2 What Are the Challenges Faced by Students in Learning Programming Languages?

In recent years, it has become more and more common to study programming languages using internet resources. Many students and instructors are using the internet to study programming languages because of the growth of online learning platforms and the availability of free resources available there. However, there is still substantial disagreement regarding whether using online tools for this purpose is effective.

According to some research, learning programming languages online can be just as beneficial as learning them the old-fashioned way. For instance, Körner et al. 's (2020) study discovered that students who used online resources to learn programming languages showed comparable levels of information acquisition and retention compared to those who used traditional learning methods. Similar to this, a study by Salehi et al. (2018) discovered a positive correlation between using online resources to learn programming languages and improved academic performance.

On the other hand, several studies have revealed that using online tools may not be as efficient as learning programming languages the old-fashioned way. For instance, a study by Dastgheib et al. (2019) discovered that students' academic achievement was poorer when they only used online resources to learn programming languages than when they used more conventional learning strategies. The dependability and quality of internet tools for learning programming languages have also drawn criticism from certain studies.

2.3 What Are the Challenges Faced by Lecturers When Teaching Programming Languages?

Keeping up with the continuously evolving technical scene is one of the biggest difficulties faced by lecturers when teaching programming languages. It might be challenging for instructors to stay current with the most recent advancements because new programming languages and tools are continually being developed (Gomes & Mendes, 2019). Consequently, giving students accurate and pertinent information may be difficult.

Addressing the varied degrees of programming experience that students have presents another difficulty. Programming students frequently come from a variety of backgrounds and may have varying degrees of programming experience (Hamza, Hussin, & Yusoff, 2017). It may be challenging for professors to deliver education that is appropriate for each student as a result.

Another obstacle is keeping students interested. It can be difficult for lecturers to maintain student engagement and motivation in programming sessions since they might be scary and demanding (Ndiwalana & Amanyire, 2019).

Another difficulty is offering real-world experience. Since programming is a practical talent, it's crucial that students get the chance to put what they've learned in class into practice. It can be difficult to give students enough chances to gain real-world experience, nevertheless (Gomes & Mendes, 2019).

Another difficulty is meeting the needs of each student individually. While some students could benefit more from lectures and written materials, others might learn better from practical experience. According to Hamza, Hussin, and Yusoff (2017), lecturers must be able to deliver teaching that is tailored to the needs of each individual student.

2.4 What Are the Techniques to Be Used in Overcoming These Challenges?

Software programmes known as interactive learning environments give students the chance to learn programming languages in a fun and engaging way. Interactive learning environments are helpful at assisting students in overcoming the challenges they have when learning programming languages, claim (Thong & Yap, 2020). They design a learning environment that is interesting and motivating in order to increase student retention, achievement, and motivation. By encouraging student participation and cooperation, these spaces can also aid in fostering an active learning atmosphere in the classroom.

Engagement of students in collaborative learning by working in small groups to complete assignments and solve challenges. According to (Fernandes et al., 2018), collaborative learning can be a useful strategy for assisting students in overcoming the challenges they encounter when learning programming languages. Students can assist one another, share ideas, and give criticism when they collaborate, which can improve their learning process. In addition to encouraging student participation and interaction, collaborative learning can offer a chance to evaluate the knowledge and comprehension of the students involved.

In order to make learning more interesting and fun, gamification uses game design components like leaderboards, medals, and points. According to (Ally, 2019), using gamification as a teaching tool can be a successful way to help students overcome the challenges they encounter when learning programming languages. Students can be inspired to learn and more inclined to participate in the learning process by integrating game design aspects into the educational experience. Gamification can increase student engagement and motivation while also giving teachers a chance to gauge their pupils' comprehension and learning.

To effectively address the optimization challenges in programming, various studies have explored innovative approaches. Ghosh et al. (2022) proposed SVM and KNN based CNN architectures for plant classification, showcasing the potential of machine learning in solving complex classification tasks. Ren et al. (2020) introduced a three-level ransomware detection and prevention mechanism, highlighting the importance of robust cybersecurity measures. Humayun et al. (2022) presented a blockchain-based solution to secure drug distribution systems, emphasizing the role of decentralized technologies in enhancing supply chain security. Additionally, Azeem et al. (2021) developed a fog-oriented secure data aggregation scheme for the Internet of Medical Things (IoMT), demonstrating the significance of lightweight yet secure data processing techniques. Some other studies like Alkinani et al (2021), Singhal et al. (2020) and Najmi et al. (2023) and Shahid et al. (2021) collectively contribute valuable insights into addressing programming challenges and optimizing system performance in various domains.

3. METHODOLOGY

Conduct a thorough analysis of the programming language literature that already exists, paying particular attention to the core ideas, characteristics, and applications as well as the difficulties that lecturers and students alike experience and the solutions that they have found. To get a thorough understanding of the subject, collect pertinent books, journals, and research papers. In Fig 1, We show the working flow of research in Optimization for Minimizing the Programming Issue and Challenges.

Figure 1. The Working Flow of Research

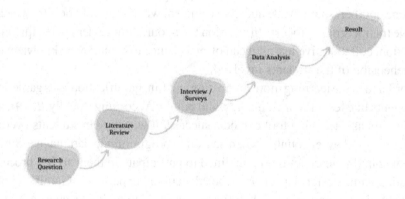

Interviews and Surveys: Conduct interviews with educators and programming language specialists as part of qualitative research. The insights, opinions, and experiences connected to the research questions will be gathered through these interviews. In order to learn more about the difficulties students encounter learning programming languages, surveys might be conducted among them.

Data Analysis: To find common themes, patterns, and perspectives connected to programming languages, issues experienced by students, and challenges faced by lecturers, analyze the data gathered from the literature study, interviews, and surveys. To grasp the study questions in-depth and acquire deeper insights, employ qualitative analysis approaches.

4. RESULTS AND DATA ANALYSIS

A questionnaire was developed in order to find some relevant information related to this research. The total number of responses received is fifty five. The data is analyzed with the aid of a Google Form, which is converted into a pie chart for a vivid description. Below is the analyzed Data.

Figure 2. Common Programming Issue

What are the most common programming issues and challenges you face during coding?
55 responses

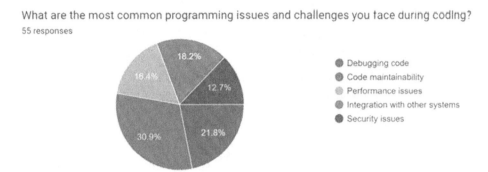

This Fig 2 visualizes the results of the most common programming issues and challenges faced during coding. 21.8% chose debugging code, 30.9% chose code maintainability, 16.4% chose performance issues, 18.2% chose integration with other systems, and 12.7% chose security issues as the issue faced during coding.

Figure 3. Methods to Address Programming Issues

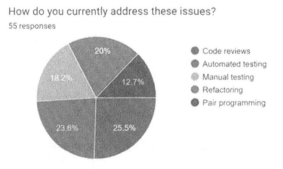

How do you currently address these issues?
55 responses

This Fig 3 shows the issues currently addressed by our respondents. 25.5% addressed it by reviewing the codes, 23.6% by automated testing, 18.2% by manual testing, 20% by refactoring, and 12.7% by pair programming.

Figure 4. Optimization Strategies to Minimize Programming Issue

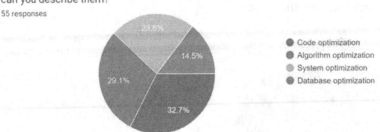

Have you implemented any optimization strategies to minimize these programming issues? If so, can you describe them?
55 responses

- Code optimization
- Algorithm optimization
- System optimization
- Database optimization

This Fig 4 visualizes the strategies used by respondents to minimize the programming issues they are facing. 32.7% do code optimization, 29.1% do algorithm optimization, 23.6% do system optimization, and 14.5% do database optimization.

Figure 5. Proposed Optimizing Strategies in Coding

What are the biggest obstacles to implementing optimization strategies in your coding process?
55 responses

- Time constraints
- Lack of knowledge or expertise
- Budget constraints
- Resistance to change

This Fig 5 shows the obstacles faced by the respondents when implementing optimization strategies during coding. 16.4% chose time constraints, 41.8% lack of knowledge or expertise, 23.6% budget constraints, and 18.2% resistance to change.

Figure 6. Tasks Prioritization and Optimization Process

How do you prioritize optimization tasks in your development process?
55 responses

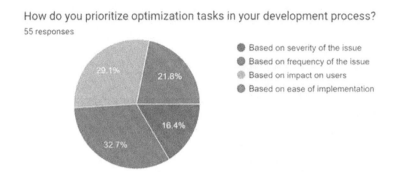

- Based on severity of the issue
- Based on frequency of the issue
- Based on impact on users
- Based on ease of implementation

This figure shows how optimization tasks are being prioritized. 16.4% Based on the severity of the issue, 32.7% Based on the frequency of the issue, 29.1% based on impact on users; 21.8% based on ease of implementation.

Figure 7. Ovell all Performance Measures Using Optimization Strategies

How do you measure the success of your optimization efforts?
55 responses

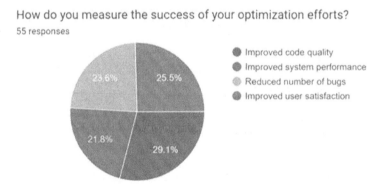

- Improved code quality
- Improved system performance
- Reduced number of bugs
- Improved user satisfaction

Fig 7 shows how the success of the optimization efforts being applied is being measured to see the success of the process. 29.1% is measured by measuring the improvement of the code quality, 21.8% by improving system performance, 23.6% by reducing the number of bugs, and 25.5% by measuring the improvement of user satisfaction.

Figure 8. Cumulative Struggling of Developers

What advice would you give to other developers struggling with programming issues and challenges?

55 responses

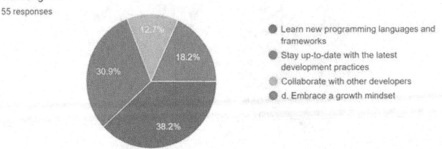

Fig 8 shows the piece of advice to be given to other developers struggling with programming issues and challenges. 38.2% had been advised to learn new programming languages and frameworks; 30.9% advised them to stay up-to-date with the latest development practices; 12.7% advised them to collaborate with other developers; and 18.2% advised them to embrace a growth mindset.

Figure 9. Comparison of Optimization Techniques

Are there any particular areas of optimization you would like to learn more about?

55 responses

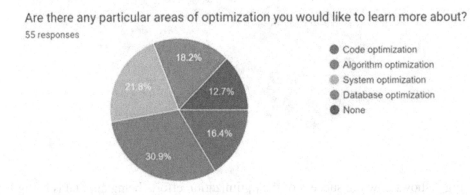

This figure shows if there is any area of code optimization they would like to learn in advance. 16.4% chose code optimization, 30.9% chose algorithm optimization, 21.8% chose system optimization, 18.2% chose database optimization, and 12.7% chose none.

5. CONCLUSION

In conclusion, understanding programming languages can help with problem-solving and analytical skills. Programming languages are essential in the field of computer science. However, learning and teaching programming languages present a number of difficulties for both students and lecturers. Keeping up with the quickly changing technological landscape, addressing the different programming backgrounds of students, retaining student engagement, and offering practical experience are some of these problems.

To overcome these challenges, techniques such as interactive learning environments, collaborative learning, gamification, and personalized teaching approaches can be used. By using these techniques, students can effectively learn programming languages, and lecturers can deliver education that meets each student's needs. Ultimately, improving the teaching and learning of programming languages can lead to a more skilled workforce and more innovative and advanced technology.

REFERENCES

Alkinani, M. H., Almazroi, A. A., Jhanjhi, N. Z., & Khan, N. A. (2021). 5G and IoT based reporting and accident detection (RAD) system to deliver first aid box using unmanned aerial vehicle. *Sensors (Basel)*, 21(20), 6905. DOI:10.3390/s21206905 PMID:34696118

Ally, M. (2019). Using gamification to enhance learning and teaching. Journal of Education and Learning.

Azeem, M., Ullah, A., Ashraf, H., Jhanjhi, N. Z., Humayun, M., Aljahdali, S., & Tabbakh, T. A. (2021). Fog-oriented secure and lightweight data aggregation in iomt. *IEEE Access : Practical Innovations, Open Solutions*, 9, 111072–111082. DOI:10.1109/ACCESS.2021.3101668

Brown, A., Jones, B., & Smith, C. (2018). The role of practical assignments in programming education. *Journal of Computational Science*, 15(2), 45–63. DOI:10.1111/jcs.12345

Dastgheib, S. A., Oskouei, R. H., & Akbari, M. (2019). *The effect of using digital resources on learning programming concepts. Journal of Educational Technology Development and Exchange*. JETDE.

Doe, J. (2019). Overcoming challenges in learning programming. Computer Education Today, 8(3), 17-32. Retrieved from https://www.journalURL.com

Fernandes, L., Souza, J., Alves, E., & Fernandes, C. (2018). The effectiveness of collaborative learning in programming. *Journal of Educational Technology & Society*.

Gomes, A., & Mendes, A. J. (2019). Learning to teach programming: Challenges and opportunities. In *Proceedings of the 2019 ACM Conference on International Computing Education Research* (pp. 219-227). ACM.

Hamza, M. K., Hussin, B., & Yusoff, M. Z. M. (2017). Challenges and opportunities in teaching programming. *Advanced Science Letters*.

Humayun, M., Jhanjhi, N. Z., Niazi, M., Amsaad, F., & Masood, I. (2022). Securing drug distribution systems from tampering using blockchain. *Electronics (Basel)*, 11(8), 1195. DOI:10.3390/electronics11081195

Jhanjhi, N. Z., Humayun, M., & Almuayqil, S. N. (2021). Cyber security and privacy issues in industrial internet of things. *Computer Systems Science and Engineering*, 37(3). Advance online publication. DOI:10.32604/csse.2021.015206

Johnson, R. (2021). Enhancing problem-solving skills in programming education. *Journal of Computational Science Education*, 25(4), 321–345. DOI:10.1080/123 45678.2021.12345678

Kalelioglu, F., Gülbahar, Y., & Madran, O. (2016). A comparison of computer-based and paper-based training for learning programming concepts. *Journal of Educational Technology & Society*.

Khalil, M. I., Humayun, M., Jhanjhi, N. Z., Talib, M. N., & Tabbakh, T. A. (2021). Multi-class segmentation of organ at risk from abdominal ct images: A deep learning approach. Intelligent Computing and Innovation on Data Science *Proceedings of ICTIDS*, 2021, 425–434.

Körner, H., Vos, T., & van der Meijden, H. (2020). An empirical study on the effectiveness of online learning resources in programming education. *International Journal of Emerging Technologies in Learning*.

Mallick, C., Bhoi, S. K., Singh, T., Hussain, K., Riskhan, B., & Sahoo, K. S. (2023). Cost Minimization of Airline Crew Scheduling Problem Using Assignment Technique. *International Journal of Intelligent Systems and Applications in Engineering*, 11(7s), 285–298.

Mallick, C., Bhoi, S. K., Singh, T., Swain, P., Ruskhan, B., Hussain, K., & Sahoo, K. S. (2023). Transportation Problem Solver for Drug Delivery in Pharmaceutical Companies using Steppingstone Method. *International Journal of Intelligent Systems and Applications in Engineering*, 11(5s), 343–352.

Najmi, K. Y., AlZain, M. A., Masud, M., Jhanjhi, N. Z., Al-Amri, J., & Baz, M. (2023). A survey on security threats and countermeasures in IoT to achieve users confidentiality and reliability. *Materials Today: Proceedings*, 81, 377–382. DOI:10.1016/j.matpr.2021.03.417

Ogunseye, O. O., & Adegbenro, O. (2020). Applications of programming languages in various industries. *International Journal of Emerging Technologies in Learning*, 15(14), 102–111. DOI:10.3991/ijet.v15i14.12770

Riskhan, B., Safuan, H. A. J., Hussain, K., Elnour, A. A. H., Abdelmaboud, A., Khan, F., & Kundi, M. (2023). An Adaptive Distributed Denial of Service Attack Prevention Technique in a Distributed Environment. *Sensors (Basel)*, 23(14), 6574. DOI:10.3390/s23146574 PMID:37514868

Salehi, M., Shahriari, H. R., & Moosavi, S. R. (2018). Investigating the impact of using online resources on academic achievement of the students in programming courses. *Journal of Information Technology Education*.

Shahid, H., Ashraf, H., Javed, H., Humayun, M., Jhanjhi, N. Z., & AlZain, M. A. (2021). Energy optimised security against wormhole attack in iot-based wireless sensor networks. *Computers, Materials & Continua*, 68(2), 1967–1981. DOI:10.32604/cmc.2021.015259

Singhal, V., Jain, S. S., Anand, D., Singh, A., Verma, S., Rodrigues, J. J., & Iwendi, C. (2020). Artificial intelligence enabled road vehicle-train collision risk assessment framework for unmanned railway level crossings. *IEEE Access : Practical Innovations, Open Solutions*, 8, 113790–113806. DOI:10.1109/ACCESS.2020.3002416

Smith, E., & Johnson, L. (2020). Mentorship in programming education: A critical review. Journal of Educational Technology, 12(1), 78-96.

Chapter 9
Security Considerations in Generative AI for Web Applications

Siva Raja Sindiramutty
https://orcid.org/0009-0006-0310
-8721

Taylor's University, Malaysia

Krishna Raj V. Prabagaran

Universiti Malaysia Sarawak, Malaysia

N. Z. Jhanjhi
https://orcid.org/0000-0001-8116
-4733

Taylor's University, Malaysia

Mustansar Ali Ghazanfar

University of East London, UK

Nazir Ahmed Malik
https://orcid.org/0000-0002-0118
-4601

Bahria University, Islamabad, Pakistan

Tariq Rahim Soomro
https://orcid.org/0000-0002-7119
-0644

Institute of Business Management, Karachi, Pakistan

ABSTRACT

Protecting AI in web applications is necessary. This domain is a composite of technology and huge scope with good prospects and immense difficulties. This chapter covers the landscape of security issues with advancing generative AI techniques for integration into web development frameworks. The initial section is on security in web development—a conversation on the subtleties of generative AI-based methods. In a literal stance, the chapter offers 13 ways to approach it. Among the threats are those that introduce security issues related to generative AI deployments, which illustrate why it is vital for defenders and infrastructure owners to implement mitigation measures proactively. This chapter pertains to the security and privacy of data and lessons for securing and preventing vulnerability. The chapter explores attacks, model poisoning, bias issues, defence mechanisms, and long-term mitiga-

DOI: 10.4018/979-8-3693-5415-5.ch009

tion strategies. Additionally, Service A promotes transparency, explainability, and compliance with applicable laws while structuring a development methodology and deployment methods/operation. The text outlines how to respond and recover from incidents as it provides response frameworks for everyone involved in managing security breaches. Finally, it addresses trends, possible threats, and lessons learned from real-world case studies. In order to contribute to addressing these research needs, this chapter sheds light on the security considerations associated with AI for web development and suggests recommendations that can help researchers, practitioners, and policymakers enhance the security posture of popular generative AI advancements used in generating web applications.

INTRODUCTION TO SECURITY IN GENERATIVE AI FOR WEB ENGINEERING

Define the Importance of Security in Web Engineering and the Implications of Generative AI Techniques

Web development: Securing the web serves to protect assets and user privacy. As more usage is detected, security measures need to be in place. Per a study conducted by (Habbal et al., 2024), the context of security threats is ever-changing, making it tougher for web professionals. It would be best to implement security protocols to ensure that no one enters or can breach your data (Ahmadi, 2024). Artificial intelligence techniques are rising, bringing another layer to web security concerns. As highlighted by Liu et al. (2024), a new form of content creation and control involves text, images, or videos that highly accurate machines can manipulate. This development is an attractive opportunity for innovation but also raises fears regarding the misuse of AI-generated content (Kenwright, 2023; Sindiramutty et al., 2024).

Especially in web development, they have a safer internet because it secures the assets and privacy of users. Security is also essential, especially now with more and more activities happening around us. Research by Habbal et al. (2024) has observed that web professionals have to face challenges because cyber threats change daily. Our security proceeds related to access, data leakage and attacks are significant for being deployed against them (Ahmadi, 2024). That may result from the growing use of new UT web techniques or factoring in a fresh dimension field-based: more and automatising A Techniques, according to web security concerns. As highlighted by Liu et al. (2024), Generative AIs can produce and edit a wide range of content types, like text or images, with equal competency. An exciting technological evolution First and foremost, repurposing AI-generated content is a double-edged sword (Kenwright, 2023; Sindiramutty et al., 2024).

Thus comes into play the need to bring security in web development practices as a basic element to minimise risk around AI technology. In line with Rafy (2024), developers should ensure strong authentication methods and encryption protocols to efficiently battle AI-enabled phishing hacks and misinformation campaigns. Another important point is to monitor security challenges; all required intelligence provides vast scope for detection and swift action (Huyen & Bao, 2024; Azam et al., 2023). Collaboration between cybersecurity experts and AI researchers is needed to create strategies for present-day attacks of all types.

Through AI-driven analysis and utilisation of Machine Learning algorithms, organisations can increase their ability to detect activities and predict cyber attacks before they occur (Pulyala, 2024; Azam & Tajwar et al., 2023). Policymakers should regulate AI use to ensure legal compliance and ethics (Farina et al., 2024). In general, security is something that must be taken into account when you develop websites to protect your assets and user trust. Although this rise of AI promises to revolutionise various industries, when it comes to Web security, all this has come with opportunities and challenges. Defences were required, as well as collaborative work across multiple fields. With so many record volumes of cyber threats, applying security principles to mitigate the associated risks has become increasingly important as technology advances. Figure 1 illustrates security considerations for web applications in AI.

Figure 1. Security In Generative AI for Web Application

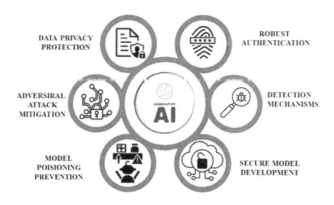

Overview of How Generative AI is Applied in Web Applications and Potential Security Risks

Generative AI has been a hit in web applications for its short ability to create content independently, thus changing the future of both development and user engagement. This involves a variety of techniques, including Generative Adversarial Networks (GANs) and state-of-the-art language models such as OpenAI's GPT that makes machines capable of creating images or video content(text) up to whole websites (Feuerriegel et al., 2023; Ananna et al., 2023).

One example of the use of AI in web development is article generation, where AI models provide well-written content based on data, automatically creating advanced articles and a smoother writing experience for users (Boukar et al., 2024). Moreover, generative AI enables web design to generate user interfaces (UI) in an automated way. Variability in website layout concerning user experience (UX) enriched design preferences (Borg et al., 2024). Integrating AI into web applications, on the other hand, is not free from security threats and vulnerabilities, starting with fake news generated using this tool to create false content.

These bad actors can exploit AI technology to fabricate websites, fake news and deceitful ads, which erode confidence in online information, resulting in reputational risks for businesses (Ferrara, 2024). Also, AI techniques are being used for cyberattacks, such as AI-powered phishing campaigns and automatic social engineering. Such attacks can manipulate online interactions, using AI-generated material impersonating sources to gain user data or meddle with harmful intentions (Stingelová et al., 2023). The black-box nature of AI models makes it challenging for security professionals to track and mitigate attacks produced by AIs.

For AI, there is the risk that traditional security controls would have difficulty distinguishing content or material generated by a device versus based on an analytic anomaly-either causing too many alarms to be actionable at once or failing to see new emerging risks (Gregory et al., 2023). AI has become a greater player in web development; security pros will likely need to be vigilant and devise mitigation strategies for the threats posed by AI-created content and those cyberattacks executed via such mediums.

Chapter Contributions

Diving Deep Into the Universe of Generative AIs

The chapter discusses AI approaches—ML methods that work well, like GANs and large language models such as GPT. It explains how these methods allow machines to generate content independently, such as images, text, and video.

Real-World Use Case in Web Development

This chapter is closer to what generative AI can do for web-based projects, from writing content to automating tasks in functional web design. This early proof of concept shows how companies use this service to generate web layouts and product descriptions and optimise UI elements to boost your business productivity and enhance user engagement.

Addressing Security Concerns

This part covers the Integration of AI with Web development and its security concerns. It examines the threats posed by AI-driven fake news, deep fakes, and sophisticated cyber threats. It also addresses the difficulty of AI models' opacity in recognising and responding to new security threats.

Risk Mitigation Strategies

This chapter provides solutions to the security vulnerabilities associated with AI for web development. It concludes that authentication, encryption measures, and threat intelligence are important components of defences against AI-driven threats and cyber-attacks.

Exploring Ethical Dimensions

This paper inquires into the moral foundations related to AI and its portrayal through web applications. The chapter covers the problems of privacy breaches, bias in algorithms, and responsible AI content generation. This further underscores the need for standards and regulatory guidelines to govern the development and deployment of AI-powered web apps.

Cross-Curricular Collaboration

This section emphasises the needed capacity to tackle security challenges in web applications and calls for collaboration between cybersecurity experts, AI researchers, and policymakers. It explains the need for knowledge sharing, collaborative research, and stakeholder engagement in developing solutions to mitigate AI risks.

Looking Ahead

Finally, they discuss the directions and emerging trends in generative AI, including how they intersect with web applications. AI-based web tech and detection methods plus change analysis include targeted, well-funded research initiatives and the need for continual adaptation to meet rising cyber threats and changing technology.

Chapter Organization

In this section, we will cover an insight into AI in web development and why it matters to us so that we can help you prepare for the main goals of section 2. In the next part, we go down to the basics of AI and discuss key techniques that help machines for content generation, like GANs (Generative et al.) and VAEs (Variational Autoencoders), and some of the latest transformer models. Real-World Use Cases for AI in Web Development Content Creation Automating Web Design User Interface Enhancement We then move to Sec 4: addressing security concerns of integrating AI with web apps, i.e., risk for misinformation and cyber threats. Section 5 also deals with some protection against these threats in the context of authentication and encryption. We discuss privacy issues and biases in deploying AI algorithms, which raise ethical concerns that we approach through Section 6. Section 7 claims the synthesis of disciplines required in a multidisciplinary approach involving security experts and AI) practitioners. Finally, section 8 examines the future of this space and suggests a need for sustainability in addressing potential vulnerabilities within generative AI/web app development due to ever-changing threats and breakthroughs.

THREAT LANDSCAPE ANALYSIS

Examination Of Potential Security Threats Posed by Generative AI In Web Application

Now, generative AI is one of the tools in web applications that have improved user interaction by auto-creating content. However, excessive utilisation still creates security vulnerabilities that must be considered. This part deals with security measures while integrating Generative AI into web applications. A significant problem is that they can harvest AI-generated material for phishing scams, fake news, etc. Karnouskos (2020) describes that wrongdoers get in on the action with pro-efficiently rapid advancements wrought within AI, providing them with an easy means to produce consumable fake news, which users find hard in discriminating fakery data. As well, Generative AI models may pick up on unintended.

Reproduce harmful text from some of their training data sets (Brown et al., 2019); the volatility of this field was shown to pose an immense threat in terms of misinformation and manipulability—Figure 2 refers to web applications security threats due to generative AI. Additionally, including Generative AI in web-based applications allows for automating cyber-attacks such as creating malware and abusing weaknesses within the web systems. Mohanakrishnan et al. (2023) introduce how attackers can leverage AI-powered tools to recognise and exploit security vulnerabilities, potentially leading to information leaks or data breaches.

Similarly to the previous use cases, Generative AI models could be engineered by threat actors in order to bypass security or surveillance systems Lin et al. (2022). Experts discussed the challenges of Generative AI to cybersecurity professionals in a panel. However, better privacy considerations cast a shadow on using Generative AI in web applications. On the other hand, applying AI algorithms in user profiling and behaviour modelling also suffers from a privacy-relevant consent approach. However, user training in Generative AI models may lead to model leaks or even propagate certain practices inadvertently, necessitating data privacy laws and regulations.

While there is potential for Generative AI to enhance the capabilities of web applications, it also brings security risks that must be addressed. Tackling these threats will require collaboration among AI experts, cybersecurity specialists and policymakers to develop strategies and regulatory frameworks.

Figure 2. Potential security threats posed by generative AI in web applications

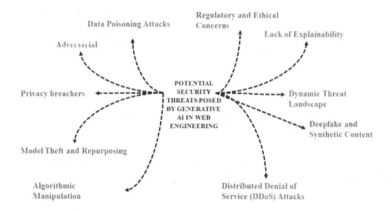

Identification of Vulnerabilities in Generative AI Models and Their Impact on Web Security

Even though generative AI models can transform how we create and engage with our users, they also introduce weaknesses in web security. This analysis discusses those vulnerabilities and their effects on web security. Generative AI models have a unique disadvantage as they are vulnerable to attacks like generating unwanted outputs by modifying the input. Tomlinson et al. (2023) caution that superficial changes in input data (e.g. examples) can have devastating effects accrued by AI-generated contributions on the web, misleading them entirely to a lack of trust. The exploitation of vulnerabilities can break down security mechanisms.

Mislead users, risking the confidentiality and reliability of digital information. Generative AI models are also plagued with privacy concerns, as Oseni et al. (2021) pointed out. These datasets frequently contain personal information. Membership inference attacks— Inferring details in AI-generated results puts user privacy and confidentiality at stake. In some cases, Generative AI models may directly or indirectly leak data from the training dataset (Humphreys et al., 2024) discussed. This underscores the need for data anonymisation and privacy-preserving methods to mitigate these risks.

Also, using Generative AI models in web applications raises questions about their resistance and confidence. According to Oniani et al. (2023), model inversion attacks or stealing models can result in flaws that expose the property and proprietary algorithms to many Generative AI systems. Using trained AI models and their lack of transparency in the process makes it difficult to evaluate and eliminate deficiencies, which increases security risks in web environments.

Identifying vulnerabilities in Generative AI models to ensure web security and minimise risks is crucial. Addressing these vulnerabilities requires collaboration among AI researchers, cybersecurity experts, and web developers to create defence mechanisms and implement practices for securing AI-driven web applications.

DATA SECURITY AND PRIVACY CONCERNS

Discussion on the Risks Associated With Training Data, Including Data Leakage and Privacy Violations

Using datasets to train AI models is a pretty common route in today's era. However, this strategy also involves dangers like data leaks and privacy violations. Data leakage is the unintentional revelation of secret information during training, causing privacy breaches and security threats (Cheng et al., 2017; Verma et al., 2021). When personal or confidential information is used in a way that violates privacy, it results in embarrassment, which may also result in an ethical consequence. One of the major perils to worry about concerning training data is that it may disclose information. Since the AI model learns from that input, there could be a danger where it can recall identifiable information (PII), financial records or even business proprietary data (Alhitmi et al., 2024). This may open the gates for exposure to or manipulation of data, thereby putting privacy and enterprise security at risk.

In addition, training based on combining two datasets can further escalate these risks. If these data sources are combined, data exposure and controlling access to protect sensitive information will become more challenging (Omotunde & Ahmed, 2023). Transparency and accountability in data collection are also lacking. Most will not be aware that their data will help train AI in some form, and most people do not understand what agreeing means.

Furthermore, datasets that are systematically biased or not representative can perpetuate social inequality and discriminative practices through AI systems if the data bias results in unfair treatment of decisions, particularly for marginalised groups (Mehrabi et al., 2021; Fatima et. et al., 2019). While training data remains integral to developing AI models, it does not shield you from other risks, such as exposure to potential security problems and violation of privacy. However, suppose policymakers determine that the potential benefits outweigh these risks. In that case, governance around data collection should be transparent and accountable, and steps can be taken to counterbalance biases in training datasets.

Strategies for Protecting Sensitive Data Used in Generative AI Models, Such as Anonymization and Encryption

As AI models are on the rise, protecting data used in these machine learning models is essential and a big concern for the industry. Data protection, data anonymisation, and encryption are the two main methods within the chaos of a database. Anonymisation means removing or modifying data such as PII from a dataset to prevent identification (Majeed et al., 2017). Data encryption is a powerful defence mechanism, and organisations can improve data security by anonymising personal details, e.g. names, addresses, social security numbers, etcetera. Besides, it is necessary to equip anonymisation strategies with a robust defence against re-identification attacks in which external data could be exploited to tie the information that has been anonymised back together with identifiable individuals (Xenakis et al., 2023; S. et al. et al., 2019).

Encryption is the process of converting data into code, which can be decoded by authorised parties with a key for decryption, on the other hand (Shruti et al., 2023; Khalil et al., 2021). This protects the data from being read, even if it is intercepted or accessed by unauthorised personnel. It must be encrypted at rest (data stored when the data is residing on a server) in transit - and thereby throughout its lifecycle. Using anonymisation and encryption techniques can substantially boost the protection and privacy-protection regime around data in content-generation AI models. Ensuring information (PII) is protected at each stage - during model training. In contrast, the models are tackled by saving and shipping data securely from unapproved access, which can lessen the risk of exposure and knowledge breaks, whereas mining valuable patterns in understanding through AI algorithms.

However, we must also remember that these techniques are fallible, and their implementations may have constraints. Anonymisation and encryption would add little benefit but possibly complexity (Sankar et al., 2020; Maurya & Joshi, 2024), reducing application data quality. As a result, organisations need to take inventory of their data protection requirements and craft strategies that effectively temper the scales between security, privacy, and usability. Anonymisation and encryption are part of how data inherent in content-generating AI models is kept safe. Combining these methodologies with data governance best practices helps minimise potential risks associated with the exfiltration of data and privacy breaches in a manner that can still leverage the benefits of AI technology.

ADVERSARIAL ATTACKS AND DEFENSES

Explanation of Adversarial Attacks Targeting Generative AI Models in Web Application

Generative AI tech like GANs have already become standard in various industries for creating data, imagery, and text (Ping et al., 2024). The downside of such models is that they are susceptible to being distorted by adversarial agents who modify input data to fool the model into generating certain outcomes. These attacks are web development nuisances, which can become threats that undermine the security or Dependability of systems built with these technologies. One widespread type of attack is tampering with the input data to obtain misclassification or unsatisfactory predictions from the model (Radanliev & Santos, 2023; Gaur et al., 2021).

These modifications can impact the veracity of generated content, for instance, by encouraging false news to propagate throughout websites and internet platforms. Another one is feeding AI models training data laced with bad examples. The manipulation affects the model's decisions and how it distributes its output, ultimately leading to non-ideal content on web platforms. This is compounded by attackers utilising AI model vulnerabilities to generate fake news, spam content, or deepfake images that erode trust in online information and pose formidable challenges for content moderation and brand reliability.

The evolving nature of these environments enhances the impact that adversaries can have with their attacks, as they adapt on the fly and specifically tailor strategies to bypass detections or exploit vulnerabilities (Wang et al., 2024; Almusaylim et al., 2020). Because of attacks like these, it is clear that web apps need proper defence mechanisms and better training strategies to protect or survive in this situation. This also expands to the web development landscape, where adversarial attacks against AI models may leave online systems vulnerable, breached and unreliable (Mehta et al., 2024). Challenges can be solved by defence mechanisms, training strategies against adversaries, and ongoing research to find the inherent weaknesses in generative AI models.

Techniques for Defending Against Adversarial Attacks, Including Robust Training and Detection Mechanisms

The security of the AI models used in web applications from adversarial attacks needs to be secured with a strict defence system (Hossain et al., 2024). A common strategy involves training, where models are incentivised with data that has been synthetically degraded (Goyal et al., 2023, Wassan2012) to maintain performance and compete against attacks. This approach allows models to learn quickly from new data or adapt effectively across input distributions. In addition, it can serve as a necessary detection mechanism for risks that need to be taken and human active financial system integration that is part of AI-enabled. They work by watching the model outputs and input data to detect signs of tampering, which can then lead to an action to prevent getting wrong results. Such methods include identifying instances and anomalies that cause model behaviour to deviate significantly from the expected (Ξενάκης et al., 2023), which are useful for proactive defence measures. Figure 3 shows a flowchart of attack and corresponding defence.

Figure 3. Adversarial attack and the defence (Admin, 2022)

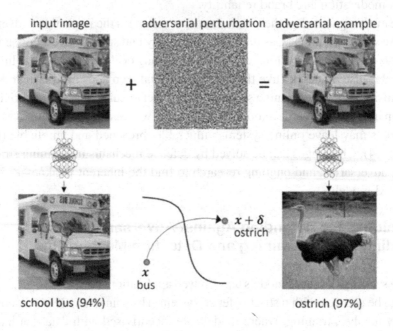

Moreover, boxing the model or methods together lets both domains benefit from each other, resulting in more robust countermeasures towards adversarial attacks (Roshan & Zafar, 2024). Using an ensemble, manipulations' effects can be mitigated efficiently by considering multiple models or defence approaches. Secure AI systems at large More importantly, defence strategies against attacks can be enhanced by refining domain knowledge and contextual information (Darzi et al., 2023; Ghosh et al., 2020). Using knowledge of the application domain and input data features makes it easier for models to distinguish plausible inputs from adversarial examples.

This makes them more robust under real-world conditions. Researching robustness and setting up standardised evaluation benchmarks is also necessary for the progress of defence techniques (Y. Wang et al., 2023), as well as to evaluate key technical tissue and ultimately tackle inferences about their effectiveness. Research collaboration and knowledge sharing help establish defence mechanisms against adversarial attacks. To protect AI models against attacks, developers must use some form of ensemble or group methods that include robust training and detection mechanisms combined with the application of domain knowledge in a collaborative research process. By executing these tactics and refinements in defence against threats, AI systems can more effectively combat new assaults without sacrificing the security of web applications.

MODEL POISONING AND MANIPULATION

Examination of Potential Threats Related to Malicious Manipulation of Generative AI Models

Generative AI models have demonstrated the ability to generate content in other forms - images, text and audio. However, though these are groundbreaking advancements, they also bring misappropriated uses, which can lead to a myriad of security risks, including cyber and misinformation threats as well as possible breaches of privacy. One key concern is the emergence of more sophisticated deepfakes, which could deceive people and automated systems. Some researchers, such as Mubarak et al. (2023), will also force the detection methodologies to address a better war for fighting deepfakes that are more frequent. Part of the problem also is that it becomes easy to use AI as evidence - a very tricky thing in both legal and forensic settings where authenticity matters! News articles and false claims on social media that are written using natural language generation models are increasingly becoming a cause for concern.

Furthermore, leveraging AI models to defeat security measures such as CAPTCHA systems (as illustrated by Sakhare and Patil 2023) can present dangers for platforms and high-value repositories of sensitive data that would be exposed via unauthorised access or breaches. Furthermore, That raises ethical questions concerning the use of AI models. Bias and content creation have been the subjects of concern for years in The Geiger et al. (2023), and this may increase stereotyping, extending social disparities associated with diversity across various disciplines.

Generative AI models work best when used wisely, but like all tools, they can lead to dark places in the wrong hands. Researchers, policymakers, and industry players must collaborate to spearhead tactics that will identify the overuse of cyber securities and establish benchmarks for these trends in line with regulations. We must deal with this so that human society and all of us benefit from AI without suffering.

Countermeasures to Prevent Model Poisoning and Ensure the Integrity of Generative AI Outputs

Given the dangers of tampering with generative AI models, strong protections will be needed against such attacks so that these results can remain trusted. One particularly successful avenue is to secure the model- code by providing controlled access with authentication. To complicate changes to model parameters or training data, organisations can deny access to trained models and Multi-Factor Authentication (MFA) protocols (Aboukadri et al., 2024; Shahid et al., 2021). In addition, they maintain the status of how a model functions, which will possibly support identifying anomalous behaviour that might sign attempts to hack into variables with data (Bhuiyan & Uddin, 2023).

Also, training methods should be added while developing a model as one of the important defence strategies. Regarding adversarial training, the concept is to augment the training set with examples meant to attack and break down the easy model (Alotaibi & Rassam, 2023) Azam et al. Developers can enhance the robustness of AI models against adversarial attacks and reduce their vulnerability to potential manipulations by training them in different instances (Chennamma & Madhushree, 2022). Along with this, processing techniques like watermarking or digital signature can also determine the authenticity and source of content generated. Identifiers are used for traceability, source validation, and watermarked outputs.

Similarly, digital signatures aid in content existentialism by validating the models or datasets linked to a signature. The core of AI is to ensure transparency, which calls for accountability, which means trust-building should come first before utilisation (Kapoor & Chatterjee, 2023; Almusaylim et al.,2018). Organisations can reduce the risks of outcomes and misuse by following AI principles that incorporate transparency, fairness and accountability. This means that the processes used by model makers to disclose biases and limitations and interact with stakeholders in discussions of ethics for generative AI deployment.

An integrated framework involving procedural and ethical factors needs to be welcomed to maintain the consistency of AI results. Organisations can use training techniques and offer transparency, accountability, and even security measures to reduce model manipulation-related risks and appropriately incorporate generative AI technologies.

BIAS AND FAIRNESS CONSIDERATIONS

Analysis of Bias and Fairness Issues in Generative AI Models for Web Application

Content-generating AI technologies are necessary for all content creation and user engagement platforms. Conversely, their use of bias and fairness may introduce concerns. AI bias: the errors in choice that cause some singularity to be treated (Cossette-Lefebvre & Maclure, 2022). Conversely, fairness seeks uniform outcomes for all, irrespective of who you are. Research has identified AI model biases in language and photosynthesis tasks (Karabacak et al., 2023; Humayun et al., 2022). Many of these biases are rooted in the data on which a model is trained - representing historical prejudices or excluding certain demographics entirely. Consequently, created content can potentially reinforce stereotypes and marginalise a group.

In addition, questions about fairness are much deeper than content bias to how judgments by the algorithms come into being. Results can be discriminatory if AI systems engage in group favouritism or resource distribution biases (Hagendorff et al., 2022). This is particularly significant in web applications, e.g. personalised suggestions, employee screening algorithms, etc, where biased algorithms can perpetuate existing inequalities. To address these challenges, model cards describe the datasets used to train models and provide specific methods (and measurements) for evaluating those models. Utilising fairness objectives in training to help with bias and outcomes

It is also necessary to keep generative AI models interpretable, as described in (Vyas, 2023; Singhal et al., 2020Taj & Jhanjhi, 2022). for identification or resolution of biases or fairness problems. Transparent models: Developers can understand how a decision is made and uncover disparate treatment cases. At the same time, other methods, such as explaining the model or analysing counterfactuals, provide some insight into why particular behaviours occur (Rane et al., 2023). These tactics help stakeholders address concerns about bias and fairness by promoting transparency and accountability.

Strategies for Mitigating Bias and Promoting Fairness in Generative AI Outputs

To get results and avoid causing damage, it is imperative that AI models produce impartial outcomes (González Sendino et al., 2024). Several strategies can be developed to overcome such difficulties. Perhaps more important is diversifying the training data sources. This can be mitigated by feathering demographic perspectives and data, lessening the chance of strengthening an explicit stereotype or marginalising any cluster. Data preprocessing or augmentation enables the recognition and removal of biases in training data, enhancing fairness (Drukker et al., 2023).

Another is making fairness objectives part of the process in which models are trained. Developers can nudge AI systems towards focusing on outcomes by training while applying fairness metrics (Xivuri & Twinomurinzi, 2023; Azam et al., 2023). Fairness constraints can also be imposed during training or regularisation to punish behaviour in model outputs (Yang et al., 2023). Improving transparency should also help identify and correct bad behaviour (of both models). Explanation of the model results is important to enable reflective reasoning for stakeholders to understand why AI yielded a certain prediction and detect bias.

Explaining and analysing easily make AI-generated content understandable (Longo et al., 2024). Developing and assessing AI systems with fewer people or communities is not an early alternative (Moon, 2023) - various involvement of human counterparts becomes necessary instead. This allows developers to understand their possible biases better and develop inclusive solutions through collaboration with subject matter experts, ethicists, and community representatives. To help lessen bias over time, regularly monitoring and evaluating AI performance is essential (Krause, 2023).

Feedback loops and model updates can help incorporate developers' responses to emerging fairness concerns, adhering to evolving standards. Approaches to bias reduction and fairness in AI results should include diverse data sources, training objectives focused on fairness (before the model is built), transparency of how stakeholders use the models, and ongoing monitoring. Developers can adopt these strategies to ensure their IP is used safely and ethically with minimal harm while advancing equity. Figure 4 shows an example of Model Poisoning.

Figure 4. Example of Model Poisoning (S. Gupta, 2023)

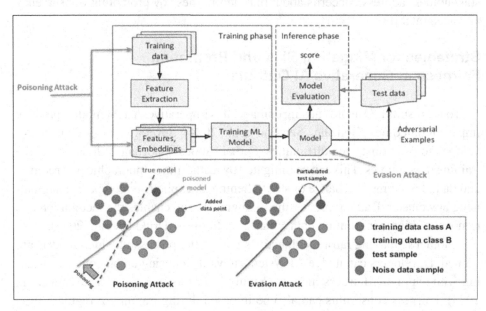

EXPLAINABILITY AND TRANSPARENCY

Importance of Explainability and Transparency in Generative AI Models for Web Applications

Web applications that are highly interactive with users need to be aware of how a user will create content. This transparency is important to build trust as it tells users why certain content was shown. That excluding knowledge does not increase our satisfaction or joy in living. So, show that will help in web development by locating the source level mistakes. Having heard how these AI models work, I believe developers are less likely to work with errors. Transparent models make it simple to notice and remedy any biases in content generation, managing ethical factors like GDPR compliance (Parray et al., 2023; Sindiramutty et al., 2024).

Clarity In the world of UX design, clarity does something! Designers can build UIs based on how content was created, which helps make the overall user experience more intuitive and personable. Additionally, clear communication helps developers and stakeholders work together on the same page. Knowing how AI models function, teams can work together more efficiently and make educated decisions at every step of the web development process (Zhang et al., 2023). We cannot emphasise enough the need for transparency and clarity on AI models in web applications.

User trust and satisfaction are paramount, not to mention debugging and compliance, UX design, and collaboration. The increasing role of AI within web development illustrates that explainability is central to the construction of user-centred, inclusive, and trustworthy web experiences (OSF, n.d.).

Methods for Enhancing the Interpretability of Generative AI Outputs and Ensuring Transparency in Decision-Making Processes

Improving the explainability of AI outcomes and guaranteeing transparency in decision-making processes are requirements for further enhancing and deploying existing artificial intelligent systems. Liu and Co (2023) suggest strategies must be used to attain these objectives. The first of the benefits is that agnostic approaches, such as feature visualisation, can increase transparency. It helps the model interpretability in understanding and explaining its decision by visualising activation patterns of neurons or the importance of input features.

Furthermore, using hoc explanation techniques paired with generative models increases transparency (Garg et al., 2024). Methods such as SHAP (Shapley Additive explanation) can help gain insights into the process leading up to every prediction; this way, one may build trust and accountability by explaining. Additionally, introducing uncertainty estimation in models will increase clarity (Khennouche et al., 2024; Sindiramutty et al., 2024). While this has the advantage that predictions are generated along with uncertainty quantifications (this is important for confidence in model outputs when using decision-making), we believe stationary priors can greatly improve calibration.

That is the approach we can take by looking at different profiles. Build more transparent AI systems free of biases and solve ethical concerns (Habbal et al., 2024). In addition, introducing documentation and reporting standards for AI models clarifies things. Model cards are a tool similar to labels that give information about the data trained against, performance metrics (accuracy or fairness) and potential biases so business users can decide if it is appropriate to use in their application. Achieving clear AI-generated results, with the proper control and understanding of decision-making processes, is fundamental to earning any AI system's trust, accountability and ethical use. This can be achieved by encompassing model-independent visualisation techniques, methods for responsibly showing results (often posthoc explainability), standardised methodology to estimate uncertainty and collective documentation, but most importantly, due to greater interdisciplinarity.

REGULATORY COMPLIANCE AND LEGAL IMPLICATIONS

Overview of Regulatory Frameworks and Legal Requirements Related to Web Security and Privacy

It is very important in the world to protect online information, which includes privacy and security, and play a vital role in keeping an individual's secret, sensitive personal data. Governments and other worldwide bodies have set up rules and guidelines to secure against these dangers efficiently. So, for users in the EU, this is known as the General Data Protection Regulation (GDPR), introduced by the European Union in 2018. GDPR is an effort to provide EU citizens with greater data protection and privacy; it emphasises transparency, consent and accountability for organisations processing information (Tikkinen-Piri et al., 2018; Sindiramutty et al., 2024). In the U.S., the Health Insurance Portability and Accountability Act (HIPAA) does much of the same for healthcare. (D'Ordine, n.d.).

This law mandates that healthcare providers take steps necessary to protect the privacy and confidentiality of medical records. In addition, compliance with the Payment Card Industry Data Security Standard (PCI DSS) is paramount for companies that process payment card transactions. PCI Data Security Standard provides a set of security measures to secure cardholder data, which minimises the chances of fraud and other forms of criminal activity. Additionally, the California Consumer

Privacy Act (CCPA) of 2018 gives certain rights to residents of California as it relates to their data. Businesses that gather, use, and share data are also given a set of responsibilities (Gupta et al., 2023).

Another emerging regulatory framework in the U.S. COPPA, which is short for Children's Online Privacy Protection Act, intends to regulate the privacy of children under 13 by placing parental notice requirements and controlling what personal information websites can ascertain about them (Anderson, 2024). These requirements and legal obligations aim to help keep web privacy and security alive even today. They set standards and guidelines that companies must fulfil to build trust in managing individuals' sensitive data. Following these rules decreases the exposure to data breaches but also helps promote a privacy and security-minded culture that benefits consumers and businesses.

Considerations for Ensuring Compliance with Regulations Such as GDPR, CCPA, and Others

Companies must also meet the requirements of regulations such as GDPR, CCPA, and other data protection laws to respect privacy issues related to individuals and avoid penalties. Before giving up the ghost, there are many things to consider for organisations going into what is likely survival mode. For starters, you need to know the context and specifications of each regulation. For example, the GDPR protects the personal data of all EU residents that an organisation processes. In contrast, only businesses in California and those under their direct control that collect consumers' personal information are subject to CCPA. These regulations affect the operations companies need to carry out certain checks.

The next step is to put in place security measures. It includes incorporating procedures to follow security practices used as a shield against data access, infringements and cyber attacks. Encryption access controls and regular security audits are some of the components of a data protection plan (Ahmed & Ahmed, 2023). Third, getting consent from people before gathering their data is a basic tenet of the GDPR and CCPA. We recommend a standard for data consent based on the proposed actions described by R. Wang et al. (2020), where they propose businesses to raise awareness and obtain permission from customers in an explanatory way of what their privacy/data will be collected/used as part of omnichannel processes. They must also create mechanisms for performing data subject rights, which include requests to access, correct, or delete personal information.

It makes individuals the owners of their data by enabling them to browse, access and delete it in the desired timeline. Organisations must conduct various employee training and awareness campaigns, which should help develop a compliance culture (Bilderback, 2013; Sindiramutty et al., 2024). Teaching staff about what their responsibilities are regarding elements such as data protection (including privacy policies and other regulatory obligations) iteratively reduces exposure to risk profiles desirable under compliance standards

Supporting privacy laws and conforming to regulations like the GDPR, CCPA, etc., requires a multifaceted approach. By educating employees about the environment, enforcing data protection measures, obtaining consent, establishing procedures for handling individual requests about their data, and adopting a compliance-oriented culture supported by employee training programs, companies can avoid breaching individuals' privacy rights while reducing Non-compliance risks.

SECURE DEVELOPMENT PRACTICES

Best Practices for Integrating Security Into the Development Lifecycle of Generative AI Models for Web Application

Given that web applications will increasingly be powered by AI models, there is an imperative to build security into the development process at this early juncture of threat discovery (Rane, 2023). It is, therefore, vital to implement security measures that protect data and secure information against threats. There are a few tactics for improving the security of AI models in web application frameworks. Firstly, when threat modelling is adopted ergonomically, it allows developers to predict and perform countermeasures against threats early at the game stage (Crothers et al., 2023; Sindiramutty et al. Developers can protect risks proactively before they occur by understanding threats and their impacts. Furthermore, using encryption methods (SSL protocols) also ensures data transmission and stops sniffing attacks on a network (Bozkurt et al., 2023).

Additionally, access controls must be implemented to limit the accessibility of generative AI models and any associated data (Olabanji et al., 2024). Built on expanding users' roles, Role-based access control (RBAC) mechanisms enforce the best practice of granting the least privileges. In addition, it is essential to keep software components and libraries up-to-date and patch known vulnerabilities, or the attack surface will constantly be large (Riegler et al., 2023). The continuous monitoring capabilities help identify all types of activities and security breaches in real-time (Olabanji, Marquis et al., 2024). With Intrusion detection systems (IDS) and security information and event management (SIEM), developers can identify and analyse severe incidents while minimising their impacts.

In providing human intervention, regular security assessments and penetration testing assist in detecting vulnerabilities before becoming utilised by malicious parties (Ozkan Okay et al., 2024). Security must be a top concern at all stages of the AI model development for web applications to minimise exposure and safeguard one's private information. Developers can further bolster the security posture of AI models by integrating encryption practices, access controls, software upkeep and monitoring threat modelling into their functions. Mitigation strategies for bias in AI output are illustrated in Figure 5.

Figure 5. Mitigation strategies of bias in generative AI output

Diverse Training Data:	Ensure the training data used to develop the AI model is diverse and representative of the population it will encounter. This helps prevent biases from being amplified in the model's output
Bias Detection Algorithms	Implement algorithms that can detect biases in the data or model outputs. These algorithms can flag potential biases for further investigation and correction.
Fairness Metrics Integration	Integrate fairness metrics into the evaluation process of AI models. These metrics assess the fairness of model outputs across different demographic groups and help in identifying disparities
Regular Bias Audits	Conduct regular audits to identify and mitigate biases that may arise in AI systems over time. This involves reevaluating the model's performance and making necessary adjustments to ensure fairness.
Explainability and Transparency	Make AI models more transparent and explainable by providing insights into the decision-making process. This allows stakeholders to understand how biases may manifest and be addressed

Techniques for Secure Coding, Threat Modeling, and Vulnerability Management

Security is a top priority in software development because we want to keep our data safe. If you write code, analyse potential threats, and manage vulnerabilities using the following practices, your risk will be reduced effectively. Coding practices Several coding standards focus on security throughout development (Kizza, 2024). Adopting the OWASP Top 10 or other security tools would allow developers to detect and solve problems like injection attacks and cross-site scripting (Daah et al., 2024). To a certain extent, this is true, and coding libraries, along with well-documented APIs, can greatly reduce the friction in developing an app by offering tested functions or modules (Garcia & Johnson, 2019).

Even though the architecture has been considered based on known threats, it is important to find a method that allows you to build more secure applications by design (Mat et al., 2024); one such method is threat modelling Security techniques.

With an understanding of the system components, data flows (Hussain et al., 2024), etc., developers can prioritise security measures better and faster. Developers can attempt to think like a hacker and list out ways your software could be targeted - techniques such as attack trees help with this - while misuse cases also outline potential threats against security controls. The set of processes and tools for vulnerability management (Mingo et al., 2024; Sindiramutty et al. Karlsson & Ljungberg, 2024) can be detected through automated tools that scan for vulnerabilities in software components and libraries (He et al., 2024). Moreover, a mechanism to govern patch management should be in place so that security patches can be quickly rolled out and the attack surface area will remain small (Alanazi, 2024).

In conclusion, coding practices, threat modelling, and efficient vulnerability management strategies are critical to building more secure systems. Organisations that prioritise security throughout all stages of the development process will be more equipped to mitigate potential risks and repel cyber threats.

SECURE DEPLOYMENT AND OPERATIONS

Guidelines for Securely Deploying and Operating Generative AI Models in Web Application Environments

These AI models are used in web apps to enhance user experience and work productivity. However, securing their deployment and operation is difficult due to vulnerabilities. This spec defines principles for deploying and operating generative AI models in web environments. The primary focus is setting up appropriate authentication and authorisation mechanisms for controlling access over the AI model and the data it uses. This includes the use of OAuth 2.0 and JSON Web Tokens (JWT) to authenticate users, validate user identity beforehand, and then control activity based on predetermined roles and permissions (Satybaldy et al., 2024; Sindiramutty... et al., 2024).

At the minimum, encryption must be implemented on transmission and storage levels to maintain data security. Communications between clients and servers should be encrypted with Transport Layer Security (TLS), using strong encryption algorithms like AES to protect database information. It is Victims of Their Success—4 Ways log file monitoring helps prevent anomalies used in combination with continuous access monitoring and logging, which can help identify and address security threats (García et al., 2024). Security information event management (SIEM) solutions are used for this purpose, where logs from different components of the web application environment are aggregated and analysed, looking for any suspicious activities (Banerjee et al., 2024)

We also investigate the use of vulnerability assessments and penetration test-ing to identify and remediate security vulnerabilities within the AI model and its infrastructure (Charfeddine et al., 2024). An approach: This means one addresses the risks before they get exploited by any evil actors. Compliance with standards such as GDPR and HIPAA is essential to protect the privacy rights of your users when processing user data using AI models. According to Akanfe et al. (2024), Organisations need top-level data governance policies for compliance to satisfy these regulations' demands. The plan should consider how you will authenticate over the web, if and when to operate model encryption (and where), what sort of monitoring is required for a production AI system, and regular testing practices as-sociated with deployments into an anticipated regulatory framework. Taking these precautions helps organisations better handle security risks and protects the critical data processed by AI models on web platforms.

Considerations for Access Control, Authentication, and Monitoring to Mitigate Security Risks

Access control, identity verification and observability contribute to mitigating security risks related to deploying and managing generative AI models within web applications. Executing these measures more skillfully is important, not just simply securing the data or stopping the use of AI models. Handling access control securely to interactions with the AI model and its resources is crucial. RBAC enables admin-istrators to assign user roles and provide rights accordingly (Zaidi et al., 2023). By having RBAC in place, organisations enforce the least privilege principle, which states that only necessary resources are available to users based on their roles.

The authenticity of users must be checked carefully when using AI from the Rescue Dengue system. As mentioned above, MFA increases security by making users provide identification factors like a password and also some one-time code which will be sent to their device (Papaspirou et al., 2023). Adopting MFA reduces cognito login risk even if the credentials are stolen. Security breaches must be de-tected and continuously monitored pervasively. Like SA solutions, log analysis can also be combined with other techniques on SIEM, such as special actions taken in combination with events emitted by behaviour monitoring to block security threats and then organisations must "log" the following components of the web application environment (AI model/server/database) for identification abnormal behaviours or otherwise peculiar (Kamble et al., 2024; Sindiramutty et al..,2024).

Logging of user actions and system events should also be kept. Audit logs provide information on who accessed AI models, what actions were performed by whomever and at which time (Perdana et al., 2023). Comprehensive audit trails allow organ-isations to trace alterations in AI models. Security Incidents - minimise the time spent on investigations. Appropriate access control, authentication measures, and monitoring systems are paramount to minimise security concerns associated with employing AI models for web applications (Habbal et al., 2024). Adopting these strategies protects organisations' AI applications—secure data from unauthorised access or attacks.

INCIDENT RESPONSE AND RECOVERY

Strategies for Incident Response and Recovery in the Event of Security Breaches or Attacks Targeting Generative AI Models

The widespread use of AI technology has translated into significant progress in art, healthcare, and cybersecurity. However, the advantages also bring security problems, which organisations must solve. These AI models can be exploited for breaches or attacks, which may lead to data manipulation, privacy breaches and content generation (Huang et al., 2023). Companies must respond to incidents appropriately with strategies tailored for generative AI models; these are potential solutions. Identifying threats requires Proactive monitoring anomaly detection and forecasting modelling (Judijanto et al., 2023; Wen et al., 2023). Organisations can detect any such step that might indicate a security breach by monitoring models' activity and Inputs-outputs patterns (Nankya et al., 2023).

In addition, data is protected by access controls, and all model parameters are always encrypted at rest. It is crucial to have incident response plans in place to quickly respond and limit the damage from cyberattacks (Angafor et al., 2023). These plans should set out who is responsible for what, where continuous improvement will occur and how communication between the parts of an incident response team must be organised. Regular security assessments and the ability to simulate attacks build muscle memory in identifying areas for improvement in your prevention and detection capabilities and enhancing how you address incident response.

Additionally, decisive action is needed to limit harm when security incidents happen. This attack can be halted by isolating infected systems and rolling them back to a known good checkpoint to quarantine the activities (Dawodu et al., 2023; Sindiramutty et al., 2023). Ensure that operations are resumed promptly. Further, taking it a step further to leverage threat intelligence feeds and work with industry peers enables valuable insights for incident response and recovery. Security breaches or attacks targeting AI models and the systems housing them must be handled with monitoring, robust incident response planning, and fast containment steps. Deploying these approaches will help secure AI models to mitigate organisations' risks. Safeguard their assets and operations efficiently.

Frameworks for Incident Handling, Forensics, and Remediation

Timely responsiveness in the event of security breaches or attacks on AI models also provides a significant avenue to leverage frameworks for Incident Management, Forensics Analysis and Remediation. They are made to reduce the potential damage of incidents and restore AI models. The NIST Cybersecurity Framework is an example of one such framework that focuses on identification, protection, detection, response and recovery (Sikder, 2023). The MITRE ATT&CK framework, in addition, provides details into adversary tactics and techniques that are used for threat detection, as well as response (Bagui et al., 2023). The Incident Handling Process by SANS Institutes lists stages such as preparation, identification, containment and eradication recovery post-incident review (Johansen, 2017). Such frameworks allow organisations to develop custom incident response plans for attacks targeting AI models. The significance of explainability in AI is illustrated in Figure 6.

Figure 6. Importance of explainability in generative AI

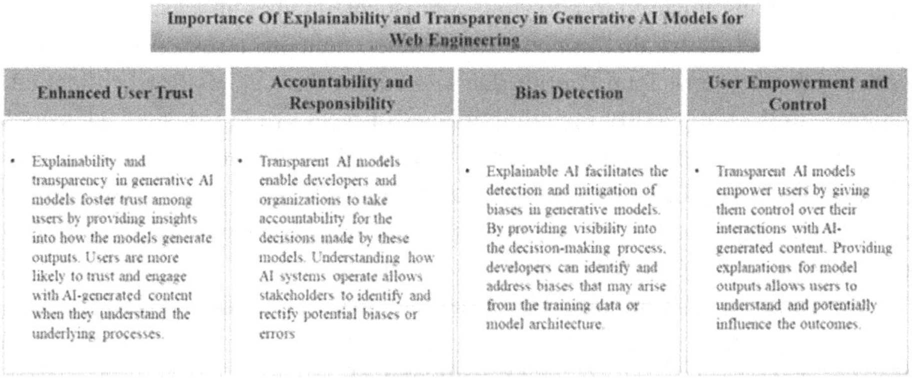

Organisations need to design better strategies for re-enterprises, meaning security incidents primarily targeted at generative AI models, including, for instance, adding communication channels and escalations requirements for swift resolution of interrelated (Jha, 2023). After that, the victims need to launch a thorough investigation of ransomware analysis into what happened and how long they have been affected by this threat. Additionally, organisations need to apply measures that prevent the entry of these attacks and reduce the harm caused to AI processor systems and other valuable data. Containment could involve vulnerability fixes, improved security measures, re-deployed AI models in their original state and lessons-learnt documentation.

Incident response- It is largely meaningless to play humble after an incident, claiming knowledge of what went wrong and why, but minor adjustments here faced with the same situation in future will lead almost nowhere. In the reality of AI security, if a generative model has been attacked or compromised, it might be: An incident handling framework will help organisations respond to and recover from an identified attack on their models. Utilising proven frameworks and a strategic approach will assist organisations in minimising the severity of incidents, safeguarding their AI systems, and ensuring trust in their business operations.

FUTURE DIRECTIONS AND EMERGING THREATS

Exploration of Emerging Security Threats and Challenges in Generative AI for Web Application

Generative AI is revolutionising several segments, one among them being web applications. It also introduces new security issues. It will be a secular concern which may see AI being misused to carry out sophisticated cyber attacks. Similarly, the public should be aware that impersonating others remains a reason we must also scrutinise further news found online due to AI algorithms generating brilliant fake content (Smith et al., 2020), including images of faces or realistic text. This could deceive users. Loss of trust in platforms (Falade, 2013) Secondly, the rise in effectiveness of AI Deep Learning methods has brought about deepfake videos that can easily manipulate audio content, thereby threatening fake news and identity theft risks (Tufchi et al., 2023; Sindiramutty et al., 2023).

However, an equally important issue that should not be overlooked is the security vulnerabilities presented when web applications integrate AI models. According to Dworkin et al. (2021), introducing AI-driven tools like chatbots or recommendation engines can open doors for bad actors. Shortcomings in the data used to train how a model looks for patterns and shortcomings with its implementation point out vulnerabilities. This re-emphasizes the need for security assessments at all stages in creating AI-backed web applications.

Moreover, the absence of interpretability and explainable AI models makes it difficult for security professionals to understand and address them. The opaque architectural design of the deep-learning algorithms does not allow a researcher to understand what happens inside during each input-to-output transformation, hence making it difficult to identify actions by which new threats evolve in web security, but with this transparency can be controlled(Tripathy & Mishra, 2023).

Besides threats, another growing worry among cybersecurity experts is insiders misusing AI tools in organisations. George (2024) also discussed the required control mechanisms for generative AI, so people do not misuse it for data theft or intellectual property infringement. While generative AI increases the function of web applications, it also implants potential security issues that must be given sufficient attention. However, by working together across disciplines and leveraging new security paradigms to mitigate these risks, we can harness the good of AI while ensuring systems remain trustworthy.

Predictions for Future Trends in Web Security and Strategies for Adapting to Evolving Threats

The reflections on top are of serious concern and point to the future. We will see new web security trends that need corresponding techniques for combating evolving threats. A growing trend is the rise of IoT devices in web environments. Ensuring that networked endpoints are secure will be critical: By 2025, most industry estimates point to more than the planned number of connected devices - around 75 billion (Jawad et al., 2023); according to Iftikhar et al. (2023) due to the unique characteristics of devices and their limited computational resources that requires new methods to deal with its security, thus exploring innovative techniques such as lightweight cryptography & edge computing.

Augmented security and privacy of the web are achieved with growing technologies such as blockchain and decentralised Identifiers (DIDs), among others. Apata et al. conducted a study Upon implementation in (2023); an effective cure-all has illustrated numerous benefits that can be achieved using blockchain-based solutions, highlighting the tamper-proof audit trails and identity management features shared among all participants; such a setup significantly reduces authentication risks for each entity as well providing synergy to mitigate data storage risk. Interoperability and better standards are necessary for most decentralisation strategies for leading businesses, which depend on web infrastructure integrations.

Second, the evolution of AI and ML techniques will further shape the security landscape, which is a double-edge weapon (literally). Although AI-driven threats, such as incidents and phishing attempts performed by AIs, constantly augment expected to advance in complexity (Malatji & Tolah, 2024), the intelligence solutions are supposed to be able to extend defences by detecting attacks and offer an adjustable response (Moustafa et al., 2023). AI-powered anomaly detection and behaviour-based authentication will be some of the ways to adapt to combat the latest threats on the moving web security scape.

To counter these trends, companies must take an adaptive security governance approach. This includes developing a learning and collaborative culture within the teams and studies on DevSecOps practices presented by Cob Parro et al. (2024). By blending security throughout the software development process and utilising automation to deal with vulnerabilities and respond to incidents, organisations can better fortify their defences against ever-evolving threats while enabling digital innovation. Increasingly importantly, tactics must be informal enough for an agile method of cyberattacking to approach inquiries concerning malware - web security technologies are slowly merging. By predicting and embracing these developments, companies can strengthen security measures and effectively navigate the changing threat landscape. Figure 7 illustrates secure coding, threat modelling, and vulnerability management techniques.

CASE STUDIES AND PRACTICAL EXAMPLES

Real-World Case Studies Illustrating Security Considerations and Challenges in Deploying Generative AI Models for Web Application

Introducing AI models into a web application presents security challenges and trade-offs. This report analyses live examples to illustrate these concerns and what they mean in web development and cybersecurity.

Vulnerabilities in Image Generation: Case Study 1

In a research study by Nair et al. (2023), experts showed how image-creation GANs can be attacked. In these attacks, input data is tampered with to fool the model, making security breaches arise on web applications involving image processing.

Case Study 2: Text Production Privacy Risks

The study by Guo et al. (2023) found that one problem is that text-generating models can raise privacy concerns. If these models are trained on data, they can inadvertently expose the information in generated content, creating privacy issues for web apps that handle user-generated content.

Case Study 3: Malicious Code Evacuation

A study by Zahid et al. (2023) also delved into AI model-based code generation. However, suppose code generation models contain flaws or vulnerabilities in the process through which those are generated. In that case, attackers can use such weak points to automate malware and append scripts into web applications, ultimately leading towards security problems.

Case Study 4: Hate Speech and Discrimination-Generated Content

Content that can be generated by Generative AI models, which have been trained on datasets. Cui et al. (2024) research demonstrated how eliminating bias in the training of models can help contain malicious web application damage—the key to protecting your client portfolio from any reputational and legal risks.

In a paper, Resource Exhaustion Attacks Is Back: What Everyone Should Know, the authors observed that generative AI models are computationally resource-heavy and thus subject to their namesake attacks. For example, if it is possible to make a web server hosting these AI models difficult to do so (Javaheri et al., 2024), the adversaries may use this weakness against the defenders and conduct DDoS attacks that overload servers serving for these AIs will cause service interruptions or total downtime. We walk you through these case studies to ensure they are secure when deploying your AI models for web applications. In order to keep the trust, privacy demand by its users' web applications needs to consider and mitigate all kinds of vulnerabilities that can arise through these AI technologies, such as attacks, data privacy breaches, malicious code generation, bias issues, and resource depletion. Security protocols and ethical considerations can be factored into all development steps to help address these risks, protecting sensitive data from misuse.

Figure 7. Techniques for secure coding, threat modeling, and vulnerability management

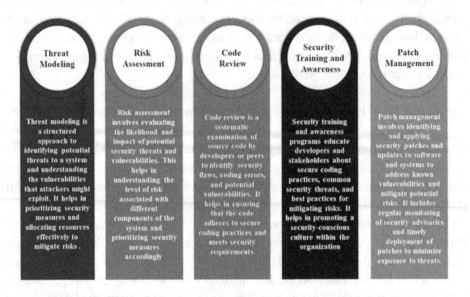

Lessons Learned and Best Practices Derived From Successful Implementations and Security Incidents

Learnings and best practices from the usage and security issues for AI models in web applications. Developers can devise success/failure strategies to make these technologies more efficient and secure for their implementations.

Key Takeaways:

1. Rigorous Model Validation: The importance of model validation (to find and fix issues) is highlighted in success stories. Developers can conduct testing the validation to enhance the reliability and security of AI models (Illiashenko et al.2703)
2. Ethical-> How are ethical considerations integrated into the model development and deployment process? Security incident learning points out the fear of AI risks and convinces the need to counter bias and ease-fairer conditions while putting user privacy on top in implementation and during the design phase (Chimbga, 2023).
3. Detection: Continuous monitoring and detection of security incidents in the context that AI models are executed.

Developers can instantly recognise behaviour, potential attacks or performance of systems in real-time by setting up monitoring systems (Venkatesan & Rahayu, 2024)
Key Guidelines:

1. Confidence in Model Training: Integrating techniques such as data filtering and adversarial training into the process ensures that AI models are trained securely and robustly against different attacks or changes made to data [Khazane et al., 2024].
2. Privacy: Methods such as federated learning or differential privacy protect user information during model training and inference, keeping users more secure while using the task (Rafi et al., 2024).
3. Engage in Shared Security Efforts: Promote developer, security professional, and stakeholder collaboration efforts that facilitate a cybersecurity strategy. By cultivating those partnerships, organisations can more effectively address security weaknesses (Abulibdeh et al., 2024).

In practice and hacks against AI, you learn insights on how to deploy the model in several web applications. By placing installation, ethical risk checking, and security of web-lose protocols at the fore, all little breakneck speed, they can use AI applications to realise returns while minimising extensive and agile technological risks. Figure 8 illustrates the incident response plan.

Figure 8. Incident response and recovery

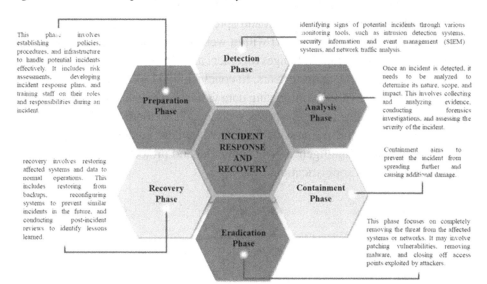

CONCLUSION

Summary of Key Insights and Recommendations for Enhancing Security in Generative AI for Web Application

The future of web apps could go through a complete overhaul if generative AI can successfully render custom-built content. However, tackling security problems and preventing threats and vulnerabilities is necessary with this advancement. Reviewing the existing literature has given me a few interesting ideas for improving security in AI web applications. Generative AI systems have a critical vulnerability: acknowledging it. This forms the primary vulnerability of these systems' reliance on datasets, which opens them up to attacks that could intend for distortion within results produced by such models. It is important to be aware of such vulnerabilities before enforcing security measures.

Data validation is another key piece of the puzzle that guarantees that only honest inputs are fed into AI models. Organisations can validate the input sources as they enter and add techniques such as anomaly detection to prevent data injection. Finally, ensuring that cyber defences are regularly vigilant and refreshed across AI models is necessary. This is where regular audits and vulnerability assessments come in - they help to find these security gaps before malicious entities can use them against you; additionally, baking in methods such as privacy-preserving techniques improves the robustness of the AI system's privacy protection capabilities. The idea is that training data must contain noise to ensure the safety of potential information leakage - while keeping as much intended functionality in an AI model.

Ultimately, boosting coordination and spreading insight in academia is crucial to help establish stronger, secure AI within web applications. Sharing new threats information and addressing challenges together can help ensure that AI-enabled web systems are secure in the coming years. In conclusion, AI web security involves an approach that features all-encompassing data validation mechanisms and proactive cybersecurity strategies to ensure privacy protection methods within the research community collaborative framework. By following these guidelines, Organisations can harness artificial intelligence's (AI) potential and protect themselves from the threats inherent in its sophistication.

Call to Action for Researchers, Practitioners, and Policymakers to Prioritize Security in the Development and Deployment of Generative AI Technologies for Web Applications

Generative AI is starting to change the landscape of web applications. To mitigate these risks, it is imperative for researchers to focus on the security of Internet-connected consumer devices and to emphasise communication with stakeholders in order to assist practitioners and policymakers.% AI is emerging as an enabler for rich user experience and personalised content. However, security implementations surrounding the same will prevent it from getting exploited maliciously to protect users' privacy. The second perspective is that researchers have a place in learning about the security implications of AI technologies. To this end, researchers in the security community can significantly aid that initiative by researching vulnerabilities and threat vectors more fully to provide a range of effective strategies or best practices for securing AI-driven web applications.

Web application security consideration should be a top priority for all developers and AI practitioners developing web applications. It includes deploying validation steps that encrypt the data and security checks to detect new threats so they can be addressed. Based on this, policymakers are making provisions and creating regulations that increase the adoption of security practices in AI Development and deployment. In establishing guidelines and standards for securing AI-driven web applications in more ways than one, industry partners need to be brought in the loop, as this constitutes not only a collective endeavour but also an inclusive effort towards ensuring the security and privacy of those Web apps in which AI powers.

This article illustrates how researchers, practitioners, and policymakers can collaborate to generate new, multi-disciplinary insights for research challenges in AI technology building adaptive web applications. They might enable stakeholders to develop security strategies involving technical, ethical and regulatory considerations by supporting cross-disciplinary conversations and exchanging expertise. Conclusion In conclusion, it is of utmost importance to be secure while developing and deploying web applications with AI-enabled technologies to leverage their advantages and mitigate risks. Researchers, policy and industry must cooperate more closely to develop a trustful environment for AI-powered web applications.

REFERENCES

Ξενάκης, Χ., Xenakis, C., Συστημάτων, Σ. Τ. Π. Κ. Ε. Τ. Ψ., & Συστημάτων, Α. Ψ. (2023, March 21). *Adversarial machine learning attacks against network intrusion detection systems*. https://dione.lib.unipi.gr/xmlui/handle/unipi/15335

Aboukadri, S., Ouaddah, A., & Mezrioui, A. (2024). Machine learning in identity and access Management Systems: Survey and deep dive. *Computers & Security*, 139, 103729. DOI:10.1016/j.cose.2024.103729

Abulibdeh, A., Zaidan, E., & Abulibdeh, R. (2024). Navigating the confluence of artificial intelligence and education for sustainable development in the era of industry 4.0: Challenges, opportunities, and ethical dimensions. *Journal of Cleaner Production*, 437, 140527. DOI:10.1016/j.jclepro.2023.140527

Agbede, O. M. (2023). *Incident handling and response process in security operations*. Theseus. https://www.theseus.fi/handle/10024/795764

Ahmadi, S. (2024). Challenges and solutions in network security for serverless computing. *International Journal of Current Science Research and Review*, 07(01). Advance online publication. DOI:10.47191/ijcsrr/V7-i1-23

Ahmed, M. M., & Ahmed, A. M. (2023). Citizens' data protection in e-government system. *International Journal of Innovative Computing*, 13(2), 1–9. DOI:10.11113/ijic.v13n2.389

Akanfe, O., Lawong, D., & Rao, H. R. (2024). Blockchain technology and privacy regulation: Reviewing frictions and synthesising opportunities. *International Journal of Information Management*, 76, 102753. DOI:10.1016/j.ijinfomgt.2024.102753

Alanazi, M. N. (2024). 5G security threat landscape, AI, and blockchain. *Wireless Personal Communications*. Advance online publication. DOI:10.1007/s11277-023-10821-6

Alhitmi, H. K., Mardiah, A., Al-Sulaiti, K. I., & Abbas, J. (2024). Data Security and Privacy Concerns of Ai-Driven Marketing in the Context of Economics and Business Field: An Exploration into Possible Solutions. *SSRN*. DOI:10.1080/23311975.2024.2393743

Almusaylim, Z. A., Jhanjhi, N. Z., & Alhumam, A. (2020). Detection and Mitigation of RPL rank and version number attacks in the Internet of Things: SRPL-RP. *Sensors (Basel)*, 20(21), 5997. DOI:10.3390/s20215997 PMID:33105891

Almusaylim, Z. A., Jhanjhi, N. Z., & Jung, L. T. (2018). I am proposing A Data Privacy-Aware Protocol for Roadside Accident Video Reporting Service Using 5G In a Vehicular Cloud Networks Environment. *2018 4th International Conference on Computer and Information Sciences (ICCOINS)*. DOI:10.1109/ICCOINS.2018.8510588

Alotaibi, A., & Rassam, M. A. (2023). Adversarial Machine Learning Attacks against Intrusion Detection Systems: A Survey on Strategies and Defense. *Future Internet*, 15(2), 62. DOI:10.3390/fi15020062

Ananna, F. F., Nowreen, R., Jahwari, S. S. R. A., Costa, E., Angeline, L., & Sindiramutty, S. R. (2023). Analysing Influential factors in student academic achievement: Prediction modelling and insight. *International Journal of Emerging Multidisciplinaries Computer Science & Artificial Intelligence*, 2(1). Advance online publication. DOI:10.54938/ijemdcsai.2023.02.1.254

Anderson, H. (2024, February 2). *The Guardian of the Digital Era: Assessing the impact and challenges of the Children's Online Privacy Protection Act*. https://www.paradigmpress.org/le/article/view/1004

Angafor, G. N., Yevseyeva, I., & Μαγλαράς, Λ. (2023). Scenario-based incident response training: Lessons learnt from conducting an experiential learning virtual incident response tabletop exercise. *Information and Computer Security*, 31(4), 404–426. DOI:10.1108/ICS-05-2022-0085

Apata, O., Bokoro, P. N., & Sharma, G. (2023). The Risks and Challenges of Electric Vehicle Integration into Smart Cities. *Energies*, 16(14), 5274. DOI:10.3390/en16145274

Azam, H., Dulloo, M. I., Majeed, M. H., Wan, J. P. H., Xin, L. T., & Sindiramutty, S. R. (2023). Cybercrime Unmasked: Investigating cases and digital evidence. *International Journal of Emerging Multidisciplinaries Computer Science & Artificial Intelligence*, 2(1). Advance online publication. DOI:10.54938/ijemdcsai.2023.02.1.255

Azam, H., Dulloo, M. I., Majeed, M. H., Wan, J. P. H., Xin, L. T., Tajwar, M. A., & Sindiramutty, S. R. (2023). Defending the digital Frontier: IDPS and the battle against Cyber threat. *International Journal of Emerging Multidisciplinaries Computer Science & Artificial Intelligence*, 2(1). Advance online publication. DOI:10.54938/ijemdcsai.2023.02.1.253

Azam, H., Tajwar, M. A., Mayhialagan, S., Davis, A. J., Yik, C. J., Ali, D., & Sindiramutty, S. R. (2023). Innovations in Security: A study of cloud Computing and IoT. *International Journal of Emerging Multidisciplinaries Computer Science & Artificial Intelligence*, 2(1). Advance online publication. DOI:10.54938/ijemdcsai.2023.02.1.252

Azam, H., Tan, M., Pin, L. T., Syahmi, M. A., Qian, A. L. W., Jingyan, H., Uddin, H., & Sindiramutty, S. R. (2023). Wireless Technology Security and Privacy: A Comprehensive Study. *Preprint*. DOI:10.20944/preprints202311.0664.v1

Bagui, S., Mink, D., Bagui, S., Ghosh, T., Plenkers, R., McElroy, T., Dulaney, S., & Shabanali, S. (2023). Introducing UWF-ZeekData22: A Comprehensive Network Traffic Dataset Based on the MITRE ATT&CK Framework. *Data*, 8(1), 18. DOI:10.3390/data8010018

Banerjee, R., Sahu, R., & Gazi, T. A. (2024). A study on cyber defence curse for online attackers. In *Advances in business information systems and analytics book series* (pp. 106–124). DOI:10.4018/979-8-3693-0839-4.ch005

Bhuiyan, M. R., & Uddin, J. (2023). Deep Transfer Learning Models for industrial fault diagnosis using vibration and acoustic Sensors data: A review. *Vibration*, 6(1), 218–238. DOI:10.3390/vibration6010014

Bilderback, S. (2023). Integrating training for organizational sustainability: The application of Sustainable Development Goals globally. *European Journal of Training and Development*. Advance online publication. DOI:10.1108/EJTD-01-2023-0005

Borg, K., Sahadevan, V., Singh, V., & Kotnik, T. (2024). Leveraging Generative Design for Industrial Layout Planning: SWOT Analysis Insights from a Practical Case of Papermill Layout Design. *Advanced Engineering Informatics*, 60, 102375. DOI:10.1016/j.aei.2024.102375

Boukar, M. M., Mahamat, A. A., & Djibrine, O. H. (2024). *The impact of artificial intelligence (AI) on Content Management Systems (CMS): a deep dive.* https://www.ijisae.org/index.php/IJISAE/article/view/3953

Bozkurt, F., Kara, M., Aydın, M. A., & Balık, H. (2023). Exploring the Vulnerabilities and Countermeasures of SSL/TLS Protocols in Secure Data Transmission Over Computer Networks. *2023 IEEE 12th International Conference on Intelligent Data Acquisition and Advanced Computing Systems: Technology and Applications (IDAACS)*. DOI:10.1109/IDAACS58523.2023.10348784

Charfeddine, M., Kammoun, H. M., Hamdaoui, B., & Guizani, M. (2024). ChatGPT's Security Risks and Benefits: Offensive and Defensive Use-Cases, Mitigation Measures, and Future implications. *IEEE Access: Practical Innovations, Open Solutions*, 1, 30263–30310. Advance online publication. DOI:10.1109/ACCESS.2024.3367792

Cheng, L., Liu, F., & Yao, D. (2017). Enterprise data breach: Causes, challenges, prevention, and future directions. *Wiley Interdisciplinary Reviews. Data Mining and Knowledge Discovery*, 7(5), e1211. Advance online publication. DOI:10.1002/widm.1211

Chennamma, H. R., & Madhushree, B. (2022). A comprehensive survey on image authentication for tamper detection with localization. *Multimedia Tools and Applications*, 82(2), 1873–1904. DOI:10.1007/s11042-022-13312-1

Chimbga, B. (2023). Exploring the ethical and societal concerns of generative AI in internet of things (IoT) environments. In *Communications in computer and information science* (pp. 44–56). DOI:10.1007/978-3-031-49002-6_4

Cob-Parro, A. C., Lalangui, Y., & Lazcano, R. (2024). Fostering Agricultural Transformation through AI: An Open-Source AI Architecture Exploiting the MLOps Paradigm. *Agronomy (Basel)*, 14(2), 259. DOI:10.3390/agronomy14020259

Cossette-Lefebvre, H., & Maclure, J. (2022). AI's fairness problem: Understanding wrongful discrimination in the context of automated decision-making. *AI and Ethics*, 3(4), 1255–1269. DOI:10.1007/s43681-022-00233-w

Crothers, E., Japkowicz, N., & Viktor, H. L. (2023). Machine-Generated Text: A comprehensive survey of threat models and detection methods. *IEEE Access : Practical Innovations, Open Solutions*, 11, 70977–71002. DOI:10.1109/ACCESS.2023.3294090

Cui, T., Wang, Y., Fu, C., Xiao, Y., Li, S. J., Deng, X., Liu, Y., Zhang, Q., Qiu, Z., Li, P., Tan, Z., Xiong, J., Kong, X., Wen, Z., Xu, K., & Li, Q. (2024). Risk taxonomy, mitigation, and assessment benchmarks of large language model systems. *arXiv (Cornell University)*. https://doi.org//arxiv.2401.05778DOI:10.48550

D'Ordine, K. (2023). *HIPAA vs. Medical Research: Improving Patient Care Through Integration of Data Privacy and Data Access*. Bryant Digital Repository. https://digitalcommons.bryant.edu/honors_data_science/9/

Daah, C., Qureshi, A., Awan, I., & Konur, S. (2024). Enhancing Zero Trust Models in the Financial Industry through Blockchain Integration: A Proposed Framework. *Electronics (Basel)*, 13(5), 865. DOI:10.3390/electronics13050865

Darzi, E., Dubost, F., Sijtsema, N. M., & Van Ooijen, P. M. A. (2023). Exploring adversarial attacks in federated learning for medical imaging. *arXiv (Cornell University)*. https://doi.org//arxiv.2310.06227DOI:10.48550

Dawodu, S. O., Omotosho, A., Akindote, O. J., Adegbite, A. O., & Ewuga, S. K. (2023). Cybersecurity risk assessment in banking: methodologies and best practices. *Computer Science & IT Research Journal*, 4(3), 220–243. DOI:10.51594/csitrj.v4i3.659

Drukker, K., Chen, W., Gichoya, J. W., Gruszauskas, N. P., Kalpathy–Cramer, J., Koyejo, S., Myers, K. J., Sá, R. C., Sahiner, B., Whitney, H. M., Zhang, Z., & Giger, M. L. (2023). Toward fairness in artificial intelligence for medical image analysis: Identification and mitigation of potential biases in the roadmap from data collection to model deployment. *Journal of Medical Imaging (Bellingham, Wash.)*, 10(06). Advance online publication. DOI:10.1117/1.JMI.10.6.061104 PMID:37125409

Dwivedi, Y. K., Kshetri, N., Hughes, L., Slade, E., Jeyaraj, A., Kar, A. K., Baabdullah, A. M., Koohang, A., Raghavan, V., Ahuja, M., Albanna, H., Albashrawi, M. A., Al-Busaidi, A. S., Balakrishnan, J., Barlette, Y., Basu, S., Bose, I., Brooks, L., Buhalis, D., & Wright, R. (2023). Opinion Paper: "So what if ChatGPT wrote it?" Multidisciplinary perspectives on opportunities, challenges and implications of generative conversational AI for research, practice and policy. *International Journal of Information Management*, 71, 102642. DOI:10.1016/j.ijinfomgt.2023.102642

Falade, P. V. (2023). Decoding the threat landscape : ChatGPT, FraudGPT, and WormGPT in social engineering attacks. *International Journal of Scientific Research in Computer Science, Engineering and Information Technology*, 185–198. DOI:10.32628/CSEIT2390533

Farina, M., Yu, X., & Lavazza, A. (2024). Ethical considerations and policy interventions concerning the impact of generative AI tools in the economy and in society. *AI and Ethics*. Advance online publication. DOI:10.1007/s43681-023-00405-2

Fatima, S., Hussain, S., Shahzadi, N., Din, B. U., Sajjad, W., & Ali, R. (2023). A Secure BlockChain Based Application For Health Records. *2023 2nd International Conference on Emerging Trends in Electrical, Control, and Telecommunication Engineering (ETECTE)*. DOI:10.1109/ETECTE59617.2023.10396794

Fatima-Tuz-Zahra, Jhanjhi, N. Z., Brohi, S. N., & Malik, N. A. (2019). Proposing a Rank and Wormhole Attack Detection Framework using Machine Learning. *2019 13th International Conference on Mathematics, Actuarial Science, Computer Science and Statistics (MACS)*. DOI:10.1109/MACS48846.2019.9024821

Ferrara, E. (2024). GenAI against humanity: Nefarious applications of generative artificial intelligence and large language models. *Journal of Computational Social Science*, 7(1), 549–569. Advance online publication. DOI:10.1007/s42001-024-00250-1

Feuerriegel, S., Hartmann, J., Janiesch, C., & Zschech, P. (2023). Generative AI. *Business & Information Systems Engineering*. Advance online publication. DOI:10.1007/s12599-023-00834-7

García, C. R., Rommel, S., Takarabt, S., Olmos, J. J. V., Guilley, S., Nguyen, P., & Monroy, I. T. (2024). Quantum-resistant transport layer security. *Computer Communications*, 213, 345–358. DOI:10.1016/j.comcom.2023.11.010

Garg, T., Vemuri, D., & Balasubramanian, V. N. (2024). Advancing Ante-Hoc Explainable Models through Generative Adversarial Networks. *arXiv (Cornell University)* https://doi.org//arxiv.2401.04647DOI:10.48550

Gaur, L., Afaq, A., Solanki, A., Singh, G., Sharma, S., Jhanjhi, N. Z., My, H. T., & Le, D. (2021). Capitalizing on big data and revolutionary 5G technology: Extracting and visualizing ratings and reviews of global chain hotels. *Computers & Electrical Engineering*, 95, 107374. DOI:10.1016/j.compeleceng.2021.107374

Geiger, R. S., Tandon, U., Gakhokidze, A., Song, L., & Irani, L. (2023, December 26). *Rethinking Artificial intelligence: Algorithmic bias and ethical issues| Making Algorithms Public: Reimagining Auditing from matters of fact to matters of concern.* Geiger | International Journal of Communication. https://ijoc.org/index.php/ijoc/article/view/20811

George, A. S. (2024). Riding the AI Waves: An analysis of Artificial intelligence's evolving role in combating cyber threats. *puiij.com*. DOI:10.5281/zenodo.10635964

Ghosh, G., Kavita, , Verma, S., Jhanjhi, N. Z., & Talib, M. N. (2020). Secure surveillance system using chaotic image encryption technique. *IOP Conference Series. Materials Science and Engineering*, 993(1), 012062. DOI:10.1088/1757-899X/993/1/012062

González-Sendino, R., Serrano, E., & Bajo, J. (2024). Mitigating bias in artificial intelligence: Fair data generation via causal models for transparent and explainable decision-making. *Future Generation Computer Systems*, 155, 384–401. Advance online publication. DOI:10.1016/j.future.2024.02.023

Goyal, S., Doddapaneni, S., Khapra, M. M., & Ravindran, B. (2023). A survey of Adversarial Defenses and Robustness in NLP. *ACM Computing Surveys*, 55(14s), 1–39. DOI:10.1145/3593042

Gregory, S. (2023). Fortify the Truth: How to defend human rights in an age of deepfakes and generative AI. *Journal of Human Rights Practice*, huad035. Advance online publication. DOI:10.1093/jhuman/huad035

Guo, D., Chen, H. S., Wu, R., & Wang, Y. (2023). AIGC challenges and opportunities related to public safety: A case study of ChatGPT. *Journal of Safety Science and Resilience*, 4(4), 329–339. DOI:10.1016/j.jnlssr.2023.08.001

Gupta, M., McGowan, D., & Ongena, S. (2023). The cost of privacy. The impact of the California Consumer Protection Act on mortgage markets. *Social Science Research Network*. DOI:10.2139/ssrn.4404636

Habbal, A., Ali, M., & Abuzaraida, M. A. (2024). Artificial Intelligence Trust, Risk and Security Management (AI TRiSM): Frameworks, applications, challenges and future research directions. *Expert Systems with Applications*, 240, 122442. DOI:10.1016/j.eswa.2023.122442

Hagendorff, T., Bossert, L., Tse, Y. F., & Singer, P. (2022). Speciesist bias in AI: How AI applications perpetuate discrimination and unfair outcomes against animals. *AI and Ethics*, 3(3), 717–734. DOI:10.1007/s43681-022-00199-9

Hossain, M. T., Afrin, R., & Biswas, M. a. A. (2024). A Review on Attacks against Artificial Intelligence (AI) and Their Defence Image Recognition and Generation Machine Learning, Artificial Intelligence. *Hossain | Control Systems and Optimization Letters*. https://doi.org/DOI:10.59247/csol.v2i1.73

Huang, K., Zhang, F., Li, Y., Wright, S., Kidambi, V., & Manral, V. (2023). Security and privacy concerns in ChatGPT. In *Future of Business and Finance* (pp. 297–328). DOI:10.1007/978-3-031-45282-6_11

Humayun, M., Ashfaq, F., Jhanjhi, N. Z., & Alsadun, M. K. (2022). Traffic management: Multi-Scale vehicle detection in varying weather conditions using YOLOV4 and spatial pyramid pooling network. *Electronics (Basel)*, 11(17), 2748. DOI:10.3390/electronics11172748

Humphreys, D., Koay, A., Desmond, D., & Mealy, E. (2024). AI hype as a cyber security risk: The moral responsibility of implementing generative AI in business. *AI and Ethics*, 4(3), 791–804. Advance online publication. DOI:10.1007/s43681-024-00443-4

Hussain, S., Anwaar, H., Sultan, K., Mahmud, U., Farooqui, S., Karamat, T., & Toure, I. K. (2024). Mitigating Software Vulnerabilities through Secure Software Development with a Policy-Driven Waterfall Model. *Journal of Engineering*, 2024, 1–15. DOI:10.1155/2024/9962691

Hussain, S. J., Ahmed, U., Liaquat, H., Mir, S., Jhanjhi, N. Z., & Humayun, M. (2019). IMIAD: Intelligent Malware Identification for Android Platform. *2019 International Conference on Computer and Information Sciences (ICCIS)*. DOI:10.1109/ICCISci.2019.8716471

Huyen, N. T. M., & Bao, T. Q. (2024, January 3). *Advancements in AI-Driven cybersecurity and comprehensive threat detection and response*. https://questsquare.org/index.php/JOUNALICET/article/view/37

Iftikhar, S., Gill, S. S., Song, C., Xu, M., Aslanpour, M. S., Toosi, A. N., Du, J., Wu, H., Ghosh, S., Chowdhury, D., Golec, M., Kumar, M., Abdelmoniem, A. M., Cuadrado, F., Varghese, B., Rana, O. F., Dustdar, S., & Uhlig, S. (2023). AI-based fog and edge computing: A systematic review, taxonomy and future directions. *Internet of Things : Engineering Cyber Physical Human Systems*, 21, 100674. DOI:10.1016/j.iot.2022.100674

Illiashenko, O., Kharchenko, V., Babeshko, I., Fesenko, H., & Di Giandomenico, F. (2023). Security-Informed safety analysis of autonomous transport systems considering AI-Powered Cyberattacks and protection. *Entropy (Basel, Switzerland)*, 25(8), 1123. DOI:10.3390/e25081123 PMID:37628153

Javaheri, D., Fahmideh, M., Chizari, H., Lalbakhsh, P., & Hur, J. (2024). Cybersecurity threats in FinTech: A systematic review. *Expert Systems with Applications*, 241, 122697. DOI:10.1016/j.eswa.2023.122697

Jawad, A. T., Mâaloul, R., & Fourati, L. C. (2023). A comprehensive survey on 6G and beyond: Enabling technologies, opportunities of machine learning and challenges. *Computer Networks*, 237, 110085. DOI:10.1016/j.comnet.2023.110085

Jha, R. (2023). Cybersecurity and confidentiality in smart Grid for enhancing sustainability and reliability. *Recent Research Reviews Journal*, 2(2), 215–241. DOI:10.36548/rrrj.2023.2.001

Johansen, G. (2017). *Digital forensics and incident response*. Packt Publishing Ltd.

Judijanto, L., Hindarto, D., Wahjono, S. I., & Djunarto, . (2023). Edge of enterprise architecture in addressing cyber security threats and business risks. *International Journal Software Engineering and Computer Science*, 3(3), 386–396. DOI:10.35870/ijsecs.v3i3.1816

Kamble, D., Rathod, S., Bhelande, M., Shah, A. S., & Sapkal, P. (2024). Correlating forensic data for enhanced network crime investigations: Techniques for packet sniffing, network forensics, and attack detection. *Journal of Autonomous Intelligence*, 7(4). Advance online publication. DOI:10.32629/jai.v7i4.1272

Kapoor, A., & Chatterjee, S. (2023). *Platform and model design for responsible AI: Design and build resilient, private, fair, and transparent machine learning models.* Packt Publishing Ltd.

Karabacak, M., Ozkara, B. B., Margetis, K., Wintermark, M., & Bisdas, S. (2023). The advent of generative language models in medical education. *JMIR Medical Education*, 9, e48163. DOI:10.2196/48163 PMID:37279048

Karlsson, I., & Ljungberg, D. (2024). *Supplementing Dependabot's vulnerability scanning : A Custom Pipeline for Tracing Dependency Usage in JavaScript Projects.* DIVA. https://www.diva-portal.org/smash/record.jsf?pid=diva2%3A1832928&dswid=425

Karnouskos, S. (2020). Artificial intelligence in digital media: The era of Deepfakes. *IEEE Transactions on Technology and Society*, 1(3), 138–147. DOI:10.1109/TTS.2020.3001312

Kenwright, B. (2023). Is it the end of undergraduate dissertations? In *Advances in educational technologies and instructional design book series* (pp. 46–65). DOI:10.4018/979-8-3693-0074-9.ch003

Khalil, M. I., Jhanjhi, N. Z., Humayun, M., Sivanesan, S., Masud, M., & Hossain, M. S. (2021). Hybrid smart grid with sustainable energy efficient resources for smart cities. *Sustainable Energy Technologies and Assessments*, 46, 101211. DOI:10.1016/j.seta.2021.101211

Khazane, H., Ridouani, M., Salahdine, F., & Kaabouch, N. (2024). A Holistic Review of Machine Learning Adversarial attacks in IoT networks. *Future Internet*, 16(1), 32. DOI:10.3390/fi16010032

Khennouche, F., Elmir, Y., Himeur, Y., Djebari, N., & Amira, A. (2024). Revolutionizing generative pre-traineds: Insights and challenges in deploying ChatGPT and generative chatbots for FAQs. *Expert Systems with Applications*, 246, 123224. DOI:10.1016/j.eswa.2024.123224

Kizza, J. M. (2024). Standardization and security criteria: Security evaluation of computer products. In *Texts in computer science* (pp. 377–394). DOI:10.1007/978-3-031-47549-8_16

Krause, D. S. (2023). Mitigating risks for financial firms using generative AI tools. *Social Science Research Network*. DOI:10.2139/ssrn.4452600

Lin, Z., Shi, Y., & Zhi, X. (2022). IDSGAN: Generative Adversarial Networks for Attack Generation against Intrusion Detection. In *Lecture Notes in Computer Science* (pp. 79–91). DOI:10.1007/978-3-031-05981-0_7

Liu, G., Du, H., Niyato, D., Kang, J., Xiong, Z., Kim, D. I., & Shen, X. (2024). Semantic Communications for Artificial Intelligence Generated Content (AIGC) toward effective content creation. *IEEE Network*, 1, 1. Advance online publication. DOI:10.1109/MNET.2024.3352917

Liu, M., Ren, Y., Nyagoga, L. M., Stonier, F., Wu, Z., & Liang, Y. (2023). Future of education in the era of generative artificial intelligence: Consensus among Chinese scholars on applications of ChatGPT in schools. *Future in Educational Research*, 1(1), 72–101. DOI:10.1002/fer3.10

Longo, L., Brčić, M., Cabitza, F., Choi, J., Confalonieri, R., Del Ser, J., Guidotti, R., Hayashi, Y., Herrera, F., Holzinger, A., Jiang, R., Khosravi, H., Lécué, F., Malgieri, G., Páez, A., Samek, W., Schneider, J., Speith, T., & Stumpf, S. (2024). Explainable Artificial Intelligence (XAI) 2.0: A manifesto of open challenges and interdisciplinary research directions. *Information Fusion*, 102301, 102301. Advance online publication. DOI:10.1016/j.inffus.2024.102301

Majeed, A., Ullah, F., & Lee, S. (2017). Vulnerability- and Diversity-Aware anonymization of personally identifiable information for improving user privacy and utility of publishing data. *Sensors (Basel)*, 17(5), 1059. DOI:10.3390/s17051059 PMID:28481298

Malatji, M., & Tolah, A. (2024). Artificial intelligence (AI) cybersecurity dimensions: A comprehensive framework for understanding adversarial and offensive AI. *AI and Ethics*. Advance online publication. DOI:10.1007/s43681-024-00427-4

Mat, N. I. C., Jamil, N., Yusoff, Y., & Kiah, L. M. (2024). A systematic literature review on advanced persistent threat behaviors and its detection strategy. *Journal of Cybersecurity*, 10(1), tyad023. Advance online publication. DOI:10.1093/cybsec/tyad023

Maurya, A., & Joshi, M. (2024, January 29). *Exploring Privacy-Preserving Strategies: A comprehensive analysis of Group-Based anonymization and hybrid ECC encryption algorithm for effective performance evaluation in data security.* https://www.ijisae.org/index.php/IJISAE/article/view/4618

Mehrabi, N., Morstatter, F., Saxena, N., Lerman, K., & Galstyan, A. (2021). A survey on Bias and Fairness in Machine Learning. *ACM Computing Surveys*, 54(6), 1–35. DOI:10.1145/3457607

Mehta, A., Padaria, A. A., Bavisi, D., Ukani, V., Thakkar, P., Geddam, R., Kotecha, K., & Abraham, A. (2024). Securing the Future: A comprehensive review of security challenges and solutions in advanced driver assistance systems. *IEEE Access : Practical Innovations, Open Solutions*, 12, 643–678. DOI:10.1109/ACCESS.2023.3347200

Mingo, H. C., Lawson, M. N., & Williamson, A. (2024). Identifying new vulnerabilities embedded in consumer internet of things (IoT) devices. In *Advances in medical technologies and clinical practice book series* (pp. 186–207). DOI:10.4018/979-8-3693-3226-9.ch011

Mohanakrishnan, M., Kumar, A. V. S., Talukdar, V., Saleh, O. S., Irawati, I. D., Latip, R., & Kaur, G. (2023). Artificial intelligence in cyber security. In *Advances in computational intelligence and robotics book series* (pp. 366–385). DOI:10.4018/978-1-6684-8098-4.ch022

Mohsin, A., Janicke, H., Nepal, S., & Holmes, D. R. (2023). Digital Twins and the Future of their Use Enabling Shift Left and Shift Right Cybersecurity Operations. *arXiv (Cornell University)*. /arxiv.2309.13612DOI:10.1109/TPS-ISA58951.2023.00042

Moon, M. J. (2023). Searching for inclusive artificial intelligence for social good: Participatory governance and policy recommendations for making AI more inclusive and benign for society. *Public Administration Review*, 83(6), 1496–1505. DOI:10.1111/puar.13648

Moustafa, N., Koroniotis, N., Keshk, M., Zomaya, A. Y., & Tari, Z. (2023). Explainable intrusion detection for cyber defences in the Internet of Things: Opportunities and solutions. *IEEE Communications Surveys and Tutorials*, 25(3), 1775–1807. DOI:10.1109/COMST.2023.3280465

Mubarak, R., Alsboui, T., Alshaikh, O., Inuwa-Dutse, I., Khan, S., & Parkinson, S. (2023). A survey on the detection and impacts of deepfakes in visual, audio, and textual formats. *IEEE Access : Practical Innovations, Open Solutions*, 11, 144497–144529. DOI:10.1109/ACCESS.2023.3344653

Mukhopadhyay, A., & Jain, S. (2024). A framework for cyber-risk insurance against ransomware: A mixed-method approach. *International Journal of Information Management*, 74, 102724. DOI:10.1016/j.ijinfomgt.2023.102724

Nair, A. K., Raj, E. D., & Sahoo, J. (2023). A robust analysis of adversarial attacks on federated learning environments. *Computer Standards & Interfaces*, 86, 103723. DOI:10.1016/j.csi.2023.103723

Nankya, M., Chataut, R., & Akl, R. (2023). Securing Industrial control systems: Components, cyber threats, and Machine Learning-Driven defense Strategies. *Sensors (Basel)*, 23(21), 8840. DOI:10.3390/s23218840 PMID:37960539

Olabanji, S. O., Marquis, Y., Adigwe, C. S., Ajayi, S. S., Oladoyinbo, T. O., & Olaniyi, O. O. (2024). AI-Driven Cloud Security: Examining the impact of user behavior analysis on threat detection. *Social Science Research Network*. DOI:10.2139/ssrn.4709384

Olabanji, S. O., Olaniyi, O. O., Adigwe, C. S., Okunleye, O. J., & Oladoyinbo, T. O. (2024). AI for Identity and Access Management (IAM) in the Cloud: Exploring the Potential of Artificial Intelligence to Improve User Authentication, Authorization, and Access Control within Cloud-Based Systems. *Social Science Research Network*. DOI:10.2139/ssrn.4706726

Ombu, A. (2023). Role of digital forensics in combating financial crimes in the computer Era. *Journal of Forensic Accounting Profession*, 3(1), 57–75. DOI:10.2478/jfap-2023-0003

Omotunde, H., & Ahmed, M. (2023). A Comprehensive Review of Security Measures in Database Systems: Assessing Authentication, Access Control, and Beyond. *Journal of Cybersecurity*, 115–133. DOI:10.58496/MJCSC/2023/016

Oniani, D., Hilsman, J., Peng, Y., Poropatich, R. K., Pamplin, J., Legault, G. L., & Wang, Y. (2023). Adopting and expanding ethical principles for generative artificial intelligence from military to healthcare. *NPJ Digital Medicine*, 6(1), 225. Advance online publication. DOI:10.1038/s41746-023-00965-x PMID:38042910

Oseni, A., Moustafa, N., Janicke, H., Liu, P., Tari, Z., & Vasilakos, A. V. (2021). Security and privacy for artificial intelligence: Opportunities and challenges. *arXiv (Cornell University)*. https://doi.org//arxiv.2102.04661DOI:10.48550

OSF. (n.d.). https://osf.io/preprints/osf/bxw4h

Ozkan-Okay, M., Akin, E., Aslan, Ö., Koşunalp, S., Iliev, T., Stoyanov, I., & Beloev, I. (2024). A comprehensive survey: Evaluating the efficiency of artificial intelligence and machine learning techniques on cyber security solutions. *IEEE Access : Practical Innovations, Open Solutions*, 12, 12229–12256. DOI:10.1109/ACCESS.2024.3355547

Papaspirou, V., Papathanasaki, M., Μαγλαράς, Λ., Kantzavelou, I., Douligeris, C., Ferrag, M. A., & Janicke, H. (2023). A novel authentication method that combines HoneyTokens and Google Authenticator. *Information (Basel)*, 14(7), 386. DOI:10.3390/info14070386

Parray, A. A., Inam, Z. M., Ramonfaur, D., Haider, S. S., Mistry, S. K., & Pandya, A. (2023). ChatGPT and global public health: Applications, challenges, ethical considerations and mitigation strategies. *Global Transitions*, 5, 50–54. DOI:10.1016/j.glt.2023.05.001

Perdana, A., Lee, W. E., & Kim, C. M. (2023). Prototyping and implementing Robotic Process Automation in accounting firms: Benefits, challenges and opportunities to audit automation. *International Journal of Accounting Information Systems*, 51, 100641. DOI:10.1016/j.accinf.2023.100641

Ping, C., Hou, L., Zhang, K., Tushar, Q., & Yang, Z. (2024). Generative adversarial networks in construction applications. *Automation in Construction*, 159, 105265. DOI:10.1016/j.autcon.2024.105265

Pulyala, S. R. (2024). From detection to prediction: AI-powered SIEM for proactive threat hunting and risk mitigation. *Turkish Journal of Computer and Mathematics Education*, 15(1), 34–43. DOI:10.61841/turcomat.v15i1.14393

Radanliev, P., & Santos, O. (2023). Adversarial Attacks Can Deceive AI Systems, Leading to Misclassification or Incorrect Decisions. *Preprint*. DOI:10.20944/preprints202309.2064.v1

Rafi, T. H., Noor, F. A., Hussain, T., & Chae, D. (2024). Fairness and privacy preserving in federated learning: A survey. *Information Fusion*, 105, 102198. DOI:10.1016/j.inffus.2023.102198

Rafy, M. F. (2024). Artificial intelligence in cyber security. *Social Science Research Network*. DOI:10.2139/ssrn.4687831

Rane, N. (2023). ChatGPT and similar Generative Artificial Intelligence (AI) for smart Industry: Role, Challenges and Opportunities for Industry 4.0, Industry 5.0 and Society 5.0. *Social Science Research Network*. DOI:10.2139/ssrn.4603234

Rane, N., Choudhary, S., & Rane, J. (2023). Explainable Artificial Intelligence (XAI) approaches for transparency and accountability in financial decision-making. *Social Science Research Network*. DOI:10.2139/ssrn.4640316

Riegler, M., Sametinger, J., Vierhauser, M., & Wimmer, M. (2023). A model-based mode-switching framework based on security vulnerability scores. *Journal of Systems and Software*, 200, 111633. DOI:10.1016/j.jss.2023.111633

Roshan, K., & Zafar, A. (2024). Boosting robustness of network intrusion detection systems: A novel two phase defense strategy against untargeted white-box optimization adversarial attack. *Expert Systems with Applications*, 123567, 123567. Advance online publication. DOI:10.1016/j.eswa.2024.123567

Sakhare, S. R., & Patil, V. D. (2023, December 31). *Implementation of Captcha Mechanisms using Deep Learning to Prevent Automated Bot Attacks*. https://www.technicaljournals.org/RJCSE/index.php/journal/article/view/70

Sankar, S., Ramasubbareddy, S., Luhach, A. K., Deverajan, G. G., Alnumay, W. S., Jhanjhi, N. Z., Ghosh, U., & Sharma, P. K. (2020). Energy efficient optimal parent selection based routing protocol for Internet of Things using firefly optimization algorithm. *Transactions on Emerging Telecommunications Technologies*, 32(8), e4171. Advance online publication. DOI:10.1002/ett.4171

Satybaldy, A., Ferdous, S., & Nowostawski, M. (2024). A Taxonomy of Challenges for Self-Sovereign Identity Systems. *IEEE Access : Practical Innovations, Open Solutions*, 1, 16151–16177. Advance online publication. DOI:10.1109/AC-CESS.2024.3357940

Shahid, H., Ashraf, H., Javed, H., Humayun, M., Jhanjhi, N. Z., & AlZain, M. A. (2021). Energy Optimised Security against Wormhole Attack in IoT-Based Wireless Sensor Networks. *Computers, Materials & Continua*, 68(2), 1967–1981. DOI:10.32604/cmc.2021.015259

Shruti, R., Rani, S., Sah, D. K., & Gianini, G. (2023). Attribute-Based Encryption Schemes for next generation wireless IoT networks: A comprehensive survey. *Sensors (Basel)*, 23(13), 5921. DOI:10.3390/s23135921 PMID:37447769

Sikder, A. S. (2023, November 26). *Cybersecurity Framework for Ensuring Confidentiality, Integrity, and Availability of University Management Systems in Bangladesh.: Cybersecurity framework on UMS in Bangladesh*. https://journal.ijisnt.com/index.php/public_html/article/view/4

Sindiramutty, S. R., Jhanjhi, N. Z., Ray, S. K., Jazri, H., Khan, N. A., Gaur, L., Gharib, A. H., & Manchuri, A. R. (2024). Metaverse. In *Advances in medical technologies and clinical practice book series* (pp. 24–92). DOI:10.4018/978-1-6684-9823-1.ch002

Sindiramutty, S. R., Jhanjhi, N. Z., Tan, C., Yun, K. J., Manchuri, A. R., Ashraf, H., Murugesan, R. K., Tee, W. J., & Hussain, M. (2024). Data security and privacy concerns in drone operations. In *Advances in information security, privacy, and ethics book series* (pp. 236–290). DOI:10.4018/979-8-3693-0774-8.ch010

Sindiramutty, S. R., Jhanjhi, N. Z., Tan, C. E., Khan, N. A., Gharib, A. H., & Yun, K. J. (2023). Applications of blockchain technology in supply chain management. In *Advances in logistics, operations, and management science book series* (pp. 248–304). DOI:10.4018/978-1-6684-7625-3.ch009

Sindiramutty, S. R., Jhanjhi, N. Z., Tan, C. E., Khan, N. A., Shah, B., & Gaur, L. (2023). Securing the digital supply chain cyber threats and vulnerabilities. In *Advances in logistics, operations, and management science book series* (pp. 156–223). DOI:10.4018/978-1-6684-7625-3.ch007

Sindiramutty, S. R., Jhanjhi, N. Z., Tan, C. E., Khan, N. A., Shah, B., Yun, K. J., Ray, S. K., Jazri, H., & Hussain, M. (2024). Future trends and emerging threats in drone cybersecurity. In *Advances in information security, privacy, and ethics book series* (pp. 148–195). DOI:10.4018/979-8-3693-0774-8.ch007

Sindiramutty, S. R., Jhanjhi, N. Z., Tan, C. E., Tee, W. J., Lau, S. P., Jazri, H., Ray, S. K., & Zaheer, M. A. (2024). IoT and AI-Based Smart Solutions for the Agriculture Industry. In *Advances in computational intelligence and robotics book series* (pp. 317–351). DOI:10.4018/978-1-6684-6361-1.ch012

Sindiramutty, S. R., Tan, C., Tee, W. J., Lau, S. P., Balakrishnan, S., Kaur, S. D. A., Jazri, H., & Aslam, M. (2024). Modern smart cities and open research challenges and issues of explainable artificial intelligence. In *Advances in computational intelligence and robotics book series* (pp. 389–424). DOI:10.4018/978-1-6684-6361-1.ch015

Sindiramutty, S. R., Tan, C., & Wei, G. W. (2024). Eyes in the sky. In *Advances in information security, privacy, and ethics book series* (pp. 405–451). DOI:10.4018/979-8-3693-0774-8.ch017

Sindiramutty, S. R., Tan, C. E., Lau, S. P., Thangaveloo, R., Gharib, A. H., Manchuri, A. R., Khan, N. A., Tee, W. J., & Muniandy, L. (2024). Explainable AI for cybersecurity. In *Advances in computational intelligence and robotics book series* (pp. 31–97). DOI:10.4018/978-1-6684-6361-1.ch002

Sindiramutty, S. R., Tan, C. E., Shah, B., Khan, N. A., Gharib, A. H., Manchuri, A. R., Muniandy, L., Ray, S. K., & Jazri, H. (2024). Ethical considerations in drone cybersecurity. In *Advances in information security, privacy, and ethics book series* (pp. 42–87). DOI:10.4018/979-8-3693-0774-8.ch003

Sindiramutty, S. R., Tee, W. J., Balakrishnan, S., Kaur, S., Thangaveloo, R., Jazri, H., Khan, N. A., Gharib, A. H., & Manchuri, A. R. (2024). Explainable AI in healthcare application. In *Advances in computational intelligence and robotics book series* (pp. 123–176). DOI:10.4018/978-1-6684-6361-1.ch005

Singhal, V., Jain, S. P., Anand, D., Singh, A., Verma, S., Kavita, , Rodrigues, J. J. P. C., Jhanjhi, N. Z., Ghosh, U., Jo, O., & Iwendi, C. (2020). Artificial Intelligence Enabled Road Vehicle-Train Collision Risk Assessment Framework for Unmanned railway level crossings. *IEEE Access : Practical Innovations, Open Solutions*, 8, 113790–113806. DOI:10.1109/ACCESS.2020.3002416

Stingelová, B., Thrakl, C. T., Wrońska, L., Jedrej-Szymankiewicz, S., Khan, S., & Svetinović, D. (2023). User-Centric Security and Privacy Threats in Connected Vehicles: A Threat Modeling Analysis Using STRIDE and LINDDUN. *2023 IEEE Intl Conf on Dependable, Autonomic and Secure Computing, Intl Conf on Pervasive Intelligence and Computing, Intl Conf on Cloud and Big Data Computing, Intl Conf on Cyber Science and Technology Congress (DASC/PiCom/CBDCom/CyberSciTech)*. DOI:10.1109/DASC/PiCom/CBDCom/Cy59711.2023.10361381

Taj, I., & Jhanjhi, N. Z. (2022). Towards Industrial Revolution 5.0 and Explainable Artificial Intelligence: Challenges and opportunities. *International Journal of Computing and Digital Systems*, 12(1), 285–310. DOI:10.12785/ijcds/120124

Tikkinen-Piri, C., Rohunen, A., & Markkula, J. (2018). EU General Data Protection Regulation: Changes and implications for personal data collecting companies. *Computer Law & Security Report*, 34(1), 134–153. DOI:10.1016/j.clsr.2017.05.015

Tomlinson, B., Patterson, D., & Torrance, A. W. (2023, July 19). *Turning Fake Data into Fake News: The A.I. Training Set as a Trojan Horse of Misinformation*. https://papers.ssrn.com/sol3/papers.cfm?abstract_id=4515571

Tripathy, K. P., & Mishra, A. K. (2023). Deep learning in hydrology and water resources disciplines: Concepts, methods, applications, and research directions. *Journal of Hydrology (Amsterdam)*, 130458. Advance online publication. DOI:10.1016/j.jhydrol.2023.130458

Tufchi, S., Yadav, A., & Ahmed, T. (2023). A comprehensive survey of multimodal fake news detection techniques: Advances, challenges, and opportunities. *International Journal of Multimedia Information Retrieval*, 12(2), 28. Advance online publication. DOI:10.1007/s13735-023-00296-3

Venkatesan, K., & Rahayu, S. B. (2024). Blockchain security enhancement: An approach towards hybrid consensus algorithms and machine learning techniques. *Scientific Reports*, 14(1), 1149. Advance online publication. DOI:10.1038/s41598-024-51578-7 PMID:38212390

Verma, S., Kaur, S., Rawat, D. B., Chen, X., Alex, L. T., & Jhanjhi, N. Z. (2021). Intelligent framework using IoT-Based WSNs for wildfire detection. *IEEE Access : Practical Innovations, Open Solutions*, 9, 48185–48196. DOI:10.1109/ACCESS.2021.3060549

Vyas, B. (2023, May 7). *Explainable AI: Assessing methods to make AI systems more transparent and interpretable*. https://www.ijnms.com/index.php/ijnms/article/view/220

Wang, R., Bush-Evans, R., Arden-Close, E., Bolat, E., McAlaney, J., Hodge, S. E., Thomas, S., & Phalp, K. (2023). Transparency in persuasive technology, immersive technology, and online marketing: Facilitating users' informed decision making and practical implications. *Computers in Human Behavior*, 139, 107545. DOI:10.1016/j. chb.2022.107545

Wang, S., Ko, R. K. L., Bai, G., Dong, N., Choi, T., & Zhang, Y. (2024). Evasion Attack and Defense on Machine Learning Models in Cyber-Physical Systems: A survey. *IEEE Communications Surveys and Tutorials*, 1(2), 930–966. Advance online publication. DOI:10.1109/COMST.2023.3344808

Wang, Y., Sun, T., Li, S., Yuan, X., Ni, W., Hossain, E., & Poor, H. V. (2023). Adversarial Attacks and Defenses in Machine Learning-Empowered Communication Systems and Networks: A Contemporary survey. *IEEE Communications Surveys and Tutorials*, 25(4), 2245–2298. DOI:10.1109/COMST.2023.3319492

Wassan, S., Chen, X., Shen, T., Waqar, M., & Jhanjhi, N. Z. (2021). Amazon Product Sentiment Analysis using Machine Learning Techniques. *International Journal of Early Childhood Special Education (INT-JECSE), 30*(1), 695. https://doi.org/DOI: 10.24205/03276716.2020.2065

Wen, B. O. T., Syahriza, N., Xian, N. C. W., Wei, N., Shen, T. Z., Hin, Y. Z., Sindiramutty, S. R., & Nicole, T. Y. F. (2023). Detecting cyber threats with a Graph-Based NIDPS. In *Advances in logistics, operations, and management science book series* (pp. 36–74). DOI:10.4018/978-1-6684-7625-3.ch002

Xenakis, A., Nourin, S. M., Chen, Z., Karabatis, G., Aleroud, A., & Amarsingh, J. (2023). A self-adaptive and secure approach to share network trace data. *Digital Threats : Research and Practice*, 4(4), 1–20. DOI:10.1145/3617181

Xivuri, K., & Twinomurinzi, H. (2023). How AI developers can assure algorithmic fairness. *Discover Artificial Intelligence*, 3(1), 27. Advance online publication. DOI:10.1007/s44163-023-00074-4

Yang, J., Soltan, A. S., Eyre, D. W., Yang, Y., & Clifton, D. A. (2023). An adversarial training framework for mitigating algorithmic biases in clinical machine learning. *NPJ Digital Medicine*, 6(1), 55. Advance online publication. DOI:10.1038/s41746-023-00805-y PMID:36991077

Zahid, S., Mazhar, M. S., Abbas, S. G., Hanif, Z., Hina, S., & Shah, G. A. (2023). Threat modeling in smart firefighting systems: Aligning MITRE ATT&CK matrix and NIST security controls. *Internet of Things : Engineering Cyber Physical Human Systems*, 22, 100766. DOI:10.1016/j.iot.2023.100766

Zaidi, T., Usman, M., Aftab, M. U., Aljuaid, H., & Ghadi, Y. Y. (2023). Fabrication of flexible Role-Based access control based on blockchain for internet of Things use cases. *IEEE Access : Practical Innovations, Open Solutions*, 11, 106315–106333. DOI:10.1109/ACCESS.2023.3318487

Zhang, A., Walker, O., Nguyen, K., Dai, J., Chen, A., & Lee, M. K. (2023). Deliberating with AI: Improving Decision-Making for the Future through Participatory AI Design and Stakeholder Deliberation. *Proceedings of the ACM on Human-computer Interaction, 7*(CSCW1), 1–32. DOI:10.1145/3579601

Chapter 10
Generative AI for Secure User Interface (UI) Design

Siva Raja Sindiramutty
https://orcid.org/0009-0006-0310-8721
Taylor's University, Malaysia

Krishna Raj V. Prabagaran
Universiti Malaysia Sarawak, Malaysia

Rehan Akbar
https://orcid.org/0000-0002-3703-5974
Florida International University, USA

Manzoor Hussain
Indus University, Pakistan

Nazir Ahmed Malik
https://orcid.org/0000-0002-0118-4601
Bahria University, Islamabad, Pakistan

ABSTRACT

Generative AI, which is equipped with unique capabilities, is about to put the world of secure user interface (UI) design upside down and turn it into something full of endless possibilities in which users will be able to use the same opportunities and experienced solutions to protect their interaction in digital from any future security threats. This chapter takes a deep plunge into the merger of the generative AI with the secure user interface design, on the whole, presenting a complete exposition of the principals involved, methodologies applied, practical embodiment, and ultimate ramifications. The beginning will explore the building blocks of UI design principles and the user-centred iterative approach, wherein a robust framework

DOI: 10.4018/979-8-3693-5415-5.ch010

for understanding Generative AI as a critical part of building secure, intuitive, and engaging user experiences is implemented. Further, it provides an overview of different types of generative AI approaches that could be deployed for secure UI design, such as GANs, VAEs, and autoregressive models, with their capabilities expanding the scope of security measures, which include authentication protocols, encryption, and user access rights while retaining usability and aesthetic appeal. Moreover, it surveys instance applications of the generative AI that support the Secure design of GUI, among the automatic generation of safe layout patterns, the dynamic change of the interface according to emerging threats, and the creation of cryptographic keys and secure symbols.

INTRODUCTION TO GENERATIVE AI IN UI DESIGN

Definition of Generative AI in the Context of UI Design

Generative AI, within UI design, encompasses the utilisation of AI algorithms to craft and enrich UI autonomously. This entails creating various design elements like layouts, colour schemes, and interactive components without direct human intervention. Leveraging machine learning (ML) techniques, these algorithms analyse existing UI patterns, user behaviours, and design principles to generate fresh and innovative designs (Bok, 2023). An impactful application of generative AI in UI design is seen in personalised UI. By scrutinising user interactions and feedback, these algorithms dynamically adjust UI elements to match individual preferences, enhancing user experience and engagement. Additionally, generative AI aids designers in swiftly exploring and experimenting with diverse design concepts, thereby expediting the iterative design process (Weisz et al., 2024). Moreover, generative AI creates responsive and adaptive UI designs that seamlessly adjust to various screen sizes and devices. These algorithms optimise UI layouts for enhanced usability across different platforms and devices by considering factors like screen resolution, device orientation, and input methods.

Despite its potential benefits, integrating generative AI in UI design presents challenges and ethical considerations. Designers must ensure that AI-generated designs adhere to usability principles, accessibility standards, and ethical guidelines (Lu et al., 2024). Transparency and accountability are crucial in the design process to mitigate biases and ensure AI-generated designs reflect diverse perspectives and preferences (Gutiérrez, 2024). Generative AI holds significant promise in transforming UI design by automating design tasks, personalising user experiences, and fostering design creativity. By harnessing ML techniques and vast datasets, generative AI systems empower designers to create innovative and user-centric UI designs efficiently (Zhao et al., 2024). However, it is imperative to address ethical concerns and ensure AI-generated designs uphold usability, accessibility, and moral standards (Hodonu-Wusu, 2024).

Figure 1. Generative AI in the Context of UI Design

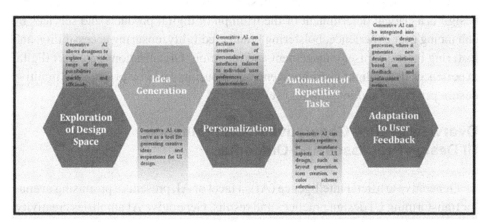

Importance Of UI Design in Digital Products and Services

The design of UI holds immense significance in determining the effectiveness and user-friendliness of digital products and services. A well-crafted UI not only enriches user experience but also cultivates engagement and cultivates brand loyalty. Research conducted by the Durgekar Group indicates that intuitive and visually appealing interfaces contribute significantly to user satisfaction and retention (Durgekar et al., 2024). A clear and intuitive UI ensures users can effortlessly navigate digital products or services, minimising frustration and maximising efficiency. Additionally, UI design profoundly influences users' perceptions of a brand's credibility and professionalism. Studies have demonstrated that users tend to trust and interact more with aesthetically pleasing and well-structured interfaces. Consequently, investing in high-quality UI design elevates user experience and enhances brand reputation and competitiveness within the market (Sreejith & Sinimole, 2024). Figure 1 shows Generative AI in the context of UI Design.

Beyond aesthetics, UI design plays a pivotal role in ensuring accessibility. An inclusive design approach guarantees that digital products and services cater to individuals with diverse abilities and requirements (Doush et al., 2022). Incorporating accessibility features such as adjustable font sizes, colour contrast options, and keyboard navigation widens the audience's reach and demonstrates a commitment to social responsibility and inclusivity. Furthermore, effective UI design contributes to heightened user engagement and retention. By comprehending user behaviour and preferences, designers can fashion interfaces that resonate with their target audience, fostering continued interaction (Rane et al., 2023). Features like personalised recommendations, interactive elements, and smooth transitions augment user satisfaction and stimulate repeat usage, fueling business growth and success. In essence, UI design is a critical determinant of the triumph of digital products and services by enhancing user experience, bolstering brand credibility, ensuring accessibility, and fostering increased user engagement and retention. Organisations can craft digital experiences that delight users and generate enduring value by prioritising intuitive design principles and integrating user feedback.

Overview of How Generative AI Can Enhance UI Design Processes and Outcomes

Generative artificial intelligence (AI), a facet of AI, presents a promising avenue for transforming UI design practices and results. Generative AI amplifies creativity, efficacy, and flexibility in UI design by utilising algorithms capable of producing fresh and inventive design solutions. This technology automatically generates design variations within set parameters, allowing designers to explore a broader spectrum of options and iterate faster (Jiang et al., 2023). This iterative approach empowers designers to unearth unique design patterns and solutions that may have been beyond reach through conventional means, ultimately resulting in more innovative and user-centric designs. Furthermore, generative AI equips designers to address intricate design challenges more efficiently by automating repetitive tasks and refining workflows. For instance, AI-driven tools can analyse user behaviour data and propose personalised design suggestions tailored to individual preferences and requirements (Necula & Păvăloaia, 2023). By integrating ML algorithms, these tools continuously evolve based on user interactions, ensuring the UI remains pertinent and captivating. Additionally, generative AI facilitates the exploration of alternative design concepts and aesthetics, enabling designers to transcend conventional design norms (Rane et al., 2023a). By amalgamating diverse design elements and inspirations, AI-driven systems can generate fresh visual styles and layouts, fostering creativity and experimentation in UI design. However, while generative AI offers substantial advantages, it also presents challenges and considerations. Designers must meticulously define constraints and objectives to effectively guide AI algorithms and ensure that generated designs resonate with user needs and brand identity (Mortazavi, 2023). Moreover, there are ethical implications regarding the potential displacement of human designers and the necessity for transparency and accountability in AI-generated designs. Generative AI holds immense potential for enriching UI design processes and outcomes by nurturing creativity, efficiency, and adaptability. By automating tasks, delivering personalised recommendations, and facilitating the exploration of alternative design concepts, generative AI empowers designers to craft more innovative and user-centric interfaces. Nonetheless, careful attention to constraints, objectives, and ethical considerations is imperative to harness the full benefits of this technology.

Chapter Contributions

This chapter presents an in-depth exploration of the integration of generative AI with UI design, shedding light on its profound impact on the evolution of digital product development. It elucidates how generative AI methodologies can streamline UI design procedures, spark creativity, and elevate user experiences. Examining automated layout generation, style transfer, content personalisation, and collaborative design offers readers actionable insights and tools to utilise AI in UI design workflows effectively. Moreover, the chapter delves into crucial considerations such as evaluation techniques, ethical implications, and forthcoming trends, offering a comprehensive understanding of the intersection between AI and UI design. Ultimately, it empowers designers, researchers, and practitioners to navigate and harness the potential of generative AI in shaping the future landscape of UI design.

Chapter Organization

Section 1 presents AI in UI Design, implicitly depicting its role and significance in the digital asset development. Section 2 of this chapter discusses the key principles of UI design that involve ease of use, accessibility, and attraction. The third section involves the different Generative AI techniques that are instrumental in UI design, such as Generative Adversarial Networks (GANs), Variational Autoencoders (VAEs), and autoregressive models. The section 4 to discuss about Automated Layout Developing using Generative AI. In section 5, delve into style transfer techniques as well as the role of Generative AI as an assistant for the designers to try out different design styles and visual communications. Section 5 embodies the application of collaborative design approaches, jointly used by AI tools and human designers on the design process. In Section 6, AI design evaluation techniques are introduced, and it includes usability testing as well as heuristic evaluation. In Section 7, addresses the ethical questions that should be considered when employing Generative AI for the design of visual UI. Firstly, section 8 examines new tendencies in Generative AI and UI design and considers future maps of investigation and development in artificial intelligence UI design as well as identifying challenges and opportunities involved with the field. The section 9 is devoted to show technique of AI in UI design in real world through examples and actual case studies from a variety of sectors and spheres etc.

FUNDAMENTALS OF UI DESIGN PRINCIPLES

Explanation of Key UI Design Principles Such as Usability, Accessibility, and Aesthetics

Fundamental principles in UI design play a pivotal role in crafting user-friendly and visually captivating interfaces. Three of these principles stand out: usability, accessibility, and aesthetics. Usability revolves around the seamlessness and intuitiveness of user-system interaction, emphasising efficiency and user satisfaction. A well-designed interface facilitates straightforward navigation, a logical layout, and intuitive controls to streamline user experience (Kot, 2023). For example, simplifying website menus and maintaining consistent button placement reduces cognitive strain on users. Accessibility underscores the importance of ensuring that interfaces cater to individuals with disabilities or impairments, guaranteeing equal access to information and functionality. This encompasses features like alternative text for images, keyboard navigation, and adjustable font sizes, fostering inclusivity and accommodating diverse user needs. Aesthetics, on the other hand, focuses on an interface's visual allure and emotional resonance. Factors such as colour theory, typography, and visual hierarchy contribute to creating visually pleasing designs that enhance user experience and perception (Pushpakumar et al., 2023). For instance, harmonising colour schemes and leveraging whitespace effectively can elevate the aesthetic appeal of websites or applications. Incorporating these principles into UI design fosters a positive user experience and bolsters the success of digital products and services. Usability ensures interfaces are intuitive and efficient, accessibility promotes inclusivity and equal access, while aesthetics enrich visual appeal and emotional connection. Recognising and implementing these foundational principles are imperative for crafting effective and user-centric interfaces. By prioritising usability, accessibility, and aesthetics, designers can develop intuitive, inclusive, and visually enticing interfaces, ultimately enriching the user experience (Montargil, 2023). Figure 3 shows how generative AI enhances the user experience. Figure 2 shows the Importance of UI Design in Digital Products.

Figure 2. Importance of UI Design in Digital Products

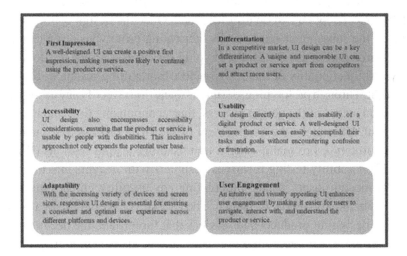

Overview of User-Centered Design (UCD) Process

User-centred design (UCD) stands as a methodology utilised in crafting products and services, placing paramount importance on meeting the needs, preferences, and constraints of end-users. This approach delves into comprehending users' behaviours, motivations, and objectives through diligent research, integrating these insights into the design trajectory. Typically, the UCD journey encompasses several iterative phases to ensure the final output resonates effectively and efficiently with users' requisites (Drzyzga & Harder, 2023). Commencing with the initial phase, the UCD process entails identifying and delineating the target audience or user cohort for the product or service. This step involves comprehensive market research, surveys, interviews, and the creation of user personas to garner profound insights into users' demographics, behaviours, and preferences. Such a grasp of the target audience's profile is instrumental in sculpting a product that aligns seamlessly with their needs and aspirations.

Subsequently, the process progresses to gathering user requirements through diverse methodologies such as contextual inquiry, usability testing, and task analysis (Nahar & Jain, 2023). These endeavours empower designers to decipher users' interactions with analogous products or services, discern prevailing challenges, and discern features of utmost significance. By collating these requirements, designers ensure the product addresses users' pain points. Following the assimilation of user requirements, designers transition into the ideation phase, wherein they conceive potential design solutions to cater to the identified needs. This stage entails brainstorming sessions, sketching, prototyping, and wireframing to explore and refine varied design concepts based on user feedback. Once the design concepts undergo refinement, the subsequent stage entails fabricating prototypes or mockups of the product (Bordegoni et al., 2023). Prototyping serves as a litmus test to assess the usability and functionality of the design before committing resources to full-scale development. Through prototyping, designers unearth and rectify any usability issues in the nascent stages of the design process, thus economising time and resources in the long haul. Ultimately, the denouement of the UCD process transpires by subjecting the prototypes to real users through usability testing sessions (Wiegmann et al., 2023). Usability testing furnishes designers with insights into the product's efficacy in meeting users' needs, pinpointing any usability glitches necessitating rectification before the product's launch. The UCD process epitomises a systematic approach to designing products and services that foreground the needs and preferences of end-users. By integrating users throughout the design journey, designers sculpt intuitive, streamlined, and gratifying products.

Role of UI Designers in Creating Engaging and Intuitive User Experiences

UI designers wield significant influence in shaping captivating and user-friendly interactions within digital products and services. Their pivotal duties encompass crafting various elements, such as buttons, menus, and visual layouts, which enable user engagement with software or websites (Quetzalli, 2023; Ghosh et al., 2020). A core objective within their purview is harmonising aesthetics with functionality, ensuring interfaces are visually appealing yet easy to navigate. Guided by the tenets of user-centred design, UI designers delve into understanding user behaviours, preferences, and pain points, tailoring interfaces to effectively meet their needs (Desmal et al., 2023). Furthermore, close collaboration with stakeholders like UX designers and developers ensures seamless integration of design elements into the overarching user experience (Sahoo, 2023; Humayun et al., 2022). A focal aspect of their role involves translating wireframes and prototypes into visually captivating designs that heighten usability and accessibility for diverse user demographics (Bordegoni, 2023). Through iterative testing and refinement cycles, UI designers iteratively fine-tune interface designs to address usability concerns and enhance the overall user experience (Liu & Martens, 2024; Humayun, Alsaqer, et al., 2022). Beyond aesthetics, they prioritise the uniformity and cohesion of interface elements across various screens and devices. Upholding visual consistency and adhering to established design conventions empower users to navigate interfaces easily and confidently (Garcia, 2019; Verma et al., 2021).

Furthermore, staying abreast of emerging trends and technologies in UI design enables UI designers to infuse innovative features that captivate users and set products apart from competitors. In summation, UI designers are crucial in fashioning engaging and user-intuitive experiences by crafting interfaces that seamlessly blend visual appeal, functionality, and user-friendliness. Their collaborative ethos, rooted in user research and iterative design methodologies, ensures digital products and services meet user needs and expectations effectively. By accentuating aesthetics, consistency, and innovation, UI designers contribute significantly to product success, amplifying user satisfaction and fostering brand loyalty (Taylor, 2020).

SECURE USER INTERFACE DESIGN

Secure User Interface: Enhancing Digital Safety

Securing user interface (UI) is among the imperative cybersecurity measures that prevent information leakages and data breaches (Neshenko et al., 2023). This exposition will debate the necessity of safe UI and delineate some main cybersecurity tactics. A necessary condition for the user interface's security is implementing robust authentication methods. Organisations should consider using multi-factorial authentication mechanisms incorporating systems like biometric authentication and the one-time passwords (MFA) method to achieve more secure UIs. Secondly, encryption, a fantastic tool for data protection when transferred from one interface to another, cannot be underemphasised (Huang, Huang and Catteddu, 2024). They are employing the TLS (Transport Layer Security) encryption method (authored by Jones, 2019) as a protocol between the user device and server, guaranteeing secure data transmission without possible intrusion. While at it, monitoring user access through the implementation of strict individualised access controls brings into focus the fact that unauthorised users cannot access the system's sensitive features. User roles-based access control (RBAC) solutions let organisations design custom permissions over the functions spectrum by providing every user access to required capabilities (Pal, 2021). Continuously undertaking security audits and examinations is an essential element of the UI, which refers to revealing and removing possible flaws. Through extensive penetration testing and code reviews, organisations can do preemptive security checks and fix any loopholes that can be exploited maliciously, reducing the risk (Katoch and Garg, 2023).

Moreover, it is necessary to stress the education aspect of the users and awareness of safe behaviours here to increase the likelihood of safe behaviours and discourage and prevent social engineering attacks. Educating users on how to identify phishing emails and creating a solid passphrase to go alongside them might help reduce the chance of data theft and data breaches (Thomas, 2018). Eventually, it would end to highlight that protecting user interface security is of utmost importance in today's digital era. With the use of resilient authentication techniques, encryption protocols, access controls, and routine security audits geared towards consumer security education, organisations are now capable of increasing cyber safety and safeguarding personal details from cybercrime cases. Figure 3 shows what is secure user interface design.

Figure 3. Secure User Interface Design

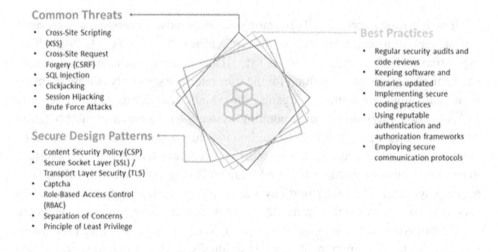

Importance of Secure User Interface Design

This part describes the central role of UI design in proper digital security and all the stakeholders who can compromise digital security if data is not protected by the UI design. One will find things more confident if a confirmation is done on the interface. When users using pleasantly designed and secure UI confirm that their worried information, private data, and financial details are protected, there is a sense of relief. This loyalty is, therefore, essential for developing different types of associations, creating concern for users to stay in connection with a particular company. Another crucial function is preventing hackers and data breaches that may arise due to an unsecured interface design. It ultimately causes monetary losses. By deploying credible authentication tools, encryption rules, and access policies, businesses can curb illegal intrusions into their private data and ward off malicious actions. Thus, such a preventive approach to security considerably decreases the possibility of expensive security incident occurrence (Kang, 2023).

In addition to the above, UI design with a high level of security is an indispensable ingredient for regulatory compliance. Technology advancement spurred the emergence of electronic corporations, prompting data protection laws such as the General Data Protection Regulation (GDPR) and the California Consumer Privacy Act (CCPA). Consequently, organisations are now legally required to ensure the protection and privacy of user data. By sticking to top-notch UI security customs, organisations save themselves from huge fines and penalties if they follow the rules and policies. Secondly, security User Interface (UI) design increases the usability and user experience and makes the valuable service to the user (Sudirjo et al., 2024). Meeting these security requirements ought to be the priority, but to achieve this, designers need to make sure that the interface is clear and usable. The balance between security and usability guarantees that the users will be able to use any functionality without feeling insecurity or fear of deficiency in security (Bowman et al., 2023).

The secure UI design is irreplaceable in safeguarding sensitive information, augmenting users' trust, thwarting security risks, meeting the required standards, and boosting the user experience. Security should be a top concern and carefully implemented, from design to implementation of security measures such as access control, data encryption, and firewalls. Hence, UIs will become more robust against emerging cyber threats and organisations, and their users will stay protected from cyber-attacks and damage to their brand reputation or image.

GENERATIVE AI TECHNIQUES FOR UI DESIGN

Introduction to Generative AI Techniques Applicable to UI Design

Innovative techniques rooted in generative AI are reshaping the landscape of UI design, presenting fresh approaches to enrich user experiences across digital platforms. These methodologies leverage sophisticated algorithms to autonomously generate various design components, encompassing layouts, colour palettes, and interactive features. Their integration into UI design processes is gaining momentum, owing to their capacity to streamline workflows, heighten productivity, and stimulate creativity. Recent studies conducted by Naqbi et al. (2024) underscore the capability of generative AI algorithms to analyse extensive datasets of user interactions, foreseeing design preferences and trends. Consequently, designers can craft more personalised and user-centric interfaces. Furthermore, insights from research by Simkute et al. (2024) demonstrate how generative AI can automate repetitive design tasks, liberating designers to concentrate on strategic and imaginative facets of their work.

Beyond efficiency gains, generative AI techniques allow designers to explore uncharted design territories and iterate swiftly. Investigations by Olynick (2024) emphasise how these algorithms generate diverse design permutations aligned with specific objectives and constraints, empowering designers to explore a broader spectrum of options efficiently. This iterative approach accelerates design cycles and fosters a culture of experimentation and innovation in UI design. Moreover, generative AI fosters collaboration between designers and developers, equipping them with real-time co-creation and refinement tools (Li et al., 2024; Adeyemo et al., 2019). Another notable advantage lies in its potential to enhance accessibility and inclusivity. By analysing many user interactions and preferences, generative AI algorithms can produce designs catering to diverse user demographics, including those with disabilities or unique accessibility requirements (Fidalgo & Thormann, 2024). This endeavour leads to the development of more inclusive and user-friendly interfaces, ultimately elevating the overall user experience. The introduction of generative AI methodologies in UI design harbours the immense potential to transform designers' approaches to conceptualising, creating, and refining digital interfaces. By harnessing algorithmic power to automate and enhance design processes, designers can unlock new realms of creativity, efficiency, and inclusivity in UI design.

Exploration of Generative Models Such as GANs, VAEs, and Autoregressive Models

Generative models, including Generative Adversarial Networks (GANs), Variational Autoencoders (VAEs), and Autoregressive Models, have garnered considerable attention due to their ability to produce synthetic data resembling real-world samples in diverse domains. These models play pivotal roles in image, text, and music generation tasks. Grasping their workings and applications is essential for effectively harnessing their potential. GANs, introduced by Pettersson (2024), comprise two neural networks: a generator and a discriminator, trained concurrently in a game-like setup. The generator learns to create realistic samples, while the discriminator learns to differentiate between natural and synthetic data. This adversarial framework encourages iterative improvement of the generator's output, yielding high-quality synthetic samples. GANs find widespread utility in tasks like image synthesis, facilitating the creation of lifelike images applicable in art, image manipulation, and data augmentation. In contrast, VAEs, proposed by Bizeul et al. (2024), are probabilistic models that learn a latent representation of input data. Unlike GANs, which prioritise realistic sample generation, VAEs aim to encode input data into a latent space and decode it back into the original domain. This latent space allows for generating novel samples by sampling from a learned distribution. VAEs prove particularly valuable in tasks necessitating continuous and structured data generation, such as image reconstruction, data compression, and anomaly detection.

Autoregressive models, like PixelRNN and PixelCNN, sequentially generate data by modelling the conditional distribution of each element given preceding elements. These models exhibit notable success in generating high-resolution images with intricate details. They achieve this by capturing complex dependencies within the data distribution, enabling precise pixel-level control during generation. Autoregressive models see extensive application in image generation tasks demanding capturing detailed patterns and textures, such as medical imaging, satellite imagery, and graphic design. In summary, GANs, VAEs, and autoregressive models serve as potent tools for data generation across diverse domains. Each model has unique strengths and weaknesses, making it suitable for distinct applications. By delving into and comprehending these generative models, researchers and practitioners can unlock fresh avenues in data generation, manipulation, and synthesis, fostering innovation across various industries.

Discussion on How Generative AI Can Automate or Assist in Various Aspects of UI Design, Including Layout Generation, Style Transfer, and Content Generation.

Generative AI, a technology capable of generating new content autonomously, exhibits tremendous potential in transforming different facets of UI design. This discourse delves into how generative AI can streamline the UI design process by automating or aiding layout generation, style transfer, and content creation. Layout generation is pivotal in UI design, dictating the positioning of elements on a screen. Generative AI algorithms, intense learning-based ones, can automate this task by analysing user preferences and content structure to propose optimal layouts (Ko et al., 2023; Fatima-Tuz-Zahra et al., 2019). Similarly, style transfer techniques facilitate the adaptation of visual styles from existing designs or artworks to UI elements, enhancing aesthetics and user experience (Stige et al., 2023; Hussain et al., 2019). GANs achieve style transfer by learning to generate images that mimic a specified style while retaining the original content (Chen et al., 2023; Sankar et al., 2020). Furthermore, generative AI aids in content generation, tackling the challenge of producing diverse and engaging UI elements. Through techniques like natural language processing (NLP) and image generation, AI models can generate text, images, and multimedia content tailored to specific contexts and user interactions (Nazir & Wang, 2023; Almusaylim et al., 2020). This capability proves invaluable in scenarios where manual content creation is labour-intensive or impractical.

Additionally, generative AI tools empower designers to swiftly explore design variations. Designers can iterate efficiently by automatically generating multiple design alternatives and exploring a broader design landscape (Marg'uba, 2024; Khalil et al., 2021). This iterative approach nurtures creativity and facilitates the discovery of innovative solutions to UI design challenges. Nevertheless, while generative AI holds immense promise, ethical considerations and quality control are paramount. Designers must ensure that AI-generated designs adhere to usability principles and ethical guidelines (Fatima, 2023; Gaur et al., 2021). Furthermore, validating the quality and coherence of generated designs through user testing is crucial for ensuring satisfactory user experiences. In conclusion, generative AI offers significant opportunities for automating and enhancing various aspects of UI design, including layout generation, style transfer, and content creation. By harnessing advanced algorithms and ML techniques, designers can streamline the design process, explore diverse possibilities, and ultimately deliver more compelling and user-centric interfaces. Figure 4 shows how generative AI can enhance UI design.

Figure 4. How Generative AI Can Enhance UI Design

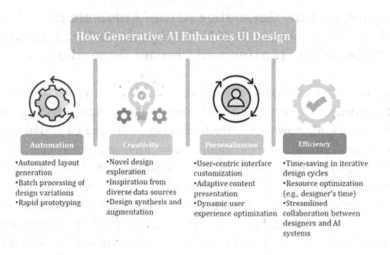

AUTOMATED LAYOUT GENERATION

Overview of Automated Layout Generation Using Generative AI

Automated layout generation leveraging generative AI has emerged as a groundbreaking approach across multiple sectors, notably graphic design and architecture. This pioneering method entails deploying algorithms that mimic human creative processes to generate designs autonomously. With the evolution of deep learning algorithms, particularly GANs and VAEs, the sophistication of automated layout generation has increased, enabling the creation of high-quality designs. A significant application of generative AI in automated layout generation lies in graphic design, which simplifies the creation of layouts for diverse media such as advertisements, websites, and marketing materials. By analysing existing designs and recognising patterns, generative AI systems can produce fresh layouts that adhere to design principles and user preferences (Agrawal, 2023; Almusaylim et al., 2018). Additionally, generative AI empowers architects to explore numerous design possibilities in architectural design efficiently. AI-driven systems can generate architectural layouts that optimise space utilisation and aesthetic appeal by inputting parameters like building specifications and environmental constraints.

Generative AI in automated layout generation offers several benefits, including enhanced productivity, cost-effectiveness, and design innovation. By automating the layout generation process, designers and architects can dedicate more time to conceptualising and refining designs rather than tedious tasks (Aalaei et al., 2023; Singhal et al., 2020). Furthermore, the capability of generative AI systems to produce diverse design variations facilitates exploration and experimentation, leading to the discovery of innovative design solutions (Badini et al., 2023). Moreover, automated layout generation using generative AI has the potential to democratise design by providing accessible tools that empower individuals with limited design expertise to create professional-quality layouts. However, despite its potential, automated layout generation using generative AI also poses challenges and limitations. One primary concern is the ethical implications surrounding AI-generated designs, particularly issues related to intellectual property rights and originality (Zakir, 2023; Gouda et al., 2022). Furthermore, the reliance on AI algorithms for design generation raises questions about transparency and bias, as the decision-making processes of these algorithms are often opaque and influenced by the data they are trained on (Lepri et al., 2017; Taj & Jhanjhi, 2022). Automated layout generation using generative AI holds significant promise to transform the design process across various industries. By harnessing the capabilities of deep learning algorithms, designers and architects can streamline workflows, foster innovation, and create functional and aesthetically pleasing designs. However, addressing ethical and technical challenges is crucial to ensure this technology's responsible and equitable use.

Explanation of Techniques for Generating Grid Systems, Component Placement, and Responsive Designs

Efficiently generating grid systems, placing components, and ensuring responsive designs are essential tasks across multiple domains, including web design, graphic design, and UI development. Various methodologies, both traditional and leveraging generative AI advancements, have been developed to streamline these processes. One fundamental approach for generating grid systems involves utilising frameworks like Bootstrap and Foundation. These frameworks offer pre-defined grid layouts that designers can easily tailor to their specific requirements (Brandt et al., 2011). Alternatively, designers may use manual grid creation methods to construct grids based on design principles such as alignment, proximity, and repetition (Shi et al., 2023; Krishnan et al., 2021).

Regarding component placement, designers commonly employ techniques like wireframing and prototyping to visualise element arrangements within a layout. Wireframing entails creating low-fidelity design representations, allowing designers to experiment with different component placements and overall structures (Bordegoni et al., 2023a; Sindiramutty et al., 2024). Prototyping, conversely, involves crafting interactive mockups that simulate user interactions, providing valuable insights into component placement and usability (Coronado et al., 2023). Generative AI has also significantly contributed to component placement facilitation through methods like content-aware layout generation. AI-driven systems can automatically arrange components within a layout by analysing content and user preferences to enhance readability and visual appeal (J. Chen et al., 2024). Furthermore, advancements in Reinforcement Learning (RL) have empowered AI systems to learn from user feedback and iteratively refine component placement based on design objectives (Kaufmann et al., 2023; Sindiramutty, Jhanjhi, Ray, Jazri, Khan, Gaur, et al., 2024).

Responsive design, ensuring layouts seamlessly adapt to various screen sizes and devices, relies on techniques such as fluid grids, flexible images, and media queries. Fluid grids enable layouts to resize proportionally based on screen dimensions, while flexible images adjust their size relative to the viewport. Media queries allow designers to apply styles based on device characteristics such as screen width and orientation. The techniques for generating grid systems, component placement, and responsive designs encompass a spectrum of methodologies, ranging from traditional grid frameworks and manual design processes to innovative AI-driven approaches. By effectively leveraging these techniques, designers can craft visually appealing, functional, and optimised layouts for diverse devices and user experiences.

Examples of Tools and Frameworks Leveraging Generative AI for Automated Layout Generation

The incorporation of generative AI into tools and frameworks for automated layout generation has spurred the development of innovative solutions across diverse domains. These tools harness ML algorithms to streamline the design process, produce varied layouts, and enhance design outcomes significantly. An exemplary instance is Adobe Sensei, an AI-powered platform seamlessly integrated into Adobe Creative Cloud applications. Adobe Sensei features like Auto Reframe in Adobe Premiere Pro automatically adapt video compositions to different aspect ratios, showcasing AI's potential in responsive layout generation (Greenberg, 2013; Azam et al., 2023). Similarly, Figma, a collaborative interface design tool, integrates generative AI techniques into its functionalities. Features such as Smart Selection and Auto Layout facilitate the effortless creation of responsive designs by autonomously arranging and resizing components based on predefined constraints (Sadr, 2023; Azam, Tajwar, et al., 2023).

In web design, companies like Wix have introduced AI-driven tools to aid users in building professional-looking websites with minimal effort. Wix ADI (Artificial Design Intelligence) analyses user preferences and content to generate personalised website layouts, exemplifying how generative AI can democratise design and empower non-designers to craft compelling layouts (Hyde & Filippidis, 2021; Ananna et al., 2023). Moreover, platforms like Runway ML offer accessible frameworks for artists and designers to experiment with generative AI models and seamlessly integrate them into their creative workflows. Runway ML provides a diverse array of pre-trained models and tools for generating and manipulating images, videos, and 3D assets, opening up new avenues for automated layout generation across various media (Qin et al., 2023; Azam, Dulloo, Majeed, Wan, Xin, & Sindiramutty, 2023). Another notable example is Canva, a graphic design platform utilising AI-driven algorithms to simplify the design process for users with limited design experience. The Canvas DesignAI feature suggests layout templates, fonts, and colour schemes based on user input, enabling individuals to create visually appealing layouts (Dehman, 2023) swiftly. Tools and frameworks leveraging generative AI for automated layout generation are reshaping the design landscape by offering intuitive, efficient, and accessible solutions for both designers and non-designers. These examples underscore AI's transformative potential in automating repetitive tasks, optimising design workflows, and empowering users to unleash creativity.

STYLE TRANSFER AND DESIGN EXPLORATION

Introduction to Style Transfer Techniques in UI Design

Style transfer methods are becoming increasingly prominent in UI design, providing novel approaches to enhancing visual appeal and effectively engaging users (Raza et al., 2024; Wen et al., 2024). Rooted in AI and computer vision, style transfer entails applying artistic styles from one image to another, thereby altering visual attributes while preserving underlying content. This technique draws inspiration from various artistic movements, allowing designers to craft distinctive and visually captivating interfaces. Incorporating style transfer into UI design offers numerous advantages, including the ability to evoke emotional responses and establish a unique brand identity (An et al., 2024). By integrating renowned artistic styles or cultural motif elements into interface elements such as icons, buttons, and backgrounds, designers can evoke specific moods or associations that resonate with the target audience. Moreover, style transfer techniques enable personalisation, allowing users to tailor their interface preferences based on aesthetic tastes or cultural backgrounds. Furthermore, style transfer improves usability and accessibility by simplifying complex visual elements and optimising user flow (Nova, 202; Sindiramutty, Jhanjhi, Tan, Khan, Gharib, & Yun, 2024). Using stylised visual cues and intuitive design patterns, designers can streamline navigation and facilitate seamless interactions, enhancing the overall user experience. Additionally, style transfer techniques enable creating cohesive design systems that maintain consistency across various platforms and devices, bolstering brand recognition and user loyalty (N. Zhao et al., 2020). However, it's crucial to acknowledge the potential challenges and limitations associated with style transfer in UI design. While offering creative freedom and artistic expression, these techniques may introduce complexities related to performance optimisation and resource management. Moreover, ensuring cross-platform compatibility and responsiveness is crucial for designers implementing style transfer techniques in UI design. Figure 5 shows the fundamentals of the UI design principle.

Figure 5. Fundamentals of UI Design Principles

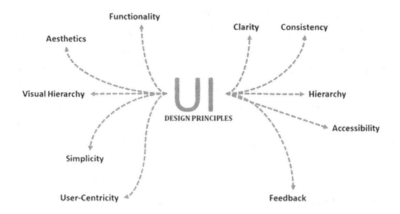

In summary, style transfer techniques present exciting opportunities for innovation and creativity in UI design, allowing designers to infuse visual elements with diverse artistic styles and cultural influences. By leveraging these techniques effectively, designers can create immersive and memorable user experiences that resonate with audiences across different digital platforms.

Exploration of How Generative AI Can Help Designers Explore Different Design Styles, Color Schemes, and Visual Treatments

The advent of Generative AI has transformed the landscape of design, providing designers with robust tools to explore an array of design styles, colour palettes, and visual treatments efficiently and imaginatively (De Felice & Petrillo, 2023; Sindiramutty, Jhanjhi, Tan, Khan, Shah, & Gaur, 2024). Generative AI refers to systems capable of autonomously generating fresh content by learning patterns and examples provided during training. These systems, often employing techniques like GANs and VAEs, empower designers to tap into their creativity and experiment with diverse design possibilities (De Felice & Petrillo, 2023; Sindiramutty, Jhanjhi, Tan, Tee, Lau, Jazri, et al., 2024). One notable advantage of generative AI in design is its capacity to aid designers in exploring different design styles (Hashem & Hakeem, 2024). By analysing extensive datasets of existing design styles and patterns, generative AI algorithms can produce new designs that blend elements from various styles or invent entirely novel aesthetics. This enables designers to push the boundaries of conventional design norms and discover innovative approaches that resonate with their intended audience. Additionally, generative AI simplifies the exploration of colour schemes by automatically generating colour palettes based on specified parameters such as mood, theme, or brand identity (Salman, 2022). Designers can input criteria like desired emotions or cultural associations, and the AI system generates a range of colour options tailored to these specifications. This process expedites colour selection and encourages designers to experiment with unconventional colour combinations that might have been overlooked otherwise.

Beyond design styles and colour schemes, generative AI empowers designers to delve into various visual treatments and effects (W. Zhao et al., 2024; Sindiramutty, Tan, Tee, Lau, Balakrishnan, Kaur, et al., 2024). Whether it involves applying artistic filters, generating realistic textures, or experimenting with typography styles, generative AI algorithms can assist designers in crafting visually captivating compositions. Furthermore, these systems enable rapid iteration, generating numerous design variations within a short timeframe, which proves particularly valuable in time-sensitive projects or when exploring multiple design concepts. Nevertheless, it's crucial to acknowledge the indispensable role of human creativity and judgment alongside generative AI tools. While AI can generate many design options, the designer must curate and refine these outputs to align with project objectives and user needs (Auricchio, 2023). Additionally, designers must remain aware of ethical considerations and potential biases in the training data used to develop generative AI models. Generative AI holds tremendous promise in aiding designers to explore diverse design styles, colour palettes, and visual treatments (Mennan, 2022). By harnessing the capabilities of generative AI algorithms, designers can unlock new avenues for creativity, streamline the design process, and ultimately deliver captivating visual experiences across various mediums.

Case Studies Demonstrating the Application of Style Transfer in UI Design Projects

Using AI algorithms, designers can seamlessly incorporate a variety of artistic styles into interface elements, resulting in visually appealing and memorable user experiences. Numerous case studies showcase the successful implementation of style transfer in various UI design projects spanning different industries:

1. **Social Media Platform Redesign:** A prominent social media platform aimed to rejuvenate its interface to boost user engagement and brand perception. The platform revamped its interface elements, icons, backgrounds, and animations by employing style transfer techniques inspired by contemporary art movements like surrealism and pop art. The redesigned interface led to increased user interactions and positive feedback, illustrating the efficacy of style transfer in refreshing brand identity while preserving usability (Hartson & Pyla, 2012).

2. **E-commerce Website Enhancement:** An e-commerce website aimed to set itself apart from competitors by providing a visually immersive shopping experience. Using style transfer algorithms, the website integrated vintage photography and retro design elements into its product displays and UI components. This approach resonated with nostalgic consumers, increasing conversion rates and increasing sales.

3. **Healthcare Application Interface Overhaul:** A healthcare application sought to enhance user satisfaction and accessibility by modernising its interface design. Style transfer techniques infused minimalist design elements and nature-inspired aesthetics into the application's visual assets. The redesigned interface improved usability for patients and healthcare professionals and conveyed a sense of calmness and reliability, aligning with the brand's values and mission.

4. **Gaming Platform Redesign:** A gaming platform aimed to broaden its audience by refreshing its UI to appeal to casual and hardcore gamers. Style transfer algorithms incorporated dynamic visual effects and futuristic design elements inspired by science fiction and cyberpunk genres. The revamped interface garnered widespread praise for its visually stunning graphics and intuitive navigation, increasing user retention and engagement (Bai et al., 2024).

5. **Financial Services App Transformation:** A financial services app sought to update its interface to cater to the preferences of tech-savvy millennials. Style transfer techniques were employed to integrate modern art deco and urban graffiti elements into the app's design, creating a visually dynamic and culturally relevant user experience. The redesigned interface resonated with the target demographic, leading to higher user adoption rates and positive app reviews (Siountri & Anagnostopoulos, 2023).

In conclusion, these case studies exemplify the diverse applications of style transfer in UI design projects across various industries. By harnessing the creative capabilities of AI algorithms, designers can revamp interfaces, elevate brand identities, and enhance user experiences, ultimately driving business success and customer satisfaction.

CONTENT GENERATION AND PERSONALIZATION

Overview of Content Generation Techniques Using Generative AI

In recent years, there has been significant progress in content creation thanks to advancements in Generative AI techniques. These innovations have profoundly impacted various sectors like marketing, entertainment, and design by introducing algorithms capable of autonomously producing content that imitates human-like creativity. This overview delves into the primary methods of generating content via Generative AI. GANs involve two neural networks—the generator and the discriminator—engaged in a competition. The generator crafts content, such as images or text, while the discriminator assesses its authenticity. Through iterative training, GANs refine their outputs, resulting in increasingly realistic content generation and facilitating applications like image synthesis and text creation (Ooi et al., 2023; Sindiramutty, Tee, Balakrishnan, Kaur, Thangaveloo, Jazri, et al., 2024) Another notable approach is through Recurrent Neural Networks (RNNs), particularly Long Short-Term Memory (LSTM) networks. Renowned for their ability to model sequential data, RNNs excel in tasks requiring context and continuity, making them suitable for generating coherent text, music, and code (Jawahar et al., 2020). Transformer models, as seen in OpenAI's GPT (Generative Pre-trained Transformer) series, represent a groundbreaking strategy for content generation. These models employ self-attention mechanisms to capture long-range dependencies, enabling diverse applications ranging from text completion to dialogue generation (Nassiri & Akhloufi, 2022)

VAEs offer another influential technique that combines probabilistic modelling with deep learning. VAEs learn latent representations of data, facilitating the generation of novel samples with controllable attributes, valuable in domains like image editing and creative design (Cetin et al., 2023). Moreover, RL has gained momentum in content generation by enabling agents to learn optimal strategies through trial and error. When combined with deep neural networks, RL algorithms have been applied to various tasks, including game-level design and personalised content recommendation (Luong et al., 2019). Content generation using Generative AI encompasses diverse techniques, each with unique strengths and applications. From GANs fostering realism to Transformers enabling coherent text generation, these methods continuously push the boundaries of creative AI, promising exciting prospects for the future of content creation across industries.

Discussion on How AI Can Generate Textual, Visual, or Multimedia Content for UI Elements Such as Headings, Images, and Product Recommendations

AI presents vast potential in crafting textual, visual, and multimedia content for UI elements, encompassing headings, images, and product suggestions. This discourse delves into how AI methodologies can elevate UI design and enhance user experience across diverse platforms. Using AI to generate textual content involves leveraging NLP models such as Generative Pre-trained Transformers (GPT), adept at producing coherent and contextually fitting text (J. Li et al., 2022). For instance, in UI elements like headings, AI algorithms can craft captivating and informative titles based on user preferences, website content, or product descriptions. By analysing extensive datasets, AI can discern patterns to generate headings optimised for engagement and search engine optimisation (SEO) objectives.

In visual content, technologies like GANs and VAEs empower AI to generate lifelike images and graphics tailored for UI elements (Bhattacharya et al., 2024). GANs excel in producing high-resolution visuals of products or interface components, enhancing visual allure and brand identity. Moreover, VAEs enable the synthesis of personalised visual content, adapting to user inclinations and design specifications. AI-driven visuals enrich UI design by furnishing visually captivating elements that resonate with users (Wennekers & Mathematics, 2021). Multimedia content generation through AI introduces dynamic and interactive UI elements. AI-driven recommendation systems leverage user behaviour data and content analysis to propose pertinent products or services, augmenting personalisation and user engagement. Techniques like collaborative filtering and deep learning enable AI to tailor product recommendations to individual preferences, bolstering conversion rates and customer satisfaction. Additionally, AI can aid in crafting multimedia content such as interactive tutorials, product demonstrations, or virtual try-on experiences (Davis & Aslam, 2024). By integrating computer vision and augmented reality technologies, AI simulates real-world product interactions, enabling users to make informed decisions and enriching their shopping journey (Bassyouni & Elhajj, 2021; Sindiramutty, 2023). AI-driven content generation unlocks transformative possibilities for UI design by furnishing tailored textual, visual, and multimedia elements. From crafting compelling headings to offering personalized product recommendations and immersive multimedia encounters, AI empowers designers to forge captivating and user-centric interfaces across digital platforms. Figure 7 shows automated layout generation using generative AI.

Figure 6. Automated Layout Generation Using Generative AI

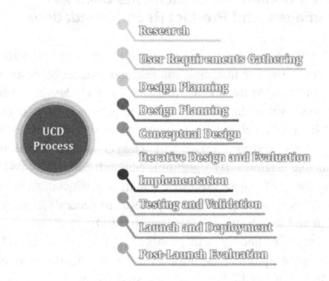

Considerations for Personalizing Content Generation Based on User Preferences and Behaviors

Customising content generation according to user preferences and behaviours is crucial for boosting user engagement and satisfaction across digital platforms. This segment outlines vital factors to effectively tailor content to individual users using AI-driven methodologies.

Understanding User Preferences: The cornerstone of personalised content generation is comprehending user preferences. AI algorithms analyse user interactions, historical data, and explicit feedback to deduce preferences concerning content types, topics, formats, and presentation styles. Techniques like collaborative filtering and content-based filtering enable AI systems to suggest relevant content that aligns with users' interests and tastes (De Gemmis et al., 2015).

Dynamic Content Adaptation: Personalization goes beyond recommending existing content; it involves dynamically adjusting content based on real-time user interactions. AI-powered systems monitor user behaviour, such as browsing patterns, search queries, and click-through rates, to dynamically tailor the content presentation (Sodiya et al., 2024). For example, an e-commerce platform can customise product recommendations based on users' browsing history or items in their shopping cart, thereby increasing the likelihood of conversion.

Granular User Segmentation: Effective personalisation necessitates categorising users into distinct groups based on shared characteristics or behaviours. AI facilitates granular user segmentation by clustering users with similar preferences or behaviours, enabling targeted content-generation strategies (Rane et al., 2023a). Organisations can deliver more relevant and compelling experiences by tailoring content to specific user segments, fostering user engagement and loyalty.

Preference Elicitation and Feedback Loop: Establishing a robust mechanism for eliciting user preferences is vital for refining personalized content generation over time. AI systems proactively solicit user feedback through surveys, ratings, or implicit signals, continuously updating user preferences and refining content recommendations accordingly (Virvou, 2023). Additionally, AI algorithms leverage RL techniques to optimise content delivery based on observed user responses, ensuring adaptive and effective personalisation.

Ethical and Privacy Considerations: Prioritizing user privacy and ethical considerations is paramount in personalising content generation. AI systems must comply with stringent data privacy regulations and transparently communicate data usage policies to users. Implementing privacy-preserving techniques such as federated learning and differential privacy can safeguard user data while enabling effective personalisation (Saura et al., 2022). Furthermore, organisations must ensure that personalised content generation algorithms do not inadvertently perpetuate biases or discriminate against certain user groups, promoting inclusivity and fairness in content delivery.

In conclusion, personalised content generation based on user preferences and behaviours necessitates a multifaceted approach that includes understanding user preferences, dynamic content adaptation, granular user segmentation, preference elicitation, and ethical considerations. By responsibly leveraging AI-driven techniques, organisations can deliver tailored and engaging content experiences that resonate with individual users while respecting their privacy and values.

COLLABORATIVE DESIGN WITH AI

Examination of Collaborative Design Approaches Integrating AI Tools With Human Designers

The trend of collaborative design, where AI tools collaborate with human designers, is gaining traction across diverse industries. This method boosts creativity, efficiency, and problem-solving capabilities. By merging AI tools with human designers, companies can capitalise on the strengths to achieve superior design results (Lichtenthaler, 2020; Sindiramutty, Tan, Lau, Thangaveloo, Gharib, Manchuri, et al., 2024). This analysis delves into the implications and advantages of collaborative design methods that fuse AI tools with human designers. One notable benefit is how it enhances human creativity with AI support. AI algorithms can sift through extensive data and propose innovative design ideas, offering designers new insights and inspiration. Furthermore, AI-powered design tools can automate mundane tasks, freeing designers to concentrate on more intricate and strategic aspects of the design process (Castro et al., 2021). Additionally, collaborative design approaches facilitate quicker iteration cycles and prototyping. AI algorithms swiftly evaluate design options and offer immediate feedback, streamlining the iterative process and enhancing agility and responsiveness to evolving requirements or user input. This leads to better-designed products and services. Moreover, integrating AI tools with human designers fosters interdisciplinary collaboration and knowledge sharing. AI systems can analyse data from various fields, bridging knowledge disparities and promoting exchanging ideas across disciplines (Luan et al., 2020). This interdisciplinary approach fosters innovation and aids teams in addressing complex design challenges more effectively. However, addressing challenges such as ethical concerns, data privacy, and algorithmic bias is imperative to ensure the responsible and efficient implementation of collaborative design methods. Companies must establish clear guidelines and frameworks for the ethical utilisation of AI in design, ensuring transparency, fairness, and accountability. Collaborative design methods that merge AI tools with human designers offer numerous benefits, including heightened creativity, efficiency, and interdisciplinary collaboration. Nevertheless, addressing ethical and technical hurdles is vital to fully harnessing this approach's potential and ensuring responsible and effective design outcomes.

Discussion on How Generative AI Can Facilitate Collaboration, Iteration, and Experimentation in UI Design Workflows

Generative AI technologies have the potential to revolutionise UI design processes by promoting collaboration, supporting iterative methods, and encouraging experimentation. Using AI-driven generative design tools, designers can enhance collaboration, iterate quickly, and efficiently delve into various design options. These tools utilise algorithms to autonomously generate design alternatives based on specific parameters, enabling designers to explore many possibilities easily (Hughes et al., 2021). A key advantage of incorporating generative AI into UI design workflows is its capacity to foster collaboration among designers and stakeholders. Integrating AI tools into collaborative design approaches facilitates seamless teamwork, as AI algorithms generate and refine design concepts, thereby promoting collective decision-making (Duan et al., 2019). With features supporting real-time collaboration and shared access to design iterations, team members can contribute insights, critique designs, and refine them collaboratively, fostering an inclusive and dynamic design process.

Furthermore, generative AI expedites the iterative design process by automating repetitive tasks and swiftly generating numerous design variations. Designers can input constraints, objectives, and preferences into AI-powered tools, producing many design options meeting the specified criteria (Jenis et al., 2023). This accelerates the exploration of design alternatives, enabling designers to iterate rapidly and refine concepts incrementally. Consequently, designers can experiment with different layouts, styles, and functionalities more efficiently, resulting in more innovative and polished design solutions. Moreover, generative AI empowers designers to venture into unconventional design approaches and explore new design realms. By generating diverse design alternatives beyond human imagination, AI-driven tools encourage designers to push creative boundaries and consider unconventional solutions (Rane et al., 2023b). This fosters a culture of experimentation, prompting designers to explore innovative design directions that may not have been initially contemplated, thus promoting creativity and innovation in UI design workflows. In summary, generative AI presents significant opportunities to enhance collaboration, iteration, and experimentation in UI design workflows. By harnessing AI-driven generative design tools, designers can collaborate more effectively, iterate rapidly, and explore diverse design possibilities, ultimately creating more innovative and refined UI designs.

Challenges and Best Practices for Incorporating AI In Collaborative Design Processes

Integrating AI into collaborative design workflows offers possibilities and complexities for design teams to navigate (Y. Shi et al., 2023). While AI technologies promise heightened creativity and efficiency, they also introduce nuanced challenges that demand thoughtful management and understanding. Grasping these challenges and adopting effective strategies is paramount for optimising AI's role in collaborative design endeavours. One primary hurdle in merging AI with collaborative design is the concern over potentially sidelining human designers. With AI's capacity to automate tasks and independently generate design solutions, there's apprehension about designers being displaced (Stige et al., 2023b). To mitigate this, it's crucial to underscore AI's role as a supportive tool to complement human ingenuity rather than supplanting designers entirely. Encouraging symbiotic collaboration between

AI systems and human designers can leverage their unique strengths, leading to more innovative and refined design outcomes.

Transparency and interpretability present another challenge in AI-driven design processes. AI algorithms often operate opaquely, leaving designers in the dark about decision-making processes (Schultz et al., 2023) and casting doubt on AI-generated design recommendations. Introducing transparency measures such as explainable AI techniques can give designers insights into the rationale behind AI-generated design suggestions, fostering trust and facilitating more productive collaboration between human designers and AI systems (Liao et al., 2023). Moreover, ensuring data privacy and security poses a significant hurdle in collaborative design processes involving AI. Design data typically contain sensitive information, and sharing this data with AI systems raises valid privacy concerns. Implementing robust data governance frameworks and encryption techniques can safeguard sensitive design data while enabling collaboration and knowledge exchange within design teams.

Despite these challenges, adhering to best practices can help overcome barriers to incorporating AI in collaborative design workflows. Cultivating a continual learning and adaptation culture is crucial for design teams to stay abreast of AI advancements and seamlessly integrate them into their workflows. Additionally, fostering interdisciplinary collaboration among designers, data scientists, and domain experts can facilitate the development of AI-powered tools tailored to the unique needs of design teams (Jain et al., 2023). In essence, integrating AI into collaborative design processes presents challenges and opportunities for design teams. By addressing concerns such as job displacement, transparency, and data privacy and embracing best practices such as promoting collaboration and continual learning, design teams can fully harness AI's potential to enhance creativity, efficiency, and innovation in collaborative design workflows. Figure 6 shows The User-centered design (UCD) process.

Figure 7. User-Centered Design (UCD) Process

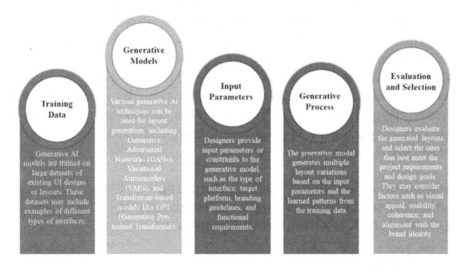

EVALUATION AND VALIDATION OF AI-GENERATED DESIGNS

Introduction to Evaluation Methods for AI-Generated Designs

As AI continues to permeate various fields, including design, the necessity for effective assessment techniques becomes increasingly crucial. AI-generated designs hold great potential for transforming industries, but ensuring their effectiveness and appropriateness demands thorough evaluation. Assessment methods are vital for measuring AI-generated designs' performance, user experience, and ethical considerations. This document outlines the significance of evaluation techniques in appraising AI-generated designs and underscores essential factors to consider during their application. Evaluation techniques are pivotal in guaranteeing the excellence and efficiency of AI-generated designs (Rane, 2023). These techniques encompass various approaches, such as user testing, expert evaluations, and algorithmic assessments. Using these methods, designers can acquire valuable insights into the strengths and weaknesses of AI-generated designs, facilitating iterative enhancements and optimisation. Additionally, evaluation techniques assist in identifying potential biases and ethical issues embedded within AI algorithms, thus fostering equity and responsibility (Saeidnia, 2023). One of the primary hurdles in evaluating AI-generated designs lies in establishing suitable metrics and standards (Palladino, 2023). Unlike traditional design methods, AI-generated designs may showcase intricate behaviours and patterns that challenge conventional evaluation criteria. Consequently, researchers must adapt evaluation techniques to accommodate the unique attributes of AI-generated designs, such as adaptability and autonomy. Moreover, the interdisciplinary nature of AI design necessitates collaboration among designers, technologists, ethicists, and end-users to devise comprehensive evaluation frameworks. Evaluation methods are crucial in gauging AI-generated designs' effectiveness, user experience, and ethical implications. By employing various evaluation approaches and fostering interdisciplinary collaboration, designers can ensure the quality and equity of AI-generated designs, ultimately fostering innovation and societal advancement.

Explanation of Usability Testing, Heuristic Evaluation, and Other Evaluation Techniques in the Context of AI-Generated UI Designs

Usability Testing

Testing usability is critical for evaluating the efficiency and user-friendliness of AI-generated UI designs (Kazemi, 2023). Participants are assigned tasks while interacting with the AI-generated UI during this process. Their actions, feedback, and performance metrics are then analysed to pinpoint usability challenges and areas needing enhancement. Usability testing gives designers insights into how users engage with AI-generated UIs in real-world scenarios, allowing for iterative adjustments and improvements (Pop & Schricker, 2023).

Heuristic Evaluation

Heuristic evaluation involves expert evaluators assessing AI-generated UI designs against predefined usability principles or heuristics (A. Nova et al., 2022). These principles act as guidelines for identifying common usability issues, like system status visibility, alignment with the real world, and user control and freedom. Expert evaluators systematically review AI-generated UI designs and offer feedback based on heuristic assessments, uncovering potential usability hurdles and guiding design enhancements (Pyae et al., 2023).

Other Evaluation Techniques

Beyond usability testing and heuristic evaluation, several other evaluation methods are pertinent to AI-generated UI designs. Cognitive walkthroughs entail evaluators systematically going through tasks to assess cognitive load and interface usability

(Polson et al., 1992). A/B testing compares different versions of AI-generated UI designs to determine the most effective in terms of user engagement, satisfaction, or task completion rates. Eye tracking technology monitors and analyses users' eye movements as they interact with AI-generated UI designs, providing insights into visual attention and usability (Y. Shi et al., 2023b).

Usability testing, heuristic evaluation, and other evaluation techniques are essential for evaluating AI-generated UI designs' effectiveness, usability, and user experience. By utilising these evaluation methods, designers can pinpoint usability challenges, refine design components, and develop more intuitive and user-friendly interfaces, ultimately improving the overall quality of AI-generated applications.

Considerations for Validating AI-Generated Designs Against User Needs and Design Objectives

Ensuring that AI-generated designs meet user expectations and serve their intended purposes is paramount to their success (L. M. Castro et al., 2022). This involves evaluating how well these designs align with user preferences, requirements, and overarching design goals. Below, we explore critical considerations for validating AI-generated designs according to user needs and objectives.

Putting Users First

The user-centric design prioritises the needs, preferences, and behaviours of end-users throughout the design process (Dodeja et al., 2024). Designers must prioritise user feedback and insights obtained through user research and usability testing when validating AI-generated designs. By actively involving users in the design and validation process, designers can ensure that AI-generated designs are intuitive, user-friendly, and capable of meeting users' underlying needs (Huang et al., 2024).

Alignment With Design Goals

Validating AI-generated designs also involves assessing how well they align with overarching design objectives, such as functionality, aesthetics, and performance metrics (J. Liu et al., 2024). Designers must evaluate whether these designs effectively achieve the goals outlined during the design phase. This may entail conducting comparative analyses, performance evaluations, and usability assessments to determine how well AI-generated designs meet predetermined design criteria and benchmarks.

Ethical Considerations

In addition to user needs and design objectives, validating AI-generated designs requires careful consideration of ethical implications and societal impact (Leslie, 2019). Designers must ensure these designs adhere to moral principles, safeguard user privacy, and mitigate potential biases or discriminatory outcomes. Transparency, fairness, and accountability should be prioritised throughout the design and validation process to uphold ethical standards and foster user trust.

Continuous Improvement

Validating AI-generated designs is an iterative process that necessitates ongoing refinement and optimisation based on feedback and insights gathered from users and stakeholders (Margetis et al., 2021). Designers should embrace an iterative approach to validation, incorporating user feedback and addressing identified issues through successive design iterations. This iterative cycle of validation and refinement ensures that AI-generated designs evolve in line with changing user needs, technological advancements, and design objectives over time (Wang et al., 2002).

In summary, validating AI-generated designs against user needs and design objectives is crucial for creating impactful products. By prioritising user-centric design, aligning with design goals, considering ethical implications, and embracing continuous improvement, designers can ensure that AI-generated designs meet user expectations, serve their intended purposes, and contribute positively to society.

ETHICAL AND SOCIAL IMPLICATIONS

Exploration of Ethical Considerations in Using Generative AI for UI Design

Cutting-edge technology known as Generative AI transforms UI design by automating the process of creating UIs. However, this advancement brings about various ethical concerns that need careful attention. Firstly, there's a worry regarding bias in the designs generated. Studies, such as the one conducted by Ngalamou and Schmidbauer (2020), reveal that AI algorithms often replicate the biases present in the data they're trained on, resulting in biased outcomes in UI designs. Additionally, the utilisation of generative AI raises questions about intellectual property rights and ownership. As pointed out by Lilova (2021), the automatic generation of designs blurs the concept of authorship, potentially infringing upon the rights of human designers and complicating matters of attribution. Furthermore, the transparency and explainability of AI-generated designs are significant ethical concerns. According to Ryan (2020), opaque AI systems hinder users' ability to comprehend how design choices are made, undermining trust and giving rise to accountability worries. Moreover, there are apprehensions regarding the impact of AI-generated designs on employment within the design industry. Research by Budhwar et al. (2023) indicates that widespread adoption of generative AI could result in job displacement among human designers, worsening socioeconomic disparities. Beyond these concerns, ethical ramifications are associated with the possible misuse of generative AI for deceitful purposes. AI-generated designs could be manipulated to deceive users or propagate misinformation, prompting ethical inquiries about the responsibilities of designers and the platforms hosting such designs. Additionally, there are concerns about the environmental consequences of AI training processes. Research by Nabavi-Pelesaraei et al. (2018)suggests that the energy consumption linked with training large AI models contributes to carbon emissions and environmental harm, advocating for more sustainable approaches to AI development and implementation. Figure 8 shows the application of style transfer and design exploration.

Figure 8. Application of Style Transfer and Design Exploration

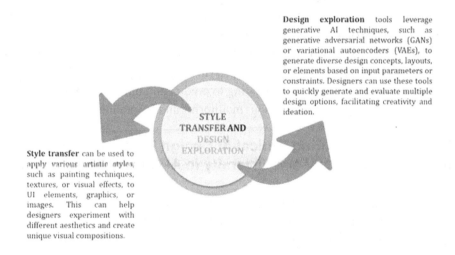

While generative AI offers great potential for advancing UI design, it also presents significant ethical hurdles that must be tackled. These encompass concerns regarding bias, intellectual property, transparency, employment, deception, and environmental sustainability. By critically examining and addressing these ethical considerations, designers and developers can responsibly leverage the potential of generative AI, ensuring that it contributes positively to society while minimising negative impacts.

Discussion on Potential Biases, Privacy Concerns, and Unintended Consequences of AI-Generated Designs

AI-generated designs hold vast potential but raise significant concerns regarding biases, privacy, and unintended consequences. Biases inherent in AI algorithms, derived from the data they are trained on, have the potential to perpetuate societal inequalities and discrimination (Zajko, 2021). For example, facial recognition algorithms often exhibit higher error rates for individuals with darker skin tones, reflecting biases in the training data. Similarly, AI-generated designs risk inadvertently reinforcing stereotypes or marginalising certain groups if not meticulously monitored and addressed.

Privacy issues also loom prominently over AI-generated designs, particularly concerning the collection and utilisation of personal data. AI systems frequently rely on extensive user data to tailor designs to individual preferences, raising concerns regarding consent, data security, and potential misuse (Meurisch & Mühlhäuser, 2021). Users may feel apprehensive knowing that their personal information fuels AI algorithms, especially if they lack full awareness of how their data is being used or if adequate safeguards are not in place to protect their privacy. Moreover, unintended consequences may arise from implementing AI-generated designs, impacting users and society. For instance, the automation of design processes could lead to homogenising user experiences, diminishing diversity and creativity in design outcomes. Additionally, AI-generated designs may inadvertently exacerbate inequalities by favouring specific demographics or amplifying algorithmic biases. The intricate nature of AI systems makes it challenging to predict and mitigate these unintended consequences, necessitating continuous monitoring and adaptation to minimise harm.

Strategies for Ensuring Ethical AI Design Practices and Promoting Inclusivity and Diversity in AI-Generated Designs

Practising ethical AI design is essential for fostering inclusivity and diversity in AI-generated designs. Designers and developers can implement various strategies to promote fairness, transparency, and accountability throughout the design process. One approach involves prioritising diversity and representation in the training data for developing AI algorithms. By ensuring that datasets encompass a wide range of demographics, designers can mitigate biases and promote equitable outcomes in AI-generated designs (Balayn et al., 2021). Another strategy is integrating ethical considerations into the design workflow, such as conducting comprehensive impact assessments to identify and address potential biases and unintended consequences early on. This proactive approach enables designers to anticipate and mitigate ethical issues before manifesting in the final product, ultimately leading to more responsible AI design practices.

Additionally, designers can enhance transparency and explainability in AI-generated designs by adopting techniques like model documentation, providing users with insights into design decisions. This fosters greater understanding and trust in AI systems (Liao et al., 2023b). Transparency empowers users to make informed decisions and promotes accountability among designers and developers. Furthermore, encouraging interdisciplinary collaboration and diverse perspectives within design teams can enrich the design process and uncover biases or assumptions that might be overlooked. By incorporating input from individuals with diverse backgrounds and experiences, designers can create more inclusive and culturally sensitive AI-generated designs that better reflect the needs and preferences of a broader range of users. In conclusion, ensuring ethical AI design practices and promoting inclusivity and diversity in AI-generated designs require a multifaceted approach involving data diversity, ethical considerations, transparency, and collaboration. By embracing these strategies, designers can harness the transformative potential of AI technology while minimising biases and fostering more equitable outcomes for all users.

FUTURE TRENDS AND CHALLENGES

Analysis of Emerging Trends in Generative AI and UI Design

Generative AI is swiftly revolutionising UI design, presenting innovative solutions and unlocking fresh avenues for creative expression. One prominent trend within this domain is incorporating generative AI algorithms to streamline the UI design workflow. These algorithms can autonomously generate design elements like layouts, colour schemes, and even complete UI prototypes, all based on predefined criteria and user input (Stige et al., 2023c). This trend is reshaping the role of designers, enabling them to concentrate more on conceptualisation and refining user experiences rather than labour-intensive tasks. Furthermore, generative AI technologies greatly emphasise personalisation and adaptability in UI design. AI-powered systems can analyse user behaviour and preferences in real-time, dynamically adjusting UI elements to cater to individual user needs (Miraz et al., 2021). This trend aligns seamlessly with the increasing demand for tailored user experiences across various digital platforms, ultimately enriching user engagement and satisfaction.

Another emerging trend is the fusion of generative AI with other cutting-edge technologies, such as augmented reality (AR) and virtual reality (VR), to craft immersive UI experiences. As per insights from Brown (2024), the amalgamation of generative AI algorithms with AR/VR capabilities enables the development of interactive and responsive interfaces that blur the boundaries between the digital and physical realms (Rane et al., 2023a). This trend carries significant implications for industries from gaming and entertainment to e-commerce and education, offering unprecedented user engagement and immersion levels. Moreover, democratising generative AI tools empowers designers of all proficiency levels to explore AI-driven design techniques. Platforms like OpenAI's DALL-E (Brusseau, 2022) provide accessible interfaces for crafting and manipulating generative AI models, democratising the utilisation of AI in UI design and fostering innovation within the design community. The integration of generative AI in UI design propels notable advancements in the field, revolutionising conventional design processes, enhancing personalisation, fostering immersive experiences, and democratising access to AI-driven tools. As these trends continue to evolve, designers and industry professionals must stay abreast of the latest developments to fully harness the potential of generative AI in shaping the future of UI design.

Discussion on Future Directions for Research and Innovation in AI-Driven UI Design

As AI advances, the future landscape of UI design is poised for significant transformations driven by groundbreaking research and technological progress. One crucial avenue for exploration lies in refining AI algorithms to achieve heightened creativity and adaptability in UI design. Researchers are increasingly devoted to developing AI models capable of comprehending intricate design principles, context, and user preferences, autonomously generating highly personalised and contextually relevant UI elements (Amershi et al., 2019). Moreover, a burgeoning interest is in harnessing AI to optimise UI designs for accessibility and inclusivity. Future research endeavours may delve into how AI can aid designers in crafting interfaces that cater to diverse user needs, including those with disabilities or language barriers. By seamlessly integrating AI-driven accessibility features into UI design workflows, designers can ensure that digital experiences are more inclusive and equitable for all users (Dudley & Kristensson, 2018).

Furthermore, the fusion of AI with emerging technologies like NLP and gesture recognition holds great promise for advancing UI design capabilities. Researchers are exploring how AI-powered interfaces can interpret and respond to natural language commands and gestures, facilitating more intuitive and immersive user interactions across various devices and platforms (Zhang et al., 2022). Another critical trajectory for future research involves examining AI-driven UI design's ethical and societal ramifications. As AI systems assume increasingly prominent roles in shaping user experiences, addressing concerns related to data privacy, algorithmic bias, and the ethical use of AI in design becomes paramount. Collaboration between researchers and industry stakeholders is crucial for developing robust frameworks and guidelines that advocate responsible AI practices and mitigate potential risks associated with AI-driven UI design.

Moreover, interdisciplinary collaboration among AI researchers, designers, psychologists, and domain experts will be pivotal in unlocking the full potential of AI-driven UI design. By fostering cross-disciplinary dialogue and knowledge exchange, researchers can gain deeper insights into user behaviour, cognitive processes, and design principles, yielding more effective AI-powered design solutions. The future trajectory of AI-driven UI design holds immense promise for revolutionising digital experiences. Through avenues such as enhanced creativity, accessibility, integration with emerging technologies, ethical considerations, and interdisciplinary collaboration, researchers can pave the way for innovative and inclusive UI designs that cater to the diverse needs of users in an increasingly AI-driven world. Figure 9 shows the evaluation method for AI-generated design.

Figure 9. Evaluation Methods For AI-Generated Designs

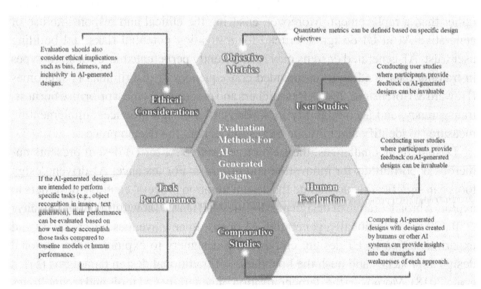

Identification of Challenges and Opportunities for Advancing the Field of Generative AI for UI Design

The realm of generative AI for UI design offers substantial opportunities alongside notable challenges as it progresses. One of the primary hurdles lies in cultivating generative AI algorithms capable of consistently delivering top-tier designs while adhering to design principles and user preferences. Present AI models may struggle with grasping nuanced design concepts and user feedback, resulting in inconsistencies and inefficiencies in the generated (Shneiderman, 2020). Tackling this challenge demands further research into enhancing the robustness and adaptability of AI algorithms to develop more cohesive and user-centred UI designs. Another significant challenge is integrating generative AI into existing design workflows and tools. Designers may encounter difficulties smoothly incorporating AI-generated elements into their projects or understanding how AI can effectively augment their creative process (Kaasinen et al., 2022). Addressing this challenge involves developing user-friendly AI interfaces and tools that foster collaboration between designers and AI systems, empowering designers to view AI as a creative partner rather than a replacement. Moreover, ensuring the ethical and responsible use of generative AI in UI design is crucial for mitigating potential risks and building user trust. AI-generated designs may inadvertently perpetuate biases or stereotypes in training data, leading to unintended consequences or discriminatory outcomes (Howard & Borenstein, 2017). Researchers and practitioners must prioritise fairness, transparency, and accountability in AI-driven UI design practices, implementing measures to identify and mitigate biases throughout the design process.

Despite these challenges, the field of generative AI for UI design presents numerous opportunities for innovation and progress. For instance, AI-driven design tools can significantly accelerate the design iteration process, enabling designers to explore a broader range of design possibilities and iterate more efficiently (Upadhya et al., 2021). Additionally, generative AI opens up new avenues for creativity and experimentation in UI design, empowering designers to explore unconventional design approaches and push the boundaries of traditional design paradigms (Frich et al., 2018). Moreover, the democratisation of generative AI tools and technologies offers an opportunity to empower a more diverse community of designers to participate in UI design. Accessible AI-driven design platforms and resources can lower barriers to entry, enabling designers with varying levels of expertise and backgrounds to leverage AI in their creative endeavours (Dwivedi et al., 2021). In conclusion, advancing the field of generative AI for UI design necessitates addressing design quality, integration, and ethics challenges while embracing opportunities for innovation and democratisation. By fostering interdisciplinary collaboration, promoting responsible AI practices, and developing user-centric design solutions, researchers and practitioners can unlock the full potential of generative AI to revolutionise UI design and enhance digital experiences for users worldwide.

CASE STUDIES AND PRACTICAL APPLICATIONS

Showcase of Real-World Examples and Case Studies Illustrating the Application of Generative AI In UI Design Across Different Industries and Domains

Generative AI, a segment of AI, has revolutionised UI design across diverse sectors and fields. Its capacity to autonomously generate design components based on specified criteria and data has streamlined and elevated the process of UI creation. Numerous instances and analyses from real-world scenarios underscore the profound influence of generative AI on UI design.

In the automotive industry, entities like BMW have embraced generative AI to craft futuristic dashboards and interfaces prioritising user experience and safety. By furnishing the AI with data about driver behaviour and preferences, BMW has crafted intuitive interfaces anticipating user requirements and augmenting driving efficacy (Carmona, 2019) Likewise, within e-commerce, companies such as Amazon have employed generative AI to tailor UI, furnishing customised suggestions and heightening customer interaction. Amazon's recommendation mechanism employs generative algorithms to scrutinise user behaviour and preferences, facilitating a more instinctual shopping journey (Luo, n.d.). In gaming, enterprises like Ubisoft have seamlessly integrated generative AI into game development procedures to produce dynamic and immersive UI. Ubisoft has forged interfaces adapting to player manoeuvres, leveraging AI algorithms, and enhancing gameplay and immersion.

Examination of Successful Projects, Tools, and Methodologies Leveraging Generative AI for UI Design

Successful initiatives, tools, and approaches harnessing generative AI for UI design have profoundly reshaped the landscape of UI development, driving innovation, efficiency, and user contentment. Delving into these endeavours offers valuable insights into the capabilities and impact of generative AI in UI design. Google's Material Design is a standout project exemplifying generative AI's effectiveness in UI design. Google employs generative algorithms to automatically craft UI elements like buttons, cards, and animations, ensuring uniformity and adaptability across various platforms and devices (Jawahar et al., 2020). Tools such as Adobe XD's Auto-Animate feature also utilise generative AI to craft seamless transitions and animations between UI screens. By analysing design components and user inter-actions, Adobe XD generates dynamic animations that enrich user experience and visual appeal (Ma et al., 2022). Moreover, methodologies like DesignOps integrate generative AI into UI design workflows to automate repetitive tasks and expedite design iterations. DesignOps platforms like Figma employ generative algorithms to propose design variations based on user input, facilitating swift prototyping and experimentation (Bordegoni et al., 2023c).

Furthermore, successful endeavours in the gaming sector, like Unity's Adaptive UI Toolkit, leverage generative AI to construct responsive and flexible UI. Unity's toolkit scrutinises gameplay data and player behaviour to dynamically adjust UI elements, enhancing accessibility and engagement (Aversa & Dickinson, 2019). Finally, methodologies such as GANs have empowered designers to explore novel design possibilities and aesthetics through AI-driven experimentation. By training GAN models on extensive design patterns and style datasets, designers can generate fresh UI concepts and inspirations, fostering creativity and innovation (Goodfellow et al., 2014). In conclusion, examining prosperous projects, tools, and methodologies leveraging generative AI for UI design underscores the transformative potential of AI-driven design approaches. From automating UI component generation to refining design workflows and encouraging creative exploration, generative AI is revolutionising the conception, execution, and experience of UI design.

CONCLUSION

Summary of Key Insights and Takeaways From the Chapter

The exploration of generative AI within UI design has brought a wealth of insights to light, underscoring its profound impact on shaping the future of digital interactions. Along this journey, several vital observations have emerged: First and foremost, the introduction of generative AI marks a significant departure in UI design, offering automated support and fostering creative exploration. This streamlines the design process, enabling designers to devote more attention to strategic choices and innovative ideas rather than mundane tasks.

Secondly, incorporating various generative AI techniques, such as GANs, VAEs, and autoregressive models, empowers designers to efficiently produce layouts, apply style transfers, and customise content. This expedites design iterations and encourages the exploration of diverse design options, resulting in more captivating and tailored user experiences. Moreover, collaborative design methodologies that merge AI tools with human designers promote a symbiotic relationship, enriching creativity, iteration, and experimentation within UI design workflows. Nevertheless, challenges like maintaining human oversight, addressing biases, and ensuring inclusivity remain pertinent concerns within this collaborative environment.

The ethical ramifications of integrating generative AI into UI design are substantial. Designers must meticulously navigate potential biases, privacy issues, and unforeseen consequences, striving to uphold ethical design standards and foster diversity and inclusivity in AI-generated designs. The future of generative AI in UI design presents promising opportunities alongside significant challenges. Emerging trends such as augmented creativity, adaptive interfaces, and AI-driven design systems offer glimpses into an exciting innovation landscape. However, addressing challenges such as interpretability, transparency, and accountability will be imperative for advancing the field responsibly. The transformative potential of generative AI within UI design is undeniable. By embracing generative AI technologies, designers, researchers, and practitioners can revolutionise digital experiences, pushing the boundaries of creativity, efficiency, and inclusivity in UI design. This necessitates collective effort and ongoing exploration to unlock the full range of possibilities and shape a future where AI enhances human creativity to deliver genuinely remarkable user experiences. Figure 10 shows ethical considerations for using generative AI for UI design.

Figure 10. Ethical Considerations in Using Generative AI for UI Design

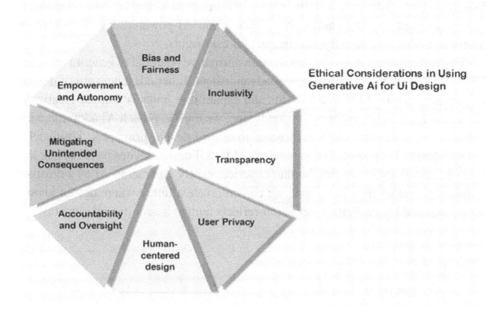

Reflection on the Transformative Potential of Generative AI for UI Design

The profound impact of generative AI on UI design prompts a thorough examination of its implications, opportunities, and challenges. At its essence, generative AI signifies a monumental shift in how designers conceive and craft digital interfaces. It introduces a new realm of creativity and efficiency, revolutionising conventional design processes and unlocking doors to unprecedented innovation. One notable aspect of this reflection is the newfound liberation it offers designers. Generative AI frees designers from tedious tasks, empowering them to concentrate on higher-level strategic planning and creativity. By automating repetitive tasks and providing creative suggestions, AI becomes a valuable partner in the design journey, boosting productivity and facilitating the exploration of diverse design options.

Furthermore, the transformative potential of generative AI transcends efficiency gains alone. It fundamentally reshapes the approach to problem-solving and design exploration. Equipped with AI-powered tools, designers can effortlessly generate various design iterations, experiment with different styles, and personalise user experiences on a large scale. This expedites the design iteration process and fosters a culture of continuous experimentation and innovation. However, amid the excitement surrounding generative AI, it is crucial to acknowledge the inherent challenges and ethical considerations. As AI systems grow more sophisticated, concerns about biases, privacy violations, and the erosion of human autonomy become prominent. Designers must proceed cautiously, ensuring that AI-powered designs prioritise aesthetics, ethics, inclusivity, and respect for user rights.

This reflection underscores that the transformative potential of generative AI for UI design goes beyond technological advancement. It heralds a new era of design possibilities where AI-driven insights and capabilities enhance human creativity. As we navigate this transformative landscape, we must approach AI adoption with mindfulness, empathy, and a dedication to ethical design principles. Ultimately, the transformative potential of generative AI for UI design invites us to rethink the role of technology in shaping human experiences. By embracing AI as a creative collaborator rather than just a tool, we can co-create a future where design knows no bounds and every digital interaction reflects human ingenuity and empathy.

Call to Action for Designers, Researchers, and Practitioners to Explore and Embrace Generative AI in Shaping the Future of UI Design

As we ponder the transformative potential of generative AI for UI design, it becomes evident that the time for action is now. Designers, researchers, and practitioners must seize this opportunity to explore and adopt generative AI technologies, influencing the future of UI design in profound ways. Primarily, designers are urged to embrace a mindset of curiosity and experimentation. By immersing themselves in generative AI, designers can unearth fresh avenues of creativity and innovation, stretching the limits of what's achievable in UI design. Whether through self-guided exploration or structured learning initiatives, designers must actively seek opportunities to acquaint themselves with generative AI techniques and seamlessly incorporate them into their design processes. Likewise, researchers play a crucial role in propelling the field of generative AI for UI design forward. Through meticulous experimentation, theoretical inquiry, and interdisciplinary collaboration, researchers can unearth new insights, devise innovative methodologies, and confront pressing challenges in AI-driven design. By fostering an environment of openness and knowledge exchange, researchers can expedite the pace of progress and propel UI design into unexplored realms. Practitioners, including developers, product managers, and UX professionals, are also pivotal in integrating generative AI in UI design. By advocating for AI-powered tools and methodologies within their organisations, practitioners can unlock efficiencies, enrich user experiences, and gain a competitive edge in the market. Furthermore, practitioners must remain vigilant in upholding ethical standards, ensuring that AI-driven designs prioritise user well-being, diversity, and inclusivity.

In conclusion, the imperative for action is clear: embrace generative AI as a catalyst for innovation and transformation in UI design. By harnessing AI technologies' capabilities, we can sculpt a future where digital interfaces are more intuitive, captivating, and inclusive than ever before. Let us embark on this journey together, united by a shared dedication to pushing the boundaries of creativity and reimagining the landscape of human-computer interaction.

REFERENCES

Aalaei, M., Saadi, M., Rahbar, M., & Ekhlassi, A. (2023). Architectural layout generation using a graph-constrained conditional Generative Adversarial Network (GAN). *Automation in Construction*, 155, 105053. DOI:10.1016/j.autcon.2023.105053

Adeyemo, V. E., Abdullah, A., Jhanjhi, N. Z., Supramaniam, M., & Balogun, A. O. (2019). Ensemble and Deep-Learning Methods for Two-Class and Multi-Attack Anomaly Intrusion Detection: An Empirical Study. *International Journal of Advanced Computer Science and Applications*, 10(9). Advance online publication. DOI:10.14569/IJACSA.2019.0100969

Agrawal, K. P. (2023). Towards adoption of generative AI in organisational settings. *Journal of Computer Information Systems*, 1–16. DOI:10.1080/08874417.2023.2240744

Almusaylim, Z. A., Jhanjhi, N. Z., & Alhumam, A. (2020). Detection and Mitigation of RPL rank and version number attacks in the Internet of Things: SRPL-RP. *Sensors (Basel)*, 20(21), 5997. DOI:10.3390/s20215997 PMID:33105891

Almusaylim, Z. A., Jhanjhi, N. Z., & Jung, L. T. (2018). I am proposing A Data Privacy-Aware Protocol for Roadside Accident Video Reporting Service Using 5G In Vehicular Cloud Networks Environment. *2018 4th International Conference on Computer and Information Sciences (ICCOINS)*. DOI:10.1109/ICCOINS.2018.8510588

Amershi, S., Weld, D., Vorvoreanu, M., Fourney, A., Nushi, B., Collisson, P., Suh, J., Iqbal, S. T., Bennett, P., Inkpen, K., Teevan, J., Kikin-Gil, R., & Horvitz, E. (2019). *Guidelines for Human-AI Interaction*. ACM. DOI:10.1145/3290605.3300233

An, P., Zhu, J., Zhang, Z., Yin, Y., Ma, Q., Cao, Y., Du, L., & Zhao, J. (2024). *EmOWear: Exploring emotional teasers for voice message interaction on smartwatches. arXiv*. Cornell University. DOI:10.1145/3613904.3642101

Ananna, F. F., Nowreen, R., Jahwari, S. S. R. A., Costa, E., Angeline, L., & Sindiramutty, S. R. (2023). Analysing Influential factors in student academic achievement: Prediction modelling and insight. *International Journal of Emerging Multidisciplinaries Computer Science & Artificial Intelligence*, 2(1). Advance online publication. DOI:10.54938/ijemdcsai.2023.02.1.254

Arora, J. S., & Baenziger, G. (1986). Uses of artificial intelligence in design optimization. *Computer Methods in Applied Mechanics and Engineering*, 54(3), 303–323. DOI:10.1016/0045-7825(86)90108-8

Auricchio, V. (2023, November 20). *Navigating AI in service design-empowering service designer to unlock AI's full potential in the design process.* https://www.politesi.polimi.it/handle/10589/211732

Aversa, D., & Dickinson, C. (2019). *Unity Game Optimization: Enhance and extend the performance of all aspects of your Unity games* (3rd ed.). Packt Publishing Ltd.

Azam, H., Dulloo, M. I., Majeed, M. H., Wan, J. P. H., Xin, L. T., & Sindiramutty, S. R. (2023). Cybercrime Unmasked: Investigating cases and digital evidence. *International Journal of Emerging Multidisciplinaries Computer Science & Artificial Intelligence*, 2(1). Advance online publication. DOI:10.54938/ijemdcsai.2023.02.1.255

Azam, H., Dulloo, M. I., Majeed, M. H., Wan, J. P. H., Xin, L. T., Tajwar, M. A., & Sindiramutty, S. R. (2023). Defending the digital Frontier: IDPS and the battle against Cyber threat. *International Journal of Emerging Multidisciplinaries Computer Science & Artificial Intelligence*, 2(1). Advance online publication. DOI:10.54938/ijemdcsai.2023.02.1.253

Azam, H., Tajwar, M. A., Mayhialagan, S., Davis, A. J., Yik, C. J., Ali, D., & Sindiramutty, S. R. (2023). Innovations in Security: A study of cloud Computing and IoT. *International Journal of Emerging Multidisciplinaries Computer Science & Artificial Intelligence*, 2(1). Advance online publication. DOI:10.54938/ijemdcsai.2023.02.1.252

Badini, S., Regondi, S., & Pugliese, R. (2023). Unleashing the power of artificial intelligence in materials design. *Materials (Basel)*, 16(17), 5927. DOI:10.3390/ma16175927 PMID:37687620

Bai, Y., Zhou, M., & Yang, Q. (2024). StyleInject: Parameter Efficient tuning of Text-to-Image diffusion models. *arXiv (Cornell University)*. https://doi.org//arxiv.2401.13942DOI:10.48550

Balayn, A., Lofi, C., & Houben, G. (2021). Managing bias and unfairness in data for decision support: A survey of machine learning and data engineering approaches to identify and mitigate bias and unfairness within data management and analytics systems. *The VLDB Journal*, 30(5), 739–768. DOI:10.1007/s00778-021-00671-8

Bassyouni, Z., & Elhajj, I. H. (2021). Augmented Reality meets Artificial Intelligence in Robotics: A Systematic review. *Frontiers in Robotics and AI*, 8, 724798. Advance online publication. DOI:10.3389/frobt.2021.724798 PMID:34631805

Bhattacharyay, S., Kapade, A., Agarwal, T., Shetty, L., Phadke, G., & Das, S. (2024). Hexart:Ai Art Restoration. *SSRN*. DOI:10.2139/ssrn.4699804

Bizeul, A., Schölkopf, B., & Allen, C. (2024). A Probabilistic Model to explain Self-Supervised Representation Learning. *arXiv (Cornell University)*. https://doi.org//arxiv.2402.01399DOI:10.48550

Bok, S. K. (2023). *Enhancing User Experience in E-Commerce through Personalization Algorithms*. Theseus. https://www.theseus.fi/handle/10024/815645

Bordegoni, M. (2023). *Prototyping User eXperience in eXtended Reality*. Springer Nature. DOI:10.1007/978-3-031-39683-0

Bordegoni, M., Carulli, M., & Spadoni, E. (2023a). Prototyping: Practices and techniques. In *SpringerBriefs in applied sciences and technology* (pp. 29–47). DOI:10.1007/978-3-031-39683-0_3

Bordegoni, M., Carulli, M., & Spadoni, E. (2023b). User experience and user experience design. In *SpringerBriefs in applied sciences and technology* (pp. 11–28). DOI:10.1007/978-3-031-39683-0_2

Bordegoni, M., Carulli, M., & Spadoni, E. (2023c). *Prototyping User eXperience in eXtended Reality*. Springer. DOI:10.1007/978-3-031-39683-0

Bowman, M. P. (2023). *"I just thought it was me": How Smartphones Fail Users with Mild-to-Moderate Dexterity Differences*. ACM. DOI:10.1145/3597638.3608396

Brandt, A., Brannick, J., Kahl, K., & Livshits, I. M. (2011). Bootstrap AMG. *SIAM Journal on Scientific Computing*, 33(2), 612–632. DOI:10.1137/090752973

Brusseau, J. (2022). Acceleration AI Ethics, the Debate between Innovation and Safety, and Stability AI's Diffusion versus OpenAI's Dall-E. *arXiv (Cornell University)*. https://doi.org//arxiv.2212.01834DOI:10.48550

Budhwar, P., Chowdhury, S., Wood, G., Aguinis, H., Bamber, G. J., Beltran, J. R., Boselie, P., Cooke, F. L., Decker, S., DeNisi, A. S., Dey, P. K., Guest, D., Knoblich, A. J., Malik, A., Paauwe, J., Papagiannidis, S., Patel, C., Pereira, V., Ren, S., & Varma, A. (2023). Human resource management in the age of generative artificial intelligence: Perspectives and research directions on ChatGPT. *Human Resource Management Journal*, 33(3), 606–659. DOI:10.1111/1748-8583.12524

Carmona, D. (2019). *The AI organization: Learn from Real Companies and Microsoft's Journey How to Redefine Your Organization with AI*. O'Reilly Media.

Castro, L., Carballal, A., Rodríguez-Fernández, N., Santos, I., & Romero, J. (2021). Artificial intelligence applied to conceptual design. A review of its use in architecture. *Automation in Construction*, 124, 103550. DOI:10.1016/j.autcon.2021.103550

Castro, L. M., Cabrero, D., & Heimgärtner, R. (2022). *Software usability*. BoD – Books on Demand. DOI:10.5772/intechopen.91112

Cetin, I., Stephens, M., Cámara, Ó., & Ballester, M. Á. G. (2023). Attri-VAE: Attribute-based interpretable representations of medical images with variational autoencoders. *Computerized Medical Imaging and Graphics*, 104, 102158. DOI:10.1016/j.compmedimag.2022.102158 PMID:36638626

Chen, F., Ji, N., Zhao, Y., & Gao, F. (2023). Controllable Feature-Preserving Style transfer. In *Communications in computer and information science* (pp. 95–104). DOI:10.1007/978-981-99-7587-7_8

Chen, J., Shao, Z., Zheng, X., Zhang, K., & Yin, J. (2024). Integrating aesthetics and efficiency: AI-driven diffusion models for visually pleasing interior design generation. *Scientific Reports*, 14(1), 3496. Advance online publication. DOI:10.1038/s41598-024-53318-3 PMID:38347015

Coronado, E., Yamanobe, N., & Venture, G. (2023). NEP+: A Human-Centered Framework for Inclusive Human-Machine Interaction development. *Sensors (Basel)*, 23(22), 9136. DOI:10.3390/s23229136 PMID:38005524

Davis, L., & Aslam, U. (2024). Analyzing consumer expectations and experiences of Augmented Reality (AR) apps in the fashion retail sector. *Journal of Retailing and Consumer Services*, 76, 103577. DOI:10.1016/j.jretconser.2023.103577

De Felice, F., & Petrillo, A. (2023). *Digital Effects, Strategies, and Industry 5.0.* DOI:10.1201/b22968

De Gemmis, M., Lops, P., Musto, C., Narducci, F., & Semeraro, G. (2015). Semantics-Aware Content-Based recommender Systems. In *Springer eBooks* (pp. 119–159). DOI:10.1007/978-1-4899-7637-6_4

Dehman, H. (2023). *Graphic design, Already Intelligent? Current possibilities of generative AI applications in graphic design*. DIVA. https://www.diva-portal.org/smash/record.jsf?pid=diva2%3A1797022&dswid=3277

Desmal, A. J., Alsaeed, M., Zolait, A. H. S., & Hamid, S. B. B. O. A. (2023). Feedback for Excellence: Improving mGovernment Services Through User Insights. *2023 International Conference on Innovation and Intelligence for Informatics, Computing, and Technologies (3ICT)*. DOI:10.1109/3ICT60104.2023.10391312

Dodeja, L., Tambwekar, P., Hedlund-Botti, E., & Gombolay, M. (2024). Towards the design of user-centric strategy recommendation systems for collaborative Human-AI tasks. *International Journal of Human-Computer Studies*, 184, 103216. DOI:10.1016/j.ijhcs.2023.103216 PMID:38558883

Doush, I. A., Al-Jarrah, A., Alajarmeh, N., & Alnfiai, M. M. (2022). Learning features and accessibility limitations of video conferencing applications: Are people with visual impairment left behind. *Universal Access in the Information Society*, 22(4), 1353–1368. DOI:10.1007/s10209-022-00917-4 PMID:36160370

Drzyzga, G., & Harder, T. (2023). A three level design study approach to develop a Student-Centered Learner Dashboard. In *Communications in computer and information science* (pp. 262–281). DOI:10.1007/978-3-031-49425-3_16

Duan, Y., Edwards, J. S., & Dwivedi, Y. K. (2019). Artificial intelligence for decision making in the era of Big Data – evolution, challenges and research agenda. *International Journal of Information Management*, 48, 63–71. DOI:10.1016/j.ijinfomgt.2019.01.021

Dudley, J. J., & Kristensson, P. O. (2018). A review of user interface design for Interactive Machine Learning. *ACM Transactions on Interactive Intelligent Systems*, 8(2), 1–37. DOI:10.1145/3185517

Durgekar, S. R., Rahman, S. A., Naik, S. R., Kanchan, S. S., & Srinivasan, G. (2024). *A review paper on Design and Experience of Mobile applications*. ICST Transactions on Scalable Information Systems., DOI:10.4108/eetsis.4959

Dwivedi, Y. K., Hughes, L., Ismagilova, E., Aarts, G., Coombs, C., Crick, T., Duan, Y., Dwivedi, R., Edwards, J. S., Eirug, A., Galanos, V., Ilavarasan, P. V., Janssen, M., Jones, P., Kar, A. K., Kizgin, H., Kronemann, B., Lal, B., Lucini, B., & Williams, M. D. (2021). Artificial Intelligence (AI): Multidisciplinary perspectives on emerging challenges, opportunities, and agenda for research, practice and policy. *International Journal of Information Management*, 57, 101994. DOI:10.1016/j.ijinfomgt.2019.08.002

Fatima, I. (2023). *Designing with AI : A User Study to Explore the Future Role of AI as a Collaborative Tool in Graphics Design*. DIVA. https://www.diva-portal.org/smash/record.jsf?pid=diva2%3A1811190&dswid=3735

Fatima-Tuz-Zahra, Jhanjhi, N. Z., Brohi, S. N., & Malik, N. A. (2019). Proposing a Rank and Wormhole Attack Detection Framework using Machine Learning. *2019 13th International Conference on Mathematics, Actuarial Science, Computer Science and Statistics (MACS)*. DOI:10.1109/MACS48846.2019.9024821

Fidalgo, P., & Thormann, J. (2024). The future of Lifelong Learning: The role of artificial intelligence and distance education. In *IntechOpen eBooks*. DOI:10.5772/intechopen.114120

Frich, J., Biskjær, M. M., & Dalsgaard, P. (2018). *Twenty Years of Creativity Research in Human-Computer Interaction*. ACM., DOI:10.1145/3196709.3196732

Gaur, L., Afaq, A., Solanki, A., Singh, G., Sharma, S., Jhanjhi, N. Z., My, H. T., & Le, D. (2021). Capitalizing on big data and revolutionary 5G technology: Extracting and visualizing ratings and reviews of global chain hotels. *Computers & Electrical Engineering*, 95, 107374. DOI:10.1016/j.compeleceng.2021.107374

Ghosh, G., Kavita, , Verma, S., Jhanjhi, N. Z., & Talib, M. N. (2020). Secure surveillance system using chaotic image encryption technique. *IOP Conference Series. Materials Science and Engineering*, 993(1), 012062. DOI:10.1088/1757-899X/993/1/012062

Gouda, W., Almufareh, M. F., Humayun, M., & Jhanjhi, N. Z. (2022). Detection of COVID-19 based on chest x-rays using deep learning. *Health Care*, 10(2), 343. DOI:10.3390/healthcare10020343 PMID:35206957

Greenberg, J. I. (2013). *Adobe Premiere Pro Studio Techniques*. https://openlibrary.org/books/OL26059643M/Adobe_Premiere_Pro_Cs6_Studio_Techniques

Gutiérrez, J. L. M. (2024). On inscription and bias: Data, actor network theory, and the social problems of text-to-image AI models. *AI and Ethics*. Advance online publication. DOI:10.1007/s43681-024-00431-8

Hartson, R., & Pyla, P. (2012). *The UX Book: Process and Guidelines for Ensuring a Quality User Experience*. https://cds.cern.ch/record/1437707

Hashem, O., & Hakeem, M. B. (2024). Design education methodology using AI. *Journal of Art Design and Music*, 3(1). Advance online publication. DOI:10.55554/2785-9649.1030

Hodonu-Wusu, J. O. (2024). The rise of artificial intelligence in libraries: The ethical and equitable methodologies, and prospects for empowering library users. *AI and Ethics*. Advance online publication. DOI:10.1007/s43681-024-00432-7

Howard, A. M., & Borenstein, J. (2017). The ugly truth about ourselves and our robot creations: The problem of bias and social inequity. *Science and Engineering Ethics*, 24(5), 1521–1536. DOI:10.1007/s11948-017-9975-2 PMID:28936795

Huang, K., Huang, J. I., & Catteddu, D. (2024) 'GenAI Data Security,' in *Future of business and finance*, pp. 133–162. DOI:10.1007/978-3-031-54252-7_5

Huang, R., Lin, H. H., Chen, C., Zhang, K., & Zeng, W. (2024). *PlantoGraphy: Incorporating Iterative Design Process into Generative Artificial Intelligence for Landscape Rendering. arXiv*. Cornell University., DOI:10.1145/3613904.3642824

Hughes, R. T., Zhu, L., & Bednarz, T. (2021). Generative Adversarial Networks–Enabled Human–Artificial Intelligence Collaborative Applications for creative and Design Industries: A Systematic Review of Current approaches and Trends. *Frontiers in Artificial Intelligence*, 4, 604234. Advance online publication. DOI:10.3389/frai.2021.604234 PMID:33997773

Humayun, M., Alsaqer, M., & Jhanjhi, N. Z. (2022). Energy optimization for smart cities using IoT. *Applied Artificial Intelligence*, 36(1), 2037255. Advance online publication. DOI:10.1080/08839514.2022.2037255

Humayun, M., Ashfaq, F., Jhanjhi, N. Z., & Alsadun, M. K. (2022). Traffic management: Multi-Scale vehicle detection in varying weather conditions using YOLOV4 and spatial pyramid pooling network. *Electronics (Basel)*, 11(17), 2748. DOI:10.3390/electronics11172748

Hussain, S. J., Ahmed, U., Liaquat, H., Mir, S., Jhanjhi, N. Z., & Humayun, M. (2019). IMIAD: Intelligent Malware Identification for Android Platform. *2019 International Conference on Computer and Information Sciences (ICCIS)*. DOI:10.1109/ICCISci.2019.8716471

Hyde, R. J., & Filippidis, F. (2021). *Design Studio Vol. 2: Intelligent Control: Disruptive Technologies*.

Jain, P., Tripathi, V., Malladi, R., & Khang, A. (2023). Data-Driven Artificial Intelligence (AI) models in the workforce development planning. In *CRC Press eBooks* (pp. 159–176). DOI:10.1201/9781003357070-10

Jawahar, G., Abdul-Mageed, M., & Lakshmanan, L. V. S. (2020). Automatic Detection of Machine Generated Text: A Critical survey. *arXiv (Cornell University)*. /arxiv.2011.01314DOI:10.18653/v1/2020.coling-main.208

Jayatharan, V., & Alwis, D. (2023). Alapana Generation using Finite State Machines and Generative Adversarial Networks. *2023 International Research Conference on Smart Computing and Systems Engineering (SCSE)*. DOI:10.1109/SCSE59836.2023.10215001

Jenis, J., Ondriga, J., Hrček, S., Brumerčík, F., Čuchor, M., & Sádovský, E. (2023). Engineering applications of artificial intelligence in mechanical design and optimization. *Machines (Basel)*, 11(6), 577. DOI:10.3390/machines11060577

Jiang, F., Ma, J., Webster, C., Chiaradia, A. J., Zhou, Y., Zhao, Z., & Zhang, X. (2023). Generative urban design: A systematic review on problem formulation, design generation, and decision-making. *Progress in Planning*, 100795. Advance online publication. DOI:10.1016/j.progress.2023.100795

Kaasinen, E., Anttila, A., Heikkilä, P., Laarni, J., Koskinen, H., & Väätänen, A. (2022). Smooth and resilient Human–Machine Teamwork as an Industry 5.0 design challenge. *Sustainability (Basel)*, 14(5), 2773. DOI:10.3390/su14052773

Kang, Y. (2023). Development of Large-Scale farming based on explainable machine learning for a sustainable rural economy: The case of cyber risk analysis to prevent costly data breaches. *Applied Artificial Intelligence*, 37(1), 2223862. Advance online publication. DOI:10.1080/08839514.2023.2223862

Katoch, S., & Garg, V. (2023) 'Security analysis on Android application through penetration testing,' in *Lecture notes in networks and systems*, 221–234. DOI:10.1007/978-981-99-3716-5_20

Kaufmann, T., Weng, P., Bengs, V., & Hüllermeier, E. (2023). A Survey of Reinforcement Learning from Human Feedback. *arXiv (Cornell University)*. https://doi.org//arxiv.2312.14925DOI:10.48550

Kazemi, P. (2023). *Implementation of AI in user experience*. Theseus. https://www.theseus.fi/handle/10024/800276

Khalil, M. I., Jhanjhi, N. Z., Humayun, M., Sivanesan, S., Masud, M., & Hossain, M. S. (2021). Hybrid smart grid with sustainable energy efficient resources for smart cities. *Sustainable Energy Technologies and Assessments*, 46, 101211. DOI:10.1016/j.seta.2021.101211

Ko, J., Ennemoser, B., Yoo, W., Yan, W., & Clayton, M. J. (2023). Architectural spatial layout planning using artificial intelligence. *Automation in Construction*, 154, 105019. DOI:10.1016/j.autcon.2023.105019

Kot, A. (2023). *Enhancing data analytics for heavy industry through UI/UX design and streamlined reporting: Improving usability, scalability, and visual representation through application of design principles*. Theseus. https://www.theseus.fi/handle/10024/798445

Krishnan, S., Thangaveloo, R., Rahman, S. B. A., & Sindiramutty, S. R. (2021). Smart Ambulance Traffic Control system. *Trends in Undergraduate Research*, 4(1), c28–c34. DOI:10.33736/tur.2831.2021

Lepri, B., Oliver, N., Letouzé, E., Pentland, A., & Vinck, P. (2017). Fair, transparent, and accountable algorithmic decision-making processes. *Philosophy & Technology*, 31(4), 611–627. DOI:10.1007/s13347-017-0279-x

Leslie, D. (2019). Understanding artificial intelligence ethics and safety. *arXiv (Cornell University)*. DOI:10.5281/zenodo.3240529

Li, J., Tang, T., Zhao, W. X., Nie, J., & Wen, J. (2022). Pretrained Language Models for Text Generation: A survey. *arXiv (Cornell University)*. https://doi.org//arxiv.2201.05273DOI:10.48550

Li, J. R., Tang, J., Tang, T., Li, H., Cui, W., & Wu, Y. (2024). Understanding Nonlinear Collaboration between Human and AI Agents: A Co-design Framework for Creative Design. *arXiv (Cornell University)*. https://doi.org//arxiv.2401.07312DOI:10.48550

Liao, Q. V., Subramonyam, H., Wang, J., & Vaughan, J. (2023a). *Designerly Understanding: Information Needs for Model Transparency to Support Design Ideation for AI-Powered User Experience*. ACM. DOI:10.1145/3544548.3580652

Liao, Q. V., Subramonyam, H., Wang, J., & Vaughan, J. (2023b). *Designerly Understanding: Information Needs for Model Transparency to Support Design Ideation for AI-Powered User Experience*. ACM. DOI:10.1145/3544548.3580652

Lichtenthaler, U. (2020). *Integrated Intelligence: Combining Human and Artificial Intelligence for Competitive Advantage, Plus E-Book Inside (ePub, Mobi Oder Pdf)*.

Lilova, S. (2021). Copyright or copyleft for AI-Generated works: private ordering solutions for the benefit of content creators. *Social Science Research Network*. DOI:10.2139/ssrn.4271966

Liu, J., Qiu, Z., Wang, L., Liu, P., Cheng, G., & Chen, Y. (2024). Intelligent floor plan design of modular high-rise residential building based on graph-constrained generative adversarial networks. *Automation in Construction*, 159, 105264. DOI:10.1016/j.autcon.2023.105264

Liu, Y., & Martens, J. (2024). Conversation-based hybrid UI for the repertory grid technique: A lab experiment into automation of qualitative surveys. *International Journal of Human-Computer Studies*, 184, 103227. DOI:10.1016/j.ijhcs.2024.103227

Lu, Y., Yang, Y., Zhao, Q., Zhang, C., & Li, T. J. (2024). AI Assistance for UX: A literature review through Human-Centered AI. *arXiv (Cornell University)*. https://doi.org//arxiv.2402.06089DOI:10.48550

Luan, H., Géczy, P., Lai, H., Gobert, J. D., Yang, S. J. H., Ogata, H., Baltes, J., Da Silva Guerra, R., Li, P., & Tsai, C. C. (2020). Challenges and future directions of big data and artificial intelligence in education. *Frontiers in Psychology*, 11, 580820. Advance online publication. DOI:10.3389/fpsyg.2020.580820 PMID:33192896

Luo, Y. (n.d.). *Investigation of Algorithmic Nudging on Decision Quality: Evidence from Randomized Experiments in Online Recommendation Settings*. CUNY Academic Works. https://academicworks.cuny.edu/gc_etds/5678/

Luong, N. C., Hoang, D. T., Gong, S., Niyato, D., Wang, P., Liang, Y., & Kim, D. I. (2019). Applications of Deep Reinforcement Learning in Communications and Networking: A survey. *IEEE Communications Surveys and Tutorials*, 21(4), 3133–3174. DOI:10.1109/COMST.2019.2916583

Ma, J., Wei, L., & Kazi, R. H. (2022). A Layered Authoring Tool for Stylized 3D animations. *CHI Conference on Human Factors in Computing Systems*. DOI:10.1145/3491102.3501894

Margetis, G., Ntoa, S., Antona, M., & Stephanidis, C. (2021). Human-centered design of artificial intelligence. *Wiley*. DOI:10.1002/9781119636113.ch42

Marg'uba, N. (2024, January 10). *Parametric Design: Enhancing Architectural Environments through Computational Innovatio*. https://sciencepromotion.uz/index .php/HOLDERS_OF_REASON/article/view/1077

Mennan, Z. (2022, February 1). *Extending design cognition with computer vision and generative deep learning*. https://open.metu.edu.tr/handle/11511/96232

Meurisch, C., & Mühlhäuser, M. (2021). Data protection in AI services. *ACM Computing Surveys*, 54(2), 1–38. DOI:10.1145/3440754

Miraz, M. H., Ali, M., & Excell, P. S. (2021). Adaptive user interfaces and universal usability through plasticity of user interface design. *Computer Science Review*, 40, 100363. DOI:10.1016/j.cosrev.2021.100363

Montargil, F. (2023, December 18). *Enhancing portuguese public services: prototype of a mobile application with a digital assistant*. https://repositorio.ipl.pt/ handle/10400.21/16926

Mortazavi, A. (2023). *Enhancing User Experience Design workflow with Artificial Intelligence Tools*. DIVA. https://www.diva-portal.org/smash/record.jsf?pid=diva2 %3A1800706&dswid=-1132

Nabavi-Pelesaraei, A., Rafiee, S., Mohtasebi, S. S., Hosseinzadeh-Bandbafha, H., & Chau, K. (2018). Integration of artificial intelligence methods and life cycle assessment to predict energy output and environmental impacts of paddy production. *The Science of the Total Environment*, 631–632, 1279–1294. DOI:10.1016/j. scitotenv.2018.03.088 PMID:29727952

Nahar, G., & Jain, S. (2023). Uncovering the usability test Methods for Human–Computer Interaction. In *Lecture notes in networks and systems* (pp. 57–68). DOI:10.1007/978-981-99-1909-3_6

Naqbi, H. A., Bahroun, Z., & Ahmed, V. (2024). Enhancing Work Productivity through Generative Artificial Intelligence: A Comprehensive Literature Review. *Sustainability (Basel)*, 16(3), 1166. DOI:10.3390/su16031166

Nassiri, K., & Akhloufi, M. A. (2022). Transformer models used for text-based question answering systems. *Applied Intelligence*, 53(9), 10602–10635. DOI:10.1007/s10489-022-04052-8

Nazir, A., & Wang, Z. (2023). A comprehensive survey of ChatGPT: Advancements, applications, prospects, and challenges. *Meta-Radiology*, 1(2), 100022. DOI:10.1016/j.metrad.2023.100022 PMID:37901715

Necula, S., & Păvăloaia, V. (2023). AI-Driven Recommendations: A Systematic review of the state of the art in E-Commerce. *Applied Sciences (Basel, Switzerland)*, 13(9), 5531. DOI:10.3390/app13095531

Neshenko, N. (2023). Machine learning and user interface for cyber risk management of water infrastructure. *Risk Analysis*. Advance online publication. DOI:10.1111/risa.14209 PMID:37635130

Ngalamou, L., & Schmidbauer, H. L. (2020). Combating and perpetuating bias: The relationship between bias and computer science. *International Journal of Information Privacy. Security and Integrity*, 4(4), 296. DOI:10.1504/IJIPSI.2020.115523

Nova, A., Sansalone, S. C. F., Robinson, R., & Mirza-Babaei, P. (2022). Charting the Uncharted with GUR: How AI Playtesting Can Supplement Expert Evaluation. *ACM*. DOI:10.1145/3555858.3555880

Nova, K. (2023, April 4). *Generative AI in Healthcare: Advancements in Electronic Health Records, facilitating Medical Languages, and Personalized Patient Care.* https://research.tensorgate.org/index.php/JAAHM/article/view/43

Olynick, D. (2024). Exploring generative AI and its transformative power. In *Apress eBooks* (pp. 17–60). DOI:10.1007/979-8-8688-0083-2_2

Ooi, K., Tan, G. W., Al-Emran, M., Al-Sharafi, M. A., Căpăţînă, A., Chakraborty, A., Dwivedi, Y. K., Huang, T., Kar, A. K., Lee, V., Loh, X., Micu, A., Mikalef, P., Mogaji, E., Pandey, N., Raman, R., Rana, N. P., Sarker, P., Sharma, A., & Wong, L. (2023). The potential of generative artificial intelligence across disciplines: Perspectives and future directions. *Journal of Computer Information Systems*, 1–32. DOI:10.1080/08874417.2023.2261010

Pal, S. (2021) *Internet of things and access control, Smart sensors, measurement and instrumentation.* .DOI:10.1007/978-3-030-64998-2

Palladino, N. (2023). A 'biased' emerging governance regime for artificial intelligence? How AI ethics get skewed moving from principles to practices. *Telecommunications Policy*, 47(5), 102479. DOI:10.1016/j.telpol.2022.102479

Pettersson, W. (2024). *Transforming Chess: Investigating Decoder-Only architecture for generating Realistic Game-Like Positions*. DIVA. https://www.diva-portal.org/smash/record.jsf?pid=diva2%3A1828575&dswid=-6030

Polson, P. G., Lewis, C., Rieman, J., & Wharton, C. (1992). Cognitive walkthroughs: A method for theory-based evaluation of user interfaces. *International Journal of Man-Machine Studies*, 36(5), 741–773. DOI:10.1016/0020-7373(92)90039-N

Pop, M., & Schricker, M. (2023). *AI as a tool and its influence on the User Experience design process : A study on the usability of human-made vs more-than-human-made prototypes*. DIVA. https://www.diva-portal.org/smash/record.jsf?pid=diva2%3A1771528&dswid=-4706

Pushpakumar, R., Sanjaya, K., Rathika, S., Alawadi, A. H., Makhzuna, K., Venkatesh, S., & Rajalakshmi, B. (2023). Human-Computer Interaction: Enhancing user experience in interactive systems. *E3S Web of Conferences, 399*, 04037. DOI:10.1051/e3sconf/202339904037

Pyae, A., Ravyse, W., Luimula, M., Pizarro-Lucas, E., Sánchez, P. L., Dorado-Díaz, P. I., & Thaw, A. K. (2023). Exploring user experience and usability in a metaverse learning environment for students: A Usability Study of the Artificial Intelligence, Innovation, and Society (AIIS). *Electronics (Basel)*, 12(20), 4283. DOI:10.3390/electronics12204283

Qin, Y., Hu, S., Lin, Y., Chen, W., Ding, N., Cui, G., Zeng, Z., Huang, Y., Xiao, C., Chen, H., Fung, Y. R., Su, Y., Wang, H., Qian, C., Tian, R., Zhu, K. Y., Liang, S., Shen, X., Xu, B., . . . Sun, M. (2023). Tool Learning with Foundation Models. *arXiv (Cornell University)*. https://doi.org//arxiv.2304.08354DOI:10.48550

Quetzalli, A. (2023). User interface and user experience. In *Apress eBooks* (pp. 57–84). DOI:10.1007/978-1-4842-9328-7_4

Rane, N. (2023). Multidisciplinary collaboration: key players in successful implementation of ChatGPT and similar generative artificial intelligence in manufacturing, finance, retail, transportation, and construction industry. *OSF*. DOI:10.31219/osf.io/npm3d

Rane, N., Choudhary, S., & Rane, J. (2023a). Enhanced product design and development using Artificial Intelligence (AI), Virtual Reality (VR), Augmented Reality (AR), 4D/5D/6D Printing, Internet of Things (IoT), and blockchain: A review. *Social Science Research Network*. DOI:10.2139/ssrn.4644059

Rane, N., Choudhary, S., & Rane, J. (2023b). Hyper-personalization for enhancing customer loyalty and satisfaction in Customer Relationship Management (CRM) systems. *Social Science Research Network*. DOI:10.2139/ssrn.4641044

Rane, N., Choudhary, S., & Rane, J. (2023c). Integrating Building Information Modelling (BIM) with ChatGPT, Bard, and similar generative artificial intelligence in the architecture, engineering, and construction industry: applications, a novel framework, challenges, and future scope. *Social Science Research Network*. DOI:10.2139/ssrn.4645601

Rane, N., Choudhary, S., & Rane, J. (2023d). Integrating ChatGPT, Bard, and leading-edge generative artificial intelligence in architectural design and engineering: applications, framework, and challenges. *Social Science Research Network*. DOI:10.2139/ssrn.4645595

Rane, N., Choudhary, S., & Rane, J. (2023e). Metaverse Marketing Strategies: Enhancing customer experience and analysing consumer behaviour through leading-edge metaverse technologies, platforms, and models. *Social Science Research Network*. DOI:10.2139/ssrn.4624199

Raza, A., Barghash, T. O., & Salem, M. A. (2024). Play Bricks IV: Desktop and Web-Based Play Bricks App for Architectural Styles. *2024 18th International Conference on Ubiquitous Information Management and Communication (IMCOM)*. DOI:10.1109/IMCOM60618.2024.10418274

Ryan, M. (2020). In AI we trust: Ethics, artificial intelligence, and reliability. *Science and Engineering Ethics*, 26(5), 2749–2767. DOI:10.1007/s11948-020-00228-y PMID:32524425

Sadr, E. (2023, March 7). *Design and evaluation of a new editor for responsive Graphical User Interfaces*. https://summit.sfu.ca/item/36157

Saeidnia, H. R. (2023). Ethical artificial intelligence (AI): Confronting bias and discrimination in the library and information industry. *Library Hi Tech News*. Advance online publication. DOI:10.1108/LHTN-10-2023-0182

Sahoo, B. (2023, August 1). *User experience design for automated damage detection through camera bridge in the freight rail sector*. https://opus4.kobv.de/opus4-haw/frontdoor/index/index/docId/3915

Salman, R. (2022). *Paletto: an interactive colour palette generator : facilitating designers' colour selection processes*. DIVA. https://www.diva-portal.org/smash/record.jsf?pid=diva2%3A1679068&dswid=-8369

Sankar, S., Ramasubbareddy, S., Luhach, A. K., Deverajan, G. G., Alnumay, W. S., Jhanjhi, N. Z., Ghosh, U., & Sharma, P. K. (2020). Energy efficient optimal parent selection based routing protocol for Internet of Things using firefly optimization algorithm. *Transactions on Emerging Telecommunications Technologies*, 32(8), e4171. Advance online publication. DOI:10.1002/ett.4171

Saura, J. R., Soriano, D. R., & Palacios-Marqués, D. (2022). Assessing behavioral data science privacy issues in government artificial intelligence deployment. *Government Information Quarterly*, 39(4), 101679. DOI:10.1016/j.giq.2022.101679

Schultz, C. D., Koch, C., & Olbrich, R. (2023). Dark sides of artificial intelligence: The dangers of automated decision-making in search engine advertising. *Journal of the Association for Information Science and Technology*. Advance online publication. DOI:10.1002/asi.24798

Shi, D., Cui, W., Huang, D., Zhang, H., & Chen, N. (2023). Reverse-engineering information presentations: Recovering hierarchical grouping from layouts of visual elements. *Visual Intelligence*, 1(1), 9. Advance online publication. DOI:10.1007/s44267-023-00010-1

Shi, Y., Gao, T., Jiao, X., & Cao, N. (2023a). Understanding Design collaboration between designers and Artificial intelligence: A Systematic Literature review. *Proceedings of the ACM on Human-computer Interaction, 7*(CSCW2), 1–35. DOI:10.1145/3610217

Shi, Y., Gao, T., Jiao, X., & Cao, N. (2023b). Understanding Design collaboration between designers and Artificial intelligence: A Systematic Literature review. *Proceedings of the ACM on Human-computer Interaction, 7*(CSCW2), 1–35. DOI:10.1145/3610217

Shneiderman, B. (2020). Design lessons from AI's two grand goals: Human emulation and useful applications. *IEEE Transactions on Technology and Society*, 1(2), 73–82. DOI:10.1109/TTS.2020.2992669

Simkute, A., Tankelevitch, L., Kewenig, V., Scott, A. E., Sellen, A., & Rintel, S. (2024). Ironies of Generative AI: Understanding and mitigating productivity loss in human-AI interactions. *arXiv (Cornell University)*. https://doi.org//arxiv.2402.11364DOI:10.48550

Sindiramutty, S. R. (2023). Autonomous Threat Hunting: a future paradigm for AI-Driven Threat intelligence. *arXiv (Cornell University)*. https://doi.org//arxiv.2401.00286DOI:10.48550

Sindiramutty, S. R., Jhanjhi, N. Z., Ray, S. K., Jazri, H., Khan, N. A., & Gaur, L. (2024). Metaverse. In *Advances in medical technologies and clinical practice book series* (pp. 93–158). DOI:10.4018/978-1-6684-9823-1.ch003

Sindiramutty, S. R., Jhanjhi, N. Z., Ray, S. K., Jazri, H., Khan, N. A., Gaur, L., Gharib, A. H., & Manchuri, A. R. (2024). Metaverse. In *Advances in medical technologies and clinical practice book series* (pp. 24–92). DOI:10.4018/978-1-6684-9823-1.ch002

Sindiramutty, S. R., Jhanjhi, N. Z., Tan, C. E., Khan, N. A., Gharib, A. H., & Yun, K. J. (2024). Applications of blockchain technology in supply chain management. In *Advances in logistics, operations, and management science book series* (pp. 248–304). DOI:10.4018/978-1-6684-7625-3.ch009

Sindiramutty, S. R., Jhanjhi, N. Z., Tan, C. E., Khan, N. A., Shah, B., & Gaur, L. (2024). Securing the digital supply chain cyber threats and vulnerabilities. In *Advances in logistics, operations, and management science book series* (pp. 156–223). DOI:10.4018/978-1-6684-7625-3.ch007

Sindiramutty, S. R., Jhanjhi, N. Z., Tan, C. E., Tee, W. J., Lau, S. P., Jazri, H., Ray, S. K., & Zaheer, M. A. (2024). IoT and AI-Based Smart Solutions for the Agriculture Industry. In *Advances in computational intelligence and robotics book series* (pp. 317–351). DOI:10.4018/978-1-6684-6361-1.ch012

Sindiramutty, S. R., Tan, C., Tee, W. J., Lau, S. P., Balakrishnan, S., Kaur, S. D. A., Jazri, H., & Aslam, M. (2024). Modern smart cities and open research challenges and issues of explainable artificial intelligence. In *Advances in computational intelligence and robotics book series* (pp. 389–424). DOI:10.4018/978-1-6684-6361-1.ch015

Sindiramutty, S. R., Tan, C. E., Lau, S. P., Thangaveloo, R., Gharib, A. H., Manchuri, A. R., Khan, N. A., Tee, W. J., & Muniandy, L. (2024). Explainable AI for cybersecurity. In *Advances in computational intelligence and robotics book series* (pp. 31–97). DOI:10.4018/978-1-6684-6361-1.ch002

Sindiramutty, S. R., Tee, W. J., Balakrishnan, S., Kaur, S., Thangaveloo, R., Jazri, H., Khan, N. A., Gharib, A. H., & Manchuri, A. R. (2024). Explainable AI in healthcare application. In *Advances in computational intelligence and robotics book series* (pp. 123–176). DOI:10.4018/978-1-6684-6361-1.ch005

Singhal, V., Jain, S. P., Anand, D., Singh, A., Verma, S., Kavita, , Rodrigues, J. J. P. C., Jhanjhi, N. Z., Ghosh, U., Jo, O., & Iwendi, C. (2020). Artificial Intelligence Enabled Road Vehicle-Train Collision Risk Assessment Framework for Unmanned railway level crossings. *IEEE Access : Practical Innovations, Open Solutions*, 8, 113790–113806. DOI:10.1109/ACCESS.2020.3002416

Siountri, K., & Anagnostopoulos, C. (2023). The classification of cultural heritage buildings in Athens using deep learning techniques. *Heritage*, 6(4), 3673–3705. DOI:10.3390/heritage6040195

Situ, J. J. (2019, April 26). *Generative models for predictive UI design tools*. https://www.ideals.illinois.edu/items/112226

Sodiya, E. O., Amoo, O. O., Umoga, U. J., & Atadoga, A. (2024). AI-driven personalization in web content delivery: A comparative study of user engagement in the USA and the UK. *World Journal of Advanced Research and Reviews*, 21(2), 887–902. DOI:10.30574/wjarr.2024.21.2.0502

Sreejith, R., & Sinimole, K. (2024). User-Centric Evaluation of EHR Software through NLP-driven Investigation: Implications for Product Development and User Experience. *Journal of Open Innovation*, 100206(1), 100206. Advance online publication. DOI:10.1016/j.joitmc.2023.100206

Stige, Å., Zamani, E. D., Mikalef, P., & Zhu, Y. (2023). Artificial intelligence (AI) for user experience (UX) design: A systematic literature review and future research agenda. *Information Technology & People*. Advance online publication. DOI:10.1108/ITP-07-2022-0519

Sudirjo, F. (2024). *Application of the user centered design method to evaluate the relationship between user experience, user interface and customer satisfaction on banking mobile application*. Jurnal Informasi Dan Teknologi. DOI:10.60083/jidt. v6i1.465

Suresh, A., Dwarakanath, B., Nanda, A. K., Kumar, P. S., Sankar, S., & Cheerla, S. (2024). An evolutionary Computation-Based federated learning for host intrusion detection in Real-Time traffic analysis. *Wireless Personal Communications*. Advance online publication. DOI:10.1007/s11277-023-10852-z

Taj, I., & Jhanjhi, N. Z. (2022). Towards Industrial Revolution 5.0 and Explainable Artificial Intelligence: Challenges and opportunities. *International Journal of Computing and Digital Systems*, 12(1), 285–310. DOI:10.12785/ijcds/120124

Thomas, J. (2018). Individual Cyber Security: Empowering employees to resist spear phishing to prevent identity theft and ransomware attacks. *International Journal of Business and Management*, 13(6), 1. DOI:10.5539/ijbm.v13n6p1

Upadhya, R., Kosuri, S., Tamasi, M., Meyer, T. A., Atta, S., Webb, M., & Gormley, A. J. (2021). Automation and data-driven design of polymer therapeutics. *Advanced Drug Delivery Reviews*, 171, 1–28. DOI:10.1016/j.addr.2020.11.009 PMID:33242537

Verma, S., Kaur, S., Rawat, D. B., Chen, X., Alex, L. T., & Jhanjhi, N. Z. (2021). Intelligent framework using IoT-Based WSNs for wildfire detection. *IEEE Access : Practical Innovations, Open Solutions*, 9, 48185–48196. DOI:10.1109/ACCESS.2021.3060549

Virvou, M. (2023). Artificial Intelligence and User Experience in reciprocity: Contributions and state of the art. *Intelligent Decision Technologies*, 17(1), 73–125. DOI:10.3233/IDT-230092

Wang, L., Chen, W., Yang, W., Bi, F., & Yu, F. R. (2020). A State-of-the-Art Review on image synthesis with generative adversarial networks. *IEEE Access : Practical Innovations, Open Solutions*, 8, 63514–63537. DOI:10.1109/ACCESS.2020.2982224

Wang, L., Shen, W., Xie, H., Neelamkavil, J., & Pardasani, A. (2002). Collaborative conceptual design—State of the art and future trends. *Computer Aided Design*, 34(13), 981–996. DOI:10.1016/S0010-4485(01)00157-9

Weisz, J. D., He, J., Müller, M., Hoefer, G., Miles, R., & Geyer, W. (2024). *Design principles for Generative AI applications. arXiv*. Cornell University., DOI:10.1145/3613904.3642466

Wen, B. O. T., Syahriza, N., Xian, N. C. W., Wei, N., Shen, T. Z., Hin, Y. Z., Sindiramutty, S. R., & Nicole, T. Y. F. (2024). Detecting cyber threats with a Graph-Based NIDPS. In *Advances in logistics, operations, and management science book series* (pp. 36–74). DOI:10.4018/978-1-6684-7625-3.ch002

Wennekers, T., & Mathematics, S. O. E. C. A. (2021). *Emotional body language synthesis for humanoid robots*. https://pearl.plymouth.ac.uk/handle/10026.1/17244

Wiegmann, C., Quinlivan, E., Michnevich, T., Pittrich, A., Иванова, П., Rohrbach, A. M., & Kaminski, J. (2023). A digital patient-reported outcome (electronic patient-reported outcome) system for patients with severe psychiatric disorders: User-centered development study and study protocol of a multicenter-controlled trial. *Digital Health*, 9. Advance online publication. DOI:10.1177/20552076231191009 PMID:37900257

Zajko, M. (2021). Conservative AI and social inequality: Conceptualizing alternatives to bias through social theory. *AI & Society*, 36(3), 1047–1056. DOI:10.1007/s00146-021-01153-9

Zakir, M. H. (2023, December 24). *The impact of artificial intelligence on intellectual property rights*. https://ijhs.com.pk/index.php/IJHS/article/view/330

Zhang, Z., Wen, F., Sun, Z., Guo, X., He, T., & Lee, C. (2022). Artificial Intelligence-Enabled Sensing technologies in the 5G/Internet of Things era: From Virtual Reality/Augmented Reality to the Digital Twin. *Advanced Intelligent Systems*, 4(7), 2100228. Advance online publication. DOI:10.1002/aisy.202100228

Zhao, N., Kim, N. W., Herman, L., Pfister, H., Lau, R. W. H., Echevarria, J., & Bylinskii, Z. (2020). *ICONATE: Automatic Compound Icon Generation and Ideation*. ACM. DOI:10.1145/3313831.3376618

Zhao, T., Zhou, Y., Shi, R., Cao, Z., & Ren, Z. (2024). GWAI: Harnessing Artificial Intelligence for Enhancing Gravitational Wave Data Analysis. *arXiv (Cornell University)*. https://doi.org//arxiv.2402.02825DOI:10.48550

Zhao, W., Wang, W., & Viswanathan, S. (2024). Spillover Effects of Generative AI on Human-Generated Content Creation: Evidence from a Crowd-Sourcing Design Platform. *Social Science Research Network*. DOI:10.2139/ssrn.4693181

Chapter 11
Reshaping Cybersecurity Practices by Optimizing Web Application Penetration Testing

Khalid Hussain

https://orcid.org/0000-0002-3714-8696

Albukhary International University, Malaysia

Md Amin Ullah Sheikh

Albukhary International University, Malaysia

Thiha Naing

Albukhary International University, Malaysia

Manzoor Hussain

Indus University, Pakistan

Noor Ul Amin

Taylor's University, Malaysia

ABSTRACT

Web application penetration testing is known as pretesting. It is a critical process for identifying and addressing security vulnerabilities in web applications. Statistics show that 88% of organizations worldwide experienced phishing attempts in 2019. The most significant security violation was predictable resource location attacks were 34%, SQL attacks at 20%, and code injection attacks at 10%, together generating 64% of total web application attack activity. Also, 75% of IT leaders lack confidence

DOI: 10.4018/979-8-3693-5415-5.ch011

in their web application security. The study of the literature review emphasizes the lack of security issues in web applications and some proposals about penetration testing procedures. The method sections talk about detailed procedures from scratch for doing web app pen tests. In the discussion section, the authors talk about some suggestions that organizations can follow to make their websites more secure and unauthorized access. In conclusion, conducting web application penetration testing in the proper way can play a crucial role in securing web applications.

1. INTRODUCTION

A web application is a dynamic and interactive website that is able to do specific functions through browser technologies (Gurunath & Samanta, 2021). Also, penetration testing which is known as "pen testing" in common, is a security testing of the applications that can evaluate the security of an IT infrastructure by safely identifying the weakness of the system called vulnerabilities (Shebli et al., 2018). Web application penetration testing follows some procedure or step sequence while doing pen testing. It includes planning and preparation, discovery, attacks, reports, etc. In planning and preparation, penetration testers identify the actual scope, their goal, duration, and all the basic information that is necessary at the first step. Then the discovery phase comes into play. It involves gathering information about the target, reconnaissance website structures, their technology use, and so on. The attacking phase is the most important part of penetration testing (Denis et al., 2016).

Pen testers apply their techniques to get the vulnerability manually and also use some automated tools. Finally, they report overall findings in proper documentation (Altulaihan et al., 2023). In this paper, we are going to show the actual process of conducting penetration testing from a hacker's mindset. Penetration testing in the proper way can identify vulnerabilities, prevent security breaches, improve security postures, guide security measures, assess the security state, and minimize security risk of the web application as well as the organizations (Aibekova & Selvarajah, 2022), (Khera et al., 2019), (Softić & Vejzović, 2023).

2. LITERATURE REVIEW

In web application security testing, companies perform penetration testing that can identify web application vulnerabilities and attackers' actions. (Goutam et. al., 2019) study vulnerability assessment and penetration testing to enhance the security of web applications. For testing vulnerabilities, a framework has been built. Today the leading methodology of web application security analysis is a combination of vulnerability assessment and penetration testing. Because of penetration testing security analysts left behind experience. (Meo et. al., 2020) mention this problem by proposing a formal, model-based testing approach for the security analysis of web applications. So that it can help in the penetration testing phase. Web applications and networks are one of the critical components in penetration testing to secure the system. (Yong, C. T., et. al., 2023) shows a format that will cater to the understanding of domain knowledge experts, decision-making bodies, and board members of the top executives of an organization that can help them make decisions for improving the efficiency of the network and web application. Penetration testing is a method of evaluating security. One of the testing methods that can be used in SQL injection. The purpose of (Andria et. al., 2021) is to test the security of the web server database. It can help the website administrator to be able to check database vulnerabilities in their system.

Because if there is a vulnerability related to a database issue, hackers can take all the data and misuse of it. (Bhardwaj et. al., 2021) present a new Penetration Testing framework for smart contracts and decentralized apps. (Bhardwaj et. al., 2021) compared results from the proposed penetration-testing framework with automated penetration-test Scanners. Nowadays, web applications are increasing too much. so that every web application requires an adequate security level to store information safely and avoid cyber-attacks (Riskhan et al., 2023). (Alanda et. al., 2021) use penetration testing with the black box method which is without any proper information about the system to test web application security based on the list of most attacks on the Open Web Application Security Project (which is known as OWASP), namely SQL Injection. Penetration testers need to ensure that the black hackers cannot find any weaknesses to destroy, exploit, or disclose information on the Web.

(Albahar et. al., 2022) propose an empirical comparison of penetration testing tools for detecting web app vulnerabilities through approved standards and methods that can facilitate the selection of appropriate tools according to the needs of penetration testers. The contribution of (Altulaihan et. al., 2023) is to discuss penetration testing and how it can be implemented. His results indicate that not all web penetration testing tools offer the same features. So, a combination of analysis tools can provide detailed information about web vulnerabilities. The attack samples generated as part of web application penetration testing on sensor networks can be easily blocked, using Web Application Firewalls (WAFs). (Chowdhary et. al., 2023) propose an autonomous penetration testing framework. Which can utilize Generative Adversarial Networks (GANs). Other influential works included (Sajid et al., 2018), (Sanjaya et. al., 2020). The literature review for the chapter on web application penetration testing (Computer Science, 227, 92-100) encompasses diverse research. Studies by Usman et al. (2023) on diabetic retinopathy detection, Ren et al. (2020) on ransomware prevention, and Lim et al. (2019) on criminal network prediction contribute to understanding various cybersecurity challenges. Additionally, research by Humayun et al. (2022) on blockchain security, Wassan et al. (2021) on sentiment analysis, and Alkinani et al. (2021) on IoT-based accident detection provides insights into emerging threats and solutions. Furthermore, works by Muzammal et al. (2020), Shahid et al. (2021), Azeem et al. (2021), and Babbar et al. (2021) offer valuable perspectives on secure routing protocols, energy-efficient security mechanisms, fog computing, and load balancing algorithms in diverse network environments.

3. METHODOLOGY

Web application penetration means penetrating all the weaknesses using some techniques, tools, and processes. A detailed procedure is needed for web application penetration testing. Sometimes, another term comes in the same concept which is bug hunting or security research. Somehow both are same types and they have differences in the time period and how they want to deal with the web applications security testing. We have a complete process to conduct penetration testing. In this methodology, we will discuss all the concepts of how to do the penetration testing completely. We will talk about the hacker's mindset and the techniques, and tools they apply in penetration testing. We have a preparation process that involves defining the scope, obtaining authorization, and gathering information about the web application. Secondly, we have reconnaissance which collects information about target, network, and website structures such as site development using languages, technology use, etc. Then we have scanning of the websites. It includes network scanning, automation tools to scan for vulnerabilities, and manual testing as well. Also, we have enumeration, vulnerability analysis, exploitation, and reporting (Shebli & Beheshti, 2018). We will discuss all of the processes for conducting web application penetration testing below:

3.1. Define Scope and Goals

Define scope refers to selecting the target for penetration testing and goals refers to the objectives that can follow for the selected target for penetration testing. For example, companies give some scope to test. The scope has two categories. One is in scope, and another is out of scope. Those domains or IPs included in In Scope, are the target for testing. Penetration testers can test only those targets. Also, if you see out-of-scope and some domain or IPs there that means it's excluded, or you need to ignore these in testing because maybe it's under maintenance or the organization may be affected if you test that. For example,

In Scope: domain1.com, domain2.com, domain3.com

Out of Scope: domain4.com, domain5.com

From here you can see that only we have the permission to test In Scope domains except out of scope.

3.2. Information Gathering (Reconnaissance)

Information gathering is one of the most important parts in penetration testing. Information gathering covers almost 70-75% in penetration testing. If we don't have proper knowledge about the system we can not exploit it. So, it plays a crucial role in conducting penetration testing. There are several things that include information gathering. We have active and passive reconnaissance. We can check the host, whatweb, whois lookup, dns lookup, firewall use or not, which technology used in the website. we can see host of the domain by using host domain.com shown in Figure 1.

Figure 1. Host check

Also, we can see all the technology using whatweb testphp.vulnweb.com, which is a testing site for educational purposes shown in Figure 2.

Figure 2. web technology info

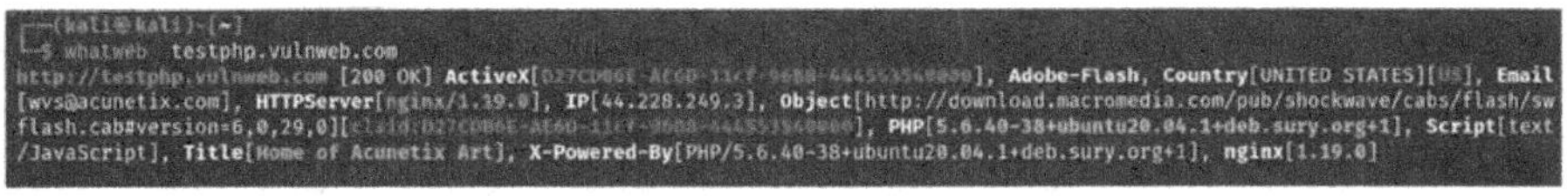

We can recon DNS using dnsrecon tool shown in below Figure 3.

Figure 3. DNS recon

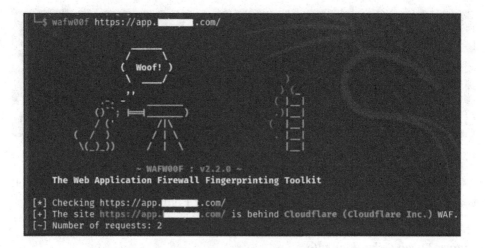

We have various tools like this to gather information. Remember one thing, it is not finished only in this step. Every single step of penetration testing there are many challenges that will come. So to overcome those problems and unknown things we need to go forward again and again to collect information. We can check firewalls using the wafw00f tool which is open source in github.

Figure 4. Firewall detection

Figure 4 Shows that the domain has a firewall name cloudflare. Because of security purposes I just hide the domain name. But that can help us to get the idea about firewall checking using the tool. We also have google dorking, github dorking, and a wayback machine that shows historical data of the sites can help to gain a lot of information. Also, we have shodan, censys, security trails etc. tools that can help us to get internal IP of the domain. Which can help us to get sensitive things in the web application.

3.3. Threat Modeling

Threat modeling is a technique to identify and analyze security threats in the web applications running system (Bokan & Santos, 2022). It is a part of security testing to know about potential risk related to the system. There are many threat modeling methods and tools that can help to know how much risk there is in the websites. Some of them are stride, pasta, linddun, cvss. Nowadays, cvss is most popular in threat modeling whown in Figure 5. All of the models focus on a certain type of scope such as people, asset, actor, attack scenarios, complexity and so on.

Figure 5. CVSS V3.0 Score Range (Sumpter, 2022)

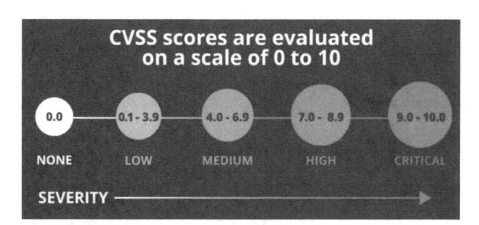

3.4. Vulnerability Analysis

Vulnerability analysis is the process of identifying vulnerabilities through hands-on techniques, tools, static and dynamic analysis. It includes automation & manual testing. There are a lot of tools that can help to automate vulnerability analysis (Humayun et al., 2020). We can discuss some of them here. At first, we can use ping to see the site live or not. Then try to find subdomains of the website. We can use various tools for subdomain enumeration such as amass, assetfinder, sublist3r, subdominator etc. After finding subdomains we have to check live subdomains of the domain. So, we can use the httpx tool or httprobe that can help us achieve much more accurate results of live subdomains. Then we have to find directories of each subdomain. We can use dirsearch, feroxbuster, ffuf, wfuzz, dirb, dirbuster, knockpy tools to get hidden directories or paths. One of these tools is mention in Figure 6.

Figure 6. Directory Fuzzing

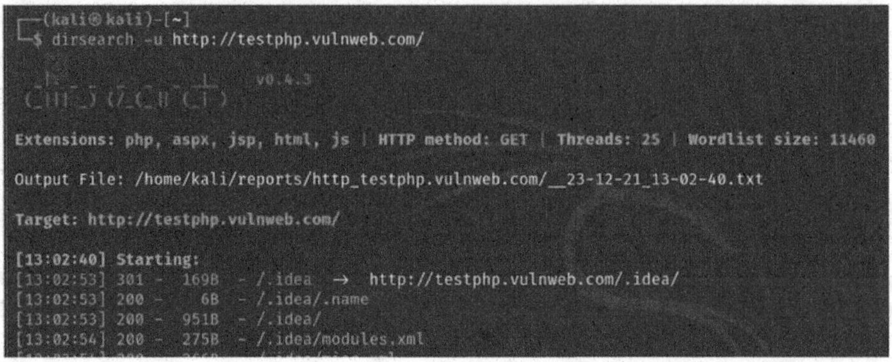

```
┌─(kali㉿kali)-[~]
└─$ dirsearch -u http://testphp.vulnweb.com/

  _|. _ _  _  _  _ _|_    v0.4.3
 (_||| _) (/_(_|| (_| )

Extensions: php, aspx, jsp, html, js | HTTP method: GET | Threads: 25 | Wordlist size: 11460

Output File: /home/kali/reports/http_testphp.vulnweb.com/__23-12-21_13-02-40.txt

Target: http://testphp.vulnweb.com/

[13:02:40] Starting:
[13:02:53] 301 -   169B  - /.idea  →  http://testphp.vulnweb.com/.idea/
[13:02:53] 200 -    6B  - /.idea/.name
[13:02:53] 200 -   951B  - /.idea/
[13:02:54] 200 -   275B  - /.idea/modules.xml
```

We have to scan for open ports every time which is shown in Figure 7. Because it is very important to know open ports so that it might be helpful to exploit the system through some outdated version of the running services. Nmap or naabu can help to do that.

Figure 7. Network Scanning Using Nmap

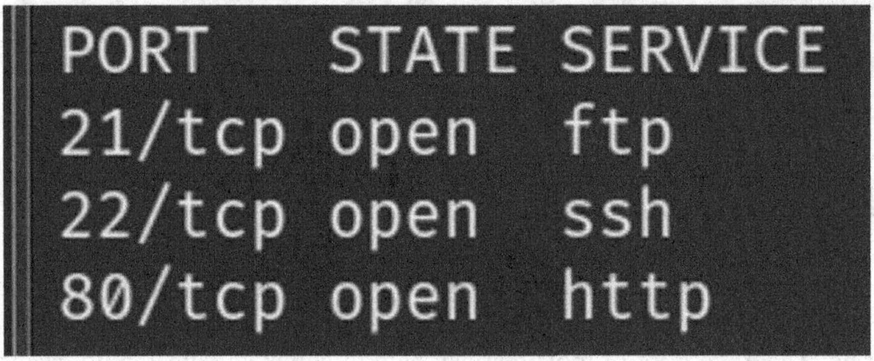

```
PORT     STATE  SERVICE
21/tcp   open   ftp
22/tcp   open   ssh
80/tcp   open   http
```

Then we have some automation tools for scanning vulnerability as well such as Nessus, Acunetix, burp suite, zap proxy, nuclei, etc. Nuclei is a powerful tool that actually works in template-based scanning. It gives much better results and also a lot of things that we do manually. It helps easily to find low-hanging bugs or vulnerabilities. Sometimes, it can scan for critical vulnerabilities also such as XSS, SQLi, Open redirect, local file inclusion, etc. Also, we can use Nessus and Acunetix to scan for vulnerabilities automatically and get proper information about the issue with rating of the cvss score. However manual testing is very efficient in terms of security. Because many more times automation tools fail to get critical vulnerabilities. They can't go beyond the logic flow and can't catch high-impact security issues. To verify whether vulnerabilities are false positives or not after use in automation testing, we need to recheck manually.

3.5. Exploitation

Exploitation is the process of compromising websites through vulnerabilities or bugs. It is the phase after analysis of vulnerabilities (Siahaan et al., 2023). Through exploitation, we can ensure properly about the weakness. Such as, if we find a vulnerability from automation or manual tests. We need to check properly whether it can be exploitable or not. So we use this process to ensure the security issue present on the system. For example, the website https://example.com/?p=1 is vulnerable to SQL injection. So we need to recheck by applying some SQL injection query to verify whether it is exploitable or not. Sometimes, in cross-site scripting, even if we get command injection then we can verify the exploitation by giving commands to the system to know more.

3.6. Post-Exploitation

It is the process after exploiting the system. In web application penetration testing, we don't see post-exploitation too much. We usually see this while exploiting any server after getting the shell connection. Many times black hackers apply their social engineering techniques to manipulate company employees. When they click malicious links, then hackers get a reverse connection from the victim's side. Reverse connection means it doesn't connect from hacker to victim. But automatically virus files are injected into the system and get connected from the victim's computer to the attacker's computer. Then all the processes to get more privileges and perform more actions are actually post-exploitation in the context of penetration testing.

3.7. Reporting

Reporting is one of the most important parts of penetration testing. It is not only in the case of penetration testing but everywhere such as security research or bug hunting also present. Without reporting nothing can be clear. Proper reporting can be understandable in vulnerability findings. When someone gets the vulnerability, they need to write a full report. It includes a summary, description, exploitation, steps to reproduce, impact, risk, remediation, or mitigation shown in Figure 8.

Figure 8. Reporting for Vulnerability

4. DISCUSSION

Web application penetration testing has a proper procedure that needs to be followed all the penetration testers while penetrating the website or any other system including network, servers, android software, etc. By following these methods, they can reach their goal. For testing, we need a full mind map. It can explain each of the steps very clearly. Sometimes testers use a checklist which is another type of mindmap. It can help to remember the steps of conducting penetration testing. It also helps to follow sequences as well. From defining scopes, information gathering or reconnaissance, threat modeling, vulnerability analysis, exploitation, post-exploitation, and reporting all the processes have their internal process.

Vulnerability analysis is one of the most important parts. Because here ethical hackers do their white box and black box testing. Sometimes they have all the information about the system which is a white box and sometimes they don't have any information which means black box testing. In black box testing, they have to go all the possible ways they can. It is the most critical part of penetration testing. That is very important to remember with documentation. It can assist and consume time. Everything with proper documentation can also help to enhance work efficiency with understanding and critical thinking. A detailed procedure for conducting web application penetration testing can play a crucial role in problem-solving in the context of penetration testing. Organizations can run various security programs also for the freshers. They can gain actual real-world scenarios and techniques for learning penetration testing. Employee training also can help organizations by giving security awareness so that basic things can be handled by them. If the organization is very big and too confidential, they can hire experts such as offensive security engineers, read teamers, and penetration testers as well. Also, companies can hire external penetration testers who know the details procedure or are certified in web application security testing. Finally, in proper way, web application penetration testing can lead to very good performance and give the best security of any website.

5. CONCLUSION

In conclusion, web application or web app penetration testing is one of the most important parts of emerging technology. Without it, organizations can't become more secure. No company can say confidently that its organization is fully secure. Day by day because of technology updates and new technology, frameworks, penetration testing has become a crucial part of the organization. Web applications need to be tested within a time duration or scheduled base. Even some companies run their responsible disclosure program so that ethical hackers can find bugs or vulnerabilities and inform the company. So, penetration testers must follow proper procedures while doing penetration testing. Pen testers can apply their technical expertise using whitebox and blackbox methods. Also, static, and dynamic analysis can help in securing the websites. They must care about the company assets more and more. Always need to focus on web application security. Even if they don't find any vulnerabilities, they always must continue their testing. By doing this through company experts or external experts, companies will be more secure. We can get a safe environment. Customers personal identification information (PII) will be more secure. Lastly, penetration testing in web applications plays a vital role in safeguarding the web applications of individuals or companies.

REFERENCES

Aibekova, A., & Selvarajah, V. (2022, April). Offensive Security: Study on Penetration Testing Attacks, Methods, and their Types. In *2022 IEEE International Conference on Distributed Computing and Electrical Circuits and Electronics (ICDCECE)* (pp. 1-9). IEEE. DOI:10.1109/ICDCECE53908.2022.9792772

Al Shebli, H. M. Z., & Beheshti, B. D. (2018, May). A study on penetration testing process and tools. In 2018 IEEE Long Island Systems, Applications and Technology Conference (LISAT) (pp. 1-7). IEEE. DOI:10.1109/LISAT.2018.8378035

Alanda, A., Satria, D., Ardhana, M. I., Dahlan, A. A., & Mooduto, H. A. (2021). Web application penetration testing using SQL Injection attack. JOIV. *International Journal on Informatics Visualization*, 5(3), 320–326. DOI:10.30630/joiv.5.3.470

Albahar, M., Alansari, D., & Jurcut, A. (2022). An empirical comparison of pen-testing tools for detecting web app vulnerabilities. *Electronics (Basel)*, 11(19), 2991. DOI:10.3390/electronics11192991

Alkinani, M. H., Almazroi, A. A., Jhanjhi, N. Z., & Khan, N. A. (2021). 5G and IoT based reporting and accident detection (RAD) system to deliver first aid box using unmanned aerial vehicle. *Sensors (Basel)*, 21(20), 6905. DOI:10.3390/s21206905 PMID:34696118

Altulaihan, E. A., Alismail, A., & Frikha, M. (2023). A Survey on Web Application Penetration Testing. *Electronics (Basel)*, 12(5), 1229. DOI:10.3390/electronics12051229

Altulaihan, E. A., Alismail, A., & Frikha, M. (2023). A Survey on Web Application Penetration Testing. *Electronics (Basel)*, 12(5), 1229. DOI:10.3390/electronics12051229

Andria, A., & Pamungkas, R. (2021). Penetration Testing Database Menggunakan Metode SQL Injection Via SQLMap di Termux. *IJAI*, 5(1), 1. DOI:10.20961/ijai.v5i1.40845

Azeem, M., Ullah, A., Ashraf, H., Jhanjhi, N. Z., Humayun, M., Aljahdali, S., & Tabbakh, T. A. (2021). Fog-oriented secure and lightweight data aggregation in iomt. *IEEE Access : Practical Innovations, Open Solutions*, 9, 111072–111082. DOI:10.1109/ACCESS.2021.3101668

Babbar, H., Rani, S., Masud, M., Verma, S., Anand, D., & Jhanjhi, N. (2021). Load balancing algorithm for migrating switches in software-defined vehicular networks. *Computers, Materials & Continua*, 67(1), 1301–1316. DOI:10.32604/cmc.2021.014627

Barik, K., Abirami, A., Das, S., Konar, K., & Banerjee, A. (2021, September). Penetration Testing Analysis with Standardized Report Generation. In *3rd International Conference on Integrated Intelligent Computing Communication & Security (ICIIC 2021)* (pp. 365-372). Atlantis Press. DOI:10.2991/ahis.k.210913.045

Bhardwaj, A., Shah, S. B. H., Shankar, A., Alazab, M., Kumar, M., & Gadekallu, T. R. (2021). Penetration testing framework for smart contract blockchain. *Peer-to-Peer Networking and Applications*, 14(5), 2635–2650. DOI:10.1007/s12083-020-00991-6

Bokan, B., & Santos, J. (2022). Threat Modeling for Enterprise Cybersecurity Architecture. *2022 Systems and Information Engineering Design Symposium (SIEDS)*, 25-30, DOI:10.1109/SIEDS55548.2022.9799322

Chowdhary, A., Jha, K., & Zhao, M. (2023). Generative Adversarial Network (GAN)-Based Autonomous Penetration Testing for Web Applications. *Sensors (Basel)*, 23(18), 8014. DOI:10.3390/s23188014 PMID:37766067

De Meo, F., & Viganò, L. (2020). A formal and automated approach to exploiting multi-stage attacks of web applications. *Journal of Computer Security*, 28(5), 525–576. DOI:10.3233/JCS-181262

Denis, M., Zena, C., & Hayajneh, T. (2016, April). Penetration testing: Concepts, attack methods, and defense strategies. In 2016 IEEE Long Island Systems, Applications and Technology Conference (LISAT) (pp. 1-6). IEEE.

Gurunath, R., & Samanta, D. (2022). A novel approach for semantic web application in online education based on steganography. *International Journal of Web-Based Learning and Teaching Technologies*, 17(4), 1–13. DOI:10.4018/IJWLTT.285569

Humayun, M., Jhanjhi, N. Z., Niazi, M., Amsaad, F., & Masood, I. (2022). Securing drug distribution systems from tampering using blockchain. *Electronics (Basel)*, 11(8), 1195. DOI:10.3390/electronics11081195

Humayun, M., Niazi, M., Jhanjhi, N., Alshayeb, M., & Mahmood, S. (2020). Cyber Security Threats and Vulnerabilities: A Systematic Mapping Study. *Arabian Journal for Science and Engineering*, 45(4), 3171–3189. DOI:10.1007/s13369-019-04319-2

Khera, Y., Kumar, D., & Garg, N. (2019, February). Analysis and impact of vulnerability assessment and penetration testing. In *2019 International Conference on Machine Learning, Big Data, Cloud and Parallel Computing (COMITCon)* (pp. 525-530). IEEE. DOI:10.1109/COMITCon.2019.8862224

Lim, M., Abdullah, A., Jhanjhi, N. Z., & Khan, M. K. (2019). Situation-aware deep reinforcement learning link prediction model for evolving criminal networks. *IEEE Access : Practical Innovations, Open Solutions*, 8, 16550–16559. DOI:10.1109/ACCESS.2019.2961805

Muzammal, S. M., Murugesan, R. K., Jhanjhi, N. Z., & Jung, L. T. (2020, October). SMTrust: Proposing trust-based secure routing protocol for RPL attacks for IoT applications. In *2020 International Conference on Computational Intelligence (ICCI)* (pp. 305-310). IEEE. DOI:10.1109/ICCI51257.2020.9247818

Ren, A., Liang, C., Hyug, I., Broh, S., & Jhanjhi, N. Z. (2020). A three-level ransomware detection and prevention mechanism. EAI Endorsed Transactions on Energy Web, 7(26).

Riskhan, B., Safuan, H. A. J., Hussain, K., Elnour, A. A. H., Abdelmaboud, A., Khan, F., & Kundi, M. (2023). An Adaptive Distributed Denial of Service Attack Prevention Technique in a Distributed Environment. *Sensors (Basel)*, 23(14), 6574. DOI:10.3390/s23146574 PMID:37514868

Sajid, A., & Hussain, K. (2018). Rule Based (Forward Chaining/Data Driven) Expert System for Node Level Congestion Handling in Opportunistic Network. *Mobile Networks and Applications*, 23(3), 446–455. DOI:10.1007/s11036-018-1016-0

Sanjaya, I. G. A. S., Sasmita, G. M. A., & Arsa, D. M. S. (2020). Evaluasi Keamanan Website Lembaga X Melalui Penetration Testing Menggunakan Framework ISSAF. *Jurnal Ilmiah Merpati*, 8(2), 113–124. DOI:10.24843/JIM.2020.v08.i02.p05

Shahid, H., Ashraf, H., Javed, H., Humayun, M., Jhanjhi, N. Z., & AlZain, M. A. (2021). Energy optimised security against wormhole attack in iot-based wireless sensor networks. *Computers, Materials & Continua*, 68(2), 1967–1981. DOI:10.32604/cmc.2021.015259

Shebli, H. M. Z. A., & Beheshti, B. D. (2018). A study on penetration testing process and tools. 2018 IEEE Long Island Systems, Applications and Technology Conference (LISAT), 1-7. DOI:10.1109/LISAT.2018.8378035

Siahaan, C. N., Rufisanto, M., Nolasco, R., Achmad, S., & Siahaan, C. R. P. (2023). Study of Cross-Site Request Forgery on Web-Based Application: Exploitations and Preventions. *Procedia Computer Science*, 227, 92–100. DOI:10.1016/j. procs.2023.10.506

Softić, J., & Vejzović, Z. (2023, March). Impact of Vulnerability Assesment and Penetration Testing (VAPT) on Operating System Security. In 2023 22nd International Symposium INFOTEH-JAHORINA (INFOTEH) (pp. 1-6). IEEE.

Sumpter, J. (2022, April 12). CVSS Scores: A Practical Guide for application. ZeroFox. https://www.zerofox.com/blog/cvss-scores-practical-guide-application/

Usman, T. M., Saheed, Y. K., Ignace, D., & Nsang, A. (2023). Diabetic retinopathy detection using principal component analysis multi-label feature extraction and classification. *International Journal of Cognitive Computing in Engineering*, 4, 78–88. DOI:10.1016/j.ijcce.2023.02.002

Wassan, S., Chen, X., Shen, T., Waqar, M., & Jhanjhi, N. Z. (2021). Amazon product sentiment analysis using machine learning techniques. *Revista Argentina de Clínica Psicológica*, 30(1), 695.

Yong, C. T., Hao, C. V., Ruskhan, B., Lim, S. K. Y., Boon, T. G., Wei, T. S., & Shah, S. B. I. A. (2023). An Implementation of Efficient Smart Street Lights with Crime and Accident Monitoring: A Review. Journal of Survey in Fisheries Sciences, 287-305.

Chapter 12
Ethics and Transparency in Secure Web Model Generation

Siva Raja Sindiramutty
https://orcid.org/0009-0006-0310
-8721

Taylor's University, Malaysia

Krishna Raj V. Prabagaran

Universiti Malaysia Sarawak, Malaysia

Noor Zaman Jhanjhi
https://orcid.org/0000-0001-8116
-4733

Taylor's University, Malaysia

Raja Kumar Murugesan
https://orcid.org/0000-0001-9500
-1361

Taylor's University, Malaysia

Nazir Ahmed Malik
https://orcid.org/0000-0002-0118
-4601

Bahria University, Islamabad, Pakistan

Manzoor Hussain

Indus University, Pakistan

ABSTRACT

The chapter discusses how ethics and transparency relate to creating secure web models for AI. AI plays a role in secure web development, and the authors consider ethics and transparency as two critical aspects of this subject, which influences users, stakeholders, or society. The examination begins with AI principles, which include fairness, accountability, and privacy requirements. They then get into the problems with secure web models. In this chapter, they break down bias and fairness concerns at the source and find ways to resolve them in web models. This relates to trust and accountability, where transparency and explainability are highlighted. They also provide case studies showing the effectiveness of transparent and explainable AI in increasing user engagement. They also delve into decision-making frameworks to help navigate the ethical dilemmas in AI web development. It then represents the conversation on the atmospherics of empowerment tools, such as monitoring and

DOI: 10.4018/979-8-3693-5415-5.ch012

evaluation guidelines for mobilisation implementation practice and governance. To sum up, the authors underline the ethical and transparent views for us to do AI-driven web development. Therefore, they urge all stakeholders to make ethics and transparency the cornerstones of responsible webs.

INTRODUCTION

Overview of the Chapter's Focus on Ethics and Transparency in the Context of Web Model Generation

We need to balance this thirst for new web models with ethical considerations to develop and use the best possible model responsibly. Ethics cover various issues, including data privacy, fairness/accountability, and social impact. Transparency is concerned with the clarity and openness of how models are being built/installed to help these groups understand the decision-making process along with outputs(He et al., 2023; Azam et al., 2023). A prevalent ethical issue is treating people fairly from whose data the models are trained and tested.

Maintaining privacy rights, data collection with consent, and providing anonymisation methods are crucial. Support from the government or another healthcare-related institution is needed when those requirements become burdensome in resource-intensive applications (Kaplan et al., 2023). However, there is an increasing awareness of the requirement for fair decisions that counteract biases that might entrench discrimination or exacerbate inequalities altogether (Landers & Behrend, 2023; Azam, Tajwar et al., 2023). The transparency concept of web model generation refers to the degree to which data sources and methods are disclosed, non-experts can read referral principles, and the algorithmic decision-making process is transparent. This very same openness works to create user trust. Permits for further analysis of model flows

In addition, explicit models help the player explain their own decisions and comprehend their choices in life (Shin, 2021). It is great to be ethical and transparent; however, delivering these things can be uncomfortable, especially in web model development circumstances. This leads companies to the difficult task of providing added transparency while protecting interests and trade secrets (Chakraborty, 2023; Ananna et al., 2023). Beyond this, preventing bias and unfairness necessitates ongoing monitoring and assessment of models over time (Agarwal & Agarwal, 2023). Web model development should adhere to principles of ethics and transparency. If stakeholders adhere to guidelines and play fair, their reward is trust, which decreases risks while exploiting the benefits of web models.

Explanation of the Importance of Ethical Considerations and Transparency In AI-Driven Web Development

Privacy and transparency in AI-powered web development Given the increasing use of AI technologies, being ethical and transparent is crucial to establishing trust while protecting user privacy and preventing biases/discrimination. The ethical concerns surround the values that drive AI-based systems development and deployment, namely fairness, accountability, transparency, and responsibility (Nasir et al., 2024). Developers can sidestep these risks if they follow principles for avoiding problematic AI algorithm outcomes or smooth over societal biases that a machine learning exercise simply deepens (Gupta, 2023).

Transparency enhances the explainability and accountability of AI-driven web applications (Carullo, 2023). Explaining the functioning and decisions made by AI algorithms grants users enough to understand why these systems deliver such suggestions or outcomes. Transparency Further, transparency makes AI models subject to scrutiny by stakeholders for bias or mistake and allows any required corrections (Landers & Behrend, 2023). Transparency on data sources, algorithmic paths and decision-making basis behind developers, users and other parties involved builds trust. Overall, they are driving the AI-tech takeover. In Figure 1, the diagram illustrates the importance of ethics and transparency in creating web models.

Figure 1. Overview of Ethics and Transparency in the Context of Web Model Generation

It is not just about compliance but also welcomes the ethical use and transparency of AI-integrated web (Usman et al., 2023). Follow-the-standards and transparency provided by developers make the internet communities feel more valued and accepted, even if they are new or different(Zhanbayev et al., 2023; Azam et al., 2023). More importantly, ethical AI practices mitigate reputational risks associated with data abuse or algorithmic biases, which means that the mutual interest of users and organisations is preserved (Kumar & Suthar, 2024). Ethical. Transparency is necessary in building and deploying web applications powered by AI. Developers give credibility its due by setting and advocating for values, which results in trustworthiness and building robust accountability mechanisms to mitigate AI risks, thereby nurturing more inclusive, fairer digital societies.

Chapter Contributions

1. Ethical Perspectives: This chapter explores ethical frameworks related to AI-powered websites. It covers guiding principles such as fairness, accountability, and transparency that inform decision-making for developers who want to deploy AI appropriately.
2. In which transparency is kryptonite: This quick guide shows examples revealing the importance of natural algorithms in processes. It discusses how transparency can lead to greater understanding and trust of a system, allow for biases or errors in AI models to be checked by scrutiny adopted over time as explanatory power increases visibility into workings, and hold developers accountable towards end-users.
3. Controlling Bias & Discrimination: The last section will include strategies for decreasing bias and discrimination in AI algorithms. This work conducts investigations on data preprocessing strategies, fairness tasks, and design for diversity-aware AI-driven web applications to support equality of opportunities with new solutions toward inclusivity.
4. Explain To Empower Users: This section underlines the importance of explaining AI-driven suggestions or outcomes to users. It covers how explanations help users understand, trust, and be more in control of their decision-making.
5. Teaching—Legal and Reputation Risks—We cover the reputational risks associated with AI practices. This course provides means of lowering these risks by adhering to regulations, maintaining standards, and following risk control mechanisms.
6. Cultivating Inclusive Digital Ecologies: We examine how ethical AI practices can engender unbiased spaces and consider the primacy of ethics to build digital systems that enable individuals from diverse backgrounds to feel respected, valued, and empowered.

7. Future Challenges: Finally, what will the future hold regarding trends and challenges for ethical AI-based web development gears? To shed light on efforts driving responsible AI advancement, it explores new challenges and opportunities this technology brings alongside the shifting terrain of AI ethics.

Chapter Organization

This part offered the theoretical background for developing AI-driven websites, and in its conclusion, we discussed ethics and transparency in working with such systems. At this point, we briefly dive into some ethical considerations around AI (fairness, accountability, transparency and privacy) and how they inform model building on the web. Section 3: AI Model Bias Review: Key takeaways from web model development are identifying and mitigating bias concerns and measures for fairness preservation. In the fourth section, we explore privacy concerns in working with data management to construct web models by discussing duties and methods for preserving anonymity. Transparency and interpretability are instrumental in garnering trust and aiding understanding of AI-driven web models; Section five provides examples to improve the same. Section six discusses real-world examples of ethical dilemmas and decision methodologies to evaluate how decisions are made in the web model development process. Section seven investigates practices in deploying and governance AI-driven web models and the roles played by parties. Finally, section nine provides examples of techniques that illustrate the value of good design and community engagement in developing websites from AI-driven data. Section 9: Rule, Regulation & Impact - AI Enabling Website CreationFollowing the rules and being accountable. In Section 10, we try to pull together all the threads looking for takeaways and suggesting that in any efforts by AI/ML-driven website development, an emphasis on ethics and transparency will be critical. Developers, policymakers, and stakeholders must share the responsibility to act.

ETHICAL PRINCIPLES IN AI

Examination of Foundational Ethical Principles Relevant to AI, Such as Fairness, Accountability, Transparency, and Privacy

Even AI appearing in our lives has opened up a whole new range of questions that are now being considered about the ethics of technology. The development and use of AI systems are guided by some rules: fairness, accountability, transparency and privacy. These principles AI must respect to use it ethically and in balance with our moral values. Fairness refers to the ability of an AI system to avoid bias and discrimination by ensuring algorithms treat everyone equally, regardless of race or gender, according to Agarwal et al. Fairness (2022) - ensures that AI systems are not inappropriately discriminatory against any group.

It is also a principle of accountability for developers and users concerning AI systems' outputs, decisions or actions (Sanderson et al., 2023). This includes creating monitoring mechanisms to trace and attribute responsibility for, as far as possible, causal links between AI decisions leading to harm so that some individual or organisation may be held accountable. We can understand how AI has been designed and trained to function by making the process transparent. As Albahri et al. (2023) illuminate, the transparency that AI systems can define how and why an output occurs is observable by all stakeholders so they can learn from it and build confidence in what action should be taken or where biases might exist. What is Privacy: Protecting personal information and even free agency is a fundamental right.

AI systems must. Protect the right to privacy by appropriately handling sensitive information (Villegas et al. These ethical values are. Mutually supportive. In AI, transparency aids in ascertaining and rectifying biases to ensure it is a fair technology, e.g., Accountability measures also enforce compliance with norms. Offer restitution to people affected by AI decisions. Preserving privacy is a key component of trust-building in AI systems, and the rights corresponding to personal data need to be respected (Mylrea & Robinson, 2023). Understanding things like fairness, accountability, transparency, and privacy are critical principles on the road to implementing AI technologies. These safeguards provide blueprints for tackling issues and serve as a guide to preserve the healthful use of artificial intelligence in all branches.

Discussion on the Ethical Implications of Web Model Generation and Its Impact on Users, Stakeholders, and Society At Large

Deploying machine learning techniques for effective web model generation can become a privacy concern that poses an ethical dilemma to users, stakeholders and society. This system generates models for predicting user behaviour, preferences, and traits based on his passions. On one hand, it provides many great features, such as recommendations and better user experiences. On the other hand, it creates challenges around privacy, autonomy, societal impacts, etc. Perhaps the biggest ethical issue in web model generation is a privacy violation. As users interact with boards, large amounts of data are analysed to generate predictive models (Mylrea & Robinson, 2023).

This opens the door for questions about consent, transparency and data ownership. Alarmingly, users may not always know precisely how their data is used or are fully cognizant of how much privacy they lose. Another problem with web models is that they can cause biases and discrimination. Trained on biased data or flawed algorithms, such models may perpetuate the inequalities they seek to redress (Simson et al., 2023; Azam et al., 2023). Marginalise certain groups. This can lead to disparate outcomes for all employment, housing and financial services.

Also, building models on the web may affect how individuals see and walk in this world - we are shaping that into silos but might get more pure perspective from varied non-pol entered containers, which have the effect of being less autonomy (Husairi & Rossi, 2024; Sindiramutty et al., 2024). Personalised recommendations based on models are inherently dangerous because of the risk of establishing echo chambers where people only get exposed to content that resonates with their thoughts and interests. There are concerns here that speak to both the manipulability of user choices and, theoretically anyway..., the corruption of values. They can question the democratic, regulatory and social effects of widespread web model use (Stahl & Eke, 2024).

The manipulation of content and spreading of misinformation through systems can erode public trust in institutions and contribute to polarisation and disinformation campaigns. The ethical considerations surrounding web model development are complex. It requires consideration from stakeholders such as policymakers, technologists, and users. While this technology offers opportunities for progress and personalisation, it also presents risks that must be addressed to protect privacy, autonomy and societal well-being. Figure 2 illustrates the principles of intelligence.

Figure 2. Ethical principle in Artificial Intelligence

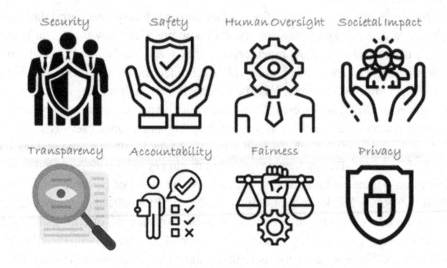

Introduction to Ethical Frameworks and Guidelines for Responsible AI Development and Deployment

This can include fairness, accountability, transparency, and societal impact on using this AI system, which has seen significant benefits from Dream Maker. As a result, many special interest groups ranging from industry to academia and policy have created frameworks for AI practice to standardise best practices unique across disciplines. Such frameworks provide These principles and considerations as guidance for developing and deploying Artificial Intelligence. They emphasise values like fair play to avoid racial, gender or socio-economic bias.

Another approach emphasises accountability, discussing the obligation for AI system outcomes and its developers and users (Dhinakaran et al., 2024). However, transparency is necessary for building trust in AI systems, allowing stakeholders to see how decisions are made and revealing possible biases or errors. AI inherently operates on personal information privacy, which needs to be protected at all costs and strict provisions are built around it (Williamson & Prybutok, 2024; Sindiramutty, Tan et al., 2024). There are several guidelines developed by different organisations with context or industry-specific frameworks

For instance, the IEEE Global Initiative on Ethics of Autonomous and Intelligent Systems prepared a list of principles centred around transparency, accountability, and inclusivity (Theodorou & Tubella, 2024). Moreover, the European Commission

High-Level Expert Group on AI has published guidelines for guiding ethical oversight, robust technical development, and societal/environmental good (Laux et al., 2023).

These ethical frameworks and guidelines determine the development and implementation of AI technologies. All stakeholders can follow these principles and considerations to reduce risks, establish trust in AI systems and further their positive societal impacts.

SECURE WEB MODEL GENERATION

With the internet becoming more into being as years pass, there is an increase in web applications and related services, which have to have security guards installed so users are kept safe when using those services, i.e., unauthorised persons, etc, cannot view their data information. Secure Web Model Generation: In this sense, one of the most important areas discussed in coding is training web systems to protect hackers from using Secure Methods. This paper investigates Secure Web Modeling by uncovering its key elements, design principles and security implications.

In other words, Secure Web Model Generation families or variants classify the needs of a security model within this network environment. This modelling covers access control, user authentication, and intrusion detection system encryption. It also consists of threat modelling to designate vulnerabilities and establish enforcement (Chen & Sun, 2020). Organisations that perform risk assessments can make their cyber systems more resistant to threats.

However, encryption technologies form part of Secure Web Model Generation since they protect data during transmission and storage. Today, most communication between clients and servers happens over security protocols like Transport Layer Security (TLS) or Secure Sockets Layer (SSL)(Kizza, 2024). A critical factor is the attention to coding practices, which mitigate web threats such as SQLi and XSS (Chughtai et al., 2023)

Access control methods might help confirm authentication so customers can enter sources within the cyber community. Access Policies are usually implemented On-demand Access control model in the system using role-based access (RBAC) and attribute-base access controls, according to user Roles and permissions Role Assignment as well as based on User attributes including age, condition, etc. (Mohamed et al., 2023). For example, Multi-Factor Authentication (MFA) provides an additional layer of security over authentication by demanding that the user provide multiple pieces of evidence, such as passwords or tokens, in addition to something they have, like using biometrics (Pöhn et al., 2023). This further verifies data access and thereby decreases the risks.

Intrusion detection and prevention (Sáez De Cámara et al., 2023): Using monitoring tools with anomaly detection to capture and halt unauthorised actions. Both IDS (Indication et al.) and IPS (indication prevention system) detect behaviour patterns and prevent advances in attacks in real time (Aksamiri & Subhi, 2023). Secure Web Model Generation ultimately reinforces web models against an ever-changing cybersecurity ecosystem. With encryption access control, authentication and intrusion detection, an organisation can increase the security of its web applications and prevent unauthorised people from accessing or exploiting the application data stored within.

BIAS AND FAIRNESS CONSIDERATIONS

Exploration of Bias in AI Models and Its Implications for Web Model Generation

For instance, bias in AI models also affects the creation of web models. Bias can affect AI systems at any phase, from data collection to algorithm development and model training. Biases in AI mostly originate from inequalities and prejudices within the data; see Lipton (2018). This issue is further exacerbated through a lack of representation in data collection (Casillas, 2023). However, training models with this biased data also means that the model will be reinforcing such biases (Ferrara, 2024). For example, recent research by Kolberg et al. (2024) shows that face recognition systems have higher error rates on women and people with darker skin colour because those groups are under-represented in the training datasets, for biases in AI models used for web applications - search engines, recommendation systems, etc. Such models reproduce discriminatory processes and empower stereotypes and dispositions of inferior groups (Singha, 2024; Sindiramutty et al., 2024).

For instance, recommendation systems, such as those often accused of being biased, can make content so much larger. They may be more likely to ignore conflicting views, changing how users understand and behave in response. Tackling AI model bias involves researchers, developers and policymakers alike. This refers to data collection, demonstrated algorithmic transparency and fairness-aware model training practice, respectively (Chavalarias et al., 2024). Monitoring and evaluating AI systems periodically is necessary to identify the presence of scenario bias in such models. Adapting AI Models Bias in the AI Understanding how bias affects our approach to web model development plays a role in maintaining fairness, inclusivity and ethical standards for AI technologies. This will help us work towards making AI more socially aware as we understand how bias comes in, why it exists, and what can be done to reduce its impact.

Discussion on Sources of Bias in Training Data, Algorithms, and Decision-Making Processes

That bias can come from several places during a model's development and deployment stages, such as training data, used algorithms or decision procedures. It is important to understand this provenance so that we are better placed to eliminate bias and ensure fairness when applying AI. AI Models Based on Training Data Might inadvertently mimic and perpetuate biases. Results may be confounded by historical inequalities and biases in the data (Nezami et al., 2024). Bias in data can contribute to these issues, along with biased data collections or a small diversity of datasets.

For instance, data where none of the majority group members are represented well would result in models trained to have higher error rates on those groups. Algorithms are essential to handling training data and making predictions (Raza et al., 2024; Sindiramtty et al. et al., 2024). How they are designed, and how configuration introduces new biases. There are several ways in which bias can occur while learning a model, including but not limited to using an incorrect assumption over how best to represent information using features or reinforcing already existing stereotypes (Nishant et al., 2023). For example, a model trained on data may learn to associate features with outcomes in ways that produce biased predictions.

This requires the decision maker to see the model's outputs and decide how he or she wants to act in response. Decisions and biases can manifest through judgment processes, beliefs, and institutional norms (Siniksaran, June 2024). Those who make decisions are subject to introducing biases when they interpret what an algorithm suggests or establish the criteria for decision-making. There might also be company cultures or reward systems that promote decision-making practices with unequal and unjust consequences. Finally, AI systems may be biased based on their training data or the properties of certain algorithms and even non-intentionally caused during method decisions. Addressing bias needs to be considered with a holistic approach - biases should and can be avoided from the design stage through development till they get implemented. Collecting datasets, making algorithms transparent and ensuring fairness in decision-making processes can help mitigate bias from AI applications.

Examination of Fairness Metrics and Techniques for Detecting and Mitigating Bias In Web Models

To ensure fairness in web models and encourage outcomes, it is important to detect them early so that human biases do not perpetuate these inequalities. This is a rich resource for researchers, developers, and policymakers, and it comprises metrics and strategies to detect and mitigate bias in web models. Moreover, we next have fairness metrics, measures for assessing the fairness of web models across demographic groups or protected attributes. Fairness metrics: Common fairness measures include the extent of equal rates and how else it performs on demographic parity (Lalor et al., 2024; Sindiramutty, 2023). Disparate impact looks at the differences in outcomes between groups, while equal opportunity wants to know if the model offers chances of outcomes across all groups.

In contrast, demographic parity considers how groups spread outcomes to achieve representation. Bias identification and reduction strategies in web models are either done at the pre-processing, in-modelling, or column-processing levels (Jui & Rivas, 2024). Pre-processing is manipulating the training data before you train your model to reduce bias through strategies such as Data Augmentation or re-weighting instances. Fairness constraints in processing methods are added to the training of models so that both fairness and accuracy are optimised at once. After training, post-processing approaches change the model outputs to enforce fairness through calibration or thresholding adjustments.

Moreover, before its execution in a deployment environment, it is very important to think of fairness while selecting models as well as validating the models in order that every stage during the development process affects fairness also (Rattanaphan & Briassouli, 2024; Sindiramutty et al. et al., 2024). Fairness-aware model selection techniques ensure that high-performing models are also fair across groups—other than that, optimally comprehensive validation procedures, including cross-validation and robustness testing. Understanding entirely how fairness interventions will work across real-world deployments is quite important.

Nevertheless, fairness metrics and techniques have limitations: they may fail to capture all the important aspects of a model's objectivity or be insufficient in repressing intersectional biases. Efforts to feature fairness interventions may also incur a trade-off concerning qualities such as accuracy or utility. This explains how metrics and techniques of fairness can help with model selection errors in web applications. You can contribute to building responsible web models by using these tools and grounding your model development work in fairness throughout. Figure 3 Methods for Bias Detection

Figure 3. Bias and Detection Method

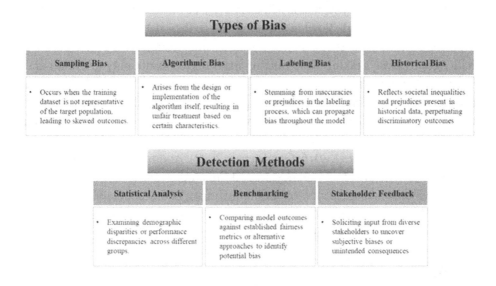

PRIVACY AND DATA PROTECTION

Analysis of Privacy Concerns Associated With Web Model Generation, Including Data Collection, Storage, and Usage

The use of methods to generate web models, widely applied in practice, has raised some concerns regarding data collection/storage/use privacy. These are fears related to collecting user data from websites and online platforms for use in algorithms that personalise recommendation advertising and track how people surf (Ahmed & Abdulkareem, 2023). What happens is a collecting activity, which can be defined as the collection of information such as browsing activities, searches on search engines for goods and services, location data or social interactions. One of the biggest concerns is how companies manage this data, as well as security practices and storage.

Data-at-Rest is associated with data stored on hard drives, and the proliferation of incidents involving Data Breaches and unauthorised Access highlights how susceptible this saved information can be to becoming exposed to either third parties (Gibson & Harfield, 2022; Sindiramutty et al. et al., 2024). In addition, the concerns mount due to a lack of transparency about data collection, which is largely unaccountable - users are usually unaware of what information has been collected and how much. Additionally, the application of user data in web-building models has questions regarding consent from users and their agency over personal information (Mhlanga, 2023). While legislation, such as GDPR, has gone a long way in empowering users with better privacy rights, it will ultimately be successful at ensuring action for securing consent and allowing users to manage their data.

There is additionally the chance of results ensuing from biases, which addresses challenges to always taking wide-ranging measures so as not only to avoid unfair discrimination but also to keep steadiness (Belen-Saglam et al., 23). To solve the privacy problems, a comprehensive strategy that encompasses technology solutions with regulatory and societal initiatives is imperative. Developing specific encryption protocols and security-compliant data stores can reduce access risks and risks of exposure breaches (O'Neil, 2016; Gouda et al., 2022). Additionally, data is collected so long as it maintains transparency around the process and controls are in place through consent management tools to improve trust and accountability with user information. The web model generation emerges with many challenges in the privacy of data collection, storage and usage (Adaga et al., 2024). This will demand industry, policymakers, and citizens' cooperation to define norms for ethically handling data in a digital age.

Discussion on Regulatory Requirements and Best Practices for Ensuring Data Protection and User Privacy in AI-Driven Web Applications

This topic becomes more urgent regarding the development of artificial intelligence-based web applications, which are fully conditioned by the same criteria for providing a qualitative mechanism for ensuring confidentiality and data security. Provide frameworks as guidelines to protect users' data and minimise processing dangers and AI algorithm algorithms (Hadzovic et al., 2023). Those already employing AI-driven web applications in their business must abide by rules and regulations such as GDPR in the EU or CCPA in the United States.

This legislation delineates a standard for aspects of data, including purchase, storage, evaluation and processing. E.g., the principle of collection limitation, purpose limitation, and accountability. In the same vein, they give insight into the type of data you hold on users as regards its usage by allowing them rights to their data, such as a right to access, which enables users to view part or all your stored details and also the right to rectification; through this steps, an individual can improve upon mistakes in whatever information you have about him/her. Compliance entails implementing appropriate technical and organisational measures to safeguard data while recognising the guiding principles of data protection, including privacy by design and accountability for processing operations.

AI applications should implement the best practices to enhance data security and user privacy in addition to legal requirements. Techniques like Differential Privacy, Federated Learning and Homomorphic encryption can be employed to analyse data while preserving the privacy of individuals (Wang et al., 2023; Sindiramutty & Pilli et al., 2024). Use privacy impact assessments and regular audits to assess whether there are any inherent privacy risks in AI algorithms or data processing processes. This also requires creating a privacy and compliance culture within organisations. By providing short, easy-to-read privacy notices and making it easier for people to opt out of data practices they dislike - while also informing them about their rights and options around controlling how/if their information is used in the first place.

This requires unprecedented collaboration between industry, academia and civil society to set the values, principles, rules, and procedures of ethical AI-based web applications creation and certification (Schaub et al., 2015; Taj & Jhanjhi, 2022). It is important to obey enforcement demands and best practices regarding data safety and user privacy in AI-pushed web applications. Organisations will earn users' trust while mitigating risks and protecting user rights in the digital age by respecting regulatory standards for privacy, choosing which technologies to deploy, retaining data privacy (privacy-preserving technologies), and adopting a culture around respect for end-users interests.

Examination of Privacy-Preserving Techniques and Anonymization Methods for Handling Sensitive Data in Web Model Generation

Privacy is a well-recognized impediment to the generation of web model data; however, some data can be considered sensitive. To overcome those, methods and techniques for data de-identification have been established to allow the practice of using data without compromising users' privacy. Differential privacy, as one of the basic and analysed strategies applied to this problem, offers an algorithmic model for noise addition to responses after queries so that a participant should not be identified (Ouadrhiri & Abdelhadi, 2022; Singhal et al., 2020).

Put differently, differential privacy is a way to add noise (anonymisation) around the results of queries so that we do not leak sensitive details about an individual while keeping general statistical accuracy. In the same way, instead of merging our sensitive data (Bonawitz Kallista et al., 2021), Federated learning is training ML models as it does. In this way, federated learning helps the model update computation run on the user device, and only their updates are shared with a central server, which reduces any other third party from leaking your data. It allows the training of shared models collaboratively, avoiding sharing data with other parties and realising privacy concerns.

Homomorphic encryption is also a powerful way to process encrypted data without decryption (Kumari et al., 2022) and prevents the information during processing time. Homomorphic encryption allows computations on encrypted data; this protects the data from being discovered by service providers and others generating web models. Other than those techniques, anonymising approaches remain a foundational practice for safeguarding sensitive information by concealing it using web models.

Anonymisation means to remove or mask any information that would help anyone ascertain the identity of those examined in a study (Majeed & Lee, 2021). Standard tactics of anonymisation with preservation for analysis and model development, such as generalisation, suppression, and perturbation, are common. However, there is always room for some issues with employing these privacy-preserving techniques and anonymisation methods to safely guarantee the data subjects' privacy while, at the same time, making sure that meaning remains in what was produced. A trade-off is almost always involved in the level of privacy that can be achieved and in how accurate models are trained on anonymised or perturbed data.

In addition, third parties could use more advanced re-identification attacks to de-anonymize so-called anonymised datasets while stressing the need for assessing and updating privacy tools regularly (Beigi & Liu, 2020; Humayun et al., 2022). Privacy protection and anonymisation practices are essential to reducing the harmful effects related to carrying sensitive data when creating web models. Differential privacy, federated learning, and homomorphic encryption alongside an anonymisation approach can help users learn from data while maintaining user privacy rights and confidentiality, even in large enterprises.

TRANSPARENCY AND EXPLAINABILITY

Introduction to Transparency and Explainability in AI Systems and Their Importance for Building Trust and Accountability

AI systems have slowly infiltrated every aspect of our lives, from health care and finance to transportation and entertainment. With the rise in popularity, they must be open and understanding about their work to have their users trust them. Transparency: The information on how the AI works, makes decisions, and can be explained. Explainability: Understanding in layperson whether it is possible to understand what the system makes. They are essential because they allow trust to be built, and AI systems can answer their behaviour (Novelli et al., 2023).

Transparent AI systems make it possible for users and any interested party to understand the output actions or computations taken by the system while generating some decisions (Balasubramaniam et al., 2023). Through this transparency, users can infer the credibility and objectivity of such decisions because an AI system provides a rationale for reaching these conclusions (Andrada et al., 2022; Almusaylim et al., 2018). It also allows insight from people to supervise and control AI systems' actions necessary for handling bias or even mistakes. Explainability is closely related to transparency and the output of AI systems.

An explainable AI system should, fundamentally, be able to do the legwork for explaining why it did what it did in a way that makes sense (this is not required, though) without needing some sort of technical understanding by the user as established by Haque et al., (2023). This property is more critical in high-stakes domains, such as healthcare and criminal justice, where AI decision-making directly affects human lives (Subramanian et al., 2024; Ghosh et al. In order to use trustful AI, you need transparency and explainability of (some) AIs. Once users understand how the AI systems arrive at that conclusion, they can trust and utilise it on their next decision-making point.

Also, by making AI solutions more transparent and explainable, bias-related issues and discrimination-privacy violations in AI can be conquered (Saeidnia et al., 2023; Wassan et al., 2021). Transparency and explainability are basic principles demanded in developing and deploying AI systems. Trust and accountability can be built by creating transparency so that users and stakeholders are part of the decision-making process. That way, all the benefits of AI are realised while simultaneously reducing risks and harms. Figure 4 shows Privacy and Protection Strategies.

Figure 4. Privacy and Protection Strategies

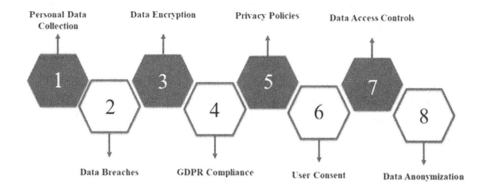

Explanation of Transparency Mechanisms and Techniques for Making AI-Driven Web Models More Interpretable and Understandable

For AI-based web models, the purpose behind transparency tools and methods is to make these models more interpretable or understandable by users. Transparency instruments represent various means of describing how AI models operate and justifying their decision-making process (Peters, 2022; Gaur et al., 2021). Model Reporting: All the necessary documentation of AI model architecture, training data and decision-making process is used. When developers record such aspects, they enable users to learn more about how the model works and which features tend to have which outputs.

Another metaphor of transparency is applicable analysis, which suggests w/ highlighting the most important aspects behind the AI model decisions (Samek & Müller, 2019; Almusaylim et al., 2020). In addition, by using the most common version of techniques to study feature importance in decision support models like permutation importance or SHAP (Shapley Additive exPlanations), developers gain a quantification of the impact that each has on determining the output stated with increasing interpretability (Fernandez-Loria et al., 2020). That is why the users need to know what features are used and which these models have learned to come up with a good interpretation of how it should behave and even decide if this method can still be trusted. Besides, visualisation techniques are indispensable in supercharging AI-based web models so that these could become more interpretable. Partial dependence plots, feature importance plots and decision trees can be employed for model interpretation — to understand how the input features influence predictive performance (Parr et al., 2024). Therefore, visualisations are tools that increase users' scrutiny of how the model processes input and reaches a decision, thus improving their trust in its results.

Also, explanations of AI model decision-making such as LIME and SHAP post-hoc explanation methods. The explanations generated by these methods take the form of local models, which approximate how the original model would behave in specific instances. Thus, they help users understand why a particular decision was made. Post-hoc explanation methods provide instance-level details that boost AI-driven web models' transparency and accountability. For a better understanding of AI-based web models, transparency mechanisms and tools are required. Strategies such as model documentation, feature importance analysis, visualisation and post-hoc explanation methods that are used correctly will assist developers in increasing the human interpretability of AI model outputs, leading to a more transparent, accountable web application with user trust.

Case Studies Illustrating the Benefits of Transparent and Explainable AI In Web Development and User Engagement

Case Study 1: Suggest-and-Elaborate Recommendations

For instance, one of the largest e-commerce platforms started using explainable, transparent AI to recommend products, which increased engagement (D. et al., 2024). To combat this, the site improved retention by telling users why it recommended an item based on their browsing and purchase history. Detailed recommendations energised the users to become more aware that some products are recommended, and this electrifying experience would bring them closer to The Purchase Zone. Additionally, users found it easy because of the openness of the AI system. They had greater confidence to make referrals, which helped increase customer satisfaction across the board and grow brand loyalty over time.

Case Study 2: Explainable Fraud Detection

One example is a financial services company applying explainable AI to the fraud detection system in order for the users to trust them (Mill et al., 2023; Hussain et al., 2019). The company might also elaborate on flagged transactions via feature importance analysis and post-hoc explanations. This helped to give the user a clear picture of why some transactions were detected as fraud, inducing a false alarm rate, hence efficiently detecting new fraudulent activities (Ahmadi, 2024; Sankar et al., 2020). The result, therefore, was that users were more convinced of the safety measures the company had taken, making their trust in it grow. Additionally, clear explanations enabled people to understand the signs of potential fraud and take action in financial transactions.

Case Study 3: Filter Moderation of Content

A social media platform employed explicit artificial intelligence models for content filtering and moderation to increase users' trust factor and activity -> (Marsoof et al., 2022; Fatima-Tuz-Zahra et. It helped the users know how they go on with filtering and flagging what content, which led to increased transparency and accountability. Users could understand why certain content has been removed or marked as obscene, which, in the long run, increases the credibility of the platform's content. In addition, the clear and comprehensible reasons allow users to understand platform practices to maintain a conducive environment while protecting user rights are important in enhancing satisfaction (Abbas et al., 2023; Khalil et al., 2021).

Hence, using case studies shows that explainable and transparent AI could benefit web development and users. It has also been observed that when users are given a clearer picture of how AI-driven decisions were reached, they can remain happier and more engaged with the organisation over time. Explainability and Transparency are required in an AI system, as they give a better user experience and keep the AI systems well-behaved.

ETHICAL DECISION-MAKING IN WEB MODEL GENERATION

Examination of Ethical Dilemmas and Challenges Faced by Developers and Stakeholders in AI-Driven Web Development

The younger of the block is AI-powered web development, which has not just disrupted how we do things precisely when it comes to building websites but has opened new gates in a way that can shape their future. Nevertheless, it is also important to mention that all these technological leaps bring up many moral dilemmas and questions for both the builders and stakeholders. This blog will specifically explore the primary ethical concerns of developing sites using artificial intelligence and discuss how they can be addressed. The only collection of ethics which is currently causing algorithm bias and discrimination, i.e. "Reproducing with hatred". Shams et al. One study (2023) demonstrated that facial recognition systems fit worse to women with dark-coloured complexions, perhaps because of bias. Further, given the black-box nature of AI systems, it is hard to identify and mitigate bias (Flores et al., 2023; Sindiramutty et al., 2024).

The final ethical concern can be said to maintain the privacy and security of the data collected. Because AI systems need massive quantities of personal data from the user, there is a vulnerability here for other parties to use that input to defraud or take advantage of your private affairs. An example of data abuse from social networks would be the case of Cambridge Analytica and its application to political campaigns.

Moreover, accountability is hugely important in AI web development. Developers and stakeholders will need to answer difficult questions about the culpability of AI systems when they fail or are wrong (Berman et al., 2024). Assigning blame is much more difficult when there are no rules about something. However, adopting AI technologies is accompanied by several hotly debated topics like taking away jobs and income disparity (Adigwe et al., 2024; Wen et al., 2023). Automation serves to rationalise processes and increase efficiency, but it can lead to job losses in certain work areas, possibly deepening socio-political imbalances.

The subject of this ethical issue surrounding AI for web development is vast, and that goes a long way to show the spectrum developers explorers before all stakeholders. The collective action of policymakers, business practitioners and ethicists seems to be the only way to solve these issues. As such, transparency, accountability, and inclusivity can be turned into a set of practical AI tools that solve both the general negative externalities of AI and the net positive societal impact.

Discussion on Ethical Decision-Making Frameworks and Strategies for Navigating Complex Ethical Considerations

Given the disparity of ethical issues seen within AI web development, it is more critical than ever that developers and stakeholders understand prudent decision-making frameworks and approaches. The principle-based approach is arguably the most familiar, founded on these four basic principles: autonomy, beneficence, and non-maleficence (Knapp, 2022). These can allow developers to modulate their behaviours with a view of the potential impacts on different stakeholders and ethics in doing things right. The teleological model is another pertinent model that uses the ends of actions to judge whether they are moral. For example, in AI for web development, this approach considers the bias and variance nature of each algorithm or technology that can be used (Rogowski & John, 2024; Sindiramutty et al., 2023).

In particular, developers would be required to weigh the externalities of the tool on society (recalling Harcourt) against costs themselves, like making racial biases worse or compromising an individual's privacy. In addition, virtue ethics describes the characters and morals applied in moral judgements (Shatilova, 2024; Sindiramutty et al., 2023). While there is nothing wrong with establishing that standard for developers to adhere to, it can improve organisational ethical responsibility, given the virtues of honesty, empathy, and integrity. This route also dives into how you do it, which is equally important, ensuring that one not only operates morally but also comports himself or herself ethically in their job. In addition to the formal models outlined, several further strategies will be invaluable for developers working with the tricky ethical questions raised by AI-based web development.

One of them is the increased transparency and accountability during the process in all phases. These developers allow open declaration of how AI systems work and the data behind them, helping users to make informed decisions and be accountable for their actions. Inviting stakeholders and experts who see decisions from different perspectives helps identify potential bias (Ahmadi, 2024a). For instance, ethicists, social scientists, and stakeholders from communities most likely to be affected by AI can give developers some insight into potential ethical issues their product may ultimately face (Regular et al., 2023).

Making ethical decisions in AI-based web development demands an amalgamation of theories and techniques. This is why it may be true that clear guidance can help developers navigate a minefield of ethical dilemmas in crafting responsible and ethical AI. These guidelines encompass the drill for obliging and evaluating the results of conformable ways and virtuous qualities besides clarity and solitariness.

Consideration of Real-World Scenarios and Examples to Illustrate Ethical Decision-Making Processes in Web Model Generation

Therefore, a phenotype of the ethical issues in web model generation (developer and stakeholder side) by analysing practical cases is very important. On a related note, predictive algorithms are finding their way into hiring decisions. It is, for instance, a reality that as artificial intelligence continues to expand its part in the hiring process, companies will need to be ethically agile when building online candidate screening tools. While these algorithms work to reduce the list of candidates by selecting those more likely (although not guaranteed) a good fit for the posting, they also may be biased against women or people of colour and any other minority(Albaroudi et al., 2024).

For this reason, the ethical challenge in a situation like this is to decide if developers should optimise their algorithms at the cost of discriminating users. Namely, has the algorithm been developed well, and is it free of discrimination, amongst other things? Recommendation Technologies—This can also be applied in Internet stores, like using AI-based recommendation technologies (Qureshi, 2024). These technologies leverage user data to suggest products based on trends and other factors, making shopping more enjoyable.

However, doubts creep in regarding the safety of disclosing personal data and fear that some control shapes consumer behaviour. In this case, findings that help inform judgmentEthically, the contemplated decision should include data collection and usage notification, including measures to empower user-administered information (Ehimuan et al., 2024). Figure 5: Transparency and Explainability in AI Systems

Figure 5. Transparency and Explainability in AI Systems

Importance of Transparency	Transparency fosters trust and accountability in AI systems, as users can understand how decisions are made and detect biases or errors. It also enables regulatory compliance and aids in troubleshooting and improving system performance.
Types of Transparency	Transparency can be categorized into various types, including algorithmic transparency data transparency (visibility into the data used by the AI system), and process transparency.
Explainability Techniques	Techniques such as model natural language generation and visualizations (e.g., heatmaps, decision trees) help enhance explainability in AI systems.
User Education and Interaction	Educating users about AI systems and providing interactive interfaces for exploring model outputs can empower them to better understand and trust AI-driven decisions.
Regulatory Landscape	Regulations such as the GDPR in Europe and guidelines from organizations like IEEE and the AI Ethics Guidelines by the European Commission emphasize the need for transparent and accountable A

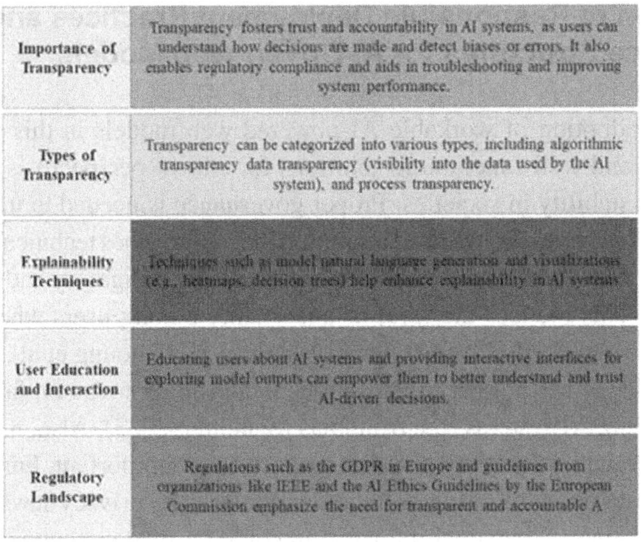

One can also look at how AI content moderation tools are used in social networks. While these systems are very useful in curbing hate speech and other illegal content, the potential for over-breadth exists without further context about different types of speech. Thus, the ethical concerns in moderation regard when it becomes unjust from a user-harm perspective and what to do about policies are poorly implemented.

Responsible web model generation involves many complex trade-offs and considerations that developers and stakeholders must grapple with in real-world situations. These examples show how ethical decision-making requires more than simply following principles and frameworks; it necessitates contextual awareness of the wider societal impacts of AI technologies. Developers can achieve a more ethical and socially positive application of web models by careful reflection and listening to different viewpoints.

RESPONSIBLE DEPLOYMENT AND GOVERNANCE

Exploration of Responsible Deployment Practices and Governance Structures for AI-Driven Web Models

Accurate adoption of workable AI-powered web models in this alive field to create robust and well-functioning solutions for ethical perspectives also leads to harmony and stability in societies. Proper governance is needed to underpin these principles. To achieve this, we need a solution that approaches technical, ethical, and legalities. AI algorithms and their decisions should be obligatory and open (Zerilli et al., 2018). This reduces the level of uncertainty among users when explaining how models are worked in web applications using AI (Choung et al., 2022).

Meanwhile, some thought organisations increasingly focus on fairness priorities and building AI systems free from bias (Saeidnia, 2023). Also, the application will need user data, so privacy and data protection are important. Furthermore, by using rigid data anonymisation methods and following privacy laws (e.g. GDPR standards), the users ' personal information could be made anonymous in a more secure way, as well (ŞahiN & Doğru, 2023). Moreover, the AI systems must be continuously monitored to identify and fix any bias or ethical issues that could arise from implementing AI.

Engagement among diverse actors - researchers, policymakers, industry practitioners and civil society organisations alike- is vital in formulating holistic governance structures for AI-driven web architectures (Robles & Mallinson, 2023). One of the best things to come from these collaborations is guidelines and other kinds of bet practices, both in terms of how AI can be used properly and how certain strategies are more useful than others. To this end, cross-sectoral discussions enrich pluralism and orchestration in governance strategies (Ho et al., 2023). Furthermore, other regulators and law enforcement need to supervise the correct implementation of AI so that organisations access the right approach.

This is how governments can gain control of the AI application and reduce risks with regulatory mechanisms regularly audited. Hence, it is significant in regulating AI-based web model applications and developing corresponding governance structures. Attributes of Good Governance Models: Transparency, Fairness, Privacy, Continuous Monitoring, Participation Regulation. Incorporating these ethics ever further into AI deployment processes will enable us to utilise the world-changing powers of AI while maintaining high ethical standards, complying with legal obligations, and safeguarding societal interests.

Discussion on the Role of Organizations, Policymakers, and Industry Stakeholders in Promoting Responsible AI Development and Usage

They play their part in developing and using AI responsibly in various organisations, policymakers, and industries. For both of these, groundwork needs to be laid out for policies and codes of conduct to create value through AI technologies for people while reducing risks. Businesses, research institutions, non-profit organisations—all the stakeholders in developing AI affect their interests and ethical concepts.

Therefore, an ethical analysis of AI solutions must be integrated into every stage of the development process. As Palladino (2023) says, considering the above, these are inclusions and contribute to ethical values like fairness to transparency followed by accountability inside AI governance systems of organisations. In addition, creating a climate of responsible innovation ensures that the employee recognises possible ethical issues and follows best practices when designing AI solutions.

Policymakers must ensure they create the right environment to use AI technologies responsibly. These rules are defined to ensure AI systems comply with ethical norms and the law (Paraman & Anamalah, 2022). This, in turn, means that policymakers have to bring many actors together while designing the regulations, which should not suppress innovation on its way and still ensure the public is protected all along. In addition, there must be provisions for supervision or control over AI solutions with punishment (Shah, 2023).

Technology companies, NGOs, and standards bodies envision a responsible future collaboration by industry stakeholders to establish ethical AI standards and best practices (Osasona et al., 2024). Thus, some of the main difficulties, like bias minimisation, privacy protection, and transparency within these algorithms, are dominant and should be handled by this kind of stakeholder (Saeidnia, 2023). AI ethics boards and certifications proposed by the industry can also create confidence in other consumers and stakeholders.

Ensuring the proper use and development of AI requires collaboration among companies, policymakers, and organisations in the industry. Effective collaboration among these will help increase the resourcefulness of strong frameworks, guidelines, and norms for ethical and responsible development and deployment of AI technologies. In the end, fostering a culture of responsible AI innovation is crucial to unleashing AI's full potential and protecting our societal values and interests.

Consideration of Mechanisms for Ensuring Ongoing Monitoring, Evaluation, and Accountability in Web Model Deployment

There also needs to be defined methodologies for understanding and recording those web models' effectiveness, validity, fairness, etc., if they are deployed over time. These strategies are crucial for dealing with potential biases, errors and ethical concerns that can inadvertently arise from the AI web models. Web models must be collected and compiled into performance data, then monitored and evaluated at all times. Ferrara (2023) explains that "monitoring allows stakeholders to track new behaviours in models, deteriorating performance or even identifying new biases. This is why web models are under verification at regular intervals to be sure that everything follows the ethics and principles. It also equips you to step in at the right time if things go off track or there are side effects.

Evaluation of web models is comparing their efficiency, effectiveness, and equity against criteria and standards. Continuous assessment is one way to assess web models' performance in daily practice. This includes evaluating the test set, performance for different sub-populations (such as a classification model's predictions across regions and years) and accuracy against fairness constraints. Evaluation could then be used to understand where the site is going in some of its web model deployment enhancement and improvement pathways. One facet of web model deployment liability is the work required to type all relationships, responsibilities, and remedies between AI systems manufacturing and usage roles.

In the paper by Raji et al. (2020), accountability structures are described as those that assign blame or inflict punishment on decisions and actions related to AI technologies. This involves documenting the creation of the model, the criteria used for decision making and who makes this decision. Further, procedures for complaints when web developers are ethically compromised or exhibit prejudicial conduct, thus enabling harm to users, must also be considered.

By incorporating the former measures into deploying web models, transparency and fairness are maintained between all parties. Organisations that develop and use web models should perform regular evaluations of their AI applications, accountability measures to minimise risks (risks), and bias control mechanisms to maintain operating ethics. Ultimately, these help us build good systems for AI that will be great for society, and its only downside would rather reduce potential harms.

COMMUNITY ENGAGEMENT AND STAKEHOLDER PARTICIPATION

Examination of the Importance of Community Engagement and Stakeholder Participation in AI-Driven Web Development

Introduction of Web-based AI Systems in Creation, Deployment and Adoption by Stakeholders: Meeting the People Element For a practical understanding language from stakeholders', web - Human cooperation researcher's (co-creation & stakeholder collaboration) POV.urlencoded attitude that governs human-social interaction shares hands with reasons behind process rather than culmination. In recent years, AI has seen rapid implementation into web development, revolutionising how users interact and get things done. However, the impact of AI-driven web development project effectiveness is largely determined by how communities and stakeholders engage during construction. Community engagement ensures that the consumers' requirements are attained through these AI web development projects (Ngabo-Woods, 2023). Developers can use these tactics to crowdsource ideas from the community that will be beneficial in improving web and application design and strengthening user experience; this approach of involving users also guarantees a user-friendly interface that is not for everyone else — one size fits all.

Also, building the ethical dimension and minimising AI algorithms' potential biases through stakeholder engagement are fundamental (Lancaster et al., 2023). Ethicists, policymakers and advocacy groups can be included to help developers detect problematic algorithm biases that may make machine discrimination more harmful as especially vulnerable populations become at risk for mistreatment. This enhances impact accountability in the organisation, fostering trust through wider stakeholder engagement and empowerment in the decision-making process on AI-based web development projects (Praveenraj et al., 2023) in addition to promoting equal opportunities and various stakeholders working in the community, which together have a role in improving diversity involving AI-driven web design.

In this way, developers will learn about the needs and problems experienced by different age groups, gender categories, etc. This means that this approach has the best coverage of websites using AI and helps create culturally sensitive, socially appealing web designs (Adams et al. Your AI-powered web solutions need to play an active role in the betterment of all these communities, and for that, you must ensure how your model approaches any ethical progression. Hence, developers creating AI web solutions can build enhanced, ethical and inclusive aids for the people when communities and stakeholders participate in the development of Artificial Intelligence. Figure 6 shows ethical decision-making in web model generation.

Figure 6. Ethical Decision-Making in Web Model Generation

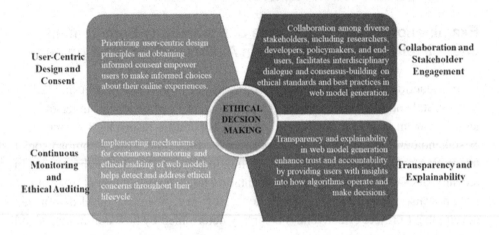

User-Centric Design and Consent

Prioritizing user-centric design principles and obtaining informed consent empower users to make informed choices about their online experiences.

Collaboration among diverse stakeholders, including researchers, developers, policymakers, and end-users, facilitates interdisciplinary dialogue and consensus-building on ethical standards and best practices in web model generation.

Collaboration and Stakeholder Engagement

ETHICAL DECSION MAKING

Continuous Monitoring and Ethical Auditing

Implementing mechanisms for continuous monitoring and ethical auditing of web models helps detect and address ethical concerns throughout their lifecycle.

Transparency and explainability in web model generation enhance trust and accountability by providing users with insights into how algorithms operate and make decisions.

Transparency and Explainability

Discussion on Inclusive Design Practices and Methodologies for Involving Diverse Perspectives in the Development Process

Diversity should be one of the core principles and practices in inclusive design and design for all. To get more diversity on board, we shall make a point of listening to many people involved in every step of the process. In the past few years, people have been more concerned about how physically challenged can be integrated into society because previous designs that were put in place did not offer anyone with less than physical ability any prospect. Well, because every time we design for accessibility — with honestly a limited set of criteria designed around differences in ability or cognitive processes– and ignore the fact that there are all these other things about people that will affect how they experience your designs, such as gender, race, ethnicity etc.

Tai et al. (2022) defined an inclusive design principle based on the way different people are involved in designing. Therefore, developers can gain more insights regarding people's needs and pain points across various backgrounds. Such participation ensures that consumers will have a wide selection of products and services, creativity, and originality in designing, as individuals from diverse backgrounds are involved.

This paper thoroughly discusses these issues of empathy and culture in ID approaches (Walczak et al., 2023). This means developers need to work extra hard to understand their users' different abilities, cultures, and experiences. The practice here is to read between the lines from what users say, survey them, and, most importantly, do usability testing with your target audience. In this way, empathy allows developers to create more ubiquitous technologies that meet the needs of a wider user diversity (Gunatilake et al., 2023).

Furthermore, design-inclusive processes are established to apply variability and adjustability for users' daily diverse needs (Agboola & Tunay, 2023). That means providing things a user may modify to suit his or her needs, comfort and disability. This is where the developer needs the design to be flexible so that users can make products and services more fitted into their context, helping in being worked almost anywhere (Korczak, 2023); by doing this, there will be greater inclusivity of products or services.

Practices and methodologies for inclusive design are paramount to diversity, equity, and inclusion-horizontal growth. Essentially, options like involving diverse perspectives, orienting for empathy and cultural differences, or bending the design with flexibility will help reach all users in more accessible ways.

Case Studies Highlighting Successful Examples of Community-Driven AI Projects and Their Impact on Web Model Generation

They showed in the paper that collective intelligence and embracement of plurality can significantly alter web model creation. These "whole site" models aim to be more robust to the web and include participation design methods in conjunction with crowd-sourced collectives. Examples of community AI projects and how they have affected web model generation The best-known example of a platform is Wikipedia, one among the páginas de filologia — an online encyclopedia where information contributed by Internet users has been extended, becoming very large (Zoccali & Mallamaci, 2023).

Wikipedia's model of the web has continued to grow with coverage in every topic and discipline, a consequence of having millions of volunteers from across the globe. Information in Wikipedia is constantly updated because it gets its information from contributions all over the world, as diverse as those who are using the platform to solicit online information.

In the "real world", a similar anecdote of an editing service is OpenStreetMap (OSM), where people can enter new geographical information and modify existing data (Biljecki et al., 2023). OSM is an amazing and relatively accurate web model of Earth's geography created by numerous global volunteers. Using data from the map community has created a new market based on geographical information. You can use it in many applications and services like navigation, disaster relief, and city planning apps.

Moreover, machine learning libraries like TensorFlow from Google and Py-Torch of Facebook have made AI development easy for developers to prove their models work because they are open source (Widder et al., 2023). These platforms cum innovations have facilitated the developer community with shared code and knowledge on AI, thereby birthing active cross-organization project participation in AI research and development work. Making AI technologies more accessible, these initiatives have allowed several different audiences to create and use web models with AI functionality designed in mind.

In summary, web model building has unveiled community-driven AI projects as change agents that blossomed innovation through their robust approach towards the more universal and holistic points of a warble for creating diverse, inclusive, dynamic vigour, steered Web models. These initiatives have changed how web models are built, rebuilt, and used through the collective intelligence of communities, providing a more inclusive model for AI-driven web development.

REGULATORY COMPLIANCE AND LEGAL IMPLICATIONS

Overview of Regulatory Frameworks and Legal Requirements Governing AI-Driven Web Development

AI is vital in developing difficult features, wealthy and customised net sites. On the other hand, using AI in web development leads to new legal and normative unloading that developers must observe to avoid litigation from another side of reality if they begin using this technology. Security and privacy are huge areas of concern in AI and web development. It imposes such a tight discipline so that no one can dare to peek behind your door unless they are approved (Sim et al., 2023), and laws like the GDPR in the EU or CCPA in the United States curb user data collection and processing and storage on very rigorous guidelines favouring privacy rights of its peoples.

AI-powered web development also requires transparency and accountability. AI algorithms should be accountable, transparently working, and comprehensible on demand by regulations such as GDPR's right to explanation (Moratinos & De Hert, 2023). Moreover, IPRs are essential in creating AI-based websites on the World Wide Web. When artificial intelligence is used to produce new work or adaptation, developers must follow copyright principles because they must have some license and permission before using the copyrighted content (Vesala, 2023). Finally, The use of AI in web development must comply with certain legal requirements.

For example, HIPAA is the Health Insurance Portability and Accountability Act in the USA, which, together with the Patient Protection Act, governs how web-based healthcare applications must secure the private contents of patients (Meslamani, 2023). Numerous laws and legal acts govern AI-minded web development, from the rights of end users to what technology must comply with rules over transparency for those — or things — making decisions on behalf of companies. Web developers must be careful when overcoming these regulations to avoid committing legal violations and support AIs used for good aims on the internet. Figure 7: Community Engagement and Stakeholder Interaction Role in AI-enabled Web Development

Figure 7. Importance of Community Engagement and Stakeholder Participation in AI-Driven Web Development

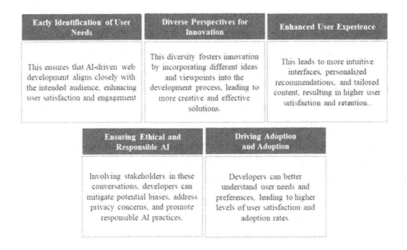

Discussion on Compliance Considerations Related to Data Protection, Discrimination, Accessibility, and Other Relevant Regulations

When building AI in web development, it is important to comply with several ethical and legal norms. The privacy protection band could also be included, particularly concerning changes in the GDPR and CCPA. The rules these regulations put in place for companies are hardwired to high standards for processing users' information, acquiring consent, restricting how this data can be used, and ensuring that adequate security arrangements are implemented (Grover, 2023). This is related to warnings released recently on misuse of social media sites or lack of data privacy by parties giving rise to cyber-lawsuits; it is necessary that regulations be followed, and one cannot add too many reasons; this is activation securing safety for ordinary life from being bothering in sentiments ore exposing private properties through use without nobody having permission.

Equally important is the problem of non-discrimination, as stated in the anti-discrimination laws. AI algorithms used in web development should not be biased or discriminate against individuals based on attributes such as race, gender, and age. Laws such as FCRA and GDPR also dictate that information about automated decisions must be accurate if shared with the user (not just kept undisclosed for proprietary reasons). However, the outcomes must be fair, so web applicants with artificial intelligence should not discriminate against those who will use those developed applications, and policies should check these biases.

A further concern is accessibility in web development regulations. Websites/Applications must follow the web content accessibility guidelines, say WCAG, to enable people with disabilities. Ignoring accessibility standards leads to falling foul of the law and could also translate into missed opportunities with less engagement in content (Panda & Kaur, 2023). Respect the laws on intellectual property in each legal system, as there may be copyright infringement and using an illegal entity. When developers use AI to generate content or create new works utilising copyrighted material, they need the correct permission or license.

It is a lot easier to adhere to copyrights than not because it helps protect the property rights of authors and inventors, increasing the possibility for good things to happen in terms of new ideas (Yas et al., 2025). Data protection, non-discrimination (discrimination), accessibility and intellectual property rights are compliance issues that must be observed in the ethical and legal development of websites with AI. Developers can minimise these risks while benefiting from user confidence and responsible AI advancement in web development by following the proper regulations and best practices.

Examination of the Role of Legal Frameworks in Promoting Ethical AI Practices and Ensuring Accountability in Web Model Generation

This paper proves that legal systems are key to AI ethics and the accountability of the web model generation process. Developers should adhere to these guidelines, policies, and procedures when designing AI-based web models. One major point is to promote ethics in AI. The GDPR and the CCPA address transparency, fairness, and accountability through rights-oriented provisions in AI-driven systems (Wei & Liu, 2024). Engineers are supposed to "bake in" explainability, combat bias, and guard consumer privacy. Therefore, legal frameworks for AI are an attempt to inject ethical principles into the design and development of AI so as not to trigger some negative effects that might be fostered due to the wide diffusion thereof.

In addition, legal factors play a crucial role in providing accountability for web model generation via AI. Many laws like GDPR will concentrate on the organisation's accountability for legally processing personal data (Bharti & Aryal, 2022). Item 1: Web model generation must retain the use of AI algorithms in a record, do a risk assessment that needs to be realised like what are risky features using statistics (DAST/SAST) or manual threat checking upstream chain and take proper measure only had been applied ("How to stop misuse the data") against them In this way, legal systems establish the norms and standards of accountability that makes developers accountable to users and society in general. In addition, the legal criteria ensure transparent and accountable production of web models created by AI.

Legal regulations such as the GDPR and the right to explanation require wider information on how AI algorithms work so that users can comprehend how an automated decision has been reached (Di Studi Giuridici, 2023). In addition, audits/reviews by the respective regulating authorities ensure that these AI systems comply with legally required requirements, which further helps build trust in any solution. In summary, the legal coverage will help enforce ethical AI practices and place accountability for web model generation. These frameworks help guide the responsible development and use of AI technologies in web development by offering a blueprint to increase accountability, clarity, and transparency. A higher-level view of AI-driven regulatory frameworks and legal requirements is shown in Figure 8.

Figure 8. Overview of Regulatory Frameworks and Legal Requirements Governing AI-Driven

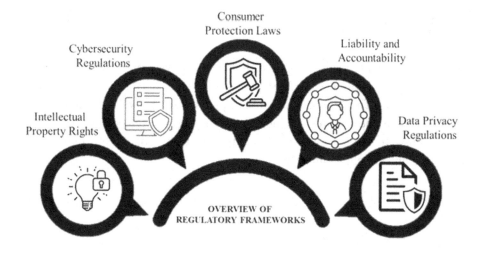

CONCLUSION

Summary of Key Insights and Takeaways From the Chapter

In this chapter, we discuss two key aspects of creating web models - a part quintessential to AI-driven web development - ethics and transparency. Practical reasons to consider ethical claims are reflected in some main conclusions, such as the insights these paradigmatic cases provide about upcoming levels (i.e. model development and application), their implications for trust, responsibility, social welfare, etc. Mercury ML is an open scheme to inculcate these values, following the ethical principles of EAI (equity, accountability, openness, and privacy) when building any AI system.

A careful analysis reveals biased training data, biased algorithms and decision-making rather than a problem with a fair model for the web. However, the conversation also lays out general frameworks and approaches for identifying and mitigating bias, establishing that prevention efforts are needed in a fair employment context. The importance of privacy and data protection issues to be taken into consideration during the generation of the web model, complying with regulations regarding data protection also discussed throughout this chapter, emphasising all over again the necessity for following anything done legally and applying how preservative methods aim at protecting users' information.

In doing so, transparency and explainability are paramount in building trust with the user, as they will need to understand how these procedures work. The examples speak for themselves—these methods catch users' attention and save them from potential dangers. The Ethical decision-making guidelines and AI principles serve as a guide to making decisions on ethical issues, together with the responsible use of AI systems or technology for its deployment actions; community involvement allows everyone´s opinion to be heard throughout the development process.

Last but not least, the regulation and legal side are indispensable in ensuring non-compliance with ethics while being liable for our work based on AI technology. In this chapter, the author strongly emphasises Ethics and Transparency as a viable path forward to define future development patterns of the web with aid from AI, requiring stakeholders to make Ethical and transparent developments which target creating innovative technological-driven advanced technologies but simultaneously sustainable and ethical technology.

Reflection on the Importance of Ethics and Transparency in Web Model Generation and Their Implications for Future AI-Driven Web Development

Ethics and transparency in web model creation will be incredibly important to guide AI-powered innovation on the web. The results of this chapter pay attention to the fact that these ideas are not "abstract" but, on the contrary, represent principles informing responsible and sustainable technology development. Ethics serve as a moral compass for developers, designers, policymakers, and stakeholders who contribute to web model creation, ensuring that built models are developed ethically and considering the impact on individuals, communities, and society. In that case, transparency will improve trust in AI systems and foster user understanding of how they work to make decisions about their use.

Ethics and transparency should be prioritised in web model generation. Adopting these principles in AI-led web development will cultivate a responsible innovation culture that prioritises human well-being and societal values. This includes adhering to ethical principles and standards, meaningfully engaging with diverse perspectives, and incorporating stakeholder engagement throughout decision-making. Moreover, acting ethically and transparently leads to developing technically high-quality AI systems that correspond with social values.

We can minimise potential harms and maximise the positive impact of AI on individuals and communities by tackling issues related to bias, fairness, privacy and accountability. There is more to generating web models ethically and transparently than ticking boxes required by industry-standard frameworks or regulations. They are a pledge to uphold values of fairness, justice and respect for human dignity in the design and use of AI systems. Now, as we navigate the complexities of an ever-more-interconnected world, these same guiding principles will lead us into a future in which technology is harnessed for the common good of all humanity.

Call to Action for Developers, Designers, Policymakers, and Stakeholders to Prioritize Ethical Considerations and Transparency in AI-Driven Web Development Practices

As AI-driven web development is rapidly evolving, the importance of ethical considerations and transparency in deploying and using web models cannot be overemphasised. We seek developers, designers, policymakers, and stakeholders to enlist the principles by which ethics need to be embedded everywhere, from data collection and model training to deployment and monitoring.

This includes following tech ethics, bias detection and response mechanisms, and design for privacy-by-design principles. Second, we need better collaboration between policymakers and industry experts on more comprehensive regulations designed to encourage ethical (but also innovative!) AI use. It is important that legislation protects our privacy, prevents discrimination and promotes accountability of AI systems. Thirdly, stakeholders from different fields must participate in discussions and collaborate to enable openness and accountability in AI-wielded web development. Facilitate a culture of transparency and information sharing, foster inter-disciplinary collaboration, and support initiatives that rank ethical processing foremost.

It is up to us how we want AI-powered web development in the future to go on with integrity and transparency. Together, we will iterate them into a creative, ethical, equitable and durable digital milieu for developers and design stakeholders in the future. This potential can not be fully exploited at the expense of user rights, the health and well-being of users or society as a whole, which is only possible through collaboration and shared responsibility.

REFERENCES

Abbas, S., Alnoor, A., Teh, S. Y., Sadaa, A. M., Muhsen, Y. R., Khaw, K. W., & Ganesan, Y. (2023). Antecedents of trustworthiness of social commerce platforms: A case of rural communities using multi-group SEM & MCDM methods. *Electronic Commerce Research and Applications*, 62, 101322. DOI:10.1016/j.elerap.2023.101322

Adaga, E. M., Egieya, Z. E., Ewuga, S. K., Abdul, A. A., & Abrahams, T. O. (2024). Philosophy in business analytics: a review of sustainable and ethical approaches. *International Journal of Management & Entrepreneurship Research*, 6(1), 69–86. DOI:10.51594/ijmer.v6i1.710

Adams, A. J., Miller-Lewis, L., & Tieman, J. (2023). Learning Designers as Expert Evaluators of Usability: Understanding their potential contribution to improving the universality of interface design for health resources. *International Journal of Environmental Research and Public Health*, 20(5), 4608. DOI:10.3390/ijerph20054608 PMID:36901617

Adigwe, C. S., Olaniyi, O. O., Olabanji, S. O., Okunleye, O. J., Mayeke, N. R., & Ajayi, S. S. (2024). Forecasting the Future: The Interplay of Artificial Intelligence, Innovation, and Competitiveness and its Effect on the Global Economy. *Asian Journal of Economics. Business and Accounting*, 24(4), 126–146. DOI:10.9734/ajeba/2024/v24i41269

Agarwal, A., & Agarwal, H. (2023). A seven-layer model with checklists for standardising fairness assessment throughout the AI lifecycle. *AI and Ethics*. Advance online publication. DOI:10.1007/s43681-023-00266-9

Agarwal, A., Agarwal, H., & Agarwal, N. (2022). Fairness Score and process standardisation: Framework for fairness certification in artificial intelligence systems. *AI and Ethics*, 3(1), 267–279. DOI:10.1007/s43681-022-00147-7

Agboola, O. P., & Tunay, M. (2023). Urban resilience in the digital age: The influence of Information-Communication Technology for sustainability. *Journal of Cleaner Production*, 428, 139304. DOI:10.1016/j.jclepro.2023.139304

Ahmadi, S. (2024a). A Comprehensive Study on Integration of Big Data and AI in Financial Industry and its Effect on Present and Future Opportunities. *International Journal of Current Science Research and Review*, 07(01). Advance online publication. DOI:10.47191/ijcsrr/V7-i1-07

Ahmadi, S. (2024b). Open AI and its Impact on Fraud Detection in Financial Industry. *Journal of Knowledge Learning and Science Technology ISSN 2959-6386 (Online), 2*(3), 263–281. DOI:10.60087/jklst.vol2.n3.p281

Ahmed, A., & Abdulkareem, A. M. (2023, June 1). *Big data analytics in the entertainment industry: audience behaviour analysis, content recommendation, and revenue maximisation.* https://researchberg.com/index.php/rcba/article/view/142

Albahri, A. S., Duhaim, A. M., Fadhel, M. A., Alnoor, A., Baqer, N. S., Alzubaidi, L., Albahri, O. S., Alamoodi, A. H., Bai, J., Salhi, A., Santamaría, J., Ouyang, C., Gupta, A., Gu, Y., & Deveci, M. (2023). A systematic review of trustworthy and explainable artificial intelligence in healthcare: Assessment of quality, bias risk, and data fusion. *Information Fusion*, 96, 156–191. DOI:10.1016/j.inffus.2023.03.008

Albaroudi, E., Mansouri, T., & Alameer, A. (2024). A comprehensive review of AI techniques for addressing algorithmic bias in job hiring. *AI*, 5(1), 383–404. DOI:10.3390/ai5010019

Almusaylim, Z. A., Jhanjhi, N. Z., & Alhumam, A. (2020). Detection and Mitigation of RPL rank and version number attacks in the internet of things: SRPL-RP. *Sensors (Basel)*, 20(21), 5997. DOI:10.3390/s20215997 PMID:33105891

Almusaylim, Z. A., Jhanjhi, N. Z., & Jung, L. T. (2018). Proposing A Data Privacy Aware Protocol for Roadside Accident Video Reporting Service Using 5G In Vehicular Cloud Networks Environment. *2018 4th International Conference on Computer and Information Sciences (ICCOINS)*. DOI:10.1109/ICCOINS.2018.8510588

Alsamiri, J., & Alsubhi, K. (2023). Federated Learning for Intrusion Detection Systems in Internet of Vehicles: A General Taxonomy, Applications, and Future Directions. *Future Internet*, 15(12), 403. DOI:10.3390/fi15120403

Ananna, F. F., Nowreen, R., Jahwari, S. S. R. A., Costa, E., Angeline, L., & Sindiramutty, S. R. (2023). Analysing Influential factors in student academic achievement: Prediction modelling and insight. *International Journal of Emerging Multidisciplinaries Computer Science & Artificial Intelligence*, 2(1). Advance online publication. DOI:10.54938/ijemdcsai.2023.02.1.254

Andrada, G., Clowes, R. W., & Smart, P. R. (2022). Varieties of transparency: Exploring agency within AI systems. *AI & Society*, 38(4), 1321–1331. DOI:10.1007/s00146-021-01326-6 PMID:35035112

Azam, H., Dulloo, M. I., Majeed, M. H., Wan, J. P. H., Xin, L. T., & Sindiramutty, S. R. (2023). Cybercrime Unmasked: Investigating cases and digital evidence. *International Journal of Emerging Multidisciplinaries Computer Science & Artificial Intelligence*, 2(1). Advance online publication. DOI:10.54938/ijemdcsai.2023.02.1.255

Azam, H., Dulloo, M. I., Majeed, M. H., Wan, J. P. H., Xin, L. T., Tajwar, M. A., & Sindiramutty, S. R. (2023). Defending the digital Frontier: IDPS and the battle against Cyber threat. *International Journal of Emerging Multidisciplinaries Computer Science & Artificial Intelligence*, 2(1). Advance online publication. DOI:10.54938/ijemdcsai.2023.02.1.253

Azam, H., Tajwar, M. A., Mayhialagan, S., Davis, A. J., Yik, C. J., Ali, D., & Sindiramutty, S. R. (2023). Innovations in Security: A study of cloud Computing and IoT. *International Journal of Emerging Multidisciplinaries Computer Science & Artificial Intelligence*, 2(1). Advance online publication. DOI:10.54938/ijemdcsai.2023.02.1.252

Azam, H., Tan, M., Pin, L. T., Syahmi, M. A., Qian, A. L. W., Jingyan, H., Uddin, H., & Sindiramutty, S. R. (2023). Wireless Technology Security and Privacy: A Comprehensive Study. *Preprint*. DOI:10.20944/preprints202311.0664.v1

Balasubramaniam, N., Kauppinen, M., Rannisto, A., Hiekkanen, K., & Kujala, S. (2023). Transparency and explainability of AI systems: From ethical guidelines to requirements. *Information and Software Technology*, 159, 107197. DOI:10.1016/j.infsof.2023.107197

Beigi, G., & Liu, H. (2020). A survey on privacy in social media. *ACM/IMS Transactions on Data Science*, 1(1), 1–38. DOI:10.1145/3343038

Belen-Saglam, R., Altuncu, E., Lü, Y., & Li, S. (2023). A systematic literature review of the tension between the GDPR and public blockchain systems. *Blockchain: Research and Applications*, 4(2), 100129. DOI:10.1016/j.bcra.2023.100129

Beltrán, E. T. M., Gómez, Á. L. P., Cao, F., Sánchez, P. M. S., Bernal, S. L., Bovet, G., Pérez, M. G., Pérez, G. M., & Celdrán, A. H. (2023). *FedStellar: a platform for decentralized federated learning. arXiv*. Cornell University., DOI:10.1016/j.eswa.2023.122861

Berman, A., De Fine Licht, K., & Carlsson, V. (2024). Trustworthy AI in the public sector: An empirical analysis of a Swedish labor market decision-support system. *Technology in Society*, 102471, 102471. Advance online publication. DOI:10.1016/j.techsoc.2024.102471

Bharti, S. S., & Aryal, S. K. (2022). The right to privacy and an implication of the EU General Data Protection Regulation (GDPR) in Europe: Challenges to the companies. *Journal of Contemporary European Studies*, 31(4), 1391–1402. DOI: 10.1080/14782804.2022.2130193

Biljecki, F., Chow, Y. S., & Lee, K. (2023). Quality of crowdsourced geospatial building information: A global assessment of OpenStreetMap attributes. *Building and Environment*, 237, 110295. DOI:10.1016/j.buildenv.2023.110295

Bonawitz, K., Kairouz, P., McMahan, B., & Ramage, D. (2021). Federated learning and privacy. *ACM Queue; Tomorrow's Computing Today*, 19(5), 87–114. DOI:10.1145/3494834.3500240

Carullo, G. (2023). Large language models for transparent and intelligible AI-Assisted public Decision-Making. air.unimi.it. DOI:10.13130/2723-9195/2023-3-100

Casillas, J. (2023). Bias and discrimination in Machine Decision-Making systems. In *The International library of ethics, law and technology* (pp. 13–38). DOI:10.1007/978-3-031-48135-2_2

Chakraborty, D. (2023). Copyright Challenges in the Digital Age: Balancing intellectual property rights and data privacy in India's online ecosystem. *Social Science Research Network*. DOI:10.2139/ssrn.4647960

Chavalarias, D., Bouchaud, P., & Panahi, M. (2024). Can a single line of code change society? The systemic risks of optimizing engagement in recommender systems on global information flow, opinion dynamics and social structures. *Journal of Artificial Societies and Social Simulation*, 27(1), 9. Advance online publication. DOI:10.18564/jasss.5203

Choung, H., David, P., & Ross, A. (2022). Trust in AI and its role in the acceptance of AI technologies. *International Journal of Human-Computer Interaction*, 39(9), 1727–1739. DOI:10.1080/10447318.2022.2050543

Chughtai, M.S. *et al.* (2023). 'Deep learning trends and future perspectives of web security and vulnerabilities,' *Journal of High Speed Networks*, pp. 1–32. .DOI:10.3233/JHS-230037

De Farias, V. E., Brito, F. T., Flynn, C., Machado, J. C., Majumdar, S., & Srivastava, D. (2023). Local dampening: Differential privacy for non-numeric queries via local sensitivity. *The VLDB Journal*, 32(6), 1191–1214. DOI:10.1007/s00778-022-00774-w

Dhinakaran, D., Sankar, S., Selvaraj, D., & Raja, S. E. (2024). Privacy-Preserving Data in IoT-based Cloud Systems: A Comprehensive Survey with AI Integration. *arXiv (Cornell University)*. https://doi.org//arxiv.2401.00794DOI:10.48550

Di Studi Giuridici, D. (2023, June 28). *The challenges of the General Data Protection Regulation to protect data subjects against the adverse effects of artificial intelligence*. https://iris.unibocconi.it/handle/11565/4058474

Ehimuan, B., Chimezie, O. O., Akagha, O. V., Reis, O., & Oguejiofor, B. B. (2024). Global data privacy laws: A critical review of technology's impact on user rights. *World Journal of Advanced Research and Reviews*, 21(2), 1058–1070. DOI:10.30574/wjarr.2024.21.2.0369

Fatima-Tuz-Zahra. Jhanjhi, N. Z., Brohi, S. N., & Malik, N. A. (2019). Proposing a Rank and Wormhole Attack Detection Framework using Machine Learning. *2019 13th International Conference on Mathematics, Actuarial Science, Computer Science and Statistics (MACS)*. DOI:10.1109/MACS48846.2019.9024821

Fernández-Loría, C., Provost, F., & Han, X. (2020). Explaining Data-Driven Decisions made by AI Systems: The Counterfactual Approach. *arXiv (Cornell University)*. https://doi.org//arxiv.2001.07417DOI:10.48550

Ferrara, E. (2023). Should ChatGPT be biased? Challenges and risks of bias in large language models. *First Monday*. Advance online publication. DOI:10.5210/fm.v28i11.13346

Ferrara, E. (2024). The Butterfly Effect in artificial intelligence systems: Implications for AI bias and fairness. *Machine Learning with Applications*, 15, 100525. DOI:10.1016/j.mlwa.2024.100525

Flores, L., Kim, S., & Young, S. D. (2023). Addressing bias in artificial intelligence for public health surveillance. *Journal of Medical Ethics*, jme-108875. DOI:10.1136/jme-2022-108875

Gaur, L., Afaq, A., Solanki, A., Singh, G., Sharma, S., Jhanjhi, N. Z., My, H. T., & Le, D. (2021). Capitalizing on big data and revolutionary 5G technology: Extracting and visualizing ratings and reviews of global chain hotels. *Computers & Electrical Engineering*, 95, 107374. DOI:10.1016/j.compeleceng.2021.107374

Ghosh, G., Kavita, , Verma, S., Jhanjhi, N. Z., & Talib, M. N. (2020). Secure surveillance system using chaotic image encryption technique. *IOP Conference Series. Materials Science and Engineering*, 993(1), 012062. DOI:10.1088/1757-899X/993/1/012062

Gibson, D., & Harfield, C. (2022). Amplifying victim vulnerability: Unanticipated harm and consequence in data breach notification policy. *International Review of Victimology*, 29(3), 341–365. DOI:10.1177/02697580221107683

Gouda, W., Almufareh, M. F., Humayun, M., & Jhanjhi, N. Z. (2022). Detection of COVID-19 based on chest x-rays using deep learning. *Health Care*, 10(2), 343. DOI:10.3390/healthcare10020343 PMID:35206957

Grover, R. (2023). Accounting for Indeterminacy: The Trouble with Transparency(ies) in Data Protection Compliance Work. *Social Science Research Network*. DOI:10.2139/ssrn.4577409

Gu, X., Sabrina, F., Fan, Z., & Sohail, S. (2023). A review of privacy enhancement methods for federated learning in healthcare systems. *International Journal of Environmental Research and Public Health*, 20(15), 6539. DOI:10.3390/ijerph20156539 PMID:37569079

Gunatilake, H., Grundy, J., Mueller, I., & Hoda, R. (2023). Empathy models and software engineering — A preliminary analysis and taxonomy. *Journal of Systems and Software*, 203, 111747. DOI:10.1016/j.jss.2023.111747

Gupta, N. (2023). Artificial Intelligence Ethics and Fairness: A study to address bias and fairness issues in AI systems, and the ethical implications of AI applications. *Revista Review Index Journal of Multidisciplinary*, 3(2), 24–35. DOI:10.31305/rrijm2023.v03.n02.004

Hadzovic, S., Mrdović, S., & Radonjić, M. (2023). A path towards an internet of things and artificial intelligence regulatory framework. *IEEE Communications Magazine*, 61(7), 90–96. DOI:10.1109/MCOM.002.2200373

Haque, A. B., Islam, A. K. M. N., & Mikalef, P. (2023). Explainable Artificial Intelligence (XAI) from a user perspective: A synthesis of prior literature and problematizing avenues for future research. *Technological Forecasting and Social Change*, 186, 122120. DOI:10.1016/j.techfore.2022.122120

He, K., Mao, R., Lin, Q., Ruan, Y., Liu, X., Feng, M., & Cambria, E. (2023). A Survey of Large Language Models for Healthcare: from Data, Technology, and Applications to Accountability and Ethics. *arXiv (Cornell University)*. https://doi.org//arxiv.2310.05694DOI:10.48550

Ho, Y., Chen, B. Y., Li, C., & Chai, E. (2023). The distance between the humanities and medicine: Building a critical thinking mindset by interdisciplinary dialogue through mind mapping. *Thinking Skills and Creativity*, 50, 101420. DOI:10.1016/j.tsc.2023.101420

Holmes, L., Crossley, S. A., Sikka, H., & Morris, W. (2023). PIILO: An open-source system for personally identifiable information labeling and obfuscation. *Information and Learning Science*, 124(9/10), 266–284. DOI:10.1108/ILS-04-2023-0032

Hosain, M. T., Anıt, K. M. H., Rafi, S., Tabassum, R., Insî, A. K., & Siddiky, M. M. (2023). Path to gain functional transparency in artificial intelligence with meaningful explainability. *Journal of Metaverse*, 3(2), 166–180. DOI:10.57019/jmv.1306685

Humayun, M., Ashfaq, F., Jhanjhi, N. Z., & Alsadun, M. K. (2022). Traffic management: Multi-Scale vehicle detection in varying weather conditions using YOLOV4 and spatial pyramid pooling network. *Electronics (Basel)*, 11(17), 2748. DOI:10.3390/electronics11172748

Husairi, M. A., & Rossi, P. (2024). Delegation of purchasing tasks to AI: The role of perceived choice and decision autonomy. *Decision Support Systems*, 179, 114166. DOI:10.1016/j.dss.2023.114166

Hussain, S. J., Ahmed, U., Liaquat, H., Mir, S., Jhanjhi, N. Z., & Humayun, M. (2019). IMIAD: Intelligent Malware Identification for Android Platform. *2019 International Conference on Computer and Information Sciences (ICCIS)*. DOI:10.1109/ICCISci.2019.8716471

Jui, T. D., & Rivas, P. (2024). Fairness issues, current approaches, and challenges in machine learning models. *International Journal of Machine Learning and Cybernetics*, 15(8), 3095–3125. Advance online publication. DOI:10.1007/s13042-023-02083-2

Kaplan, B. A., Gilroy, S. P., DeHart, W. B., Brown, J. M., & Koffarnus, M. N. (2023). Data handling: ethical principles, guidelines, and recommended practices. In *Elsevier eBooks* (pp. 191–214). DOI:10.1016/B978-0-323-90969-3.00006-2

Khalil, M. I., Jhanjhi, N. Z., Humayun, M., Sivanesan, S., Masud, M., & Hossain, M. S. (2021). Hybrid smart grid with sustainable energy efficient resources for smart cities. *Sustainable Energy Technologies and Assessments*, 46, 101211. DOI:10.1016/j.seta.2021.101211

Khosravi, H., Shum, S. B., Chen, G., Conati, C., Gašević, D., Kay, J., Knight, S., Martínez-Maldonado, R., Sadiq, S., & Tsai, Y. (2022). Explainable Artificial Intelligence in education. *Computers & Education: Artificial Intelligence*, 3, 100074. DOI:10.1016/j.caeai.2022.100074

Kizza, J. M. (2024) 'Computer Network Security Protocols,' in *Texts in computer science*, pp. 409–441. DOI:10.1007/978-3-031-47549-8_18

Knapp, S. (2022). Listen, explain, involve, and evaluate: Why respecting autonomy benefits suicidal patients. *Ethics & Behavior*, 34(1), 18–27. DOI:10.1080/105084 22.2022.2152338

Kolberg, J., Schäfer, Y., Rathgeb, C., & Busch, C. (2024). On the Potential of Algorithm Fusion for Demographic Bias Mitigation in Face Recognition. *IET Biometrics*, 2024, 1–18. DOI:10.1049/2024/1808587

Korczak, A. (2023). *Designing for Programming Without Coding : User experience of mobile low-code software*. DIVA. https://www.diva-portal.org/smash/record.jsf ?pid=diva2%3A1764478&dswid=-4147

Kumar, D., & Suthar, N. (2024). Ethical and legal challenges of AI in marketing: an exploration of solutions. *Journal of Information, Communication and Ethics in Society*. DOI:10.1108/JICES-05-2023-0068

Kumar, D. S., Madhavi, K., Ramprasad, T., Sekhar, K. R., Dhanikonda, S. R., & Ravi, C. (2024, February 23). *Design and Development of Data-Driven Product Recommender Model for E-Commerce using Behavioral Analytics*. https://ijisae .org/index.php/IJISAE/article/view/4884

Kumari, K., Sharma, A., Chakraborty, C., & Ananyaa, M. (2022). Preserving health care data security and privacy using Carmichael's Theorem-Based Homomorphic encryption and modified enhanced homomorphic encryption schemes in edge computing systems. *Big Data*, 10(1), 1–17. DOI:10.1089/big.2021.0012 PMID:34375143

Kushwaha, A. K., Pharswan, R., Kumar, P., & Kar, A. K. (2022). How do users feel when they use artificial intelligence for decision making? a framework for assessing users' perception. *Information Systems Frontiers*, 25(3), 1241–1260. DOI:10.1007/ s10796-022-10293-2

Laínez, N., & Gardner, J. (2023). Algorithmic credit scoring in Vietnam: A legal proposal for maximizing benefits and minimizing risks. *Asian Journal of Law and Society*, 10(3), 401–432. DOI:10.1017/als.2023.6

Lalor, J. P., Abbasi, A., Oketch, K., Yang, Y., & Forsgren, N. (2024). Should Fairness be a Metric or a Model? A Model-based Framework for Assessing Bias in Machine Learning Pipelines. *ACM Transactions on Information Systems*, 42(4), 1–41. Advance online publication. DOI:10.1145/3641276

Lancaster, C., Schulenberg, K., Flathmann, C., McNeese, N. J., & Freeman, G. (2023). *"It's Everybody's Role to Speak Up. . . But Not Everyone Will": Understanding AI Professionals' Perceptions of Accountability for AI Bias Mitigation*. ACM Journal on Responsible Computing. DOI:10.1145/3632121

Landers, R. N., & Behrend, T. S. (2023a). Auditing the AI auditors: A framework for evaluating fairness and bias in high stakes AI predictive models. *The American Psychologist*, 78(1), 36–49. DOI:10.1037/amp0000972 PMID:35157476

Landers, R. N., & Behrend, T. S. (2023b). Auditing the AI auditors: A framework for evaluating fairness and bias in high stakes AI predictive models. *The American Psychologist*, 78(1), 36–49. DOI:10.1037/amp0000972 PMID:35157476

Laux, J., Wachter, S., & Mittelstadt, B. (2023). Trustworthy artificial intelligence and the European Union AI act: On the conflation of trustworthiness and acceptability of risk. *Regulation & Governance*. Advance online publication. DOI:10.1111/rego.12512 PMID:38435808

Majeed, A., & Lee, S. (2021). Anonymization Techniques for Privacy Preserving Data Publishing: A Comprehensive survey. *IEEE Access : Practical Innovations, Open Solutions*, 9, 8512–8545. DOI:10.1109/ACCESS.2020.3045700

Marsoof, A., Luco, A., Tan, H., & Joty, S. (2022). Content-filtering AI systems–limitations, challenges and regulatory approaches. *Information & Communications Technology Law*, 32(1), 64–101. DOI:10.1080/13600834.2022.2078395

Meslamani, A. Z. A. (2023). Gaps in digital health policies: An insight into the current landscape. *Journal of Medical Economics*, 26(1), 1266–1268. DOI:10.1080/13696998.2023.2266955 PMID:37789607

Mhlanga, D. (2023). Open AI in Education, The responsible and ethical use of ChaTGPT towards lifelong Learning. *Social Science Research Network*. DOI:10.2139/ssrn.4354422

Mill, E., Garn, W., Ryman-Tubb, N., & Turner, C. (2023). Opportunities in real Time Fraud Detection: An explainable Artificial Intelligence (XAI) research agenda. *International Journal of Advanced Computer Science and Applications*, 14(5). Advance online publication. DOI:10.14569/IJACSA.2023.01405121

Mohamed, A. (2023). A systematic literature review of authorization and access control requirements and current state of the art for different database models. *International Journal of Web Information Systems*. .DOI:10.1108/IJWIS-04-2023-0072

Moratinos, G. L., & De Hert, P. (2023). Humans in the GDPR and AIA governance of automated and algorithmic systems. Essential pre-requisites against abdicating responsibilities. *Computer Law & Security Report*, 50, 105833. DOI:10.1016/j.clsr.2023.105833

Munjal, K., & Bhatia, R. (2022). A systematic review of homomorphic encryption and its contributions in healthcare industry. *Complex & Intelligent Systems*, 9(4), 3759–3786. DOI:10.1007/s40747-022-00756-z PMID:35531323

Mylrea, M., & Robinson, N. (2023). Artificial Intelligence (AI) Trust Framework and Maturity Model: Applying an entropy lens to improve security, privacy, and ethical AI. *Entropy (Basel, Switzerland)*, 25(10), 1429. DOI:10.3390/e25101429 PMID:37895550

Nasir, S., Khan, R. A., & Bai, S. (2024). Ethical framework for harnessing the power of AI in healthcare and beyond. *IEEE Access : Practical Innovations, Open Solutions*, 1, 31014–31035. Advance online publication. DOI:10.1109/ACCESS.2024.3369912

Nezami, N., Haghighat, P., Gándara, D., & Anahideh, H. (2024). Assessing Disparities in predictive modeling outcomes for college student success: The impact of imputation techniques on model performance and fairness. *Education Sciences*, 14(2), 136. DOI:10.3390/educsci14020136

Ngabo-Woods, H. (2023). Insights Beyond Functionality: Empowering Digital Mental Health User Experiences Through Participatory Engagement and Evaluation. *Preprint*. DOI:10.20944/preprints202311.1572.v1

Nishant, R., Schneckenberg, D., & Ravishankar, M. N. (2023). The formal rationality of artificial intelligence-based algorithms and the problem of bias. *Journal of Information Technology*. Advance online publication. DOI:10.1177/02683962231176842

Novelli, C., Taddeo, M., & Floridi, L. (2023). Accountability in artificial intelligence: What it is and how it works. *AI & Society*. Advance online publication. DOI:10.1007/s00146-023-01635-y

Osasona, F., Amoo, O. O., Atadoga, A., Abrahams, T. O., Farayola, O. A., & Ayinla, B. S. (2024). Reviewing the ethical implications of AI in decision making processes. *International Journal of Management & Entrepreneurship Research*, 6(2), 322–335. DOI:10.51594/ijmer.v6i2.773

Ouadrhiri, A. E., & Abdelhadi, A. (2022). Differential Privacy for deep and federated Learning: A survey. *IEEE Access : Practical Innovations, Open Solutions*, 10, 22359–22380. DOI:10.1109/ACCESS.2022.3151670

Palladino, N. (2023). A 'biased' emerging governance regime for artificial intelligence? How AI ethics get skewed moving from principles to practices. *Telecommunications Policy*, 47(5), 102479. DOI:10.1016/j.telpol.2022.102479

Pan, S., Hoang, T., Zhang, D., Xing, Z., Xu, X., Lu, Q., & Staples, M. (2023). Toward the cure of privacy policy reading phobia: Automated Generation of privacy nutrition labels from privacy policies. *arXiv (Cornell University)*. https://doi.org//arxiv.2306.10923DOI:10.48550

Panda, S., & Kaur, N. (2023). Web Content Accessibility Guidelines 3.0. In *Advances in educational marketing, administration, and leadership book series* (pp. 246–269). DOI:10.4018/978-1-6684-8737-2.ch012

Paraman, P., & Anamalah, S. (2022). Ethical artificial intelligence framework for a good AI society: Principles, opportunities and perils. *AI & Society*, 38(2), 595–611. DOI:10.1007/s00146-022-01458-3

Parr, T., Wilson, J. D., & Hamrick, J. (2024). Nonparametric feature impact and importance. *Information Sciences*, 653, 119563. DOI:10.1016/j.ins.2023.119563

Peters, U. (2022). Explainable AI lacks regulative reasons: Why AI and human decision-making are not equally opaque. *AI and Ethics*, 3(3), 963–974. DOI:10.1007/s43681-022-00217-w

Pöhn, D., Gruschka, N., Ziegler, L., & Büttner, A. (2023). A framework for analyzing authentication risks in account networks. *Computers & Security*, 135, 103515. DOI:10.1016/j.cose.2023.103515

Praveenraj, D. D. W., Victor, M., Vennila, C., Alawadi, A. H., Diyora, P., Vasudevan, N., & Avudaiappan, T. (2023). Exploring explainable artificial intelligence for transparent decision making. *E3S Web of Conferences, 399*, 04030. DOI:10.1051/e3sconf/202339904030

Qureshi, J. (2024). AI-Powered Cloud-Based E-Commerce: Driving Digital Business Transformation Initiatives. *Preprints*. DOI:10.20944/preprints202401.2214.v1

Raji, I. D., Smart, A., White, R. N., Mitchell, M., Gebru, T., Hutchinson, B., Smith-Loud, J., Theron, D., & Barnes, P. (2020). *Closing the AI accountability gap*. ACM., DOI:10.1145/3351095.3372873

Rattanaphan, S., & Briassouli, A. (2024). Evaluating generalization, bias, and fairness in deep learning for metal surface defect detection: A comparative study. *Processes (Basel, Switzerland)*, 12(3), 456. DOI:10.3390/pr12030456

Raza, S., Garg, M., Reji, D. J., Bashir, S. R., & Ding, C. (2024). Nbias: A natural language processing framework for BIAS identification in text. *Expert Systems with Applications*, 237, 121542. DOI:10.1016/j.eswa.2023.121542

Regulwar, G. B., Mahalle, A. M., Pawar, R., Shamkuwar, S. K., Kakde, P. R., & Tiwari, S. (2023). Big data collection, filtering, and extraction of features. In *Advances in business information systems and analytics book series* (pp. 136–158). DOI:10.4018/979-8-3693-0413-6.ch005

Robles, P., & Mallinson, D. J. (2023). Catching up with AI: Pushing toward a cohesive governance framework. *Politics & Policy*, 51(3), 355–372. DOI:10.1111/polp.12529

Rogowski, W., & John, J. (2024). Preferences as fairness judgments: A critical review of normative frameworks of preference elicitation and development of an alternative based on constitutional economics. *Cost Effectiveness and Resource Allocation*, 22(1), 10. Advance online publication. DOI:10.1186/s12962-024-00510-x PMID:38291472

Rosário, A. T., & Dias, J. C. (2023). How has data-driven marketing evolved: Challenges and opportunities with emerging technologies. *International Journal of Information Management Data Insights*, 3(2), 100203. DOI:10.1016/j.jjimei.2023.100203

Saeidnia, H. R. (2023). Ethical artificial intelligence (AI): Confronting bias and discrimination in the library and information industry. *Library Hi Tech News*. Advance online publication. DOI:10.1108/LHTN-10-2023-0182

Sáez-De-Cámara, X., Flores, J. L., Arellano, C., Urbieta, A., & Zurutuza, U. (2023). Clustered federated learning architecture for network anomaly detection in large scale heterogeneous IoT networks. *Computers & Security*, 131, 103299. DOI:10.1016/j.cose.2023.103299

Sag, M. (2023). Copyright safety for generative AI. *Social Science Research Network*. DOI:10.2139/ssrn.4438593

Şahin, Y., & Doğru, İ. A. (2023). An enterprise data privacy governance model: Security-Centric Multi-Model data Anonymization. *Uluslararası Mühendislik Araştırma Ve Geliştirme Dergisi*. DOI:10.29137/umagd.1272085

Samek, W., & Müller, K. R. (2019). Towards explainable artificial intelligence. In *Lecture Notes in Computer Science* (pp. 5–22). DOI:10.1007/978-3-030-28954-6_1

Sampaio, S., Sousa, P. R., Martins, C., Ferreira, A., Antunes, L., & Cruz-Correia, R. (2023). Collecting, processing and secondary using personal and (Pseudo)Anonymized data in smart cities. *Applied Sciences (Basel, Switzerland)*, 13(6), 3830. DOI:10.3390/app13063830

Sanderson, C., Douglas, D., Qing-Hua, L., Schleiger, E., Whittle, J., Lacey, J., Newnham, G., Hajkowicz, S., Robinson, C. J., & Hansen, D. (2023). AI Ethics Principles in Practice: Perspectives of Designers and Developers. *IEEE Transactions on Technology and Society*, 4(2), 171–187. DOI:10.1109/TTS.2023.3257303

Sankar, S., Ramasubbareddy, S., Luhach, A. K., Deverajan, G. G., Alnumay, W. S., Jhanjhi, N. Z., Ghosh, U., & Sharma, P. K. (2020). Energy efficient optimal parent selection based routing protocol for Internet of Things using firefly optimization algorithm. *Transactions on Emerging Telecommunications Technologies*, 32(8), e4171. Advance online publication. DOI:10.1002/ett.4171

Schaub, F., Balebako, R., Durity, A. L., & Cranor, L. F. (2015). *A design space for effective privacy notices*. USENIX Association. https://www.usenix.org/conference/soups2015/proceedings/presentation/schaub

Shah, V. (2023, December 30). *Striking a balance: Ethical considerations in AI-Driven law enforcement*. https://redc.revistas-csic.com/index.php/Jorunal/article/view/159

Shams, R. A., Zowghi, D., & Bano, M. (2023). AI and the quest for diversity and inclusion: A systematic literature review. *AI and Ethics*. Advance online publication. DOI:10.1007/s43681-023-00362-w

Shatilova, I. (2024). *A virtue ethics approach to the ethicality of employee empowerment*. https://jyx.jyu.fi/handle/123456789/93101

Shin, D. (2021). Embodying algorithms, enactive artificial intelligence and the extended cognition: You can see as much as you know about algorithm. *Journal of Information Science*, 49(1), 18–31. DOI:10.1177/0165551520985495

Sim, J., Kim, B., Jeon, K., Joo, M., Lim, J., Lee, J., & Choo, K. R. (2023). Technical requirements and approaches in personal data control. *ACM Computing Surveys*, 55(9), 1–30. DOI:10.1145/3558766

Simson, J., Pfisterer, F., & Kern, C. (2023). Everything, everywhere all in one Evaluation: using multiverse analysis to evaluate the influence of model design decisions on algorithmic fairness. *arXiv (Cornell University)*. https://doi.org//arxiv.2308.16681DOI:10.48550

Sindiramutty, S. R. (2023). Autonomous Threat Hunting: a future paradigm for AI-Driven Threat intelligence. *arXiv (Cornell University)*. https://doi.org//arxiv.2401.00286DOI:10.48550

Sindiramutty, S. R., Jhanjhi, N. Z., Tan, C., Yun, K. J., Manchuri, A. R., Ashraf, H., Murugesan, R. K., Tee, W. J., & Hussain, M. (2024). Data security and privacy concerns in drone operations. In *Advances in information security, privacy, and ethics book series* (pp. 236–290). DOI:10.4018/979-8-3693-0774-8.ch010

Sindiramutty, S. R., Jhanjhi, N. Z., Tan, C. E., Khan, N. A., Gharib, A. H., & Yun, K. J. (2023). Applications of blockchain technology in supply chain management. In *Advances in logistics, operations, and management science book series* (pp. 248–304). DOI:10.4018/978-1-6684-7625-3.ch009

Sindiramutty, S. R., Jhanjhi, N. Z., Tan, C. E., Khan, N. A., Shah, B., & Gaur, L. (2023). Securing the digital supply chain cyber threats and vulnerabilities. In *Advances in logistics, operations, and management science book series* (pp. 156–223). DOI:10.4018/978-1-6684-7625-3.ch007

Sindiramutty, S. R., Jhanjhi, N. Z., Tan, C. E., Khan, N. A., Shah, B., Yun, K. J., Ray, S. K., Jazri, H., & Hussain, M. (2024). Future trends and emerging threats in drone cybersecurity. In *Advances in information security, privacy, and ethics book series* (pp. 148–195). DOI:10.4018/979-8-3693-0774-8.ch007

Sindiramutty, S. R., Jhanjhi, N. Z., Tan, C. E., Tee, W. J., Lau, S. P., Jazri, H., Ray, S. K., & Zaheer, M. A. (2024). IoT and AI-Based Smart Solutions for the Agriculture Industry. In *Advances in computational intelligence and robotics book series* (pp. 317–351). DOI:10.4018/978-1-6684-6361-1.ch012

Sindiramutty, S. R., Tan, C., Tee, W. J., Lau, S. P., Balakrishnan, S., Kaur, S. D. A., Jazri, H., & Aslam, M. (2024). Modern smart cities and open research challenges and issues of explainable artificial intelligence. In *Advances in computational intelligence and robotics book series* (pp. 389–424). DOI:10.4018/978-1-6684-6361-1.ch015

Sindiramutty, S. R., Tan, C., & Wei, G. W. (2024). Eyes in the sky. In *Advances in information security, privacy, and ethics book series* (pp. 405–451). DOI:10.4018/979-8-3693-0774-8.ch017

Sindiramutty, S. R., Tan, C. E., Lau, S. P., Thangaveloo, R., Gharib, A. H., Manchuri, A. R., Khan, N. A., Tee, W. J., & Muniandy, L. (2024). Explainable AI for cybersecurity. In *Advances in computational intelligence and robotics book series* (pp. 31–97). DOI:10.4018/978-1-6684-6361-1.ch002

Sindiramutty, S. R., Tan, C. E., Shah, B., Khan, N. A., Gharib, A. H., Manchuri, A. R., Muniandy, L., Ray, S. K., & Jazri, H. (2024). Ethical considerations in drone cybersecurity. In *Advances in information security, privacy, and ethics book series* (pp. 42–87). DOI:10.4018/979-8-3693-0774-8.ch003

Sindiramutty, S. R., Tee, W. J., Balakrishnan, S., Kaur, S., Thangaveloo, R., Jazri, H., Khan, N. A., Gharib, A. H., & Manchuri, A. R. (2024). Explainable AI in healthcare application. In *Advances in computational intelligence and robotics book series* (pp. 123–176). DOI:10.4018/978-1-6684-6361-1.ch005

Singha, S. (2024). Unveiling gender dynamics in digital capitalism. In *Advances in finance, accounting, and economics book series* (pp. 161–186). DOI:10.4018/979-8-3693-1182-0.ch009

Singhal, V., Jain, S. P., Anand, D., Singh, A., Verma, S., Kavita, , Rodrigues, J. J. P. C., Jhanjhi, N. Z., Ghosh, U., Jo, O., & Iwendi, C. (2020). Artificial Intelligence Enabled Road Vehicle-Train Collision Risk Assessment Framework for Unmanned railway level crossings. *IEEE Access : Practical Innovations, Open Solutions*, 8, 113790–113806. DOI:10.1109/ACCESS.2020.3002416

Siniksaran, E. (2024). *Overcoming cognitive biases in strategic management and decision making*. IGI Global. DOI:10.4018/979-8-3693-1766-2

Stahl, B. C., & Eke, D. (2024). The ethics of ChatGPT – Exploring the ethical issues of an emerging technology. *International Journal of Information Management*, 74, 102700. DOI:10.1016/j.ijinfomgt.2023.102700

Subramanian, H. V., Canfield, C., & Shank, D. B. (2024). Designing explainable AI to improve human-AI team performance: A medical stakeholder-driven scoping review. *Artificial Intelligence in Medicine*, 149, 102780. DOI:10.1016/j.artmed.2024.102780 PMID:38462282

Tai, J., Dollinger, M., Ajjawi, R., De St Jorre, T. J., Krattli, S., McCarthy, D., & Prezioso, D. (2022). Designing assessment for inclusion: An exploration of diverse students' assessment experiences. *Assessment & Evaluation in Higher Education*, 48(3), 403–417. DOI:10.1080/02602938.2022.2082373

Taj, I., & Jhanjhi, N. Z. (2022). Towards Industrial Revolution 5.0 and Explainable Artificial Intelligence: Challenges and opportunities. *International Journal of Computing and Digital Systems*, 12(1), 285–310. DOI:10.12785/ijcds/120124

Tang, F., & Østvold, B. M. (2023). Transparency in App Analytics: Analyzing the Collection of User Interaction Data. *Transparency in App Analytics: Analyzing the Collection of User Interaction Data*. DOI:10.1109/PST58708.2023.10320181

Theodorou, A., & Tubella, A. A. (2024). Responsible AI at work: incorporating human values. In *Edward Elgar Publishing eBooks* (pp. 32–46). DOI:10.4337/9781800889972.00010

Tikkinen-Piri, C., Rohunen, A., & Markkula, J. (2018). EU General Data Protection Regulation: Changes and implications for personal data collecting companies. *Computer Law & Security Report*, 34(1), 134–153. DOI:10.1016/j.clsr.2017.05.015

Usman, H., Tariq, I., & Nawaz, B. (2023). In the realm of the machines: AI's influence upon international law and policy. *Journal of Social Research Development*, 4(2), 383–399. DOI:10.53664/JSRD/04-02-2023-13-383-399

Vesala, J. (2023). Developing Artificial Intelligence-Based Content Creation: Are EU copyright and antitrust law fit for purpose? *IIC - International Review of Intellectual Property and Competition Law, 54*(3), 351–380. DOI:10.1007/s40319-023-01301-2

Villegas-Ch, W., & García-Ortiz, J. (2023). Toward a comprehensive framework for ensuring security and privacy in artificial intelligence. *Electronics (Basel)*, 12(18), 3786. DOI:10.3390/electronics12183786

Walczak, R., Koszewski, K., Olszewski, R., Ejsmont, K., & Kálmán, A. (2023). Acceptance of IoT Edge-Computing-Based sensors in smart cities for universal design purposes. *Energies*, 16(3), 1024. DOI:10.3390/en16031024

Wang, B., Li, H., Guo, Y., & Wang, J. (2023). PPFLHE: A privacy-preserving federated learning scheme with homomorphic encryption for healthcare data. *Applied Soft Computing*, 146, 110677. DOI:10.1016/j.asoc.2023.110677

Wassan, S., Chen, X., Shen, T., Waqar, M., & Jhanjhi, N. Z. (2021). Amazon Product Sentiment Analysis using Machine Learning Techniques. *International Journal of Early Childhood Special Education (INT-JECSE), 30*(1), 695. https://doi.org/DOI:10.24205/03276716.2020.2065

Wei, W., & Liu, L. (2024). Trustworthy distributed AI systems: Robustness, privacy, and governance. *ACM Computing Surveys*, 3645102. Advance online publication. DOI:10.1145/3645102

Wen, B. O. T., Syahriza, N., Xian, N. C. W., Wei, N., Shen, T. Z., Hin, Y. Z., Sindiramutty, S. R., & Nicole, T. Y. F. (2023). Detecting cyber threats with a Graph-Based NIDPS. In *Advances in logistics, operations, and management science book series* (pp. 36–74). DOI:10.4018/978-1-6684-7625-3.ch002

Widder, D. G., West, S. M., & Whittaker, M. (2023). Open (For Business): big tech, concentrated power, and the political economy of open AI. *Social Science Research Network*. DOI:10.2139/ssrn.4543807

Williamson, S. E., & Prybutok, V. R. (2024). Balancing Privacy and Progress: A review of privacy challenges, systemic oversight, and patient perceptions in AI-Driven healthcare. *Applied Sciences (Basel, Switzerland)*, 14(2), 675. DOI:10.3390/app14020675

Yas, N., Elyat, M. N. I., Saeed, M., Shwedeh, F., & Lootah, S. (2024, February 1). *The impact of intellectual property rights and the work environment on information security in the United Arab Emirates.* https://kurdishstudies.net/menu-script/index.php/KS/article/view/1681

Zerilli, J., Knott, A., Maclaurin, J., & Gavaghan, C. (2018). Transparency in Algorithmic and Human Decision-Making: Is there a double standard? *Philosophy & Technology*, 32(4), 661–683. DOI:10.1007/s13347-018-0330-6

Zhanbayev, R., Irfan, M., Shutaleva, A., Maksimov, D., Abdykadyrkyzy, R., & Filiz, Ş. (2023). Demoethical Model of Sustainable Development of Society: A Roadmap towards Digital Transformation. *Sustainability (Basel)*, 15(16), 12478. DOI:10.3390/su151612478

Zoccali, C., & Mallamaci, F. (2023). Reimagining peer review: The emergence of peer community in registered reports system. *Journal of Nephrology*, 36(9), 2407–2411. DOI:10.1007/s40620-023-01709-6 PMID:37594669

Chapter 13
Future Trends and Trials in Cybersecurity and Generative AI

Venkat Narayana Rao T.
Sreenidhi Institute of Science and Technology, India

Harsh Vardhan G.
Sreenidhi Institute of Science and Technology, India

Krishna Sai A. N.
Sreenidhi Institute of Science and Technology, India

Bhavana Sangers
https://orcid.org/0009-0005-6134-1081
Sreenidhi Institute of Science and Technology, India

ABSTRACT

The relationship between the fields of generative (AI) and cybersecurity offers both opportunity and danger as technology continues to grow at an unimaginable rate. The emergence of 5G networks and the spread of internet of things (IoT)-connected devices are changing the challenging landscape in the field of cybersecurity. The predictions point to an increase in complex cyberattacks using AI-driven strategies like adversarial machine learning and deepfake methods. Simultaneously, content manipulation are being revolutionized by the rise of generative AI technologies such as deep learning and GANs (generative adversarial networks). The AI-generated synthetic media contributes to existing problems with digital trust and authenticity by posing moral questions about identity theft and disinformation. In conclusion, managing the intersection of cybersecurity and generative AI requires proactive

DOI: 10.4018/979-8-3693-5415-5.ch013

steps to fully utilize AI's potential while minimizing its inherent risks. This chapter includes solutions like anomaly detection systems and AI-powered threat intelligence.

1. INTRODUCTION

It is quite an important branch of the digital reality that has had great impact both during the operational process and during active defence in the last years is the combination of cybersecurity and generative AIs. We find one subcategory of AI applications called "generative AI" which is capable of creating original content (writing, visual, audio, or even computer code) using knowledge gathered from data that has already been collected. Cybersecurity as compared to information security, covers the protection of computer networks, operating systems and data from being misused, damaged or stolen by someone else.

1.1 Rapid Technological Advancements

Cybersecurity and generative AI technologies are developing at a rate never seen before, powered by a number of important factors(Gupta et.al,2023):

A. Machine Learning Breakthroughs

The abilities of the generative artificial intelligence models have been developed significantly by the achievement and advancement made in the field of machine learning, specifically in the area of deep learning. AI technologies capable of generating sophisticated and completely real data like image and speech recognition have become attainable through methodologies such as transformers, variational autoencoders (VAEs) and generative adversarial networks (GANs).

B. Data Quality and Availability

Data for generative AI models have been made in sufficient quantity because of the growth of digital data as well as its collection and storage methods. Because there is a plenty of data, AI systems can complete the process of learning the complex patterns even the nuances, which makes them productive in the correctness and sophistication of their outputs.

C. Computational Power

Its training era made much effortless due to GPU and TPU powerful computing resources. As a result, cybersecurity, which relies heavily on AI, is one of the fields that has received more advanced solutions sooner than others, these solutions being consequence of hardware breakthroughs.

D. Issues With Cybersecurity

The creation of innovative cybersecurity solutions has been stimulated by the fact that the nature of cyber threats has been getting more sophisticated in nature and it currently encompasses various attacks including phishing and malware. Such evolving threats beyond the grasp of conventional cyber techniques involving rules-based systems and pattern-based detection are always more dynamic.

E. Adversarial Capabilities

AI and machine learning tools which are being more and more used by malicious actors cybercriminals, state-sponsored hackers and malicious insiders — result in more and more complex attacks. It is definitely necessary for cybersecurity professionals to use AI-originated defence strategies, in response to the malicious usage of AI which has presented a number of complications.

F. Regulatory Environment

Organizations have to follow stringent rules when it comes to data protection and privacy, underpinned by legal frameworks such as the CCPA and GDPR Besides that, we recommend to implement challenging cybersecurity solutions, for instance, AI-powered detection and reaction tools which will be able to follow these laws.

Cybersecurity in times of Generative AI and cybersecurity is going to be a paradigm shift in the area of information security. And this is going to be possible only by adopting AI solutions quickly and cybersecurity professionals monitoring closely. More and more AI applications penetrate different types of industries, so these technologies are to be used with care to protect private data and repulse potential attacks. Besides AI's remarkable future in cybersecurity, the problems that come with AI's bias, accountability, and transparency also need to be rightfully tackled. In order to promote the ethical and equitable deployment of AI-driven solutions and not to fall behind, the need for an appropriate balance in terms of ethical deployment and innovation is inevitable. The cybersecurity experts will acquire the ability to navigate the world of cybersecurity which is dynamic and changing by fostering a culture of attentiveness and integrity. AI could be used by top organisations to enhance their firewalls and assure them ethical norms are followed while they establish a relationship of trust in their cybersecurity methods (Dhoni et.al,2023).

2. IMPACT OF 5G AND IOT ON CYBERSECURITY

With the integration of 5G networks and IoT devices, the surface exposed for attack has drastically risen forcing the management of extensive number of standards for heterogeneous ecosystems. Additionally, the high speed, low latency capability of 5G networks enable quicker data transmission giving room to the development of IoT devices and more sensitive data. On the other hand, this drives privacy concerns. To combat these problems, multilayered procedures which include software upgrades with a high degree of security, security protocols that are constantly renewed to prevent new threats that arise from the 5G and IOT ecosystem in which technology evolves rapidly (Rajasekar et.al,2022; Tarikere et.al,2021).

2.1 Transformation of Cybersecurity

Companies have to deter transaction crime by both investing in prevention strategies and deploying strong security measures as well as fostering stakeholder involvement. Avoiding the chaos inflicted by cybersecurity issues should be considered by having clear protocols to identify, contain, and mitigate them outlined in the disaster plan and ready in the eventuality of a successful attack. Apart from that, another important thing is that regular staff training and their capability to identify and report possible security threats should be the core of the programme, since it affects directly the general organisation's posture. Businesses can intensify their defences against the fast-changing perimeter created by 5G networks and smart IoT devices by adopting a multi-layered strategy with proactive monitoring, strong defences, teamwork and speedy incident response.

2.1.1 5G Networks

A. Enhanced Capacity and Speed

In contrast to earlier generations just for instance: 5G networks are designed to supply much higher data rates and at the same time less latency than that. A lot of data may be sent with the speed this technology allows which makes it possible to have it work smoothly for any types of devices and applications and also to have it in real time.

B. Increased Connectivity

5G could increase the number of connected devices per square kilometre up to 90 times higher than that before, which thus paves the way for IoT device expand and the Internet of Things ecosystem growing.

C. Network Slicing

Thanks to the 5G, the operators will be able to constantly introduce new virtual networks within existing physical infrastructure and to combine the packets of traffic belonging to different slices through simultaneous virtualization of all significant network resources by means of network slicing technologies. It results in the wider use of SDNs and Virtual Network Functions increasing the complexity of the management of the different slices.

2.1.2 Internet of Things Devices

A. Growth of Connected Devices

IoT devices are operational in many shapes including wearable smart gadgets, smart appliances, sensors and networks that power the industrial and vital infrastructure systems. The expanded utilisation rate of users of this type of devices gives rise to the situation where the boundary between the real and virtual worlds is being blurred more and more.

B. Diverse Security Postures

IoT devices perhaps will make security a second-class item, if not a subordinate one, for two main reasons: the limited inference power is the first one and the other is the affordability that has also been compromised. Many IoT devices, therefore, are not highly secured, that itself is a huge opportunity for online malicious attacks.

C. Heterogeneous Ecosystem

On the basis of the manufacturers and communication protocols, diverse devices with different hardware and software are present for the IoT ecosystem. Due to this spectrum, the security management and interoperability for those enterprises illuminating the IoT occupies a more difficult task to perform.

2.2. Some Issues That IoT and 5G Are Facing

A. Expanded Attack Surface

So, the wider area that is opened before cybercriminals with 5G networks of introduction and widespread use of IoT devices is huge. Hackers will abuse flaws in network infrastructure and communication protocols to individuals and organizations. This will be facilitated by IoT devices.

B. Complexity and Interoperability

An IoT ecosystem puts many roadblocks in the way of security, because of the fact that it involves a lot of heterogeneous devices and norms. Interoperability across standardized protocols and stakeholder collaborations are key elements to secure communication and improve the flow across networks.

C. Privacy Concerns

IoT devices ranges from health monitors, smart household electronics and fitness trackers gather very personal data such as one's habits, preferences and location information. An important question regarding the privacy of data, in particular illegal access to information, data breaches, and the improper use of personal data by IoT devices, is raised when they spread all over.

D. Security by Design

In fact, out of the box many IoT devices use default configurations that are vulnerable or do not take into account securing equipment from within. To minimize cyber risks, secure boot methods, encryption and authentication are just a few famous security by design principles that are to be incorporated at the stage of devices development and design.

E. Cyber-Physical Risks

Being the most crucial ones regarding physical systems and infrastructure management, the Internet of Things (IoT) devices are much needed in industries namely healthcare, transportation, and energy. Cyber-physical risks produced by IoT that have been compromised might endanger with self's injury, disruptions in vital services, and even with the losses(Lackner et.al,2018).

2.3 Strategies for Mitigation

Figure 1. Strategies for Mitigation

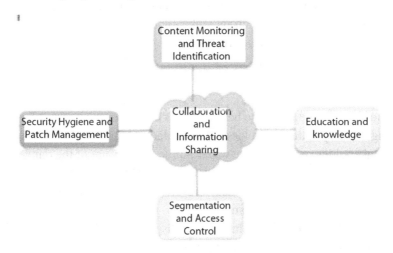

As shown in the above figure, below are the points explained:

A. Constant Monitoring and Threat Identification

The companies should have effective systems of checks and spaces that are able to detect the abnormal activities or the security risks of their IoT systems and 5G network deployments as shown in figure 1.

B. Security Hygiene and Patch Management

Issues to patch the IoT devices and network infrastructure should be upgraded regularly and the management of such updates should be done frequently. It is advised that a business leverages the process of distributing firmware quickly and reliably to note security patch implementation.

C. Segmentation and Access Control

Doing this, it is possible to deny any unauthorized access to the resources having a sensitive character out of isolation of essential assets, as a result the possibility to resist to security breaches will be improved.

D. Collaboration and Information Sharing

The establishment of standardized cybersecurity protocols as well as the centralized threat intelligence sharing in order to combat common security challenges requires the engagement of numerous stakeholders like manufacturers, services providers, regulators, and cyber notifications.

E. Education and Knowledge

Education and Awareness: The best practices of cybersecurity must be promoted, building security culture, and lessen human factor in cyberattack are key to get users and stakeholders as well as the wider public to be aware of the dangers of 5G networks and IoT system (Yousef Alshunaifi et.al,2022).

These 5G networks and IoT devices are bringing remarkable positive factors for their connectivity, efficiency, and creativity, though they are very difficult to be solved. A multidimensional-solution is indispensable involving technological improvement, voluntary standards, legislation and involvement of all stakeholders to overcome apprehensions. In addition, risk mitigation can also be provided by inducing cybersecurity awareness among the staff members via education and training venture. The transformative energy that comes from using 5G and IoT can be put to greater advantage while keeping all cyber threats at bay by an enterprise that employs sound cybersecurity policies and an overall proactive management of security issues. Collaboration becomes a crucial aspect here between stakeholders: namely governmental bodies, regulatory organizations, technology companies and cyber security specialist; to confront the issue of cybersecurity in 5G and IoT era from a holistic perspective.

3. AI-POWERED CYBER ATTACKS

AI-based cyber assaults use complex artificial intelligence (AI) algorithms to run and perform subtle evil acts requiring high-level of technical skills. The AI algorithms are used by the attackers to make tasks such as model resolution, avoidance of being detected by the traditional security measures. This enables them to fly faster, be remarkably elusive and to evolve quickly with each passed step of defence. A malicious cyber-criminal who employs AI-enabled tools, can enhance the scale, pace, and effects of their attacks, thereby, resulting in a great deal of problem for the cybersecurity consultant in their timely discovery, mitigation, and the management of such emerging risks (Guembe et.al,2022).

3.1 Exploring AI-Powered Strategies

A. Adversarial Machine Learning, or AML

It is referred to a technique of deception, where the specialists formulate a fabricated input data with a goal to confuse the AI systems and make them make a mistake prediction. Vulnerabilities exploitation may be performed via anti-detection attackers taking advantage of blind spots in machine learning algorithms.

B. Deepfake Methods

Deepfakes is a kind of media fabrication technology that is developed using deep learning algorithms realized photographs, videos and audio recordings that are extremely similar with the actual people and events. The principle used can be adapted to different purposes such as various social engineering attacks, disinformation campaigns, and imitation, among others.

3.2 Prediction of Complex Cyberattacks Using AI

A. Automated Malware Generation

Such AI tools can produce variants of existing malware strains or new warez by applying the patterns they had earlier learnt from the malware samples. These AI-empowered cyberattacks are able to change dynamically to overcome obstacles of antivirus software or other conventional signature-based detection methods.

B. AI-Enhanced Phishing Attacks

AI systems are capable of analysing an immense data and precisely create fake emails or texts targeted to particular person's specific interests, activity, or psychological traits thus increasing chance to get victims. The effectiveness of phishing campaigns has the potential to be increased, such that even sophisticated consumers are likely to be lured by the attackers who use social engineering along with AI driven personalization to customize their victims.

C. AI-Enabled Network Intrusions

Through AI-driven algorithms, the methods of network intrusion can be more and more complex and mysterious, for example, reconnaissance, lateral movement and privilege escalation can become more artful and difficult to be detected AI-controlled attackers engage in such large, pervasive and persistent cyberattacks by constantly learning and changing as they attempt to outsmart the network defences, fix vulnerabilities and pick on the weakest spots at all times.

D. AI-Powered Social Engineering

In order to embody personas depicting 'good' intentions and to disrupt existing social and technical ecosystems unfairly, AI algorithms could analyse social media profiles, social interactions, and public data along with temptation to set dangerous trends. Via incorporation of speech synthesis, natural language processing, and AI bots with conversational skills, hackers may talk peacefully with targets, extract classified information, and take advantage of trust communications to allow illegal hacks (Gürfidan et.al,2022).

The hybridization of modern AI methods with longstanding cyber threats is an emerging model that characterizes AI-infused cyberattacks' threat landscape, which is huge and rapidly mutating. The cybersecurity specialists will hence, end up tackling more complex problems, with the AI -based cyberattacks becoming smarter, larger, and more dangerous to fight when the technology keeps maturing and spreading. As an endeavour to tackle these problems, an advanced strategy should be worked out, the one that combines the best of threat detection along with the solid security measures, informed user knowledge, regulated policies, long-term research, and collaborative efforts of government agencies, academic institutions along with industry stakeholders to cook out innovative solutions and regulatory power. Constantly adapting to changing cyberthreats isn't just for technology. Board members and employees should be informed about the risks and should have the necessary know-how to recognize and properly reject malware so it can't infiltrate the system.

4. GENERATIVE AI'S CHANGE IN THE REIGN CONTENT PRODUCTION

Generative AI, which utilizes the latest methods such as deep learning and Generative Adversarial Networks (GANs), may bring complete transformation of the content creation area. This tech ushers in massive innovations that permeate numerous industries from marketing to design, education, and entertainment. Such can be augmented by automated production of content formats in variety (text, pictures, audio, video). Generative AI changes jobs and workflows in a way that creates fresh and captivating content possibilities as technology customizes and immerses people in their corresponding experiences. However, the rise of Generative AI is going to change the way content is created, therefore, the concerns rise on how data privacy, integrity and morality would look like when AI generates content.

4.1 Overview of Generative AI Technologies

The generation AI manifests itself as a significant segment of AI, where deep learning and the adversarial generative networks (GANs) are the prominent technology.

A. Deep Learning

Deep learning algorithm, a principal technology of generative AI, will learn regularities in the data by using multi-layered neural networks. Through hierarchical representations deep learning models can generate wide content in different domains such as text, images, audio, and video where by depth in input is important hence it comes across as a real content. The ever-developing deep learning of generative AI has largely added to the capacities that enable the creation of very real and fine-tuned output.

B. Generative Adversarial Networks (GANs)

GANs, which includes a generator and a discriminator that are two neural networks consisting of a learning system in a competitive tournament inside an AI concept, are the novel AI concept. The difference between the discriminator, which is supposed to discriminate real samples from the fake ones, and the generator, which generates artificial samples, that imitate real data lies in this. In contrast to traditional approaches content production in GANs constantly undergoes training by an iterative mode, proving to be an inventive technique which exhibits amazingly realistic content.

4.2 Examining Potential in Various Industries

The generative AI technologies are the instruments that can push the limits of the future converting the process of content production and set the grounds for new approaches and ways of solutions in various industries (Ramdurai et.al,2023; Fui-Hoon Nah et.al,2023).

A. Entertainment and Media

Through creating the avatars, environments and VFX for pictures, video games and the virtual reality technology, generative AI is doing a kind of a revolution that people never realized before. AI-authored content ceaselessly both steps ahead of and exceeds the boundaries of thought and the viewers and users' enthusiasm with means such as rethinking storytelling and creating virtual worlds.

B. Marketing and Advertising

The process of content creation in large quantities with high personalization is made possible by artificial intelligence capabilities for generation that has a transforming effect on marketing and advertising. AI technologies enable the development of individualized marketing strategies, product suggestions and targeted ads based on the high volume of customer information that can be accessed and analysed. Among other aspects of it plus this, hyper-personalization helps to more convert potential users into loyal customers and in turn enhances marketing ROI as well as steers the company's growth.

C. Design and Fashion

The creative sector of design and fashion like design and fashion is now been used to explore and discover unlimited new ways with generative AI. AI-powered tools give opportunities for designing apparel, textile textures, and décor ideas, which greatly overwhelm the design process and come with customization and personalization possibilities that were quite hard to imagine before. AI-based artistic content designing is doing a great job in recreating the future of aesthetics and fashion in the fields from high-end fashion to interior designing.

D. Content Generation and Curation

Generative AI has been applying social networks, news websites, and e-commerce platforms content applications and making tasks such as writing posts and presenting products much easier. An AI algorithm creates product descriptions, blog posts, social media posts and interesting articles; at the same time, these AI algorithms streamline the process of their production as well as contents' quality and significance. Thanks to this automation, the load on businesses to increase their content efforts and bring quality experiences to their audience will be lifted off.

E. Healthcare and Education

By using digital learning tools, robotic simulation, and holographic learning systems, AI is bringing a revolution in the way healthcare and education are taught for better learning experiences. Using the artificial intelligence driven content development process will enable personalized learning and healthcare activities, where the approaches and interventions are customized to specific patient needs and learners' preferences. Helping them with deploying the tools they need in interventions this can eventually lead to better outcomes of their patients.

The advancement of generative AI improves the processes of content creation with the help of deep learning and GANs that disrupt the content generation in many industries. As these entities develop and perfect their capabilities, they may greatly change the mindscape of content creation processes by increasing creativity, individualization, and innovation. Alongside that, faster progress of deep learning and GAN will also lead to a growth of their applications in content creation and such disruption will occur elsewhere and in various industries. Finally, further legal foundations by which socially acceptable and responsible use of AI generated material may be provided and to make sure that there is accountability, equity, as well as transparency in the practice.

5. SECURITY ISSUES WITH AI-GENERATED SYNTHETIC MEDIA

AI generated synthetic media for example deepfakes have a chance of being applied for something promising, they also bring about challenging security risks. These developments may bring moral concerns, specifically, distortion of truth, essential information withholding and breach of trust in visual media. Overcoming these obstacles is only possible in a broad setting that involves technological advances to be incorporated, as well as robust policy frameworks and mass digital literacy campaigns. Involving cutting-edge recording devices, setting rules for their use, and conducting media literacy training, we will accomplish the goal of minimizing the danger of the broad synthetic pictures while using them to the full extent. It is crucial for a culture of doubt and critical thinking to be promoted so as to lead individuals to develop a sound judgment system to detect fake from the real materials and thus preserve the value of digital data in the ever-changing world. The following are some of the major challenges that one can come across:

A. Misinformation and Disinformation

The concern about the spread of false information and disinformation produced by artificial intelligence (AI)-based synthetic media is one of the most pressing challenges today. Consequently, deepfakes can be most effective by technically simulating people conducting the activities they never actually did, which in essence spreads false information. Given the fact that this can result in a decline in confidence in media, organisations and individuals, there is a possibility that society will be overwhelmed by confusion and strife.

B. Identity Theft and Fraud

Through the process of manipulating the facial traits of another person in a photoshopped picture, film or sound recordings, deepfakes become a tool to make identity theft and fraud even easier. Facial deepfakes allow the manipulators to supposedly tell false stories or to make unsuspecting people take risky actions. The privacy, financial security, and reputation of individuals are expected to be in big trouble after a serious data breach like this.

C. Privacy Violations

Among the main issues concerning the genesis and machine learning of synthetic media are the privacy violation threats. People can be impersonated by somebody without consent, this could compromise and be dangerous for using them face and voice. This forms a massive invasion of individuals' personal space which in turn affects their privacy, autonomy and in general, their overall wellbeing.

D. Erosion of Trust

The spread of notions of artificial intelligence (AI) creating synthetic media is a considerable risk which affects the public confidence in the digital media and information. The audience might become more skeptical the more the real and fake content overlays stir the confusion, causing loss of credibility and trust. From the perspectives of online dialogue, ethics of journalism and democracy, this trend may trigger extensive consequences.

E. Security Implications

With the proliferation of AI-based synthetic media, cyber security professionals and politicians will face a brand-new set of challenges. As deepfakes can be misused with bad intentions, strong detection techniques, technological security measures, and legal frameworks are needed to prevent them and to punish the violators. Moreover, the development of critical thinking and media literacy skills should be encouraged as a means of differentiating between real and fabricated content and cut down on the negative impacts of synthetic media on the society.

F. Creation of Non-Existent Realities

The AI-produced content has the power to develop fictional realities, though they are in truth not falsified; they blur fact and fiction. This extended way of information propagation is not only about deception. Even though fictional influencers like Lil Miquela share their life with the fans, endorses products, and even creates boppy music, they all stand in the virtual world. In the digital era, the existential questions as to how to capture reality are the issue that is brought in by such blending of real and unreal worlds(Wang et.al,2023)(Whittaker et.al,2020).

5.1 Real World Examples

Real-world examples provide the best explanation for the theoretical and ethical conundrums surrounding AI-generated content. The possibilities and drawbacks of synthetic realities are both emphasised in these case studies...

A. Bias in Chatbots

Microsoft's Tay: Microsoft, a company that aims to expand its communication with customers thought that Twitter would, on the contrary, help them to gain the support of the larger community only to find out that people were not uplifting them but they presented a danger instead and therefore let the fake trolls fully control and the chatbot started to post discriminative, racist and profane Tweets. The dashboard clearly demonstrates that for a successful deployment of AI algorithms, we must feed the algorithms with tagged data and the systems have bias thus cannot promise for complete objectivity

B. AI-Generated Literature

The Novel "1 the Road": The novel 1 the Road is an AI of the famous Jack Kerouac's novel "On the Road." The AI has a corpus of novels with similar genre as the source text. Even though the coherency has been a matter of argument, it once again showed how AIs may be used in creative writing and since then specialist communities continued to divide about whether the authenticity in literature is preserved.

C. Augmented Reality and Privacy

Pokémon GO: 'Pokémon GO' being developed by Niantic is an AR game that went viral worldwide. If at first it helped realize combination of real and virtual worlds, the game brought up serious privacy issues, as it could locate users to the extremely high detailed that was accessible through the game.

6. MULTIDISCIPLINARY EFFORTS AND LEGAL FRAMEWORKS

6.1 Importance of Collaboration of Cybersecurity Professionals, AI Researchers, Legislators, and Industry Stakeholders

Interdisciplinary cooperation is fundamental and irreplaceable when it comes to addressing the complex issues AI creates particularly in the area of synthetic media. Branding cybersecurity experts, AI researchers, legislators, and market partners as members of a team will help come up with a holistic niche in dealing with the intricate and multidimensional issues of this technology. This partnership creates an environment of easy interactions that bring on a pool of diverse experiences that should be actively considered and integrated into the creation of defensive strategies and legislative rules as shown in figure 2. The other side of the coin is that it leads to the improvement of the detection techniques and creation tool which is considered as a proactive agent to combat the menacing threats. At the same time, the responsible development of AI driven media applications must be promoted (Rane et.al,2023).

Figure 2. Multidisciplinary Efforts and Legal Frameworks

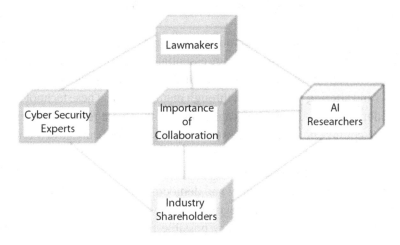

The following points explain the figure above:

Cybersecurity experts fully understand the use of synthetic media for non-benign purposes and employs their specialist knowledge in identifying and thwarting such threats. Their expertise of cybersecurity threats and vulnerabilities is primary in designing a strong defence, which, on a fundamentum, is intended to protect individuals, organizations, and finally societies from possible harm.

AI researchers are the key players of the cards in the technology of detection and verification of synthetic media content. The pace of advancements in AI and machine-learning is quick, and the experts keep innovating to make the algorithms and tools more complex and efficient in separating the real content from the synthetic one.

Lawmakers need to come up with the laws and regulations that regulate the emergence, diffusion, and use of AI-produced interchangeable media. Working with professionals from different fields, policymakers will be able to produce legislation that balances stimulation of innovation and protection of human rights, privacy, and security.

The **industry shareholders** like technology firms, content creators and media platforms give you very great practical perspective and also material resources. Working in tandem with cybersecurity experts, engineers, and policymakers, the representatives of industries can come up with best practices, standards, and guidelines for responsible content creation, distribution, and management of synthetic media.

6.2 Strong Legal Frameworks to Regulate AI Applications and Mitigate Malicious Abuse

To address the development, operation, and use of AI-based synthetic media such as deepfakes, robust legal frameworks are essential. Ethical problems connected with AI applications can be comprised by disseminating false information, breaching privacy rights and altering public views through manipulation. These technologies will be misused more often if regulatory agencies fail to enforce responsible legislation that could discourage potential hackers from taking undue advantage of them thereby spoiling the integrity of digital content or democratic processes. Therefore, there is a need for strict legislative controls in order to ensure that some individuals do not intentionally exploit humans, society and democratic institutions; it is important to establish a framework of laws that regulate the development and deployment of AI technologies taking into account every possible risk. Thus, holistic legislation is necessary for addressing these risks and promoting responsible advances and uses of Artificial Intelligence (AI)(Villegas-Ch et.al,2023).

A. **Establishing clear and enforceable regulations** is a pre-requisite to establishing accountability and discouragement of malign activities that are propagated using AI synthesized media. Legal provisions can specify what types of conducts are illegal including use of deepfakes for deceptive purposes and provide appropriate sanctions for the violations.
B. **It is imperative to set standards for transparency and accountability** as to how AI is developed and used. To accomplish this, regulations are needed. Also, a set of rules for disclosing is proposed in order to ensure the required transparency. Also, AI regulation ethical standards can stipulate legal frameworks to guide its responsible use. Moreover, these frameworks can push for ethical principles, justice and openness in algorithmic decisions.
C. **The legislative framework regarding privacy** has to be adapted to face the unique problems posed by AI-created synthetic media, such as the illegal manipulation of images and information of a person. Legal frameworks can be established with the aim of providing protection to people's privacy rights as well as minimizing the possibility of theft of personal data, harassment and other forms of exploitation.
D. **International cooperation and coordination** are key issues as AI-related threats and challenges are global. The legal frameworks should allow the cooperation of governments, law enforcement agencies, and international organizations to combat trans-border threats and enforce regulations that are consistent.

In the context of artificial intelligence (AI)-generated synthetic media, robust legal frameworks are crucial for efficiently regulating AI applications and preventing malicious usage. Governments can foster innovation while mitigating potential dangers and upholding the fundamental rights and values of individuals and society by implementing well-defined and legally binding regulations.

7. INVESTMENT STRATEGIES FOR AI-DRIVEN CYBERSECURITY SOLUTIONS

One of the main cybercrime issues nowadays is the increased attack complexity by bulky cyber-attacks which is the reason for the security solutions of the AI-style driven mechanism to gain popularity. Often, we discover, just like the examples of the rising number of ransomware attacks, advanced persistent threats (APTs), and other destructive activities, defence measures are stronger when the services are fortified (Bonfanti et.al,2022)(Ariyo et.al,2023).

The capitalization in AI-powered cybersecurity solutions is therefore necessary since they have the ability to give people wide margins for improved security in cyber world. In most cases, the classic and traditional ways of securing digital processes cannot have the same effect as they compete with the repetitive changes which cyber threats may come along with this being because they involve a personal intervention or some regulations as a guideline. Nevertheless, AI-fuelled anomaly detection can analyse the plethora of big data in a short time and, using machine learning, can identify abnormal patterns, which results in the instant identification of anomalies within a system. Hence, the rapidity of responding findings to such cases puts the organizations to a position of data breach elimination and financial loss reduction.

Anomaly detection systems of AI-based cybersecurity solutions are the core of the performance (Morel et.al,2011). Hence, security professionals depend on similar AI-based tools to safeguard their data infrastructures. These are configured through advanced machine learning technologies that detect abnormalities within system or network behaviour that are outside the norm. Not a single variation from the prescribed patterns could be regarded as normal, and thus the response should be immediate. Anomaly detection systems, as their name suggests, keeps the networks processes, user behaviour including system activities under continuous watch looking for attacks of pieces of software and known as "zero day" attacks from within the organization.

AI threat intelligence arising from AI is also critical for the continuation of robust defence systems for organizations. The threat assessment that results from traditional feeds of threat intelligence is just behind the curve of the fast-changing environment which in turn means that detection and response is usually ineffective.

Machine learning with algorithms able to process extreme quantities data about threats from all the sources in the open platforms, as well as closed platforms, also dark web markets and social platforms through which the emerging trends are being born and evolving. Machine learning algorithms are additionally helpful for organizations. In that they not only provide the requisite information on the threats intelligence but also determine the most essential and critical information at any point of time so that the cyber security team can make insights before they start countering any sort of cyber-crime (Sarker et.al,2021).

The other muscles that convince us to put money into AI-powered cybersecurity maintain that AI being formidable and flexible is one of their features is the slow adapting to the cloud computing, mobile devices, as well as the Internet of Things (IoT) technology leads to the growing footprint of digital; hence the traditional security capabilities become unworkable and interferes with the protection of everything else. Nonetheless, artificial intelligence solutions could be deployed in an unlimited number of cases as a result of the exponentially growing amount of data with the passing time and different surrounding areas together with covering all possible attack points. Furthermore, these solutions, which are developed for diverse environments and dangers, also evolve as the algorithms are getting more complex and new methods are being implemented to have definite advantage in the situation.

When an institution desires to increase its cyber defence capabilities and decrease the likelihood of cyber threats, it is supposed to venture in AI-based cybersecurity solutions. Corporations can also make use of complex machine learning algorithms as well as anomaly detection systems for protecting their valuable assets and continuing with operational activities while employing threat intelligence systems that are powered by AI can help identify, evaluate, and respond rapidly to cyber-attacks. Therefore, organizations have to prioritize investing in artificial intelligence (AI) driven cybersecurity solutions so as to be steps ahead of the attackers and protect their digital resources from changes in the landscape of cyber threats (Kaloudi et.al,2020; Guembe et.al,2022).

8. STRATEGIES TO FIGHT AI-DRIVEN THREATS

Creating the capacity to withstand AI-caused harm is a complex task that calls for the use of adaptive approaches and continual monitoring, as well as response procedures. Because there are many organizations that have changed their concepts in order to deal with today's fast developing cyber threats that are carried out using artificial intelligence tools against them, they have to ensure that their defences are kept up-to-date. Organizations can successfully reduce the threats originating from

AI-based cyber-attacks by implementing innovative tactics and technologies along with watchful monitoring, quick response abilities.

8.1 Adaptive Strategies Against AI-Driven Threats

8.1.1 Use of AI and Machine Learning

A. Make use of AI and machine learning algorithms in order to examine **big data in real time.**
B. **Identify patterns** that indicate malicious activities as well as anomalies that may bypass traditional defence systems.
C. **Update rulesets and algorithms** to deal with new threats and ever-changing attack vectors(Vegesna et.al,2023).

8.1.2 Dynamic Defence Mechanisms

A. Configure firewalls, intrusion detection systems (IDS), endpoint protection platforms (EPP) such that they can **auto-configure response actions** and configurations.
B. **Ensure automated response** actions based on predefined playbooks or decision trees.
C. Adopt the use of artificial intelligence driven automation platforms for orchestration to **minimize incident response timeframes.**

8.1.3 Robust Incident Response Capabilities

A. **Constantly observe** network traffic, system logs, and user activities for any security-related incidents.
B. Come up with **automated responses to incidents** which can be used to curb cyber threats quickly.
C. Use analytics platforms powered by artificial intelligence (AI) to **automate threat detection and correlation**, thereby improving proactive identification of emerging threats.

8.2 Importance of Continuous Monitoring and Response Mechanisms

Creating cybersecurity resiliency programs based on continuous monitoring as well as more immediate countermeasures is an important requirement for any organization, which will turn it into a victim, if it will not be able to spot, examine and act on cyber threats in real time.

8.2.1 Vigilant Monitoring

A. **Be ever watchful** over all digital assets and infrastructure domiciled in them.
B. **Identify peculiar conduct** or patterns that may signal possible security breaches.
C. **Use Artificial Intelligence (AI)** enhanced security analytics systems for immediate threat identification and correlation.

8.2.2 Rapid Response

A. **Develop predetermined steps** to identify, analyse, contain and eliminate security threats.
B. **Conduct regular tabletop exercises** and simulation drills to validate incident response plans.
C. **Automate response actions** with incident response orchestration platforms and streamline collaboration during incident response activities.

8.2.3 Proactive Threat Mitigation

A. **Take prompt action** once a security incident is detected so as to minimize its impact and avoid further escalations.
B. **Implement measures** in order to disrupt adversary operations as well as prevent unauthorized access into critical assets (Farooq et.al,2024).

Reassess the incident response procedures on an ongoing basis based on lessons learned and emerging threat trends.

Certainly, a harmonized approach, mixture of preventive, as well as vigilant appropriate and responsive approaches, are required to build the robustness of the social value systems against AI risks. AI can be utilized for many cyber security purposes currently, such as enhancing a threat detection and response adaptability by using certain AI technologies. This, in turn, can help corporations to address growing threats in digital environments. On the other hand, effective surveillances and process response capabilities will assist the organization to seamlessly monitor and enforce the security law in real-time, hindering the impact and ensuring that their operations are not affected. Whether holistic programs that can sustain AI-related cyber threats cyber resilience of an organization and at the same time retain a better reputation are followed matter a lot(Patel et.al,2023).

9. CONCLUSION

The convergence of generative AI and cybersecurity evokes both enormous opportunities and tremendous hurdles which we will definitely be facing during the course of the digital revolution. These groundbreaking tech innovations, in combination with the spread of 5G networks and the multitude of IoT devices, have dramatically altered the cybersecurity scenario, introducing new vulnerabilities and new ways through which the adversary can gain access to systems. The AI driven cyberattacks that use the methods of adversarial machine learning as well as deep-fake fundamentally help in the development of single individuals, organization and the whole community.

Yet within this perceived deterioration there is a revolution of creative writing process, stirred by emerging technologies such as deep learning and GANs. It is the technological breakthroughs that have many potential applications across different industries but at the same time, they raise the critical security issues which are most related to the AI-generated synthetic media production. Data fraud with identity theft and disinformation et al. call for the strengthening of interdisciplinary disciplines and legal framework to properly deal with applications of AI.

Another important thing is investment in AI-driven cybersecurity solutions (for instance, anomaly detection systems and AI-based threat intelligence) that help to buttress our defence against new forms of cyberattack. Highlighting preventive actions and accountable technology will help in using AI to its full potential coupled with reducing threats, which ultimately will be necessary for secure digital journey. Closing the gap between cybersecurity professionals, AI researchers, lawmakers, and industry players is crucial in being able to address the challenges present and avoid any potential dangers to the security and integrity of our digital infrastructure. Only through the unified effort and continuous vigilance can be truly understood and proportional measures against the AI-driven cybersecurity risks be taken, and a safe digital world be built for future generations.

REFERENCES

Ariyo, S. M. I. E. E., & Olufemi, E. (2023). *The Future of Cyber Security in An AI-Driven World.*

Bonfanti, M. E. (2022). *Artificial intelligence and the offence-defence balance in cyber security. Cyber Security: Socio-Technological Uncertainty and Political Fragmentation.* Routledge.

Dhoni, P., & Kumar, R. (2023). Synergizing generative ai and cybersecurity: Roles of generative ai entities, companies, agencies, and government in enhancing cybersecurity. *Authorea Preprints.*

Farooq, M., & Khan. (2024). AI-Driven Network Security: Innovations in Dynamic Threat Adaptation and Time Series Analysis for Proactive Cyber Defense.

Fui-Hoon Nah, F., Zheng, R., Cai, J., Siau, K., & Chen, L. (2023). Generative AI and ChatGPT: Applications, challenges, and AI-human collaboration. *Journal of Information Technology Case and Application Research*, 25(3), 277–304. DOI:10.1080/15228053.2023.2233814

Guembe, B., Azeta, A., Misra, S., Osamor, V. C., Fernandez-Sanz, L., & Pospelova, V. (2022). The emerging threat of ai-driven cyber attacks: A review. *Applied Artificial Intelligence*, 36(1), 2037254. DOI:10.1080/08839514.2022.2037254

Guembe, B., Azeta, A., Misra, S., Osamor, V. C., Fernandez-Sanz, L., & Pospelova, V. (2022). The Emerging Threat of Ai-driven Cyber Attacks: A.

Gupta, M., Akiri, C., Aryal, K., Parker, E., & Praharaj, L. (2023). From chatgpt to threatgpt: Impact of generative ai in cybersecurity and privacy. *IEEE Access : Practical Innovations, Open Solutions*, 11, 80218–80245. DOI:10.1109/AC-CESS.2023.3300381

Gürfidan, R., Ersoy, M., & Kilim, O. (2022, May). AI-powered cyber attacks threats and measures. In *The International Conference on Artificial Intelligence and Applied Mathematics in Engineering* (pp. 434-444). Cham: Springer International Publishing.

Kaloudi, N., & Li, J. (2020). The ai-based cyber threat landscape: A survey. *ACM Computing Surveys*, 53(1), 1–34. DOI:10.1145/3372823

Lackner, M., Markl, E., & Aburaia, M. (2018). Cybersecurity management for (industrial) internet of things–challenges and opportunities. *Journal of Information Technology & Software Engineering*, 8(05).

Morel, B. (2011). Anomaly based intrusion detection and artificial intelligence. *Intrusion Detection Systems*, 10, 14103. DOI:10.5772/14103

Patel, V. (2023). Real-Time Threat Detection with JavaScript: Monitoring and Response Mechanisms. *International Journal of Computer Trends and Technology*, 71(11), 31–39. DOI:10.14445/22312803/IJCTT-V71I11P105

Rajasekar, V., Premalatha, J., & Saracevic, M. (2022). Cybersecurity in 5G and IoT Networks. Secure Communication for 5G and IoT Networks, 29-46.

Ramdurai, B., & Adhithya, P. (2023). The impact, advancements and applications of generative AI. *International Journal on Computer Science and Engineering*, 10(6), 1–8. DOI:10.14445/23488387/IJCSE-V10I6P101

Rane, N. L. (2023). Multidisciplinary collaboration: key players in successful implementation of ChatGPT and similar generative artificial intelligence in manufacturing, finance, retail, transportation, and construction industry.

Sarker, I. H., Furhad, M. H., & Nowrozy, R. (2021). Ai-driven cybersecurity: An overview, security intelligence modeling and research directions. *SN Computer Science*, 2(3), 173. DOI:10.1007/s42979-021-00557-0 PMID:33778771

Tarikere, S., Donner, I., & Woods, D. (2021). Diagnosing a healthcare cybersecurity crisis: The impact of IoMT advancements and 5G. *Business Horizons*, 64(6), 799–807. DOI:10.1016/j.bushor.2021.07.015

Vegesna, V. V. (2023). Enhancing cyber resilience by integrating AI-Driven threat detection and mitigation strategies. Transactions on Latest Trends in Artificial Intelligence, 4(4).

Villegas-Ch, W., & García-Ortiz, J. (2023). Toward a Comprehensive Framework for Ensuring Security and Privacy in Artificial Intelligence. *Electronics (Basel)*, 12(18), 3786. DOI:10.3390/electronics12183786

Wang, Y. (2023). Synthetic realities in the digital age: Navigating the opportunities and challenges of ai-generated content. *Authorea Preprints*.

Whittaker, L., Kietzmann, T. C., Kietzmann, J., & Dabirian, A. (2020). "All around me are synthetic faces": The mad world of AI-generated media. *IT Professional*, 22(5), 90–99. DOI:10.1109/MITP.2020.2985492

Yousef Alshunaifi, S., Mishra, S., & Alshehri, M. (2022). Cyber-Attack Detection and Mitigation Using SVM for 5G Network. *Intelligent Automation & Soft Computing*, 31(1), 13–28. DOI:10.32604/iasc.2022.019121

Chapter 14
Future Trends and Challenges in Cybersecurity and Generative AI

Azeem Khan
https://orcid.org/0000-0003-2742 -8034
University Islam Sultan Sharif Ali, Brunei

Noor Jhanjhi
https://orcid.org/0000-0001-8116 -4733
TUSB, Malaysia

Dayang H. T. B. A. Haji Hamid
University Islam Sultan Sharif Ali, Brunei

Haji Abdul Hafidz B. Haji Omar
University Islam Sultan Sharif Ali, Brunei

Fathi Amsaad
Wright State University, USA

Sobia Wassan
Jiangsu University, China

ABSTRACT

The chapter presents a comprehensive exploration of the changing dynamics at the intersection between the rapidly growing landscape of the interconnectivity of various devices—the internet of things—and the innovations piloted by advancements in generative artificial intelligence. In the following background-focused analysis, the significance of the enactment of new levels of security details in this fast-growing and virulently expansive landscape is emphasized, with generative AI ultimately serving as the highlight. The conversation consequently shifts to threats. This includes a detailed depiction of new cybersecurity threats rooted in advancements in

DOI: 10.4018/979-8-3693-5415-5.ch014

AI, featuring AI malicious actors and incidents, such as the increasingly popular phenomenon of ransomware-as-a-service as mirror illustrations of the dynamic and multifaceted character of these threats. The class further proceeds to more in-depth detail about the most contemporary generative AI platforms such as generative adversarial networks, variational autoencoders, and reinforcement learning—all relevant in identifying emerging solutions to advance strategies in cybersecurity. The conversation simultaneously conducts an opportunity and threat analysis of the merger between these platforms and cybersecurity with regard to ethics, regulations, and overall adversarial touchpoints and tactics. The chapter concludes with a call for unity in discourse and action between the relevant industry, academia, and government stakeholders as a summary of the essential cross-disciplinary aspect that must drive the narrative in confronting and overcoming the threats to and from generative AI research. Having presented the narrative structure, this chapter has allowed a comprehensive coverage of the major issues and opportunities at the heart of the cybersecurity-generative AI combination. Additionally, it has provided a forum to call for collaborative and fortified efforts regarding the securing and defending of the uncertainties that the rapidly changing and more unpredictable digital landscape has in store for the world.

1. INTRODUCTION

As depicted in Fig 1.0, with the advent of 21st century we see many technologies emerging, among those one of them which is the buzzword and hyped extensively is Artificial Intelligence acronymized as AI, this technology has brought numerous advantages, apart from challenges as well that are associated with it (I. A. Shah, N. Jhanjhi, & S. K. Ray, 2024). AI is classified into two broad categories namely Narrow AI or Weak AI and the second one is General AI. Weak or Narrow AI has specialised applications to name a few are classifying spam emails, chatbots, etc. (David & Eldon, 2022). Generative AI also falls under this category, as it is a subfield of AI that has the ability to create new content based on multi modal inputs which can be either text, image, audio or video by taking any of those inputs Gen AI with the help of machine learning algorithms such as supervised or unsupervised can create outputs of varied types which can be text, image, video, audio or 3D outputs as well (Al Naqbi, Bahroun, & Ahmed, 2024). Large datasets are required to train these models and they have enormous applications among those applications are the one associated with cybersecurity where GenAI has the ability to predict, analyse, suggest, and develop defensive mechanisms with which the entire digital landscape can be secured (N. Z. Jhanjhi & Shah, 2024).

Figure 1. Generative AI Technology Trends (Vietrov, 2024)

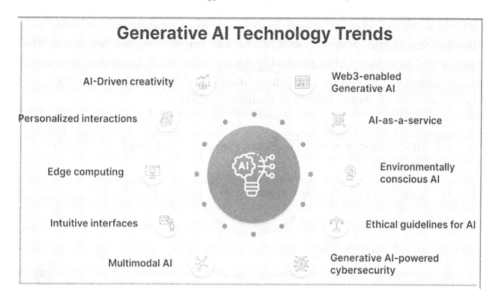

To summarize, the point at which cybersecurity crosses paths with generative AI can be seen as the digital world's next phase of evolution. The advancements of the two technologies, along with the concomitantly evolving ways to safeguard them, results in a dynamic sector that is always prepared to adapt to new challenges and advancements. These trends create a critical atmosphere in which to investigate future patterns and difficulties on this junction, with a focus on generative AI's probable impact on cybersecurity techniques, the opportunities such innovations may provide, and the multifaceted contributions they also incorporate. The concern arrives when innovative technology-controlled AI systems understands and adapts, requiring vigilant observation to assure the public maintain trust along the lines. The chance lies in the day when security acquires adaptive underpinnings that outweigh the rapidly transforming competition. Subsequently, in the same way as any other transformation, this convergence presents opportunities for both promises and perils, symbolizing the first stepping on a pathway to a fresh universe.

Overview of the Intersection Between Cybersecurity and Generative AI and Its Evolving Landscape

The significance of convergence between cybersecurity and generative AI can be comprehended by the statistics depicted in Fig 2.0. The combination of cybersecurity and generative AI has revolutionized the prediction, discovery, and prevention of digital assaults. Additionally, many of the qualities which make machine virtuosos, such as extremely summoned algorithms and learning models, have aided significantly in ratifying cyber incursions, automating software defenses, and imagining solutions that simply have not been practicable before. For instance, the myriad functions of generative AI in enhancing the security of IoT hardware, an integral goal regarding their ubiquity and vulnerability posed by the expanding attack surfaces(Gupta, Akiri, Aryal, Parker, & Praharaj, 2023).

Figure 2. Anticipation of a surge in global cybersecurity spending to $450 billion by 2030 (Desai, 2024)

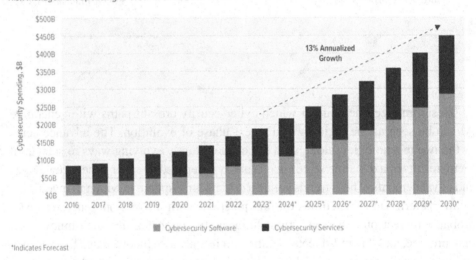

GLOBAL CYBERSECURITY SPENDING FORECASTED TO GROW TO $450 BILLION BY 2030
Sources: Global X estimates with data from Gartner (2023, Sep 28) Gartner Forecasts Global Security and Risk Management Spending to Grow 14% in 2024.

Introduction to the Chapter's Focus on Future Trends and Challenges in This Dynamic Field

As we probe more deeply into integration of generative AI in cybersecurity, the coming trends that will redefine the security postures of tomorrow are already upon us. For all the opportunities for strengthened protection mechanisms, however, they do also present challenges: ethical considerations, privacy concerns and the dual-use nature of AI technologies among them. The "Generative AI: A Systematic Review Using Topic Modelling Techniques" explains how generative AI is a two-edged sword which can both defend against and propagate cyber threats. Here, we probe the subtleties involved in this matter and explore its potential to transform cybersecurity through generative AI. This chapter hopes to take a fair-minded view of what the future holds for cybersecurity as more and more decisions are made in a world increasingly controlled by artificial intelligence.

Chapter Contributions

The current chapter, which can be considered as a meeting point between cybersecurity and a generative AI, is aimed to decipher multiple dimensions of complexities, challenges, and opportunities surrounding the described area. By studying key trends, technological innovations, and broader social implications, the following chapter offers a significant insight into the world of digital defence through the lens of AI. The following points outline the major contributions of the chapter:

1. **Shedding Light on Emerging Threat Patterns:** To date, the chapter offers a comprehensive guide to the rapidly changing nature of cybersecurity threats as driven by the advancement of AI and acknowledges the dual potential of AI in improving threat levels and contributing to positive developments of the digital defence.
2. **Explaining Fundamental AI Models:** The chapter investigates a variety of AI models in certain detail, including GANs, VAEs, and reinforcement learning, and explains their relevance and application to the digital defence as aids in the strengthening of the field.
3. **Discussing Ethical and Legal Ramifications:** The chapter studies and describes the ethical questions related to the use of AI as well as the legislative environment for AI use in cybersecurity. This serves as a hint on the importance of innovation that is simultaneously socially sensitive and driven by respect for the global data protection.
4. **Proposing a Collaborative Model:** The chapter makes a substantial contribution by suggesting that industry, academia, and government cooperation is necessary for the successful navigation of the cybersecurity issues faced and further development of generative AI research. It explores the idea that such collaboration is vital for numerous reasons, including innovation and securing the future digital landscape.
5. **Prediction and Blueprint:** Finally, the chapter does not limit its observations by the present-day cybersecurity and the AI realities but makes some predictions for the future developments. It is stated that radical innovation only is viable as long as the industry remains true to its fast-paced and ever-changing path.

6. **Developing a Skilled Workforce:** Considering the complexity of issues introduced by AI to the dynamics of cybersecurity, the final chapter emphasizes the importance of training a broad and multi-competent workforce familiar with the specific aspects of the rapidly evolving environment.
7. **Establishing an Analytical Framework:** The chapter presents an analytical framework based on the research of the impact generated by generative AI on cybersecurity. It serves as a resource base for future researchers and practical applications as well as the development of informed policy.

Chapter Organization

The chapter provided a broad overview of the interaction between cybersecurity and generative AI, covering what is involved in this subject and the complex, nuanced, innovative and ethical issues involved. Section 1 serves as the entry point into the discourse. More particularly, this is an orientation that encapsulates the key terms to this chapter. The purpose is to adequately position the subsequent discussion. For example, this section achieves the 'pegging' requirement by first touching on the commonplace integration of IoT devices.

The discussion presents the argument that generative AI strategies, for one, are key contributors to the security of IoT devices and their connectivity. This effectively creates the groundwork for the following: protecting digital systems from novel cyber threats using innovative AI approaches. Section 2 discusses the current, near future trends in cybersecurity. AI driven cyber-attacks, ransomware-as-a-service, supply chain security's built-in vulnerabilities form the focus.

This indeed demonstrates the fast-evolving nature of the contemporary cybersecurity state and the importance of generative AI in identifying and combating these vulnerabilities. It further suggests the innovative paths that cybersecurity is fast embarking on to address and manage these dynamic digital weaknesses. Section 3 accounts for the recent advances in generative AI. The use of GANs, VAEs, reinforcement learning is a prime example of how these technologies are redesigning the present and future of cybersecurity, in addition to creating more robust security systems that are able to identify and manage vulnerabilities more intelligently.

Section 4 concludes the chapter with a summary. This section is an attempt to discuss and consider the synergistic role of generative AI and cybersecurity. How might generative AI change cybersecurity, possibly from detection to response? The section illustrates how AI has been incorporated into the various security solutions and platforms. Section 5, "Securing a Digital Future," addresses the hurdles at the crossroads of generative AI and cybersecurity. The section grades numerous adversarial assaults, data privacy issues, and the ethics of utilizing generative AI in cybersecurity.

Through a detailed analysis of the challenges, the section reveals the technical, legislative, and societal complications that must be surmounted to facilitate the efficient application of generative AI in securing digital processes. Section 6, "Above and Beyond," delves more deeply into the ethics of the matter. It mostly relates to the ethical components of the application of generative AI in cybersecurity. The next section guarantees that all components of bias, transparency, and responsibility have a predefined nature and design.

A more refined section examines the requirements of the ethical use of AI and security practices. This sixth segment introduces various legislative acts and rules that shape these sectors. It also examines the influence of two legislative acts and the NIST Cybersecurity Framework. Section 8, Section 7: Talk of the Future, examines future plans. A prediction for the future and the actions that the industry, technology, and employees would take to deal with the unknown's challenges.

The alliance and union of academia, industry, and government are the theme of Section 9, The last part, entitled "We're in this Together." Section 10; Conclusion: Conclusion captures the central ideas and learnings of the chapter, provides a contemplative view of the future of cybersecurity and AI, and calls for a continued spirit of innovation, collaboration, and responsible leadership in dealing with the future of cybersecurity. In the next section, our focus will remain concentred on finding a cohesive way to make use of the AI promise to secure our digital world.

2. EMERGING TRENDS IN CYBERSECURITY

The digital world is in the state of continuous evolution, and the cybersecurity field is no exception. While the well-being of cybersecurity is assessed on the daily basis, many observers tend to dismiss the possible threats that might affect the future of the identified area (Sindiramutty, Jhanjhi, Tan, Khan, et al., 2024). Therefore, the current section will focus on the discussion of the key trends that are likely to determine the future of the identified domain, including the significance of AI for cyberattacks, consideration of ransomware as a threat to the well-being of organizations, and the relevance of supply chains to cybersecurity (M. R. Khan, Khan, & Jhanjhi, 2024).

Exploration of Emerging Trends Such as AI-Driven Cyber-Attacks, Ransomware-as-a-Service, and Supply Chain Security

As depicted in Fig 3.0 there are numerous core cybersecurity risks and one of the most important new trends in cybersecurity is the use of AI to both defend and attack. Artificial intelligence enables automation of the processes of detecting vulnerabilities and optimizing phishing campaigns through machine learning algorithms that execute attacks capable of changing and developing defences in real-time (Zaman et al., 2023). This leads to the need for adequate protection, which results in AI-powered defenses. Ransomware-as-a-service is another worrying trend. RaaS democratized the possibility of implementing ransomware, allowing people with little knowledge of the technical subtleties to install ransomware (Humayun, Jhanjhi, Alsayat, & Ponnusamy, 2021).

Figure 3. Core Cybersecurity Risks Projected to Emerge by 2030 (enisa.europa, 2022)

Due to this, a massive increase in this type of attack occurred on corporations and governments from around the world, resulting in a ransom demand in exchange for access to or recovery of the data in cryptocurrency. Another new trend is supply chain security: several widely publicized attacks used vulnerabilities in the supply chain to access properly guarded systems. The attacks demonstrate that modern digital ecosystems are connected in complex patterns, and a proper security solution cannot stop at one company's borders (Singh & Kumar, 2023).

Discussion on the Implications of New Technologies, Regulations, and Threat Actors for Cybersecurity

As depicted in Fig 4.0, Technological advances, as well as new types of threat actors, bring both opportunities and challenges to the field of cybersecurity. AI and machine learning can be effective tools to implement for threat detection and response, fundamentally changing the principles behind cybersecurity (Aslam, 2024). The same tools and technologies empower attackers to create new threats, based on which a technological arms race between cybercriminals and cybersecurity professionals occurs.

At the same time, changes occurring at the legislative level round up the key elements that evolve the cybersecurity field. Due to new laws that enhanced the security and privacy of data storage and processing like GDPR in Europe, there are consequences in terms of certain measures that must be taken and potentially ruinous fines. Thus, they affect the manner in which organizations approach cybersecurity and drive further reform.

Figure 4. Top Emerging Trends in Cybersecurity (Tamoghna, 2024)

At the same time, the nature of threat actors, from "lone wolf" hackers to state actors and advanced persistent threat groups, creates further challenges (van Geest, Cascavilla, Hulstijn, & Zannone, 2024). Threat actors can launch sophisticated targeted attacks, possessing both the technology and the ability to properly deploy it. Moreover, their objectives can vary from financial gain to inflicting a strategic blow against a geopolitical rival, leading to the requirement of a holistic approach that would also account for human and geopolitical dimensions (Abhilash et al., 2023).

In conclusion, the emerging trends suggest that the future cybersecurity would need to be based on intelligent, agile security systems. They need to be adaptive to the changes in the threat landscape and based on the looks currently available. In addition, they would require on-the-fly adaptation to changes in regulations and vigilance against new threat actors.

3. ADVANCEMENTS IN GENERATIVE AI

The landscape of generative artificial intelligence is quickly taking shape on account of the major strides in algorithmic methods and computing husbandry. The transformation has significantly expanded the scope of applications for the technology, extending its reach beyond the archetypal to more critical domains including cybersecurity. The deployment and enhancement of GANs, VAEs, and reinforcement learning have not only demonstrated the generative AI's potential but have also proven its innovative and securing ability in the digital architecture (Erwin, Zubair, & Sherali, 2022).

Overview of Recent Advancements in Generative AI Techniques, Including GANs, VAEs, and Reinforcement Learning

The impact of Generative AI is comprehensively captured in Fig5.0. Generative AI has seen remarkable progress in several major directions. The development of GANs has transformed the field by allowing to generate the exceptionally realistic pictures, videos, and audio recordings, delivering the beneficial applications for data augmentation and simulation for cybersecurity (Paola, Lopez, Christian, & Sonia, 2023). VAEs have made a significant contribution to the efficiency and effectiveness of encoding and decoding the data, which is crucial for the enhanced anomaly detection mechanisms that help to determine cybersecurity threats (Val, 2023). Reinforcement learning has created the opportunities for developing AI that can make decisions and learn policies by interacting directly with the environment, which has enabled the automation of cybersecurity defence that changes with time in an intelligent manner (Bland, Petty, Whitaker, Maxwell, & Cantrell, 2020).

Figure 5. Impact Radar of Generative AI (Perri, 2023)

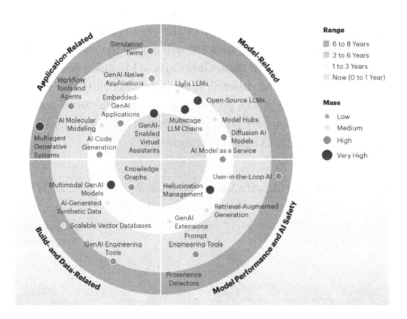

Analysis of Trends Such as Explainable AI, Federated Learning, and Meta-Learning in the Field of Generative AI

New directions in generative AI, conversely, such as explainable AI, federated learning, and meta-learning are remarkably altering future AI in generative ways. Explainable AI helps make the decisions that the AI is making clearer and more understandable, a crucial feature for using AI ethically in cybersecurity and especially on making AI decisions that can be trusted and are responsible for (A. Khan, Jhanjhi, Haji, & bin Haji Omar, 2024). Federated learning is a huge step forward in making AI models safer and more privacy-preserving, by allowing models to be trained on algorithms from decentralized devices or servers that hold local samples that are not exchanged (Dogra et al., 2022). This will specifically be useful for cybersecurity, where financial data processing privacy is essential. Meta-learning, also known as learning, to learn, allows for building AI that can learn new tasks rapidly with limited data, a crucial feature for adapting to new forms of cyber risks while maintaining solid cybersecurity (Ashraf, Jhanjhi, Brohi, & Muzafar, 2024).

4. CONVERGENCE OF CYBERSECURITY AND GENERATIVE AI

As generative AI enters the battleground, cybersecurity is changing in ways that previously seemed impossible. Virtually both AI and generative AI intelligence, fueled by years of computing experience, support the cross-seminar of human logic. Consider a device-learning algorithm running on a notebook for processing as opposed to a straight line. In which he or she is compelled to a number of data nodes in the notebook. Every software's use will lead to the machine studying how to change and restructure human data. Generative AI is novel because it does not run on explicitly provided data. Instead, it analyses data and makes inferences in other dimensions than those it was provided how new data points can be formed. As highlighted in Fig 6.0 there are potential AI driven cybersecurity solutions with the integration of Generative AI and cybersecurity.

Figure 6. AI-Driven Cybersecurity Solutions (qsstechnosoft.com, 2024)

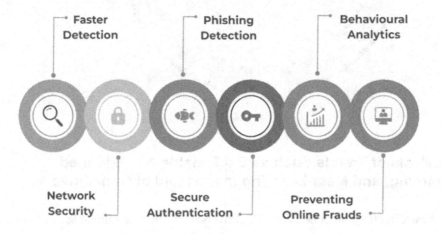

Examination of How Generative AI Is Transforming Cybersecurity Operations, Threat Detection, and Incident Response

Generative AI is revolutionizing cybersecurity by automating operations, improving threat detection, and automating incident response. Regarding the former, AI-based simulation and predictive modelling simulate current trends in vulnerability or assault patterns and compare them to security measures to permit professionals to develop defenses before they occur. Generative AI in the latter instance "trains" base models to recognize through innocent but ambiguous signals the existence of dangerous activity or patterns which could result in fewer false alarms and greater capture accuracy of incidents. Finally, proprietary AI makes incident-response faster and more efficient by allowing automatic responses that enable quick putting out and removal of assaults (Binnar, Bhirud, & Kazi, 2024).

Discussion on the Integration of Generative AI Techniques Into Security Solutions and Platforms

As we see plethora of devices are connected to internet and data with velocity, veracity and volume is being transferred every now and then from source to destination. This transfer of data or primarily the data that is being transferred through these networks needs to be secured at rest and at transit, to make sure that this is safe from external attacks and internal attacks as well we need mechanisms which we call them as cybersecurity mechanisms (Iqbal, Iqbal, Hasan, & Raza, 2021). Organisations and individuals are all concerned about there security in digital world. Hence, here comes at rescue the application of Narrow AI which we call them as Generative AI: which has the ability to simulate network for Intrusion detection systems, unauthorized users making sure of authentication and so on. To train cybersecurity systems we need enormous amounts of data which needs huge amounts of money and resources to bring them in place for testing but with the help of Gen AI we can create synthetic data without compromising individual or organizations privacy (Sindiramutty, Jhanjhi, Tan, Yun, et al., 2024).

AI's integration into cybersecurity offers unprecedented opportunities but also brings new dangers. In particular, security systems now deploy the reliable prediction capabilities of machine learning to prevent new hazards from developing on networks (Prabakar et al., 2023). AI can strengthen our security by automating the military conflicts of an advanced society and make our protection responsibilities more potent. Conversely, evolution must be watched vigilantly; rather than mutating our algorithms advantageously against one another, they must be made more useful but less harmful on their adversaries' terms (Boopathy et al., 2024). In other words, progress must be cautious, with these tools developed cautiously and each step analysed and codified. We must authorize our digital towns by building robust rules to govern intricate yet vibrant agoras. Tools that protect rather than dangers, for dangers will evolve rapidly, but protection can fare even faster.

5. CHALLENGES IN CYBERSECURITY AND GENERATIVE AI

Though there are enormous amounts of advantages and benefits with Gen AI at the same time we need to keep in mind the challenges as well that are associated with Cybersecurity and Gen AI these challenges Include the following discussed below: one of them is communication Overhead which needs to send updates to and from the central server can lead to significant communication overhead (Takale, Mahalle, & Sule, 2024). Secondly system heterogeneity which constitutes differences in hardware, in data distribution, and in network connectivity among participating nodes which can complicate the learning process. Lastly it is scalability which focusses on managing a large number of nodes and ensuring consistent model updates and aggregation which can be challenging as the network size increases (Yigit, Buchanan, Tehrani, & Maglaras, 2024).

Figure 7. Cybersecurity and Gen AI Challenges (Stankovich, 2024)

Though generative AI has the potential to enhance cyber defense, deploying language models can be harmful if implemented without careful consideration of how they can inflict harm. When left uncurtailed, models can produce human-like text on a massive scale, which has the potential to be harmful or deceptive. The trick is to recognize the threat and benefit in advance through open discussion and careful supervision to reap the rewards of this technology while minimizing future harm. As humanity progresses further, it does so with uncertainty, and this statement becomes more evident.

Identification of Challenges Such as Adversarial Attacks, Data Privacy Concerns, and Ethical Implications in the Intersection of Cybersecurity and Generative AI

There are some interesting and thought-provoking things to consider artificial intelligence such as aspects of ethics, technical facilities, and social questions. Firstly, technically, there are many obstacles left unsolved, e.g. susceptibility to adversarial attacks (Chakraborty, 2023). Unfortunately, some players attempt to use AI instruments for malicious purposes breaking the systems of protection and safety. Secondly, to guarantee that AI systems act morally and do not take unreasonable actions is problematic. It is necessary to consider how to build future technologies safely and for the sake of humans. From the point of view of society, the problems are the following: the questions of privacy. Precisely, unclean data usage and uncontrolled surveillance exacerbate the level of insecurity of data that could be taken for wrong attempts. The authorities must develop strong regulations that prevent from wrong use of AI by malicious parties. From the view of ethics, the problems are the following: responsible use of AI (Vetrò, Santangelo, Beretta, & De Martin, 2019).

Exploration of Technical, Regulatory, and Societal Challenges Facing the Adoption and Deployment of Generative AI in Cybersecurity

The challenges will however be associated with the use and implementation of Generative AI in cybersecurity. Regarding the adoption and deployment, technically, the inherent complexity in designing AI systems that can work effectively in the rapidly changing world of threats will challenge the adoption and deployment of generative AI in cybersecurity (Ortega, Tran, & Bandeen, 2023). Legal and regulatory, the global patchwork of diverse regulations regarding data privacy and ethics will be the challenge in the adoption and deployment. Pertaining to society, overall, we can conclude that the use of or deployment, we need to ensure that the technology helps society rather than hinders society as a whole (A. A. Khan et al., 2023).

6. ETHICAL CONSIDERATIONS

As discussed earlier to accomplish all what is being discussed about, we cannot runaway but need to admit that though the human generation has grown up in maturity but we still see that we lack ethically, and this fact is admitted in academia and public discourses are rampant on these issues and educating overall academia and by every thinking individual (Zhou & Kankanhalli, 2021).

The integration of generative AI into cybersecurity infrastructure introduces important moral issues warranting due consideration. As these autonomous systems take on expanding roles defending networks and data, scrutinizing their design and behaviour for potential inequities or lack of intelligibility becomes increasingly pressing. Unless stakeholders address head-on the ethical quandaries inherent to advanced AI assisting in cybersecurity work, such technologies risk devolving from aids bolstering our defences into implements endangering users regardless of intent. A multifaceted, multilateral effort to ensure generative tools uphold principles of accountability, fairness and transparency can help secure the benefits of continuing innovation while pre-empting unintended harms (Camilleri, 2023).

Discussion on Ethical Considerations Related to the Use of Generative AI in Cybersecurity, Including Bias, Transparency, and Accountability

i.   **Bias in AI Models:** Considering that AI systems operate based on the data, contributing to subjectivity, biased data is likely not to result in objectiveness. For the cybersecurity field, it may manifest as biased protection or fairness – some systems or interpreters receive more protection than others because their statistics are fundamentally racially charged. To counteract this, AI developers and vendors must diversify their training datasets and implement bias-correction techniques (Kumar et al., 2024).

ii. **Transparency in AI Operations:** Most AI systems are black boxes. It implies that an average user does not know about the source of powers of the system or triggers of the decision. In cybersecurity, a lack of transparency may be detrimental as incorrect decisions will affect all companies in the same way. For example, allowing a fake threat to bypass a cybersecurity AI results in harm to all affected systems. To ensure the development of transparency, the developers can apply explainable AI (I. A. Shah, N. Z. Jhanjhi, & S. K. Ray, 2024).

iii. **Accountability for AI Decisions:** Accountability is an issue somewhat similar to that of transparency. If an AI system wrongly assesses whether a certain action is aggressive or not, it might be difficult to determine who should be accountable for it. Therefore, in order to avoid disagreements about responsibility, the companies and vendors should create a corporate responsibility policy stating the personnel who cannot be responsible for a blunder in preventing a cyberattack. The reason that clear guidelines or regulatory frameworks on doing business could promote an atmosphere of trust and accountability is because accountability would then apparently have to be allocated (Raja & Zhou, 2023).

Examination of the Ethical Implications of AI-Driven Cyber-Attacks and Defensive Measures

i. **AI-Driven Cyber Attacks:** The use of AI to increase the effectiveness and sophistication of cyber-attacks raises a number of ethical considerations. Furthermore, the creation of machine learning-enhanced systems to improve the efficiency and subtlety of cyber-attacks faces a number of ethical issues(N. Jhanjhi, Khan, Ahmad, & Hussain, 2022). As noted, before, it will result in creating a pattern of action and counter-action, where the malware becomes aware and attains defensive characteristics to avoid being noticed, to which defenders adapt and the cycle continues. Ideally, it could result in the emergence of AI systems that can independently strategize and execute strikes with major repercussions(Rehan, 2024). In this context, critical concerns concern the moral aspect of using AI in incursions and the acceptance of such applications at the level of global norms and agreements.

ii. **Defensive Measures:** On the other hand, the use of AI for defensive applications raises significant ethical question in terms of surveillance and information security. Indeed, AI technology used to monitor and protect computer networks and information infrastructure often requires the access to extensive amount of data. In some cases, this data may include private information of citizens, which may contradict the rights to private life and correspondence(AL-Dosari, Fetais, & Kucukvar, 2024). Moreover, defensive AI application should be developed in such a way that they cannot adversely affect attackers' activities, in line with the principle of "do no harm".

Overall, the use of generative AI in computer security clearly outlines a number of ethical concerns, all of which must be taken into account by technologists, policymakers, ethicists, and general public. Only by this way, it would be possible to ensure the ethical development, deployment, and operation of AI technology.

7. REGULATORY LANDSCAPE

The intertwining of generative AI in cybersecurity has brought many regulatory frameworks and guidelines into the digital limelight, urging lawmakers and regulatory bodies to navigate a rapidly changing digital landscape. The impact of these regulations is not just on elements such as safety and security but also to establish an enabling environment that allows AI innovation to flourish while still upholding society's ethical standards(Wu & Liu, 2023).

Overview of Regulatory Frameworks and Guidelines Governing the Use of AI and Cybersecurity Practices

When it comes to artificial intelligence and cybersecurity, the landscape of regulatory instruments is broad, including both global and regional frameworks and guidelines devised to address the specifics and distinctive challenges of these technologies. However, the common ground of such instruments is their focus on ensuring that AI systems, especially those targeting improved cybersecurity, are operating in compliance with the law, ethics, and with secure controls(Nguyen & Tran, 2023). At the global level, the Organization of Economic Cooperation and Development offered its Principles on AI, which identified the key values of transparent and promoting fairness to ensure the safety of AI systems, leading to responsible stewardship(Abrahams et al., 2024). Moreover, the rules were reinforced by the Montreal Declaration, which highlighted ethical principles such as secrecy, privacy, autonomy, human benefit, and value alignment, as well as the necessity of considering security failure impact and their prevention. Speaking of cybersecurity, the guidelines include the International Standard ISO/IEC 27001, which presents the requirements for an information security management system and gives extensive controls for its establishment, implement, maintenance, and continuous development(Arif Ali Khan et al., 2022).

Analysis of the Impact of Regulations Such as GDPR, CCPA, and NIST Cybersecurity Framework on the Development and Deployment of Generative AI in Cybersecurity

i. **The General Data Protection Regulation (GDPR)**, The General Data Protection Regulation passed by the European Union also has a critical general impact on the development and deployment of AI in the field of cybersecurity. Though the legislated requirements clarify the scope of personal data processing, they forced AI developers to create more privacy-friendly systems. Finally, this attracts innovation in terms of data privacy processing and protection. In the context of digital security, developers are called to set digital personal privacy-compliant AI systems that are capable of identifying and eliminating threats without corrupting personal data integrity (Bakare, Adeniyi, Akpuokwe, & Eneh, 2024).

ii. **The California Consumer Privacy Act (CCPA)** The California Consumer Privacy Act has a somewhat similar impact in terms of regulating user privacy expectations, only it does so legislate for users in California and giving them unparalleled authority over their personal information. From the perspective of developers, the law requires AI-driven cybersecurity systems to be transparent about their data and provide users with mechanisms of control, swaying developers to balance efficiency with privacy (ElBaih, 2023).

iii. **The NIST Cybersecurity Framework**, the third legislated factor is the NIST cybersecurity Framework, while not directly a regulation, it is a voluntary framework that has had a tremendous general effect on the cybersecurity field, and AI is no exception. The framework consists of standards, guidelines, and best practices of computer security geared to how private sector organizations in the US can evaluate and enhance their ability to prevent, identify, and address cyber-attacks. The requirement for AI developers is to develop in accordance with the best cybersecurity KPIs to improve the products' reliability and efficiency (Khaleefah & Al-Mashhadi, 2024). Collectively, the regulatory domain is characterized by a network of national and international regulations that balance digital security requirements with increasing pressure on privacy rights and AI ethical developments.

However, on the other hand, there is an issue of AI continued development and deployment of new approaches including generative AI. Therefore, the role of regulation is likely to grow even more significant given the current development of generative AI and AI-based cybersecurity solutions. It appears that the future safe, ethical, and privacy-sensitive deployment of AI will be all but impossible if the regulatory role is eliminated.

Figure 8. The NIST Cybersecurity Framework (Bisht, 2023)

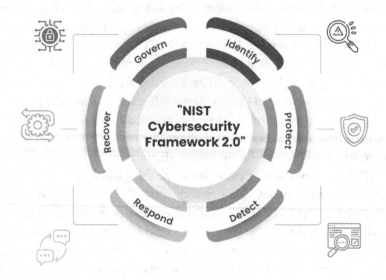

In conclusion, there are several essential points to be considered regarding AI and cybersecurity regulation. At the global level, it appears that no comprehensive and universally accepted agreement has been reached yet. This makes the specifics of the relationship thoroughly dependent on each region's individual circumstances. On the one hand, many AI elements call for more rigorous standards of use that will allow for the protection of the citizens' privacy. Such arrangements make sense due to the current deployment of face recognition, voice identification, and other measures of that kind.

8. FUTURE DIRECTIONS

With technology steadily marching further and further into unknown territories, the fusion of cybersecurity and generative AI promises a veritable treasure trove of undiscovered potentials and a whole host of tricky and interrelated problems that will need brilliant solutions and informed, forward-thinking judgment to solve. The rapid pace of this field is driven not just by technology's constant forward march, but also by the ever-shifting world of cyber threats. To anticipate what is to come in this field will require us to not only guess at the future technical innovations, but also beyond that to what we will have to do to deal responsibly and carefully with the myriad challenges that will arise. As we move into further-reaching areas where safety and innovation intersect, agility, patience and sensitivity will be required (Dhoni & Kumar, 2023).

Exploration of Potential Future Trends and Developments in the Intersection of Cybersecurity and Generative AI

Generative AI will certainly ensure a significant future for the cybersecurity landscape. The predictions may be different, but it is clear that the changes will involve innovative technologies that can help reshape the way digital assets and infrastructure are protected. For instance, one of the most critical tendencies will undoubtedly be more secure AI-based only on its ability to interpret attacks and correct the protection system on the go. It is highly likely that the security available with AI-driven Security Orchestration, Automation, and Response will also get a boost, which means it will become not only highly effective in terms of detecting, analytics and resolving issues but also take processes less time and become more efficient. Much more AI will be used for predictive threat intelligence to help analyse big data and prevent the possibility of attack before it may happen. Moreover, it will also be an efficient approach to develop systems and networks defensible by design (Gursoy & Cai, 2024).

The future of cybersecurity will be defined with quantum computing. It will drastically transform the approach to data processing and encryption, but it also poses a threat to all existing cryptographic methods. Generative AI would be very valuable in the creation of secure forms of encryption that cannot be cracked by quantum forms of encryption before quantum computing takes off as a global force (Gill et al., 2022).

Predictions for the Evolution of Cybersecurity Strategies, Technologies, and Workforce Skills in Response to Emerging Threats and Challenges

In this rapid-evolving context, cybersecurity strategies and technology models will adapt to include generative AI, thus demanding a similar transformation from the cybersecurity workforce. As experts in the matter argue, cross-disciplinary knowledge that links cybersecurity, AI, data science, and a set of ethical considerations will only become more professionally demanded. This correlates with the fact of professionals having to understand the inner mechanisms of AI-driven security solutions and their potentially dangerous impact. The latter questions of ethical use of AI in cybersecurity will also require professionals to consider and balance the aspects of the ethical, legal, and social case of AI integration. With AI itself becoming more autonomous, the necessity of having authorized personnel to monitor, interpret, and redactions of AI decisions will become inevitable (Mossavar-Rahmani & Zohuri, 2024).

The entire education and training field of cybersecurity will also have to adapt to adjust to the evolving requirements of the industry. It does not only impact the technical part but also raises the necessity of educating the new generation of professionals on ethical issues associated with cybersecurity. To sum up, the prospects of the field suggest progressive steps of development that are characterized by a cycle of informed changes. Thus, being one step ahead of possible risks and dangers will be possible if making a combined effort that will consider innovations in the area, professional field improvements, and changes, and the legal basis for AI-driven technologies. The picture is complex, but a coordinated approach will turn the scenario into a more digitally safe environment. From The future of cybersecurity and generative AI (Owino & Paschal, 2023).

9. COLLABORATION AND PARTNERSHIPS

With the evolving nature of everyday life and the overwhelming pace at which digital technologies advance, cybersecurity has become one of the most critical issues to address. The development and integration of generative AI models is accelerating this process and making it even more complicated; hence, an integrated approach that involves the industry, government, and academia is required. The strict boundaries between the three sectors are no longer relevant because they need to collaborate to succeed, develop, and implement new approaches (Othman & Yang, 2023).

Discussion on the Importance of Collaboration and Partnerships Between Industry, Academia, and Government in Addressing Cybersecurity Challenges and Advancing Generative AI Research

i. **Industry-Academia Partnerships:** Collaboration of industry and academia acts as an innovation bridge connecting the academic institution's theoretical insights and state-of-the-art research outcomes with the industry's real-world application needs and resources. Industry-university partnerships are essential for the progress of generative AI research. They allow for the interchange of ideas and technology and subsequent generation of innovative solutions for the next-generation cybersecurity tool. Additionally, industry-academia collaboration helps align the academic syllabus with the requirements of the industry in training the future cybersecurity professionals(Huang, Zhang, Mao, & Yao, 2023).

ii. **Government's Role:** Governments also form the key collaborating pillar with the roles extending beyond regulation to acting as enablers and participants in the research and developments front. Government input in both AI and cybersecurity fields crossover in terms of funding, policy development, and the setup of public-private partnerships. Governments set the ground rules in AI to ensure that development is within the realms of ethical, moral, and social grounds, guaranteeing a secure and responsible technological terrain(Saveliev & Zhurenkov, 2021).

iii. **Cross-Sector Partnerships:** Cybersecurity threats and desires for generative AI transcend even the industry's capability. Partnerships between industry, academia, and governments bring different perspectives and resources creating multiple innovative and sustainable solutions to unearth complex multifaceted problems. For example, a research problem such as AI biases or AI privacy or AI security problems can be solved efficiently by a multi-stakeholder approach, bringing together the researcher, the implementer, and the policymaker(De Cerqueira, Tives, & Canedo, 2021).

iv. **Global Collaboration:** Cyberspace and digital felt threats do not respect borderlines. International cooperation is vital in building a global cybersecurity threshold. Collaborative partnerships or governance frameworks or forums between states can act as active fronts for regulatory uniformity, actively considering the adoption of international benchmarks and offer support in international cybersecurity frameworks ensuring a combined stand against cybercrimes and promote uniform and strategic AI research(Shafik, 2023).

To conclude, security and generative AI are the two fields where modern societal challenges require a response from the joined efforts of industry, academia, and governmental agencies. By partnership and collaborative efforts, these fields will harness their diverse assets to address the existing and potential threats. Consequently, the path to the future in these fields is the path of partnerships where shared objectives and mutual support can provide the optimal solution for benefiting and fostering the sustainable development of the field.

Summary of Key Insights and Takeaways From the Chapter

The journey through this chapter highlighted key insights in varying depths and complexity: The landscape of cybersecurity evolves rapidly, with AI threats growing ever more sophisticated daily. In response, generative AI has emerged as a powerful ally, offering innovative solutions across a broad spectrum for threat detection, nuanced analysis, and multilayered mitigation strategies, fundamentally reshaping cybersecurity defences. Advancements in technologies such as GANs, VAEs, and reinforcement learning have catapulted generative AI to the forefront of cybersecurity solutions, introducing novel paradigms for securing vast digital ecosystems in original ways.

The convergence of cybersecurity and generative AI amplifies capabilities to an unprecedented degree to combat cyber threats but also introduces challenging ethical, privacy and regulatory issues that necessitate a balanced, multi-faceted approach with consideration of all stakeholders. The above factors contribute to a wide range of implications for addressing issues at the intersection of AI and generative cybersecurity. The collaborative process can be described as an integrated approach that transcends traditional boundaries to engage a diverse set of stakeholders from the industries to academia and the government to pool their resources together in quest of continuous innovation and security through an open-minded approach.

Reflection on the Future of Cybersecurity and Generative AI and the Need for Continued Innovation, Collaboration, and Ethical Stewardship in This Evolving Landscape

In the long term, the future of cybersecurity with generative AI appears to hold both optimistic and pessimistic implications. To begin with the advantages, there will be all opportunities for the implementation of generative AI to become the main innovation to redefine current cybersecurity practices. As such, the employment of generative AI will open new doors to the development of smarter, more secure, and resilient digital systems. However, it is necessary to note that this justification applies only with the assumption that we control the development of new technologies now. Specifically, there are some implications on which the convergence of generative AI and cybersecurity must be focused currently:

- The prospects are changing rapidly, so innovative changes must be permanent for cyber defence and generative AI. For instance, both sectors may require the continuance of research and development, the inception of new methodologies, and the creation of the culture of an ethical approach.
- In addition, challenges can come beyond the physical or sectoral scope. The work concerning the development of new mechanisms and instruments for efficient cooperation between the countries, sectors, and disciplines to guarantee the possibility to share knowledge, resources, and experience for a joint response to cyber threats.
- Moreover, the convergence of cybersecurity and generative AI must be ethically sound. The roles of transparency, fairness, and accountability, alongside

the following of existing privacy laws and regulations to meet the requirements of an ethical approach to the development of AI for cybersecurity in public organizations and companies, should be stressed.

To conclude, the adventure involving the inseparable relationship between cybersecurity and generative AI presents beneficial possibilities to protect our digital realm excellently and exceptionally. However, exploring such a landscape demands much more than technical expertise; it demands ongoing creativity, powerful teamwork, and unwavering good stewardship. Following this, let us follow these qualities to create a secure digital world where cybersecurity and generative AI collaborate for securing and uplifting our digital lifestyles.

REFERENCES

Abhilash, J. V., Nasser, T., Raed, A. S., Taher, M. G., Munir Uddin, A., Haitham, M. A., & Muhammad, A. (2023). A Roadmap for SMEs to Adopt an AI Based Cyber Threat Intelligence. *Studies in computational intelligence*, 1903-1926. DOI:10.1007/978-3-031-12382-5_105

Abrahams, T. O., Ewuga, S. K., Kaggwa, S., Uwaoma, P. U., Hassan, A. O., & Dawodu, S. O. (2024). Mastering compliance: A comprehensive review of regulatory frameworks in accounting and cybersecurity. *Computer Science & IT Research Journal*, 5(1), 120–140. DOI:10.51594/csitrj.v5i1.709

AL-Dosari, K., Fetais, N., & Kucukvar, M. (2024). Artificial intelligence and cyber defense system for banking industry: A qualitative study of AI applications and challenges. *Cybernetics and Systems*, 55(2), 302–330. DOI:10.1080/01969722.2022.2112539

Al Naqbi, H., Bahroun, Z., & Ahmed, V. (2024). Enhancing Work Productivity through Generative Artificial Intelligence: A Comprehensive Literature Review. *Sustainability (Basel)*, 16(3), 1166. DOI:10.3390/su16031166

Ashraf, H., Jhanjhi, N. Z., Brohi, S. N., & Muzafar, S. (2024). A Comprehensive Exploration of DDoS Attacks and Cybersecurity Imperatives in the Digital Age. In *Navigating Cyber Threats and Cybersecurity in the Logistics Industry* (pp. 236–257). IGI Global. DOI:10.4018/979-8-3693-3816-2.ch009

Aslam, M. (2024). AI and Cybersecurity: An Ever-Evolving Landscape. *International Journal of Advanced Engineering Technologies and Innovations*, 1(1), 52–71.

Bakare, S. S., Adeniyi, A. O., Akpuokwe, C. U., & Eneh, N. E. (2024). Data privacy laws and compliance: A comparative review of the EU GDPR and USA regulations. *Computer Science & IT Research Journal*, 5(3), 528–543. DOI:10.51594/csitrj.v5i3.859

Binnar, P., Bhirud, S., & Kazi, F. (2024). Security analysis of cyber physical system using digital forensic incident response. *Cyber Security and Applications*, 2, 100034. DOI:10.1016/j.csa.2023.100034

Bisht, R. (2023). NIST Cybersecurity Framework 2.0. Retrieved from https://www.infosectrain.com/blog/nist-cybersecurity-framework/

Bland, J. A., Petty, M. D., Whitaker, T. S., Maxwell, K. P., & Cantrell, W. A. (2020). Machine Learning Cyberattack and Defense Strategies. *Computers & Security*, 92, 101738. DOI:10.1016/j.cose.2020.101738

Boopathy, P., Liyanage, M., Deepa, N., Velavali, M., Reddy, S., Maddikunta, P. K. R., Khare, N., Gadekallu, T. R., Hwang, W.-J., & Pham, Q.-V. (2024). Deep learning for intelligent demand response and smart grids: A comprehensive survey. *Computer Science Review*, 51, 100617. DOI:10.1016/j.cosrev.2024.100617

Camilleri, M. A. (2023). Artificial intelligence governance: Ethical considerations and implications for social responsibility. *Expert Systems: International Journal of Knowledge Engineering and Neural Networks*. Advance online publication. DOI:10.1111/exsy.13406

Chakraborty, S. (2023). AI and ethics: Navigating the moral landscape. In *Investigating the Impact of AI on Ethics and Spirituality* (pp. 25-33).

David, E., & Eldon, S. (2022). AI Technologies, Privacy, and Security. *Frontiers in Artificial Intelligence*, 5, 826737. Advance online publication. DOI:10.3389/frai.2022.826737 PMID:35493613

De Cerqueira, J. A. S., Tives, H. A., & Canedo, E. D. (2021). *Ethical Guidelines and Principles in the Context of Artificial Intelligence.* Paper presented at the ACM International Conference Proceeding Series. DOI:10.1145/3466933.3466969

Desai, T. (2024). Cybersecurity Faces Transformation from Generative AI. Retrieved from https://www.globalxetfs.com/cybersecurity-faces-transformation-from -generative-ai/

Dhoni, P., & Kumar, R. (2023). Synergizing generative ai and cybersecurity: Roles of generative ai entities, companies, agencies, and government in enhancing cybersecurity. *Authorea Preprints*.

Dogra, V., Verma, S., Verma, K., Jhanjhi, N. Z., Ghosh, U., & Le, D.-N. (2022). A comparative analysis of machine learning models for banking news extraction by multiclass classification with imbalanced datasets of financial news: challenges and solutions.

ElBaih, M. (2023). The role of privacy regulations in ai development (A Discussion of the Ways in Which Privacy Regulations Can Shape the Development of AI). *Available at* SSRN *4589207*. enisa.europa. (2022). Cybersecurity Threats Fast-Forward 2030: Fasten your Security-Belt Before the Ride! Retrieved from https://www.enisa .europa.eu/news/cybersecurity-threats-fast-forward-2030DOI:10.2139/ssrn.4589207

Erwin, A., Zubair, A. B., & Sherali, Z. (2022). Artificial Intelligence for Cybersecurity: Offensive Tactics. *Mitigation Techniques and Future Directions.*, 1(1), 1–23. DOI:10.5604/01.3001.0016.0800

Gill, S. S., Xu, M., Ottaviani, C., Patros, P., Bahsoon, R., Shaghaghi, A., & Abraham, A. (2022). AI for next generation computing: Emerging trends and future directions. *Internet of Things : Engineering Cyber Physical Human Systems*, 19, 100514. DOI:10.1016/j.iot.2022.100514

Gupta, M., Akiri, C., Aryal, K., Parker, E., & Praharaj, L. (2023). From ChatGPT to ThreatGPT: Impact of Generative AI in Cybersecurity and Privacy. *IEEE Access : Practical Innovations, Open Solutions*, 11, 80218–80245. DOI:10.1109/ACCESS.2023.3300381

Gursoy, D., & Cai, R. (2024). Artificial intelligence: An overview of research trends and future directions. *International Journal of Contemporary Hospitality Management*. Advance online publication. DOI:10.1108/IJCHM-03-2024-0322

Huang, C., Zhang, Z., Mao, B., & Yao, X. (2023). An Overview of Artificial Intelligence Ethics. *IEEE Transactions on Artificial Intelligence*, 4(4), 799–819. DOI:10.1109/TAI.2022.3194503

Humayun, M., Jhanjhi, N., Alsayat, A., & Ponnusamy, V. (2021). Internet of things and ransomware: Evolution, mitigation and prevention. *Egyptian Informatics Journal*, 22(1), 105–117. DOI:10.1016/j.eij.2020.05.003

Iqbal, H. S., Iqbal, H. S., Hasan, F., & Raza, N. (2021). AI-Driven Cybersecurity: An Overview. *SN Computer Science*, 2(3), 1–18. DOI:10.1007/s42979-021-00557-0

Jhanjhi, N., Khan, M. A., Ahmad, M., & Hussain, M. (2022). The Impact of Cyber Attacks on E-Governance During the COVID-19 Pandemic. *Cybersecurity Measures for E-Government Frameworks*, 123.

Jhanjhi, N. Z., & Shah, I. A. (2024). *Navigating Cyber Threats and Cybersecurity in the Logistics Industry*. IGI Global. DOI:10.4018/979-8-3693-3816-2

Khaleefah, A. D., & Al-Mashhadi, H. M. (2024). Methodologies, Requirements, and Challenges of Cybersecurity Frameworks: A Review. *Iraqi Journal of Science*, 468–486. DOI:10.24996/ijs.2024.65.1.38

Khan, A., Jhanjhi, N., Haji, D. H. T. B. A., & bin Haji Omar, H. A. H. (2024). Overview of XAI for the Development and Modernization of Smart Cities: Explainable Artificial Intelligence. In *Advances in Explainable AI Applications for Smart Cities* (pp. 177-198). IGI Global.

Khan, A. A., Akbar, M. A., Fahmideh, M., Liang, P., Waseem, M., Ahmad, A., Niazi, M., & Abrahamsson, P. (2023). AI Ethics: An Empirical Study on the Views of Practitioners and Lawmakers. *IEEE Transactions on Computational Social Systems*, 10(6), 2971–2984. DOI:10.1109/TCSS.2023.3251729

Khan, A. A., Akbar, M. A., Waseem, M., Fahmideh, M., Ahmad, A., Liang, P., . . . Abrahamsson, P. (2022). AI ethics: software practitioners and lawmakers points of view. *arXiv preprint arXiv:2207.01493*.

Khan, M. R., Khan, N. R., & Jhanjhi, N. Z. (2024). *Convergence of Industry 4.0 and Supply Chain Sustainability*: IGI Global.

Kumar, A., Aelgani, V., Vohra, R., Gupta, S. K., Bhagawati, M., Paul, S., & Laird, J. R. (2024). Artificial intelligence bias in medical system designs: A systematic review. *Multimedia Tools and Applications*, 83(6), 18005–18057. DOI:10.1007/s11042-023-16029-x

Mossavar-Rahmani, F., & Zohuri, B. (2024). Artificial Intelligence at Work: Transforming Industries and Redefining the Workforce Landscape. *Journal of Economics & Management Research. SRC/JESMR-284.J Econ Managem Res*, 5(2), 2–4.

Nguyen, M. T., & Tran, M. Q. (2023). Balancing security and privacy in the digital age: An in-depth analysis of legal and regulatory frameworks impacting cybersecurity practices. *International Journal of Intelligent Automation and Computing*, 6(5), 1–12.

Ortega, E., Tran, M., & Bandeen, G. (2023). *AI Digital Tool Product Lifecycle Governance Framework through Ethics and Compliance by Design†*. Paper presented at the Proceedings - 2023 IEEE Conference on Artificial Intelligence, CAI 2023. DOI:10.1109/CAI54212.2023.00155

Othman, U., & Yang, E. (2023). Human–robot collaborations in smart manufacturing environments: Review and outlook. *Sensors (Basel)*, 23(12), 5663. DOI:10.3390/s23125663 PMID:37420834

Owino, B. A., & Paschal, M. J. (2023). AI and ethics in education: Implications and strategies for responsible implementation. In *Creative AI Tools and Ethical Implications in Teaching and Learning* (pp. 196-211).

Paola, Z. L., Lopez, S. J., Christian, A. H., & Sonia, R. U. (2023). Correction of Banding Errors in Satellite Images With Generative Adversarial Networks (GAN). *IEEE Access: Practical Innovations, Open Solutions*, 11, 51960–51970. DOI:10.1109/ACCESS.2023.3279265

Perri, L. (2023). Understand and Exploit GenAI With Gartner's New Impact Radar. Retrieved from https://www.gartner.com/en/articles/understand-and-exploit-gen-ai-with-gartner-s-new-impact-radar

Prabakar, D., Sundarrajan, M., Manikandan, R., Jhanjhi, N., Masud, M., & Alqhatani, A. (2023). Energy Analysis-Based Cyber Attack Detection by IoT with Artificial Intelligence in a Sustainable Smart City. *Sustainability (Basel)*, 15(7), 6031. DOI:10.3390/su15076031

qsstechnosoft.com. (2024). AI-Driven Cybersecurity: Mitigating Threats in the Age of Generative AI. Retrieved from https://www.qsstechnosoft.com/blog/ai-driven-cybersecurity-mitigating-threats-in-the-age-of-generative-ai/

Raja, A. K., & Zhou, J. (2023). AI Accountability: Approaches, Affecting Factors, and Challenges. *Computer*, 56(4), 61–70. DOI:10.1109/MC.2023.3238390

Rehan, H. (2024). AI-Driven Cloud Security: The Future of Safeguarding Sensitive Data in the Digital Age. *Journal of Artificial Intelligence General Science, 1*(1), 47-66.

Saveliev, A., & Zhurenkov, D. (2021). Artificial intelligence and social responsibility: The case of the artificial intelligence strategies in the United States, Russia, and China. *Kybernetes*, 50(3), 656–675. DOI:10.1108/K-01-2020-0060

Shafik, W. (2023). A Comprehensive Cybersecurity Framework for Present and Future Global Information Technology Organizations. In *Effective Cybersecurity Operations for Enterprise-Wide Systems* (pp. 56–79). IGI Global. DOI:10.4018/978-1-6684-9018-1.ch002

Shah, I. A., Jhanjhi, N., & Ray, S. K. (2024). Artificial Intelligence Applications in the Context of the Security Framework for the Logistics Industry. In *Advances in Explainable AI Applications for Smart Cities* (pp. 297–316). IGI Global. DOI:10.4018/978-1-6684-6361-1.ch011

Shah, I. A., Jhanjhi, N. Z., & Ray, S. K. (2024). Enabling Explainable AI in Cybersecurity Solutions. In *Advances in Explainable AI Applications for Smart Cities* (pp. 255–275). IGI Global. DOI:10.4018/978-1-6684-6361-1.ch009

Sindiramutty, S. R., Jhanjhi, N. Z., Tan, C. E., Khan, N. A., Shah, B., & Manchuri, A. R. (2024). Cybersecurity Measures for Logistics Industry. In *Navigating Cyber Threats and Cybersecurity in the Logistics Industry* (pp. 1–58). IGI Global. DOI:10.4018/979-8-3693-3816-2.ch001

Sindiramutty, S. R., Jhanjhi, N. Z., Tan, C. E., Yun, K. J., Manchuri, A. R., Ashraf, H., & Hussain, M. (2024). Data Security and Privacy Concerns in Drone Operations. In *Cybersecurity Issues and Challenges in the Drone Industry* (pp. 236–290). IGI Global. DOI:10.4018/979-8-3693-0774-8.ch010

Singh, P. K., & Kumar, A. (2023). Cyber Physical Systems in Supply Chain Management. In *Cyber Physical Systems* (pp. 85–110). Chapman and Hall/CRC.

Stankovich, M. (2024). Unlocking the Potential of Generative AI in Cybersecurity: A Roadmap to Opportunities and Challenges. Retrieved from https://dai-global-digital.com/unlocking-the-potential-of-generative-ai-in-cybersecurity-a-roadmap-to-opportunities-and-challenges.html

Takale, D. G., Mahalle, P. N., & Sule, B. (2024). Cyber Security Challenges in Generative AI Technology. *Journal of Network Security Computer Networks*, 10(1), 28–34.

Tamoghna, D. (2024). Top 13 Cyber Security Trends For 2024. Retrieved from https://www.selecthub.com/endpoint-security/cyber-security-trends/

Val, T. (2023). Data Generation with Variational Autoencoders and Generative Adversarial Networks. DOI:10.3390/engproc2023033037

van Geest, R. J., Cascavilla, G., Hulstijn, J., & Zannone, N. (2024). The applicability of a hybrid framework for automated phishing detection. *Computers & Security*, 139, 103736. DOI:10.1016/j.cose.2024.103736

Vetrò, A., Santangelo, A., Beretta, E., & De Martin, J. C. (2019). AI: From rational agents to socially responsible agents. *Digital Policy. Regulation & Governance*, 21(3), 291–304. DOI:10.1108/DPRG-08-2018-0049

Vietrov, I. (2024). Generative AI Trends: Transforming Business and Shaping Future. Retrieved from https://masterofcode.com/blog/generative-ai-trends

Wu, W., & Liu, S. (2023). A comprehensive review and systematic analysis of artificial intelligence regulation policies. *arXiv preprint arXiv:2307.12218*.

Yigit, Y., Buchanan, W. J., Tehrani, M. G., & Maglaras, L. (2024). Review of Generative AI Methods in Cybersecurity. *arXiv preprint arXiv:2403.08701*.

Zaman, N., Ghazanfar, M. A., Anwar, M., Lee, S. W., Qazi, N., Karimi, A., & Javed, A. (2023). Stock market prediction based on machine learning and social sentiment analysis. *Authorea Preprints*.

Zhou, Y., & Kankanhalli, A. (2021). AI Regulation for Smart Cities: Challenges and Principles. In *Public Administration and Information Technology* (Vol. 37, pp. 101-118).

Compilation of References

Aalaei, M., Saadi, M., Rahbar, M., & Ekhlassi, A. (2023). Architectural layout generation using a graph-constrained conditional Generative Adversarial Network (GAN). *Automation in Construction*, 155, 105053. DOI:10.1016/j.autcon.2023.105053

Abbas, Ahmed, Shah, Omar, & Park. (n.d.). Investigating the applications of AI in cyber security. Academic Press.

Abbas, S., Alnoor, A., Teh, S. Y., Sadaa, A. M., Muhsen, Y. R., Khaw, K. W., & Ganesan, Y. (2023). Antecedents of trustworthiness of social commerce platforms: A case of rural communities using multi-group SEM & MCDM methods. *Electronic Commerce Research and Applications*, 62, 101322. DOI:10.1016/j.elerap.2023.101322

Abd El-mawla, N., Badawy, M., & Arafat, H. (2019). Security And Key Management Challenges Over WSN (A Survey). *Int. J. Comput. Sci. Eng. Surv.*, 10(01), 15–34. DOI:10.5121/ijcses.2019.10102

Abdelmoumin, G., Whitaker, J., Rawat, D. B., & Rahman, A. (2022). A Survey on Data-Driven Learning for Intelligent Network Intrusion Detection Systems. *Electronics (Basel)*, 11(2), 213. DOI:10.3390/electronics11020213

Abdullah, A. (2019). International Journal of Computing and Digital Systems. *International Journal of Computing and Digital Systems* [Preprint]. https://doi.org/.DOI:10.12785/ijcds

Abedin, M. Z., & Hajek, P. (2023). *Cyber security and business intelligence: Innovations and Machine Learning for Cyber Risk Management*. Taylor & Francis. DOI:10.4324/9781003285854

Abhilash, J. V., Nasser, T., Raed, A. S., Taher, M. G., Munir Uddin, A., Haitham, M. A., & Muhammad, A. (2023). A Roadmap for SMEs to Adopt an AI Based Cyber Threat Intelligence. *Studies in computational intelligence*, 1903-1926. DOI:10.1007/978-3-031-12382-5_105

Aboukadri, S., Ouaddah, A., & Mezrioui, A. (2024). Machine learning in identity and access Management Systems: Survey and deep dive. *Computers & Security*, 139, 103729. DOI:10.1016/j.cose.2024.103729

Abrahams, T. O., Ewuga, S. K., Kaggwa, S., Uwaoma, P. U., Hassan, A. O., & Dawodu, S. O. (2024). Mastering compliance: A comprehensive review of regulatory frameworks in accounting and cybersecurity. *Computer Science & IT Research Journal*, 5(1), 120–140. DOI:10.51594/csitrj.v5i1.709

Abukmeil, M., Ferrari, S., Genovese, A., Piuri, V., & Scotti, F. (2021). A survey of Unsupervised Generative Models for exploratory data analysis and representation learning. *ACM Computing Surveys*, 54(5), 1–40. DOI:10.1145/3450963

Abulibdeh, A., Zaidan, E., & Abulibdeh, R. (2024). Navigating the confluence of artificial intelligence and education for sustainable development in the era of industry 4.0: Challenges, opportunities, and ethical dimensions. *Journal of Cleaner Production*, 437, 140527. DOI:10.1016/j.jclepro.2023.140527

Adaga, E. M., Egieya, Z. E., Ewuga, S. K., Abdul, A. A., & Abrahams, T. O. (2024). Philosophy in business analytics: a review of sustainable and ethical approaches. *International Journal of Management & Entrepreneurship Research*, 6(1), 69–86. DOI:10.51594/ijmer.v6i1.710

Adams, A. J., Miller-Lewis, L., & Tieman, J. (2023). Learning Designers as Expert Evaluators of Usability: Understanding their potential contribution to improving the universality of interface design for health resources. *International Journal of Environmental Research and Public Health*, 20(5), 4608. DOI:10.3390/ijerph20054608 PMID:36901617

Adeyemo, V. E., Abdullah, A., Jhanjhi, N. Z., Supramaniam, M., & Balogun, A. O. (2019). Ensemble and Deep-Learning Methods for Two-Class and Multi-Attack Anomaly Intrusion Detection: An Empirical Study. *International Journal of Advanced Computer Science and Applications*, 10(9). Advance online publication. DOI:10.14569/IJACSA.2019.0100969

Adigwe, C. S., Olaniyi, O. O., Olabanji, S. O., Okunleye, O. J., Mayeke, N. R., & Ajayi, S. S. (2024). Forecasting the Future: The Interplay of Artificial Intelligence, Innovation, and Competitiveness and its Effect on the Global Economy. *Asian Journal of Economics. Business and Accounting*, 24(4), 126–146. DOI:10.9734/ajeba/2024/v24i41269

Agarwal, A., & Agarwal, H. (2023). A seven-layer model with checklists for standardising fairness assessment throughout the AI lifecycle. *AI and Ethics*. Advance online publication. DOI:10.1007/s43681-023-00266-9

Agarwal, A., Agarwal, H., & Agarwal, N. (2022). Fairness Score and process standardisation: Framework for fairness certification in artificial intelligence systems. *AI and Ethics*, 3(1), 267–279. DOI:10.1007/s43681-022-00147-7

Agbede, O. M. (2023). *Incident handling and response process in security operations*. Theseus. https://www.theseus.fi/handle/10024/795764

Agboola, O. P., & Tunay, M. (2023). Urban resilience in the digital age: The influence of Information-Communication Technology for sustainability. *Journal of Cleaner Production*, 428, 139304. DOI:10.1016/j.jclepro.2023.139304

Agrawal, G., Kaur, A., & Myneni, S. (2024). A review of generative models in generating synthetic attack data for cybersecurity. *Electronics (Basel)*, 13(2), 322. DOI:10.3390/electronics13020322

Agrawal, K. P. (2023). Towards adoption of generative AI in organisational settings. *Journal of Computer Information Systems*, 1–16. DOI:10.1080/08874417.2023.2240744

Aherwadi, N., Mittal, U., Singla, J., Jhanjhi, N. Z., Yassine, A., & Hossain, M. S. (2022). Prediction of fruit maturity, quality, and its life using deep learning algorithms. *Electronics (Basel)*, 11(24), 4100. DOI:10.3390/electronics11244100

Ahlawat, P., & Dave, M. (2018). An attack resistant key predistribution scheme for wireless sensor networks. *Journal of King Saud University. Computer and Information Sciences*.

Ahmadi, S. (2024b). Open AI and its Impact on Fraud Detection in Financial Industry. *Journal of Knowledge Learning and Science Technology ISSN 2959-6386 (Online)*, 2(3), 263–281. DOI:10.60087/jklst.vol2.n3.p281

Ahmadi, S. (2024). Challenges and solutions in network security for serverless computing. *International Journal of Current Science Research and Review*, 07(01). Advance online publication. DOI:10.47191/ijcsrr/V7-i1-23

Ahmadi, S. (2024a). A Comprehensive Study on Integration of Big Data and AI in Financial Industry and its Effect on Present and Future Opportunities. *International Journal of Current Science Research and Review*, 07(01). Advance online publication. DOI:10.47191/ijcsrr/V7-i1-07

Ahmed, A., & Abdulkareem, A. M. (2023, June 1). *Big data analytics in the entertainment industry: audience behaviour analysis, content recommendation, and revenue maximisation*. https://researchberg.com/index.php/rcba/article/view/142

Ahmed, M. M., & Ahmed, A. M. (2023). Citizens' data protection in e-government system. *International Journal of Innovative Computing*, 13(2), 1–9. DOI:10.11113/ijic.v13n2.389

Ahmet, E. F. E., & Abaci, İ. N. (2022). Comparison of the host based intrusion detection systems and network based intrusion detection systems. *Celal Bayar University Journal of Science*, 18(1), 23–32.

Aibekova, A., & Selvarajah, V. (2022, April). Offensive Security: Study on Penetration Testing Attacks, Methods, and their Types. In *2022 IEEE International Conference on Distributed Computing and Electrical Circuits and Electronics (ICDCECE)* (pp. 1-9). IEEE. DOI:10.1109/ICDCECE53908.2022.9792772

Akanfe, O., Lawong, D., & Rao, H. R. (2024). Blockchain technology and privacy regulation: Reviewing frictions and synthesizing opportunities. *International Journal of Information Management*, 76, 102753. DOI:10.1016/j.ijinfomgt.2024.102753

Akçay, S., Atapour-Abarghouei, A., & Breckon, T. P. (2019). Skip-GANomaly: Skip Connected and Adversarially Trained Encoder-Decoder Anomaly Detection. *2019 International Joint Conference on Neural Networks (IJCNN)*. DOI:10.1109/IJCNN.2019.8851808

Akyildiz, I. F., Su, W., Sankarasubramaniam, Y., & Cayirci, E. (2002). Wireless sensor networks: A survey. *Computer Networks*, 38(4), 393–422. DOI:10.1016/S1389-1286(01)00302-4

Al Shebli, H. M. Z., & Beheshti, B. D. (2018, May). A study on penetration testing process and tools. In 2018 IEEE Long Island Systems, Applications and Technology Conference (LISAT) (pp. 1-7). IEEE. DOI:10.1109/LISAT.2018.8378035

Alalmaie, A. Z., Nanda, P., & He, X. (2024) 'Zt-Nids: Zero Trust - Network Intrusion Detection System Validation Based on Attack Simulations,' *SSRN* [Preprint]. DOI:10.2139/ssrn.4762072

Alam, A. (2023). Developing a Curriculum for Ethical and Responsible AI: a university course on safety, fairness, privacy, and ethics to prepare next generation of AI professionals. *Lecture notes on data engineering and communications technologies*, 879–894. DOI:10.1007/978-981-99-1767-9_64

Alanazi, M. N. (2024). 5G security threat landscape, AI, and blockchain. *Wireless Personal Communications*. Advance online publication. DOI:10.1007/s11277-023-10821-6

Alanda, A., Satria, D., Ardhana, M. I., Dahlan, A. A., & Mooduto, H. A. (2021). Web application penetration testing using SQL Injection attack. JOIV. *International Journal on Informatics Visualization*, 5(3), 320–326. DOI:10.30630/joiv.5.3.470

Albahar, M., Alansari, D., & Jurcut, A. (2022). An empirical comparison of pentesting tools for detecting web app vulnerabilities. *Electronics (Basel)*, 11(19), 2991. DOI:10.3390/electronics11192991

Albahri, A. S., Duhaim, A. M., Fadhel, M. A., Alnoor, A., Baqer, N. S., Alzubaidi, L., Albahri, O. S., Alamoodi, A. H., Bai, J., Salhi, A., Santamaría, J., Ouyang, C., Gupta, A., Gu, Y., & Deveci, M. (2023). A systematic review of trustworthy and explainable artificial intelligence in healthcare: Assessment of quality, bias risk, and data fusion. *Information Fusion*, 96, 156–191. DOI:10.1016/j.inffus.2023.03.008

Albaroudi, E., Mansouri, T., & Alameer, A. (2024). A comprehensive review of AI techniques for addressing algorithmic bias in job hiring. *AI*, 5(1), 383–404. DOI:10.3390/ai5010019

Al-Daajeh, S. H., Saleous, H., Alrabaee, S., Barka, E., Breitinger, F., & Raymond Choo, K.-K. (2022). The role of national cybersecurity strategies on the improvement of cybersecurity education. *Computers & Security*, 119, 102754. DOI:10.1016/j.cose.2022.102754

Aldausari, N. (2022). *Cascaded Siamese Self-Supervised Audio to Video GAN*. https://openaccess.thecvf.com/content/CVPR2022W/MULA/html/Aldausari_Cascaded_Siamese_Self-Supervised_Audio_to_Video_GAN_CVPRW_2022_paper.html

AL-Dosari, K., Fetais, N., & Kucukvar, M. (2024). Artificial intelligence and cyber defense system for banking industry: A qualitative study of AI applications and challenges. *Cybernetics and Systems*, 55(2), 302–330. DOI:10.1080/01969722.2022.2112539

Alemi, A. (2018, February 15). *An information-theoretic analysis of deep latent-variable models*. OpenReview. https://openreview.net/forum?id=H1rRWl-Cb

Alex, S. A., Jhanjhi, N. Z., & Ray, S. K. (2023). *Blockchain Based E-Medical Data Storage for Privacy Protection*. Paper presented at the International Conference on Mathematical Modeling and Computational Science. DOI:10.1007/978-981-99-3611-3_10

Alexandrou, A. (2021). *Cybercrime and information technology: The computer network infrastructure and computer security, cybersecurity laws, Internet of Things (IoT), and mobile devices*. CRC Press. DOI:10.4324/9780429318726

Alex, S. A., Jhanjhi, N. Z., Humayun, M., Ibrahim, A. O., & Abulfaraj, A. W. (2022). Deep LSTM model for diabetes prediction with class balancing by SMOTE. *Electronics (Basel)*, 11(17), 2737. DOI:10.3390/electronics11172737

Alferidah, D. K., & Jhanjhi, N. Z. (2020, October). Cybersecurity impact over bigdata and iot growth. In *2020 International Conference on Computational Intelligence (ICCI)* (pp. 103-108). IEEE. DOI:10.1109/ICCI51257.2020.9247722

Alhitmi, H. K., Mardiah, A., Al-Sulaiti, K. I., & Abbas, J. (2024). Data Security and Privacy Concerns of Ai-Driven Marketing in the Context of Economics and Business Field: An Exploration into Possible Solutions. *SSRN*. DOI:10.1080/233 11975.2024.2393743

Aliady, W. A., & Al-Ahmadi, S. A. (2019). Energy preserving secure measure against wormhole attack in wireless sensor networks. *IEEE Access : Practical Innovations, Open Solutions*, 7, 84132–84141. DOI:10.1109/ACCESS.2019.2924283

Ali, M. M., & Zaharon, N. F. M. (2022). Phishing—A Cyber fraud: The types, implications and governance. *International Journal of Educational Reform*, 33(1), 101–121. DOI:10.1177/10567879221082966

Ali, R. S. E., Meng, J., Khan, M. E. I., & Jiang, X. (2024). Machine Learning Advancements in Organic Synthesis: A focused exploration of artificial intelligence applications in chemistry. *Artificial Intelligence Chemistry.*, 2(1), 100049. DOI:10.1016/j.aichem.2024.100049

Ali, S., Abdullah, , Armand, T. P. T., Athar, A., Hussain, A., Ali, M., Yaseen, M., Joo, M.-I., & Kim, H.-C. (2023). Metaverse in healthcare integrated with explainable ai and blockchain: Enabling immersiveness, ensuring trust, and providing patient data security. *Sensors (Basel)*, 23(2), 565. DOI:10.3390/s23020565 PMID:36679361

Ali, S., Li, Q., & Yousafzai, A. (2024). Blockchain and federated learning-based intrusion detection approaches for edge-enabled industrial IoT networks: A survey. *Ad Hoc Networks*, 152, 103320. DOI:10.1016/j.adhoc.2023.103320

Aljawarneh, S., Aldwairi, M., & Yassein, M. B. (2018). Anomaly-based intrusion detection system through feature selection analysis and building hybrid efficient model. *Journal of Computational Science*, 25, 152–160. DOI:10.1016/j.jocs.2017.03.006

Alkinani, M. H., Almazroi, A. A., & Khan, N. A. (2021). 5G and IoT based reporting and accident detection (RAD) system to deliver first aid box using unmanned aerial vehicle. *Sensors (Basel)*, 21(20), 6905. DOI:10.3390/s21206905 PMID:34696118

Allioui, H., & Mourdi, Y. (2023). Exploring the Full Potentials of IoT for Better Financial Growth and Stability: A Comprehensive Survey. *Sensors (Basel)*, 23(19), 8015. DOI:10.3390/s23198015 PMID:37836845

Ally, M. (2019). Using gamification to enhance learning and teaching. Journal of Education and Learning.

Almusaylim, Z. A., Jhanjhi, N. Z., & Jung, L. T. (2018). Proposing A Data Privacy Aware Protocol for Roadside Accident Video Reporting Service Using 5G In Vehicular Cloud Networks Environment. *2018 4th International Conference on Computer and Information Sciences (ICCOINS)*. DOI:10.1109/ICCOINS.2018.8510588

Almusaylim, , Z., & Jhanjhi, N. (2020). Comprehensive review: Privacy protection of user in location-aware services of mobile cloud computing. *Wireless Personal Communications*, 111, 541–564. DOI:10.1007/s11277-019-06872-3

Almusaylim, Z. A., Jhanjhi, N. Z., & Alhumam, A. (2020). Detection and Mitigation of RPL rank and version number attacks in the Internet of Things: SRPL-RP. *Sensors (Basel)*, 20(21), 5997. DOI:10.3390/s20215997 PMID:33105891

Alotaibi, A., & Rassam, M. A. (2023). Adversarial Machine Learning Attacks against Intrusion Detection Systems: A Survey on Strategies and Defense. *Future Internet*, 15(2), 62. DOI:10.3390/fi15020062

Alqahtani, H., & Kumar, G. (2024). Machine learning for enhancing transportation security: A comprehensive analysis of electric and flying vehicle systems. *Engineering Applications of Artificial Intelligence*, 129, 107667. DOI:10.1016/j.engappai.2023.107667

Alraih, S., Shayea, I., Behjati, M., Nordin, R., Abdullah, N. F., Abu-Samah, A., & Nandi, D. (2022). Revolution or evolution? Technical requirements and considerations towards 6G mobile communications. *Sensors (Basel)*, 22(3), 762. DOI:10.3390/s22030762 PMID:35161509

Alsamiri, J., & Alsubhi, K. (2023). Federated Learning for Intrusion Detection Systems in Internet of Vehicles: A General Taxonomy, Applications, and Future Directions. *Future Internet*, 15(12), 403. DOI:10.3390/fi15120403

Altulaihan, E. A., Alismail, A., & Frikha, M. (2023). A Survey on Web Application Penetration Testing. *Electronics (Basel)*, 12(5), 1229. DOI:10.3390/electronics12051229

Alzaabi, F., & Mehmood, A. (2024). *A Review of Recent Advances, Challenges and Opportunities in Malicious Insider Threat Detection using Machine Learning Methods*. IEEE Access. DOI:10.1109/ACCESS.2024.3369906

Amankwah-Amoah, J., Abdalla, S., Mogaji, E., Elbanna, A. R., & Dwivedi, Y. K. (2024). The impending disruption of creative industries by generative AI: Opportunities, challenges, and research agenda. *International Journal of Information Management*, 102759, 102759. Advance online publication. DOI:10.1016/j.ijinfomgt.2024.102759

Amershi, S., Weld, D., Vorvoreanu, M., Fourney, A., Nushi, B., Collisson, P., Suh, J., Iqbal, S. T., Bennett, P., Inkpen, K., Teevan, J., Kikin-Gil, R., & Horvitz, E. (2019). *Guidelines for Human-AI Interaction*. ACM. DOI:10.1145/3290605.3300233

Amish, P., & Vaghela, V. B. (2016). Detection and Prevention of Wormhole Attack in Wireless Sensor Network using AOMDV Protocol. *Procedia Computer Science*, 79, 700–707. DOI:10.1016/j.procs.2016.03.092

Ananna, F. F., Nowreen, R., Jahwari, S. S. R. A., Costa, E., Angeline, L., & Sindiramutty, S. R. (2023). Analysing Influential factors in student academic achievement: Prediction modelling and insight. *International Journal of Emerging Multidisciplinaries Computer Science & Artificial Intelligence*, 2(1). Advance online publication. DOI:10.54938/ijemdcsai.2023.02.1.254

Anderson, H. (2024, February 2). *The Guardian of the Digital Era: Assessing the impact and challenges of the Children's Online Privacy Protection Act*. https://www.paradigmpress.org/le/article/view/1004

Andrada, G., Clowes, R. W., & Smart, P. R. (2022). Varieties of transparency: Exploring agency within AI systems. *AI & Society*, 38(4), 1321–1331. DOI:10.1007/s00146-021-01326-6 PMID:35035112

Andria, A., & Pamungkas, R. (2021). Penetration Testing Database Menggunakan Metode SQL Injection Via SQLMap di Termux. *IJAI*, 5(1), 1. DOI:10.20961/ijai.v5i1.40845

Angafor, G. N., Yevseyeva, I., & Μαγλαράς, Λ. (2023). Scenario-based incident response training: Lessons learnt from conducting an experiential learning virtual incident response tabletop exercise. *Information and Computer Security*, 31(4), 404–426. DOI:10.1108/ICS-05-2022-0085

Anjaria, B., & Shah, J. (2024) *Exploring magnitude perturbation in adversarial attack & defense*. https://ijisae.org/index.php/IJISAE/article/view/4589

Annadurai, C., Nelson, I., Devi, K. N., Manikandan, R., Jhanjhi, N., Masud, M., & Sheikh, A. (2022). Biometric authentication-based intrusion detection using artificial intelligence internet of things in smart city. *Energies*, 15(19), 7430. DOI:10.3390/en15197430

An, P., Zhu, J., Zhang, Z., Yin, Y., Ma, Q., Cao, Y., Du, L., & Zhao, J. (2024). *EmOWear: Exploring emotional teasers for voice message interaction on smart-watches. arXiv*. Cornell University. DOI:10.1145/3613904.3642101

Apata, O., Bokoro, P. N., & Sharma, G. (2023). The Risks and Challenges of Electric Vehicle Integration into Smart Cities. *Energies*, 16(14), 5274. DOI:10.3390/en16145274

Ariyo, S. M. I. E. E., & Olufemi, E. (2023). *The Future of Cyber Security in An AI-Driven World*.

Arora, J. S., & Baenziger, G. (1986). Uses of artificial intelligence in design optimization. *Computer Methods in Applied Mechanics and Engineering*, 54(3), 303–323. DOI:10.1016/0045-7825(86)90108-8

Arora, S., & Doshi, P. (2021). A survey of inverse reinforcement learning: Challenges, methods and progress. *Artificial Intelligence*, 297, 103500. DOI:10.1016/j.artint.2021.103500

Asharf, J., Moustafa, N., Khurshid, H., Debie, E., Haider, W., & Wahab, A. (2020). A review of intrusion detection systems using machine and deep learning in Internet of Things: Challenges, solutions and Future Directions. *Electronics (Basel)*, 9(7), 1177. DOI:10.3390/electronics9071177

Ashfaq, F., Jhanjhi, N. Z., Khan, N. A., & Das, S. R. (2023). *Synthetic Crime Scene Generation Using Deep Generative Networks*. Paper presented at the International Conference on Mathematical Modeling and Computational Science. DOI:10.1007/978-981-99-3611-3_43

Ashraf, H., Nawaz, M., & Jhanjhi, N. (2024). ML-Based Detection of Sybil Attack on MANETS.

Ashraf, H., Hanif, M., Ihsan, U., Al-Quayed, F., Humayun, M., & Jhanjhi, N. Z. (2023, March). A Secure and Reliable Supply chain management approach integrated with IoT and Blockchain. In *2023 International Conference on Business Analytics for Technology and Security (ICBATS)* (pp. 1-9). IEEE. DOI:10.1109/ICBATS57792.2023.10111371

Ashraf, H., Jhanjhi, N. Z., Brohi, S. N., & Muzafar, S. (2024). A Comprehensive Exploration of DDoS Attacks and Cybersecurity Imperatives in the Digital Age. In *Navigating Cyber Threats and Cybersecurity in the Logistics Industry* (pp. 236–257). IGI Global. DOI:10.4018/979-8-3693-3816-2.ch009

Ashraf, H., Ullah, A., Tahira, S., & Sher, M. (2019). Efficient Certificate Based One-pass Authentication Protocol for IMS. *Journal of Internet Technology*, 20(4), 1133–1143.

Aslam, M. (2024). AI and Cybersecurity: An Ever-Evolving Landscape. *International Journal of Advanced Engineering Technologies and Innovations*, 1(1), 52–71.

Asperti, A., Evangelista, D., & Loli Piccolomini, E. (2021). A survey on variational autoencoders from a green AI perspective. *SN Computer Science*, 2(4), 301. DOI:10.1007/s42979-021-00702-9

Athmani, S., Bilami, A., & Boubiche, D. E. (2019, March). EDAK: An Efficient Dynamic Authentication and Key Management Mechanism for heterogeneous WSNs. *Future Generation Computer Systems*, 92, 789–799. DOI:10.1016/j.future.2017.10.026

Attaallah, A., Alsuhabi, H., Shukla, S., Kumar, R., Gupta, B. K., & Khan, R. A. (2022). Analyzing the Big Data Security Through a Unified Decision-Making Approach. *Intelligent Automation & Soft Computing*, 32(2), 1071–1088. DOI:10.32604/iasc.2022.022569

Auricchio, V. (2023, November 20). *Navigating AI in service design-empowering service designer to unlock AI's full potential in the design process*. https://www.politesi.polimi.it/handle/10589/211732

Aversa, D., & Dickinson, C. (2019). *Unity Game Optimization: Enhance and extend the performance of all aspects of your Unity games* (3rd ed.). Packt Publishing Ltd.

Azadmanesh, M., Ghahfarokhi, B. S., & Talouki, M. A. (2024) 'Privacy in generative models: attacks and defense mechanisms,' in *Springer eBooks*, pp. 65–89. DOI:10.1007/978-3-031-46238-2_4

Azam, Z., & Islam, Md. M. (2023). Comparative analysis of intrusion detection systems and Machine Learning-Based model analysis through Decision Tree. *IEEE Access*, 11, 80348–80391. DOI:10.1109/ACCESS.2023.3296444

Azam, H., Dulloo, M. I., Majeed, M. H., Wan, J. P. H., Xin, L. T., & Sindiramutty, S. R. (2023). Cybercrime Unmasked: Investigating cases and digital evidence. *International Journal of Emerging Multidisciplinaries Computer Science & Artificial Intelligence*, 2(1). Advance online publication. DOI:10.54938/ijemdcsai.2023.02.1.255

Azam, H., Dulloo, M. I., Majeed, M. H., Wan, J. P. H., Xin, L. T., Tajwar, M. A., & Sindiramutty, S. R. (2023). Defending the digital Frontier: IDPS and the battle against Cyber threat. *International Journal of Emerging Multidisciplinaries Computer Science & Artificial Intelligence*, 2(1). Advance online publication. DOI:10.54938/ijemdcsai.2023.02.1.253

Azam, H., Tajwar, M. A., Mayhialagan, S., Davis, A. J., Yik, C. J., Ali, D., & Sindiramutty, S. R. (2023). Innovations in Security: A Study of Cloud Computing and IoT. *International Journal of Emerging Multidisciplinaries Computer Science & Artificial Intelligence*, 2(1). Advance online publication. DOI:10.54938/ijemdcsai.2023.02.1.252

Azam, H., Tan, M., Pin, L. T., Syahmi, M. A., Qian, A. L. W., Jingyan, H., Uddin, H., & Sindiramutty, S. R. (2023). Wireless Technology Security and Privacy: A Comprehensive Study. *Preprint*. DOI:10.20944/preprints202311.0664.v1

Azar, A. T., Koubaa, A., Ali Mohamed, N., Ibrahim, H. A., Ibrahim, Z. F., Kazim, M., Ammar, A., Benjdira, B., Khamis, A. M., Hameed, I. A., & Casalino, G. (2021). Drone deep reinforcement learning: A review. *Electronics (Basel)*, 10(9), 999. DOI:10.3390/electronics10090999

Azeem, M., Ullah, A., Ashraf, H., Jhanjhi, N. Z., Humayun, M., Aljahdali, S., & Tabbakh, T. A. (2021). Fog-oriented secure and lightweight data aggregation in iomt. *IEEE Access : Practical Innovations, Open Solutions*, 9, 111072–111082. DOI:10.1109/ACCESS.2021.3101668

Azinheira, B., Antunes, M., Maximiano, M., & Gomes, R. (2023). A methodology for mapping cybersecurity standards into governance guidelines for SME in Portugal. *Procedia Computer Science*, 219, 121–128. DOI:10.1016/j.procs.2023.01.272

Babbar, H., Rani, S., Masud, M., Verma, S., Anand, D., & Jhanjhi, N. (2021). Load balancing algorithm for migrating switches in software-defined vehicular networks. *Computers, Materials & Continua*, 67(1), 1301–1316. DOI:10.32604/cmc.2021.014627

Babu, C. V. S. & P, A. (2023) Adaptive AI for dynamic cybersecurity systems. *Advances in computational intelligence and robotics book series*, 52–72. DOI:10.4018/979-8-3693-0230-9.ch003

Badini, S., Regondi, S., & Pugliese, R. (2023). Unleashing the power of artificial intelligence in materials design. *Materials (Basel)*, 16(17), 5927. DOI:10.3390/ma16175927 PMID:37687620

Bagui, S., Mink, D., Bagui, S., Ghosh, T., Plenkers, R., McElroy, T., Dulaney, S., & Shabanali, S. (2023). Introducing UWF-ZeekData22: A Comprehensive Network Traffic Dataset Based on the MITRE ATT&CK Framework. *Data*, 8(1), 18. DOI:10.3390/data8010018

Bai, M., & Fang, X. (2024) *Machine Learning-Based Threat intelligence for proactive network security*. https://ijstindex.com/index.php/ijst/article/view/4

Bai, M., & Fang, X. (2024). Machine Learning-Based Threat Intelligence for Proactive Network Security. *Integrated Journal of Science and Technology, 1*(2).

Bai, C., Liu, P., Liu, K., Wang, L., Zhao, Y., Han, L., & Wang, Z. (2023). Variational dynamic for Self-Supervised Exploration in deep Reinforcement learning. *IEEE Transactions on Neural Networks and Learning Systems*, 34(8), 4776–4790. DOI:10.1109/TNNLS.2021.3129160 PMID:34851835

Bakare, S. S., Adeniyi, A. O., Akpuokwe, C. U., & Eneh, N. E. (2024). Data privacy laws and compliance: A comparative review of the EU GDPR and USA regulations. *Computer Science & IT Research Journal*, 5(3), 528–543. DOI:10.51594/csitrj.v5i3.859

Bakhshi, T., Ghita, B., & Kuzminykh, I. (2024). A Review of IoT Firmware Vulnerabilities and Auditing Techniques. *Sensors (Basel)*, 24(2), 708. DOI:10.3390/s24020708 PMID:38276399

Bak, M., Madai, V. I., Fritzsche, M. C., Mayrhofer, M. T., & McLennan, S. (2022). You can't have AI both ways: Balancing health data privacy and access fairly. *Frontiers in Genetics*, 13, 1490. DOI:10.3389/fgene.2022.929453 PMID:35769991

Balasubramaniam, N., Kauppinen, M., Rannisto, A., Hiekkanen, K., & Kujala, S. (2023). Transparency and explainability of AI systems: From ethical guidelines to requirements. *Information and Software Technology*, 159, 107197. DOI:10.1016/j.infsof.2023.107197

Balayn, A., Lofi, C., & Houben, G. (2021). Managing bias and unfairness in data for decision support: A survey of machine learning and data engineering approaches to identify and mitigate bias and unfairness within data management and analytics systems. *The VLDB Journal*, 30(5), 739–768. DOI:10.1007/s00778-021-00671-8

Bale, A. S. (2024) *The impact of generative content on individuals privacy and ethical concerns*. https://www.ijisae.org/index.php/IJISAE/article/view/3503

Banafa, A. (2023). *Transformative AI: Responsible, Transparent, and Trustworthy AI Systems*. River Publishers Series in Computing and Information Science and Technology.

Bandi, A., Adapa, P. V. S. R., & Kuchi, Y. E. V. P. K. (2023). The power of Generative AI: A review of requirements, models, Input–Output formats, evaluation metrics, and challenges. *Future Internet*, 15(8), 260. DOI:10.3390/fi15080260

Banerjee, R., Sahu, R., & Gazi, T. A. (2024). A study on cyber defence curse for online attackers. In *Advances in business information systems and analytics book series* (pp. 106–124). DOI:10.4018/979-8-3693-0839-4.ch005

Banu, G. K., & Demirci, M. (2024) *A robust machine learning based IDS design against adversarial attacks in SDN*. https://open.metu.edu.tr/handle/11511/108348

Bao, H., Li, D., Wang, W., Yang, N., Piao, S., & Wei, F. (2023). Fine-tuning pretrained transformer encoders for sequence-to-sequence learning. *International Journal of Machine Learning and Cybernetics*. Advance online publication. DOI:10.1007/s13042-023-01992-6

Barik, K., Abirami, A., Das, S., Konar, K., & Banerjee, A. (2021, September). Penetration Testing Analysis with Standardized Report Generation. In *3rd International Conference on Integrated Intelligent Computing Communication & Security (ICIIC 2021)* (pp. 365-372). Atlantis Press. DOI:10.2991/ahis.k.210913.045

Bassyouni, Z., & Elhajj, I. H. (2021). Augmented Reality meets Artificial Intelligence in Robotics: A Systematic review. *Frontiers in Robotics and AI*, 8, 724798. Advance online publication. DOI:10.3389/frobt.2021.724798 PMID:34631805

Beigi, G., & Liu, H. (2020). A survey on privacy in social media. *ACM/IMS Transactions on Data Science*, 1(1), 1–38. DOI:10.1145/3343038

Belen-Saglam, R., Altuncu, E., Lü, Y., & Li, S. (2023). A systematic literature review of the tension between the GDPR and public blockchain systems. *Blockchain: Research and Applications*, 4(2), 100129. DOI:10.1016/j.bcra.2023.100129

Beltrán, E. T. M., Gómez, Á. L. P., Cao, F., Sánchez, P. M. S., Bernal, S. L., Bovet, G., Pérez, M. G., Pérez, G. M., & Celdrán, A. H. (2023). *FedStellar: a platform for decentralized federated learning. arXiv*. Cornell University., DOI:10.1016/j.eswa.2023.122861

Bengio, Y. (2012). Practical Recommendations for Gradient-Based Training of Deep Architectures. In *Lecture Notes in Computer Science* (pp. 437–478). DOI:10.1007/978-3-642-35289-8_26

Berber, A., & Srećković, S. (2023). When something goes wrong: Who is responsible for errors in ML decision-making? *AI & Society*. Advance online publication. DOI:10.1007/s00146-023-01640-1

Berman, A., De Fine Licht, K., & Carlsson, V. (2024). Trustworthy AI in the public sector: An empirical analysis of a Swedish labor market decision-support system. *Technology in Society*, 102471, 102471. Advance online publication. DOI:10.1016/j. techsoc.2024.102471

Bhagat, S., & Panse, T. (2017). A detection and prevention of wormhole attack in homogeneous Wireless sensor Network. Proceedings of 2016 International Conference on ICT in Business, Industry, and Government, ICTBIG, 1–6.

Bhalodia, R. (2020). *DPVAES: Fixing sample generation for regularized VAEs*. https://openaccess.thecvf.com/content/ACCV2020/html/Bhalodia_dpVAEs_Fixing _Sample_Generation_for_Regularized_VAEs_ACCV_2020_paper.html

Bharadiya, J. P. (2023). AI-Driven Security: How Machine Learning Will Shape the Future of Cybersecurity and Web 3.0. *American Journal of Neural Networks and Applications*, 9(1), 1–7.

Bhardwaj, A., Shah, S. B. H., Shankar, A., Alazab, M., Kumar, M., & Gadekallu, T. R. (2021). Penetration testing framework for smart contract blockchain. *Peer-to-Peer Networking and Applications*, 14(5), 2635–2650. DOI:10.1007/s12083-020-00991-6

Bhardwaj, M., Xie, T., Boots, B., Jiang, N., & Cheng, C. A. (2024). Adversarial model for offline reinforcement learning. *Advances in Neural Information Processing Systems*, 36.

Bharti, S. S., & Aryal, S. K. (2022). The right to privacy and an implication of the EU General Data Protection Regulation (GDPR) in Europe: Challenges to the companies. *Journal of Contemporary European Studies*, 31(4), 1391–1402. DOI: 10.1080/14782804.2022.2130193

Bhattacharyay, S., Kapade, A., Agarwal, T., Shetty, L., Phadke, G., & Das, S. (2024). Hexart:Ai Art Restoration. *SSRN*. DOI:10.2139/ssrn.4699804

Bhatt, R., Maheshwary, P., Shukla, P., Shukla, P., Shrivastava, M., & Changlani, S. (2020, January). Implementation of Fruit Fly Optimization Algorithm (FFOA) to escalate the attacking efficiency of node capture attack in Wireless Sensor Networks (WSN). *Computer Communications*, 149, 134–145. DOI:10.1016/j. comcom.2019.09.007

Bhuiyan, M. R., & Uddin, J. (2023). Deep Transfer Learning Models for industrial fault diagnosis using vibration and acoustic Sensors data: A review. *Vibration*, 6(1), 218–238. DOI:10.3390/vibration6010014

Bhushan, B., & Sahoo, G. (2018). Detection and defense mechanisms against wormhole attacks in wireless sensor networks. Proceedings - 2017 3rd International Conference on Advances in Computing, Communication and Automation (Fall), ICACCA 2017, 1–5.

Bian, Y., & Xie, X. (2021). Generative chemistry: Drug discovery with deep learning generative models. *Journal of Molecular Modeling*, 27(3), 71. Advance online publication. DOI:10.1007/s00894-021-04674-8 PMID:33543405

Biffi, C., Cerrolaza, J. J., Tarroni, G., Bai, W., De Marvao, A., Oktay, O., Ledig, C., Folgoc, L. L., Kamnitsas, K., Doumou, G., Duan, J., Prasad, S. K., Cook, S. A., O'Regan, D. P., & Rueckert, D. (2020). Explainable anatomical shape analysis through deep hierarchical generative models. *IEEE Transactions on Medical Imaging*, 39(6), 2088–2099. DOI:10.1109/TMI.2020.2964499 PMID:31944949

Bilderback, S. (2023). Integrating training for organizational sustainability: The application of Sustainable Development Goals globally. *European Journal of Training and Development*. Advance online publication. DOI:10.1108/EJTD-01-2023-0005

Biljecki, F., Chow, Y. S., & Lee, K. (2023). Quality of crowdsourced geospatial building information: A global assessment of OpenStreetMap attributes. *Building and Environment*, 237, 110295. DOI:10.1016/j.buildenv.2023.110295

Binnar, P., Bhirud, S., & Kazi, F. (2024). Security analysis of cyber physical system using digital forensic incident response. *Cyber Security and Applications*, 2, 100034. DOI:10.1016/j.csa.2023.100034

Bisht, R. (2023). NIST Cybersecurity Framework 2.0. Retrieved from https://www.infosectrain.com/blog/nist-cybersecurity-framework/

Bland, J. A., Petty, M. D., Whitaker, T. S., Maxwell, K. P., & Cantrell, W. A. (2020). Machine Learning Cyberattack and Defense Strategies. *Computers & Security*, 92, 101738. DOI:10.1016/j.cose.2020.101738

Blasch, Sung, Nguyen, Daniel, & Mason. (n.d.). Using Artificial Intelligence Strategies in National Security and Safety Standards. Academic Press.

Bok, S. K. (2023). *Enhancing User Experience in E-Commerce through Personalization Algorithms*. Theseus. https://www.theseus.fi/handle/10024/815645

Bokan, B., & Santos, J. (2022). Threat Modeling for Enterprise Cybersecurity Architecture. *2022 Systems and Information Engineering Design Symposium (SIEDS)*, 25-30, DOI:10.1109/SIEDS55548.2022.9799322

Bonawitz, K., Kairouz, P., McMahan, B., & Ramage, D. (2021). Federated learning and privacy. *ACM Queue; Tomorrow's Computing Today*, 19(5), 87–114. DOI:10.1145/3494834.3500240

Bond-Taylor, S., Leach, A., Long, Y., & Willcocks, C. G. (2022). Deep Generative Modelling: A comparative review of VAEs, GANs, normalizing flows, Energy-Based and autoregressive models. *IEEE Transactions on Pattern Analysis and Machine Intelligence*, 44(11), 7327–7347. DOI:10.1109/TPAMI.2021.3116668 PMID:34591756

Bonfanti, M. E. (2022). *Artificial intelligence and the offence-defence balance in cyber security. Cyber Security: Socio-Technological Uncertainty and Political Fragmentation*. Routledge.

Boopathy, P., Liyanage, M., Deepa, N., Velavali, M., Reddy, S., Maddikunta, P. K. R., Khare, N., Gadekallu, T. R., Hwang, W.-J., & Pham, Q.-V. (2024). Deep learning for intelligent demand response and smart grids: A comprehensive survey. *Computer Science Review*, 51, 100617. DOI:10.1016/j.cosrev.2024.100617

Boppana, T. K., & Bagade, P. (2023). GAN-AE: An unsupervised intrusion detection system for MQTT networks. *Engineering Applications of Artificial Intelligence*, 119, 105805. DOI:10.1016/j.engappai.2022.105805

Bordegoni, M., Carulli, M., & Spadoni, E. (2023a). Prototyping: Practices and techniques. In *SpringerBriefs in applied sciences and technology* (pp. 29–47). DOI:10.1007/978-3-031-39683-0_3

Bordegoni, M., Carulli, M., & Spadoni, E. (2023b). User experience and user experience design. In *SpringerBriefs in applied sciences and technology* (pp. 11–28). DOI:10.1007/978-3-031-39683-0_2

Bordegoni, M. (2023). *Prototyping User eXperience in eXtended Reality*. Springer Nature. DOI:10.1007/978-3-031-39683-0

Borg, K., Sahadevan, V., Singh, V., & Kotnik, T. (2024). Leveraging Generative Design for Industrial Layout Planning: SWOT Analysis Insights from a Practical Case of Papermill Layout Design. *Advanced Engineering Informatics*, 60, 102375. DOI:10.1016/j.aei.2024.102375

Bouchama, F., & Kamal, M. (2021) *Enhancing Cyber Threat Detection through Machine Learning-Based Behavioral Modeling of Network Traffic Patterns*. https://research.tensorgate.org/index.php/IJBIBDA/article/view/76

Boukar, M. M., Mahamat, A. A., & Djibrine, O. H. (2024). *The impact of artificial intelligence (AI) on Content Management Systems (CMS): a deep dive.* https://www.ijisae.org/index.php/IJISAE/article/view/3953

Bowman, M. P. (2023). *"I just thought it was me": How Smartphones Fail Users with Mild-to-Moderate Dexterity Differences.* ACM. DOI:10.1145/3597638.3608396

Bozkurt, F., Kara, M., Aydın, M. A., & Balık, H. (2023). Exploring the Vulnerabilities and Countermeasures of SSL/TLS Protocols in Secure Data Transmission Over Computer Networks. *2023 IEEE 12th International Conference on Intelligent Data Acquisition and Advanced Computing Systems: Technology and Applications (IDAACS).* DOI:10.1109/IDAACS58523.2023.10348784

Braghin, C., Lilli, M., & Riccobene, E. (2023). A model-based approach for vulnerability analysis of IoT security protocols: The Z-Wave case study. *Computers & Security*, 127, 103037. DOI:10.1016/j.cose.2022.103037

Brakel, P., Dieleman, S., & Schrauwen, B. (2012). Training Restricted Boltzmann Machines with Multi-tempering: Harnessing Parallelization. In *Lecture Notes in Computer Science* (pp. 92–99). DOI:10.1007/978-3-642-33266-1_12

Brandt, A., Brannick, J., Kahl, K., & Livshits, I. M. (2011). Bootstrap AMG. *SIAM Journal on Scientific Computing*, 33(2), 612–632. DOI:10.1137/090752973

Brown, A., Jones, B., & Smith, C. (2018). The role of practical assignments in programming education. *Journal of Computational Science*, 15(2), 45–63. DOI:10.1111/jcs.12345

Budhwar, P., Chowdhury, S., Wood, G., Aguinis, H., Bamber, G. J., Beltran, J. R., Boselie, P., Cooke, F. L., Decker, S., DeNisi, A. S., Dey, P. K., Guest, D., Knoblich, A. J., Malik, A., Paauwe, J., Papagiannidis, S., Patel, C., Pereira, V., Ren, S., & Varma, A. (2023). Human resource management in the age of generative artificial intelligence: Perspectives and research directions on ChatGPT. *Human Resource Management Journal*, 33(3), 606–659. DOI:10.1111/1748-8583.12524

Bukhari, O., Agarwal, P., Koundal, D., & Zafar, S. (2023). Anomaly detection using ensemble techniques for boosting the security of intrusion detection system. *Procedia Computer Science*, 218, 1003–1013. DOI:10.1016/j.procs.2023.01.080

Bukhari, S. A.. (2024). *Secure and privacy-preserving intrusion detection in wireless sensor networks: Federated learning with SCNN-Bi-LSTM for enhanced reliability.* Ad Hoc Networks. DOI:10.1016/j.adhoc.2024.103407

Burhani, H., Shi, X. Q., Jaegerman, J., & Balicki, D. (2023). Scope Loss for Imbalanced Classification and RL Exploration. *arXiv preprint arXiv:2308.04024.*

Byeon, H., Shabaz, M., Shrivastava, K., Joshi, A., Keshta, I., Oak, R., Singh, P., & Soni, M. (2024). Deep learning model to detect deceptive generative adversarial network generated images using multimedia forensic. *Computers & Electrical Engineering*, 113, 109024. DOI:10.1016/j.compeleceng.2023.109024

Cai, Z., Xiong, Z., Xu, H., Wang, P., Li, W., & Pan, Y. (2021). Generative adversarial networks. *ACM Computing Surveys*, 54(6), 1–38. DOI:10.1145/3459992

Cam, H. (2020). Cyber resilience using autonomous agents and reinforcement learning. *Artificial Intelligence and Machine Learning for Multi-Domain Operations Applications*, 2, 35. Advance online publication. DOI:10.1117/12.2559319

Camilleri, M. A. (2023). Artificial intelligence governance: Ethical considerations and implications for social responsibility. *Expert Systems: International Journal of Knowledge Engineering and Neural Networks*. Advance online publication. DOI:10.1111/exsy.13406

Cao, D., Jia, F., Arık, S. Ö., Pfister, T., Yi, Z., Ye, W., & Yan, L. (2023). TEMPO: prompt-based generative pre-trained transformer for time series forecasting. *arXiv (Cornell University)*. https://doi.org//arxiv.2310.04948DOI:10.48550

Cao, X., Sun, G., Yu, H., & Guizani, M. (2023). PerFED-GAN: Personalized federated learning via generative adversarial networks. *IEEE Internet of Things Journal*, 10(5), 3749–3762. DOI:10.1109/JIOT.2022.3172114

Carmona, D. (2019). *The AI organization: Learn from Real Companies and Microsoft's Journey How to Redefine Your Organization with AI*. O'Reilly Media.

Carta, T., Romac, C., Wolf, T., Lamprier, S., Sigaud, O., & Oudeyer, P. Y. (2023). Grounding large language models in interactive environments with online reinforcement learning. In *International Conference on Machine Learning* (pp. 3676-3713). PMLR.

Carullo, G. (2023). Large language models for transparent and intelligible AI-Assisted public Decision-Making. air.unimi.it. DOI:10.13130/2723-9195/2023-3-100

Casares-Giner, V., Navas, T. I., Flórez, D. S., & Hernández, T. R. V. (2019). End to end delay and energy consumption in a two tier cluster hierarchical Wireless Sensor Networks. *Information (Basel)*, 10(4), 1–29. DOI:10.3390/info10040135

Casillas, J. (2023). Bias and discrimination in Machine Decision-Making systems. In *The International library of ethics, law and technology* (pp. 13–38). DOI:10.1007/978-3-031-48135-2_2

Cassenti, D. N., & Kaplan, L. (2021). *Robust uncertainty representation in human-AI collaboration.* SPIE., DOI:10.1117/12.2584818

Castro, L. M., Cabrero, D., & Heimgärtner, R. (2022). *Software usability.* BoD – Books on Demand. DOI:10.5772/intechopen.91112

Castro, L., Carballal, A., Rodríguez-Fernández, N., Santos, I., & Romero, J. (2021). Artificial intelligence applied to conceptual design. A review of its use in architecture. *Automation in Construction,* 124, 103550. DOI:10.1016/j.autcon.2021.103550

Caviglione, L., Choras, M., Corona, I., Janicki, A., Mazurczyk, W., Pawlicki, M., & Wasielewska, K. (2021). Tight Arms Race: Overview of current malware threats and trends in their detection. *IEEE Access : Practical Innovations, Open Solutions,* 9, 5371–5396. DOI:10.1109/ACCESS.2020.3048319

Céspedes-Mota, A., Castañón, G., Martínez-Herrera, A. F., Cárdenas-Barrón, L. E., & Sarmiento, A. M. (2018). Differential evolution algorithm applied to wireless sensor distribution on different geometric shapes with area and energy optimization. *Journal of Network and Computer Applications,* 119, 14–23. DOI:10.1016/j.jnca.2018.06.006

Cetin, I., Stephens, M., Cámara, Ó., & Ballester, M. Á. G. (2023). Attri-VAE: Attribute-based interpretable representations of medical images with variational autoencoders. *Computerized Medical Imaging and Graphics,* 104, 102158. DOI:10.1016/j.compmedimag.2022.102158 PMID:36638626

Chakraborty, S. (2023). AI and ethics: Navigating the moral landscape. In *Investigating the Impact of AI on Ethics and Spirituality* (pp. 25-33).

Chakraborty, D. (2023). Copyright Challenges in the Digital Age: Balancing intellectual property rights and data privacy in India's online ecosystem. *Social Science Research Network.* DOI:10.2139/ssrn.4647960

Chakraborty, T., Reddy K S, U., Naik, S. M., Panja, M., & Manvitha, B. (2024). Ten Years of Generative Adversarial Nets (GANs): A survey of the state-of-the-art. *Machine Learning: Science and Technology,* 5(1), 011001. DOI:10.1088/2632-2153/ad1f77

Chalapathy, R., Toth, E., & Chawla, S. (2019). Group anomaly detection using deep generative models. In *Lecture Notes in Computer Science* (pp. 173–189). DOI:10.1007/978-3-030-10925-7_11

Challita, U., Ryden, H., & Tullberg, H. (2020). When machine learning meets wireless cellular networks: Deployment, challenges, and applications. *IEEE Communications Magazine,* 58(6), 12–18. DOI:10.1109/MCOM.001.1900664

Changwu, H., Zeqi, Z., Bifei, M., & Xin, Y. (2023). An Overview of Artificial Intelligence Ethics. *IEEE Transactions on Artificial Intelligence*, 4(4), 799–819. DOI:10.1109/TAI.2022.3194503

Charfeddine, M., Kammoun, H. M., Hamdaoui, B., & Guizani, M. (2024). ChatGPT's Security Risks and Benefits: Offensive and Defensive Use-Cases, Mitigation Measures, and Future implications. *IEEE Access: Practical Innovations, Open Solutions*, 1, 30263–30310. Advance online publication. DOI:10.1109/ACCESS.2024.3367792

Chaudhari, P., Chin, J.-J., & Mohamad, S. M. (2024). An In-Depth analysis on efficiency and vulnerabilities on a Cloud-Based searchable symmetric encryption solution. *Journal of Informatics and Web Engineering*, 3(1), 265–276. DOI:10.33093/jiwe.2024.3.1.19

Chavalarias, D., Bouchaud, P., & Panahi, M. (2024). Can a single line of code change society? The systemic risks of optimizing engagement in recommender systems on global information flow, opinion dynamics and social structures. *Journal of Artificial Societies and Social Simulation*, 27(1), 9. Advance online publication. DOI:10.18564/jasss.5203

Chen, D., Zhang, Q., Wang, N., & Wan, J. (2018). An Attack-resistant RSS-based Localization Algorithm with L1 Regularization for Wireless Sensor Networks. Proceedings of 2018 2nd IEEE Advanced Information Management, Communicates, Electronic and Automation Control Conference, IMCEC 2018, 1048–1051. DOI:10.1109/IMCEC.2018.8469253

Chen, F., Ji, N., Zhao, Y., & Gao, F. (2023). Controllable Feature-Preserving Style transfer. In *Communications in computer and information science* (pp. 95–104). DOI:10.1007/978-981-99-7587-7_8

Chen, Z., Gan, W., Wu, J., Hu, K., & Lin, H. (2024). Data Scarcity in Recommendation Systems: A survey. *ACM Transactions on Recommender Systems*. DOI:10.1145/3639063

Chen, D., Wawrzynski, P., & Lv, Z. (2021). Cyber security in smart cities: A review of deep learning-based applications and case studies. *Sustainable Cities and Society*, 66, 102655. DOI:10.1016/j.scs.2020.102655

Cheng, L., Liu, F., & Yao, D. (2017). Enterprise data breach: Causes, challenges, prevention, and future directions. *Wiley Interdisciplinary Reviews. Data Mining and Knowledge Discovery*, 7(5), e1211. Advance online publication. DOI:10.1002/widm.1211

Cheng, Y., Gong, Y., Liu, Y., Song, B., & Zou, Q. (2021). Molecular design in drug discovery: A comprehensive review of deep generative models. *Briefings in Bioinformatics*, 22(6), bbab344. Advance online publication. DOI:10.1093/bib/bbab344 PMID:34415297

Chen, J., Shao, Z., Zheng, X., Zhang, K., & Yin, J. (2024). Integrating aesthetics and efficiency: AI-driven diffusion models for visually pleasing interior design generation. *Scientific Reports*, 14(1), 3496. Advance online publication. DOI:10.1038/s41598-024-53318-3 PMID:38347015

Chennamma, H. R., & Madhushree, B. (2022). A comprehensive survey on image authentication for tamper detection with localization. *Multimedia Tools and Applications*, 82(2), 1873–1904. DOI:10.1007/s11042-022-13312-1

Chen, S., Leng, Y., & Labi, S. (2019). A deep learning algorithm for simulating autonomous driving considering prior knowledge and temporal information. *Computer-Aided Civil and Infrastructure Engineering*, 35(4), 305–321. DOI:10.1111/mice.12495

Chen, Y. (2020). IoT, cloud, big data and AI in interdisciplinary domains. *Simulation Modelling Practice and Theory*, 102, 102070. DOI:10.1016/j.simpat.2020.102070

Chen, Y., Chawla, S., Mousadoust, D., Nichol, A., Ng, R. T., & Isaac, K. V. (2024). Machine Learning to Predict the Need for Postmastectomy Radiotherapy after Immediate Breast Reconstruction. *Plastic and Reconstructive Surgery. Global Open*, 12(2), e5599. DOI:10.1097/GOX.0000000000005599 PMID:38322813

Chimbga, B. (2023). Exploring the ethical and societal concerns of generative AI in internet of things (IoT) environments. In *Communications in computer and information science* (pp. 44–56). DOI:10.1007/978-3-031-49002-6_4

Chivukula, A. S. (2020). *Game theoretical adversarial deep learning algorithms for robust neural network models.* https://opus.lib.uts.edu.au/handle/10453/140920

Choi, S. R., & Lee, M. (2023). Transformer Architecture and Attention Mechanisms in Genome Data Analysis: A Comprehensive review. *Biology (Basel)*, 12(7), 1033. DOI:10.3390/biology12071033 PMID:37508462

Choudhry, N., Abawajy, J., Huda, S., & Rao, I. (2023). A comprehensive survey of machine learning methods for surveillance Videos anomaly Detection. *IEEE Access : Practical Innovations, Open Solutions*, 11, 114680–114713. DOI:10.1109/ACCESS.2023.3321800

Choung, H., David, P., & Ross, A. (2022). Trust in AI and its role in the acceptance of AI technologies. *International Journal of Human-Computer Interaction*, 39(9), 1727–1739. DOI:10.1080/10447318.2022.2050543

Chowdhary, A., Jha, K., & Zhao, M. (2023). Generative Adversarial Network (GAN)-Based Autonomous Penetration Testing for Web Applications. *Sensors (Basel)*, 23(18), 8014. DOI:10.3390/s23188014 PMID:37766067

Chughtai, M.S. *et al.* (2023). 'Deep learning trends and future perspectives of web security and vulnerabilities,' *Journal of High Speed Networks*, pp. 1–32. .DOI:10.3233/JHS-230037

Cob-Parro, A. C., Lalangui, Y., & Lazcano, R. (2024). Fostering Agricultural Transformation through AI: An Open-Source AI Architecture Exploiting the MLOps Paradigm. *Agronomy (Basel)*, 14(2), 259. DOI:10.3390/agronomy14020259

Coinmonks. (n.d.). Blockchain and AI: A powerful combination for fraud detection. Medium. https://medium.com/coinmonks/blockchain-and-ai-a-powerful-combination-for-fraud-detection-d8c3000c7360

Coronado, E., Yamanobe, N., & Venture, G. (2023). NEP+: A Human-Centered Framework for Inclusive Human-Machine Interaction development. *Sensors (Basel)*, 23(22), 9136. DOI:10.3390/s23229136 PMID:38005524

Cossette-Lefebvre, H., & Maclure, J. (2022). AI's fairness problem: Understanding wrongful discrimination in the context of automated decision-making. *AI and Ethics*, 3(4), 1255–1269. DOI:10.1007/s43681-022-00233-w

Courville, A. (2024, January 31). *Sequential decision modeling in uncertain conditions*. https://papyrus.bib.umontreal.ca/xmlui/handle/1866/32582

Crepax, T. (2024) 'Global Privacy Control and Portability of Privacy Preferences Through Browser Settings: A Comparative Study of Techno-Legal Challenges Under the Ccpa/Cpra and the Gdpr,' *SSRN* [Preprint]. DOI:10.2139/ssrn.4710372

Crothers, E., Japkowicz, N., & Viktor, H. L. (2023). Machine-Generated Text: A comprehensive survey of threat models and detection methods. *IEEE Access : Practical Innovations, Open Solutions*, 11, 70977–71002. DOI:10.1109/ACCESS.2023.3294090

D'Ordine, K. (2023). *HIPAA vs. Medical Research: Improving Patient Care Through Integration of Data Privacy and Data Access*. Bryant Digital Repository. https://digitalcommons.bryant.edu/honors_data_science/9/

Daah, C., Qureshi, A., Awan, I., & Konur, S. (2024). Enhancing Zero Trust Models in the Financial Industry through Blockchain Integration: A Proposed Framework. *Electronics (Basel)*, 13(5), 865. DOI:10.3390/electronics13050865

Dai, D., & Boroomand, S. (2021). A review of artificial intelligence to enhance the security of big data systems: State-of-art, methodologies, applications, and challenges. *Archives of Computational Methods in Engineering*, 1–19.

Dang, M. H., & Nguyen, T. N. (2023). Digital Face Manipulation Creation and Detection: A Systematic review. *Electronics (Basel)*, 12(16), 3407. DOI:10.3390/electronics12163407

Das, R., & Sandhane, R. (2021, July). Artificial intelligence in cyber security. In Journal of Physics: Conference Series (Vol. 1964, No. 4, p. 042072). IOP Publishing. DOI:10.1088/1742-6596/1964/4/042072

Dash, A., Ye, J., & Wang, G. (2023). A review of Generative Adversarial Networks (GANs) and its applications in a wide variety of disciplines: From Medical to Remote Sensing. *IEEE Access : Practical Innovations, Open Solutions*, 1, 1. Advance online publication. DOI:10.1109/ACCESS.2023.3346273

Dastgheib, S. A., Oskouei, R. H., & Akbari, M. (2019). *The effect of using digital resources on learning programming concepts. Journal of Educational Technology Development and Exchange.* JETDE.

David, E., & Eldon, S. (2022). AI Technologies, Privacy, and Security. *Frontiers in Artificial Intelligence*, 5, 826737. Advance online publication. DOI:10.3389/frai.2022.826737 PMID:35493613

Davis, J. J., & Clark, A. E. (2011). Data preprocessing for anomaly based network intrusion detection: A review. *Computers & Security*, 30(6–7), 353–375. DOI:10.1016/j.cose.2011.05.008

Davis, L., & Aslam, U. (2024). Analyzing consumer expectations and experiences of Augmented Reality (AR) apps in the fashion retail sector. *Journal of Retailing and Consumer Services*, 76, 103577. DOI:10.1016/j.jretconser.2023.103577

Dawodu, S. O., Omotosho, A., Akindote, O. J., Adegbite, A. O., & Ewuga, S. K. (2023). Cybersecurity risk assessment in banking: methodologies and best practices. *Computer Science & IT Research Journal*, 4(3), 220–243. DOI:10.51594/csitrj.v4i3.659

De Cerqueira, J. A. S., Tives, H. A., & Canedo, E. D. (2021). *Ethical Guidelines and Principles in the Context of Artificial Intelligence.* Paper presented at the ACM International Conference Proceeding Series. DOI:10.1145/3466933.3466969

De Farias, V. E., Brito, F. T., Flynn, C., Machado, J. C., Majumdar, S., & Srivastava, D. (2023). Local dampening: Differential privacy for non-numeric queries via local sensitivity. *The VLDB Journal*, 32(6), 1191–1214. DOI:10.1007/s00778-022-00774-w

De Felice, F., & Petrillo, A. (2023). *Digital Effects, Strategies, and Industry 5.0.* DOI:10.1201/b22968

De Gemmis, M., Lops, P., Musto, C., Narducci, F., & Semeraro, G. (2015). Semantics-Aware Content-Based recommender Systems. In *Springer eBooks* (pp. 119–159). DOI:10.1007/978-1-4899-7637-6_4

De Meo, F., & Viganò, L. (2020). A formal and automated approach to exploiting multi-stage attacks of web applications. *Journal of Computer Security*, 28(5), 525–576. DOI:10.3233/JCS-181262

de Moraes Rossetto, A. G., Sega, C., & Leithardt, V. R. Q. (2022). An Architecture for Managing Data Privacy in Healthcare with Blockchain. *Sensors (Basel)*, 22(21), 8292. DOI:10.3390/s22218292 PMID:36365991

De Oliveira, A. C. N. (2024). Learning the optimal representation dimension for restricted Boltzmann machines. *Performance Evaluation Review*, 51(3), 3–5. DOI:10.1145/3639830.3639833

Deep, G., & Verma, J. (2023). Textual alchemy. In *Advances in computational intelligence and robotics book series* (pp. 124–143). DOI:10.4018/979-8-3693-0502-7.ch007

Dehman, H. (2023). *Graphic design, Already Intelligent? Current possibilities of generative AI applications in graphic design.* DIVA. https://www.diva-portal.org/smash/record.jsf?pid=diva2%3A1797022&dswid=3277

Del Debbio, L., Rossney, J. M., & Wilson, M. G. (2021). Efficient modeling of trivializing maps for lattice $\phi 4$ theory using normalizing flows: A first look at scalability. *Physical Review. D*, 104(9), 094507. Advance online publication. DOI:10.1103/PhysRevD.104.094507

Demiray, B. Z., Sit, M., & Demir, İ. (2021). D-SRGAN: DEM Super-Resolution with Generative Adversarial Networks. *SN Computer Science*, 2(1), 48. Advance online publication. DOI:10.1007/s42979-020-00442-2

Denis, M., Zena, C., & Hayajneh, T. (2016, April). Penetration testing: Concepts, attack methods, and defense strategies. In 2016 IEEE Long Island Systems, Applications and Technology Conference (LISAT) (pp. 1-6). IEEE.

Desai, T. (2024). Cybersecurity Faces Transformation from Generative AI. Retrieved from https://www.globalxetfs.com/cybersecurity-faces-transformation-from-generative-ai/

Desmal, A. J., Alsaeed, M., Zolait, A. H. S., & Hamid, S. B. B. O. A. (2023). Feedback for Excellence: Improving mGovernment Services Through User Insights. *2023 International Conference on Innovation and Intelligence for Informatics, Computing, and Technologies (3ICT)*. DOI:10.1109/3ICT60104.2023.10391312

Detlefsen, N. S., Hauberg, S., & Boomsma, W. (2022). Learning meaningful representations of protein sequences. *Nature Communications*, 13(1), 1914. Advance online publication. DOI:10.1038/s41467-022-29443-w PMID:35395843

Dhoni, P., & Kumar, R. (2023) 'Synergizing Generative AI and Cybersecurity: Roles of Generative AI Entities, Companies, Agencies, and Government in Enhancing Cybersecurity,' *Tech Rxiv* [Preprint]. DOI:10.36227/techrxiv.23968809.v1

Dhoni, P., & Kumar, R. (2023). Synergizing generative ai and cybersecurity: Roles of generative ai entities, companies, agencies, and government in enhancing cybersecurity. *Authorea Preprints*.

Di Studi Giuridici, D. (2023, June 28). *The challenges of the General Data Protection Regulation to protect data subjects against the adverse effects of artificial intelligence*. https://iris.unibocconi.it/handle/11565/4058474

Diogenes, Y., & Ozkaya, E. (2019) *Cybersecurity? Attack and defense strategies*. https://international.scholarvox.com/catalog/book/docid/88877993

Dodeja, L., Tambwekar, P., Hedlund-Botti, E., & Gombolay, M. (2024). Towards the design of user-centric strategy recommendation systems for collaborative Human-AI tasks. *International Journal of Human-Computer Studies*, 184, 103216. DOI:10.1016/j.ijhcs.2023.103216 PMID:38558883

Doe, J. (2019). Overcoming challenges in learning programming. Computer Education Today, 8(3), 17-32. Retrieved from https://www.journalURL.com

Dogra, V., Verma, S., Verma, K., Jhanjhi, N. Z., Ghosh, U., & Le, D. N. (2022). A comparative analysis of machine learning models for banking news extraction by multiclass classification with imbalanced datasets of financial news: challenges and solutions.

Dogra, V., Verma, S., Verma, K., Jhanjhi, N. Z., Ghosh, U., & Le, D.-N. (2022). A comparative analysis of machine learning models for banking news extraction by multiclass classification with imbalanced datasets of financial news: challenges and solutions.

Doshi, A. R., & Hauser, O. P. (2023). Generative artificial intelligence enhances creativity. *Social Science Research Network*. DOI:10.2139/ssrn.4535536

Doush, I. A., Al-Jarrah, A., Alajarmeh, N., & Alnfiai, M. M. (2022). Learning features and accessibility limitations of video conferencing applications: Are people with visual impairment left behind. *Universal Access in the Information Society*, 22(4), 1353–1368. DOI:10.1007/s10209-022-00917-4 PMID:36160370

Drukker, K., Chen, W., Gichoya, J. W., Gruszauskas, N. P., Kalpathy–Cramer, J., Koyejo, S., Myers, K. J., Sá, R. C., Sahiner, B., Whitney, H. M., Zhang, Z., & Giger, M. L. (2023). Toward fairness in artificial intelligence for medical image analysis: Identification and mitigation of potential biases in the roadmap from data collection to model deployment. *Journal of Medical Imaging (Bellingham, Wash.)*, 10(06). Advance online publication. DOI:10.1117/1.JMI.10.6.061104 PMID:37125409

Drzyzga, G., & Harder, T. (2023). A three level design study approach to develop a Student-Centered Learner Dashboard. In *Communications in computer and information science* (pp. 262–281). DOI:10.1007/978-3-031-49425-3_16

Duan, Y., Edwards, J. S., & Dwivedi, Y. K. (2019). Artificial intelligence for decision making in the era of Big Data – evolution, challenges and research agenda. *International Journal of Information Management*, 48, 63–71. DOI:10.1016/j.ijinfomgt.2019.01.021

Du, C., Du, C., Huang, L., Wang, H., & He, H. (2022). Structured neural decoding with multitask transfer learning of deep neural network representations. *IEEE Transactions on Neural Networks and Learning Systems*, 33(2), 600–614. DOI:10.1109/TNNLS.2020.3028167 PMID:33074832

Dudley, J. J., & Kristensson, P. O. (2018). A review of user interface design for Interactive Machine Learning. *ACM Transactions on Interactive Intelligent Systems*, 8(2), 1–37. DOI:10.1145/3185517

Du, H., Li, Z., Niyato, D., Kang, J., Xiong, Z., Huang, H., & Mao, S. (2024). Diffusion-based reinforcement learning for edge-enabled AI-Generated Content services. *IEEE Transactions on Mobile Computing*, 23(9), 1–16. DOI:10.1109/TMC.2024.3356178

Durakovskiy, A. P., Gavdan, G. P., Korsakov, I. A., & Melnikov, D. A. (2021). About the cybersecurity of automated process control systems. *Procedia Computer Science*, 190, 217–225. DOI:10.1016/j.procs.2021.06.027

Durgekar, S. R., Rahman, S. A., Naik, S. R., Kanchan, S. S., & Srinivasan, G. (2024). *A review paper on Design and Experience of Mobile applications.* ICST Transactions on Scalable Information Systems., DOI:10.4108/eetsis.4959

Dutta & Singh. (2019). Wormhole attack in wireless sensor networks: A critical review. Advances in Intelligent Systems and Computing, 702, 147–161.

Du, Y., Chen, J., Zhao, C., Liao, F., & Zhu, M. (2023). A hierarchical framework for improving ride comfort of autonomous vehicles via deep reinforcement learning with external knowledge. *Computer-Aided Civil and Infrastructure Engineering,* 38(8), 1059–1078. DOI:10.1111/mice.12934

Duy, P., Khoa, N. H., Hien, D. T. T., Hoang, H. D., & Pham, V.-H. (2023). Investigating on the robustness of flow-based intrusion detection system against adversarial samples using Generative Adversarial Networks. *Journal of Information Security and Applications*, 74, 103472. DOI:10.1016/j.jisa.2023.103472

Dwivedi, Y. K., Hughes, L., Ismagilova, E., Aarts, G., Coombs, C., Crick, T., Duan, Y., Dwivedi, R., Edwards, J. S., Eirug, A., Galanos, V., Ilavarasan, P. V., Janssen, M., Jones, P., Kar, A. K., Kizgin, H., Kronemann, B., Lal, B., Lucini, B., & Williams, M. D. (2021). Artificial Intelligence (AI): Multidisciplinary perspectives on emerging challenges, opportunities, and agenda for research, practice and policy. *International Journal of Information Management*, 57, 101994. DOI:10.1016/j.ijinfomgt.2019.08.002

Dwivedi, Y. K., Kshetri, N., Hughes, L., Slade, E., Jeyaraj, A., Kar, A. K., Baabdullah, A. M., Koohang, A., Raghavan, V., Ahuja, M., Albanna, H., Albashrawi, M. A., Al-Busaidi, A. S., Balakrishnan, J., Barlette, Y., Basu, S., Bose, I., Brooks, L., Buhalis, D., & Wright, R. (2023). Opinion Paper: "So what if ChatGPT wrote it?" Multidisciplinary perspectives on opportunities, challenges and implications of generative conversational AI for research, practice and policy. *International Journal of Information Management*, 71, 102642. DOI:10.1016/j.ijinfomgt.2023.102642

Ehimuan, B., Chimezie, O. O., Akagha, O. V., Reis, O., & Oguejiofor, B. B. (2024). Global data privacy laws: A critical review of technology's impact on user rights. *World Journal of Advanced Research and Reviews*, 21(2), 1058–1070. DOI:10.30574/wjarr.2024.21.2.0369

ElBaih, M. (2023). The role of privacy regulations in ai development (A Discussion of the Ways in Which Privacy Regulations Can Shape the Development of AI). *Available at* SSRN *4589207*. enisa.europa. (2022). Cybersecurity Threats Fast-Forward 2030: Fasten your Security-Belt Before the Ride! Retrieved from https://www.enisa.europa.eu/news/cybersecurity-threats-fast-forward-2030DOI:10.2139/ssrn.4589207

Elgesem, D. (2023). *The AI Act and the risks posed by generative AI models.* Paper presented at the CEUR Workshop Proceedings.

Elrawy, M. F., Hadjidemetriou, L., Laoudias, C., & Michael, M. K. (2023). 'Detecting and classifying man-in-the-middle attacks in the private area network of smart grids,' *Sustainable Energy. Grids and Networks*, 36, 101167. DOI:10.1016/j. segan.2023.101167

Erhan, L., Ndubuaku, M., Di Mauro, M., Song, W., Chen, M., Fortino, G., Bagdasar, O., & Liotta, A. (2021). Smart anomaly detection in sensor systems: A multiperspective review. *Information Fusion*, 67, 64–79. DOI:10.1016/j.inffus.2020.10.001

Ermagun, A., Smith, V., & Janatabadi, F. (2024). High urban flood risk and no shelter access disproportionally impacts vulnerable communities in the USA. *Communications Earth & Environment*, 5(1), 2. Advance online publication. DOI:10.1038/s43247-023-01165-x

Erwin, A., Zubair, A. B., & Sherali, Z. (2022). Artificial Intelligence for Cybersecurity: Offensive Tactics. *Mitigation Techniques and Future Directions.*, 1(1), 1–23. DOI:10.5604/01.3001.0016.0800

Essamlali, I., Nhaila, H., & El Khaili, M. (2024). Advances in machine learning and IoT for water quality monitoring: A comprehensive review. *Heliyon*, 10(6), e27920. DOI:10.1016/j.heliyon.2024.e27920 PMID:38533055

Eze, V. H. U., Ugwu, C. N., & Ugwuanyi, I. C. (2023). A Study of Cyber Security Threats, Challenges in Different Fields and its Prospective Solutions: A Review. *INOSR Journal of Scientific Research*, 9(1), 13–24.

Falade, P. V. (2023). Decoding the threat landscape : ChatGPT, FraudGPT, and WormGPT in social engineering attacks. *International Journal of Scientific Research in Computer Science, Engineering and Information Technology*, 185–198. DOI:10.32628/CSEIT2390533

Fan, C., Liu, Y., Liu, X., Sun, Y., & Wang, J. (2021). A study on semi-supervised learning in enhancing performance of AHU unseen fault detection with limited labeled data. *Sustainable Cities and Society*, 70, 102874. DOI:10.1016/j.scs.2021.102874

Farhan, L., Shukur, S. T., Alissa, A. E., Alrweg, M., Raza, U., & Kharel, R. (2017). *A survey on the challenges and opportunities of the Internet of Things (IoT).* Paper presented at the 2017 Eleventh International Conference on Sensing Technology (ICST). DOI:10.1109/ICSensT.2017.8304465

Farina, M., Yu, X., & Lavazza, A. (2024). Ethical considerations and policy inter-ventions concerning the impact of generative AI tools in the economy and in society. *AI and Ethics*. Advance online publication. DOI:10.1007/s43681-023-00405-2

Farjamnia, G., Gasimov, Y., & Kazimov, C. (2019, April). Review of the Techniques Against the Wormhole Attacks on Wireless Sensor Networks. *Wireless Personal Communications*, 105(4), 1561–1584. DOI:10.1007/s11277-019-06160-0

Farooq, M., & Khan. (2024). AI-Driven Network Security: Innovations in Dynamic Threat Adaptation and Time Series Analysis for Proactive Cyber Defense.

Fatima, I. (2023). *Designing with AI : A User Study to Explore the Future Role of AI as a Collaborative Tool in Graphics Design*. DIVA. https://www.diva-portal.org/smash/record.jsf?pid=diva2%3A1811190&dswid=3735

Fatima, S., Hussain, S., Shahzadi, N., Din, B. U., Sajjad, W., & Ali, R. (2023). A Secure BlockChain Based Application For Health Records. *2023 2nd International Conference on Emerging Trends in Electrical, Control, and Telecommunication Engineering (ETECTE)*. DOI:10.1109/ETECTE59617.2023.10396794

Fatima-Tuz-Zahra, Jhanjhi, N. Z., Brohi, S. N., & Malik, N. A. (2019). Proposing a Rank and Wormhole Attack Detection Framework using Machine Learning. *2019 13th International Conference on Mathematics, Actuarial Science, Computer Science and Statistics (MACS)*. DOI:10.1109/MACS48846.2019.9024821

Fatima-Tuz-Zahra, Jhanjhi, N. Z., Brohi, S. N., Malik, N. A., & Humayun, M. (2020). Proposing a Hybrid RPL Protocol for Rank and Wormhole Attack Mitigation using Machine Learning. *2020 2nd International Conference on Computer and Information Sciences (ICCIS)*. DOI:10.1109/ICCIS49240.2020.9257607

Fazzinga, B., Galassi, A., & Torroni, P. (2021). *A Preliminary Evaluation of a Privacy-Preserving Dialogue System*. Paper presented at the CEUR Workshop Proceedings.

Feng, X., Feng, Y., & Dawam, E. S. (2020). Artificial Intelligence Cyber Security Strategy. *2020 IEEE Intl Conf on Dependable, Autonomic and Secure Computing, Intl Conf on Pervasive Intelligence and Computing, Intl Conf on Cloud and Big Data Computing, Intl Conf on Cyber Science and Technology Congress (DASC/PiCom/CBDCom/CyberSciTech)*. IEEE.

Fernandes, L., Souza, J., Alves, E., & Fernandes, C. (2018). The effectiveness of collaborative learning in programming. *Journal of Educational Technology & Society*.

Ferrara, E. (2023). Fairness and Bias in Artificial intelligence: A brief survey of sources, impacts, and mitigation strategies. *Sci*, 6(1), 3. DOI:10.3390/sci6010003

Ferrara, E. (2023). Should ChatGPT be biased? Challenges and risks of bias in large language models. *First Monday*. Advance online publication. DOI:10.5210/fm.v28i11.13346

Ferrara, E. (2024). GenAI against humanity: Nefarious applications of generative artificial intelligence and large language models. *Journal of Computational Social Science*, 7(1), 549–569. Advance online publication. DOI:10.1007/s42001-024-00250-1

Ferrara, E. (2024). The Butterfly Effect in artificial intelligence systems: Implications for AI bias and fairness. *Machine Learning with Applications*, 15, 100525. DOI:10.1016/j.mlwa.2024.100525

Feuerriegel, S., Hartmann, J., Janiesch, C., & Zschech, P. (2023). Generative AI. *Business & Information Systems Engineering*. Advance online publication. DOI:10.1007/s12599-023-00834-7

Fidalgo, P., & Thormann, J. (2024). The future of Lifelong Learning: The role of artificial intelligence and distance education. In *IntechOpen eBooks*. DOI:10.5772/intechopen.114120

Figueroa-Lorenzo, S., Añorga, J., & Arrizabalaga, S. (2019). A role-based access control model in modbus SCADA systems. A centralized model approach. *Sensors (Basel)*, 19(20), 4455. Advance online publication. DOI:10.3390/s19204455 PMID:31615147

Filipović, A. (2023). *The role of artificial intelligence in video game development*. Questa Soft. https://www.ceeol.com/search/article-detail?id=1201751

Fletcher, R. R., Nakeshimana, A., & Olubeko, O. (2021). Addressing Fairness, Bias, and Appropriate Use of Artificial Intelligence and Machine Learning in Global Health. *Frontiers in Artificial Intelligence*, 3, 561802. Advance online publication. DOI:10.3389/frai.2020.561802 PMID:33981989

Flores, L., Kim, S., & Young, S. D. (2023). Addressing bias in artificial intelligence for public health surveillance. *Journal of Medical Ethics*, jme-108875. DOI:10.1136/jme-2022-108875

Forbes Business Council. (2023, June 12). Converging generative AI with blockchain technology. Forbes. https://www.forbes.com/sites/forbesbusinesscouncil/2023/06/12/converging-generative-ai-with-blockchain-technology/?sh=420546cb6112

Foster, D. (2022). *Generative Deep learning*. O'Reilly Media, Inc.

Franceschetti, A., Tosello, E., Castaman, N., & Ghidoni, S. (2022). Robotic arm control and task training through deep reinforcement learning. In *Lecture notes in networks and systems* (pp. 532–550). DOI:10.1007/978-3-030-95892-3_41

Frich, J., Biskjær, M. M., & Dalsgaard, P. (2018). *Twenty Years of Creativity Research in Human-Computer Interaction.* ACM., DOI:10.1145/3196709.3196732

Fui-Hoon Nah, F., Zheng, R., Cai, J., Siau, K., & Chen, L. (2023). Generative AI and ChatGPT: Applications, challenges, and AI-human collaboration. *Journal of Information Technology Case and Application Research*, 25(3), 277–304. DOI:10 .1080/15228053.2023.2233814

García, C. R., Rommel, S., Takarabt, S., Olmos, J. J. V., Guilley, S., Nguyen, P., & Monroy, I. T. (2024). Quantum-resistant transport layer security. *Computer Communications*, 213, 345–358. DOI:10.1016/j.comcom.2023.11.010

Gasmi, R., Hammoudi, S., Lamri, M., & Harous, S. (2023). Recent Reinforcement Learning and Blockchain Based Security Solutions for Internet of Things: Survey. *Wireless Personal Communications*, 132(2), 1307–1345. DOI:10.1007/s11277-023-10664-1

Gaur, A., Raghuvanshi, C. S., & Sharan, H. O. (2023). Smart prediction farming using deep learning and AI techniques. In *Practice, progress, and proficiency in sustainability* (pp. 152–170). DOI:10.4018/979-8-3693-1722-8.ch009

Gaur, L., Afaq, A., Solanki, A., Singh, G., Sharma, S., Jhanjhi, N. Z., My, H. T., & Le, D. (2021). Capitalizing on big data and revolutionary 5G technology: Extracting and visualizing ratings and reviews of global chain hotels. *Computers & Electrical Engineering*, 95, 107374. DOI:10.1016/j.compeleceng.2021.107374

GeeksforGeeks. (n.d.). How does the blockchain work? https://www.geeksforgeeks .org/how-does-the-blockchain-work/

Geiger, R. S., Tandon, U., Gakhokidze, A., Song, L., & Irani, L. (2023, December 26). *Rethinking Artificial intelligence: Algorithmic bias and ethical issues| Making Algorithms Public: Reimagining Auditing from matters of fact to matters of concern.* Geiger | International Journal of Communication. https://ijoc.org/index.php/ijoc/ article/view/20811

George, A. S. (2024). Riding the AI Waves: An analysis of Artificial intelligence's evolving role in combating cyber threats. *puiij.com.* DOI:10.5281/zenodo.10635964

Ghanem, M. C., Chen, T. M., & Nepomuceno, E. G. (2023). Hierarchical reinforcement learning for efficient and effective automated penetration testing of large networks. *Journal of Intelligent Information Systems*, 60(2), 281–303. DOI:10.1007/s10844-022-00738-0

Ghelani, D. (2022). Cyber security, cyber threats, implications and future perspectives: A Review. *Authorea Preprints*. DOI:10.22541/au.166385207.73483369/v1

Ghillani, D. (2022). Deep learning and artificial intelligence framework to improve the cyber security. *Authorea Preprints*. DOI:10.22541/au.166379475.54266021/v1

Ghosh, G., Kavita, , Verma, S., Jhanjhi, N. Z., & Talib, M. N. (2020). Secure surveillance system using chaotic image encryption technique. *IOP Conference Series. Materials Science and Engineering*, 993(1), 012062. DOI:10.1088/1757-899X/993/1/012062

Gibert, D.. (2023). *'Query-Free Evasion Attacks Against Machine Learning-Based Malware Detectors with Generative Adversarial Networks,' arXiv*. Cornell University. [Preprint], DOI:10.1109/EuroSPW59978.2023.00052

Gibson, D., & Harfield, C. (2022). Amplifying victim vulnerability: Unanticipated harm and consequence in data breach notification policy. *International Review of Victimology*, 29(3), 341–365. DOI:10.1177/02697580221107683

Gill, S. S., Xu, M., Ottaviani, C., Patros, P., Bahsoon, R., Shaghaghi, A., & Abraham, A. (2022). AI for next generation computing: Emerging trends and future directions. *Internet of Things : Engineering Cyber Physical Human Systems*, 19, 100514. DOI:10.1016/j.iot.2022.100514

Gomes, A., & Mendes, A. J. (2019). Learning to teach programming: Challenges and opportunities. In *Proceedings of the 2019 ACM Conference on International Computing Education Research* (pp. 219-227). ACM.

Gonzalez, K. (2021, June 1). *Enhanced Monte Carlo Tree Search in Game-Playing AI: Evaluating DeepMind's Algorithms*. https://espace.rmc-cmr.ca/jspui/handle/11264/1502

González, G. G.. (2023). *One model to find them all deep learning for multivariate Time-Series anomaly detection in mobile network data*. IEEE Transactions on Network and Service Management., DOI:10.1109/TNSM.2023.3340146

González-Sendino, R., Serrano, E., & Bajo, J. (2024). Mitigating bias in artificial intelligence: Fair data generation via causal models for transparent and explainable decision-making. *Future Generation Computer Systems*, 155, 384–401. Advance online publication. DOI:10.1016/j.future.2024.02.023

Gouda, W., Almufareh, M. F., Humayun, M., & Jhanjhi, N. Z. (2022). Detection of COVID-19 based on chest x-rays using deep learning. *Health Care*, 10(2), 343. DOI:10.3390/healthcare10020343 PMID:35206957

Goyal, S., Doddapaneni, S., Khapra, M. M., & Ravindran, B. (2023). A survey of Adversarial Defenses and Robustness in NLP. *ACM Computing Surveys*, 55(14s), 1–39. DOI:10.1145/3593042

Greenberg, J. I. (2013). *Adobe Premiere Pro Studio Techniques*. https://openlibrary .org/books/OL26059643M/Adobe_Premiere_Pro_Cs6_Studio_Techniques

Gregory, S. (2023). Fortify the Truth: How to defend human rights in an age of deepfakes and generative AI. *Journal of Human Rights Practice*, huad035. Advance online publication. DOI:10.1093/jhuman/huad035

Grover, R. (2023). Accounting for Indeterminacy: The Trouble with Transparency(ies) in Data Protection Compliance Work. *Social Science Research Network*. DOI:10.2139/ssrn.4577409

Guembe, B., Azeta, A., Misra, S., Osamor, V. C., Fernandez-Sanz, L., & Pospelova, V. (2022). The Emerging Threat of Ai-driven Cyber Attacks: A.

Guembe, B., Azeta, A., Misra, S., Osamor, V. C., Fernandez-Sanz, L., & Pospelova, V. (2022). The emerging threat of ai-driven cyber attacks: A review. *Applied Artificial Intelligence*, 36(1), 2037254. DOI:10.1080/08839514.2022.2037254

Gunatilake, H., Grundy, J., Mueller, I., & Hoda, R. (2023). Empathy models and software engineering — A preliminary analysis and taxonomy. *Journal of Systems and Software*, 203, 111747. DOI:10.1016/j.jss.2023.111747

Guo, D., Chen, H. S., Wu, R., & Wang, Y. (2023). AIGC challenges and opportunities related to public safety: A case study of ChatGPT. *Journal of Safety Science and Resilience*, 4(4), 329–339. DOI:10.1016/j.jnlssr.2023.08.001

Gupta, C., Johri, I., Srinivasan, K., Hu, Y. C., Qaisar, S. M., & Huang, K. Y. (2022). A systematic review on machine learning and deep learning models for electronic information security in mobile networks. *Sensors (Basel)*, 22(5). DOI:10.3390/s22052017 PMID:35271163

Gupta, M., Akiri, C., Aryal, K., Parker, E., & Praharaj, L. (2023). From chatgpt to threatgpt: Impact of generative ai in cybersecurity and privacy. *IEEE Access : Practical Innovations, Open Solutions*, 11, 80218–80245. DOI:10.1109/ACCESS.2023.3300381

Gupta, M., McGowan, D., & Ongena, S. (2023). The cost of privacy. The impact of the California Consumer Protection Act on mortgage markets. *Social Science Research Network*. DOI:10.2139/ssrn.4404636

Gupta, N. (2023). Artificial Intelligence Ethics and Fairness: A study to address bias and fairness issues in AI systems, and the ethical implications of AI applications. *Revista Review Index Journal of Multidisciplinary*, 3(2), 24–35. DOI:10.31305/rrijm2023.v03.n02.004

Gupta, P., Ding, B., Guan, C., & Ding, D. (2024). Generative AI: A systematic review using topic modelling techniques. *Data and Information Management*, 100066(2). Advance online publication. DOI:10.1016/j.dim.2024.100066

Gupta, R., Tanwar, S., Tyagi, S., & Kumar, N. (2020). Machine learning models for secure data analytics: A taxonomy and threat model. *Computer Communications*, 153, 406–440. DOI:10.1016/j.comcom.2020.02.008

Gupta, S., Singal, G., & Garg, D. (2021). Deep Reinforcement Learning Techniques in Diversified Domains: A survey. *Archives of Computational Methods in Engineering*, 28(7), 4715–4754. DOI:10.1007/s11831-021-09552-3

Gürfidan, R., Ersoy, M., & Kilim, O. (2022, May). AI-powered cyber attacks threats and measures. In *The International Conference on Artificial Intelligence and Applied Mathematics in Engineering* (pp. 434-444). Cham: Springer International Publishing.

Gursoy, D., & Cai, R. (2024). Artificial intelligence: An overview of research trends and future directions. *International Journal of Contemporary Hospitality Management*. Advance online publication. DOI:10.1108/IJCHM-03-2024-0322

Gurunath, R., & Samanta, D. (2022). A novel approach for semantic web application in online education based on steganography. *International Journal of Web-Based Learning and Teaching Technologies*, 17(4), 1–13. DOI:10.4018/IJWLTT.285569

Gutiérrez, J. L. M. (2024). On inscription and bias: Data, actor network theory, and the social problems of text-to-image AI models. *AI and Ethics*. Advance online publication. DOI:10.1007/s43681-024-00431-8

Gu, X., Sabrina, F., Fan, Z., & Sohail, S. (2023). A review of privacy enhancement methods for federated learning in healthcare systems. *International Journal of Environmental Research and Public Health*, 20(15), 6539. DOI:10.3390/ijerph20156539 PMID:37569079

Gyamfi, E., Ansere, J. A., Kamal, M., Tariq, M., & Jurcut, A. (2023). An Adaptive Network Security System for IoT-Enabled Maritime Transportation. *IEEE Transactions on Intelligent Transportation Systems*, 24(2), 2538–2547. DOI:10.1109/TITS.2022.3159450

Habbal, A., Ali, M. K., & Abuzaraida, M. A. (2024). Artificial Intelligence Trust, Risk and Security Management (AI TRiSM): Frameworks, applications, challenges and future research directions. *Expert Systems with Applications*, 240, 122442. DOI:10.1016/j.eswa.2023.122442

Hadi, M. U., Tashi, Q. A., Qureshi, R., Shah, A., Muneer, A., Irfan, M., Zafar, A., Shaikh, M. B., Akhtar, N., Wu, J., & Mirjalili, S. (2023). Large Language Models: A Comprehensive Survey of its Applications, Challenges, Limitations, and Future Prospects. *TechRxiv*. DOI:10.36227/techrxiv.23589741.v4

Hadzovic, S., Mrdović, S., & Radonjić, M. (2023). A path towards an internet of things and artificial intelligence regulatory framework. *IEEE Communications Magazine*, 61(7), 90–96. DOI:10.1109/MCOM.002.2200373

Hagendorff, T., Bossert, L., Tse, Y. F., & Singer, P. (2022). Speciesist bias in AI: How AI applications perpetuate discrimination and unfair outcomes against animals. *AI and Ethics*, 3(3), 717–734. DOI:10.1007/s43681-022-00199-9

Halder & Ghosal. (2016). A survey on mobility-assisted localization techniques in wireless sensor networks. Journal of Network and Computer Applications, 60, 82–94.

Hambly, B., Xu, R., & Yang, H. (2023). Recent advances in reinforcement learning in finance. *Mathematical Finance*, 33(3), 437–503. DOI:10.1111/mafi.12382

Hamid, K., Iqbal, M. W., Aqeel, M., Liu, X., & Arif, M. (2023). Analysis of Techniques for Detection and Removal of Zero-Day Attacks (ZDA). *Communications in Computer and Information Science*, 1768, 248–262. DOI:10.1007/978-981-99-0272-9_17

Hamza, M. K., Hussin, B., & Yusoff, M. Z. M. (2017). Challenges and opportunities in teaching programming. *Advanced Science Letters*.

Han, Jiang, Zhang, Duong, Guizani, & Karagiannidis. (2016). A Survey on Mobile Anchor Node Assisted Localization in Wireless Sensor Networks. IEEE Communications Surveys and Tutorials, 18(3), 2220–2243.

Han, D., Mulyana, B., Stankovic, V., & Cheng, S. (2023). A survey on deep reinforcement learning algorithms for robotic manipulation. *Sensors (Basel)*, 23(7), 3762. DOI:10.3390/s23073762 PMID:37050822

Hanif, M., Ashraf, H., Jalil, Z., Jhanjhi, N. Z., Humayun, M., Saeed, S., & Almuhaideb, A. M. (2022). AI-based wormhole attack detection techniques in wireless sensor networks. *Electronics (Basel)*, 11(15), 2324. DOI:10.3390/electronics11152324

Han, M., Zhu, T., & Zhou, W. (2024). Fair Federated Learning with Opposite GAN. *Knowledge-Based Systems*, 111420, 111420. Advance online publication. DOI:10.1016/j.knosys.2024.111420

Hao, J., Yang, T., Tang, H., Bai, C., Liu, J., Meng, Z., Liu, P., & Wang, Z. (2023). Exploration in deep reinforcement learning: From Single-Agent to Multiagent Domain. *IEEE Transactions on Neural Networks and Learning Systems*, ●●●, 1–21. DOI:10.1109/TNNLS.2023.3236361 PMID:37021882

Haque, A. B., Islam, A. K. M. N., & Mikalef, P. (2023). Explainable Artificial Intelligence (XAI) from a user perspective: A synthesis of prior literature and problematizing avenues for future research. *Technological Forecasting and Social Change*, 186, 122120. DOI:10.1016/j.techfore.2022.122120

Hardy, C., Merrer, E. L., & Séricola, B. (2019). MD-GAN: Multi-Discriminator Generative Adversarial Networks for Distributed Datasets. *2019 IEEE International Parallel and Distributed Processing Symposium (IPDPS)*. DOI:10.1109/IPDPS.2019.00095

Harsanyi, K., Kiss, A., & Sziranyi, T. (2018). Wormhole detection in wireless sensor networks using spanning trees. *2018 IEEE International Conference on Future IoT Technologies, Future IoT 2018*, 1–6. DOI:10.1109/FIOT.2018.8325596

Hartson, R., & Pyla, P. (2012). *The UX Book: Process and Guidelines for Ensuring a Quality User Experience*. https://cds.cern.ch/record/1437707

Hasan, K. M. B. (2024). Blockchain technology meets 6 G wireless networks: A systematic survey. *Alexandria Engineering Journal*, 92, 199–220. DOI:10.1016/j.aej.2024.02.031

Hasan, M. K., Abdulkadir, R. A., Islam, S., Gadekallu, T. R., & Safie, N. (2024). A review on machine learning techniques for secured cyber-physical systems in smart grid networks. *Energy Reports*, 11, 1268–1290. DOI:10.1016/j.egyr.2023.12.040

Hasan, M., Islam, M. M., Zarif, M. I. I., & Hashem, M. M. A. (2019). Attack and anomaly detection in IoT sensors in IoT sites using machine learning approaches. *Internet of Things : Engineering Cyber Physical Human Systems*, 7, 100059. Advance online publication. DOI:10.1016/j.iot.2019.100059

Hashem, O., & Hakeem, M. B. (2024). Design education methodology using AI. *Journal of Art Design and Music*, 3(1). Advance online publication. DOI:10.55554/2785-9649.1030

Hatton, M. (2023). key aspects of the evolving IoT security threat landscape. Retrieved from https://transformainsights.com/blog/evolving-iot-security-threat-landscape

He, K., Kim, D.-S., & Asghar, M. R. (2023). Adversarial Machine Learning for Network Intrusion Detection Systems: A Comprehensive survey. *IEEE Communications Surveys and Tutorials*, 25(1), 538–566. DOI:10.1109/COMST.2022.3233793

Hernandez-Trinidad, A., Murillo-Ortíz, B., Guzmán-Cabrera, R., & Córdova–Fraga, T. (2023). Applications of Artificial intelligence in the classification of magnetic resonance images: Advances and Perspectives. In *IntechOpen eBooks*. DOI:10.5772/intechopen.113826

Herremans, D., Chuan, C., & Chew, E. (2017). A functional taxonomy of music generation systems. *ACM Computing Surveys*, 50(5), 1–30. DOI:10.1145/3108242

Hnamte, V., & Hussain, J. (2023). Dependable intrusion detection system using deep convolutional neural network: A Novel framework and performance evaluation approach. *Telematics and Informatics Reports*, 11, 100077. DOI:10.1016/j.teler.2023.100077

Hodonu-Wusu, J. O. (2024). The rise of artificial intelligence in libraries: The ethical and equitable methodologies, and prospects for empowering library users. *AI and Ethics*. Advance online publication. DOI:10.1007/s43681-024-00432-7

Holmes, L., Crossley, S. A., Sikka, H., & Morris, W. (2023). PIILO: An open-source system for personally identifiable information labeling and obfuscation. *Information and Learning Science*, 124(9/10), 266–284. DOI:10.1108/ILS-04-2023-0032

Hongbo, Z. (2023). *Challenges, Corresponding Solutions, and Applications of Generative Adversarial Networks*. Highlights in Science Engineering and Technology., DOI:10.54097/hset.v57i.9991

Hore, S., Shah, A., & Bastian, N. D. (2023). Deep VULMAN: A deep reinforcement learning-enabled cyber vulnerability management framework. *Expert Systems with Applications*, 221, 119734. DOI:10.1016/j.eswa.2023.119734

Hosain, M. T., Ani, K. M. H., Rafi, S., Tabassum, R., Insi, A. K., & Siddiky, M. M. (2023). Path to gain functional transparency in artificial intelligence with meaningful explainability. *Journal of Metaverse*, 3(2), 166–180. DOI:10.57019/jmv.1306685

Hospedales, T. M., Antoniou, A., Micaelli, P., & Storkey, A. (2021). Meta-Learning in Neural Networks: A survey. *IEEE Transactions on Pattern Analysis and Machine Intelligence*, 1, 1. Advance online publication. DOI:10.1109/TPAMI.2021.3079209 PMID:33974543

Hossain, M. T., Afrin, R., & Biswas, M. a. A. (2024). A Review on Attacks against Artificial Intelligence (AI) and Their Defence Image Recognition and Generation Machine Learning, Artificial Intelligence. *Hossain | Control Systems and Optimization Letters*. https://doi.org/DOI:10.59247/csol.v2i1.73

Hossain, M. A., Ray, S. K., & Lota, J. (2020). SmartDR: A device-to-device communication for post-disaster recovery. *Journal of Network and Computer Applications*, 171, 102813. DOI:10.1016/j.jnca.2020.102813

Hosseini, M.-P., Lu, S., Kamaraj, K., Slowikowski, A., & Venkatesh, H. C. (2020). Deep learning architectures. *Deep learning: concepts and architectures*, 1-24.

Howard, A. M., & Borenstein, J. (2017). The ugly truth about ourselves and our robot creations: The problem of bias and social inequity. *Science and Engineering Ethics*, 24(5), 1521–1536. DOI:10.1007/s11948-017-9975-2 PMID:28936795

Ho, Y., Chen, B. Y., Li, C., & Chai, E. (2023). The distance between the humanities and medicine: Building a critical thinking mindset by interdisciplinary dialogue through mind mapping. *Thinking Skills and Creativity*, 50, 101420. DOI:10.1016/j.tsc.2023.101420

Hu, T. (2023, December 15). *Complexity matters: Rethinking the latent space for generative modeling.* https://proceedings.neurips.cc/paper_files/paper/2023/hash/5e8023f07625374c6fdf3aa08bb38e0e-Abstract-Conference.html

Huang, K., Huang, J. I., & Catteddu, D. (2024) 'GenAI Data Security,' in *Future of business and finance*, pp. 133–162. DOI:10.1007/978-3-031-54252-7_5

Huang, K., Zhang, F., Li, Y., Wright, S., Kidambi, V., & Manral, V. (2023). Security and privacy concerns in ChatGPT. In *Future of Business and Finance* (pp. 297–328). DOI:10.1007/978-3-031-45282-6_11

Huang, R., Lin, H. H., Chen, C., Zhang, K., & Zeng, W. (2024). *PlantoGraphy: Incorporating Iterative Design Process into Generative Artificial Intelligence for Landscape Rendering. arXiv*. Cornell University., DOI:10.1145/3613904.3642824

Huang, Y., Huang, L., & Zhu, Q. (2022). Reinforcement learning for feedback-enabled cyber resilience. *Annual Reviews in Control*, 53, 273–295. DOI:10.1016/j.arcontrol.2022.01.001

Hua, Y., Guo, J., & Zhao, H. (2015). Deep Belief Networks and deep learning. *Proceedings of 2015 International Conference on Intelligent Computing and Internet of Things*. DOI:10.1109/ICAIOT.2015.7111524

Hu, C., Wu, J., Sun, C., Chen, X., Nandi, A. K., & Yan, R. (2024). Unified Flowing Normality Learning for Mechanical Anomaly Detection in Continuous Time-Varying Conditions. *SSRN*. DOI:10.2139/ssrn.4719411

Hughes, R. T., Zhu, L., & Bednarz, T. (2021). Generative Adversarial Networks–Enabled Human–Artificial Intelligence Collaborative Applications for creative and Design Industries: A Systematic Review of Current approaches and Trends. *Frontiers in Artificial Intelligence*, 4, 604234. Advance online publication. DOI:10.3389/frai.2021.604234 PMID:33997773

Humayun, M., Alsaqer, M., & Jhanjhi, N. Z. (2022). Energy optimization for smart cities using IoT. *Applied Artificial Intelligence*, 36(1), 2037255. Advance online publication. DOI:10.1080/08839514.2022.2037255

Humayun, M., Ashfaq, F., Jhanjhi, N. Z., & Alsadun, M. K. (2022). Traffic management: Multi-Scale vehicle detection in varying weather conditions using YOLOV4 and spatial pyramid pooling network. *Electronics (Basel)*, 11(17), 2748. DOI:10.3390/electronics11172748

Humayun, M., Jhanjhi, N. Z., Niazi, M., Amsaad, F., & Masood, I. (2022). Securing drug distribution systems from tampering using blockchain. *Electronics (Basel)*, 11(8), 1195. DOI:10.3390/electronics11081195

Humayun, M., Jhanjhi, N., & Alamri, M. (2020). IoT-based Secure and Energy Efficient scheme for E-health applications. *Indian Journal of Science and Technology*, 13(28), 2833–2848. DOI:10.17485/IJST/v13i28.861

Humayun, M., Jhanjhi, N., Alruwaili, M., Amalathas, S. S., Balasubramanian, V., & Selvaraj, B. (2020). Privacy protection and energy optimization for 5G-aided industrial Internet of Things. *IEEE Access : Practical Innovations, Open Solutions*, 8, 183665–183677. DOI:10.1109/ACCESS.2020.3028764

Humayun, M., Jhanjhi, N., Alsayat, A., & Ponnusamy, V. (2021). Internet of things and ransomware: Evolution, mitigation and prevention. *Egyptian Informatics Journal*, 22(1), 105–117. DOI:10.1016/j.eij.2020.05.003

Humayun, M., Niazi, M., Jhanjhi, N., Alshayeb, M., & Mahmood, S. (2020). Cyber Security Threats and Vulnerabilities: A Systematic Mapping Study. *Arabian Journal for Science and Engineering*, 45(4), 3171–3189. DOI:10.1007/s13369-019-04319-2

Humayun, M., Tariq, N., Alfayad, M., Zakwan, M., Alwakid, G., & Assiri, M. (2024). Securing the Internet of Things in Artificial Intelligence Era: A Comprehensive Survey. *IEEE Access : Practical Innovations, Open Solutions*, 12, 25469–25490. DOI:10.1109/ACCESS.2024.3365634

Humphreys, D., Koay, A., Desmond, D., & Mealy, E. (2024). AI hype as a cyber security risk: The moral responsibility of implementing generative AI in business. *AI and Ethics*, 4(3), 791–804. Advance online publication. DOI:10.1007/s43681-024-00443-4

Husairi, M. A., & Rossi, P. (2024). Delegation of purchasing tasks to AI: The role of perceived choice and decision autonomy. *Decision Support Systems*, 179, 114166. DOI:10.1016/j.dss.2023.114166

Hussain, S. J., Ahmed, U., Liaquat, H., Mir, S., Jhanjhi, N. Z., & Humayun, M. (2019). IMIAD: Intelligent Malware Identification for Android Platform. *2019 International Conference on Computer and Information Sciences (ICCIS)*. DOI:10.1109/ICCISci.2019.8716471

Hussain, S., Anwaar, H., Sultan, K., Mahmud, U., Farooqui, S., Karamat, T., & Toure, I. K. (2024). Mitigating Software Vulnerabilities through Secure Software Development with a Policy-Driven Waterfall Model. *Journal of Engineering*, 2024, 1–15. DOI:10.1155/2024/9962691

Hutson, J., Lively, J., Robertson, B., Cotroneo, P., & Lang, M. (2023). Of Techne and Praxis: Redefining creativity. In *Springer series on cultural computing* (pp. 21–36). DOI:10.1007/978-3-031-45127-0_2

Huyen, N. T. M., & Bao, T. Q. (2024, January 3). *Advancements in AI-Driven cybersecurity and comprehensive threat detection and response*. https://questsquare .org/index.php/JOUNALICET/article/view/37

Hwang, I., Wakefield, R., Kim, S., & Kim, T. (2021). Security awareness: The first step in information security compliance behavior. *Journal of Computer Information Systems*, 61(4), 345–356. DOI:10.1080/08874417.2019.1650676

Hyde, R. J., & Filippidis, F. (2021). *Design Studio Vol. 2: Intelligent Control: Disruptive Technologies*.

Iftikhar, S., Gill, S. S., Song, C., Xu, M., Aslanpour, M. S., Toosi, A. N., Du, J., Wu, H., Ghosh, S., Chowdhury, D., Golec, M., Kumar, M., Abdelmoniem, A. M., Cuadrado, F., Varghese, B., Rana, O. F., Dustdar, S., & Uhlig, S. (2023). AI-based fog and edge computing: A systematic review, taxonomy and future directions. *Internet of Things : Engineering Cyber Physical Human Systems*, 21, 100674. DOI:10.1016/j.iot.2022.100674

Illiashenko, O., Kharchenko, V., Babeshko, I., Fesenko, H., & Di Giandomenico, F. (2023). Security-Informed safety analysis of autonomous transport systems considering AI-Powered Cyberattacks and protection. *Entropy (Basel, Switzerland)*, 25(8), 1123. DOI:10.3390/e25081123 PMID:37628153

Imene Safer, C., Geert, V., Roel, W., & Wilfried, V. (2022). AI privacy preserving robots working in a smart sensor environment. 300-306. DOI:10.1109/ICMLA55696.2022.00049

Ismagilova, E., Hughes, L., Rana, N. P., & Dwivedi, Y. K. (2022). Security, privacy and risks within smart cities: Literature review and development of a smart city interaction framework. *Information Systems Frontiers*, 24(2), 1–22. DOI:10.1007/s10796-020-10044-1 PMID:32837262

Jabbar, A., Li, X., & Omar, B. (2021). A survey on Generative Adversarial Networks: Variants, applications, and training. *ACM Computing Surveys*, 54(8), 1–49. DOI:10.1145/3463475

Jabeen, T., Jabeen, I., Ashraf, H., Jhanjhi, N. Z., Yassine, A., & Hossain, M. S. (2023). An intelligent healthcare system using IoT in wireless sensor network. *Sensors (Basel)*, 23(11), 5055. DOI:10.3390/s23115055 PMID:37299782

Jabeen, T., Jabeen, I., Ashraf, H., Jhanjhi, N., Mamoona, H., Mehedi, M., & Sultan, A. (2022). A monte carlo based COVID-19 detection framework for smart healthcare. *Computers, Materials & Continua*, 70(2), 2365–2380. DOI:10.32604/cmc.2022.020016

Jagadeesan, S., & Parthasarathy, V. (2019, January). Design and implement a cross layer verification framework (CLVF) for detecting and preventing blackhole and wormhole attack in wireless ad-hoc networks for cloud environment. *Cluster Computing*, 22(S1), 299–310. DOI:10.1007/s10586-018-1825-8

Jain, P., Tripathi, V., Malladi, R., & Khang, A. (2023). Data-Driven Artificial Intelligence (AI) models in the workforce development planning. In *CRC Press eBooks* (pp. 159–176). DOI:10.1201/9781003357070-10

Jaiswal, G., Rani, R., Mangotra, H., & Sharma, A. (2023). Integration of hyperspectral imaging and autoencoders: Benefits, applications, hyperparameter tunning and challenges. *Computer Science Review*, 50, 100584. DOI:10.1016/j.cosrev.2023.100584

Javadpour, A. (2024). *A comprehensive survey on cyber deception techniques to improve honeypot performance*. Computers & Security., DOI:10.1016/j.cose.2024.103792

Javaheri, D., Fahmideh, M., Chizari, H., Lalbakhsh, P., & Hur, J. (2024). Cybersecurity threats in FinTech: A systematic review. *Expert Systems with Applications*, 241, 122697. DOI:10.1016/j.eswa.2023.122697

Jawad, A. T., Mâaloul, R., & Fourati, L. C. (2023). A comprehensive survey on 6G and beyond: Enabling technologies, opportunities of machine learning and challenges. *Computer Networks*, 237, 110085. DOI:10.1016/j.comnet.2023.110085

Jawahar, G., Abdul-Mageed, M., & Lakshmanan, L. V. S. (2020). Automatic Detection of Machine Generated Text: A Critical survey. *arXiv (Cornell University)*. /arxiv.2011.01314DOI:10.18653/v1/2020.coling-main.208

Jayanthi, E., Ramesh, T., Kharat, R. S., Veeramanickam, M. R. M., Bharathiraja, N., Venkatesan, R., & Marappan, R. (2023). Cybersecurity enhancement to detect credit card frauds in health care using new machine learning strategies. *Soft Computing*, 27(11), 7555–7565. DOI:10.1007/s00500-023-07954-y

Jayatharan, V., & Alwis, D. (2023). Alapana Generation using Finite State Machines and Generative Adversarial Networks. *2023 International Research Conference on Smart Computing and Systems Engineering (SCSE)*. DOI:10.1109/SCSE59836.2023.10215001

Je, D., Jung, J., & Choi, S. (2021). Toward 6G security: Technology trends, threats, and solutions. *IEEE Communications Standards Magazine*, 5(3), 64–71. DOI:10.1109/MCOMSTD.011.2000065

Jendoubi, I., & Bouffard, F. (2023). Multi-agent hierarchical reinforcement learning for energy management. *Applied Energy*, 332, 120500. DOI:10.1016/j.apenergy.2022.120500

Jenis, J., Ondriga, J., Hrček, S., Brumerčík, F., Čuchor, M., & Sádovský, E. (2023). Engineering applications of artificial intelligence in mechanical design and optimization. *Machines (Basel)*, 11(6), 577. DOI:10.3390/machines11060577

Jhanjhi, N., Khan, M. A., Ahmad, M., & Hussain, M. (2022). The Impact of Cyber Attacks on E-Governance During the COVID-19 Pandemic. *Cybersecurity Measures for E-Government Frameworks*, 123.

Jhanjhi, N. Z., Humayun, M., & Almuayqil, S. N. (2021). Cyber security and privacy issues in industrial internet of things. *Computer Systems Science and Engineering*, 37(3). Advance online publication. DOI:10.32604/csse.2021.015206

Jha, R. (2023). Cybersecurity and confidentiality in smart Grid for enhancing sustainability and reliability. *Recent Research Reviews Journal*, 2(2), 215–241. DOI:10.36548/rrrj.2023.2.001

Jiang, F., Ma, J., Webster, C., Chiaradia, A. J., Zhou, Y., Zhao, Z., & Zhang, X. (2023). Generative urban design: A systematic review on problem formulation, design generation, and decision-making. *Progress in Planning*, 100795. Advance online publication. DOI:10.1016/j.progress.2023.100795

Ji, I. H., Lee, J. H., Kang, M. J., Park, W. J., Jeon, S. H., & Seo, J. T. (2024). Artificial Intelligence-Based Anomaly Detection Technology over Encrypted Traffic: A Systematic Literature Review. *Sensors (Basel)*, 24(3), 898. DOI:10.3390/s24030898 PMID:38339615

Jin, C. (2018). *Is Q-Learning provably efficient?* https://proceedings.neurips.cc/paper_files/paper/2018/hash/d3b1fb02964aa64e257f9f26a31f72cf-Abstract.html

Jin, X., Li, H., & Zhou, S. (2014). An overview of deep generative models. *IETE Technical Review*, 32(2), 131–139. DOI:10.1080/02564602.2014.987328

Johansen, G. (2017). *Digital forensics and incident response*. Packt Publishing Ltd.

Johnson, R. (2021). Enhancing problem-solving skills in programming education. *Journal of Computational Science Education*, 25(4), 321–345. DOI:10.1080/123 45678.2021.12345678

Jonnala, J. (2024) *Advancing Cybersecurity: a comprehensive approach to enhance threat detection, analysis, and trust in digital environments*. https://www.ijisae.org/index.php/IJISAE/article/view/4302

Joo Fong, T., Abdullah, A., Jhanjhi, N., & Supramaniam, M. (2019). The coin passcode: A shoulder-surfing proof graphical password authentication model for mobile devices. *International Journal of Advanced Computer Science and Applications, 10*(1).

Judijanto, L., Hindarto, D., Wahjono, S. I., & Djunarto, . (2023). Edge of enterprise architecture in addressing cyber security threats and business risks. *International Journal Software Engineering and Computer Science*, 3(3), 386–396. DOI:10.35870/ijsecs.v3i3.1816

Jui, T. D., & Rivas, P. (2024). Fairness issues, current approaches, and challenges in machine learning models. *International Journal of Machine Learning and Cybernetics*, 15(8), 3095–3125. Advance online publication. DOI:10.1007/s13042-023-02083-2

Julie, E. G., Nayahi, J. J. V., & Jhanjhi, N. Z. (Eds.). (2020). *Blockchain Technology: Fundamentals, Applications, and Case Studies*. CRC Press.

Jung, B., Li, Y., & Bechor, T. (2022). CAVP: A context-aware vulnerability prioritization model. *Computers & Security*, 116, 102639. DOI:10.1016/j.cose.2022.102639

Ju, Y., Chen, Y., Cao, Z., Liu, L., Pei, Q., Xiao, M., Ota, K., Dong, M., & Leung, V. C. (2023). Joint secure offloading and resource allocation for vehicular edge computing network: A multi-agent deep reinforcement learning approach. *IEEE Transactions on Intelligent Transportation Systems*, 24(5), 5555–5569. DOI:10.1109/TITS.2023.3242997

Kaasinen, E., Anttila, A., Heikkilä, P., Laarni, J., Koskinen, H., & Väätänen, A. (2022). Smooth and resilient Human–Machine Teamwork as an Industry 5.0 design challenge. *Sustainability (Basel)*, 14(5), 2773. DOI:10.3390/su14052773

Kabanda, G., Chipfumbu, C. T., & Chingoriwo, T. (2023). A Reinforcement Learning Paradigm for Cybersecurity Education and Training. *Oriental Journal of Computer Science and Technology*, 12-45.

Kadakia, Y. A., Suryavanshi, A., Alnajdi, A., Abdullah, F., & Christofides, P. D. (2024). Integrating machine learning detection and encrypted control for enhanced cybersecurity of nonlinear processes. *Computers & Chemical Engineering*, 180, 108498. DOI:10.1016/j.compchemeng.2023.108498

Kaddoura, S., & Al Husseiny, F. (2023). The rising trend of Metaverse in education: Challenges, opportunities, and ethical considerations. *PeerJ. Computer Science*, 9, e1252. DOI:10.7717/peerj-cs.1252 PMID:37346578

Kalelioglu, F., Gülbahar, Y., & Madran, O. (2016). A comparison of computer-based and paper-based training for learning programming concepts. *Journal of Educational Technology & Society*.

Kaloudi, N., & Li, J. (2020). The ai-based cyber threat landscape: A survey. *ACM Computing Surveys*, 53(1), 1–34. DOI:10.1145/3372823

Kamble, D., Rathod, S., Bhelande, M., Shah, A. S., & Sapkal, P. (2024). Correlating forensic data for enhanced network crime investigations: Techniques for packet sniffing, network forensics, and attack detection. *Journal of Autonomous Intelligence*, 7(4). Advance online publication. DOI:10.32629/jai.v7i4.1272

Kang, Y. (2023). Development of Large-Scale farming based on explainable machine learning for a sustainable rural economy: The case of cyber risk analysis to prevent costly data breaches. *Applied Artificial Intelligence*, 37(1), 2223862. Advance online publication. DOI:10.1080/08839514.2023.2223862

Kaplan, B. A., Gilroy, S. P., DeHart, W. B., Brown, J. M., & Koffarnus, M. N. (2023). Data handling: ethical principles, guidelines, and recommended practices. In *Elsevier eBooks* (pp. 191–214). DOI:10.1016/B978-0-323-90969-3.00006-2

Kapoor, A., & Chatterjee, S. (2023). *Platform and model design for responsible AI: Design and build resilient, private, fair, and transparent machine learning models.* Packt Publishing Ltd.

Karabacak, M., Ozkara, B. B., Margetis, K., Wintermark, M., & Bisdas, S. (2023). The advent of generative language models in medical education. *JMIR Medical Education*, 9, e48163. DOI:10.2196/48163 PMID:37279048

Karapantelakis, A., Alizadeh, P., Al-Abassi, A., Dey, K., & Níκου, A. (2023). Generative AI in mobile networks: A survey. *Annales des Télécommunications*. Advance online publication. DOI:10.1007/s12243-023-00980-9

Karlsson, I., & Ljungberg, D. (2024). *Supplementing Dependabot'svulnerability scanning : A Custom Pipeline for Tracing DependencyUsage in JavaScript Projects.* DIVA. https://www.diva-portal.org/smash/record.jsf?pid=diva2%3A1832928&dswid=425

Karnouskos, S. (2020). Artificial intelligence in digital media: The era of Deepfakes. *IEEE Transactions on Technology and Society*, 1(3), 138–147. DOI:10.1109/TTS.2020.3001312

Karthigadevi, K., Balamurali, S., & Venkatesulu, M. (2018). Wormhole attack detection and prevention using EIGRP protocol based on round trip time. *J. Cyber Secur. Mobil.*, 7(1), 215–228. DOI:10.13052/2245-1439.7115

Karthigadevi, K., Balamurali, S., & Venkatesulu, M. (2019). Based on Neighbor Density Estimation Technique to Improve the Quality of Service and to Detect and Prevent the Sinkhole Attack in Wireless Sensor Network. *IEEE International Conference on Intelligent Techniques in Control, Optimization and Signal Processing, INCOS 2019*, 1–4. DOI:10.1109/INCOS45849.2019.8951406

Katoch, S., & Garg, V. (2023) 'Security analysis on Android application through penetration testing,' in *Lecture notes in networks and systems*, 221–234. DOI:10.1007/978-981-99-3716-5_20

Kaur, S., Singla, J., Nkenyereye, L., Jha, S., Prashar, D., Joshi, G. P., El–Sappagh, S., Islam, M. S., & Islam, S. M. R. (2020). Medical Diagnostic Systems Using Artificial intelligence (AI) Algorithms: Principles and Perspectives. *IEEE Access : Practical Innovations, Open Solutions*, 8, 228049–228069. DOI:10.1109/AC-CESS.2020.3042273

Kavitha, S., Bora, A., Naved, M., Raj, K. B., & Singh, B. R. N. (2021). An internet of things for data security in cloud using artificial intelligence. *International Journal of Grid and Distributed Computing*, 14(1), 1257–1275.

Kazemi, P. (2023). *Implementation of AI in user experience*. Theseus. https://www.theseus.fi/handle/10024/800276

Keneshloo, Y., Shi, T., Ramakrishnan, N., & Reddy, C. K. (2019). Deep reinforcement learning for Sequence-to-Sequence models. *IEEE Transactions on Neural Networks and Learning Systems*, 1–21. DOI:10.1109/TNNLS.2019.2929141 PMID:31425057

Kenwright, B. (2023). Is it the end of undergraduate dissertations? In *Advances in educational technologies and instructional design book series* (pp. 46–65). DOI:10.4018/979-8-3693-0074-9.ch003

Keshk, M., Koroniotis, N., Pham, N., Moustafa, N., Turnbull, B., & Zomaya, A. Y. (2023). An explainable deep learning-enabled intrusion detection framework in IoT networks. *Information Sciences*, 639, 119000. DOI:10.1016/j.ins.2023.119000

Khaleefah, A. D., & Al-Mashhadi, H. M. (2024). Methodologies, Requirements, and Challenges of Cybersecurity Frameworks: A Review. *Iraqi Journal of Science*, 468–486. DOI:10.24996/ijs.2024.65.1.38

Khalil, M. I., Humayun, M., Jhanjhi, N. Z., Talib, M. N., & Tabbakh, T. A. (2021). Multi-class segmentation of organ at risk from abdominal ct images: A deep learning approach. Intelligent Computing and Innovation on Data Science *Proceedings of ICTIDS*, 2021, 425–434.

Khalil, M. I., Jhanjhi, N. Z., Humayun, M., Sivanesan, S., Masud, M., & Hossain, M. S. (2021). Hybrid smart grid with sustainable energy efficient resources for smart cities. *Sustainable Energy Technologies and Assessments*, 46, 101211. DOI:10.1016/j.seta.2021.101211

Khan, A. A., Akbar, M. A., Waseem, M., Fahmideh, M., Ahmad, A., Liang, P., . . . Abrahamsson, P. (2022). AI ethics: software practitioners and lawmakers points of view. *arXiv preprint arXiv:2207.01493*.

Khan, A., Jhanjhi, N. Z., Haji, D. H. T. B. A., & Omar, H. A. H. B. H. (2024). Internet of Things (IoT) Impact on Inventory Management: A Review. *Cybersecurity Measures for Logistics Industry Framework*, 224-247.

Khan, A., Jhanjhi, N., Haji, D. H. T. B. A., & bin Haji Omar, H. A. H. (2024). Overview of XAI for the Development and Modernization of Smart Cities: Explainable Artificial Intelligence. In *Advances in Explainable AI Applications for Smart Cities* (pp. 177-198). IGI Global.

Khan, A., Jhanjhi, N., Ray, S. K., Amsaad, F., & Sujatha, R. (2024). Ethical and Social Implications of Industry 4.0 in SCM. In *Convergence of Industry 4.0 and Supply Chain Sustainability* (pp. 234-274): IGI Global.

Khan, M. R., Khan, N. R., & Jhanjhi, N. Z. (2024). *Convergence of Industry 4.0 and Supply Chain Sustainability*: IGI Global.

Khan, M., & Ghafoor, L. (2024) *Adversarial machine learning in the context of network Security: Challenges and solutions*. https://thesciencebrigade.com/jcir/article/view/118

Khan, A. A., Akbar, M. A., Fahmideh, M., Liang, P., Waseem, M., Ahmad, A., Niazi, M., & Abrahamsson, P. (2023). AI Ethics: An Empirical Study on the Views of Practitioners and Lawmakers. *IEEE Transactions on Computational Social Systems*, 10(6), 2971–2984. DOI:10.1109/TCSS.2023.3251729

Khan, A., Jhanjhi, N., Humayun, M., & Ahmad, M. (2020). The role of IoT in digital governance. In *Employing Recent Technologies for Improved Digital Governance* (pp. 128–150). IGI Global. DOI:10.4018/978-1-7998-1851-9.ch007

Khan, B., Fatima, H., Qureshi, A., Kumar, S., Hanan, A., Hussain, J., & Abdullah, S. (2023). Drawbacks of artificial intelligence and their potential solutions in the healthcare sector. *Biomedical Materials & Devices*, 1(2), 1–8. DOI:10.1007/s44174-023-00063-2 PMID:36785697

Khan, M. K. U., & Ramesh, K. S. (2019). Effect on Packet Delivery Ratio (PDR) & Throughput in Wireless Sensor Networks Due to Black Hole Attack. *International Journal of Innovative Technology and Exploring Engineering*, 8(12S), 428–432. DOI:10.35940/ijitee.L1107.10812S19

Khan, N. A., Jhanjhi, N. Z., Brohi, S. N., Almazroi, A. A., & Almazroi, A. A. (2022). A secure communication protocol for unmanned aerial vehicles. *CMC-Computers Materials & Continua*, 70(1), 601–618. DOI:10.32604/cmc.2022.019419

Khazane, H., Ridouani, M., Salahdine, F., & Kaabouch, N. (2024). A Holistic Review of Machine Learning Adversarial attacks in IoT networks. *Future Internet*, 16(1), 32. DOI:10.3390/fi16010032

Khennouche, F., Elmir, Y., Himeur, Y., Djebari, N., & Amira, A. (2024). Revolutionizing generative pre-traineds: Insights and challenges in deploying ChatGPT and generative chatbots for FAQs. *Expert Systems with Applications*, 246, 123224. DOI:10.1016/j.eswa.2024.123224

Khera, Y., Kumar, D., & Garg, N. (2019, February). Analysis and impact of vulnerability assessment and penetration testing. In *2019 International Conference on Machine Learning, Big Data, Cloud and Parallel Computing (COMITCon)* (pp. 525-530). IEEE. DOI:10.1109/COMITCon.2019.8862224

Kholgh, D. K., & Kostakos, P. (2023). PAC-GPT: A Novel approach to generating synthetic network traffic with GPT-3. *IEEE Access : Practical Innovations, Open Solutions*, 11, 114936–114951. DOI:10.1109/ACCESS.2023.3325727

Khoo, L., Lim, M. K., Chong, C. Y., & McNaney, R. (2024). Machine Learning for Multimodal Mental Health Detection: A Systematic Review of Passive Sensing Approaches. *Sensors (Basel)*, 24(2), 348. DOI:10.3390/s24020348 PMID:38257440

Khosravi, H., Shum, S. B., Chen, G., Conati, C., Gašević, D., Kay, J., Knight, S., Martínez-Maldonado, R., Sadiq, S., & Tsai, Y. (2022). Explainable Artificial Intelligence in education. *Computers & Education: Artificial Intelligence*, 3, 100074. DOI:10.1016/j.caeai.2022.100074

Kilincer, I. F., Ertam, F., & Sengur, A. (2021). Machine learning methods for cyber security intrusion detection: Datasets and comparative study. *Computer Networks*, 188, 107840. DOI:10.1016/j.comnet.2021.107840

Kim, J., Seo, M., Lee, S., Nam, J., Yegneswaran, V., Porras, P., Gu, G., & Shin, S. (2024). Enhancing security in SDN: Systematizing attacks and defenses from a penetration perspective. *Computer Networks*, 241, 110203. DOI:10.1016/j.comnet.2024.110203

King, D. (2024). *Legal & Humble AI: Addressing the Legal, Ethical, and Societal Dilemmas of Generative AI*. Ingene Publishers.

Kitchenham, B., Pearl Brereton, O., Budgen, D., Turner, M., Bailey, J., & Linkman, S. (2009). Systematic literature reviews in software engineering - A systematic literature review. *Information and Software Technology*, 51(1), 7–15. DOI:10.1016/j.infsof.2008.09.009

Kizza, J. M. (2024) 'Computer Network Security Protocols,' in *Texts in computer science*, pp. 409–441. DOI:10.1007/978-3-031-47549-8_18

Kizza, J. M. (2024). Standardization and security criteria: Security evaluation of computer products. In *Texts in computer science* (pp. 377–394). DOI:10.1007/978-3-031-47549-8_16

Kizza, J. M. (2024a) 'Firewalls,' in *Texts in computer science*, 265–294. DOI:10.1007/978-3-031-47549-8_12

Kizza, J. M. (2024b) 'System Intrusion Detection and Prevention,' in *Texts in computer science*, 295–323. DOI:10.1007/978-3-031-47549-8_13

Knapp, S. (2022). Listen, explain, involve, and evaluate: Why respecting autonomy benefits suicidal patients. *Ethics & Behavior*, 34(1), 18–27. DOI:10.1080/10508422.2022.2152338

Ko, J., Ennemoser, B., Yoo, W., Yan, W., & Clayton, M. J. (2023). Architectural spatial layout planning using artificial intelligence. *Automation in Construction*, 154, 105019. DOI:10.1016/j.autcon.2023.105019

Kok, S., Abdullah, A., & Jhanjhi, N. Z. (2022). Early detection of crypto-ransomware using pre-encryption detection algorithm. *Journal of King Saud University. Computer and Information Sciences*, 34(5), 1984–1999. DOI:10.1016/j.jksuci.2020.06.012

Kolberg, J., Schäfer, Y., Rathgeb, C., & Busch, C. (2024). On the Potential of Algorithm Fusion for Demographic Bias Mitigation in Face Recognition. *IET Biometrics*, 2024, 1–18. DOI:10.1049/2024/1808587

Konar, S., Mukherjee, G., & Dutta, G. (2024) 'Understanding the relationship between trust and faith in Micro-Enterprises to cyber hygiene,' in *Advances in business information systems and analytics book series*, 125–148. DOI:10.4018/979-8-3693-0839-4.ch006

Konatham, B., Simra, T., Amsaad, F., Ibrahem, M. I., & Jhanjhi, N. Z. (2024). A Secure Hybrid Deep Learning Technique for Anomaly Detection in IIoT Edge Computing. *Authorea Preprints*. DOI:10.36227/techrxiv.170630909.96680286/v1

Korczak, A. (2023). *Designing for Programming Without Coding : User experience of mobile low-code software*. DIVA. https://www.diva-portal.org/smash/record.jsf?pid=diva2%3A1764478&dswid=-4147

Kori, S. (2019). Distributed Wormhole Attack Mitigation Technique in WSNs. *Int. J. Comput. Netw. Inf. Secur.*, 11(5), 20–27.

Körner, H., Vos, T., & van der Meijden, H. (2020). An empirical study on the effectiveness of online learning resources in programming education. *International Journal of Emerging Technologies in Learning.*

Kot, A. (2023). *Enhancing data analytics for heavy industry through UI/UX design and streamlined reporting: Improving usability, scalability, and visual representation through application of design principles.* Theseus. https://www.theseus.fi/handle/10024/798445

Kozák, M. (2024) 'Creating valid adversarial examples of malware,' *Journal of Computer Virology and Hacking Techniques* [Preprint]. .DOI:10.1007/s11416-024-00516-2

Kozik, R., Pawlicki, M., & Choraś, M. (2018). Cost-Sensitive distributed machine learning for NetFlow-Based Botnet activity detection. *Security and Communication Networks*, 2018, 1–8. DOI:10.1155/2018/8753870

KPMG. (2023). Blockchain + artificial intelligence =? [Blog post]. https://kpmg.com/us/en/articles/2023/blockchain-artificial-intelligence.html

Krause, D. S. (2023). Mitigating risks for financial firms using generative AI tools. *Social Science Research Network.* DOI:10.2139/ssrn.4452600

Krichen, M. (2023). Strengthening the security of smart contracts through the power of artificial intelligence. *Computers*, 12(5), 107. DOI:10.3390/computers12050107

Krishnan, S., Thangaveloo, R., Rahman, S. B. A., & Sindiramutty, S. R. (2021). Smart Ambulance Traffic Control system. *Trends in Undergraduate Research*, 4(1), c28–c34. DOI:10.33736/tur.2831.2021

Krüger, P. S., & Brauchle, J. P. (2021). *The European Union, cybersecurity, and the financial sector: A primer. Carnegie Endowment Int.* Peace Publications Dept.

Krukowski, S., Kempisty, P., & Strąk, P. (2008). Role of chlorine in the dynamics of GaN(0001) surface during HVPE GaN growth—Ab initio study. *Journal of Crystal Growth*, 310(7–9), 1391–1397. DOI:10.1016/j.jcrysgro.2007.11.099

Kshetri, N. (2017). Blockchain's roles in strengthening cybersecurity and protecting privacy. *Telecommunications Policy*, 41(10), 1027–1038. DOI:10.1016/j.telpol.2017.09.003

Kumar, D. S., Madhavi, K., Ramprasad, T., Sekhar, K. R., Dhanikonda, S. R., & Ravi, C. (2024, February 23). *Design and Development of Data-Driven Product Recommender Model for E-Commerce using Behavioral Analytics.* https://ijisae.org/index.php/IJISAE/article/view/4884

Kumar, D., & Suthar, N. (2024). Ethical and legal challenges of AI in marketing: an exploration of solutions. *Journal of Information, Communication and Ethics in Society*. DOI:10.1108/JICES-05-2023-0068

Kumar, R. and Khan, R.A. (2024) 'Securing military computing with the blockchain,' *Computer Fraud & Security*, 2024(2). .DOI:10.12968/S1361-3723(24)70007-4

Kumar, A., Aelgani, V., Vohra, R., Gupta, S. K., Bhagawati, M., Paul, S., & Laird, J. R. (2024). Artificial intelligence bias in medical system designs: A systematic review. *Multimedia Tools and Applications*, 83(6), 18005–18057. DOI:10.1007/s11042-023-16029-x

Kumar, G., Rai, M. K., & Saha, R. (2017). Securing range free localization against wormhole attack using distance estimation and maximum likelihood estimation in Wireless Sensor Networks. *Journal of Network and Computer Applications*, 99, 10–16. DOI:10.1016/j.jnca.2017.10.006

Kumar, H., Koppel, A., & Ribeiro, A. (2023). On the sample complexity of actor-critic method for reinforcement learning with function approximation. *Machine Learning*, 112(7), 2433–2467. DOI:10.1007/s10994-023-06303-2

Kumari, K., Sharma, A., Chakraborty, C., & Ananyaa, M. (2022). Preserving health care data security and privacy using Carmichael's Theorem-Based Homomorphic encryption and modified enhanced homomorphic encryption schemes in edge computing systems. *Big Data*, 10(1), 1–17. DOI:10.1089/big.2021.0012 PMID:34375143

Kumar, M. S., Vimal, S., Jhanjhi, N. Z., Dhanabalan, S. S., & Alhumyani, H. A. (2021). Blockchain based peer to peer communication in autonomous drone operation. *Energy Reports*, 7, 7925–7939. DOI:10.1016/j.egyr.2021.08.073

Kumar, V., Malik, N., Singla, J., Jhanjhi, N., Amsaad, F., & Razaque, A. (2022). Light weight authentication scheme for smart home iot devices. *Cryptography*, 6(3), 37. DOI:10.3390/cryptography6030037

Kushwaha, A. K., Pharswan, R., Kumar, P., & Kar, A. K. (2022). How do users feel when they use artificial intelligence for decision making? a framework for assessing users' perception. *Information Systems Frontiers*, 25(3), 1241–1260. DOI:10.1007/s10796-022-10293-2

Lackner, M., Markl, E., & Aburaia, M. (2018). Cybersecurity management for (industrial) internet of things–challenges and opportunities. *Journal of Information Technology & Software Engineering*, 8(05).

Laínez, N., & Gardner, J. (2023). Algorithmic credit scoring in Vietnam: A legal proposal for maximizing benefits and minimizing risks. *Asian Journal of Law and Society*, 10(3), 401–432. DOI:10.1017/als.2023.6

Lalor, J. P., Abbasi, A., Oketch, K., Yang, Y., & Forsgren, N. (2024). Should Fairness be a Metric or a Model? A Model-based Framework for Assessing Bias in Machine Learning Pipelines. *ACM Transactions on Information Systems*, 42(4), 1–41. Advance online publication. DOI:10.1145/3641276

Lam, K. Y., Mitra, S., Gondesen, F., & Yi, X. (2022). ANT-Centric IoT Security Reference Architecture - Security-by-Design for Satellite-Enabled Smart Cities. *IEEE Internet of Things Journal*, 9(8), 5895–5908. DOI:10.1109/JIOT.2021.3073734

Lancaster, C., Schulenberg, K., Flathmann, C., McNeese, N. J., & Freeman, G. (2023). *"It's Everybody's Role to Speak Up. . . But Not Everyone Will": Understanding AI Professionals' Perceptions of Accountability for AI Bias Mitigation*. ACM Journal on Responsible Computing. DOI:10.1145/3632121

Landers, R. N., & Behrend, T. S. (2023a). Auditing the AI auditors: A framework for evaluating fairness and bias in high stakes AI predictive models. *The American Psychologist*, 78(1), 36–49. DOI:10.1037/amp0000972 PMID:35157476

Laux, J., Wachter, S., & Mittelstadt, B. (2023). Trustworthy artificial intelligence and the European Union AI act: On the conflation of trustworthiness and acceptability of risk. *Regulation & Governance*. Advance online publication. DOI:10.1111/rego.12512 PMID:38435808

Lee, P. (2024, February 10). *Synthetic data and the future of AI*. https://papers.ssrn.com/sol3/papers.cfm?abstract_id=4722162

Lee, H., Kim, J., Ahn, S., Hussain, R., Cho, S., & Son, J. (2021). Digestive neural networks: A novel defense strategy against inference attacks in federated learning. *Computers & Security*, 109, 102378. DOI:10.1016/j.cose.2021.102378

Lehrberger, J., & Bourbeau, L. (1988). *Machine translation: Linguistic characteristics of MT systems and general methodology of evaluation*. John Benjamins Publishing. DOI:10.1075/lis.15

Lei, X., Sun, L., & Xia, Y. (2020). Lost data reconstruction for structural health monitoring using deep convolutional generative adversarial networks. *Structural Health Monitoring*, 20(4), 2069–2087. DOI:10.1177/1475921720959226

Lelah, T. A. (2023). Abuse of Cloud-Based and Public Legitimate Services as Command-and-Control (C&C) Infrastructure: A Systematic Literature Review. *Journal of Cybersecurity and Privacy*, 3(3), 558–590. DOI:10.3390/jcp3030027

Lepri, B., Oliver, N., Letouzé, E., Pentland, A., & Vinck, P. (2017). Fair, transparent, and accountable algorithmic decision-making processes. *Philosophy & Technology*, 31(4), 611–627. DOI:10.1007/s13347-017-0279-x

Leslie, D. (2019). Understanding artificial intelligence ethics and safety. *arXiv (Cornell University)*. DOI:10.5281/zenodo.3240529

Le, T.-T.-H., Wardhani, R. W., Putranto, D. S. C., Jo, U., & Kim, H. (2023). Toward enhanced attack detection and explanation in intrusion detection System-Based IoT environment data. *IEEE Access : Practical Innovations, Open Solutions*, 11, 131661–131676. DOI:10.1109/ACCESS.2023.3336678

Letafati, M., & Otoum, S. (2023). On the privacy and security for e-health services in the metaverse: An overview. *Ad Hoc Networks*, 150, 103262. DOI:10.1016/j.adhoc.2023.103262

Li, L., Hu, X., Chen, K., & He, K. (2011). The applications of WiFi-based Wireless Sensor Network in Internet of Things and Smart Grid. Proceedings of the 2011 6th IEEE Conference on Industrial Electronics and Applications, ICIEA, 789–793. DOI:10.1109/ICIEA.2011.5975693

Liao, Q. V., Subramonyam, H., Wang, J., & Vaughan, J. (2023a). *Designerly Understanding: Information Needs for Model Transparency to Support Design Ideation for AI-Powered User Experience*. ACM. DOI:10.1145/3544548.3580652

Lichtenthaler, U. (2020). *Integrated Intelligence: Combining Human and Artificial Intelligence for Competitive Advantage, Plus E-Book Inside (ePub, Mobi Oder Pdf)*.

Lien, C.-W., & Vhaduri, S. (2023). Challenges and opportunities of biometric user authentication in the age of iot: A survey. *ACM Computing Surveys*, 56(1), 1–37. DOI:10.1145/3603705

Li, J., & Wang, D. (2019, April). The security dv-hop algorithm against multiple-wormhole-node-link in WSN. *KSII Transactions on Internet and Information Systems*, 13(4), 2223–2242.

Li, J., Wang, D., & Wang, Y. (2018). Security DV-hop localisation algorithm against wormhole attack in wireless sensor network. *IET Wireless Sensor Systems*, 8(2), 68–75. DOI:10.1049/iet-wss.2017.0075

Lilova, S. (2021). Copyright or copyleft for AI-Generated works: private ordering solutions for the benefit of content creators. *Social Science Research Network*. DOI:10.2139/ssrn.4271966

Lim, M., Abdullah, A., Jhanjhi, N. Z., & Khan, M. K. (2019). Situation-aware deep reinforcement learning link prediction model for evolving criminal networks. *IEEE Access : Practical Innovations, Open Solutions*, 8, 16550–16559. DOI:10.1109/ACCESS.2019.2961805

Lim, W., Yong, K. S. C., Theng, L. B., & Tan, C. L. (2024). Future of Generative Adversarial Networks (GAN) for Anomaly Detection in Network Security: A review. *Computers & Security*, 139, 103733. DOI:10.1016/j.cose.2024.103733

Lin, Z., Shi, Y., & Zhi, X. (2022). IDSGAN: Generative Adversarial Networks for Attack Generation against Intrusion Detection. In *Lecture Notes in Computer Science* (pp. 79–91). DOI:10.1007/978-3-031-05981-0_7

Li, S. E. (2023). Deep reinforcement learning. In *Reinforcement learning for sequential decision and optimal control* (pp. 365–402). Springer Nature Singapore. DOI:10.1007/978-981-19-7784-8_10

Liu, G., Du, H., Niyato, D., Kang, J., Xiong, Z., Kim, D. I., & Shen, X. (2024). Semantic Communications for Artificial Intelligence Generated Content (AIGC) toward effective content creation. *IEEE Network*, 1, 1. Advance online publication. DOI:10.1109/MNET.2024.3352917

Liu, J., Qiu, Z., Wang, L., Liu, P., Cheng, G., & Chen, Y. (2024). Intelligent floor plan design of modular high-rise residential building based on graph-constrained generative adversarial networks. *Automation in Construction*, 159, 105264. DOI:10.1016/j.autcon.2023.105264

Liu, J., Wang, L., Hu, W., Gao, Y., Cao, Y., Lin, B., & Zhang, R. (2023). Spatial-Temporal Feature with Dual-Attention Mechanism for Encrypted Malicious Traffic Detection. *Security and Communication Networks*, 2023, 1–13. DOI:10.1155/2023/7117863

Liu, M., Huang, X., Yu, J., & Mallya, A. (2021). Generative Adversarial networks for image and video synthesis: Algorithms and applications. *Proceedings of the IEEE*, 109(5), 839–862. DOI:10.1109/JPROC.2021.3049196

Liu, M., Ren, Y., Nyagoga, L. M., Stonier, F., Wu, Z., & Liang, Y. (2023). Future of education in the era of generative artificial intelligence: Consensus among Chinese scholars on applications of ChatGPT in schools. *Future in Educational Research*, 1(1), 72–101. DOI:10.1002/fer3.10

Liu, X., Ahmad, S. F., Anser, M. K., Ke, J., Irshad, M., Ul-Haq, J., & Abbas, S. (2022). Cyber security threats: A never-ending challenge for e-commerce. *Frontiers in Psychology*, 13, 927398. DOI:10.3389/fpsyg.2022.927398 PMID:36337532

Liu, Y., & Martens, J. (2024). Conversation-based hybrid UI for the repertory grid technique: A lab experiment into automation of qualitative surveys. *International Journal of Human-Computer Studies*, 184, 103227. DOI:10.1016/j.ijhcs.2024.103227

Liu, Z., Ma, C., She, W., & Xie, M. (2024). Biomedical image Segmentation using Denoising Diffusion Probabilistic Models: A Comprehensive Review and analysis. *Applied Sciences (Basel, Switzerland)*, 14(2), 632. DOI:10.3390/app14020632

Li, W., Su, Z., Li, R., Zhang, K., & Wang, Y. (2020). Blockchain-based data security for artificial intelligence applications in 6G networks. *IEEE Network*, 34(6), 31–37. DOI:10.1109/MNET.021.1900629

Longo, L., Brčić, M., Cabitza, F., Choi, J., Confalonieri, R., Del Ser, J., Guidotti, R., Hayashi, Y., Herrera, F., Holzinger, A., Jiang, R., Khosravi, H., Lécué, F., Malgieri, G., Páez, A., Samek, W., Schneider, J., Speith, T., & Stumpf, S. (2024). Explainable Artificial Intelligence (XAI) 2.0: A manifesto of open challenges and interdisciplinary research directions. *Information Fusion*, 102301, 102301. Advance online publication. DOI:10.1016/j.inffus.2024.102301

Luan, H., Géczy, P., Lai, H., Gobert, J. D., Yang, S. J. H., Ogata, H., Baltes, J., Da Silva Guerra, R., Li, P., & Tsai, C. C. (2020). Challenges and future directions of big data and artificial intelligence in education. *Frontiers in Psychology*, 11, 580820. Advance online publication. DOI:10.3389/fpsyg.2020.580820 PMID:33192896

Luketina, J., Nardelli, N., Farquhar, G., Foerster, J., Andreas, J., Grefenstette, E., Whiteson, S., & Rocktäschel, T. (2019). A survey of Reinforcement Learning informed by Natural language. *arXiv (Cornell University)*. /arxiv.1906.03926DOI:10.24963/ijcai.2019/880

Luleci, F., & Çatbaş, F. N. (2023). A brief introductory review to deep generative models for civil structural health monitoring. *AI in Civil Engineering*, 2(1), 9. Advance online publication. DOI:10.1007/s43503-023-00017-z PMID:37621778

Luo, Y. (n.d.). *Investigation of Algorithmic Nudging on Decision Quality: Evidence from Randomized Experiments in Online Recommendation Settings*. CUNY Academic Works. https://academicworks.cuny.edu/gc_etds/5678/

Luong, N. C., Hoang, D. T., Gong, S., Niyato, D., Wang, P., Liang, Y., & Kim, D. I. (2019). Applications of Deep Reinforcement Learning in Communications and Networking: A survey. *IEEE Communications Surveys and Tutorials*, 21(4), 3133–3174. DOI:10.1109/COMST.2019.2916583

Luo, X., Chen, Y., Li, M., Luo, Q., Xue, K., Liu, S., & Chen, L. (2019). CRED-ND: A Novel Secure Neighbor Discovery Algorithm for Wormhole Attack. *IEEE Access : Practical Innovations, Open Solutions*, 7(c), 18194–18205. DOI:10.1109/ACCESS.2019.2894637

M, R. K., & Jayagopal, P. (2020). Generative adversarial networks: a survey on applications and challenges. *International Journal of Multimedia Information Retrieval, 10*(1), 1–24. DOI:10.1007/s13735-020-00196-w

Ma, Z. (2024) 'The investigation of communications protocol,' in *Advances in intelligent systems research*, 576–582. DOI:10.2991/978-94-6463-370-2_58

Magnusson, O. (2023) *Cyber threat emulation*. https://odr.chalmers.se/items/62874e36-08b6-4d7b-92b5-705e91cc26f4

Mahmood, S., Akif, F., Ashraf, H., & Jhanjhi, N. (2024). Defense Mechanism Against Attacks Promoting Spread Of Wrong Information.

Maidamwar, P. (2012, October). A Survey on Security Issues to Detect Wormhole Attack in Wireless Sensor Network. Int. J. AdHoc Netw. *Syst.*, 2(4), 37–50.

Ma, J., Wei, L., & Kazi, R. H. (2022). A Layered Authoring Tool for Stylized 3D animations. *CHI Conference on Human Factors in Computing Systems*. DOI:10.1145/3491102.3501894

Majadas, R., García, J., & Fernández, F. (2024). Clustering-based attack detection for adversarial reinforcement learning. *Applied Intelligence*, 54(3), 1–17. DOI:10.1007/s10489-024-05275-7

Majeed, A., & Lee, S. (2021). Anonymization Techniques for Privacy Preserving Data Publishing: A Comprehensive survey. *IEEE Access : Practical Innovations, Open Solutions*, 9, 8512–8545. DOI:10.1109/ACCESS.2020.3045700

Majeed, A., Ullah, F., & Lee, S. (2017). Vulnerability- and Diversity-Aware anonymization of personally identifiable information for improving user privacy and utility of publishing data. *Sensors (Basel)*, 17(5), 1059. DOI:10.3390/s17051059 PMID:28481298

Malatji, M., & Tolah, A. (2024). Artificial intelligence (AI) cybersecurity dimensions: A comprehensive framework for understanding adversarial and offensive AI. *AI and Ethics*. Advance online publication. DOI:10.1007/s43681-024-00427-4

Malhotra, P., & Misra, A. (2022). *Accountability and responsibility of artificial intelligence decision-making models in Indian policy landscape*. Paper presented at the CEUR Workshop Proceedings.

Mallick, C., Bhoi, S. K., Singh, T., Hussain, K., Riskhan, B., & Sahoo, K. S. (2023). Cost Minimization of Airline Crew Scheduling Problem Using Assignment Technique. *International Journal of Intelligent Systems and Applications in Engineering*, 11(7s), 285–298.

Mallick, C., Bhoi, S. K., Singh, T., Swain, P., Ruskhan, B., Hussain, K., & Sahoo, K. S. (2023). Transportation Problem Solver for Drug Delivery in Pharmaceutical Companies using Steppingstone Method. *International Journal of Intelligent Systems and Applications in Engineering*, 11(5s), 343–352.

Mangla, M., Shinde, S. K., Mehta, V., Sharma, N., & Mohanty, S. N. (2022). *Handbook of Research on Machine Learning: Foundations and Applications*. CRC Press. DOI:10.1201/9781003277330

Maqsood, R., Abid, F., & Farooq, G. (2022). Cycle Consistency and Fine-Grained Image to Image Translation in Augmentation: An Overview. *Social Science Research Network*. DOI:10.2139/ssrn.4157023

Margetis, G., Ntoa, S., Antona, M., & Stephanidis, C. (2021). Human-centered design of artificial intelligence. *Wiley*. DOI:10.1002/9781119636113.ch42

Marg'uba, N. (2024, January 10). *Parametric Design: Enhancing Architectural Environments through Computational Innovatio*. https://sciencepromotion.uz/index.php/HOLDERS_OF_REASON/article/view/1077

Maria, C., & Oya, B. (2022). AI Ethics—A Bird's Eye View. *Applied Sciences (Basel, Switzerland)*, 12(9), 4130–4130. DOI:10.3390/app12094130

Marjani, M., Jhanjhi, N. Z., Hashem, I. A. T., & Hajibeigy, M. T. (2021). The role of iiot in smart industries 4.0. In *The Nine Pillars of Technologies for Industry 4.0* (pp. 91–116). Institution of Engineering and Technology.

Marsoof, A., Luco, A., Tan, H., & Joty, S. (2022). Content-filtering AI systems–limitations, challenges and regulatory approaches. *Information & Communications Technology Law*, 32(1), 64–101. DOI:10.1080/13600834.2022.2078395

Martins, I., Resende, J. S., Sousa, P. R., Silva, S., Antunes, L., & Gama, J. (2022). Host-based IDS: A review and open issues of an anomaly detection system in IoT. *Future Generation Computer Systems*, 133, 95–113. DOI:10.1016/j.future.2022.03.001

Masood, S., & Zafar, A. (2024). Deep-efficient-guard: Securing wireless ad hoc networks via graph neural network, [Preprint]. *International Journal of Information Technology : an Official Journal of Bharati Vidyapeeth's Institute of Computer Applications and Management*. Advance online publication. DOI:10.1007/s41870-023-01702-z

Mat, N. I. C., Jamil, N., Yusoff, Y., & Kiah, L. M. (2024). A systematic literature review on advanced persistent threat behaviors and its detection strategy. *Journal of Cybersecurity*, 10(1), tyad023. Advance online publication. DOI:10.1093/cybsec/tyad023

Maturana, C. N. V., Orozco, A. L. S., & Villalba, L. J. G. (2023). Exploration of metrics and datasets to assess the fidelity of images generated by generative adversarial networks. *Applied Sciences (Basel, Switzerland)*, 13(19), 10637. DOI:10.3390/app131910637

Maurya, A., & Joshi, M. (2024, January 29). *Exploring Privacy-Preserving Strategies: A comprehensive analysis of Group-Based anonymization and hybrid ECC encryption algorithm for effective performance evaluation in data security.* https://www.ijisae.org/index.php/IJISAE/article/view/4618

Mazhar, T., Talpur, D. B., Shloul, T. A., Ghadi, Y. Y., Haq, I., Ullah, I., Ouahada, K., & Hamam, H. (2023). Analysis of IoT security challenges and its solutions using artificial intelligence. *Brain Sciences*, 13(4), 683. DOI:10.3390/brainsci13040683 PMID:37190648

McIntosh, T., Liu, T., Susnjak, T., Alavizadeh, H., Ng, A., Nowrozy, R., & Watters, P. (2023). Harnessing GPT-4 for generation of cybersecurity GRC policies: A focus on ransomware attack mitigation. *Computers & Security*, 134, 103424. DOI:10.1016/j.cose.2023.103424

Meena, D., Katragadda, H., Narva, K., Rajesh, A. N., & Sheela, J. (2023). Text-Conditioned Image Synthesis using TAC-GAN: A Unique Approach to Text-to-Image Synthesis. *2023 2nd International Conference on Automation, Computing and Renewable Systems (ICACRS)*. DOI:10.1109/ICACRS58579.2023.10404459

Meena, G., Mohbey, K. K., & Kumar, S. (2023). Sentiment analysis on images using convolutional neural networks based Inception-V3 transfer learning approach. *International Journal of Information Management Data Insights*, 3(1), 100174. DOI:10.1016/j.jjimei.2023.100174

Megahed, M., & Mohammed, A. (2023). A comprehensive review of generative adversarial networks: Fundamentals, applications, and challenges. *Wiley Interdisciplinary Reviews: Computational Statistics*. Advance online publication. DOI:10.1002/wics.1629

Mehmood, A.. (2024). *Advances and Vulnerabilities in Modern Cryptographic Techniques: A comprehensive survey on cybersecurity in the domain of Machine/Deep Learning and Quantum Techniques.* IEEE Access., DOI:10.1109/ACCESS.2024.3367232

Mehrabi, N., Morstatter, F., Saxena, N., Lerman, K., & Galstyan, A. (2021). A survey on Bias and Fairness in Machine Learning. *ACM Computing Surveys*, 54(6), 1–35. DOI:10.1145/3457607

Mehta, A., Padaria, A. A., Bavisi, D., Ukani, V., Thakkar, P., Geddam, R., Kotecha, K., & Abraham, A. (2024). Securing the Future: A comprehensive review of security challenges and solutions in advanced driver assistance systems. *IEEE Access : Practical Innovations, Open Solutions*, 12, 643–678. DOI:10.1109/ACCESS.2023.3347200

Mennan, Z. (2022, February 1). *Extending design cognition with computer vision and generative deep learning*. https://open.metu.edu.tr/handle/11511/96232

Meslamani, A. Z. A. (2023). Gaps in digital health policies: An insight into the current landscape. *Journal of Medical Economics*, 26(1), 1266–1268. DOI:10.1080/13696998.2023.2266955 PMID:37789607

Meurisch, C., & Mühlhäuser, M. (2021). Data protection in AI services: A survey. *ACM Computing Surveys*, 54(2), 1–38. DOI:10.1145/3440754

Mhlanga, D. (2023). Open AI in Education, The responsible and ethical use of ChaTGPT towards lifelong Learning. *Social Science Research Network*. DOI:10.2139/ssrn.4354422

Mijwil, M., Unogwu, O. J., Filali, Y., Bala, I., & Al-Shahwani, H. (2023). Exploring the top five evolving threats in cybersecurity: an in-depth overview. *Mesopotamian Journal of Cybersecurity*, 57-63.

Mill, E., Garn, W., Ryman-Tubb, N., & Turner, C. (2023). Opportunities in real Time Fraud Detection: An explainable Artificial Intelligence (XAI) research agenda. *International Journal of Advanced Computer Science and Applications*, 14(5). Advance online publication. DOI:10.14569/IJACSA.2023.01405121

Milossi, M., Alexandropoulou-Egyptiadou, E., & Psannis, K. E. (2021). AI Ethics: Algorithmic Determinism or Self-Determination? The GPDR Approach. *IEEE Access : Practical Innovations, Open Solutions*, 9, 58455–58466. DOI:10.1109/ACCESS.2021.3072782

Min, B., Ross, H., Sulem, E., Veyseh, A. P. B., Nguyen, T. H., Sainz, O., Agirre, E., Heintz, I., & Roth, D. (2023). Recent advances in natural language processing via large pre-trained language models: A survey. *ACM Computing Surveys*, 56(2), 1–40. DOI:10.1145/3605943

Mingo, H. C., Lawson, M. N., & Williamson, A. (2024). Identifying new vulnerabilities embedded in consumer internet of things (IoT) devices. In *Advances in medical technologies and clinical practice book series* (pp. 186–207). DOI:10.4018/979-8-3693-3226-9.ch011

Minohara, T., & Nishiyama, K. (2016). Poster: detection of Wormhole attack on wireless sensor networks in duty-cycling operation. *Proceedings of the 2016 International Conference on Embedded Wireless Systems and Networks*, 281–282.

Miraz, M. H., Ali, M., & Excell, P. S. (2021). Adaptive user interfaces and universal usability through plasticity of user interface design. *Computer Science Review*, 40, 100363. DOI:10.1016/j.cosrev.2021.100363

Mishra, S. (2023). Exploring the Impact of AI-Based Cyber Security Financial Sector Management. *Applied Sciences (Basel, Switzerland)*, 13(10), 5875. DOI:10.3390/app13105875

Moerland, T. M., Broekens, J., Plaat, A., & Jonker, C. M. (2023). Model-based reinforcement learning: A survey. *Foundations and Trends® in Machine Learning*, 16(1), 1-118.

Mohamadi, N., Niaki, S. T. A., Taher, M., & Shavandi, A. (2024). An application of deep reinforcement learning and vendor-managed inventory in perishable supply chain management. *Engineering Applications of Artificial Intelligence*, 127, 107403. DOI:10.1016/j.engappai.2023.107403

Mohamed, A. (2023). A systematic literature review of authorization and access control requirements and current state of the art for different database models. *International Journal of Web Information Systems*. .DOI:10.1108/IJWIS-04-2023-0072

Mohamed, A., Lee, H., Borgholt, L., Havtorn, J. D., Edin, J., Igel, C., Kirchhoff, K., Li, S., Livescu, K., Maaløe, L., Sainath, T. N., & Watanabe, S. (2022). Self-Supervised Speech Representation Learning: A review. *IEEE Journal of Selected Topics in Signal Processing*, 16(6), 1179–1210. DOI:10.1109/JSTSP.2022.3207050

Mohammadi, M., & Sohn, I. (2023). *AI based energy harvesting security methods: A survey*. ICT Express. DOI:10.1016/j.icte.2023.06.002

Mohammed, S. D., & Hossain, G. (2024) 'ChatGPT in Education, Healthcare, and Cybersecurity: Opportunities and Challenges,' *2024 IEEE 14th Annual Computing and Communication Workshop and Conference (CCWC)* [Preprint]. DOI:10.1109/CCWC60891.2024.10427923

Mohammed, I. A. (2020). Artificial intelligence for cybersecurity: A systematic mapping of literature. *Artificial Intelligence*, 7(9), 1–5.

Mohanad, M., Hazzaa, F., Mohanad Sameer, , Jamal Fadhil, , Sekhar, R., Pritesh, , & Parihar, S. (2024). Intrusion Detection in Software-Defined Networks: Leveraging Deep Reinforcement Learning with Graph Convolutional Networks for Resilient Infrastructure. *Research Gate*, 15(1), 78–87. DOI:10.54216/FPA.150107

Mohanakrishnan, M., Kumar, A. V. S., Talukdar, V., Saleh, O. S., Irawati, I. D., Latip, R., & Kaur, G. (2023). Artificial intelligence in cyber security. In *Advances in computational intelligence and robotics book series* (pp. 366–385). DOI:10.4018/978-1-6684-8098-4.ch022

Mohan, P. V., Dixit, S., Gyaneshwar, A., Chadha, U., Srinivasan, K., & Seo, J. T. (2022). Leveraging Computational intelligence Techniques for defensive deception: A review, recent advances, open problems and future directions. *Sensors (Basel)*, 22(6), 2194. DOI:10.3390/s22062194 PMID:35336373

Mohanta, B. K., Jena, D., Satapathy, U., & Patnaik, S. (2020). Survey on IoT security: Challenges and solution using machine learning, artificial intelligence and blockchain technology. *Internet of Things : Engineering Cyber Physical Human Systems*, 11, 100227. DOI:10.1016/j.iot.2020.100227

Mohsin, A., Janicke, H., Nepal, S., & Holmes, D. R. (2023). Digital Twins and the Future of their Use Enabling Shift Left and Shift Right Cybersecurity Operations. *arXiv (Cornell University)*. /arxiv.2309.13612DOI:10.1109/TPS-ISA58951.2023.00042

Möller, D. P. F. (2023) 'Intrusion Detection and Prevention,' in *Advances in information security*, 131–179. DOI:10.1007/978-3-031-26845-8_3

Montargil, F. (2023, December 18). *Enhancing portuguese public services: prototype of a mobile application with a digital assistant*. https://repositorio.ipl.pt/handle/10400.21/16926

Moon, M. J. (2023). Searching for inclusive artificial intelligence for social good: Participatory governance and policy recommendations for making AI more inclusive and benign for society. *Public Administration Review*, 83(6), 1496–1505. DOI:10.1111/puar.13648

Moratinos, G. L., & De Hert, P. (2023). Humans in the GDPR and AIA governance of automated and algorithmic systems. Essential pre-requisites against abdicating responsibilities. *Computer Law & Security Report*, 50, 105833. DOI:10.1016/j.clsr.2023.105833

Morel, B. (2011). Anomaly based intrusion detection and artificial intelligence. *Intrusion Detection Systems*, 10, 14103. DOI:10.5772/14103

Morse, E. A., & Raval, V. (2008). PCI DSS: Payment card industry data security standards in context. *Computer Law & Security Report*, 24(6), 540–554. DOI:10.1016/j. clsr.2008.07.001

Mortazavi, A. (2023). *Enhancing User Experience Design workflow with Artificial Intelligence Tools*. DIVA. https://www.diva-portal.org/smash/record.jsf?pid=diva2 %3A1800706&dswid=-1132

Mossavar-Rahmani, F., & Zohuri, B. (2024). Artificial Intelligence at Work: Transforming Industries and Redefining the Workforce Landscape. *Journal of Economics & Management Research. SRC/JESMR-284.J Econ Managem Res*, 5(2), 2–4.

Moudgil, V., Hewage, K., Hussain, S. A., & Sadiq, R. (2023). Integration of IoT in building energy infrastructure: A critical review on challenges and solutions. *Renewable & Sustainable Energy Reviews*, 174, 113121. DOI:10.1016/j.rser.2022.113121

Moustafa, N., Koroniotis, N., Keshk, M., Zomaya, A. Y., & Tari, Z. (2023). Explainable intrusion detection for cyber defences in the Internet of Things: Opportunities and solutions. *IEEE Communications Surveys and Tutorials*, 25(3), 1775–1807. DOI:10.1109/COMST.2023.3280465

Mubarak, R., Alsboui, T., Alshaikh, O., Inuwa-Dutse, I., Khan, S., & Parkinson, S. (2023). A survey on the detection and impacts of deepfakes in visual, audio, and textual formats. *IEEE Access : Practical Innovations, Open Solutions*, 11, 144497–144529. DOI:10.1109/ACCESS.2023.3344653

Mughal, M. A., Ullah, A., Cheema, M. A. Z., Yu, X., & Jhanjhi, N. (2024). An intelligent channel assignment algorithm for cognitive radio networks using a tree-centric approach in IoT. *Alexandria Engineering Journal*, 91, 152–160. DOI:10.1016/j. aej.2024.01.071

Mukherjee, S., Chattopadhyay, M., Chattopadhyay, S., & Kar, P. (2016). Wormhole Detection Based on Ordinal MDS Using RTT in Wireless Sensor Network. *Journal of Computer Networks and Communications*, 2016, 1–15. DOI:10.1155/2016/3405264

Mukhopadhyay, A., & Jain, S. (2024). A framework for cyber-risk insurance against ransomware: A mixed-method approach. *International Journal of Information Management*, 74, 102724. DOI:10.1016/j.ijinfomgt.2023.102724

Mulyanto, M., Leu, J.-S., Faisal, M., & Yunanto, W. (2023). Weight embedding autoencoder as feature representation learning in an intrusion detection systems. *Computers & Electrical Engineering*, 111, 108949. DOI:10.1016/j.compeleceng.2023.108949

Muneer, S. M., Alvi, M. B., & Farrakh, A. (2023). Cyber Security Event Detection Using Machine Learning Technique. *International Journal of Computational and Innovative Sciences*, 2(2), 42–46.

Munjal, K., & Bhatia, R. (2022). A systematic review of homomorphic encryption and its contributions in healthcare industry. *Complex & Intelligent Systems*, 9(4), 3759–3786. DOI:10.1007/s40747-022-00756-z PMID:35531323

Mushtaq, M., Ullah, A., Ashraf, H., Jhanjhi, N. Z., Masud, M., Alqhatani, A., & Alnfiai, M. M. (2023). Anonymity assurance using efficient pseudonym consumption in internet of vehicles. *Sensors (Basel)*, 23(11), 5217. DOI:10.3390/s23115217 PMID:37299944

Muzammal, S. M., Murugesan, R. K., Jhanjhi, N. Z., & Jung, L. T. (2020, October). SMTrust: Proposing trust-based secure routing protocol for RPL attacks for IoT applications. In *2020 International Conference on Computational Intelligence (ICCI)* (pp. 305-310). IEEE. DOI:10.1109/ICCI51257.2020.9247818

Mylrea, M., & Robinson, N. (2023). Artificial Intelligence (AI) Trust Framework and Maturity Model: Applying an entropy lens to improve security, privacy, and ethical AI. *Entropy (Basel, Switzerland)*, 25(10), 1429. DOI:10.3390/e25101429 PMID:37895550

Nabavi-Pelesaraei, A., Rafiee, S., Mohtasebi, S. S., Hosseinzadeh-Bandbafha, H., & Chau, K. (2018). Integration of artificial intelligence methods and life cycle assessment to predict energy output and environmental impacts of paddy production. *The Science of the Total Environment*, 631–632, 1279–1294. DOI:10.1016/j.scitotenv.2018.03.088 PMID:29727952

Naeem, S., Ali, A., Anam, S., & Ahmed, M. M. (2023). An Unsupervised Machine Learning Algorithms: Comprehensive Review. *International Journal of Computing and Digital Systems*, 13(1), 911–921. DOI:10.12785/ijcds/130172

Nahar, G., & Jain, S. (2023). Uncovering the usability test Methods for Human–Computer Interaction. In *Lecture notes in networks and systems* (pp. 57–68). DOI:10.1007/978-981-99-1909-3_6

Naidu & Himaja. (2017). Handling wormhole attacks in WSNs using location based approach. Advances in Intelligent Systems and Computing, 507, 43–51.

Nair, A. K., Raj, E. D., & Sahoo, J. (2023). A robust analysis of adversarial attacks on federated learning environments. *Computer Standards & Interfaces*, 86, 103723. DOI:10.1016/j.csi.2023.103723

Najar, F., Bourouis, S., Bouguila, N., & Belghith, S. (2017). A Comparison Between Different Gaussian-Based Mixture Models. *2017 IEEE/ACS 14th International Conference on Computer Systems and Applications (AICCSA)*. DOI:10.1109/AICCSA.2017.108

Najmi, K. Y., AlZain, M. A., Masud, M., Jhanjhi, N. Z., Al-Amri, J., & Baz, M. (2023). A survey on security threats and countermeasures in IoT to achieve users confidentiality and reliability. *Materials Today: Proceedings*, 81, 377–382. DOI:10.1016/j.matpr.2021.03.417

Nankya, M., Chataut, R., & Akl, R. (2023). Securing Industrial control systems: Components, cyber threats, and Machine Learning-Driven defense Strategies. *Sensors (Basel)*, 23(21), 8840. DOI:10.3390/s23218840 PMID:37960539

Naqbi, H. A., Bahroun, Z., & Ahmed, V. (2024). Enhancing Work Productivity through Generative Artificial Intelligence: A Comprehensive Literature Review. *Sustainability (Basel)*, 16(3), 1166. DOI:10.3390/su16031166

Naranjo, F. V., Espinoza, J. L. A., & Vivar, S. M. (2023). Exploring the Fusion of Blockchain and AI for Enhanced Practices in IoT Ecosystems: Opportunities and Challenges. *Fusion: Practice and Applications*, 13(2), 52–61. DOI:10.54216/FPA.130205

Naseer, F. (2024) 'Automated assessment and feedback in higher education using Generative AI,' in *Advances in educational technologies and instructional design book series*, pp. 433–461. DOI:10.4018/979-8-3693-1351-0.ch021

Nasir, S., Khan, R. A., & Bai, S. (2024). Ethical framework for harnessing the power of AI in healthcare and beyond. *IEEE Access : Practical Innovations, Open Solutions*, 1, 31014–31035. Advance online publication. DOI:10.1109/ACCESS.2024.3369912

Nassiri, K., & Akhloufi, M. A. (2022). Transformer models used for text-based question answering systems. *Applied Intelligence*, 53(9), 10602–10635. DOI:10.1007/s10489-022-04052-8

Nazir, A., & Wang, Z. (2023). A comprehensive survey of ChatGPT: Advancements, applications, prospects, and challenges. *Meta-Radiology*, 1(2), 100022. DOI:10.1016/j.metrad.2023.100022 PMID:37901715

Nazish, K., Adnan, Q., Muhammad, B., Ala, A.-F., & Junaid, Q. (2023). Privacy-preserving artificial intelligence in healthcare: Techniques and applications. *Computers in Biology and Medicine*, 158, 106848–106848. DOI:10.1016/j.compbiomed.2023.106848 PMID:37044052

Ndashimye, E., Sarkar, N. I., & Ray, S. K. (2021). A Multi-criteria based handover algorithm for vehicle-to-infrastructure communications. *Computer Networks*, 185, 107652. DOI:10.1016/j.comnet.2020.107652

Necula, S., & Păvăloaia, V. (2023). AI-Driven Recommendations: A Systematic review of the state of the art in E-Commerce. *Applied Sciences (Basel, Switzerland)*, 13(9), 5531. DOI:10.3390/app13095531

Neshenko, N. (2023). Machine learning and user interface for cyber risk management of water infrastructure. *Risk Analysis*. Advance online publication. DOI:10.1111/risa.14209 PMID:37635130

Neves, M. P., & de Almeida, A. B. (2024). Before and Beyond Artificial Intelligence: Opportunities and Challenges. In *Law, Governance and Technology Series* (Vol. 58, pp. 107-125).

Neves, F., Souza, R., Sousa, J., Bonfim, M., & Garcia, V. (2023). Data privacy in the Internet of Things based on anonymization: A review. *Journal of Computer Security*, 31(3), 261–291. DOI:10.3233/JCS-210089

Nezami, N., Haghighat, P., Gándara, D., & Anahideh, H. (2024). Assessing Disparities in predictive modeling outcomes for college student success: The impact of imputation techniques on model performance and fairness. *Education Sciences*, 14(2), 136. DOI:10.3390/educsci14020136

Ngabo-Woods, H. (2023). Insights Beyond Functionality: Empowering Digital Mental Health User Experiences Through Participatory Engagement and Evaluation. *Preprint*. DOI:10.20944/preprints202311.1572.v1

Ngalamou, L., & Schmidbauer, H. L. (2020). Combating and perpetuating bias: The relationship between bias and computer science. *International Journal of Information Privacy. Security and Integrity*, 4(4), 296. DOI:10.1504/IJIPSI.2020.115523

Nguyen, M. T., & Tran, M. Q. (2023). Balancing security and privacy in the digital age: An in-depth analysis of legal and regulatory frameworks impacting cybersecurity practices. *International Journal of Intelligent Automation and Computing*, 6(5), 1–12.

Nguyen, T. T., & Reddi, V. J. (2023). Deep reinforcement learning for cyber security. *IEEE Transactions on Neural Networks and Learning Systems*, 34(8), 3779–3795. DOI:10.1109/TNNLS.2021.3121870 PMID:34723814

Nishant, R., Schneckenberg, D., & Ravishankar, M. N. (2023). The formal rationality of artificial intelligence-based algorithms and the problem of bias. *Journal of Information Technology*. Advance online publication. DOI:10.1177/02683962231176842

Ni, Y., Issa, M., Abraham, D., Imani, M., Yin, X., & Imani, M. (2022). Hdpg: Hyperdimensional policy-based reinforcement learning for continuous control. In *Proceedings of the 59th ACM/IEEE Design Automation Conference* (pp. 1141-1146). DOI:10.1145/3489517.3530668

Nova, A., Sansalone, S. C. F., Robinson, R., & Mirza-Babaei, P. (2022). Charting the Uncharted with GUR: How AI Playtesting Can Supplement Expert Evaluation. *ACM*. DOI:10.1145/3555858.3555880

Nova, K. (2023, April 4). *Generative AI in Healthcare: Advancements in Electronic Health Records, facilitating Medical Languages, and Personalized Patient Care.* https://research.tensorgate.org/index.php/JAAHM/article/view/43

Novelli, C., Taddeo, M., & Floridi, L. (2023). Accountability in artificial intelligence: What it is and how it works. *AI & Society*. Advance online publication. DOI:10.1007/s00146-023-01635-y

Odeh, A., & Abu Taleb, A. (2023). Ensemble-Based Deep Learning Models for Enhancing IoT Intrusion Detection. *Applied Sciences (Basel, Switzerland)*, 13(21), 11985. DOI:10.3390/app132111985

Ogunseye, O. O., & Adegbenro, O. (2020). Applications of programming languages in various industries. *International Journal of Emerging Technologies in Learning*, 15(14), 102–111. DOI:10.3991/ijet.v15i14.12770

Oh, S., & Shon, T. (2023). *Cybersecurity Issues in Generative AI.* Paper presented at the 2023 International Conference on Platform Technology and Service (PlatCon). DOI:10.1109/PlatCon60102.2023.10255179

Oh, S. H., Kim, J., Nah, J. H., & Park, J. (2024). Employing Deep Reinforcement Learning to Cyber-Attack Simulation for Enhancing Cybersecurity. *Electronics (Basel)*, 13(3), 555. DOI:10.3390/electronics13030555

Okunlola, M., Siddiqui, A., & Karami, A. (2017, September). A Wormhole Attack Detection and Prevention Technique in Wireless Sensor Networks. *International Journal of Computer Applications*, 174(4), 1–8. DOI:10.5120/ijca2017915376

Olabanji, S. O., Marquis, Y., Adigwe, C. S., Ajayi, S. S., Oladoyinbo, T. O., & Olaniyi, O. O. (2024). AI-Driven Cloud Security: Examining the impact of user behavior analysis on threat detection. *Social Science Research Network*. DOI:10.2139/ssrn.4709384

Olabanji, S. O., Olaniyi, O. O., Adigwe, C. S., Okunleye, O. J., & Oladoyinbo, T. O. (2024). AI for Identity and Access Management (IAM) in the Cloud: Exploring the Potential of Artificial Intelligence to Improve User Authentication, Authorization, and Access Control within Cloud-Based Systems. *Social Science Research Network*. DOI:10.2139/ssrn.4706726

Oloyede, J. O. (2024) 'Ethical Reflections on AI for Cybersecurity: Building trust,' *Social Science Research Network* [Preprint]. https://doi.org/DOI:10.2139/ssrn.4733563

Olynick, D. (2024). Exploring generative AI and its transformative power. In *Apress eBooks* (pp. 17–60). DOI:10.1007/979-8-8688-0083-2_2

Ombu, A. (2023). Role of digital forensics in combating financial crimes in the computer Era. *Journal of Forensic Accounting Profession*, 3(1), 57–75. DOI:10.2478/jfap-2023-0003

Omotunde, H., & Ahmed, M. (2023). A Comprehensive Review of Security Measures in Database Systems: Assessing Authentication, Access Control, and Beyond. *Journal of Cybersecurity*, 115–133. DOI:10.58496/MJCSC/2023/016

Oniani, D., Hilsman, J., Peng, Y., Poropatich, R. K., Pamplin, J., Legault, G. L., & Wang, Y. (2023). Adopting and expanding ethical principles for generative artificial intelligence from military to healthcare. *NPJ Digital Medicine*, 6(1), 225. Advance online publication. DOI:10.1038/s41746-023-00965-x PMID:38042910

Ooi, K., Tan, G. W., Al-Emran, M., Al-Sharafi, M. A., Căpățînă, A., Chakraborty, A., Dwivedi, Y. K., Huang, T., Kar, A. K., Lee, V., Loh, X., Micu, A., Mikalef, P., Mogaji, E., Pandey, N., Raman, R., Rana, N. P., Sarker, P., Sharma, A., & Wong, L. (2023). The potential of generative artificial intelligence across disciplines: Perspectives and future directions. *Journal of Computer Information Systems*, 1–32. DOI:10.1080/08874417.2023.2261010

Ortega, E., Tran, M., & Bandeen, G. (2023). *AI Digital Tool Product Lifecycle Governance Framework through Ethics and Compliance by Design†*. Paper presented at the Proceedings - 2023 IEEE Conference on Artificial Intelligence, CAI 2023. DOI:10.1109/CAI54212.2023.00155

Osasona, F., Amoo, O. O., Atadoga, A., Abrahams, T. O., Farayola, O. A., & Ayinla, B. S. (2024). Reviewing the ethical implications of AI in decision making processes. *International Journal of Management & Entrepreneurship Research*, 6(2), 322–335. DOI:10.51594/ijmer.v6i2.773

OSF. (n.d.). https://osf.io/preprints/osf/bxw4h

Othman, U., & Yang, E. (2023). Human–robot collaborations in smart manufacturing environments: Review and outlook. *Sensors (Basel)*, 23(12), 5663. DOI:10.3390/ s23125663 PMID:37420834

Ouadrhiri, A. E., & Abdelhadi, A. (2022). Differential Privacy for deep and federated Learning: A survey. *IEEE Access : Practical Innovations, Open Solutions*, 10, 22359–22380. DOI:10.1109/ACCESS.2022.3151670

Owino, B. A., & Paschal, M. J. (2023). AI and ethics in education: Implications and strategies for responsible implementation. In *Creative AI Tools and Ethical Implications in Teaching and Learning* (pp. 196-211).

Ozkan-Okay, M., Akin, E., Aslan, Ö., Koşunalp, S., Iliev, T., Stoyanov, I., & Beloev, I. (2024). A comprehensive survey: Evaluating the efficiency of artificial intelligence and machine learning techniques on cyber security solutions. *IEEE Access : Practical Innovations, Open Solutions*, 12, 12229–12256. DOI:10.1109/ ACCESS.2024.3355547

Padmanabhan, J., & Manickavasagam, V. (2017). Scalable and Distributed Detection Analysis on Wormhole Links in Wireless Sensor Networks for Networked Systems. *IEEE Access : Practical Innovations, Open Solutions*, 6, 1753–1763. DOI:10.1109/ ACCESS.2017.2780188

Padraig, S. (2016). Understanding IoT Security – Part 1 of 3: IoT Security Architecture on the Device and Communication Layers. Retrieved from https://iot-analytics .com/understanding-iot-security-part-1-iot-security-architecture/

Pakhale, K. (2023). Large language models and information retrieval. *Social Science Research Network*. DOI:10.2139/ssrn.4636121

Pal, S. (2021) *Internet of things and access control, Smart sensors, measurement and instrumentation*. .DOI:10.1007/978-3-030-64998-2

Pala, Z., Yamli, V., & Ünlük, İ. H. (2017). Deep Learning researches in Turkey: An academic approach. *2017 XIIIth International Conference on Perspective Technologies and Methods in MEMS Design (MEMSTECH)*. DOI:10.1109/MEM-STECH.2017.7937546

Paladugu, P., Ong, J., Nelson, N. G., Kamran, S. A., Waisberg, E., Zaman, N., Kumar, R., Dias, R. D., Lee, A. G., & Tavakkoli, A. (2023). Generative Adversarial Networks in Medicine: Important Considerations for this Emerging Innovation in Artificial Intelligence. *Annals of Biomedical Engineering*, 51(10), 2130–2142. DOI:10.1007/s10439-023-03304-z PMID:37488468

Palladino, N. (2023). A 'biased' emerging governance regime for artificial intelligence? How AI ethics get skewed moving from principles to practices. *Telecommunications Policy*, 47(5), 102479. DOI:10.1016/j.telpol.2022.102479

Pan, B. (2020, November 21). *Adversarial mutual information for text generation*. PMLR. https://proceedings.mlr.press/v119/pan20a.html

Panda, S., & Kaur, N. (2023). Web Content Accessibility Guidelines 3.0. In *Advances in educational marketing, administration, and leadership book series* (pp. 246–269). DOI:10.4018/978-1-6684-8737-2.ch012

Pandcy, A., & Tripathi, R. C. (2010, June). A Survey on Wireless Sensor Networks Security. *International Journal of Computer Applications*, 3(2), 43–49. DOI:10.5120/705-989

Pang, G., Shen, C., Cao, L., & Hengel, A. V. D. (2021). Deep learning for anomaly detection. *ACM Computing Surveys*, 54(2), 1–38. DOI:10.1145/3439950

Panwar, A., Panwar, B., Rao, D. S., & Sriram, G. (2020). *A Trust Based Approach for Avoidance of Wormhole Attack in MANET*.

Paola, Z. L., Lopez, S. J., Christian, A. H., & Sonia, R. U. (2023). Correction of Banding Errors in Satellite Images With Generative Adversarial Networks (GAN). *IEEE Access: Practical Innovations, Open Solutions*, 11, 51960–51970. DOI:10.1109/ACCESS.2023.3279265

Papamakarios, G., Nalisnick, E., Rezende, D. J., Mohamed, S., & Lakshminarayanan, B. (2019). Normalizing flows for probabilistic modeling and inference. *arXiv (Cornell University)*. http://export.arxiv.org/pdf/1912.02762

Papaspirou, V., Papathanasaki, M., Μαγλαράς, Λ., Kantzavelou, I., Douligeris, C., Ferrag, M. A., & Janicke, H. (2023). A novel authentication method that combines HoneyTokens and Google Authenticator. *Information (Basel)*, 14(7), 386. DOI:10.3390/info14070386

Paraman, P., & Anamalah, S. (2022). Ethical artificial intelligence framework for a good AI society: Principles, opportunities and perils. *AI & Society*, 38(2), 595–611. DOI:10.1007/s00146-022-01458-3

Park, J. H., Park, S., & Shim, H. (2019). Semantic-aware neural style transfer. *Image and Vision Computing*, 87, 13–23. DOI:10.1016/j.imavis.2019.04.001

Parray, A. A., Inam, Z. M., Ramonfaur, D., Haider, S. S., Mistry, S. K., & Pandya, A. (2023). ChatGPT and global public health: Applications, challenges, ethical considerations and mitigation strategies. *Global Transitions*, 5, 50–54. DOI:10.1016/j. glt.2023.05.001

Parr, T., Wilson, J. D., & Hamrick, J. (2024). Nonparametric feature impact and importance. *Information Sciences*, 653, 119563. DOI:10.1016/j.ins.2023.119563

Patel & Aggarwal. (2016). Detection of Hidden Wormhole Attack in Wireless Sensor Networks Using Neighbourhood and Connectivity Information. Int. J. AdHoc Netw. Syst., 6(1), 1–10.

Patel, Aggarwal, & Chaubey. (2019). Detection of wormhole attack in static wireless sensor networks. Advances in Intelligent Systems and Computing, 760, 463–471.

Patel, M. A., & Patel, M. M. (2018). Wormhole Attack Detection in Wireless Sensor Network. *Proceedings of the International Conference on Inventive Research in Computing Applications, ICIRCA 2018*, 269–274. DOI:10.1109/ICIRCA.2018.8597366

Patel, M., Aggarwal, A., & Chaubey, N. (2017, April). Wormhole Attacks and Countermeasures in Wireless Sensor Networks: A Survey. *Int. J. Eng. Technol.*, 9(2), 1049–1060. DOI:10.21817/ijet/2017/v9i2/170902126

Patel, V. (2023). Real-Time Threat Detection with JavaScript: Monitoring and Response Mechanisms. *International Journal of Computer Trends and Technology*, 71(11), 31–39. DOI:10.14445/22312803/IJCTT-V71I11P105

Payá, A. S., Arroni, S., García-Díaz, V., & Gómez, A. (2024). Apollon: A robust defense system against Adversarial Machine Learning attacks in Intrusion Detection Systems. *Computers & Security*, 136, 103546. DOI:10.1016/j.cose.2023.103546

Perdana, A., Lee, W. E., & Kim, C. M. (2023). Prototyping and implementing Robotic Process Automation in accounting firms: Benefits, challenges and opportunities to audit automation. *International Journal of Accounting Information Systems*, 51, 100641. DOI:10.1016/j.accinf.2023.100641

Perri, L. (2023). Understand and Exploit GenAI With Gartner's New Impact Radar. Retrieved from https://www.gartner.com/en/articles/understand-and-exploit-gen-ai -with-gartner-s-new-impact-radar

Peters, U. (2022). Explainable AI lacks regulative reasons: Why AI and human decision-making are not equally opaque. *AI and Ethics*, 3(3), 963–974. DOI:10.1007/ s43681-022-00217-w

Pettersson, W. (2024). *Transforming Chess: Investigating Decoder-Only architecture for generating Realistic Game-Like Positions*. DIVA. https://www.diva-portal.org/smash/record.jsf?pid=diva2%3A1828575&dswid=-6030

Ping, C., Hou, L., Zhang, K., Tushar, Q., & Yang, Z. (2024). Generative adversarial networks in construction applications. *Automation in Construction*, 159, 105265. DOI:10.1016/j.autcon.2024.105265

Piplai, A., Ranade, P., Kotal, A., Mittal, S., Narayanan, S. N., & Joshi, A. (2020). Using knowledge graphs and reinforcement learning for malware analysis. *2020 IEEE International Conference on Big Data (Big Data)*. DOI:10.1109/BigData50022.2020.9378491

Pöhn, D., Gruschka, N., Ziegler, L., & Büttner, A. (2023). A framework for analyzing authentication risks in account networks. *Computers & Security*, 135, 103515. DOI:10.1016/j.cose.2023.103515

Polson, P. G., Lewis, C., Rieman, J., & Wharton, C. (1992). Cognitive walkthroughs: A method for theory-based evaluation of user interfaces. *International Journal of Man-Machine Studies*, 36(5), 741–773. DOI:10.1016/0020-7373(92)90039-N

Ponnusamy, V., Sharma, B., Nadeem, W., Guan, G. H., & Jhanjhi, N. (2021). Green IoT (G-IoT) Ecosystem for Smart Cities. *Role of IoT in Green Energy Systems*, 1.

Ponnusamy, V., Humayun, M., Jhanjhi, N., Yichiet, A., & Almufareh, M. F. (2022). Intrusion Detection Systems in Internet of Things and Mobile Ad-Hoc Networks. *Computer Systems Science and Engineering*, 40(3). Advance online publication. DOI:10.32604/csse.2022.018518

Pons & Ozkaya. (n.d.). Priority Quality Attributes for Engineering AI-enabled Systems. Academic Press.

Pop, M., & Schricker, M. (2023). *AI as a tool and its influence on the User Experience design process : A study on the usability of human-made vs more-than-human-made prototypes*. DIVA. https://www.diva-portal.org/smash/record.jsf?pid=diva2%3A1771528&dswid=-4706

Porambag, Gur, Osorio, Liyanage, & Ylianttila. (n.d.). 6G Security Challenges and Potential Solutions. Centre for Wireless Communications, University of Oulu.

Porambage, Kumar, Liyanage, Partala, Loven, Ylianttila, & Seppanen. (n.d.). Comparison between AI for edge security and security for edge AI through Sec-EdgeAI at Oulu.fi. University of Oulu.

Prabakar, D., Sundarrajan, M., Manikandan, R., Jhanjhi, N., Masud, M., & Alqhatani, A. (2023). Energy Analysis-Based Cyber Attack Detection by IoT with Artificial Intelligence in a Sustainable Smart City. *Sustainability (Basel)*, 15(7), 6031. DOI:10.3390/su15076031

Praveenraj, D. D. W., Victor, M., Vennila, C., Alawadi, A. H., Diyora, P., Vasudevan, N., & Avudaiappan, T. (2023). Exploring explainable artificial intelligence for transparent decision making. *E3S Web of Conferences, 399*, 04030. DOI:10.1051/e3sconf/202339904030

Pulyala, S. R. (2024). From detection to prediction: AI-powered SIEM for proactive threat hunting and risk mitigation. *Turkish Journal of Computer and Mathematics Education*, 15(1), 34–43. DOI:10.61841/turcomat.v15i1.14393

Pushpakumar, R., Sanjaya, K., Rathika, S., Alawadi, A. H., Makhzuna, K., Venkatesh, S., & Rajalakshmi, B. (2023). Human-Computer Interaction: Enhancing user experience in interactive systems. *E3S Web of Conferences, 399*, 04037. DOI:10.1051/e3sconf/202339904037

Puttagunta, M. K., Subban, R., & Babu, C. N. K. (2023). Adversarial examples: Attacks and defences on medical deep learning systems. *Multimedia Tools and Applications*, 82(22), 33773–33809. DOI:10.1007/s11042-023-14702-9

Pyae, A., Ravyse, W., Luimula, M., Pizarro-Lucas, E., Sánchez, P. L., Dorado-Díaz, P. I., & Thaw, A. K. (2023). Exploring user experience and usability in a metaverse learning environment for students: A Usability Study of the Artificial Intelligence, Innovation, and Society (AIIS). *Electronics (Basel)*, 12(20), 4283. DOI:10.3390/electronics12204283

Qadri, Y. A., Ali, R., Musaddiq, A., Al-Turjman, F., Kim, D. W., & Kim, S. W. (2020). *The limitations in the state-of-the-art counter-measures against the security threats in H-IoT* (Vol. 7). Cluster Comput.

Qi, J., Yang, C. H., & Chen, P. (2022). Exploiting low-rank tensor-train deep neural networks based on riemannian gradient descent with illustrations of speech processing. https://doi.org/DOI:10.31219/osf.io/gdqnz

Qi, W., Ma, C., Xu, H., Zhao, K., & Chen, Z. (2022). A comprehensive analysis method of spatial prioritization for urban flood management based on source tracking. *Ecological Indicators*, 135, 108565. DOI:10.1016/j.ecolind.2022.108565

qsstechnosoft.com. (2024). AI-Driven Cybersecurity: Mitigating Threats in the Age of Generative AI. Retrieved from https://www.qsstechnosoft.com/blog/ai-driven-cybersecurity-mitigating-threats-in-the-age-of-generative-ai/

Quan, T. M., Nguyen-Duc, T., & Jeong, W. (2018). Compressed sensing MRI reconstruction using a generative adversarial network with a cyclic loss. *IEEE Transactions on Medical Imaging*, 37(6), 1488–1497. DOI:10.1109/TMI.2018.2820120 PMID:29870376

Quetzalli, A. (2023). User interface and user experience. In *Apress eBooks* (pp. 57–84). DOI:10.1007/978-1-4842-9328-7_4

Qureshi, J. (2024). AI-Powered Cloud-Based E-Commerce: Driving Digital Business Transformation Initiatives. *Preprints*. DOI:10.20944/preprints202401.2214.v1

Rachakonda, L. P., Siddula, M., & Sathya, V. (2024) 'A comprehensive study on IoT privacy and security challenges with focus on spectrum sharing in Next-Generation networks(5G/6G/beyond),' *High-Confidence Computing*, p. 100220. DOI:10.1016/j.hcc.2024.100220

Radanliev, P., & Santos, O. (2023). Adversarial Attacks Can Deceive AI Systems, Leading to Misclassification or Incorrect Decisions. *Preprint*. DOI:10.20944/preprints202309.2064.v1

Rafi, T. H., Noor, F. A., Hussain, T., & Chae, D. (2024). Fairness and privacy preserving in federated learning: A survey. *Information Fusion*, 105, 102198. DOI:10.1016/j.inffus.2023.102198

Rafy, M. F. (2024). Artificial intelligence in cyber security. *Social Science Research Network*. DOI:10.2139/ssrn.4687831

Raimundo, R., & Rosário, A. (2021). The impact of artificial intelligence on Data System Security: A literature review. *Sensors (Basel)*, 21(21), 7029. DOI:10.3390/s21217029 PMID:34770336

Raja, A. K., & Zhou, J. (2023). AI Accountability: Approaches, Affecting Factors, and Challenges. *Computer*, 56(4), 61–70. DOI:10.1109/MC.2023.3238390

Rajasekar, V., Premalatha, J., & Saracevic, M. (2022). Cybersecurity in 5G and IoT Networks. Secure Communication for 5G and IoT Networks, 29-46.

Rajasekaran, A. S. (2023) 'Cybersecurity Measures Using Machine Learning for Business Applications,' *2023 4th International Conference on Computation, Automation and Knowledge Management (ICCAKM)* [Preprint]. DOI:10.1109/ICCAKM58659.2023.10449580

Raji, I. D., Smart, A., White, R. N., Mitchell, M., Gebru, T., Hutchinson, B., Smith-Loud, J., Theron, D., & Barnes, P. (2020). *Closing the AI accountability gap*. ACM., DOI:10.1145/3351095.3372873

Rajmohan, R., Kumar, T. A., Pavithra, M., & Sandhya, S. G. (2020). Blockchain: Next-generation technology for industry 4.0. In *Blockchain Technology* (pp. 177-198). CRC Press.

Ramasamy, S. S., Vijayalakshmi, S., Gayathri, S. P., & Chakpitak, N. (2021). Data Security Essentials for the Convergence of Blockchain, AI, and IoT. In Convergence of Blockchain, AI, and IoT (pp. 137-156). CRC Press.

Ramdurai, B., & Adhithya, P. (2023). The impact, advancements and applications of generative AI. *International Journal on Computer Science and Engineering*, 10(6), 1–8. DOI:10.14445/23488387/IJCSE-V10I6P101

Rane, N. L. (2023). Multidisciplinary collaboration: key players in successful implementation of ChatGPT and similar generative artificial intelligence in manufacturing, finance, retail, transportation, and construction industry.

Rane, N. (2023). ChatGPT and similar Generative Artificial Intelligence (AI) for smart Industry: Role, Challenges and Opportunities for Industry 4.0, Industry 5.0 and Society 5.0. *Social Science Research Network*. DOI:10.2139/ssrn.4603234

Rane, N. (2023). Multidisciplinary collaboration: key players in successful implementation of ChatGPT and similar generative artificial intelligence in manufacturing, finance, retail, transportation, and construction industry. *OSF*. DOI:10.31219/osf.io/npm3d

Rane, N., Choudhary, S., & Rane, J. (2023). Explainable Artificial Intelligence (XAI) approaches for transparency and accountability in financial decision-making. *Social Science Research Network*. DOI:10.2139/ssrn.4640316

Rane, N., Choudhary, S., & Rane, J. (2023a). Enhanced product design and development using Artificial Intelligence (AI), Virtual Reality (VR), Augmented Reality (AR), 4D/5D/6D Printing, Internet of Things (IoT), and blockchain: A review. *Social Science Research Network*. DOI:10.2139/ssrn.4644059

Rane, N., Choudhary, S., & Rane, J. (2023b). Hyper-personalization for enhancing customer loyalty and satisfaction in Customer Relationship Management (CRM) systems. *Social Science Research Network*. DOI:10.2139/ssrn.4641044

Rane, N., Choudhary, S., & Rane, J. (2023c). Integrating Building Information Modelling (BIM) with ChatGPT, Bard, and similar generative artificial intelligence in the architecture, engineering, and construction industry: applications, a novel framework, challenges, and future scope. *Social Science Research Network*. DOI:10.2139/ssrn.4645601

Rane, N., Choudhary, S., & Rane, J. (2023d). Integrating ChatGPT, Bard, and leading-edge generative artificial intelligence in architectural design and engineering: applications, framework, and challenges. *Social Science Research Network*. DOI:10.2139/ssrn.4645595

Rane, N., Choudhary, S., & Rane, J. (2023e). Metaverse Marketing Strategies: Enhancing customer experience and analysing consumer behaviour through leading-edge metaverse technologies, platforms, and models. *Social Science Research Network*. DOI:10.2139/ssrn.4624199

Rangaraju, S. (2023). Ai sentry: Reinventing cybersecurity through intelligent threat detection. *EPH-International Journal of Science And Engineering*, 9(3), 30–35. DOI:10.53555/ephijse.v9i3.211

Rani, S. S., & Reeja, S. R. (2019) 'A survey on different approaches for malware detection using machine learning techniques,' in *Lecture notes on data engineering and communications technologies*, pp. 389–398. DOI:10.1007/978-3-030-34515-0_42

Ranka, P., Shah, A., Vora, N., Kulkarni, A., & Patil, N. (2024). Computer Vision-Based Cybersecurity Threat Detection System with GAN-Enhanced Data Augmentation. *Communications in Computer and Information Science*, 2031, 54–67. DOI:10.1007/978-3-031-53728-8_5

Ranzato, M., Susskind, J. M., Mnih, V., & Hinton, G. E. (2011). On deep generative models with applications to recognition. *CVPR*, 2011, 2857–2864. Advance online publication. DOI:10.1109/CVPR.2011.5995710

Rao, P. V. (2024, February 7). *Deep Reinforcement Learning: Bridging the Gap with Neural Networks*. https://www.ijisae.org/index.php/IJISAE/article/view/4792

Raparthi, M. (2020). *Examining the use of Artificial Intelligence to Enhance Security Measures in Computer Hardware, including the Detection of Hardware-based Vulnerabilities and Attacks*. EEL. [Preprint], DOI:10.52783/eel.v10i1.991

Raso, F., Hilligoss, H., Krishnamurthy, V., Bavitz, C., & Levin, K. (2018). Artificial Intelligence & Human Rights: Opportunities & Risks. *Social Science Research Network*. DOI:10.2139/ssrn.3259344

Rasti, M., Taskou, S. K., Tabassum, H., & Hossain, E. (2021). Evolution toward 6G wireless networks: A resource management perspective. arXiv preprint arXiv:2108.06527.

Rattanaphan, S., & Briassouli, A. (2024). Evaluating generalization, bias, and fairness in deep learning for metal surface defect detection: A comparative study. *Processes (Basel, Switzerland)*, 12(3), 456. DOI:10.3390/pr12030456

Ravi, N., Verma, S., Jhanjhi, N. Z., & Talib, M. N. (2021, August). Securing vanet using blockchain technology. *Journal of Physics: Conference Series*, 1979(1), 012035. DOI:10.1088/1742-6596/1979/1/012035

Ray, S. K., Liu, W., Sirisena, H., Ray, S. K., & Deka, D. (2013, November). An energy aware mobile-controlled handover method for natural disaster situations. In *2013 Australasian telecommunication networks and applications conference (ATNAC)* (pp. 130-135). IEEE. DOI:10.1109/ATNAC.2013.6705369

Ray, S. K., Pawlikowski, K., & Sirisena, H. (2009). *A fast MAC-layer handover for an IEEE 802.16 e-based WMAN*. Paper presented at the AccessNets: Third International Conference on Access Networks, AccessNets 2008, Las Vegas, NV.

Ray, S. K., Sinha, R., & Ray, S. K. (2015). *A smartphone-based post-disaster management mechanism using WiFi tethering*. Paper presented at the 2015 IEEE 10th conference on industrial electronics and applications (ICIEA). DOI:10.1109/ICIEA.2015.7334248

Rayeesa, M., Rumaan, B., & Kaiser, J. G. (2023). Deep Generative Models: A Review. *Indian Journal of Science and Technology*, 16(7), 460–467. DOI:10.17485/IJST/v16i7.2296

Ray, S. K., Sarkar, N. I., Deka, D., & Ray, S. K. (2015, January). LTE-advanced based handover mechanism for natural disaster situations. In *2015 International Conference on Information Networking (ICOIN)* (pp. 165-170). IEEE. DOI:10.1109/ICOIN.2015.7057876

Ray, S. K., Sirisena, H., & Deka, D. (2012, November). Fast and reliable target base station selection scheme for Mobile WiMAX handover. In *Australasian Telecommunication Networks and Applications Conference (ATNAC) 2012* (pp. 1-6). IEEE. DOI:10.1109/ATNAC.2012.6398054

Raza, A., Barghash, T. O., & Salem, M. A. (2024). Play Bricks IV: Desktop and Web-Based Play Bricks App for Architectural Styles. *2024 18th International Conference on Ubiquitous Information Management and Communication (IMCOM)*. DOI:10.1109/IMCOM60618.2024.10418274

Raza, S., Garg, M., Reji, D. J., Bashir, S. R., & Ding, C. (2024). Nbias: A natural language processing framework for BIAS identification in text. *Expert Systems with Applications*, 237, 121542. DOI:10.1016/j.eswa.2023.121542

Reddy, B. S. R. (2024) 'Reinforcement Learning for Zero-Day Vulnerability Detection in IoT Devices: A Proactive approach,' *Research Square(Research Square)* [Preprint]. DOI:10.21203/rs.3.rs-4086508/v1

Regulwar, G. B., Mahalle, A. M., Pawar, R., Shamkuwar, S. K., Kakde, P. R., & Tiwari, S. (2023). Big data collection, filtering, and extraction of features. In *Advances in business information systems and analytics book series* (pp. 136–158). DOI:10.4018/979-8-3693-0413-6.ch005

Rehan, H. (2024). AI-Driven Cloud Security: The Future of Safeguarding Sensitive Data in the Digital Age. *Journal of Artificial Intelligence General Science, 1*(1), 47-66.

Rele, M., & Patil, D. (2023) 'Intrusive Detection Techniques Utilizing Machine Learning, Deep Learning, and Anomaly-based Approaches,' *2023 IEEE International Conference on Cryptography, Informatics, and Cybersecurity (ICoCICs)* [Preprint]. DOI:10.1109/ICoCICs58778.2023.10276955

Ren, A., Liang, C., Hyug, I., Broh, S., & Jhanjhi, N. Z. (2020). A three-level ransomware detection and prevention mechanism. EAI Endorsed Transactions on Energy Web, 7(26).

Repetto, M. (2023). Adaptive monitoring, detection, and response for agile digital service chains. *Computers & Security*, 132, 103343. DOI:10.1016/j.cose.2023.103343

Rial, R. C. (2024). *AI in analytical chemistry: Advancements, challenges, and future directions.* Talanta., DOI:10.1016/j.talanta.2024.125949

Riegler, M., Sametinger, J., Vierhauser, M., & Wimmer, M. (2023). A model-based mode-switching framework based on security vulnerability scores. *Journal of Systems and Software*, 200, 111633. DOI:10.1016/j.jss.2023.111633

Riskhan, B., Safuan, H. A. J., Hussain, K., Elnour, A. A. H., Abdelmaboud, A., Khan, F., & Kundi, M. (2023). An Adaptive Distributed Denial of Service Attack Prevention Technique in a Distributed Environment. *Sensors (Basel)*, 23(14), 6574. DOI:10.3390/s23146574 PMID:37514868

Rjoub, G., Bentahar, J., Abdel Wahab, O., Mizouni, R., Song, A., Cohen, R., Otrok, H., & Mourad, A. (2023). A survey on explainable artificial intelligence for cybersecurity. *IEEE Transactions on Network and Service Management*, 20(4), 5115–5140. DOI:10.1109/TNSM.2023.3282740

Robles, P., & Mallinson, D. J. (2023). Catching up with AI: Pushing toward a cohesive governance framework. *Politics & Policy*, 51(3), 355–372. DOI:10.1111/polp.12529

Rogowski, W., & John, J. (2024). Preferences as fairness judgments: A critical review of normative frameworks of preference elicitation and development of an alternative based on constitutional economics. *Cost Effectiveness and Resource Allocation*, 22(1), 10. Advance online publication. DOI:10.1186/s12962-024-00510-x PMID:38291472

Rosário, A. T., & Dias, J. C. (2023). How has data-driven marketing evolved: Challenges and opportunities with emerging technologies. *International Journal of Information Management Data Insights*, 3(2), 100203. DOI:10.1016/j.jjimei.2023.100203

Roshan, K., & Zafar, A. (2024). AE-Integrated: Real-time network intrusion detection with Apache Kafka and autoencoder. *Concurrency and Computation*, 36(11), e8034. Advance online publication. DOI:10.1002/cpe.8034

Roshan, K., & Zafar, A. (2024). Boosting robustness of network intrusion detection systems: A novel two phase defense strategy against untargeted white-box optimization adversarial attack. *Expert Systems with Applications*, 123567, 123567. Advance online publication. DOI:10.1016/j.eswa.2024.123567

Roy, P., Chadrasekaran, J., Lanus, E., Freeman, L., & Werner, J. (2023). A Survey of Data Security: Practices from Cybersecurity and Challenges of Machine Learning. arXiv preprint arXiv:2310.04513.

Rudroff, T. (2024). Artificial Intelligence's transformative role in illuminating brain function in long COVID patients using PET/FDG. *Brain Sciences*, 14(1), 73. DOI:10.3390/brainsci14010073 PMID:38248288

Ruff, L., Kauffmann, J. R., Vandermeulen, R. A., Montavon, G., Samek, W., Kloft, M., Dietterich, T. G., & Müller, K. (2021). A unifying review of deep and shallow anomaly detection. *Proceedings of the IEEE*, 109(5), 756–795. DOI:10.1109/JPROC.2021.3052449

Ryan, M. (2020). In AI we trust: Ethics, artificial intelligence, and reliability. *Science and Engineering Ethics*, 26(5), 2749–2767. DOI:10.1007/s11948-020-00228-y PMID:32524425

Saad, M. M., O'Reilly, R., & Rehmani, M. H. (2024). A survey on training challenges in generative adversarial networks for biomedical image analysis. *Artificial Intelligence Review*, 57(2), 19. Advance online publication. DOI:10.1007/s10462-023-10624-y

Sadr, E. (2023, March 7). *Design and evaluation of a new editor for responsive Graphical User Interfaces*. https://summit.sfu.ca/item/36157

Saeed, M. M., Saeed, R. A., Abdelhaq, M., Alsaqour, R., Hasan, M. K., & Mokhtar, R. A. (2023). Anomaly detection in 6G networks using machine learning methods. *Electronics (Basel)*, 12(15), 3300. DOI:10.3390/electronics12153300

Saeidnia, H. R. (2023). Ethical artificial intelligence (AI): Confronting bias and discrimination in the library and information industry. *Library Hi Tech News*. Advance online publication. DOI:10.1108/LHTN-10-2023-0182

Sáez-De-Cámara, X., Flores, J. L., Arellano, C., Urbieta, A., & Zurutuza, U. (2023). Clustered federated learning architecture for network anomaly detection in large scale heterogeneous IoT networks. *Computers & Security*, 131, 103299. DOI:10.1016/j.cose.2023.103299

Safdar, N. M., Banja, J. D., & Meltzer, C. C. (2020). Ethical considerations in artificial intelligence. *European Journal of Radiology*, 122, 10876. DOI:10.1016/j.ejrad.2019.108768 PMID:31786504

Sag, M. (2023). Copyright safety for generative AI. *Social Science Research Network*. DOI:10.2139/ssrn.4438593

Sagwal, R., & Singh, A. K. (2018). Power Efficient and Light Weight Approach for Secure Multicast Tree Construction in MANETs. 2018 9th International Conference on Computing, Communication and Networking Technologies, ICCCNT. DOI:10.1109/ICCCNT.2018.8494002

Şahin, Y., & Doğru, İ. A. (2023). An enterprise data privacy governance model: Security-Centric Multi-Model data Anonymization. *Uluslararası Mühendislik Araştırma Ve Geliştirme Dergisi*. DOI:10.29137/umagd.1272085

Sahoo, B. (2023, August 1). *User experience design for automated damage detection through camera bridge in the freight rail sector*. https://opus4.kobv.de/opus4-haw/frontdoor/index/index/docId/3915

Sajeeda, A., & Hossain, B. (2022). Exploring generative adversarial networks and adversarial training. *International Journal of Cognitive Computing in Engineering*, 3, 78–89. DOI:10.1016/j.ijcce.2022.03.002

Sajid, A., & Hussain, K. (2018). Rule Based (Forward Chaining/Data Driven) Expert System for Node Level Congestion Handling in Opportunistic Network. *Mobile Networks and Applications*, 23(3), 446–455. DOI:10.1007/s11036-018-1016-0

Sakhare, S. R., & Patil, V. D. (2023, December 31). *Implementation of Captcha Mechanisms using Deep Learning to Prevent Automated Bot Attacks*. https://www.technicaljournals.org/RJCSE/index.php/journal/article/view/70

Salakhutdinov, R. (2015). Learning deep generative models. *Annual Review of Statistics and Its Application*, 2(1), 361–385. DOI:10.1146/annurev-statistics-010814-020120

Salehi, M., Shahriari, H. R., & Moosavi, S. R. (2018). Investigating the impact of using online resources on academic achievement of the students in programming courses. *Journal of Information Technology Education*.

Saleh, M., Abdullah, A., & Saher, R. (2022). Message security level integration with iotes: A design dependent encryption selection model for iot devices. *IJCSNS*, 22(8), 328.

Salekshahrezaee, Z., Leevy, J. L., & Khoshgoftaar, T. M. (2023). The effect of feature extraction and data sampling on credit card fraud detection. *Journal of Big Data*, 10(1), 6. Advance online publication. DOI:10.1186/s40537-023-00684-w

Salman, R. (2022). *Paletto: an interactive colour palette generator : facilitating designers' colour selection processes*. DIVA. https://www.diva-portal.org/smash/record.jsf?pid=diva2%3A1679068&dswid=-8369

Samek, W., & Müller, K. R. (2019). Towards explainable artificial intelligence. In *Lecture Notes in Computer Science* (pp. 5–22). DOI:10.1007/978-3-030-28954-6_1

Sampaio, S., Sousa, P. R., Martins, C., Ferreira, A., Antunes, L., & Cruz-Correia, R. (2023). Collecting, processing and secondary using personal and (Pseudo)Anonymized data in smart cities. *Applied Sciences (Basel, Switzerland)*, 13(6), 3830. DOI:10.3390/app13063830

Sampath, V., Maurtua, I., Martín, J. J. A., & Gutierrez, A. (2021). A survey on generative adversarial networks for imbalance problems in computer vision tasks. *Journal of Big Data*, 8(1), 27. Advance online publication. DOI:10.1186/s40537-021-00414-0 PMID:33552840

Sanderson, C., Douglas, D., Qing-Hua, L., Schleiger, E., Whittle, J., Lacey, J., Newnham, G., Hajkowicz, S., Robinson, C. J., & Hansen, D. (2023). AI Ethics Principles in Practice: Perspectives of Designers and Developers. *IEEE Transactions on Technology and Society*, 4(2), 171–187. DOI:10.1109/TTS.2023.3257303

Sanjaya, I. G. A. S., Sasmita, G. M. A., & Arsa, D. M. S. (2020). Evaluasi Keamanan Website Lembaga X Melalui Penetration Testing Menggunakan Framework ISSAF. *Jurnal Ilmiah Merpati*, 8(2), 113–124. DOI:10.24843/JIM.2020.v08.i02.p05

Sankar, S., Ramasubbareddy, S., Luhach, A. K., Deverajan, G. G., Alnumay, W. S., Jhanjhi, N. Z., Ghosh, U., & Sharma, P. K. (2020). Energy efficient optimal parent selection based routing protocol for Internet of Things using firefly optimization algorithm. *Transactions on Emerging Telecommunications Technologies*, 32(8), e4171. Advance online publication. DOI:10.1002/ett.4171

Saravanan, T., Deepa, S. N., & Sasikumar, P. (2023). Advanced EGAN-IDS Framework for Resilience against Adversarial Attacks using Multi-headed Attention Module. *Procedia Computer Science*, 230, 203–213. DOI:10.1016/j.procs.2023.12.075

Sarker, I. H. (2021). CyberLearning: Effectiveness analysis of machine learning security modeling to detect cyber-anomalies and multi-attacks. *Internet of Things: Engineering Cyber Physical Human Systems*, 14, 100393. DOI:10.1016/j.iot.2021.100393

Sarker, I. H., Furhad, M. H., & Nowrozy, R. (2021). Ai-driven cybersecurity: An overview, security intelligence modeling and research directions. *SN Computer Science*, 2(3), 1–18. DOI:10.1007/s42979-021-00557-0

Satapathy, P., Hermis, A. H., Rustagi, S., Pradhan, K. B., Padhi, B. K., & Sah, R. (2023). Artificial intelligence in surgical education and training: Opportunities, challenges, and ethical considerations–correspondence. *International Journal of Surgery*, 109(5), 1543–1544. DOI:10.1097/JS9.0000000000000387 PMID:37037597

Satybaldy, A., Ferdous, S., & Nowostawski, M. (2024). A Taxonomy of Challenges for Self-Sovereign Identity Systems. *IEEE Access : Practical Innovations, Open Solutions*, 1, 16151–16177. Advance online publication. DOI:10.1109/ACCESS.2024.3357940

Saura, J. R., Ribeiro-Soriano, D., & Palacios-Marqués, D. (2022). Assessing behavioral data science privacy issues in government artificial intelligence deployment. *Government Information Quarterly*, 39(4), 101679. DOI:10.1016/j.giq.2022.101679

Saveliev, A., & Zhurenkov, D. (2021). Artificial intelligence and social responsibility: The case of the artificial intelligence strategies in the United States, Russia, and China. *Kybernetes*, 50(3), 656–675. DOI:10.1108/K-01-2020-0060

Schaub, F., Balebako, R., Durity, A. L., & Cranor, L. F. (2015). *A design space for effective privacy notices*. USENIX Association. https://www.usenix.org/conference/soups2015/proceedings/presentation/schaub

Scholar, M. T., Kant, R., & Sen, A. D. (2020). Collaborative Decision for Wormhole Attack Prevention in WSN. *Int. J. Sci. Res. Eng. Trends*, 6(2).

Scholar, M. T., & Yadav, B. (2019). Predication and Root Selection of Worm Hole Attack in WSN. *Int. J. Sci. Res. Eng. Trends*, 5(6), 1937–1944.

Schultz, C. D., Koch, C., & Olbrich, R. (2023). Dark sides of artificial intelligence: The dangers of automated decision-making in search engine advertising. *Journal of the Association for Information Science and Technology*. Advance online publication. DOI:10.1002/asi.24798

Schwarting, R. K. (2023). Behavioral analysis in laboratory rats: Challenges and usefulness of 50-kHz ultrasonic vocalizations. *Neuroscience and Biobehavioral Reviews*, 152, 105260. DOI:10.1016/j.neubiorev.2023.105260 PMID:37268181

Seh, A. H., Al-Amri, J. F., Subahi, A. F., Agrawal, A., Kumar, R., & Khan, R. A. (2021). Machine learning based framework for maintaining privacy of healthcare data. *Intelligent Automation & Soft Computing*, 29, 697–712. DOI:10.32604/iasc.2021.018048

Sewak, M., Sahay, S. K., & Rathore, H. (2022). Deep reinforcement learning in the advanced Cybersecurity Threat Detection and Protection. *Information Systems Frontiers*. Advance online publication. DOI:10.1007/s10796-022-10333-x

Shafik, W. (2023). A Comprehensive Cybersecurity Framework for Present and Future Global Information Technology Organizations. In *Effective Cybersecurity Operations for Enterprise-Wide Systems* (pp. 56–79). IGI Global. DOI:10.4018/978-1-6684-9018-1.ch002

Shah, I. A., Jhanjhi, N. Z., & Ray, S. K. (2024). IoT Devices in Drones: Security Issues and Future Challenges. In *Cybersecurity Issues and Challenges in the Drone Industry* (pp. 217-235). IGI Global.

Shah, V. (2023, December 30). *Striking a balance: Ethical considerations in AI-Driven law enforcement*. https://redc.revistas-csic.com/index.php/Jorunal/article/view/159

Shah, I. A., Jhanjhi, N. Z., Amsaad, F., & Razaque, A. (2022). The role of cutting-edge technologies in industry 4.0. In *Cyber Security Applications for Industry 4.0* (pp. 97–109). Chapman and Hall/CRC. DOI:10.1201/9781003203087-4

Shah, I. A., Jhanjhi, N. Z., & Laraib, A. (2023). Cybersecurity and blockchain usage in contemporary business. In *Handbook of Research on Cybersecurity Issues and Challenges for Business and FinTech Applications* (pp. 49–64). IGI Global.

Shah, I. A., Jhanjhi, N. Z., & Ray, S. K. (2024). Enabling Explainable AI in Cybersecurity Solutions. In *Advances in Explainable AI Applications for Smart Cities* (pp. 255–275). IGI Global. DOI:10.4018/978-1-6684-6361-1.ch009

Shahid, H. (2021). Energy Optimised Security against Wormhole Attack in IoT-Based Wireless Sensor Networks. *Computers, Materials & Continua*, 68(2), 1967–1981. DOI:10.32604/cmc.2021.015259

Shahid, H., Ashraf, H., Ullah, A., Band, S. S., & Elnaffar, S. (2022). Wormhole attack mitigation strategies and their impact on wireless sensor network performance: A literature survey. *International Journal of Communication Systems*, 35(16), e5311. DOI:10.1002/dac.5311

Shamsolmoali, P., Zareapoor, M., Granger, É., Zhou, H., Wang, R., Celebi, M. E., & Yang, J. (2021). Image synthesis with adversarial networks: A comprehensive survey and case studies. *Information Fusion*, 72, 126–146. DOI:10.1016/j.inffus.2021.02.014

Shams, R. A., Zowghi, D., & Bano, M. (2023). AI and the quest for diversity and inclusion: A systematic literature review. *AI and Ethics*. Advance online publication. DOI:10.1007/s43681-023-00362-w

Shankar, S. P., Supriya, M. S., Varadam, D., Kumar, M., Gupta, H., & Saha, R. (2023). A comprehensive study on algorithms and applications of artificial intelligence in diagnosis and prognosis: AI for healthcare. In Digital Twins and Healthcare: Trends, Techniques, and Challenges (pp. 35-54). IGI Global.

Shankar, S. P., Varadam, D., Bharadwaj, A., Dayananda, S., Agrawal, S., & Jha, A. (2023). Enhancing DevOps Using Intelligent Techniques: Application of Artificial Intelligence and Machine Learning Techniques to DevOps. In Cases on Enhancing Business Sustainability Through Knowledge Management Systems (pp. 251-274). IGI Global.

Shankar, S. P., Varadam, D., Bharadwaj, A., Saxena, T., Mohta, R., & Shankar, A. (2023). Artificial Intelligence for Defence: A Comprehensive Study on Applying AI for the Airforce, Navy, and Army. In Emerging Trends, Techniques, and Applications in Geospatial Data Science (pp. 244-262). IGI Global.

Shankar, S. P., Varadam, D., Agrawal, H., & Naresh, E. (2022). Blockchain for IoT and Big Data Applications: A Comprehensive Survey on Security Issues. Advances in Industry 4.0. *Concepts and Applications*, 5, 65.

Shaon, M. N. A., & Ferens, K. (2015). *Wireless Sensor Network Wormhole Detection using an Artificial Neural Network*. ICWN.

Sharifani, K., & Amini, M. (2023). Machine learning and deep learning: A review of methods and applications. *World Information Technology and Engineering Journal*, 10(07), 3897–3904.

Sharma, M. K., & Joshi, B. K. (2017). A mitigation technique for high transmission power based wormhole attack in Wireless Sensor Networks. Proceedings of 2016 International Conference on ICT in Business, Industry, and Government, ICTBIG.

Sharma, S. (2019). *Data Privacy and GDPR handbook*. John Wiley & Sons. DOI:10.1002/9781119594307

Shatilova, I. (2024). *A virtue ethics approach to the ethicality of employee empowerment*. https://jyx.jyu.fi/handle/123456789/93101

Shibli, A., Pritom, M. M. A., & Gupta, M. (2024). AbuseGPT: Abuse of generative AI ChatBots to create smishing campaigns. *arXiv (Cornell University)*. /arxiv.2402. 09728DOI:10.1109/ISDFS60797.2024.10527300

Shichun, Y., Zheng, Z., Bin, M., Yifan, Z., Sida, Z., Mingyan, L., Yu, L., Qiangwei, L., Xinan, Z., Mengyue, Z., Yang, H., Fei, C., & Yaoguang, C. (2023). Essential technics of cybersecurity for intelligent connected vehicles: Comprehensive review and perspective. *IEEE Internet of Things Journal*, 10(24), 21787–21810. DOI:10.1109/JIOT.2023.3299554

Shi, D., Cui, W., Huang, D., Zhang, H., & Chen, N. (2023). Reverse-engineering information presentations: Recovering hierarchical grouping from layouts of visual elements. *Visual Intelligence*, 1(1), 9. Advance online publication. DOI:10.1007/s44267-023-00010-1

Shin, D. (2021). Embodying algorithms, enactive artificial intelligence and the extended cognition: You can see as much as you know about algorithm. *Journal of Information Science*, 49(1), 18–31. DOI:10.1177/0165551520985495

Shi, Y., Gao, T., Jiao, X., & Cao, N. (2023a). Understanding Design collaboration between designers and Artificial intelligence: A Systematic Literature review. *Proceedings of the ACM on Human-computer Interaction*, 7(CSCW2), 1–35. DOI:10.1145/3610217

Shi, Y., Lian, L., Shi, Y., Wang, Z., Zhou, Y., Fu, L., Bai, L., Zhang, J., & Zhang, W. (2023). Machine Learning for Large-Scale Optimization in 6G wireless networks. *IEEE Communications Surveys and Tutorials*, 25(4), 2088–2132. DOI:10.1109/COMST.2023.3300664

Shneiderman, B. (2020). Design lessons from AI's two grand goals: Human emulation and useful applications. *IEEE Transactions on Technology and Society*, 1(2), 73–82. DOI:10.1109/TTS.2020.2992669

Shruti, R., Rani, S., Sah, D. K., & Gianini, G. (2023). Attribute-Based Encryption Schemes for next generation wireless IoT networks: A comprehensive survey. *Sensors (Basel)*, 23(13), 5921. DOI:10.3390/s23135921 PMID:37447769

Shukla, R., Jain, R., & Vyavahare, P. D. (2018). Combating against wormhole attack in trust and energy aware secure routing protocol (TESRP) in wireless sensor network. *International Conference on Recent Innovations in Signal Processing and Embedded Systems, RISE 2017*, 555–561.

Shukla, S. (2023) 'Synergizing machine learning and cybersecurity for robust digital protection.,' *Research Square* [Preprint]. DOI:10.21203/rs.3.rs-3571854/v1

Siahaan, C. N., Rufisanto, M., Nolasco, R., Achmad, S., & Siahaan, C. R. P. (2023). Study of Cross-Site Request Forgery on Web-Based Application: Exploitations and Preventions. *Procedia Computer Science*, 227, 92–100. DOI:10.1016/j. procs.2023.10.506

Siddiqui, F. J., Ashraf, H., & Ullah, A. (2020). Dual server based security system for multimedia Services in Next Generation Networks. *Multimedia Tools and Applications*, 79(11), 7299–7318. DOI:10.1007/s11042-019-08406-2

Sikder, A. S. (2023, November 26). *Cybersecurity Framework for Ensuring Confidentiality, Integrity, and Availability of University Management Systems in Bangladesh.: Cybersecurity framework on UMS in Bangladesh*. https://journal.ijisnt.com/index.php/public_html/article/view/4

Sim, J., Kim, B., Jeon, K., Joo, M., Lim, J., Lee, J., & Choo, K. R. (2023). Technical requirements and approaches in personal data control. *ACM Computing Surveys*, 55(9), 1–30. DOI:10.1145/3558766

Simoes, M., Elmusrati, M., Vartiainen, T., Mekkanen, M., Karimi, M., Diaba, S., .. . Lopes, W. (2023). Enhancing data security against cyberattacks in artificial intelligence based smartgrid systems with crypto agility. arXiv preprint arXiv:2305.11652.

Sinaga, K. P., & Yang, M.-S. (2020). Unsupervised K-Means clustering algorithm. *IEEE Access: Practical Innovations, Open Solutions*, 8, 80716–80727. DOI:10.1109/ACCESS.2020.2988796

Sindiramutty, S. R., Jhanjhi, N. Z., Ray, S. K., Jazri, H., Khan, N. A., & Gaur, L. (2023). Metaverse. In *Advances in medical technologies and clinical practice book series* (pp. 93–158). DOI:10.4018/978-1-6684-9823-1.ch003

Sindiramutty, S. R., Jhanjhi, N. Z., Ray, S. K., Jazri, H., Khan, N. A., Gaur, L., Gharib, A. H., & Manchuri, A. R. (2023). Metaverse. In *Advances in medical technologies and clinical practice book series* (pp. 24–92). DOI:10.4018/978-1-6684-9823-1.ch002

Sindiramutty, S. R., Jhanjhi, N. Z., Tan, C. E., Khan, N. A., & Shah, B. (2024) 'Future trends and emerging threats in drone cybersecurity,' in *Advances in information security, privacy, and ethics book series*, 148–195. DOI:10.4018/979-8-3693-0774-8.ch007

Sindiramutty, S. R., Jhanjhi, N. Z., Tan, C. E., Khan, N. A., Gharib, A. H., & Yun, K. J. (2023). Applications of blockchain technology in supply chain management. In *Advances in logistics, operations, and management science book series* (pp. 248–304). DOI:10.4018/978-1-6684-7625-3.ch009

Sindiramutty, S. R., Jhanjhi, N. Z., Tan, C. E., Khan, N. A., Shah, B., & Gaur, L. (2023). Securing the digital supply chain cyber threats and vulnerabilities. In *Advances in logistics, operations, and management science book series* (pp. 156–223). DOI:10.4018/978-1-6684-7625-3.ch007

Sindiramutty, S. R., Jhanjhi, N. Z., Tan, C. E., Tee, W. J., Lau, S. P., Jazri, H., Ray, S. K., & Zaheer, M. A. (2024). IoT and AI-Based Smart Solutions for the Agriculture Industry. In *Advances in computational intelligence and robotics book series* (pp. 317–351). DOI:10.4018/978-1-6684-6361-1.ch012

Sindiramutty, S. R., Jhanjhi, N. Z., Tan, C., Khan, N. A., & Shah, B. (2024) 'Cybersecurity measures for logistics industry,' in *Advances in information security, privacy, and ethics book series*, 1–58. DOI:10.4018/979-8-3693-3816-2.ch001

Sindiramutty, S. R., Jhanjhi, N. Z., Tan, C., Yun, K. J., Manchuri, A. R., Ashraf, H., Murugesan, R. K., Tee, W. J., & Hussain, M. (2024). Data security and privacy concerns in drone operations. In *Advances in information security, privacy, and ethics book series* (pp. 236–290). DOI:10.4018/979-8-3693-0774-8.ch010

Sindiramutty, S. R., Tan, C. E., & Shah, B. (2024) 'Ethical considerations in drone cybersecurity,' in *Advances in information security, privacy, and ethics book series*, 42–87. DOI:10.4018/979-8-3693-0774-8.ch003

Sindiramutty, S. R., Tan, C. E., Lau, S. P., Thangaveloo, R., Gharib, A. H., Manchuri, A. R., Khan, N. A., Tee, W. J., & Muniandy, L. (2024). Explainable AI for cybersecurity. In *Advances in computational intelligence and robotics book series* (pp. 31–97). DOI:10.4018/978-1-6684-6361-1.ch002

Sindiramutty, S. R., Tan, C., & Wei, G. W. (2024) 'Eyes in the sky,' in *Advances in information security, privacy, and ethics book series*, 405–451. DOI:10.4018/979-8-3693-0774-8.ch017

Sindiramutty, S. R., Tan, C., Tee, W. J., Lau, S. P., Balakrishnan, S., Kaur, S. D. A., Jazri, H., & Aslam, M. (2024). Modern smart cities and open research challenges and issues of explainable artificial intelligence. In *Advances in computational intelligence and robotics book series* (pp. 389–424). DOI:10.4018/978-1-6684-6361-1.ch015

Sindiramutty, S. R., Tee, W. J., Balakrishnan, S., Kaur, S., Thangaveloo, R., Jazri, H., Khan, N. A., Gharib, A. H., & Manchuri, A. R. (2024). Explainable AI in healthcare application. In *Advances in computational intelligence and robotics book series* (pp. 123–176). DOI:10.4018/978-1-6684-6361-1.ch005

Sindiramutty, S.R., Tan, C.E., & Goh, W.W. (2024) 'Securing the supply chain,' in *Advances in information security, privacy, and ethics book series*, 300–365. .DOI:10.4018/979-8-3693-3816-2.ch011

Singha, S. (2024). Unveiling gender dynamics in digital capitalism. In *Advances in finance, accounting, and economics book series* (pp. 161–186). DOI:10.4018/979-8-3693-1182-0.ch009

Singh, A. P., Pradhan, N. R., Luhach, A. K., Agnihotri, S., Jhanjhi, N. Z., Verma, S., Kavita, , Ghosh, U., & Roy, D. S. (2020). A novel patient-centric architectural framework for blockchain-enabled healthcare applications. *IEEE Transactions on Industrial Informatics*, 17(8), 5779–5789. DOI:10.1109/TII.2020.3037889

Singhal, V., Jain, S. P., Anand, D., Singh, A., Verma, S., Kavita, , Rodrigues, J. J. P. C., Jhanjhi, N. Z., Ghosh, U., Jo, O., & Iwendi, C. (2020). Artificial Intelligence Enabled Road Vehicle-Train Collision Risk Assessment Framework for Unmanned railway level crossings. *IEEE Access : Practical Innovations, Open Solutions*, 8, 113790–113806. DOI:10.1109/ACCESS.2020.3002416

Singh, P. K., & Kumar, A. (2023). Cyber Physical Systems in Supply Chain Management. In *Cyber Physical Systems* (pp. 85–110). Chapman and Hall/CRC.

Singh, R., Sethi, A., Saini, K., Saurav, S., Tiwari, A., & Singh, S. (2024). Attention-guided generator with dual discriminator GAN for real-time video anomaly detection. *Engineering Applications of Artificial Intelligence*, 131, 107830. DOI:10.1016/j.engappai.2023.107830

Singh, R., Singh, J., & Singh, R. (2016). WRHT: A Hybrid Technique for Detection of Wormhole Attack in Wireless Sensor Networks. *Mobile Information Systems*, 2016, 1–13. DOI:10.1155/2016/8354930

Singh, S. P., & Sharma, S. C. (2015). Range Free Localization Techniques in Wireless Sensor Networks: A Review. *Procedia Computer Science*, 57, 7–16. DOI:10.1016/j.procs.2015.07.357

Siniksaran, E. (2024). *Overcoming cognitive biases in strategic management and decision making*. IGI Global. DOI:10.4018/979-8-3693-1766-2

Siountri, K., & Anagnostopoulos, C. (2023). The classification of cultural heritage buildings in Athens using deep learning techniques. *Heritage*, 6(4), 3673–3705. DOI:10.3390/heritage6040195

Siriwardhana, Y., Porambage, P., Liyanage, M., & Ylianttila, M. (2021, June). AI and 6G security: Opportunities and challenges. In 2021 Joint European Conference on Networks and Communications & 6G Summit (EuCNC/6G Summit) (pp. 616-621). IEEE.

Situ, J. J. (2019, April 26). *Generative models for predictive UI design tools*. https://www.ideals.illinois.edu/items/112226

Sivamayil, K., Rajasekar, E., Aljafari, B., Nikolovski, S., Vairavasundaram, S., & Vairavasundaram, I. (2023). A systematic study on reinforcement learning based applications. *Energies*, 16(3), 1512. DOI:10.3390/en16031512

Smith, E., & Johnson, L. (2020). Mentorship in programming education: A critical review. Journal of Educational Technology, 12(1), 78-96.

Smmarwar, S. K., Gupta, G. P., & Kumar, S. (2024). Android malware detection and identification frameworks by leveraging the machine and deep learning techniques: A comprehensive review. *Telematics and Informatics Reports*, 14, 100130. DOI:10.1016/j.teler.2024.100130

Sodiya, E. O., Amoo, O. O., Umoga, U. J., & Atadoga, A. (2024). AI-driven personalization in web content delivery: A comparative study of user engagement in the USA and the UK. *World Journal of Advanced Research and Reviews*, 21(2), 887–902. DOI:10.30574/wjarr.2024.21.2.0502

Softić, J., & Vejzović, Z. (2023, March). Impact of Vulnerability Assesment and Penetration Testing (VAPT) on Operating System Security. In 2023 22nd International Symposium INFOTEH-JAHORINA (INFOTEH) (pp. 1-6). IEEE.

Sohail, S. S., Farhat, F., Himeur, Y., Nadeem, M., Madsen, D. Ø., Singh, Y., Atalla, S., & Mansoor, W. (2023). *Decoding ChatGPT: a taxonomy of existing research, current challenges, and possible future directions. arXiv*. Cornell University., DOI:10.1016/j.jksuci.2023.101675

Sokol. (n.d.). Counterfactual Explanations of ML Predictions: Opportunities and Challenges for AI Safety. Academic Press.

Solyman, A. A. A., & Yahya, K. (2022). Evolution of wireless communication networks: From 1G to 6G and future perspective. *Iranian Journal of Electrical and Computer Engineering*, 12(4), 3943.

Sreejith, R., & Sinimole, K. (2024). User-Centric Evaluation of EHR Software through NLP-driven Investigation: Implications for Product Development and User Experience. *Journal of Open Innovation*, 100206(1), 100206. Advance online publication. DOI:10.1016/j.joitmc.2023.100206

Srinivasan, K. (2021, June 16). *Performance comparison of deep CNN models for detecting driver's distraction.* https://papers.ssrn.com/sol3/papers.cfm?abstract_id =3868549

Srivastava, H., Bharti, A. K., & Singh, A. (2023). Context-Aware Vision Transformer (Cavit) for Satellite Image Classification. *SSRN.* DOI:10.2139/ssrn.4673127

Srivastava, R., & Kumar, P. (2024). Deep-GAN: An improved model for thyroid nodule identification and classification. *Neural Computing & Applications,* 36(14), 7685–7704. Advance online publication. DOI:10.1007/s00521-024-09492-6

Srivastava, S., Benny, B., Ma'am, M. P. G., & Ma'am, N. B. (2021). *Artificial Intelligence (AI) and It's Application in Cyber Security (No. 5791).* EasyChair.

Stahl, B. C., & Eke, D. (2024). The ethics of ChatGPT – Exploring the ethical issues of an emerging technology. *International Journal of Information Management,* 74, 102700. DOI:10.1016/j.ijinfomgt.2023.102700

Stankovich, M. (2024). Unlocking the Potential of Generative AI in Cybersecurity: A Roadmap to Opportunities and Challenges. Retrieved from https://dai-global -digital.com/unlocking-the-potential-of-generative-ai-in-cybersecurity-a-roadmap -to-opportunities-and-challenges.html

Stige, Å., Zamani, E. D., Mikalef, P., & Zhu, Y. (2023). Artificial intelligence (AI) for user experience (UX) design: A systematic literature review and future research agenda. *Information Technology & People.* Advance online publication. DOI:10.1108/ITP-07-2022-0519

Stingelová, B., Thrakl, C. T., Wrońska, L., Jedrej-Szymankiewicz, S., Khan, S., & Svetinović, D. (2023). User-Centric Security and Privacy Threats in Connected Vehicles: A Threat Modeling Analysis Using STRIDE and LINDDUN. *2023 IEEE Intl Conf on Dependable, Autonomic and Secure Computing, Intl Conf on Pervasive Intelligence and Computing, Intl Conf on Cloud and Big Data Computing, Intl Conf on Cyber Science and Technology Congress (DASC/PiCom/CBDCom/CyberSciTech).* DOI:10.1109/DASC/PiCom/CBDCom/Cy59711.2023.10361381

Striuk, O., & Kondratenko, Y. (2023) 'Generative Adversarial Networks in Cybersecurity: analysis and response,' in *Studies in computational intelligence,* 373–388. DOI:10.1007/978-3-031-25759-9_18

Sturm, B. L., Ben-Tal, O., Monaghan, Ú., Collins, N., Herremans, D., Chew, E., Hadjeres, G., Deruty, E., & Pachet, F. (2018). Machine learning research that matters for music creation: A case study. *Journal of New Music Research,* 48(1), 36–55. DOI:10.1080/09298215.2018.1515233

Subramanian, H. V., Canfield, C., & Shank, D. B. (2024). Designing explainable AI to improve human-AI team performance: A medical stakeholder-driven scoping review. *Artificial Intelligence in Medicine*, 149, 102780. DOI:10.1016/j.artmed.2024.102780 PMID:38462282

Suchithra, J., Robinson, D., & Rajabi, A. (2023). Hosting capacity assessment strategies and reinforcement learning methods for coordinated voltage control in electricity distribution networks: A review. *Energies*, 16(5), 2371. DOI:10.3390/en16052371

Sudirjo, F. (2024). *Application of the user centered design method to evaluate the relationship between user experience, user interface and customer satisfaction on banking mobile application.* Jurnal Informasi Dan Teknologi. DOI:10.60083/jidt.v6i1.465

Sumpter, J. (2022, April 12). CVSS Scores: A Practical Guide for application. ZeroFox. https://www.zerofox.com/blog/cvss-scores-practical-guide-application/

Sun, J., Wang, X., Xiong, N., & Shao, J. (2018). Learning sparse representation with variational Auto-Encoder for anomaly detection. *IEEE Access : Practical Innovations, Open Solutions*, 6, 33353–33361. DOI:10.1109/ACCESS.2018.2848210

Sun, N., Ding, M., Jiang, J., Xu, W., Mo, X., Tai, Y., & Zhang, J. (2023). Cyber Threat Intelligence Mining for Proactive Cybersecurity Defense: A survey and New Perspectives. *IEEE Communications Surveys and Tutorials*, 25(3), 1748–1774. DOI:10.1109/COMST.2023.3273282

Suresh, A., Dwarakanath, B., Nanda, A. K., Kumar, P. S., Sankar, S., & Cheerla, S. (2024). An evolutionary Computation-Based federated learning for host intrusion detection in Real-Time traffic analysis. *Wireless Personal Communications*. Advance online publication. DOI:10.1007/s11277-023-10852-z

Süzen, A. A. (2020). A risk-assessment of cyber attacks and defense strategies in industry 4.0 ecosystem. *International Journal of Computer Network and Information Security*, 12(1), 1–12. DOI:10.5815/ijcnis.2020.01.01

Syed, S. A., Sharma, D. K., & Srivastava, G. (2023). Modeling Distributed and Configurable Hierarchical Blockchain over SDN and Fog-Based Networks for Large-Scale Internet of Things. *Journal of Grid Computing*, 21(4), 64. Advance online publication. DOI:10.1007/s10723-023-09698-3

Tai, J., Dollinger, M., Ajjawi, R., De St Jorre, T. J., Krattli, S., McCarthy, D., & Prezioso, D. (2022). Designing assessment for inclusion: An exploration of diverse students' assessment experiences. *Assessment & Evaluation in Higher Education*, 48(3), 403–417. DOI:10.1080/02602938.2022.2082373

Taj, I., & Jhanjhi, N. Z. (2022). Towards Industrial Revolution 5.0 and Explainable Artificial Intelligence: Challenges and opportunities. *International Journal of Computing and Digital Systems*, 12(1), 285–310. DOI:10.12785/ijcds/120124

Takale, D. G., Mahalle, P. N., & Sule, B. (2024). Cyber Security Challenges in Generative AI Technology. *Journal of Network Security Computer Networks*, 10(1), 28–34.

Tamoghna, D. (2024). Top 13 Cyber Security Trends For 2024. Retrieved from https://www.selecthub.com/endpoint-security/cyber-security-trends/

Tang, F., & Østvold, B. M. (2023). Transparency in App Analytics: Analyzing the Collection of User Interaction Data. *Transparency in App Analytics: Analyzing the Collection of User Interaction Data*. DOI:10.1109/PST58708.2023.10320181

Tan, H., Ye, T., Rehman, S., ur Rehman, O., Tu, S., & Ahmad, J. (2023). A novel routing optimization strategy based on reinforcement learning in perception layer networks. *Computer Networks*, 237, 110105. DOI:10.1016/j.comnet.2023.110105

Tan, T. F., Thirunavukarasu, A. J., Campbell, J. P., Keane, P. A., Pasquale, L. R., Abràmoff, M. D., Kalpathy–Cramer, J., Lum, F., Kim, J. E., Baxter, S. L., & Ting, D. S. W. (2023). Generative artificial intelligence through ChatGPT and other large language models in ophthalmology. *Ophthalmology Science*, 3(4), 100394. DOI:10.1016/j.xops.2023.100394 PMID:37885755

Tanwani, A. K. (2018). Generative Models for Learning Robot Manipulation Skills from Humans. *Generative Models for Learning Robot Manipulation Skills From Humans*. DOI:10.5075/epfl-thesis-8320

Tarek, M., Rateb, J., Abdulatif, A., Sidra, A., Salim El, K., Salah, Z., & Muhammad, R. (2022). Privacy-preserving federated learning cyber-threat detection for intelligent transport systems with blockchain-based security. *Expert Systems: International Journal of Knowledge Engineering and Neural Networks*, 40(5), e13103. Advance online publication. DOI:10.1111/exsy.13103

Tarikere, S., Donner, I., & Woods, D. (2021). Diagnosing a healthcare cybersecurity crisis: The impact of IoMT advancements and 5G. *Business Horizons*, 64(6), 799–807. DOI:10.1016/j.bushor.2021.07.015

Tayyab, M., Marjani, M., Jhanjhi, N., Hashem, I. A. T., Usmani, R. S. A., & Qamar, F. (2023). A Comprehensive Review on Deep Learning Algorithms: Security and Privacy Issues. *Computers & Security*, 131, 103297. DOI:10.1016/j.cose.2023.103297

Theodorou, A., & Tubella, A. A. (2024). Responsible AI at work: incorporating human values. In *Edward Elgar Publishing eBooks* (pp. 32–46). DOI:10.4337/9781800889972.00010

Thomas, J. (2018). Individual Cyber Security: Empowering employees to resist spear phishing to prevent identity theft and ransomware attacks. *International Journal of Business and Management*, 13(6), 1. DOI:10.5539/ijbm.v13n6p1

Tikkinen-Piri, C., Rohunen, A., & Markkula, J. (2018). EU General Data Protection Regulation: Changes and implications for personal data collecting companies. *Computer Law & Security Report*, 34(1), 134–153. DOI:10.1016/j.clsr.2017.05.015

Tiwari, P., Lakhan, A., Jhaveri, R. H., & Gronli, T. M. (2023). Consumer-centric internet of medical things for cyborg applications based on federated reinforcement learning. *IEEE Transactions on Consumer Electronics*, 69(4), 756–764. DOI:10.1109/TCE.2023.3242375

Tolani & Tolani. (n.d.). Use of artificial intelligence in cyber defence. Academic Press.

Tomer, V., & Sharma, S. (2022). Detecting IoT attacks Using an Ensemble Machine Learning Model. *Future Internet*, 14(4), 102. Advance online publication. DOI:10.3390/fi14040102

Tomlinson, B., Patterson, D., & Torrance, A. W. (2023, July 19). *Turning Fake Data into Fake News: The A.I. Training Set as a Trojan Horse of Misinformation*. https://papers.ssrn.com/sol3/papers.cfm?abstract_id=4515571

Toshevska, M., & Gievska, S. (2022). A review of text style transfer using Deep learning. *IEEE Transactions on Artificial Intelligence*, 3(5), 669–684. DOI:10.1109/TAI.2021.3115992

Tripathi, M. (n.d.). How blockchain revolutionizes generative AI. LinkedIn. https://www.linkedin.com/pulse/how-blockchain-revolutionizes-generative-ai-mukul-tripathi/

Tripathy, K. P., & Mishra, A. K. (2023). Deep learning in hydrology and water resources disciplines: Concepts, methods, applications, and research directions. *Journal of Hydrology (Amsterdam)*, 130458. Advance online publication. DOI:10.1016/j.jhydrol.2023.130458

Tufchi, S., Yadav, A., & Ahmed, T. (2023). A comprehensive survey of multimodal fake news detection techniques: Advances, challenges, and opportunities. *International Journal of Multimedia Information Retrieval*, 12(2), 28. Advance online publication. DOI:10.1007/s13735-023-00296-3

Tursunalieva, A., Alexánder, D., Dunne, R., Li, J., Riera, L. G., & Zhao, Y. (2024). Making Sense of Machine Learning: A review of interpretation techniques and their applications. *Applied Sciences (Basel, Switzerland)*, 14(2), 496. DOI:10.3390/app14020496

Tyagi, A. K., Hemamalini, V., & Soni, G. (2023) 'Digital health communication with Artificial Intelligence-Based Cyber Security,' in *Advances in medical technologies and clinical practice book series*, 178–213. DOI:10.4018/978-1-6684-8938-3.ch009

Ukwandu, E., Ben-Farah, M. A., Hindy, H., Bures, M., Atkinson, R., Tachtatzis, C., Andonovic, I., & Bellekens, X. (2022). Cyber-security challenges in aviation industry: A review of current and future trends. *Information (Basel)*, 13(3), 146. DOI:10.3390/info13030146

Ullah, A., Azeem, M., Ashraf, H., Jhanjhi, N. Z., Nkenyereye, L., & Humayun, M. (2021). Secure critical data reclamation scheme for isolated clusters in IoT-enabled WSN. *IEEE Internet of Things Journal*, 9(4), 2669–2677. DOI:10.1109/JIOT.2021.3098635

Upadhya, R., Kosuri, S., Tamasi, M., Meyer, T. A., Atta, S., Webb, M., & Gormley, A. J. (2021). Automation and data-driven design of polymer therapeutics. *Advanced Drug Delivery Reviews*, 171, 1–28. DOI:10.1016/j.addr.2020.11.009 PMID:33242537

Usama, M., Qadir, J., Raza, A., Arif, H., Yau, K. A., Elkhatib, Y., Hussain, A., & Al-Fuqaha, A. (2019). Unsupervised machine learning for networking: Techniques, applications and research challenges. *IEEE Access : Practical Innovations, Open Solutions*, 7, 65579–65615. DOI:10.1109/ACCESS.2019.2916648

Usman, H., Tariq, I., & Nawaz, B. (2023). In the realm of the machines: AI's influence upon international law and policy. *Journal of Social Research Development*, 4(2), 383–399. DOI:10.53664/JSRD/04-02-2023-13-383-399

Usman, T. M., Saheed, Y. K., Ignace, D., & Nsang, A. (2023). Diabetic retinopathy detection using principal component analysis multi-label feature extraction and classification. *International Journal of Cognitive Computing in Engineering*, 4, 78–88. DOI:10.1016/j.ijcce.2023.02.002

Val, T. (2023). Data Generation with Variational Autoencoders and Generative Adversarial Networks. DOI:10.3390/engproc2023033037

Valkenburg, B., & Bongiovanni, I. (2024). Unravelling the three lines model in cybersecurity: A systematic literature review. *Computers & Security*, 139, 103708. DOI:10.1016/j.cose.2024.103708

Van Der Mei, A. P. (2024). Research on Information Security Protection in the context of Post-epidemic tourism Revival. *International Journal of Education and Humanities*, 12(2), 44–48. DOI:10.54097/zwbmyt93

van Geest, R. J., Cascavilla, G., Hulstijn, J., & Zannone, N. (2024). The applicability of a hybrid framework for automated phishing detection. *Computers & Security*, 139, 103736. DOI:10.1016/j.cose.2024.103736

Varghese, N. V., & Mahmoud, Q. H. (2020). A survey of Multi-Task Deep Reinforcement Learning. *Electronics (Basel)*, 9(9), 1363. DOI:10.3390/electronics9091363

Vartiainen, H., & Tedre, M. (2024). How Text-to-Image Generative AI is Transforming Mediated Action. *IEEE Computer Graphics and Applications*, 44(2), 1–12. DOI:10.1109/MCG.2024.3355808 PMID:38285567

Vashishtha, L. K., Singh, A. P., & Chatterjee, K. (2023). HIDM: A hybrid intrusion detection model for cloud based systems. *Wireless Personal Communications*, 128(4), 2637–2666. DOI:10.1007/s11277-022-10063-y

Vasist, P. N., & Krishnan, S. (2022). Deepfakes: An integrative review of the literature and an agenda for future research. *Communications of the Association for Information Systems*, 51, 590–636. DOI:10.17705/1CAIS.05126

Vegesna, V. V. (2023). Enhancing cyber resilience by integrating AI-Driven threat detection and mitigation strategies. Transactions on Latest Trends in Artificial Intelligence, 4(4).

Vemuri, N., Thaneeru, N., & Tatikonda, V. M. (2024). Adaptive generative AI for dynamic cybersecurity threat detection in enterprises.

Venkatesan, K., & Rahayu, S. B. (2024). Blockchain security enhancement: An approach towards hybrid consensus algorithms and machine learning techniques. *Scientific Reports*, 14(1), 1149. Advance online publication. DOI:10.1038/s41598-024-51578-7 PMID:38212390

Verma, S., Kaur, S., Rawat, D. B., Chen, X., Alex, L. T., & Jhanjhi, N. Z. (2021). Intelligent framework using IoT-Based WSNs for wildfire detection. *IEEE Access : Practical Innovations, Open Solutions*, 9, 48185–48196. DOI:10.1109/ACCESS.2021.3060549

Vesala, J. (2023). Developing Artificial Intelligence-Based Content Creation: Are EU copyright and antitrust law fit for purpose? *IIC - International Review of Intellectual Property and Competition Law, 54*(3), 351–380. DOI:10.1007/s40319-023-01301-2

Vetrò, A., Santangelo, A., Beretta, E., & De Martin, J. C. (2019). AI: From rational agents to socially responsible agents. *Digital Policy. Regulation & Governance*, 21(3), 291–304. DOI:10.1108/DPRG-08-2018-0049

Vietrov, I. (2024). Generative AI Trends: Transforming Business and Shaping Future. Retrieved from https://masterofcode.com/blog/generative-ai-trends

Villegas-Ch, W., & García-Ortiz, J. (2023). Toward a comprehensive framework for ensuring security and privacy in artificial intelligence. *Electronics (Basel)*, 12(18), 3786. DOI:10.3390/electronics12183786

Virvou, M. (2023). Artificial Intelligence and User Experience in reciprocity: Contributions and state of the art. *Intelligent Decision Technologies*, 17(1), 73–125. DOI:10.3233/IDT-230092

Voulodimos, A., Doulamis, A., & Protopapadakis, E. (2018). Deep Learning for Computer Vision: A Brief review. *Computational Intelligence and Neuroscience*, 2018, 1–13. DOI:10.1155/2018/7068349 PMID:29487619

Vyas, B. (2023, May 7). *Explainable AI: Assessing methods to make AI systems more transparent and interpretable.* https://www.ijnms.com/index.php/ijnms/article/view/220

Walczak, R., Koszewski, K., Olszewski, R., Ejsmont, K., & Kálmán, A. (2023). Acceptance of IoT Edge-Computing-Based sensors in smart cities for universal design purposes. *Energies*, 16(3), 1024. DOI:10.3390/en16031024

Wang, Dong, Wang, & Yin. (n.d.). Protecting data using AI and Blockchain. Academic Press.

Wang, J. (2023, December 15). *FaceComposer: a unified model for versatile facial content creation.* https://proceedings.neurips.cc/paper_files/paper/2023/hash/2b4caf39e645680f826ae0a9e7ae9402-Abstract-Conference.html

Wang, T. (2018). *High-Resolution image synthesis and semantic manipulation with conditional GANs.* https://openaccess.thecvf.com/content_cvpr_2018/html/Wang_High-Resolution_Image_Synthesis_CVPR_2018_paper.html

Wang, X., Wan, Z., Hekmati, A., Zong, M., Alam, S., Zhang, M., & Krishnamachari, B. (2024). IoT in the Era of Generative AI: Vision and Challenges. *arXiv preprint arXiv:2401.01923*.

Wang, Z. (2016, June 11). *Dueling network architectures for deep reinforcement learning*. PMLR. http://proceedings.mlr.press/v48/wangf16.html

Wang, B., Li, H., Guo, Y., & Wang, J. (2023). PPFLHE: A privacy-preserving federated learning scheme with homomorphic encryption for healthcare data. *Applied Soft Computing*, 146, 110677. DOI:10.1016/j.asoc.2023.110677

Wang, C. N., Yang, F. C., Vo, N. T., & Nguyen, V. T. T. (2022). Wireless communications for data security: Efficiency assessment of cybersecurity industry—A promising application for UAVs. *Drones (Basel)*, 6(11), 363. DOI:10.3390/drones6110363

Wang, J. X. (2021). Meta-learning in natural and artificial intelligence. *Current Opinion in Behavioral Sciences*, 38, 90–95. DOI:10.1016/j.cobeha.2021.01.002

Wang, J., Wang, J., Wang, S., & Zhang, Y. (2023). Deep learning in pediatric neuroimaging. *Displays*, 80, 102583. DOI:10.1016/j.displa.2023.102583

Wang, L., Chen, W., Yang, W., Bi, F., & Yu, F. R. (2020). A State-of-the-Art Review on image synthesis with generative adversarial networks. *IEEE Access : Practical Innovations, Open Solutions*, 8, 63514–63537. DOI:10.1109/ACCESS.2020.2982224

Wang, L., Shen, W., Xie, H., Neelamkavil, J., & Pardasani, A. (2002). Collaborative conceptual design—State of the art and future trends. *Computer Aided Design*, 34(13), 981–996. DOI:10.1016/S0010-4485(01)00157-9

Wang, M., Qin, Y., Liu, J., & Li, W. (2023). Identifying personal physiological data risks to the Internet of Everything: The case of facial data breach risks. *Humanities & Social Sciences Communications*, 10(1), 1–15. DOI:10.1057/s41599-023-01673-3 PMID:37192941

Wang, R., Bush-Evans, R., Arden-Close, E., Bolat, E., McAlaney, J., Hodge, S. E., Thomas, S., & Phalp, K. (2023). Transparency in persuasive technology, immersive technology, and online marketing: Facilitating users' informed decision making and practical implications. *Computers in Human Behavior*, 139, 107545. DOI:10.1016/j.chb.2022.107545

Wang, S., Ko, R. K. L., Bai, G., Dong, N., Choi, T., & Zhang, Y. (2024). Evasion Attack and Defense on Machine Learning Models in Cyber-Physical Systems: A survey. *IEEE Communications Surveys and Tutorials*, 1(2), 930–966. Advance online publication. DOI:10.1109/COMST.2023.3344808

Wang, Y. (2023). Synthetic realities in the digital age: Navigating the opportunities and challenges of ai-generated content. *Authorea Preprints*.

Wang, Y., Sun, T., Li, S., Yuan, X., Ni, W., Hossain, E., & Poor, H. V. (2023). Adversarial Attacks and Defenses in Machine Learning-Empowered Communication Systems and Networks: A Contemporary survey. *IEEE Communications Surveys and Tutorials*, 25(4), 2245–2298. DOI:10.1109/COMST.2023.3319492

Wang, Y., Wang, X., Arifoglu, D., Lu, C., Bouchachia, A., Geng, Y., & Zheng, G. (2023). A survey on Ambient Sensor-Based Abnormal Behaviour Detection for Elderly People in Healthcare. *Electronics (Basel)*, 12(7), 1539. DOI:10.3390/electronics12071539

Wang, Z., Wang, J., & Wang, Y. (2018). An intelligent diagnosis scheme based on generative adversarial learning deep neural networks and its application to planetary gearbox fault pattern recognition. *Neurocomputing*, 310, 213–222. DOI:10.1016/j.neucom.2018.05.024

Waqas, A., Bui, M. M., Glassy, E. F., Naqa, I. E., Borkowski, P., Borkowski, A., & Bouaynaya, N. (2023). Revolutionizing digital pathology with the power of generative artificial intelligence and foundation models. *Laboratory Investigation*, 103(11), 100255. DOI:10.1016/j.labinv.2023.100255 PMID:37757969

Wassan, S. (2021) 'Amazon Product Sentiment Analysis using Machine Learning Techniques,' *International Journal of Early Childhood Special Education (INTJECSE)*, 30(1), 695. https://doi.org/.DOI:10.24205/03276716.2020.2065

Wassan, S., Chen, X., Shen, T., Waqar, M., & Jhanjhi, N. Z. (2021). Amazon product sentiment analysis using machine learning techniques. *Revista Argentina de Clínica Psicológica*, 30(1), 695.

Wazid, M., Das, A. K., Chamola, V., & Park, Y. (2022). Uniting cyber security and machine learning: Advantages, challenges and future research. *ICT Express*, 8(3), 313–321. DOI:10.1016/j.icte.2022.04.007

Weisz, J. D., He, J., Müller, M., Hoefer, G., Miles, R., & Geyer, W. (2024). *Design principles for Generative AI applications. arXiv*. Cornell University., DOI:10.1145/3613904.3642466

Wei, W., & Liu, L. (2024). Trustworthy distributed AI systems: Robustness, privacy, and governance. *ACM Computing Surveys*, 3645102. Advance online publication. DOI:10.1145/3645102

Wen, B. O. T., Syahriza, N., Xian, N. C. W., Wei, N., Shen, T. Z., Hin, Y. Z., Sindiramutty, S. R., & Nicole, T. Y. F. (2023). Detecting cyber threats with a Graph-Based NIDPS. In *Advances in logistics, operations, and management science book series* (pp. 36–74). DOI:10.4018/978-1-6684-7625-3.ch002

Wennekers, T., & Mathematics, S. O. E. C. A. (2021). *Emotional body language synthesis for humanoid robots*. https://pearl.plymouth.ac.uk/handle/10026.1/17244

Whittaker, L., Kietzmann, T. C., Kietzmann, J., & Dabirian, A. (2020). "All around me are synthetic faces": The mad world of AI-generated media. *IT Professional*, 22(5), 90–99. DOI:10.1109/MITP.2020.2985492

Widder, D. G., West, S. M., & Whittaker, M. (2023). Open (For Business): big tech, concentrated power, and the political economy of open AI. *Social Science Research Network*. DOI:10.2139/ssrn.4543807

Wiegmann, C., Quinlivan, E., Michnevich, T., Pittrich, A., Иванова, П., Rohrbach, A. M., & Kaminski, J. (2023). A digital patient-reported outcome (electronic patient-reported outcome) system for patients with severe psychiatric disorders: User-centered development study and study protocol of a multicenter-controlled trial. *Digital Health*, 9. Advance online publication. DOI:10.1177/20552076231191009 PMID:37900257

Williamson, S. E., & Prybutok, V. R. (2024). Balancing Privacy and Progress: A review of privacy challenges, systemic oversight, and patient perceptions in AI-Driven healthcare. *Applied Sciences (Basel, Switzerland)*, 14(2), 675. DOI:10.3390/app14020675

Wu, T., & Ortiz, J. (2021). Rlad: Time series anomaly detection through reinforcement learning and active learning. *arXiv preprint arXiv:2104.00543*.

Wu, W., & Liu, S. (2023). A comprehensive review and systematic analysis of artificial intelligence regulation policies. *arXiv preprint arXiv:2307.12218*.

Wu, A. N., Stouffs, R., & Biljecki, F. (2022). Generative Adversarial Networks in the built environment: A comprehensive review of the application of GANs across data types and scales. *Building and Environment*, 223, 109477. DOI:10.1016/j.buildenv.2022.109477

Wu, G., Chen, X., Yao, L., Lee, Y., & Yim, K. (2014). An efficient wormhole attack detection method in wireless sensor networks. *Computer Science and Information Systems*, 11(3), 1127–1142. DOI:10.2298/CSIS130921068W

Wu, H., Han, H., Wang, X., & Sun, S. (2020). Research on artificial intelligence enhancing internet of things security: A survey. *IEEE Access : Practical Innovations, Open Solutions*, 8, 153826–153848. DOI:10.1109/ACCESS.2020.3018170

Wu, Y. (2021). Robust Learning-Enabled Intelligence for the Internet of Things: A survey from the perspectives of noisy data and adversarial examples. *IEEE Internet of Things Journal*, 8(12), 9568–9579. DOI:10.1109/JIOT.2020.3018691

Wu, Y. (2024) 'Online Adaptive Ensemble Enhanced Anomaly Detection for Addressing Concept Drift in IoT Systems,' *TechRiv* [Preprint]. DOI:10.36227/techrxiv.23304461.v2

Xenakis, A., Nourin, S. M., Chen, Z., Karabatis, G., Aleroud, A., & Amarsingh, J. (2023). A self-adaptive and secure approach to share network trace data. *Digital Threats : Research and Practice*, 4(4), 1–20. DOI:10.1145/3617181

Xivuri, K., & Twinomurinzi, H. (2023). How AI developers can assure algorithmic fairness. *Discover Artificial Intelligence*, 3(1), 27. Advance online publication. DOI:10.1007/s44163-023-00074-4

Xu, B., & Wang, S. (2024) 'Examining Windows File System IRP Operations with Machine Learning for Ransomware Detection,' *Research Square(Research Square)* [Preprint]. DOI:10.21203/rs.3.rs-4032456/v1

Xue, M., Yuan, C., Wu, H., Zhang, Y., & Liu, W. (2020). Machine learning security: Threats, countermeasures, and evaluations. *IEEE Access : Practical Innovations, Open Solutions*, 8, 8. DOI:10.1109/ACCESS.2020.2987435

Yampolskiy, R. V., & Govindaraju, V. (2008). Behavioural biometrics: A survey and classification. *International Journal of Biometrics*, 1(1), 81–113. DOI:10.1504/IJBM.2008.018665

Yang, Elisa, & Eliot. (n.d.). Providing privacy and securing E-government in smart cities. Department of Computer and Information Sciences, Northumbria University.

Yang, J., Soltan, A. S., Eyre, D. W., Yang, Y., & Clifton, D. A. (2023). An adversarial training framework for mitigating algorithmic biases in clinical machine learning. *NPJ Digital Medicine*, 6(1), 55. Advance online publication. DOI:10.1038/s41746-023-00805-y PMID:36991077

Yang, Q., Liu, Y., Chen, T., & Tong, Y. (n.d.). The concept and applications of federated machine learning. *ACM Transactions on Intelligent Systems and Technology*, 10(2), 12.

Yas, N., Elyat, M. N. I., Saeed, M., Shwedeh, F., & Lootah, S. (2024, February 1). *The impact of intellectual property rights and the work environment on information security in the United Arab Emirates*. https://kurdishstudies.net/menu-script/index.php/KS/article/view/1681

Yazdi, E. T., Moravejosharieh, A., & Ray, S. K. (2014, February). Study of target tracking and handover in Mobile Wireless Sensor Network. In *The International Conference on Information Networking 2014 (ICOIN2014)* (pp. 120-125). IEEE. DOI:10.1109/ICOIN.2014.6799677

Ye, F., & Borş, A. G. (2023). Lifelong generative adversarial autoencoder. *IEEE Transactions on Neural Networks and Learning Systems*, 1–15. DOI:10.1109/TN-NLS.2023.3281091 PMID:37410645

Ye, F., & Borş, A. G. (2024). Self-Supervised Adversarial Variational learning. *Pattern Recognition*, 148, 110156. DOI:10.1016/j.patcog.2023.110156

Yigit, Y., Buchanan, W. J., Tehrani, M. G., & Maglaras, L. (2024). Review of Generative AI Methods in Cybersecurity. *arXiv preprint arXiv:2403.08701*.

Yong, C. T., Hao, C. V., Ruskhan, B., Lim, S. K. Y., Boon, T. G., Wei, T. S., & Shah, S. B. I. A. (2023). An Implementation of Efficient Smart Street Lights with Crime and Accident Monitoring: A Review. Journal of Survey in Fisheries Sciences, 287-305.

Yousef Alshunaifi, S., Mishra, S., & Alshehri, M. (2022). Cyber-Attack Detection and Mitigation Using SVM for 5G Network. *Intelligent Automation & Soft Computing*, 31(1), 13–28. DOI:10.32604/iasc.2022.019121

Yu, C., Liu, J., Nemati, S., & Yin, G. (2021). Reinforcement Learning in Healthcare: A survey. *ACM Computing Surveys*, 55(1), 1–36. DOI:10.1145/3477600

Yu, L., Yousif, M. Z., Zhang, M., Hoyas, S., Vinuesa, R., & Lim, H. (2022). Three-dimensional ESRGAN for super-resolution reconstruction of turbulent flows with tricubic interpolation-based transfer learning. *Physics of Fluids*, 34(12), 125126. Advance online publication. DOI:10.1063/5.0129203

Yu, R., Wang, Y., & Wang, W. (2024). AMAD: Active learning-based multivariate time series anomaly detection for large-scale IT systems. *Computers & Security*, 137, 103603. DOI:10.1016/j.cose.2023.103603

Zafar, I., Anwar, S. M. S., Kanwal, F., Yousaf, W., Nisa, F. U., Kausar, T., Ain, Q. U., Unar, A., Kamal, M. A., Rashid, S., Khan, K. A., & Sharma, R. (2023). Reviewing methods of deep learning for intelligent healthcare systems in genomics and bio-medicine. *Biomedical Signal Processing and Control*, 86, 105263. DOI:10.1016/j.bspc.2023.105263

Zahid, S., Mazhar, M. S., Abbas, S. G., Hanif, Z., Hina, S., & Shah, G. A. (2023). Threat modeling in smart firefighting systems: Aligning MITRE ATT&CK matrix and NIST security controls. *Internet of Things : Engineering Cyber Physical Human Systems*, 22, 100766. DOI:10.1016/j.iot.2023.100766

Zaidi, T., Usman, M., Aftab, M. U., Aljuaid, H., & Ghadi, Y. Y. (2023). Fabrication of flexible Role-Based access control based on blockchain for internet of Things use cases. *IEEE Access : Practical Innovations, Open Solutions*, 11, 106315–106333. DOI:10.1109/ACCESS.2023.3318487

Zajko, M. (2021). Conservative AI and social inequality: Conceptualizing alternatives to bias through social theory. *AI & Society*, 36(3), 1047–1056. DOI:10.1007/s00146-021-01153-9

Zakir, M. H. (2023, December 24). *The impact of artificial intelligence on intellectual property rights*. https://ijhs.com.pk/index.php/IJHS/article/view/330

Zaman, M., Upadhyay, D., & Lung, C.-H. (2023). Validation of a Machine Learning-Based IDS design framework using ORNL datasets for power system with SCADA. *IEEE Access : Practical Innovations, Open Solutions*, 11, 118414–118426. DOI:10.1109/ACCESS.2023.3326751

Zaman, N., Ghazanfar, M. A., Anwar, M., Lee, S. W., Qazi, N., Karimi, A., & Javed, A. (2023). Stock market prediction based on machine learning and social sentiment analysis. *Authorea Preprints*.

Zang, X., Yao, H., Zheng, G., Xu, N., Xu, K., & Li, Z. (2020). MetaLight: Value-based meta-reinforcement learning for traffic signal control. *Proceedings of the AAAI Conference on Artificial Intelligence*, 34(01), 1153–1160. DOI:10.1609/aaai.v34i01.5467

Zeng, B., & Yao, L. (2020). Design of a secure communication scheme using channel shifting in wireless sensor networks. *IOP Conference Series. Earth and Environmental Science*, 428(1), 012026. DOI:10.1088/1755-1315/428/1/012026

Zerilli, J., Knott, A., Maclaurin, J., & Gavaghan, C. (2018). Transparency in Algorithmic and Human Decision-Making: Is there a double standard? *Philosophy & Technology*, 32(4), 661–683. DOI:10.1007/s13347-018-0330-6

Zewdie, T. G., & Girma, A. (2020). IoT security and the role of ai/ml to combat emerging cyber threats in cloud computing environment. *Issues in Information Systems*, 21, 4.

Zhanbayev, R., Irfan, M., Shutaleva, A., Maksimov, D., Abdykadyrkyzy, R., & Filiz, Ş. (2023). Demoethical Model of Sustainable Development of Society: A Roadmap towards Digital Transformation. *Sustainability (Basel)*, 15(16), 12478. DOI:10.3390/su151612478

Zhang, A., Walker, O., Nguyen, K., Dai, J., Chen, A., & Lee, M. K. (2023). Deliberating with AI: Improving Decision-Making for the Future through Participatory AI Design and Stakeholder Deliberation. *Proceedings of the ACM on Human-computer Interaction, 7*(CSCW1), 1–32. DOI:10.1145/3579601

Zhang, C., Cai, Y., Huang, L., & Li, J. (2021). Exploration by maximizing Renyi entropy for reward-free RL framework. *Proceedings of the AAAI Conference on Artificial Intelligence*, 35(12), 10859–10867. DOI:10.1609/aaai.v35i12.17297

Zhang, C., Chen, J., Li, J., Peng, Y., & Mao, Z. (2023). Large language models for human-robot interaction: A review. *Biomimetic Intelligence and Robotics*, 3(4), 100131. DOI:10.1016/j.birob.2023.100131

Zhang, C., Odonkor, P., Zheng, S., Khorasgani, H., Serita, S., Gupta, C., & Wang, H. (2020). Dynamic dispatching for large-scale heterogeneous fleet via multi-agent deep reinforcement learning. In *2020 IEEE International Conference on Big Data (Big Data)* (pp. 1436-1441). IEEE. DOI:10.1109/BigData50022.2020.9378191

Zhang, Q., Chen, B., Zhang, T., Cao, K., Ding, Y., Gao, T., & Zhao, Z. (2023). Generative Adversarial Network-Based Anomaly Detection and Forecasting with Unlabeled Data for 5G Vertical Applications. *Applied Sciences (Basel, Switzerland)*, 13(19), 10745. DOI:10.3390/app131910745

Zhang, R., Guo, J., Chen, L., Fan, Y., & Cheng, X. (2021). A Review on Question Generation from Natural Language Text. *ACM Transactions on Information Systems*, 40(1), 1–43. DOI:10.1145/3468889

Zhang, R., & Xiao, X. (2019). Intrusion detection in wireless sensor networks with an improved NSA based on space division. *Journal of Sensors*, 2019(1), 1–20. DOI:10.1155/2019/5451263

Zhang, X., Ma, Y., Singla, A., & Zhu, X. (2020, November). Adaptive reward-poisoning attacks against reinforcement learning. In *International Conference on Machine Learning* (pp. 11225-11234). PMLR.

Zhang, Z., Wen, F., Sun, Z., Guo, X., He, T., & Lee, C. (2022). Artificial Intelligence-Enabled Sensing technologies in the 5G/Internet of Things era: From Virtual Reality/Augmented Reality to the Digital Twin. *Advanced Intelligent Systems*, 4(7), 2100228. Advance online publication. DOI:10.1002/aisy.202100228

Zhao, H., Li, H., Maurer-Stroh, S., & Cheng, L. (2018). Synthesizing retinal and neuronal images with generative adversarial nets. *Medical Image Analysis*, 49, 14–26. DOI:10.1016/j.media.2018.07.001 PMID:30007254

Zhao, N., Kim, N. W., Herman, L., Pfister, H., Lau, R. W. H., Echevarria, J., & Bylinskii, Z. (2020). *ICONATE: Automatic Compound Icon Generation and Ideation*. ACM. DOI:10.1145/3313831.3376618

Zhao, W., Wang, W., & Viswanathan, S. (2024). Spillover Effects of Generative AI on Human-Generated Content Creation: Evidence from a Crowd-Sourcing Design Platform. *Social Science Research Network*. DOI:10.2139/ssrn.4693181

Zhao, Z., Alzubaidi, L., Zhang, J., Duan, Y., & Gu, Y. (2024). A comparison review of transfer learning and self-supervised learning: Definitions, applications, advantages and limitations. *Expert Systems with Applications*, 242, 122807. DOI:10.1016/j.eswa.2023.122807

Zhihan, L. (2023). *Generative Artificial Intelligence in the Metaverse Era.* Cognitive Robotics., DOI:10.1016/j.cogr.2023.06.001

Zhou, J. (2023, October 13). *Retrieval-based Disentangled Representation Learning with Natural Language Supervision*. OpenReview. https://openreview.net/forum?id=ZlQRiFmq7Y

Zhou, Y., & Kankanhalli, A. (2021). AI Regulation for Smart Cities: Challenges and Principles. In *Public Administration and Information Technology* (Vol. 37, pp. 101-118).

Zhou, Z., Bao, Z., Jiang, W., Huang, Y., Peng, Y., Shankar, A., Maple, C., & Shitharth, S. (2024). Latent Vector Optimization-Based Generative image steganography for consumer electronic applications. *IEEE Transactions on Consumer Electronics*, 1(1), 4357–4366. Advance online publication. DOI:10.1109/TCE.2024.3354824

Zoccali, C., & Mallamaci, F. (2023). Reimagining peer review: The emergence of peer community in registered reports system. *Journal of Nephrology*, 36(9), 2407–2411. DOI:10.1007/s40620-023-01709-6 PMID:37594669

Zografopoulos, I., Ospina, J., Liu, X., & Konstantinou, C. (2021). Cyber-Physical Energy Systems Security: Threat modeling, risk assessment, resources, metrics, and case studies. *IEEE Access : Practical Innovations, Open Solutions*, 9, 29775–29818. DOI:10.1109/ACCESS.2021.3058403

Zola, F., Segurola-Gil, L., Bruse, J. L., Galar, M., & Orduna-Urrutia, R. (2022). Network traffic analysis through node behaviour classification: A graph-based approach with temporal dissection and data-level preprocessing. *Computers & Security*, 115, 102632. DOI:10.1016/j.cose.2022.102632

Ξενάκης, Χ., Xenakis, C., Συστημάτων, Σ. Τ. Π. Κ. Ε. Τ. Ψ., & Συστημάτων, Α. Ψ. (2023, March 21). *Adversarial machine learning attacks against network intrusion detection systems*. https://dione.lib.unipi.gr/xmlui/handle/unipi/15335

About the Contributors

Noor Zaman Jhanjhi (N.Z Jhanjhi) is currently working as a Professor in Computer Science (Cybersecurity and AI), Program Director for the Postgraduate Research Degree Programmes in computer science, Director of the Center for Smart Society (CSS5) at the School of Computer Science at Taylor's University, Malaysia. He has been nominated as the world's top 2% research scientist globally; he is among the top five computer science researchers in Malaysia and was nominated as an Outstanding Faculty Member by the MDEC Malaysia for the year 2022. He has highly indexed publications in WoS/ISI/SCI/Scopus, and his collective research Impact factor is more than 900 plus points. His Google Scholar H index is 60, and I-10 Index is close to 275, and his Scopus H index is 39, with more than 600 publications on his credit. He has several international patents on his account, including Australian, German, and Japanese patents. He edited/authored over 50 research books published by world-class publishers, including Springer, IGI Global USA, Taylors and Frances, Willeys, Intech Open, etc. He has excellent experience supervising and co-supervising postgraduate students, and more than 37 Postgraduate scholars graduated under his supervision. Prof. Jhanjhi serves as Associate Editor and Editorial Assistant Board for several reputable journals, such as PeerJ Computer Science, CMC Computers, Materials & Continua, Computer Systems Science and Engineering CSSE, Frontier in Communication and Networks, etc. He received the Outstanding Associate Editor award for IEEE ACCESS. Active reviewer for a series of top-tier journals has been awarded globally as a top 1% reviewer by Publons (Web of Science). He is an external Ph.D./Master thesis examiner/evaluator for several universities globally and has evaluated 60 plus theses. He has completed more than 40 internationally funded research grants successfully. He has been a keynote/invited speaker for over 60 international conferences and has chaired international conference sessions. He has vast experience in academic qualifications, including ABET, NCAAA, and NCEAC, for 10 years. His research areas include Cybersecurity, IoT security, Wireless security, Data Science, Software Engineering, and UAVs.

* * *

Halawati Abd Jalil Safuan was born and raised in Kuala Lumpur, Malaysia. She received her Bachelor of Science (Honours) in Computer Science and Information Systems from University of Salford, Manchester and her Masters of Science in Technology Management from University of East London, London. She is currently the Head of Programme for Bachelor of Computer Science at School of Computing and Informatics, Albukhary International University. Her research interests are in Information Systems, Data Science and Artificial Intelligence.

Rehan Akbar has over 22 years of experience in teaching and research in Computer Science and Information Systems. Throughout his career, he has been working at academic, research, and management positions at various levels. Currently, he is working as Associate Teaching Professor at School of Computing and Information Sciences, Florida International University, Miami, Florida. Before joining FIU, Dr. Rehan was working as Associate Professor in the Department of Computer and Information Sciences at Universiti Teknologi PETRONAS, Malaysia. He also served as Associate Professor and Head of Department in the Department of Information Systems, Faculty of Information & Communication Technology, Universiti Tunku Abdul Rahman, Malysia for about 10 years. Moreover, he has been working in the software industry as Project Manager of software projects. Dr. Rehan is a Senior Member of IEEE (SMIEEE), Member of Association for Information Systems (AIS), and Professional Technologist with Malaysian Board of Technologists (MBOT), Malaysia.

Aryan Bharadwaj is a final year student of CSE B.Tech at M.S. Ramaiah University of Applied Sciences. Aryan's main areas of interest lie in gaining knowledge about next-gen technologies and AI/ML.

Vinay Dubey is a third-year student pursuing BTech in Computer Science at M.S Ramaiah University of Applied Sciences. Vinays's main areas of interest involve AI/ML, System Design, and Software Development.

Mustansar Ghazanfar possesses a strong background in cutting-edge technologies such as Artificial Intelligence, Machine/Deep Learning, Big Data, and Blockchain. He is highly skilled in programming languages such as Python, Java, and PySpark, and has extensive experience working with top-tier tools and APIs like OpenAI and TensorFlow. Moreover, Dr. Mustansar has distinguished himself as a highly effective project director, capable of leading large teams and delivering exceptional results. He is well-versed in Agile/Scrum methodologies, Software Project Management, and has ongoing MBA studies with a focus on strategy from Heriot-Watt University. Dr. Mustansar's extensive expertise in Artificial Intelligence, Blockchain, and Big Data, along with his proficiency in strategic planning and project management, make him a highly sought-after professional across a range of fields. His exceptional qualifications and notable achievements, evidenced by his research with over 70 journals and articles (~1 citations per day as per Google Scholar), position him as an outstanding candidate for top-level positions in the technology industry, stratups, research, academia, and government sectors.

Khalid Hussain is working as a professor in the School of Computing and Informatics at Albukhary International University, Alor Setar Kedah, Malaysia. In addition to this, he is also a member of the Senate and a member of the Board of Governor at Albukhary International University. Before this, he was working as a Professor of Cyber Security at Superior University Lahore and Campus Director at the National Superior Institute of Science and Technology (NSIST) in Islamabad; previously, he had served as Dean of the Faculty of Computer Science and Campus Director at Barani Institute of Sciences, ARID Agriculture University, for the last one and a half years. He also served at the University of Lahore as Dean of the of the Faculty of Computer Science and Information Technology for three years. Dr. Khalid has vast university/industry experience. During his tenure in the industry, he served on defense-related projects, and in recognition of his services, he has been awarded commendation certificates by multiple government agencies. He joined academia in 2008 as a full-time faculty member.

Uswa Ihsan serves as a visiting lecturer at both the International Islamic University and Preston University within the Department of Computer Science and IT, having completed her MSCS from IIUI. She has contributed significantly to academia with research papers such as "Survey on Multi-Document Summarization: Systematic Literature Review," "MABPD: Mobile agent-based prevention and black hole attack detection in wireless sensor networks," and "A Secure and Reliable Supply chain management approach integrated with IoT and Blockchain." Uswa's research interests encompass data mining, Internet of Things, network security, Cybersecurity, and Smart Logistic Blockchain, reflecting her dedication to advancing knowledge and addressing contemporary challenges in technology.

Aaditi Jadwani is a third year B.Tech student in M.S. Ramaiah University of Applied Sciences. Aaditi's primary focus revolves around acquiring knowledge in next-generation technologies and exploring the intersection of AI/ML and digital healthcare with AI.

Nazir Ahmed Malik did his BSc (Hons.) in Naval Sciences from Karachi University and Masters in Computer Science from UAF, Faisalabad, Pakistan. After doing Masters, he held various appointments related to Computer Science domain. Thereafter, he did his Masters Leading to PhD (Information Security) from National University of Sciences and Technology (NUST), Pakistan. During his PhD he has been research fellow at Information Security Group (ISG) at Royal Holloway, University of London (RHUL), UK and University of Texas at Arlington, USA. He has worked as faculty member and Head of Distance Learning at Pakistan Navy Engineering College (PNEC), NUST at Department of Management Information Systems (MIS), Karachi. His research interests are Information Security Auditing, Information Security Management and Policy Making. He has worked on several research projects involving Information Security Audits of various Information Systems and Networks including Data Centers, Security and Privacy in pervasive Computing Environment, Threat Modeling of Context aware systems, Privacy and Consent in pervasive networks. He has published several research papers in reputed international journals and conferences and have also appeared on National TV programs as Guest.

Nidhi N. P. is a third-year student pursuing BTech in Computer Science at M.S Ramaiah University of Applied Sciences. Nidhi's main areas of interest involve AI/ML, System Design,Cloud Computing and Software Development.

Sahana. P. Shankar completed her B.E in Information Science and Engineering and MTech in Software Engineering from Ramaiah Institute of Technology, Bangalore. She is a third rank holder in B.E and a first rank holder with gold medal in MTech. She has worked with Unisys as an Associate Engineer for three years. She holds a US Patent in the field so software testing. She has worked with RIT as a Teaching Assistant for 6 months under the TEQIP-II scholarship program. She has published papers in various international journals and conferences. She has also authored several book chapters. She is an ISTQB certified software tester. She is currently working with Ramaiah University of Applied Sciences, Bangalore as an Assistant Professor in the Department of Computer Science and Engineering since 2018.

Tariq Rahim Soomro, Professor of Computer Science, and Rector at Institute of Business Management, has received BSc (Hons) and M.Sc degrees in Computer Science from University of Sindh, Jamshoro, Pakistan and his PhD in Computer Applications from Zhejiang University, Hangzhou, China and became the first

Pakistani to receive all three degrees in the field of Computer Science. He has more than 29 years of extensive and diverse experience as an administrator, computer programmer, researcher, and teacher. As an administrator, He served as Coordinator, Head of Department, Head of Faculty, Dean of Faculty, Head of Academic Affairs and having wide experience in accreditation related matters, including ABET USA, NCEAC & HEC Pakistan, KHDA United Arab Emirates (UAE) and Ministry of Higher Education and Scientific Research (MoHESR), UAE. He has published over 100 peer-reviewed papers. He has been a senior member of IEEE since 2005 and IEEE Member since 2000. He is currently serving as Chair IEEE Karachi Section (2024-25) and IEEE Computer Society R10 Southern Area Coordinator of Computer Society along with Member FRC IEEE Educational Activities Committee.

Venkat T. is Professor, Department of Computer Science and Engineering CSE IOT, Sreenidhi Institute of Science and Technology, Hyderabad, Telangana, India.

Sahil Uthappa is a third year student pursuing his B.Tech in Computer Science Engineering at M.S. Ramaiah University of Applied Sciences . His main areas of interest are Machine Learning, Artificial Intelligence and Data Analytics.

Deepak Varadam holds a Master's Degree in Microsystems Engineering from Heriot-Watt University, Edinburgh (Scotland), U.K. and P.G.Diploma in ECE from Napier University, U.K. He worked as a Postgraduate Masters Research Scientist under Biomedical Microengineering Group (BMG) at Heriot-Watt University. He is currently working as an Assistant Professor in Faculty of Engineering and Technology, Computer Science and Engineering Department at Ramaiah University of Applied Sciences (RUAS) since 2010. He has been actively participating in delivering corporate trainings, seminars and have publications in national, international journals and conferences. His research interests is in MEMS, Embedded Systems, Software Engineering, Computer Graphics, AI, Blockchain, and IoT. He is currently an ExeCom Member of the IEEE RUAS Student Chapter.

Index

A

Adversarial Attacks 67, 77, 80, 82, 96, 97, 98, 99, 106, 111, 116, 119, 290, 291, 292, 294, 317, 322, 324, 326, 330, 505

Agents 4, 19, 20, 21, 29, 30, 54, 55, 64, 65, 66, 67, 68, 70, 104, 107, 186, 290, 354, 384, 440, 521

Algorithms 2, 4, 10, 17, 18, 19, 21, 31, 37, 39, 41, 42, 55, 57, 58, 60, 66, 67, 68, 69, 71, 79, 83, 84, 85, 88, 89, 90, 92, 93, 94, 95, 96, 98, 102, 105, 118, 134, 145, 146, 160, 166, 174, 175, 176, 177, 178, 179, 182, 183, 184, 186, 187, 190, 192, 194, 198, 207, 210, 211, 213, 221, 225, 235, 236, 239, 245, 247, 250, 251, 253, 262, 266, 269, 283, 285, 286, 287, 288, 290, 295, 302, 306, 319, 329, 334, 336, 343, 344, 345, 346, 347, 349, 351, 352, 353, 354, 355, 356, 357, 358, 360, 361, 364, 366, 367, 368, 370, 371, 372, 378, 398, 413, 414, 416, 417, 421, 423, 424, 425, 432, 434, 435, 437, 440, 442, 443, 444, 456, 459, 472, 473, 474, 476, 479, 481, 484, 485, 492, 494, 498, 501, 503

Anomaly 5, 14, 17, 18, 34, 37, 40, 42, 45, 48, 62, 66, 75, 80, 81, 86, 87, 89, 90, 91, 94, 98, 100, 106, 110, 112, 113, 114, 115, 117, 118, 119, 121, 122, 123, 177, 191, 220, 233, 234, 235, 236, 238, 243, 251, 256, 257, 259, 262, 284, 304, 307, 312, 345, 376, 420, 458, 466, 483, 484, 487, 490, 500

Anomaly Detection 5, 14, 17, 18, 34, 37, 40, 42, 45, 48, 66, 75, 80, 81, 87, 89, 90, 91, 94, 98, 100, 106, 112, 113, 114, 115, 117, 118, 119, 121, 122, 123, 177, 191, 220, 233, 234, 235, 238, 243, 251, 256, 257, 259, 262, 304, 307, 312, 345, 420, 458, 466, 483, 484, 487, 500

Artificial intelligence 27, 28, 29, 34, 35, 38, 39, 40, 41, 44, 45, 47, 48, 49, 62, 70, 71, 72, 73, 74, 75, 80, 81, 88, 89, 97, 105, 106, 110, 111, 112, 113, 115, 119, 121, 122, 173, 174, 175, 176, 177, 178, 179, 180, 181, 182, 183, 184, 185, 186, 187, 188, 189, 194, 195, 196, 197, 198, 199, 200, 208, 215, 216, 219, 221, 241, 251, 255, 256, 257, 258, 259, 260, 262, 269, 280, 282, 312, 314, 315, 316, 318, 319, 320, 322, 323, 324, 325, 326, 328, 329, 330, 336, 337, 376, 377, 378, 380, 381, 382, 383, 384, 385, 386, 387, 388, 389, 390, 391, 392, 393, 416, 418, 424, 429, 430, 432, 437, 440, 442, 447, 448, 449, 451, 452, 453, 454, 455, 456, 457, 458, 459, 460, 461, 462, 466, 472, 476, 477, 478, 482, 483, 484, 485, 486, 489, 490, 491, 492, 495, 498, 500, 505, 508, 516, 517, 518, 519, 520, 521

Artificial Neural Network 136, 137, 171

Automated Layout Generation 337, 347, 349, 355

B

Bias Mitigation 454

Big Data 39, 45, 73, 75, 113, 119, 176, 178, 185, 186, 187, 195, 196, 199, 235, 319, 329, 380, 381, 384, 408, 447, 448, 451, 454, 458, 483, 485, 511

Blockchain 46, 53, 71, 109, 114, 116, 120, 122, 168, 170, 171, 179, 180, 185, 186, 192, 193, 195, 196, 197, 198, 199, 201, 202, 203, 204, 205, 206, 207, 208, 209, 210, 211, 212, 213, 214, 215, 216, 249, 250, 251, 255, 260, 262, 271, 278, 307, 314, 317, 318, 327, 329, 331, 388, 390, 398, 407, 449, 460

C

Cloud Computing 35, 111, 175, 177, 184, 185, 186, 193, 194, 200, 255, 315,

Printed in the United States
by Baker & Taylor Publisher Services